A level, BTEC and first degree

COMPUTING

Nick Waites BSc, MSc, Cert Ed

Geoffrey Knott BA (Open), AIB, Cert Ed

New College Durham

Business Education Publishers Limited
1992

© NICK WAITES and GEOFFREY KNOTT 1992

ISBN 0 907679 40 4

First published in 1992
Reprinted 1993
Reprinted 1994

Published in Great Britain by Business Education Publishers Limited
Leighton House 10 Grange Crescent Stockton Road
Sunderland Tyne and Wear SR2 7BN

Tel. 091 567 4963 Fax. 091 514 3277

British Cataloguing-in-Publications Data
A catalogue record for this book is available from the British Library

Printed in Great Britain by M and A Thomson Litho Limited
East Kilbride Glasgow

Preface

This text has been specifically designed to cover the Advanced Level Computing syllabuses of the major examining boards. It is also highly suitable as a first-year study text for students following Higher Education Courses in Computing or studying for the Part 1 examination of the British Computer Society. The material is organized into seven sections, titled as follows.

Fundamental Concepts

Computer Hardware

Computer Software

Systems Analysis

Data Processing

Program Design and Implementation

Computers and Society

The logical grouping of related topics facilitates access to particular areas of interest as well as providing a framework for a teaching or self-study programme.

Examination practice is also provided through a range of actual examination questions selected from a number of major examining boards. A tutor's manual containing suggested solutions to these questions is available from the publisher for centres which adopt the book.

A disk produced by *Microfile*, the educational software house, containing software to supplement a number of selected topics from the text, can be purchased from Business Education Publishers Ltd. The disk includes an integrated suite of programs for an assembler specifically designed for educational use, a number of programs to illustrate data structures and the source listings of a number of sorting programs described in the book.

Acknowledgements

This book has been produced with the help of a number of people who deserve particular mention. Special thanks go to Jim Morton for his excellent technical editing and general comments upon the material, and to Alun Knott who meticulously produced most of the diagrams in the book. Moira Page and Caroline White were responsible for the production editing and managed this with their usual calm and good humour. Mr. Yunas Nadiadi of Silicon Vision kindly allowed us to use a number of graphics illustrations from one of his company's CAD products.

We would like to record thanks to the following examination Boards for their kind permission to reproduce selected questions set from recent past papers:

The Associated Examining Board

Joint Matriculation Board

University of Cambridge Local Examination Syndicate

University of London Examinations and Assessment Council

Welsh Joint Education Committee

Acknowledgement is made by each question reproduced to the relevant Examination Board.

All errors and omissions should have been spotted; if they were not then they remain the responsibility of the authors.

Durham, June 1992.

Table of Contents

Section VII *Computers and Society*

Chapter 30 *Organizational Aspects of Computerization*

Chapter 31 *Applications and Benefits of Computerization*

Chapter 32 *Computers and Employment*

Chapter 33 *Personal Privacy and Computer Fraud*

1 *Number Systems*

Although the denary number system has proved to be the simplest for humans to use, it is more convenient for computers to use the binary number system. As is explained in more detail in Chapter 2, the electronic components used in computers can be in one of two physical states, which can be used to represent 0 and 1, the two digits of the binary number system. This chapter explains the basis of this and other number systems relevant to the subject of computing.

The Radix or Base of a Number System

First consider the denary system. There are ten symbols, 0 to 9 and the base or radix of a number system is simply the number of different symbols it uses. Thus, the denary number system has a radix or base of 10.

Place Value

Each symbol can be given a weight or place value, according to its position within a number. In the denary system, each place value is a power of ten. Thus, for denary integers the place values (starting from the least significant digit on the right) are units, tens, hundreds, thousands etc. The concept of place value can be illustrated with the following example of an integer number, 1263:

Power of ten 10^3	10^2	10^1	10^0
thousands	hundreds	tens	units
1	2	6	3

Figure 1.1

The normal representation of 1263 can be seen as:

$$1 \times 1000 + 2 \times 100 + 6 \times 10 + 3 \times 1$$

It should be noted that any number raised to the power of zero is 1.

The fractional component of a number (*Figure 1.2*) is also determined by position, except that the power is negative.

Power of ten	10^{-1}	10^{-2}
	tenths	hundredths
	3	2
	$\frac{3}{10}$	$\frac{2}{100}$

Figure 1.2

The normal representation of $0 \cdot 75$ or $\frac{3}{4}$ can be seen as:

$$7 \times \frac{1}{10} + 5 \times \frac{1}{100} = \frac{75}{100} = \frac{3}{4}$$

The Binary System

The binary system uses two symbols, 0 and 1. Thus, it has a base or radix of 2. The denary system uses powers of ten and the binary system powers of two. Each binary digit (bit) is weighted with a power of two according to its position within a number. Some of the place values are shown below in *Figure 1.3*.

Power of two	2^4	2^3	2^2	2^1	2^0	2^{-1}	2^{-2}	2^{-3}
	16	8	4	2	1	$\frac{1}{2}$	$\frac{1}{4}$	$\frac{1}{8}$

Integers   Fractions

Figure 1.3

Thus the binary number $11001 \cdot 11$ is equivalent to:

$$1 \times 2^4 + 1 \times 2^3 + 0 \times 2^2 + 0 \times 2^1 + 1 \times 2^0 + 1 \times 2^{-1} + 1 \times 2^{-2}$$

which equals denary $25\frac{3}{4}$

Figure 1.4 shows the binary equivalents of 1 to 10 in the denary system:

Denary	Binary
1	0 0 0 1
2	0 0 1 0
3	0 0 1 1
4	0 1 0 0
5	0 1 0 1
6	0 1 1 0
7	0 1 1 1
8	1 0 0 0
9	1 0 0 1
10	1 0 1 0

Figure 1.4

Using the place values for the binary system shown earlier, it is easy to see how each of the denary numbers in the table equates with its binary representation.

Binary - Rules of Arithmetic

Addition Rules   *Examples*

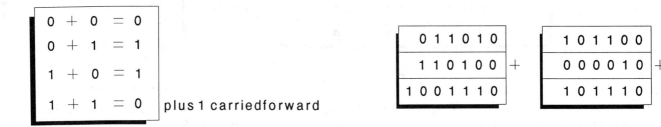

```
0 + 0 = 0
0 + 1 = 1
1 + 0 = 1
1 + 1 = 0   plus 1 carried forward
```

Figure 1.5

The rules for binary addition are needed when studying computer arithmetic in Chapter 2.

Octal and Hexadecimal Numbers

These number systems are often used as a shorthand method for representing binary numbers. As can be seen from the binary numbers listed above, they are very confusing to the eye and it is difficult, even with small groupings, to distinguish one pattern from another. Where it is necessary for the computer's binary codes to be written or read by programmers, for example, then it is invariably more convenient to use alternative coding methods. Octal and hexadecimal (hex) notations are used in preference to denary because they are more readily converted to or from binary.

It must be emphasized that computers can only handle binary forms of coding. Therefore octal and hexadecimal codes must be converted to binary before they can be handled by the computer.

Octal Coding

The octal number system has a base of 8, using 0 to 7 as its symbols. Some of the place values are shown in *Figure 1.6*.

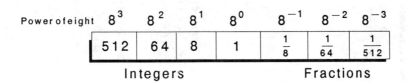

Figure 1.6

The coding of binary numbers in octal is straightforward. Three binary digits will allow 8 (2^3) different patterns of bits, sufficient to represent each of the octal symbols. These are given in *Figure 1.7*.

Octal	Binary
0	0 0 0
1	0 0 1
2	0 1 0
3	0 1 1
4	1 0 0
5	1 0 1
6	1 1 0
7	1 1 1

Binary number	0	1 1 1	0 0 1	1 0 1	1 0 0	1 1 0	(16 bits)
Octal coding	0	7	1	5	4	6	

Figure 1.7

A binary number can be split into groups of 3 bits, starting from the right-hand side, as the example shows. Because the 16 bits will not divide exactly into groups of 3, the left-most or Most Significant Bit (MSB) can only take the values 0 or 1.

A more commonly used system is the hexadecimal coding system.

Hexadecimal Coding

The hexadecimal number system has a base of 16, and uses the following symbols:

0 to 9 and A to F (used for the numbers 10 to 15 in the denary system)

The letters A, B, C, D, E and F are used to bring the number of unique symbols up to sixteen. The place values can be illustrated as follows:

Power of sixteen	16^3	16^2	16^1	16^0	16^{-1}	16^{-2}	16^{-3}
	4096	256	16	1	$\frac{1}{16}$	$\frac{1}{256}$	$\frac{1}{4096}$
		Integers				Fractions	

Figure 1.8

A group of 4 bits will provide 16 possible unique patterns, the number required to represent all the symbols of the hexadecimal number system. These are given in *Figure 1.9*.

Binary	Hex	Binary	Hex
0 0 0 0	0	1 0 0 0	8
0 0 0 1	1	1 0 0 1	9
0 0 1 0	2	1 0 1 0	A
0 0 1 1	3	1 0 1 1	B
0 1 0 0	4	1 1 0 0	C
0 1 0 1	5	1 1 0 1	D
0 1 1 0	6	1 1 1 0	E
0 1 1 1	7	1 1 1 1	F

Figure 1.9

Therefore, a binary number can be coded by grouping the bits into groups of four, starting from the right-hand side and using the appropriate hexadecimal symbol for each group, as the following example shows:

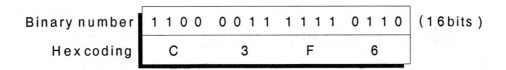

Figure 1.10

Hexadecimal coding is more commonly used because computers organize their internal memory in 8-bit groupings (bytes) or multiples of bytes. These groupings conveniently divide into 4-bit 'nibbles' which can be coded in the 'shorthand' of hexadecimal.

A knowledge of hexadecimal is essential for the interpretation of computer manufacturers' manuals, which use the coding system extensively to specify memory and backing storage features. Programmers using low level languages, such as assembly code, also need to be familiar with this number system.

2 *Data Representation*

Data, in the context of this chapter, is a general term which covers any data or information which is capable of being handled by the computer's internal circuitry, or of being stored on backing storage media such as magnetic tape or disk. To be processed by computer, data must be in a form which the computer can handle; it must be *machine-sensible*.

Forms of Coding

To be 'machine-sensible', data has to be in *binary* format. In Chapter 1, it is explained that the binary number system uses only two digits, 0 and 1. Both the main memory and external storage media, such as magnetic disk and tape, use electrical/magnetic patterns representing the digits 0 and 1 to record data and instructions.

Why Binary? - Bi-stable Devices

Computer storage uses two-state or bi-stable devices to indicate the presence of a 0 or a 1. The circuits inside a computer represent these two states by being either conducting or non-conducting, that is, current is either flowing or is not flowing through the circuit. A simple example of a bi-stable device is an electric light bulb. At any one time it must be in one or other of two states, on or off. Magnetic storage media use magnetic fields of two possible polarities (north and south) as bi-stable devices to represent 0 and 1.

To understand the benefits of using binary representation, consider the electronic requirements which would be necessary if the decimal (denary) system were used. To record the digits 0 - 9, a computer's circuitry would have to use and accommodate ten clearly defined physical electronic states. This would require extremely reliable components to avoid the machine confusing one physical state with another. With bi-stable devices, slight changes in performance do not prevent differentiation between the two physical states which represent 0 and 1.

Character and Numeric Codes

Much of the data processed by computer and stored on backing storage is represented by *character* codes. The codes used inside the computer are referred to as *internal* codes, whereas those used by various peripherals are termed *external* codes. Data transferred between peripheral devices and the processor may utilize a variety of binary character codes, but when processing data the processor will tend to use a particular internal code, which will vary with machines of different manufacture. Sometimes, an external character code may continue to be used for storage of data in main memory; alphabetic data remains in character code form during computer processing. On the other hand, numeric data presented by a peripheral in character code form is converted to one of a number of numeric codes for processing purposes. Code conversion may be executed within a peripheral, within the interface device between a peripheral and the processor, or within the processor itself.

Characters may be grouped according to the following categories:

    ☐ alphabetic (upper and lower case);

    ☐ numeric (0 to 9);

    ☐ special characters (apostrophe, comma, etc);

    ☐ control characters and codes.

Control characters are used in data transmission, perhaps to indicate the start or end of a block of data; *control codes* can be used to affect the display of data on a VDU screen and include those which cause, for example, carriage return, delete, highlight or blinking. Control characters and codes do not form part of the data which is to be usefully processed, but are necessary for its control.

The range of characters which can be represented by a computer system is known as its *character set*. The ASCII (American Standard Code for Information Interchange) code uses seven binary digits (bits) to represent a full range of characters. Data passing between a peripheral and the computer is usually in character code, typically ASCII or EBCDIC (Extended Binary Coded Decimal Interchange Code). This latter 8-bit character code has a 256 character set and is generally used with IBM and IBM-compatible equipment.

ASCII Character Set (Extract)

Character	ASCII code	Character	ASCII code
0	0110000	I	1001001
1	0110001	J	1001010
2	0110010	K	1001011
3	0110011	L	1001100
4	0110100	M	1001101
5	0110101	N	1001110
6	0110110	O	1001111
7	0110111	P	1010000
8	0111000	Q	1010001
9	0111001	R	1010010
A	1000001	S	1010011
B	1000010	T	1010100
C	1000011	U	1010101
D	1000100	V	1010110
E	1000101	W	1010111
F	1000110	X	1011000
G	1000111	Y	1011001
H	1001000	Z	1011010

Figure 2.1

Extended Binary Coded Decimal Interchange Code (EBCDIC) (Extract)

Character	EBCDIC code	Character	EBCDIC code
0	11110000	I	11001001
1	11110001	J	11010001
2	11110010	K	11010010
3	11110011	L	11010011
4	11110100	M	11010100
5	11110101	N	11010101
6	11110110	O	11010110
7	11110111	P	11010111
8	11111000	Q	11011000
9	11111001	R	11011001
A	11000001	S	11100010
B	11000010	T	11100011
C	11000011	U	11100100
D	11000100	V	11100101
E	11000101	W	11100110
F	11000110	X	11100111
G	11000111	Y	11101000
H	11001000	Z	11101001

Figure 2.2

Parity Checking of Codes

The ASCII code shown in *Figure 2.1* is a 7-bit code. An additional bit in the left-most (most significant bit) position is used for detecting single bit errors which may occur during data transfer. Such errors may result from a peripheral fault or from corruption of data on storage media.

The scheme used for detecting errors is simple. There are two types of parity, namely odd and even, though it is of little significance which is used. To record odd parity, the parity bit is set to 1 or 0 in order that there are an odd number of bit 1s in the group. Conversely, even parity requires that the parity bit is set so that there are an even number of bit 1s in the group.

Examples of these two methods are shown in *Figure 2.3*.

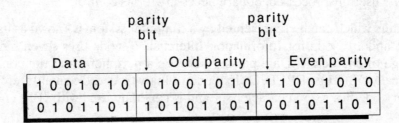

Figure 2.3

If even parity is being used and the main store receives the grouping 10010100 then the presence of an odd number of bit 1s indicates an error in transmission. Provided an odd number of bits are corrupted all transmission errors will be detected. However, an even number of bits in error will not affect the parity condition and additional controls can be implemented which make use of parity checks on blocks of characters; known as *block check characters* (BCC) and used extensively in data transmission control, they are described in the Chapter on Data Communications.

Data Storage in Main Memory

Character codes, such as the ASCII code (*Figure 2.1*), are primarily of use during data transfer between a peripheral and the main memory. They are also generally used to represent non-numeric data inside the computer. Numeric data is usually converted to one of a number of numeric codes.

Internal Parity Checks

Most mini and mainframe computers use parity bits to detect and sometimes correct, data transfer errors within the computer, so the actual length of codes is extended accordingly.

Binary Coded Decimal (BCD)

As the name suggests, BCD uses a binary code to represent the decimal digits. It is a 4-bit code and is only used for the representation of numeric values. Each of the ten digits used in the decimal system is coded with its binary equivalent as in *Figure 2.4*.

Decimal Digit	0	1	2	3	4	5	6	7	8	9
BCD Code	0000	0001	0010	0011	0100	0101	0110	0111	1000	1001

Figure 2.4

In this way, any number can be represented by coding each digit separately. For example, a decimal value of 624 would be coded as in *Figure 2.5*.

Decimal	6	2	4
BCD Code	0110	0010	0100

Figure 2.5

BCD Arithmetic

Floating point arithmetic (dealt with later in this chapter) can introduce small inaccuracies which can be a problem in financial data processing applications. For example, an amount of $120 \cdot 50$ stored in floating point form may return a value of $120 \cdot 499999$; although the application of rounding algorithms can adjust the figure to the required number of significant figures, the rounding is being carried out on the binary representation, when it is the decimal form which should be rounded.

For BCD numbers, each decimal character is separately coded and their addition cannot be accomplished with the normal ADD instruction; more complex electronics are needed to carry out arithmetic on data in BCD form than are necessary for pure binary numbers. BCD numbers also take more memory space than pure binary numbers. For example, with a 16-bit word the maximum BCD number is 9999_{10}, while using binary it is 65535_{10}.

Numbers with a fractional element are represented with an implied decimal point which can be located between any of the 4-bit groupings.

Boolean Values

Apart from characters and numeric values, binary words can also represent the Boolean values of *true* or *false* (Chapter 4), the former by 1 and the latter by 0. Boolean variables can be used to indicate, for example, the condition of a *busy* register during programmed input/output (Chapter 7), the occurrence of an overflow condition after an arithmetic operation, or an interrupt (Chapter 7) from a peripheral indicating its need for servicing by the processor.

Bit-mapped Graphics

Chapter 6 on Peripherals refers to bit-mapping for the pixel-level control of displayed output; thus a monochrome VDU screen with a *resolution* of 720 pixels by 350 rows needs 252,000 bits of memory, each bit being set to 1 or 0 as required to indicate a pixel as being on or off. Colour screens need to use more bits for each pixel, to allow the setting of a variety of colours, one byte per pixel permitting 256 (2^8) separate colours to be used. By definition, bit-mapped device control is inflexible and very device-dependent, but its use is essential for graphical work, word processing and text output which uses a variety of sophisticated fonts. Since large amounts of memory are needed, particularly for high resolution colour display, graphics adaptor cards provide additional RAM for screen memory.

Gray or Cyclic Code

Gray code is used in mechanical systems, for example shaft encoders, which generate a binary number according to the angle of the disk, but is of no use for arithmetic operations. *Figure 2.6* illustrates a 3-bit Gray code and shaft encoder with 8 segments, each corresponding to one of the code's patterns.

A normal 3-bit binary number would, according to the place values of each bit and beginning with the least significant bit, have a 421 weighting. To convert each of the Gray codes in *Figure 2.6*, take these 421 weightings and transform each by 2n-1, n being the normal binary weighting. Then, ignoring zeroes and working from the most significant to the least significant digit, alternately add and subtract the new weighted values.

An examination of the codes will reveal that if any individual code is incremented or decremented, only one bit changes, thus removing any prospect of ambiguity when the encoded disk crosses the boundary between two segments. Obviously, an increased number of bits will allow a larger number of unique codes with the consequent ability to determine the position of an increased number of segments on the shaft encoder's disk. Gray Code can also be used in disk drives for identifying sectors on magnetic disk.

Denary	Weighting binary (n) Gray (2n-1)	4 7	2 3	1 1	
0		0	0	0	
1		0	0	1	
2		0	1	1	3 less 1
3		0	1	0	3
4		1	1	0	7 less 3
5		1	1	1	7 less 3 plus 1
6		1	0	1	7 less 1
7		1	0	0	7

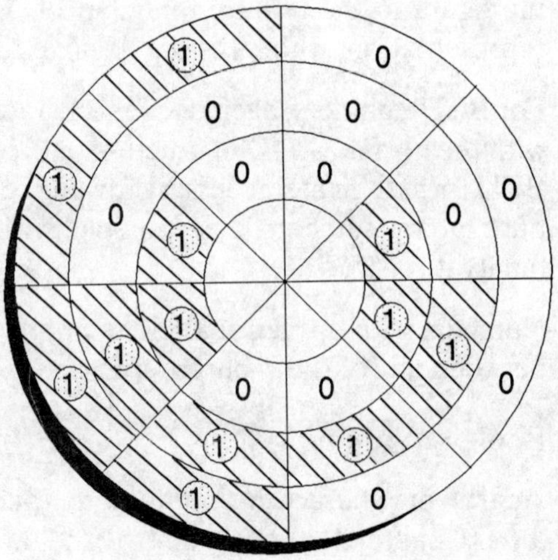

Figure 2.6

The Structure of Main Memory

Main memory is divided into a number of cells or *locations*, each of which has a unique name or *address* and is capable of holding a unit or grouping of bits which may represent data or an instruction. More is said about instructions in Chapter 3. Memory locations are normally addressed using whole numbers from zero upwards.

Size of Locations

The size of memory location used varies from one make of computer to another and is related to the coding methods used and the number of bits it is designed to handle as a unit.

Memory Words

A memory word is a given number of bits in memory, addressable as a unit. The addresses of memory locations run consecutively, starting with address 0 and running up to the largest address. Each location contains a *word* which can be retrieved by specification of its address. Similarly, an instruction to write to a location results in the storage of a word into the quoted address. For example, the word 01100110 may be stored in location address 15 and the word 11000110 in location address 16. A memory word may represent data or an instruction. The topic of memory addressing is dealt with in Chapter 3. The number of bits which is stored in a location is known as the memory's *word length*. Thus, memory which handles memory words of 16 bits is known as 16-bit memory, whilst that which makes use of 32-bit words is known as 32-bit memory. In practice, a machine may use memory words of different lengths for different operations. Word length is one of the most important design characteristics of computers, in that it can be fundamental to the efficiency and speed of the computer. Generally, the larger and more powerful the computer, the greater the word length. Until recently, 32-bit and 64-bit words were largely used by mainframe and minicomputer systems exclusively. When first introduced, microcomputers were 4-bit or 8-bit machines, but advances in technology have made 16-bit and 32-bit microcomputers commonplace.

Bytes

Words can usually be broken down into smaller units called *bytes*. An 8-bit unit is called a byte. In an 8-bit computer, the terms 'byte' and 'word' are interchangeable. A 16-bit computer, for example, may be able to access a 16-bit memory word in two 8-bit bytes.

Nibbles

In 4-bit microprocessors, the 4-bit word is known as a *nibble*, two nibbles forming a byte.

The need to refer to bytes arises from the fact that a location may contain more than one separate grouping of bits, each of which has a separate purpose and as explained above, the coding systems used for numeric and non-numeric data are different and thus need different storage requirements. This has led to a number of different memory structures, based on different word lengths, which have sufficient flexibility to accommodate the requirements of both numeric and non-numeric data.

Alternative Memory Structures

Byte Machines

In byte machines each location has a fixed length of 8 bits, making possible 256 different bit patterns ($2^8 = 256$). Thus, the full ASCII character set (*Figure 2.1*) can be represented and in addition, two 4-bit BCD numeric characters can be fitted into each 8-bit location.

Word Machines (Fixed Word Length Computer)

In this design, data is handled a word at a time; one word = one location. The unit of transfer between the processor and the main memory is always the same size, word lengths including 16, 24, 32 and 64 bits.

Several characters may be packed into one word, for example, four 4-bit BCD digits or two 8-bit EBCDIC characters in a 16-bit word. Frequently, storage is wasted if only part of a word is occupied, for example, when one 8-bit EBCDIC character is held in a 16-bit word.

Variable Word Length Computers

This type of computer allows a word to be of variable length by using one or more locations at the time of data transfer. If, for example, the characters 'CAT' were to be stored, the word length could be set to one and each character referred to separately, or, alternatively, the word length could be set to three to allow 'CAT' to be accessed as a single unit. The byte machine provides an example of a variable word length computer.

Number Representation Inside the Computer

To be of practical use, a computer must be able to store, manipulate and differentiate between positive and negative numbers.

There are a number of different ways this can be done. The most common are:

☐ sign and magnitude;

☐ complementation.

Before describing these methods convention states that, in common with other number systems, the right-most digit in a binary number is the Least Significant Bit (LSB) and the bits increase in significance until the Most Significant Bit (MSB) in the left-most position.

Sign and Magnitude

With this method, the MSB position is occupied by a bit 0 or a bit 1 to indicate, respectively, either a positive or negative sign. The remainder of the binary word holds the *absolute* (independent of the sign) magnitude of the number. The examples in *Figure 2.7* illustrate this method in a 16-bit word:

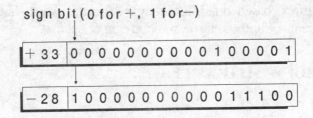

Figure 2.7

Complementation

Complementation enables a computer to carry out subtraction by addition.

The two's complement of a binary number is generated by the following stages:

(i) The number is converted to its one's complement representation by inverting the values of all the bits in the number. In other words all ones are 'flipped' to zeroes and all zeroes are 'flipped' to ones. The examples in *Figure 2.8* illustrate the one's complements of some binary numbers:

Binary number	One's complement
0 0 1 1 0 1	1 1 0 0 1 0
1 0 0 1 0 0	0 1 1 0 1 1
0 0 1 0 0 1 1 0 0	1 1 0 1 1 0 0 1 1

Figure 2.8

(ii) The one's complement of the binary number is then converted to two's complement by adding 1. For example:

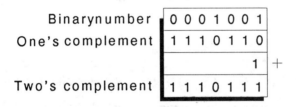

Binary number	0 0 0 1 0 0 1
One's complement	1 1 1 0 1 1 0
	1 +
Two's complement	1 1 1 0 1 1 1

Figure 2.9

To follow the computer arithmetic examples in this chapter, the rules for binary addition need to be understood and these are listed in Chapter 1 on Number Systems.

Binary Subtraction

Subtraction can be carried out by negating the second number (known as the *subtrahend*), in this case by conversion to two's complement form and adding it to the first number (called the *minuend*). The ease with which binary numbers can be switched from positive to negative and vice-versa by complementation, makes subtraction by addition suitable for computers. Consider the examples in *Figures 2.10* and *2.11*, assuming a 6-bit word length.

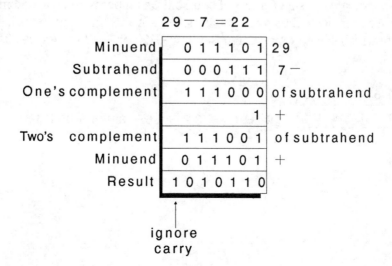

$$29 - 7 = 22$$

Minuend	0 1 1 1 0 1	29
Subtrahend	0 0 0 1 1 1	7 −
One's complement	1 1 1 0 0 0	of subtrahend
	1	+
Two's complement	1 1 1 0 0 1	of subtrahend
Minuend	0 1 1 1 0 1	+
Result	1 0 1 0 1 1 0	

ignore
carry

Figure 2.10

The answer 010110 converts to decimal as $0 + 16 + 0 + 4 + 2 + 0$, which equals 22.

Consider the example in *Figure 2.11* where the minuend is smaller than the subtrahend, resulting in a negative answer:

$$7 - 9 = -2$$

Minuend	0 0 0 1 1 1	7
Subtrahend	0 0 1 0 0 1	9 −
One's complement	1 1 0 1 1 0	of subtrahend
	1	+
Two's complement	1 1 0 1 1 1	of subtrahend
Minuend	0 0 0 1 1 1	+
Result	1 1 1 1 1 0	

Figure 2.11

The answer converts to decimal as $-32 + 16 + 8 + 4 + 2 + 0$, which equals -2.

The MSB is the sign bit which, in two's complement, is part of the number. No provision is needed for separate explicit sign representation. The sign is implicit, unlike sign and magnitude representation which uses the sign bit explicitly to indicate a positive or negative value.

As the examples in *Figures 2.10* and *2.11* show, a positive value is indicated by a 0 and a negative value by a 1 in the MSB position. Thus, a 1 in the MSB position means its positional value is negative (in *Figure 2.11*, it is −32). The addition of those lower significance positional values which contain a bit 1 results in a negative value (in the above example, $-32 + 16 + 8 + 4 + 2 + 0 = -2$).

Arithmetic Overflow

The *number range* of a word in a computer is limited by the number of bits in the word and the fact that the MSB is needed to indicate the sign (unless of course the number is an unsigned integer). This applies whatever method is used to indicate the sign of numbers. Thus in an 8-bit computer using two's complement, the maximum number which can be represented is either +127 or − 128 as *Figures 2.12* and *2.13* show:

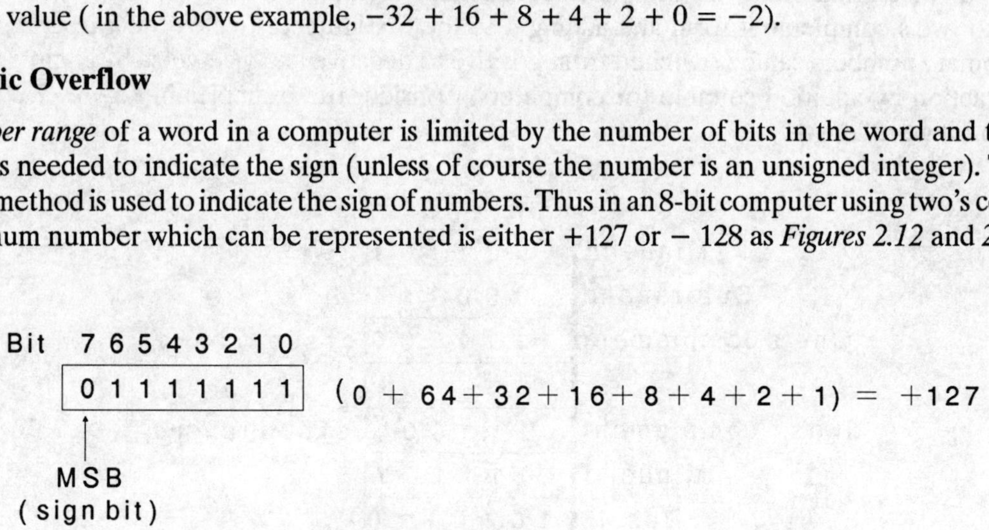

Bit   7 6 5 4 3 2 1 0

| 0 1 1 1 1 1 1 1 | $(0 + 64 + 32 + 16 + 8 + 4 + 2 + 1) = +127$

MSB
(sign bit)

Figure 2.12

Bit 7 6 5 4 3 2 1 0

$$\boxed{1\ 0\ 0\ 0\ 0\ 0\ 0\ 0}\ (-128)$$

MSB
(sign bit)

Figure 2.13

With sign and magnitude, the maximum negative value is -127.

Bit 7 6 5 4 3 2 1 0

$$\boxed{1\ 1\ 1\ 1\ 1\ 1\ 1\ 1}\ -(64+32+16+8+4+2+1)=-127$$

MSB
(sign bit – not part of
the number)

Figure 2.14

Detection of Overflow

If the result of an operation involving two numbers exceeds the maximum permitted by the word, then overflow occurs. For example, in an 8-bit word machine using integer arithmetic any result outside the range -128 to $+127$ would produce overflow.

This needs to be detected by the computer so that an incorrect result is not overlooked. The hardware in the ALU detects an overflow condition by comparing the states of the *carry in to*, and the *carry out from*, the sign bit. If they are not equal, overflow has occurred and the answer is incorrect.

Consider the two's complement examples in *Figures 2.15, 2.16* and *2.17*, assuming an 8-bit word:

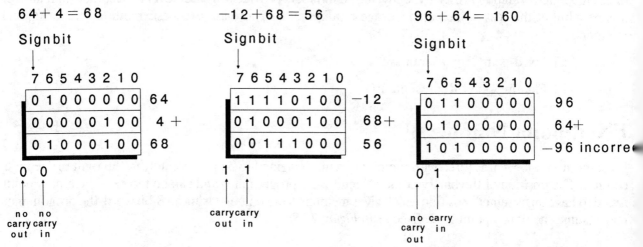

$64+4=68$

Signbit

7 6 5 4 3 2 1 0
| 0 1 0 0 0 0 0 0 | 64
| 0 0 0 0 0 1 0 0 | 4 +
| 0 1 0 0 0 1 0 0 | 68

0 0

no   no
carry carry
out   in

Figure 2.15

$-12+68=56$

Signbit

7 6 5 4 3 2 1 0
| 1 1 1 1 0 1 0 0 | -12
| 0 1 0 0 0 1 0 0 | 68 +
| 0 0 1 1 1 0 0 0 | 56

1 1

carry carry
out   in

Figure 2.16

$96+64=160$

Signbit

7 6 5 4 3 2 1 0
| 0 1 1 0 0 0 0 0 | 96
| 0 1 0 0 0 0 0 0 | 64 +
| 1 0 1 0 0 0 0 0 | -96 incorre

0 1

no   carry
carry in
out

Figure 2.17

Figures 2.15 and *2.16* do not indicate any overflow. *Figure 2.17* appears to result in a negative sum, a consequence of overflow, indicated by the carry in and carry out values.

Overflow will also occur when two negative numbers are added to produce a sum beyond the range of the word.

An overflow 'flag' (a single bit) in the condition codes or *status register* is set as soon as an overflow occurs. Thus, following the execution of an arithmetic process, a programmer can include a single test on the overflow flag to determine whether or not incorrect results are due to arithmetic overflow. Other machines may use the flag to implement an *interrupt* (which interrupts the CPU operation) to suspend processing and display an error message.

The problem of limited number range and the need for accuracy can be overcome by the use of two or more words of memory to store a single number.

Integer Numbers

Earlier in this chapter, it is pointed out that the word length of a particular machine places limits on the range of numbers which can be stored. The example of an 8-bit machine (*Figures 2.12, 2.13*) was used to illustrate a two's complement number range restricted from -127 to $+128$. Similarly, a machine which uses a 16-bit word length can only store two's complement numbers ranging from $+32767$ ($2^{16} - 1$) to -32768. These number ranges also assume that machine use is limited to whole or *integer* numbers (which have no fractional element). Although a programmer could choose to restrict numbers to integer format, machines without the facility to handle fractions are uncommon.

Real Numbers

Real numbers include all the integers and fractions of a number system, that is, all numbers above and below zero and including zero.

Many computer applications require the use of numbers with a fractional element, that is, real numbers. Such numbers are represented in binary with a binary point to separate the integer and fractional parts of the number, for example, 1101.11. Clearly, mixed numbers provide a greater level of accuracy than integer numbers but at the cost of increased storage requirements. There are two basic methods of storing real numbers:

- ☐ Fixed-point Representation
- ☐ Floating-point Representation

Fixed-point Numbers

Fixed-point numbers are stored with the binary point imagined to be immediately to the right of the units column. The position of the binary point is fixed by the programmer and can be moved. The binary point is said to have an 'assumed' position which gives meaning to a number. Using an 8-bit word, the programmer may assume the binary point to be fixed as in *Figure 2.18*:

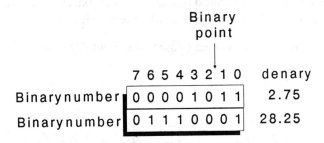

Figure 2.18

If the binary point is assumed to be as in *Figure 2.19* then the same binary groupings take on different values (shifting the point one place to the left halves the number, whilst a single shift to the right doubles it - for clarification of this, refer to the Chapter on Instructions and Memory Addressing):

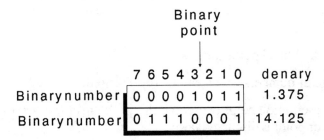

Figure 2.19

Therefore, a programmer must keep track of the point position in order to know the value of stored numbers. This problem is of concern to the programmer using low level languages.

Consider a 16-bit word with the binary point assumed to be between bits 4 and 5 and sign and magnitude format where the sign bit occupies the most significant bit position, leaving 10 bits for the *integral* part and 5 bits for the *fractional* part of the number. The *absolute* (positive or negative) number range which can be represented is limited to that given in *Figure 2.20*.

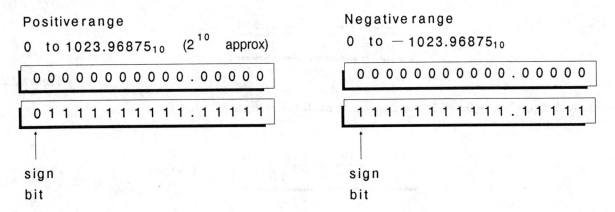

Figure 2.20

Precision is limited by the number of bits allocated to the fractional part of the number and no matter what word length is used, some loss of precision is, occasionally, inevitable.

Consider the multiplication of two denary values (*Figure 2.21*), where only 3 places are available for the fractional parts.

$$\boxed{1 \cdot 363 \quad \times \quad 1 \cdot 112} \quad \text{gives} \quad 1.515656$$

Figure 2.21

The fractional part of the product has overflowed and by rounding, the computer stores the result as $1 \cdot 516$, which is $0 \cdot 000344$ greater than the product, accurate to 6 decimal places.

Given a particular word length for fixed point numbers, the allocation of more bits to the fractional part improves precision but at the cost of reduced number range; conversely, number range can be improved at the cost of reduced precision.

However, the main drawback of fixed point form is

☐ the small range of numbers which can be represented.

Floating-point number representation helps overcome this problem at the cost of *slower computation* and *decreased accuracy*; this latter point is discussed later.

Arithmetic Underflow

This condition occurs when a number (which will be a fraction) is too small to fit into a given length word.

Floating-point Numbers

A *mantissa* and *exponent* can be used to represent a number. The number 6,800,000, for example, can be written as in *Figure 2.22*.

$$\begin{array}{cc} \text{Mantissa} & \text{Exponent} \\ \boxed{0.68 \quad \times \quad 10^7} \end{array}$$

Figure 2.22

Similarly the number, $0 \cdot 0000564$ can be written as shown in *Figure 2.23*:

$$\begin{array}{cc} \text{Mantissa} & \text{Exponent} \\ \boxed{0.564 \quad \times \quad 10^{-4}} \end{array}$$

Figure 2.23

The above decimal examples make use of what is referred to as Standard Index Form.

Binary numbers are similarly represented in *Figure 2.24*:

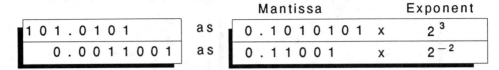

Figure 2.24

In floating-point notation, the point is not fixed by the programmer. Instead it remains in a position at the left of the mantissa, as shown in the above examples. Floating-point notation is based on the expression:

$$m \times r^e \text{ where } m \text{ is } + \text{ or } - \text{ and } e \text{ is } + \text{ or } -$$

'*m*' is the mantissa, '*r*' is the radix (base) and '*e*' is the exponent (power). In binary the radix (r) is 2.

Fixed-point numbers can be converted to floating-point numbers by a process called *normalization*. As the above examples show, if the number is greater than 1 then the point 'floats' to a position immediately before the most significant bit. This part becomes the mantissa (m). The point in *Figure 2.25* has moved 4 places and the exponent (e) is therefore, 4.

Figure 2.25

If the number is a fraction and a bit 1 does not immediately follow the point, then the point 'floats' to the right of any leading zeros, until the first non-zero bit is reached, as in *Figure 2.26*:

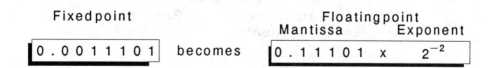

Figure 2.26

With normalized positive numbers the binary point must not be followed immediately by a zero. Conversely, normalized negative numbers require that the binary point is not followed immediately by a one. Any normalized binary mantissa must be a fraction falling within the range +0.5 to less than +1 for positive values and −1 to greater than −0.5 for negative values. The range of possible normalized mantissas, given a 4-bit allocation, is shown in *Figure 2.27*.

Positive mantissas	Denary equivalent
0 . 1 0 0	$+\frac{1}{2}$
0 . 1 0 1	$+\frac{5}{8}$
0 . 1 1 0	$+\frac{3}{4}$
0 . 1 1 1	$+\frac{7}{8}$

Negative mantissas	Denary equivalent
1 . 0 0 0	-1
1 . 0 0 1	$-\frac{7}{8}$
1 . 0 1 0	$-\frac{3}{4}$
1 . 0 1 1	$-\frac{5}{8}$

Figure 2.27

The decimal values shown assume a zero exponent.

Storage of Floating-point Numbers

Floating-point numbers are always stored in two parts:

- [ ] The *mantissa*, the length of which is determined by the precision to which numbers are represented. Clearly, if fewer bits are allocated to the mantissa (which is always a left-justified fraction) then less precision is possible.

- [ ] The *exponent*, which is usually allocated one-third to one-half of the number of bits used for the mantissa.

Figure 2.28 is based on an 8-bit machine, where two words are used to store each floating-point number in two's complement form.

Of the 16 bits available, 12 bits are used for the mantissa and 4 bits for the exponent.

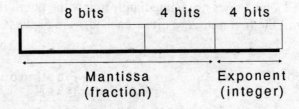

Figure 2.28

The binary point in the mantissa fraction is immediately to the right of the sign bit, which is 0 for a positive and 1 for a negative floating-point number. *Figures 2.29* and *2.30* illustrate these features.

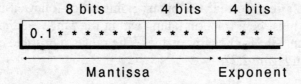

Figure 2.29

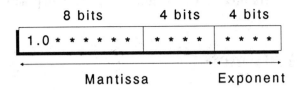

Figure 2.30

In two's complement form, the most significant digit to the right of the binary point is 1 for a positive and 0 for a negative floating-point number. It should be noticed that the sign bit and the most significant non-sign bit differ in both cases. As is explained earlier, any representation where they are the same indicates that the mantissa needs to be normalized. This may be necessary after any floating-point arithmetic operation.

Floating-point Conversion

To obtain the denary equivalent of a floating-point representation requires the mantissa to be multiplied by 2 raised to the power of e, which has the value stored in the exponent part of the number. Thus, if e has the value 5:

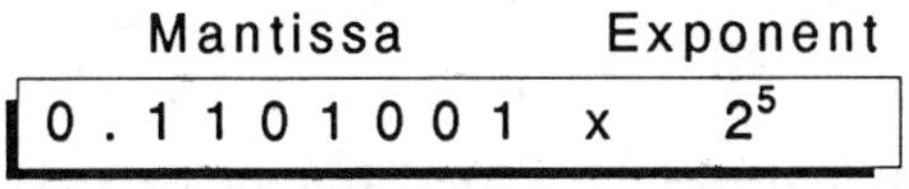

$$
\begin{array}{cc}
\text{Mantissa} & \text{Exponent} \\
0.1101001 \times & 2^5
\end{array}
$$

Figure 2.31

Converted to denary, this becomes:

$$(\tfrac{1}{2} + \tfrac{1}{4} + 0 + \tfrac{1}{16} + 0 + 0 + \tfrac{1}{128}) \times 2^5$$
$$= \tfrac{105}{128} \times 32 = 26\tfrac{1}{4}$$

Figure 2.32

or in fixed-point binary, $11010 \cdot 01$

In *Figure 2.31*, 4 bits are allocated to the exponent which allows e to have a value between $+7$ and -8 (assuming two's complement form).

Alternatively, in a 16-bit machine, two words with a total of 32 bits may be used to store each floating-point number. The mantissa may occupy 24 bits, leaving 8 bits for the exponent. In such a representation, the exponent e could have a value between $+127$ and -128 (assuming two's complement).

Alternative Floating-point Forms

Different machines use different methods for coding floating-point numbers. The mantissa may be coded in two's complement, as described previously, or it may be stored as sign and magnitude. The advantage for machine arithmetic of storing numbers in two's complement form has already been identified, but machines with the circuitry to handle floating-point numbers may also have the facility to carry out subtraction without two's complement representation. The above illustrations of floating-point numbers assume that the exponent is also stored in two's complement form. In practice, the exponent is often stored in sign and magnitude.

Floating-point Arithmetic

Addition

To add two floating-point numbers, they must both have the same value exponent. If they differ, the necessary scaling is effected by *shifting* to the right the mantissa of the number with the smaller exponent and incrementing the exponent at every shift until the exponents are equal. The shifting process follows the rules for arithmetic shifts, which are described in Chapter 3. *Figures 2.33* to *2.37*, assume a 6-bit mantissa and illustrate the floating-point addition procedure:

$$6.75 + 12.5 = 19.25$$

	Mantissa		Exponent
6.75	0 . 1 1 0 1 1	x	2^3
12.50	0 . 1 1 0 0 1	x	2^4

Figure 2.33

The mantissa with the smaller exponent is right-shifted and the exponent incremented thus:

Mantissa		Exponent			Mantissa		Exponent
0 . 1 1 0 1 1	x	2^3	becomes		0 . 0 1 1 0 1	x	2^4

Figure 2.34

As a result a bit 1 is lost from the least significant bit position.

The mantissas are added:

	Mantissa	Exponent
	0 . 0 1 1 0 1	2^4
+	0 . 1 1 0 0 1	2^4
=	1 . 0 0 1 1 0	2^4

Figure 2.35

This is clearly incorrect as the sign bit is now 1, indicating a negative value, when the result should be positive. The method by which the computer detects this type of error is explained earlier in this chapter.

The mantissa is beyond the permitted range (see previous section) for a positive number and normalization is required; the mantissa is shifted one place to the right and the exponent is incremented accordingly:

$$\text{Mantissa} \qquad \text{Exponent}$$
$$0 \,.\, 1\ 0\ 0\ 1\ 1 \quad \times \quad 2^5$$

Figure 2.36

This floating-point value represents:

$$\text{Mantissa} \qquad \text{Exponent}$$
$$0 \,.\, 1\ 0\ 0\ 1\ 1 \quad \times \quad 32$$

$$= (\tfrac{1}{2} + 0 + 0 + \tfrac{1}{16} + \tfrac{1}{32}) \times 32$$
$$= 19$$

Figure 2.37

Some loss of accuracy has resulted (19 instead of $19 \cdot 25$). The loss of accuracy results from the right-shift operation required to equalize the exponents; a significant bit is lost when the binary value for $6 \cdot 75$, $0 \cdot 11011$ became $0 \cdot 01101$. The decimal value of this discarded bit is its fractional value of $^1/_{32}$ multiplied by the exponent (before scaling) of $2^3(8)$, giving a result of $0 \cdot 25$. Although a further right-shift is needed to normalize the result, the discarded bit is a 0 and does not produce any additional inaccuracy.

Subtraction

The procedures for subtraction are the same as for addition except that the mantissas are subtracted. This can be achieved by negating the subtrahend and then adding it to the minuend. Consider the following example in *Figures 2.38* to *2.42*, assuming a 6-bit word and a two's complement mantissa and exponent.

$$12 \cdot 5 - 6 \cdot 75 = 5 \cdot 75$$

This can be expressed as $12 \cdot 5 + (-6 \cdot 75) = 5 \cdot 75$

$$\text{Mantissa} \qquad \text{Exponent}$$
$$6.75 \quad 0 \,.\, 1\ 1\ 0\ 1\ 1 \quad \times \quad 2^3$$
$$12.50 \quad 0 \,.\, 1\ 1\ 0\ 0\ 1 \quad \times \quad 2^4$$

Figure 2.38

Right-shift the mantissa with the smaller exponent and increment the exponent, repeatedly if necessary, until the exponents of the two numbers are equalized. In this case, only one right-shift is needed.

$$\text{Mantissa} \qquad \text{Exponent}$$
$$0 \,.\, 1\ 1\ 0\ 1\ 1 \quad \times \quad 2^3 \qquad \text{becomes} \qquad 0 \,.\, 0\ 1\ 1\ 0\ 1 \quad \times \quad 2^4$$

Figure 2.39

Note that the right-shift of one place has resulted in the loss of a bit 1 from the LSB position and thus some loss of accuracy.

Negate the subtrahend (*Figure 2.40*) by finding the two's complement of its mantissa and then add the mantissas (*Figure 2.41*):

6.75	0 .	0	1	1	0	1	
One's complement	1 .	1	0	0	1	0	
						1	+
Two's complement	1 .	1	0	0	1	1	

Figure 2.40

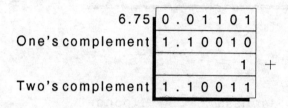

Mantissa	Exponent
0 . 1 1 0 0 1	2^4
1 . 1 0 0 1 1	2^4
1 0 . 0 1 1 0 0	2^4

↑
ignore
carry

Figure 2.41

If necessary, normalize the result. In this case, the answer is not in normal form because the sign bit and the most significant bit to the right of the binary point are the same (this is explained with *Figures 2.29* and *2.30*). The result can be normalized by carrying out a left-shift of one on the mantissa and decrementing the exponent accordingly, to produce:

Mantissa	Exponent
0 . 1 1 0 0 0 x	2^3

$$= (\tfrac{1}{2} + \tfrac{1}{4}) \times 8$$
$$= 6$$

Figure 2.42

Note that a zero is inserted into the least significant bit position. The floating point process has resulted in some significant loss of accuracy (6 as opposed to 5·75).

Fixed Point versus Floating Point Representation

Accuracy. As stated earlier, given a particular word length, fixed point representation allows greater accuracy than is possible with floating point form. Consider, for example, a word length of six bits used to store wholly fractional numbers. In fixed point form, all the bit positions can be used by significant digits, but in floating point form, if two bits are reserved for the exponent, this leaves only four bits for the mantissa and thus a maximum of four figure accuracy.

Range. As is demonstrated in the previous section, a major advantage of floating point form is the facility for storing an increased number range.

Maintenance of Floating Point Arithmetic Precision

Floating-point arithmetic precision can be improved by:

☐ increasing the number of bits allocated to the mantissa;

☐ rounding;

☐ double precision numbers and arithmetic.

Mantissa Length

Increasing the number of bits allocated to the *mantissa* will improve precision but inaccuracies can never be completely eliminated. In practice, memory words are much longer than those used for illustration here and where memory words are of insufficient length to ensure acceptable accuracy, two adjacent locations may be used. Machines which make use of this method are providing what is referred to as *double-precision floating-point* facilities.

Rounding

The subtraction example in *Figures 2.38* to *2.42* demonstrates a loss of accuracy through *truncation*; a significant bit is lost when the mantissa is shifted one place to the right, in order to equalize the exponents of the minuend and the subtrahend. If a computer process requires a series of calculations, each using the results of previous ones, repeated truncation may accrue considerable inaccuracy and this will be reflected in the final result. As can be seen from the example of floating-point addition in *Figures 2.33* to *2.37*, the process of normalizing the result also requires the shifting or justification of the mantissa. Consider the example in *Figure 2.43*, which only shows the mantissas to illustrate the normalization process:

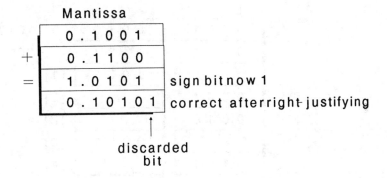

Figure 2.43

Normalization has resulted in the loss of a bit 1 from the least significant bit position and consequent loss of accuracy. Rounding dictates that if the last bit to be discarded (the most significant of those which are lost) during an arithmetic shift is a 1, then 1 is added to the least significant retained bit. Consider an 8-bit mantissa rounded as in *Figure 2.44*.

1 0 1 0 1 1 0 1	rounded to 7 bits becomes	1 0 1 0 1 1 1
1 0 1 0 1 1 0 1	rounded to 6 bits becomes	1 0 1 0 1 1
1 0 1 0 1 1 0 1	rounded to 5 bits becomes	1 0 1 1 0
1 0 1 0 1 1 0 1	rounded to 4 bits becomes	1 0 1 1

Figure 2.44

The accumulated errors caused by repeated truncation of values during a lengthy arithmetic process can partially, though not entirely, be avoided by rounding. In practice, rounding can sometimes result in greater inaccuracies than would result without rounding. Many rounding algorithms exist to try to overcome this problem and the type of inaccuracy which occasionally occurs will depend on the rounding algorithm used.

Double Precision Numbers

As the term (also known as *double length numbers*) suggests, where a single memory word is of insufficient length to accommodate a number, two contiguous words are used. Double precision numbers may be used to increase accuracy or when the product of a multiplication operation will not fit into a single location.

Double Precision Arithmetic. The pseudocode algorithm in *Listing 2.1* and example addition in *Figure 2.45* provides a basic idea of double precision arithmetic; in the example, each number occupies two contiguous 4-bit nibbles, with the following format:

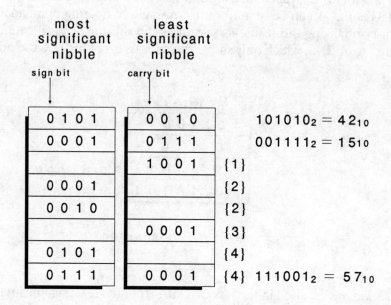

Figure 2.45

```
algorithm double precision
add least significant halves of numbers   {1}
if carry = 1 then
 add 1 to most significant half {2}
 set carry bit to 0   {3}
endif
add most significant halves of numbers {4}
end
```

Listing 2.1

Floating-point Multiplication and Division

To multiply two floating-point numbers, the mantissas are multiplied and their exponents are added.

For the sake of simplicity, the multiplication process is best illustrated using denary numbers, but the principles are the same for binary floating point numbers. Consider *Figures 2.46* to *2.48*.

$$300_{10} \quad \times \quad 2000_{10}$$

Mantissa	Exponent		Mantissa	Exponent
$(0.3 \quad \times \quad 10^3)$		$\times$	$(0.2 \quad \times \quad 10^4)$	

Figure 2.46

multiply mantissas and add exponents to give

Mantissa	Exponent
$(0.06 \quad \times \quad 10^7)$	

Figure 2.47

normalize the result (the exponent is *decremented* each time the point is moved one position to the right).

Mantissa	Exponent
$(0.6 \quad \times \quad 10^6)$	

Figure 2.48

Figures 2.49 to *2.51* provide a second example.

$$23.7_{10} \quad \text{x} \quad 415_{10}$$

Mantissa	Exponent		Mantissa	Exponent
$(0.237 \quad \text{x}$	$10^2)$	x	$(0.415 \quad \text{x}$	$10^3)$

Figure 2.49

multiply mantissas and add exponents to give

Mantissa	Exponent
$(0.098355 \quad \text{x}$	$10^5)$

Figure 2.50

normalize the result (the exponent is *decremented* each time the point is moved one position to the *right*).

Mantissa	Exponent
$(0.98355 \quad \text{x}$	$10^4)$

Figure 2.51

Floating-point division is carried out by dividing the mantissas and subtracting their exponents.

Hardware and Software Control of Computer Arithmetic

The execution of computer arithmetic operations often involves a mixture of hardware and software control. Increasingly, to improve processing efficiency, many computers are equipped with additional circuitry to handle floating-point numbers directly.

Excess Codes

An excess code involves the addition of an excess to the value to be represented. Thus, for example, an 8-bit excess 128 code would produce the value representations for +26 and −42 in *Figure 2.52*.

+26	`0 0 0 1 1 0 1 0`
Excess +128	`1 0 0 0 0 0 0 0`
Code for +26	`1 0 0 1 1 0 1 0` = 154

−42	`1 1 0 1 0 1 1 0`
Excess +128	`1 0 0 0 0 0 0 0`
Code for −42	`0 1 0 1 0 1 1 0` = 86

Figure 2.52

The sum of the two numbers in the same code is given in *Figure 2.53*.

154	1 0 0 1 1 0 1 0	+ 26
86	0 1 0 1 0 1 1 0	− 42
	1 1 1 1 0 0 0 0	
Subtract 128	1 0 0 0 0 0 0 0	because 128 included twice in this sum
= 112	0 1 1 1 0 0 0 0	− 16 in excess128

Figure 2.53

An 8-bit unsigned number can represent values between 0 and 255, but with the excess 128 code values from −128 to +127 can be stored. Excess codes are used for:

- ☐ storage of exponents in floating point numbers;

- ☐ the representation of decimal numbers.

A 4-bit excess 3 code is sometimes used for the storage of BCD numbers. The digits 0 to 9 are represented with the excess values of 3 to 12. Thus, for example, the BCD number 537 in excess 3 code is

BCD + 537	0 1 0 1	0 0 1 1	0 1 1 1
Excess + 333	0 0 1 1	0 0 1 1	0 0 1 1
BCD 537 in excess 3	1 0 0 0	0 1 1 0	1 0 1 0

Figure 2.54

Although the excess 3 code provides some benefits (not of concern here) in the process of BCD arithmetic, the more usual BCD format, illustrated in *Figures 2.4* and *2.5*, is generally used.

3 *Instructions and Memory Addressing*

This chapter deals with activity of the Central Processing Unit (CPU) and the ways in which computer program instructions are stored, decoded and executed in order that the computer can perform its tasks.

In Chapter 2 it is stated that data can take various forms when stored as a memory word, namely:

- pure binary;
- coded binary, for example, binary-coded decimal (BCD);
- character codes, for example, ASCII.

All the above are considered to be data and can be interpreted as such by the CPU, but in order to perform any tasks, it has to have access to computer instructions. During processing, data currently being processed and the instructions needed to process the data are stored in main memory.

Thus a memory word can also form an instruction, in which case, it is referred to as an *instruction word*; one formed of data is known as a *data word*.

The Central Processing Unit (CPU)

The CPU has a number of registers which it can use to temporarily store a number of words read from memory. These registers are used to apply meaning to memory words. It should be noted that memory words cannot be determined as being data or instructions simply by examination of the code. The CPU differentiates between data and instructions by locating:

- instructions in an *instruction register*;
- data in *data registers*.

A computer program stored in main memory comprises a sequence of instructions, each of which is transferred, in turn, into the CPU's instruction register, thus identifying the next operation the CPU is to perform. The instructions are retrieved from consecutive memory locations, unless the last instruction executed requires the next instruction to be fetched from a different location. Instructions dealing with the latter circumstance are called *branch* or *jump* instructions. The various types of instruction are described later. The process of fetching, interpreting and executing instructions is called the *fetch-execute cycle* but may also be referred to as the *instruction cycle* or *automatic sequence control*.

As indicated in Chapter 5, the control unit has the function of governing all hardware operations, including the activities of the CPU itself. To understand the fetch-execute cycle it is necessary to be aware of the names and functions of the various CPU registers used.

The Program Counter (PC)

The PC keeps track of the locations where instructions are stored. At any one time during a program's execution the PC holds the memory address of the next instruction to be executed. Its operation is possible because, in all computer systems, the instructions forming a program are stored in adjacent memory locations, so that the next instruction will normally (except when a branch instruction is executed) be stored in an address a single increment more than the address of the last instruction to be fetched. By incrementing the address in the PC each time an instruction is received, the PC always has the address of the next instruction to be retrieved.

The program counter is also known by a variety of other names, including the Sequence Control Register (SCR) and the Instruction Address Register (IAR).

Memory Buffer Register (MBR)

Whenever the contents of a memory word are to be transferred into or out of main memory, they pass through the MBR. This applies to both data and instructions.

Memory Address Register (MAR)

The MAR provides the location address of the specific memory word (both instructions and data) to be read from or written to memory via the MBR.

Current Instruction Register (CIR)

As the name suggests, the function of the CIR is to store the current instruction for decoding and execution.

Accumulators and General-purpose Registers

These registers are situated within the arithmetic/logic unit (ALU) and provide a working area for data fetched from memory. Values about to be added or subtracted can be copied, via the MBR, into the accumulators. The arithmetic result can be placed in one accumulator and copied from there into a main memory location.

All communications between the CPU and the memory take place via the MAR and the MBR, as *Figure 3.1* illustrates.

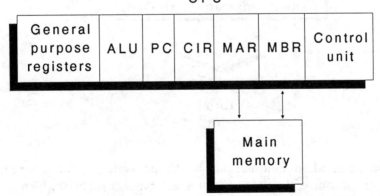

Figure 3.1

In order to fetch an instruction from memory the CPU places the address of the instruction in the MAR and then carries out a memory read; the instruction is then copied into the MBR and from there, into the CIR. Similarly, an instruction which itself requires the reading of a particular data word causes the address of the data word to be placed into the MAR. The execution of the memory read then results in the copying of the addressed data word into the MBR, from where it can be accessed by the processor. The MBR acts as the point of transfer for both data and instructions passing, in either direction, between the main memory and the CPU.

Fetch-execute Cycle

The instruction fetch-execute cycle can be described as follows:

Fetch phase - common to all instructions.

☐ the contents of the PC are copied into the MAR. The MAR now contains the location address of the next instruction and a memory read is initiated to copy the instruction word from memory into the MBR.

☐ the PC is incremented and now contains the address of the next instruction.

☐ the instruction word is then copied from the MBR into the CIR.

Execute phase - the action taken is unique to the instruction.

☐ the instruction in the CIR is decoded

☐ the instruction in the CIR is executed.

☐ unless the instruction is a STOP instruction, then the cycle is repeated.

The cycle can be illustrated with a flowchart, as shown in *Figure 3.2*.

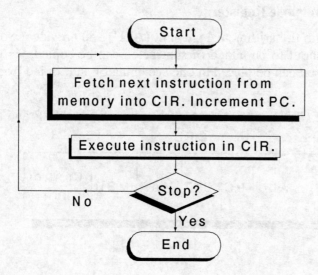

Figure 3.2

The fetch-execute cycle is carried out automatically by the hardware and the programmer cannot control its sequence of operation. Of course, the programmer does have control over which instructions are stored in memory and the order in which they are executed.

Types of Instruction

All the instructions available on a particular machine are known collectively as the *instruction set* of that machine. There are certain types of instruction commonly available in most computer systems. They can be classified according to their function as follow:

- [ ] arithmetic and logical operations on data;

- [ ] input and output of data;

- [ ] changing the sequence of program execution (branch instructions);

- [ ] transfer of data between memory and the CPU registers;

- [ ] transfer of data between registers within the CPU.

Examples of these instructions and their effects are given in Chapter 28 on Assembly Language Programming.

Instruction Format

An instruction usually consists of two main components, the function or *operation code* (opcode) and the *operand*. The opcode part of the instruction defines the operation to be performed, for example to add or to move data and the operand defines the location address in memory of the data to be operated upon. The storage of an instruction is illustrated in *Figure 3.3* using a 16-bit memory word:

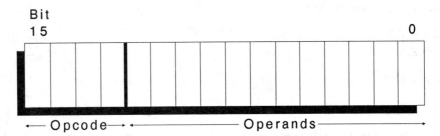

Figure 3.3

Thus, the most significant 4 bits determine the type of instruction and the remaining 12 bits specify the operand or operands to be used.

Three-address Instruction

If an expression requiring the use of three memory variables is to be accommodated by one instruction, then the instruction word will need to contain the address of each variable, that is three operands. An addition instruction can be expressed symbolically as,

> **ADD Z,X,Y**

that is, add the contents of X to the contents of Y and store the result in Z.

The instruction word needs to be large enough to accommodate the three addresses and can be illustrated as follows in *Figure 3.4*.

OPCODE	ADDRESS	ADDRESS	ADDRESS

Figure 3.4

Because of the large number of bits required this format is not often used.

Two-address Instruction

With this format, only two addresses are available in the instruction, so it is implicit that the result is to be stored in one of the operands (X or Y). This means that one of the original numbers is overwritten by the result.

If only one instruction is used, then adding the contents of X and Y and placing the result in X is expressed symbolically as,

ADD X,Y

and the instruction word format is illustrated in *Figure 3.5*.

Figure 3.5

In order to place the result in Z (as in the first expression) and to preserve the original contents of X, a preceding instruction could be used to copy the contents of X to Z. Assuming that a MOVE instruction has this effect, then the two expressions

MOVE Z,X
ADD Z,Y

will effect the addition.

One-Address Instruction

It should be obvious that this format only allows an opcode to refer to one operand and that two assumptions regarding storage are implicit. Firstly, as with the two-address format, it must be assumed that the result is to be stored in Z. Secondly, if only one operand can be referred to, the addition process must use another storage area for the second operand. Generally, a CPU general-purpose register, called the *accumulator*, is used. The single-address instruction is used where there is only a single accumulator, so the instruction does not need to refer to the accumulator. The instruction word format is illustrated in *Figure 3.6*.

Figure 3.6

The processes needed to achieve the required result may be:

1. Copy the contents of one operand, X, into the accumulator. This operation uses a LOAD (accumulator) instruction.

2. ADD the contents of operand Y, placing the result in the accumulator. At the time of the addition, the contents of operand Y are in the MBR, having been read from memory as part of the instruction. An ADD instruction usually has this effect.

3. Copy the result from the accumulator into address Z using a STORE command.

The assembly language coding for the above process may be as follows:

Instruction	Effect
LDA X	copies the content of X, via the MBR, into the accumulator;
ADD Y	reads the content of Y into the MBR, adds it to the accumulator and leaves the result in the accumulator;
STA Z	copies the result from the accumulator into memory address Z, via the MBR.

One-and-a-half-Address Instruction

Where there is more than one accumulator, an instruction using the accumulator must indicate which one is to be used. Since the number of accumulators is generally small, the number of bits needed to refer to a single accumulator is usually less than the number needed for a memory location address. The processes for carrying out the example sum are the same as for the one-address format, except that a specified accumulator is used. The instruction word format is illustrated in *Figure 3.7*

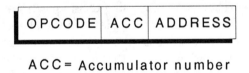

ACC = Accumulator number

Figure 3.7

Zero-Address Instruction

This type of instruction is particularly popular with small machines because of its economy in size. Many microcomputer systems operate with a combination of one-address and zero-address instructions. A zero-address instruction does not specify any operands within it and relies on the use of a memory-based data structure called a *stack*, to provide the operands.

A stack consists of a group of adjacent memory locations, the contents of which are addressed by a stack pointer, a register that contains the address of the current top of stack. Values can only be added (*pushed*) to or removed (*popped*) from the top of the stack, which is indicated by the current position of the *stack pointer*. The value of the stack pointer is incremented or decremented when an item is pushed or popped. A value located below the top item on the stack (as indicated by the stack pointer) cannot be removed until any values above it have been removed.

Consider, for example, an ADD instruction which requires the addition of two operands, X and Y. The operands X and then Y are pushed onto the stack; Y is thus at the top of the stack and is the first one which can be removed. The ADD instruction causes the popping of Y and X from the stack; they are added and the sum is pushed onto the top of the stack.

Although this instruction format is extremely short, additional instructions are needed in order to transfer operands from memory to the stack and from the stack to memory; obviously these instructions need to be longer in order to allow specification of memory addresses. They are similar to single instruction words, except that operands are copied to and from the stack rather than to and from the accumulator.

Instruction Format and Memory Size

Given a particular *word length* (the number of bit positions in a memory word), single-address instructions can directly address (specify the actual memory address) a larger number of memory locations than one-and-a-half or multiple-address formats because all the address bits can be used for one address. Many computers allow a *variable length* instruction word so that the number of bits available for the address portion of the instruction can be increased, to allow a larger number of memory locations to be directly addressed. If, for example, there are 16 bits for the address, then the highest location which can be directly addressed is:

$$2^{16} - 1 = 65,535$$

Therefore, 65,536 locations can be addressed, numbered 0 to 65,535 (computer memory sizes are quoted in nK, K being 1024 and 'n' being a variable) and this example illustrates a 64K memory, that is, 64 × 1024 which equals 65,536.

By increasing the number of bits available for the address to, say 20, the number of locations which can be addressed is over a million, although in practice, not all memory words need to be addressed directly. For example, to enable the direct addressing of all locations in a 256K (256 × 1024 = 262,144) memory requires the use of 18 bits (2^{18} = 262,144). There are addressing techniques to reduce the number of bits needed for a memory address and some of these are described later in the chapter. An increase in word size also allows an increase in the number of bits available for the opcode and the possibility of an increase in the size of the instruction set. It has to be said, however, that a recent development in computer architecture, namely that of the RISC (Reduced Instruction Set Computer) processor, is making this latter benefit somewhat less relevant.

A Typical Instruction Set

The range of instructions available for any particular machine depends on the machine's architecture, in terms of word length and the number and types of registers used. For this reason it is only possible to list some typical types of instruction (the names LOAD etc are not actual mnemonic opcodes) some of which were used in the earlier example:

Load - copies the contents of a specified location into a register.

Add - adds the contents of a specified memory location to the contents of a register.

Subtract - subtracts the contents of a specified memory location from the contents of a register.

Store - copies the contents of a register into a specified memory location.

Branch - switches control to another instruction address other than the next in sequence.

Register-register - moves contents from one register to another.

Shift - moves bits in a memory location to the left or to the right for arithmetic purposes or for pattern manipulation.

Input/output - effects data transfers between peripherals and memory.

Logical operations (AND, OR, NOT, NAND and so on) which combine the contents of a register and a specified memory location or register. These operations are described in Chapter 4 on Computer Logic. The first four instruction types in this list have already been explained in the earlier addition example, so the following sections deal with those remaining.

Branch Instructions

These instructions cause the program to divert from the normal sequence dictated by contiguous memory locations containing program instructions. A branch instruction causes the value of the Program Counter (PC) to be altered, to direct the next instruction to be fetched from a location which is not physically adjacent to the current instruction. A branch may be *conditional* (dependent on some condition) or *unconditional*. In the latter case, the branch is always made, whereas in the former, the branch only occurs if a specified condition occurs. The conditions tested usually include tests on CPU register contents for zero, non-zero, negative and positive number values. The branch or jump may be to a specified address or simply to 'skip' the next instruction (or several instructions). In either case the program counter must be altered accordingly to change its contents to the address specified by the branch instruction. Branching can be used to repeat a sequence of instructions in a loop. Usually this is conditional to avoid an infinite program iteration.

Program Control

A branch instruction to jump or skip to a specified instruction address does not necessarily involve a return to the original sequence once the branch has been made. To provide for such a return requires a special form of branching. There are circumstances when a group of instructions referred to as a *subprogram* needs to be executed more than once during a program's execution. It may be necessary, for example, to carry out a particular sequence of calculations at different points in a program. Instead of coding the instructions at each point where they are required, the coding can be written as a subprogram.

Whenever a subprogram is used or called, there must be a mechanism for returning control to the original program sequence. One method is to save the current contents of the PC in the first location of the subprogram before the branch to it is made. Upon completion the contents of the first location can be loaded into the PC and control returned to the calling program. The process of branching and then returning to continue the instruction sequence is illustrated in *Figure 3.8*.

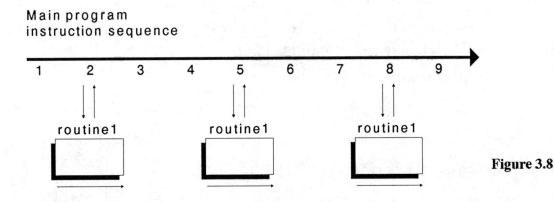

Figure 3.8

Alternatively, the return address may be placed on a stack (a memory facility described earlier in this chapter) and copied back into the PC to allow a resumption of the normal program sequence. The stack is particularly useful where subprograms are 'nested', which means that a call may be made from within another subprogram. The return addresses are placed onto the stack and removed in reverse order so that the last return address is the first to be removed. The technique is described in detail in Chapter 26 on Data Structures. Subprograms called in this way are referred to as *closed*, but where one is inserted, as and when required, as part of the main program, it is referred to as *open*.

Register-Register Instructions

As the name suggests, instructions of this type are used to transfer the contents of one register to another. Its format is similar to that of the two-address instruction and is illustrated in *Figure 3.9*.

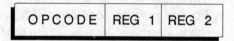

| OPCODE | REG 1 | REG 2 |

Figure 3.9

Although operands to address memory are not used, the instruction allows two operands to address the registers involved. The number of registers available will tend to be small, perhaps two or three, so that a single byte may be sufficient to contain the two operands. In an 8-bit machine, such instructions may be two bytes long, one for the opcode and one for the two register addresses. Data transfers between registers within the CPU are carried out via the processor *bus* system which is a subdivision of the computer system's architecture (Chapter 5).

Shift Instructions

A shift operation moves the bits in a register to new positions in the register, can be either to the left or to the right and may be logical or arithmetic. Consider *Figure 3.10* which illustrates the concept of logical shifting.

```
                    Bit   5 4 3 2 1 0
    Initial register contents  0 0 1 1 0 1
  Shift contents LEFT 1 place  0 1 1 0 1 0   0 lost from MSB
                                             0 moved into LSB
```

```
                    Bit   5 4 3 2 1 0
    Initial register contents  0 0 1 1 0 1
  Shift contents RIGHT 1 place 0 0 0 1 1 0   1 lost from LSB
                                             0 moved into MSB
```

Figure 3.10

The instruction format is shown in *Figure 3.11*.

Figure 3.11

The opcode indicates the type of shift, which may be one of the following:

Logical Shifts

Logical shifts are used for pattern manipulation of data and are not concerned with arithmetic operations. Thus the above examples illustrate logical shifts. Another type of logical shift involves rotation of bits in a register or location and is called a rotational or cyclic shift.

Rotational Shifts

A rotational shift can be either to the left or to the right, as the examples in *Figures 3.12* and *3.13* illustrate:

A RIGHT rotational shift of 1

Figure 3.12

The 1 in the LSB position is moved to the MSB position as each bit moves one place to the right.

A LEFT rotational shift of 1

Figure 3.13

The 1 in the MSB position is moved to the LSB position as each bit moves one place to the left.

Arithmetic Shifts

Left and right shift operations are used for multiply and divide operations but arithmetic meaning must be maintained. A left shift of one doubles the number and a right shift of one halves the number. Computer multiplication can be carried out through a sequence of additions and shifts, and division by a sequence of subtractions and shifts. Some examples of arithmetic shifts using twos complement notation are provided in *Figures 3.14* and *3.15*.

A left shift of 1 (zeros are inserted into the LSB position)

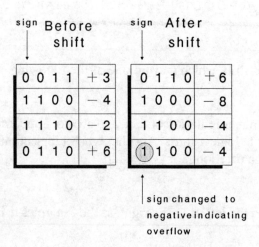

Figure 3.14

Note that in the last example above the sign has been changed from positive to negative by the left shift operation. In these circumstances an overflow signal would be set.

A right shift of 1 (where necessary, a 1 is shifted into the sign bit to preserve the sign)

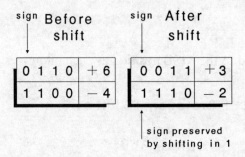

Figure 3.15

Input/Output Instructions

Input/output (I/O) instructions are concerned with the transfer of data between peripherals and memory or between peripherals and registers in the CPU. Chapter 7 on Input/Output Control deals with this topic.

Memory Addressing Methods

The physical memory addresses ultimately used by the hardware are the *absolute* addresses. As explained earlier, addressing memory locations *directly* restricts the size of useable memory and for this reason a computer's instruction set will normally include facilities for addressing locations beyond those directly addressable with a given address length. Thus, absolute addresses may be referenced in a variety of ways and the addressing mode used is indicated in the operand of an instruction word (*Figure 3.16*).

| OPCODE | ADDRESSING MODE | ADDRESS |

Figure 3.16

The following addressing modes are common to most machines:

Immediate Addressing

With this method, the operand to be accessed by the instruction is stored in the instruction word or in the word immediately following it in memory. In the former case, the operand would be fetched with the instruction and no separate memory read would then be necessary. In the latter case, an ADD instruction which employed this method of addressing would indicate that the operand is to be found immediately after the opcode in memory. In a byte organized machine, the first byte would contain the opcode, the execution of which would involve the fetching of the next byte in memory which contained the required operand. Computers based on the Intel 8080 or Motorola 6800 processor use this latter method for immediate addressing. The Intel 8080 provides the opcode ADI (add immediate) as part of its instruction set. Immediate addressing is useful when small constants or literals are required in a program, for example, a set value of 3 to be subtracted from the contents of a register at some stage in the program. It is inappropriate to use this method if there is any need for the value to be changed as this would require changing the program coding.

Direct Addressing

As the name suggests, this addressing mode specifies the actual or effective memory address containing the required operand, in the address field of the instruction word. The addressed memory location specified must be accessed to obtain the operand.

Indirect Addressing

With this method, the location address in the instruction word does not contain the operand. Instead, it contains the address of another location which itself contains the address of the data item. Thus, an indirect address is, in effect, a pointer to the address containing the operand. For example, IAD 156 (indirect add) indicates that the address 156 contains the address of the required operand. If specific indirect addressing instructions are not provided, an instruction word may contain a 'flag' bit to indicate whether or not an operand is an indirect or direct address; the flag bit may be set to 1 if the address is indirect and to 0 if it is direct. In this way, an LDA (load accumulator) instruction is able to refer to a direct or indirect address by the appropriate setting of the flag bit. *Figure 3.17* illustrates the principle of indirect addressing.

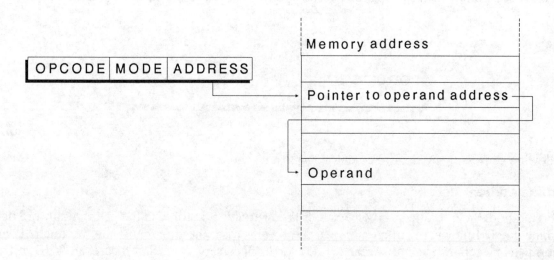

Figure 3.17

Indirect addressing is generally slower in execution than direct addressing as an extra *memory cycle* is needed each time the actual address is deferred. Indirect addressing is also known as *deferred* addressing and if the address is deferred more than once it is known as a *multi-level* address.

Relative Addressing

With relative addressing, the instruction word contains an *offset* address which indicates the location of the operand relative to the position of the instruction in memory (sometimes known as self-relative addressing). Thus, if an instruction is stored in address N and the offset is 5, then the operand is in address N + 5. It is a useful technique for branching a program, in which case the offset address will indicate the relative address of the next instruction to be fetched, rather than a data item. The program counter (PC), together with the offset, is used to calculate the effective address, taking into account the fact that the PC contains the address of the next instruction. The instruction set usually contains instructions which allow such program jumps to be made. Absolute addresses may also be determined as being relative to a *base* address and as is explained in the chapter on Operating Systems, by alteration of this base address, programs can be *relocated* rather than be tied to particular absolute addresses each time they are loaded. Multi-programming techniques demand that programs are relocatable.

Indexed Addressing

With this method, the effective address is calculated by the addition of an index value to the address given in the instruction. The index value is usually stored in either a general-purpose CPU register or a special index register.

The method can be employed by a programmer when an ordered block of data is to be accessed and each data item is to be processed in the same way. If the value of the index is N and the address in the instruction is X, then the effective address for an operand is N + X. The register is set to an initial value and incremented as the instructions step through the memory locations. A branch instruction is used to create a program loop to repeat the same set of instructions needed for each item of data in the block.

4

Computer Logic

In Chapter 2 it was explained that data and instructions in a digital computer are represented by the binary numbering system. Internal registers and locations within the memory of the computer must be able to 'remember' data and instructions as sequences of binary digits. The ALU (Arithmetic and Logic Unit) must be able to perform arithmetic on numbers held in this form, and the decoding circuitry of the Control Unit must be able to recognise and interpret program instructions represented by binary numbers. All of these functions, and many more, are performed by logic circuits.

Computer logic is based on a branch of mathematical logic called *Boolean Algebra* (named after the English mathematician George Boole) which allows the symbolic manipulation of logical variables in a manner very similar to the manipulation of 'unknowns' in an ordinary algebraic expression of the form

$$x.(y+z) \text{ or } x.y + x.z$$

Just as laws are needed for ordinary algebraic expressions, fundamental laws exist for the manipulation of Boolean expressions. By means of these laws, complex logical expressions, representing logic circuits, can be analysed or designed.

This chapter introduces the foundations of Boolean Algebra, its relevance to computer circuitry, and the processes by which such circuitry may be designed and analysed. The chapter concludes with a brief discussion of the evolution of integrated circuits.

Boolean Variables

A Boolean variable has one of two values, normally represented by 1 and 0. In terms of computer circuitry, a Boolean variable represents a voltage on a line which may be an input to a logic circuit or an output from a logic circuit. For instance, a value of 1 might represent five volts and a value of 0, zero volts. Boolean variables are denoted by letters of the alphabet. Thus the variables X, Y, Z, P, Q, R are each able to represent a value of 1 or 0.

Gates

The term *gate* is used to describe the members of a set of basic electronic components which, when combined with each other, are able to perform complex logical and arithmetic operations. These are the types of operations associated with the ALU of the CPU. For present purposes, the physical construction of the gates is of no direct concern, and the discussion will be restricted to their functions only.

The *OR* Gate

Gates have one or more inputs but only a single output. The nature of the gate determines what the output should be given the current inputs. For example, the OR gate could be defined as follows:

X	Y	X OR Y
0	0	0
0	1	1
1	0	1
1	1	1

The output is 1 if the X input OR the Y input is 1

X and Y are Boolean variables capable at any time of having the value 1 or 0. Thus at any instant X could have a value of 0 and Y a value of 1, or X could have a value of 1 and Y could have a value of 1; there are four such combinations of the values of X and Y as shown in the table above. With an OR gate, when there is at least one 1 in the input variables, the output is 1. The third column of the table shows the output produced by each combination of the two inputs. The complete table is known as a *truth table* and completely defines the operation of the OR gate for every combination of inputs. As will be shown throughout this chapter, truth tables are extremely useful for describing logic circuits.

Symbolically, the combination of X and Y using an OR gate is written

$$X \ OR \ Y \quad or \quad X + Y \quad (read \ as \ `X \ or \ Y')$$

Both forms mean that X and Y are inputs to an OR gate. The second form is that required for Boolean Algebra and the ' + ' is known as the OR operator.

The symbol used when drawing an OR gate in a logic circuit is shown in *Figure 4.1*.

Figure 4.1

Gates are the physical realisations of simple Boolean expressions. The design of logic circuits is performed symbolically using Boolean Algebra. A Boolean algebraic expression can then be converted very easily into a logic circuit consisting of combinations of gates.

The OR gate is only one of several which are used to produce logic circuits. The other gates of interest are AND, NOT, XOR, NAND and NOR. The first two, in conjunction with the OR gate, are of the greatest importance since these three are directly related to the Boolean operators used in Boolean Algebra.

The *AND* Gate

The AND gate is defined by the following truth table:

X	Y	X AND Y
0	0	0
0	1	0
1	0	0
1	1	1

The output is 1 when the
X input AND the Y input are 1s

This time, the gate only produces an output of 1 when both inputs are 1s. The Boolean operator equivalent to the AND gate is the AND operator '.', and is written

X.Y (read as 'X and Y')

The symbol for the AND gate is shown in *Figure 4.2.*

Figure 4.2

The *NOT* Gate

The third important gate is the NOT gate which has the truth table

X	NOT X
0	1
1	0

This gate only has a single input which is inverted at the output. A NOT gate is often called an "inverter" for this reason.

The symbol for a NOT gate is shown in *Figure 4.3.*

Figure 4.3

and it is written $\overline{X}$ or $\sim X$ in Boolean expressions.

Example of a Useful Logic Circuit

At this point it is worth considering an example of a widely used logic circuit to illustrate the relevance of this chapter. The circuit, which is called a *half adder*, performs the addition of two binary digits to give a sum term, S and a carry term, C, both being Boolean variables. The inputs to the circuit are X and Y representing the two binary digits to be added. The rules for binary addition are

$$0 + 0 = 0 \text{ carry } 0 \quad (00)$$
$$0 + 1 = 1 \text{ carry } 0 \quad (01)$$
$$1 + 0 = 1 \text{ carry } 0 \quad (01)$$
$$1 + 1 = 0 \text{ carry } 1 \quad (10)$$

The equivalent truth table is

X	Y	S	C
0	0	0	0
0	1	1	0
1	0	1	0
1	1	0	1

The requirement is for a combination of AND/OR/NOT gates to give two separate outputs for (S)um and (C)arry given any two binary digits represented by X and Y. The circuit is shown in *Figure 4.4*.

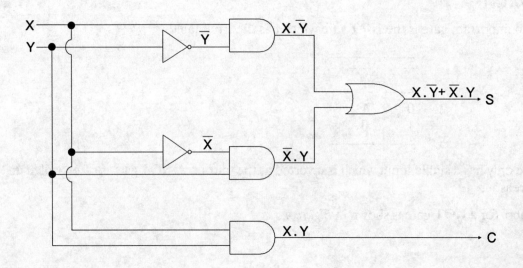

Figure 4.4

and the equivalent Boolean expressions for S and C are

$$S = X.\overline{Y} + \overline{X}.Y$$
$$C = X.Y$$

To prove that the circuit actually works a truth table is constructed showing the output from every component in the circuit from stage to stage, given the inputs to that stage:

X	Y	$\overline{X}$	$\overline{Y}$	$X.\overline{Y}$	$\overline{X}.Y$	$X.\overline{Y}+\overline{X}.Y$ (S)	X.Y (C)
0	0	1	1	0	0	0	0
0	1	1	0	0	1	1	0
1	0	0	1	1	0	1	0
1	1	0	0	0	0	0	1

Thus if X=0 and Y=0, $\overline{Y}$=1 and using the truth table for the AND gate, $X.\overline{Y}$ = 0.1 = 0 and $\overline{X}.Y$ = 1.0 = 0. The rightmost OR gate in the diagram has inputs $X.\overline{Y}$ and $\overline{X}.Y$, that is, 0 and 0 , and using the truth table for the OR gate, it can be seen that this results in an output of 0 for S. Similarly, if X=0 and Y=0, the truth table for the AND gate shows that X.Y=0, that is C=0 for this combination of inputs.

Following this type of argument for the remaining rows in the truth table, it can be seen that the circuit produces exactly the right output for each combination of inputs to perform binary addition on the input bits. Thus a combination of a few elementary components has produced a most important circuit. A truth table allowed the operation of the circuit to be confirmed. Later it will be shown how the Boolean expressions representing the circuit can be derived directly from the first truth table defining the required operation of the circuit.

The Derivation of Boolean Expressions from Truth Tables

Suppose that it is required to produce a suitable logic circuit from the following circuit specification:

> A circuit has two binary inputs, X and Y. The output from the circuit is 1 when the two inputs are the same; otherwise the output is 0.

The first step is to produce a truth table to define the circuit fully:

X	Y	OUTPUT
0	0	1
0	1	0
1	0	0
1	1	1

Each possible combination of X and Y has been listed. Where X and Y are the same, OUTPUT has been assigned a value of 1; where X and Y are different, OUTPUT has been assigned a value of 0.

The next step is to define, for each entry in the OUTPUT column having a value of 1, a Boolean expression involving X and Y which uniquely defines that value. So for the first row in the table, where X=0 and Y=0, the expression $\overline{X}.\overline{Y}$ has a value of 1; for any other combination of X and Y it has a value of 0. The expression therefore satisfies the requirement of uniquely defining this combination of values. The expression X.Y has a value of 1 only when X=1 and Y=1, otherwise it has a value of 0, and so it uniquely defines the last row in the truth table. Together the expressions $\overline{X}.\overline{Y}$ and X.Y will produce an output of 1 when X=0 and Y=0 or when X=1 and Y=1. Hence

$$OUTPUT = \overline{X}.\overline{Y} + X.Y$$

The following truth table confirms this result:

X	Y	$\overline{X}$	$\overline{Y}$	$\overline{X}.\overline{Y}$	X.Y	$\overline{X}.\overline{Y} + X.Y$
0	0	1	1	1	0	1
0	1	1	0	0	0	0
1	0	0	1	0	0	0
1	1	0	0	0	1	1

=OUTPUT

The circuit is shown in *Figure 4.5*.

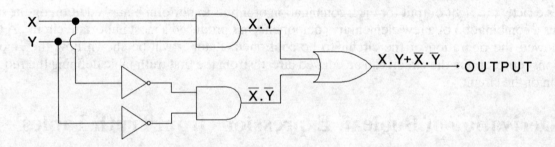

Figure 4.5

The process of converting a truth table to a Boolean expression is summarised as follows:

(a) Consider only the rows of the truth table for which the output is to be 1.

(b) Take each of these rows in turn and write alongside the row an expression containing the input variables connected by the AND operator. If the value of an input variable is 0 then it will appear inverted in the expression.

(c) Combine these expressions using the OR operator.

To provide another illustration of the process suppose that three binary signals, A, B and C, are required to represent a number in the range 0 to 4. The variable A represents the most significant digit of the binary number ABC, B is the next significant digit, and C is the least significant digit. A circuit is required to detect an illegal combination (that is the numbers 5 to 7) by producing an output of 1. The truth table is

A	B	C		OUTPUT	
0	0	0	(0)	0	
0	0	1	(1)	0	
0	1	0	(2)	0	
0	1	1	(3)	0	
1	0	0	(4)	0	
1	0	1	(5)	1	$A.\overline{B}.C$
1	1	0	(6)	1	$A.B.\overline{C}$
1	1	1	(7)	1	$A.B.C$

Therefore

$$OUTPUT = A.\overline{B}.C + A.B.\overline{C} + A.B.C$$

and the required circuit is shown in *Figure 4.6*.

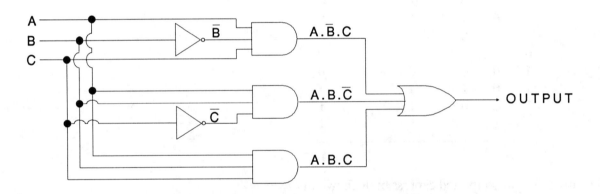

Figure 4.6

As an exercise, use a truth table to prove that the Boolean expression above does indeed produce the required outputs.

The Laws of Boolean Algebra

Though the circuit above does perform as specified, it is very inefficient; it uses more gates than are absolutely necessary to produce the required outputs. In fact rather than six gates, only two are necessary because, as the truth tables following show,

$$A.\overline{B}.C + A.B.\overline{C} + A.B.C = A.(B + C)$$

A	B	C	$\bar{B}$	$\bar{C}$	A.$\bar{B}$.C	A.B.$\bar{C}$	A.B.C	(A.$\bar{B}$.C + A.B.$\bar{C}$ + A.B.C)
0	0	0	1	1	0	0	0	0
0	0	1	1	0	0	0	0	0
0	1	0	0	1	0	0	0	0
0	1	1	0	0	0	0	0	0
1	0	0	1	1	0	0	0	0
1	0	1	1	0	1	0	0	1
1	1	0	0	1	0	1	0	1
1	1	1	0	0	0	0	1	1

=OUTPUT

A	B	C	B + C	A.(B + C)
0	0	0	0	0
0	0	1	1	0
0	1	0	1	0
0	1	1	1	0
1	0	0	0	0
1	0	1	1	1
1	1	0	1	1
1	1	1	1	1

=OUTPUT

The circuit for the simplified expression is shown in *Figure 4.7*.

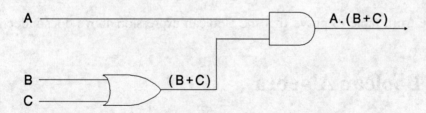

Figure 4.7

The laws of Boolean Algebra enable Boolean expressions such as that in the example to be transformed and, where possible, simplified. The most useful of these laws are as follows:

1. Commutative Laws.

(a) X+Y=Y+X;   (b) X.Y=Y.X

2. Associative Laws.

(a) $X+(Y+Z) = (X+Y)+Z$;   (b) $X.(Y.Z) = (X.Y).Z$

3. Distributive Laws.

(a) $X.(Y+Z) = X.Y + X.Z$;   (b) $X + Y.Z = (X+Y).(X+Z)$

4. De Morgan's Laws.

(a) $\overline{(X + Y)} = \overline{X}.\overline{Y}$;   (b) $\overline{(X.Y)} = \overline{X} + \overline{Y}$

5. Laws of Absorption.

(a) $X + X.Y = X$;   (b) $X.(X + Y) = X$

6. Laws of Tautology.

(a) $X + X = X$;   (b) $X.X = X$

7. Law of Complementation.

$\overline{\overline{X}} = X$

8. Other useful identities.

(a) $X + \overline{X} = 1$;   (b) $X.\overline{X} = 0$

(c) $X + 1 = 1$;   (d) $X.1 = X$

(e) $X + 0 = X$;   (f) $X.0 = 0$

Notice that with each of the first six laws, there is a connection between (a) and (b). Given one of these rules, the other may be derived by replacing the '+' operator with the '.' operator or vice-versa. Thus if it is known that $X + X.Y = X$, then the *dual* of the rule, that $X.(X+Y)$, is also true. All identities in Boolean Algebra have this useful property.

To illustrate the use of these laws in the simplification of Boolean expressions, consider the expression derived earlier:

$$A.\overline{B}.C + A.B.\overline{C} + A.B.C$$

Simplification of this expression could proceed as follows:

(i) $A.\overline{B}.C + A.B.\overline{C} + A.B.C = A.\overline{B}.C + (A.B.\overline{C} + A.B.C)$

   Rule 1 allows us to deal with terms in any order.

(ii)   Considering the bracketed pair of terms,

   $A.B.\overline{C} + A.B.C = A.B.(\overline{C} + C)$ by rule 3(a)

   Here A.B is treated as if it were a single variable, and the expression is therefore of the form

   $X.\overline{C} + X.C = X.(\overline{C} +C)$ where X represents A.B

(iii) Rule 8(a) shows that $\overline{C} + C = 1$, so that

$$A.B.(\overline{C} + C) = A.B.1$$

and by rule 8(d),

$$A.B.1 = A.B$$

(iv) Hence,

$$A.\overline{B}.C + (A.B.\overline{C} + A.B.C) = A.\overline{B}.C + A.B$$

(v) Again using rule 3(a),

$$A.\overline{B}.C + A.B = A.(\overline{B}.C + B)$$

This is of the form

$$X.Y + X.Z = X.(Y + Z)$$

(vi) Now consider the term $\overline{B}.C + B$.

Using rule 1(a), this can be rewritten $B + \overline{B}.C$, and now using rule 3(b),

$$B + \overline{B}.C = (B + \overline{B}).(B + C)$$

As in step (iii), $(B + \overline{B}) = 1$ and $1.(B+C) = (B+C)$.

Hence $B + \overline{B}.C = (B + C)$ and therefore

$$A.(B + \overline{B}.C) = A.(B+C)$$

Thus the original expression has been considerably simplified and confirms the identity stated earlier.

Fortunately, the process of simplifying expressions involving AND terms separated by OR operators can be performed in a much simpler way using the Karnaugh Map method. This method, as well as being quicker and less prone to error, is also more likely to result in the best simplification possible, particularly where four variables are involved. In certain cases, however, a knowledge of the laws of Boolean Algebra are required. Examples of such instances will be provided later.

Karnaugh Maps

A Karnaugh map consists of a two-dimensional grid which is used to represent a Boolean expression in such a way that it can be simplified with great ease. For example, consider the expression

$$\overline{X}.Y + X.\overline{Y} + X.Y$$

This expression involves two Boolean variables, X and Y. The number of different terms possible with two variable is four, and therefore the Karnaugh map for expressions involving two variables is a 2 × 2 grid (*Figure 4.8*).

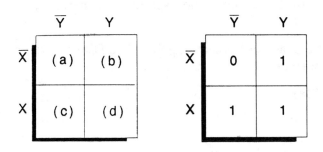

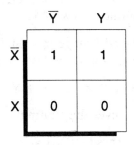

Figure 4.8　　　　　　　　　**Figure 4.9**　　　　　　　　　**Figure 4.10**

Each cell in the grid may be regarded as having a co-ordinate formed from a combination of X and Y. Thus the cell labelled (a) has the co-ordinate $\overline{X}.\overline{Y}$, (b) has the co-ordinate $\overline{X}.Y$, (c) has the co-ordinate $X.\overline{Y}$, and (d) has the co-ordinate X.Y. When entered onto the map, the expression quoted above translates to the map in *Figure 4.9*.

Each '1' on the map indicates the presence of the term corresponding to its cell co-ordinate in the expression, and each '0' indicates its absence.

Using a further example, the expression $X.Y + \overline{X}.\overline{Y}$ translates to the map shown in *Figure 4.10*.

Having drawn the appropriate Karnaugh map, the next stage is to attempt to identify a simplified expression. The procedure is as follows:

　(i)　Identify all pairs of adjacent '1's on the map. (Horizontally and vertically).

　(ii)　Draw loops around each pair.

　(iii)　Attempt to include every '1' on the map in at least one loop; it is allowable to have the same '1' in two different loops.

　(iv)　The aim is to include each '1' in at least one loop, but using as few loops as possible.

Thus the expression $\overline{X}.Y + X.\overline{Y} + X.Y$ becomes the map shown in *Figure 4.11*.

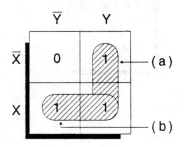

Figure 4.11

　(v)　Take each loop in turn and write down the term represented: the loop labelled (a) in *Figure 4.11* spans both X and $\overline{X}$, but Y remains constant. The loop is therefore given the value Y. In the loop labelled (b), both Y co-ordinates are covered but X remains constant. This loop has the value X.

(vi) The loop values are ORed together. In the example, the expression is therefore equivalent to X + Y.

Karnaugh maps take advantage of a small number of the laws of Boolean Algebra. The Distributive Law allows terms with common variables to be grouped together:

$$X.\overline{Y} + X.Y = X.(\overline{Y} + Y) \quad (\text{see rule 3(a)})$$

Another law (8(a)) gives the identity $\overline{Y} + Y = 1$.

And finally, law 8(d) says that $X.1 = X$.

The Karnaugh map allows this sequence of applications of laws to be performed in a single step:

the loop (b) representing $X.\overline{Y} + X.Y$ becomes X.

'1's may be included in more than one loop because of the Law of Tautology (Tautology is saying the same thing twice). Thus X + X = X, and conversely, X = X + X. In other words, any term in an expression may be duplicated as many times as desired without affecting the value of the expression. So, given the expression

$$\overline{X}.Y + X.\overline{Y} + X.Y,$$

the term X.Y may be duplicated to give the equivalent expression

$$\overline{X}.Y + X.Y + X.\overline{Y} + X.Y,$$

where loop (a) is $\overline{X}.Y + X.Y$, and loop (b) is $X.\overline{Y} + X.Y$.

As a further example, the expression

$$\overline{X}.\overline{Y} + \overline{X}.Y + X.Y$$

gives the map in *Figure 4.12*

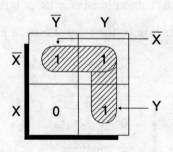

Figure 4.12

and the equivalent expression is $\overline{X} + Y$.

Karnaugh Maps for Three Variables

Expressions containing three variables can contain up to eight terms. The 3-variable map is drawn as follows shown in *Figure 4.13*.

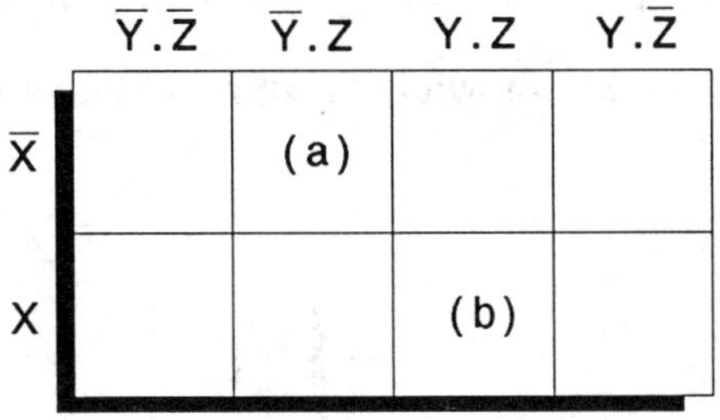

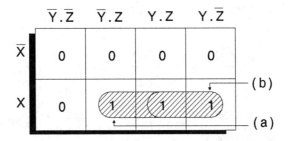

Figure 4.13

This time a co-ordinate pair comprises an X variable and a YZ term.

For example, the cell (a) represents the term $\overline{X}.\overline{Y}.Z$, and (b) represents $X.Y.Z$.

The map in *Figure 4.14* represents the expression $X.\overline{Y}.Z + X.Y.\overline{Z} + X.Y.Z$.

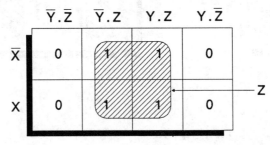

Figure 4.14

In loop (a), X and Z are common factors, but Y changes ($\overline{Y}.Z + Y.Z$). The loop has the value X.Z. In loop (b), X and Y are constant but Z changes ($Y.Z + Y.\overline{Z}$). Thus (b) has value X.Y. The expression therefore simplifies to

$$X.Y + X.Z$$

and a further application of law 3(a) gives the final solution

$$X.\overline{Y}.Z + X.Y.\overline{Z} + X.Y.Z = X.(Y + Z)$$

With a 3-variable map, as well as looping pairs of '1's, it is necessary to look for groups of four '1's. For example, the map shown in *Figure 4.15* could represent the expression

$$X.Y.Z + \overline{X}.\overline{Y}.Z + \overline{X}.Y.Z + X.\overline{Y}.Z$$

Figure 4.15

The single loop spans the X co-ordinate completely, and so X can be removed from the simplified expression. In the YZ terms spanned, Y changes and Z is constant. The simplified expression is merely Z.

Two further examples of groups of four are shown in *Figures 4.16* and *4.17*.

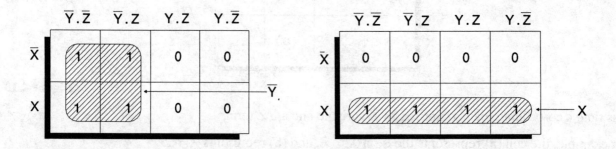

Figure 4.16   Figure 4.17

In *Figure 4.18* the group of four is formed from opposite sides of the grid.

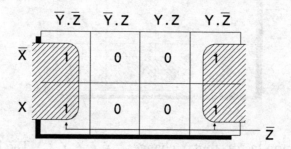

Figure 4.18

Figures 4.19 to *4.22* show some further examples with combinations of different types of loops illustrated.

Note that the largest groups are identified first, and then sufficient smaller groups so that every '1' is in at least one loop.

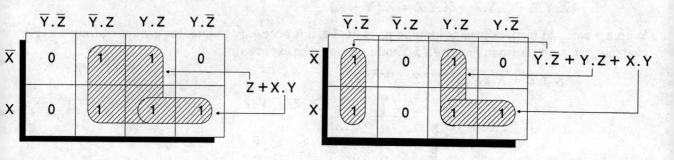

Figure 4.19   Figure 4.20

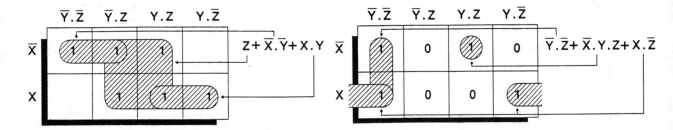

Figure 4.21   **Figure 4.22**

Karnaugh Maps for Four Variables

With four variables there can be up to sixteen different terms involved, and the 4-variable map is a 4 × 4 grid as shown in *Figure 4.23*.

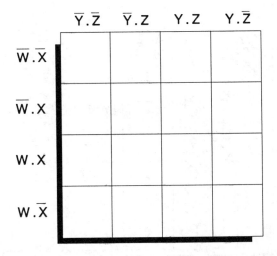

Figure 4.23

It is necessary to look for groupings of 8, 4 and 2 with the 4-variable map. *Figures 4.24 to 4.27* illustrate a number of possible groupings, including some that occur on the edges of the maps and which are sometimes difficult to recognise. Again, to determine the term equivalent to the loop, look for the variables that remain common to the co-ordinates of the loop's range horizontally and vertically.

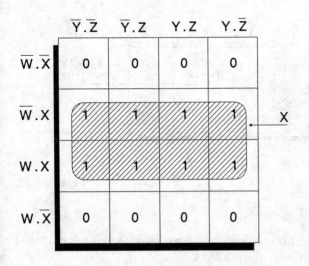

Figure 4.24

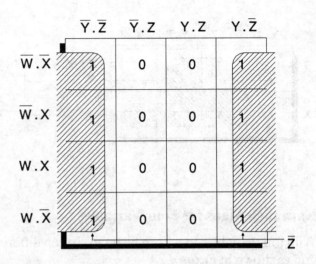

Figure 4.25

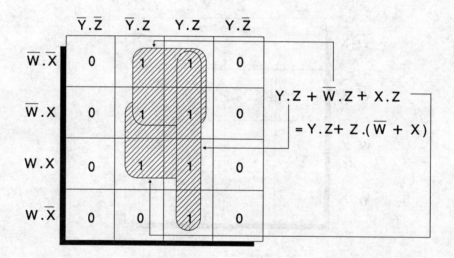

Figure 4.26

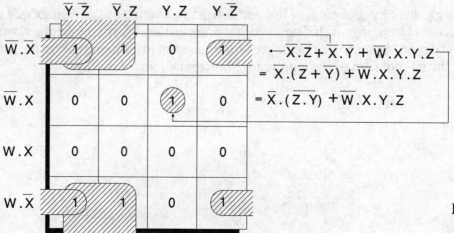

Figure 4.27

The Design of Logic Circuits

The complete process of designing a logic circuit may be summarized as follows:

- (i) Identify Boolean variables equivalent to the inputs to the circuit required.

- (ii) Identify the outputs from the circuit.

- (iii) Draw a truth table to define the output required for each possible combination of the input variables.

- (iv) Derive an expression from the truth table for the output in terms of the input variables.

- (v) Simplify this expression using a Karnaugh map.

- (vi) Examine the simplified expression for possible further simplifications using direct applications of the laws of Boolean Algebra.

- (vii) Draw the circuit using the appropriate gate symbols.

The following problem illustrates the process.

> Four binary signals A, B, C, D represent a single Binary Coded Decimal (BCD) digit. A logic circuit is required to output logic 1 on the occurrence of an invalid combination of the signals, that is, when they represent a number in the range 10 to 15.

- (i) The inputs to the circuit are clearly defined and it is assumed that A is the most significant digit and D the least significant digit.

- (ii) The single output is to be 1 when the binary number represented by ABCD is in the range 10 to 15, that is, 1010 to 1111 in binary.

- (iii) The truth table has 16 entries, representing the numbers 0 to 15.

A	B	C	D	OUTPUT		
0	0	0	0	(0)	0	
0	0	0	1	(1)	0	
0	0	1	0	(2)	0	
0	0	1	1	(3)	0	
0	1	0	0	(4)	0	
0	1	0	1	(5)	0	
0	1	1	0	(6)	0	
0	1	1	1	(7)	0	
1	0	0	0	(8)	0	
1	0	0	1	(9)	0	
1	0	1	0	(10)	1	$A.\bar{B}.C.\bar{D}$
1	0	1	1	(11)	1	$A.\bar{B}.C.D$
1	1	0	0	(12)	1	$A.B.\bar{C}.\bar{D}$
1	1	0	1	(13)	1	$A.B.\bar{C}.D$
1	1	1	0	(14)	1	$A.B.C.\bar{D}$
1	1	1	1	(15)	1	$A.B.C.D$

(iv) The expression for the output is given by

OUTPUT = $A.\bar{B}.C.\bar{D} + A.\bar{B}.C.D + A.B.\bar{C}.\bar{D} + A.B.\bar{C}.D + A.B.C.\bar{D} + A.B.C.D$

(v) The Karnaugh map is shown in *Figure 4.28*.

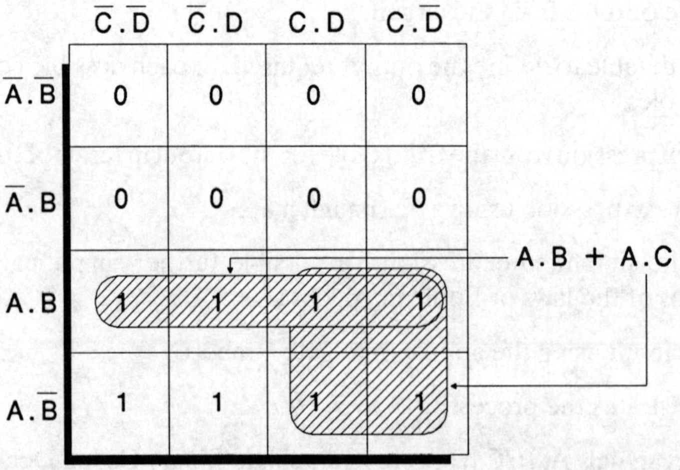

	$\bar{C}.\bar{D}$	$\bar{C}.D$	$C.D$	$C.\bar{D}$
$\bar{A}.\bar{B}$	0	0	0	0
$\bar{A}.B$	0	0	0	0
$A.B$	1	1	1	1
$A.\bar{B}$	1	1	1	1

A.B + A.C

Figure 4.28

(vi) Using the Distributive law, 3(a), the expression A.B + A.C may be written A.(B + C).

(vii) This expression translates to the logic diagram shown in *Figure 4.29*.

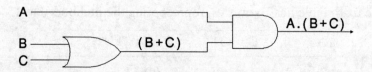

Figure 4.29

More Logic Gates

The gates that have yet to be defined are the NOR(Not OR), NAND(Not AND) and XOR (eXclusive OR) gates.

The truth table for the NOR gate shows that its outputs are the inverse of those for the OR gate:

X	Y	X NOR Y
0	0	1
0	1	0
1	0	0
1	1	0

Algebraically, the NOR gate is written $\overline{(X+Y)}$. Thus the gate appears to be formed from one OR gate and one NOT gate inverting the output from the OR gate. In practice, however, the OR gate outputs are generated from a single simple circuit and not by the combination of an OR gate followed by a NOT gate.

The symbol for the NOR gate is shown in *Figure 4.30(a)*.

(a) NOR gate   **(b)NAND gate**

Figure 4.30

The truth table for the NAND gate shows that its outputs are the inverse of those for the AND gate:

X	Y	X NAND Y
0	0	1
0	1	1
1	0	1
1	1	0

In Boolean Algebra, the gate is written $\overline{(X.Y)}$. The comments above regarding the construction of the NOR gate similarly apply here: the NAND gate is not constructed from an AND gate followed by a NOT gate, but consists of a single circuit no more complex than the other gates.

The symbol for the NAND gate is shown in *Figure 4.30(b)*.

The Importance of the NAND gate and NOR gate

The importance of these gates may be attributed to two factors:

(i)   each may be manufactured cheaply and easily;

(ii)   each can be used in the production of any circuit using AND/OR/NOT logical components. In other words, NOR gates and NAND gates can be used in the place of AND, OR or NOT gates.

These two properties mean that a logic circuit using, for instance, NOR gates only, can be produced easier and cheaper than the same circuit using combinations of three different types of components (AND, OR and NOT gates). A unit using a number of the same component is much easier to manufacture than one using several different components.

Figure 4.31 shows how NOR gates may be used to represent the functions of NOT, AND and OR gates.

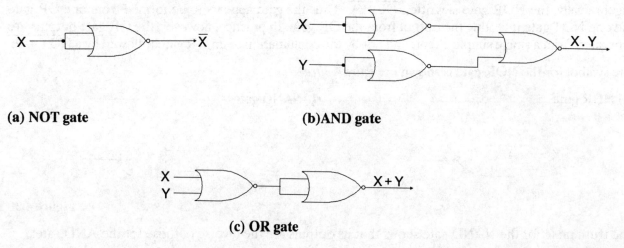

(a) NOT gate   **(b)AND gate**

(c) OR gate

Figure 4.31

Figure 4.32 shows how NAND gates may be used to represent the functions of NOT, AND OR gates.

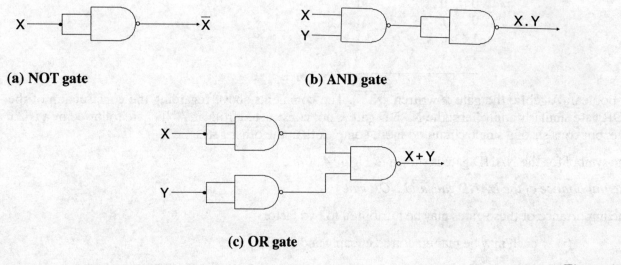

(a) NOT gate   **(b) AND gate**

(c) OR gate

Figure 4.32

(As an exercise, write down Boolean expressions equivalent to the circuits shown above and prove their validity using truth tables).

It may appear from *Figures 4.31* and *4.32* that circuits using NAND or NOR gates will generally require more gates than when using AND/OR /NOT components. This may be true on occasions, but at other times fewer gates may be required. The number of gates required often may be reduced by transforming the Boolean expression into a more suitable form. For example, the following expression, when implemented directly using NOR gates, uses more gates than the expression requires using AND/OR/NOT logic:

$$X.\overline{Y} + \overline{X}.Y \quad (2 \text{ AND gates, } 2 \text{ NOT gates, } 1 \text{ OR gate} = 5 \text{ gates})$$

However, it can be shown that the following identity is true:

$$X.\overline{Y} + \overline{X}.Y = \overline{\overline{(\overline{X} + \overline{Y})} + \overline{(X + Y)}}$$

which may not look very helpful but, in fact, shows that the original expression can be transformed into one much more suited to implementation by NOR gates. The circuit based on this transformed expression has only five NOR gates. (See *Figure 4.33*)

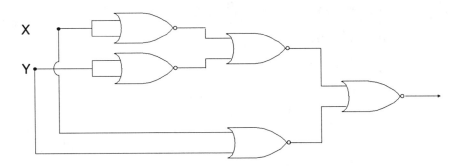

Figure 4.33

The Exclusive OR gate

This is usually abbreviated to XOR or EOR. The XOR gate has the following truth table:

X	Y	X XOR Y
0	0	0
0	1	1
1	0	1
1	1	0

The exclusive OR gate is so named because, of its output values, the case where both inputs are logic 1 is excluded; in the OR gate these inputs produce an output of 1. In effect, the XOR gate has an output of logic 1 when the inputs are different; when the inputs are the same, the output is logic 0.

Algebraically, the XOR gate is $X.\overline{Y} + \overline{X}.Y$ and the symbol that is frequently used is shown in *Figure 4.34*.

Figure 4.34

As an example of its use, suppose that it is required to generate an even parity bit for a four bit word ABCD. The truth table for this problem is as follows:

A	B	C	D		Parity Bit
0	0	0	0	0	
0	0	0	1	1	$\overline{A}.\overline{B}.\overline{C}.D$
0	0	1	0	1	$\overline{A}.\overline{B}.C.\overline{D}$
0	0	1	1	0	
0	1	0	0	1	$\overline{A}.B.\overline{C}.\overline{D}$
0	1	0	1	0	
0	1	1	0	0	
0	1	1	1	1	$\overline{A}.B.C.D$
1	0	0	0	1	$A.\overline{B}.\overline{C}.\overline{D}$
1	0	0	1	0	
1	0	1	0	0	
1	0	1	1	1	$A.\overline{B}.C.D$
1	1	0	0	0	
1	1	0	1	1	$A.B.\overline{C}.D$
1	1	1	0	1	$A.B.C.\overline{D}$
1	1	1	1	0	

The expression for even parity is thus

Parity bit = $\overline{A}.\overline{B}.\overline{C}.D + \overline{A}.\overline{B}.C.\overline{D} + \overline{A}.B.\overline{C}.\overline{D} + \overline{A}.B.C.D + A.\overline{B}.\overline{C}.\overline{D} + A.\overline{B}.C.D + A.B.\overline{C}.D + A.B.C.\overline{D}$

and the Karnaugh map representation is shown in *Figure 4.35(a)*.

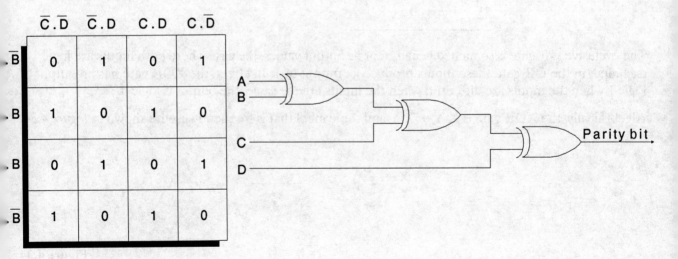

(a)Karnaugh map   **(b) Circuit using XOR gates**

Figure 4.35

As the map shows, there is no way of simplifying the expression. However, if the terms are grouped together as follows, a pattern begins to emerge:

Parity bit = $\overline{A}.\overline{B}.(\overline{C}.D + C.\overline{D}) + \overline{A}.B.(C.D + \overline{C}.\overline{D}) +$

$\overline{A}.B.(\overline{C}.\overline{D} + C.D) + A.B.(\overline{C}.D + C.\overline{D})$

Rearranging the terms,

Parity bit = $\overline{A}.\overline{B}.(\overline{C}.D + C.\overline{D}) + A.B.(\overline{C}.D + C.\overline{D}) +$

$\overline{A}.B.(C.D + \overline{C}.\overline{D}) + A.\overline{B}.(C.D + \overline{C}.\overline{D})$

Again, using the Distributive law, the first two and the last two terms can be grouped together to give

Parity bit = $(\overline{A}.\overline{B} + A.B).(\overline{C}.D + C.\overline{D}) + (\overline{A}.B + A.\overline{B}).(\overline{C}.\overline{D} + C.D)$

Notice that two of the terms in brackets are immediately recognisable as XOR functions. In addition it can be shown that

$$\overline{\overline{X}.Y + X.\overline{Y}} = (\overline{X}.\overline{Y} + X.Y)$$

Using this identity, the expression for parity becomes

Parity bit = $(\overline{A}.B + A.\overline{B}).(\overline{C}.D + C.\overline{D}) + \overline{(\overline{A}.B + A.\overline{B})}.\overline{(\overline{C}.D + C.\overline{D})}$

Now each bracketed term looks like an XOR gate and, treating each bracketed term as a unit, the complete expression has the form

$\overline{X}.Y + X.\overline{Y}$, where $X = (\overline{A}.B + A.\overline{B})$ and $Y = (\overline{C}.D + C.\overline{D})$

Thus the whole expression, and every term within it, represent XOR gates.

The equivalent circuit is shown in *Figure 4.35(b)*.

Logic Circuits for Binary Addition

The logic circuits which perform the function of addition in the Arithmetic and Logic Unit of the Central Processing Unit are called *adders*. A unit which adds two binary digits is called a *half adder* and one which adds together three binary digits is called a *full adder*. In this section each of these units will be examined in detail, and it will be shown how such units are combined to add binary numbers.

Half Adders

Earlier in this chapter, the function of a half adder was explained in order to illustrate the relevance of computer logic. Remember that the function of a half adder is to add two binary digits and produce as output the Sum term and Carry term. The operation of the half adder is defined by the following truth table:

X	Y	Sum		Carry	
0	0	0		0	
0	1	1	$\overline{X}.Y$	0	
1	0	1	$X.\overline{Y}$	0	
1	1	0		1	$X.Y$

Thus, the expressions for the Sum and Carry terms are given by:

$$Sum = \overline{X}.Y + X.\overline{Y}$$
$$Carry = X.Y$$

The circuit equivalent to these expressions was presented earlier in *Figure 4.4*.

The symbol shown in *Figure 4.36* will henceforth be used for a half adder

Figure 4.36

Full Adders

The truth table for the addition of three binary digits is

X	Y	Z	Sum		Carry	
0	0	0	0		0	
0	0	1	1	$\overline{X}.\overline{Y}.Z$	0	
0	1	0	1	$\overline{X}.Y.\overline{Z}$	0	
0	1	1	0		1	$\overline{X}.Y.Z$
1	0	0	1	$X.\overline{Y}.\overline{Z}$	0	
1	0	1	0		1	$X.\overline{Y}.Z$
1	1	0	0		1	$X.Y.\overline{Z}$
1	1	1	1	$X.Y.Z$	1	$X.Y.Z$

Considering the Sum term first, the expression derived from the truth table is

$$Sum = \overline{X}.\overline{Y}.Z + \overline{X}.Y.\overline{Z} + X.\overline{Y}.\overline{Z} + X.Y.Z$$

Grouping together the first and fourth terms, and the middle two terms gives

$$Sum = \overline{Z}.(\overline{X}.Y + X.\overline{Y}) + Z.(\overline{X}.\overline{Y} + X.Y)$$

Using the identity

$$\overline{\overline{X}.Y + X.\overline{Y}} = (\overline{X}.\overline{Y} + X.Y)$$ (the proof for this has been given earlier)

the Sum term can be written

$$\text{Sum} = \overline{Z}.(\overline{X}.Y + X.\overline{Y}) + Z.(\overline{\overline{X}.Y + X.\overline{Y}})$$

which is of the form

$$\overline{Z}.S + Z.\overline{S} \text{ where } S = \overline{X}.Y + X.\overline{Y}$$

In other words, S is the sum term from a half adder with inputs X and Y, and Sum is one of the outputs from a half adder with inputs Z and S.

The Sum term can now be produced using two half adders; as shown in *Figure 4.37*.

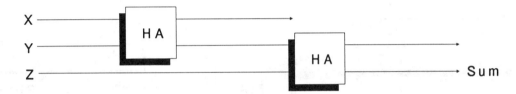

Figure 4.37

Returning to the Carry term, the expression derived from the truth table is

$$\text{Carry} = \overline{X}.Y.Z + X.\overline{Y}.Z + X.Y.\overline{Z} + X.Y.Z$$

Again gathering terms,

$$\text{Carry} = Z.(\overline{X}.Y + X.\overline{Y}) + X.Y.(\overline{Z} + Z)$$
$$= Z.(\overline{X}.Y + X.\overline{Y}) + X.Y \quad \text{since } \overline{Z} + Z = 1 \text{ and } X.Y.1 = X.Y$$

Substituting S for $\overline{X}.Y + X.\overline{Y}$ as before, the expression becomes

$$\text{Carry} = Z.S + X.Y$$

Both of these terms look like the carry term from a half adder: Z.S is the carry term from a half adder with inputs Z and S (the carry term from the second half adder in the diagram above); X.Y is the carry output from the first half adder in the diagram. The two carry outputs merely need to be ORed together: to give the final circuit shown in *Figure 4.38*.

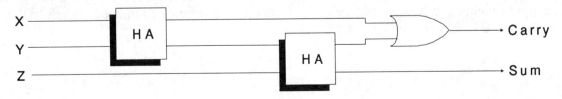

Figure 4.38

Adding Binary Numbers

So far, the circuits for addition have only been capable of adding two or three binary digits; more complex schemes are necessary in order to add two binary numbers each comprising several digits. Two approaches will be considered. The first adds numbers bit by bit, one pair of bits after another and is termed *serial addition*; the other accepts as inputs all pairs of bits in the two numbers simultaneously and is called *parallel addition*.

Serial Addition

Suppose that the numbers to be added have a four-bit wordlength, and the two numbers A and B have digits $a_3 a_2 a_1 a_0$ and $b_3 b_2 b_1 b_0$ respectively. The circuit for a four-bit serial adder is shown in *Figure 4.39*.

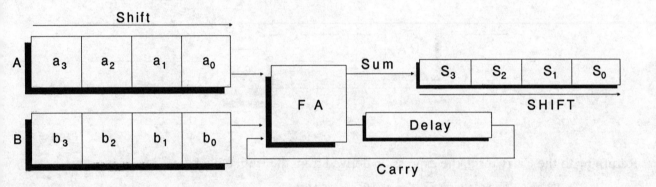

Figure 4.39

In this particular design, a single full adder is presented with pairs of bits from the two numbers in the sequence $a_0 b_0$, $a_1 b_1$, $a_2 b_2$, $a_3 b_3$. As each pair of bits is added, the sum term is transmitted to a shift register to hold the result, and the carry term is delayed so that it is added in to the next addition operation.

Though this method is cheap in terms of hardware requirements, it is not often (if at all) used in modern digital computers because of its slow operation. The degree to which hardware prices have dropped in recent years has resulted in the almost universal adoption of parallel addition.

Parallel Addition

In parallel addition, a separate adder is used for the addition of each digit pair. Thus for the addition of two four-digit numbers, one half adder and three full adders would be used. In this type of circuit, all the digits are input simultaneously, with the carry term from each stage being connected directly to the input of the next stage. This is shown in *Figure 4.40*.

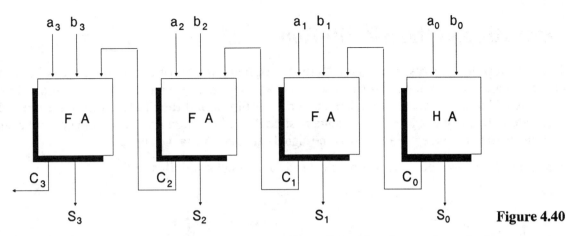

Figure 4.40

Though faster than serial addition, one fault of the type of parallel adder shown above is the successive carry out to carry in connections which cause relatively long delays; more elaborate schemes are capable of overcoming this problem (at the expense of added circuitry).

The efficiency of the addition circuits is of particular importance in microprocessors where the functions of multiplication and division, as well as subtraction, often use these circuits. Larger computers (and many of the more recent 16 and 32 bit microprocessors) have special purpose circuitry for multiplication and division.

Flip-flops

One of the fundamental functions performed by digital computers is the storage of data in memory. The electronic component which is usually used for this purpose is called a *flip-flop*. Other names for the same device are *bistable*, *latch* and *toggle*, but flip-flop is the most commonly used name.

A flip-flop is capable of storing, in electrical form, a single binary digit. Thus, a collection of eight flip-flops can store a byte of data. As well as being used for memory, flip-flops form the basis of other useful CPU components, such as *shift registers* and *binary counters*.

Flip-flops are frequently constructed with gates, but using *sequential logic* rather than the *combinational logic* described in the previous part of this chapter. As we have seen, a combinational logic circuit produces an output which is entirely dependent on the current inputs; with sequential logic, because of the use of feedback, the output from a sequential logic circuit depends on its current state in addition to the current inputs. In other words, the output from a sequential logic circuit is partly determined by the previous inputs it received.

In this section we describe the operational characteristics of the simplest type of flip-flop, the *SR flip-flop*, before going on to show how it may be constructed using NAND gates. We then discuss the synchronous version of the SR flip-flop, the *clocked SR flip-flop* before showing how shift registers, binary counters and memory units may be fabricated using them.

Though there are a number of different types of flip-flops in common use, including JK, Master-Slave and D-type flip-flops, essentially they are all based on the SR flip-flop, and it is beyond the scope of this book to discuss the precise differences between them and why one type is preferred over another for certain types of application.

Operation of the SR flip-flop

The term flip-flop derives from its characteristic of being in one of two stable states at any instant, and hence the alternative name, *bistable*. These two states we conveniently designate 0 and 1. In state 1, the device is said to be *set*, and in state 0, *reset*, hence *SR* flip-flop. If the flip-flop is in state 1, it will remain in that state until an input causes it to change to state 0, in which state it will also remain until changed. Thus it "remembers" its current state until some signal causes it to change state.

Figure 4.41(a) shows the symbol generally used for an unclocked SR flip-flop.

(a) Unclocked   **(b) Clocked**

Figure 4.41

The two outputs are labelled Q and $\overline{Q}$ because each is the complement of the other. The current state of the device is by convention that of the Q output. The input lines, S and R, are used to control the state of the flip-flop. If a signal is applied to the S line, the flip-flop is set (ie Q=1); a signal on the R line resets it (ie Q=0). The absence of any signal leaves the state of the flip-flop unchanged. Applying a signal to both lines simultaneously is not allowed. The following table illustrates these rules with a sequence of input signals and the resulting state of the flip-flop:

S	R	Q	Q'	Effect of input
1	0	1	0	Set
0	0	1	0	Remains in same state
0	0	1	0	
0	1	0	1	Reset
0	0	0	1	Remains in same state
1	0	1	0	Set
1	0	1	0	Already set so no effect
0	1	0	1	Reset
0	1	0	1	Already set so no effect

Construction of the SR flip-flop

A simple form of an SR flip-flop may be implemented using two NAND gates connected as shown in Figure 4.42.

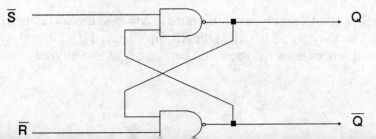

Figure 4.42

The operation of this flip-flop is defined by the following table:

S	R	Q'
0	0	Q
0	1	1
1	0	1
1	1	Not defined

The current state of the circuit is denoted by Q and the resulting state, due to the two inputs, is Q'. We can verify the operation of the circuit by tracing each pair of inputs and comparing them with the outputs shown:

(i) $\overline{S}=1$, $\overline{R}=1$ and Q=1. This corresponds to the null input, self-sustaining state. The inputs to the lower NAND gate are both 1, producing an output, Q', of 0. This means that the inputs to the upper NAND gate are 1 and 0, producing an output of 1 - no change in the outputs. If the current state is Q=0, the lower gate has inputs 0 and 1, producing an output of 1, and the upper gate now has both inputs at logic-1, producing an output of 0 - again no change.

(ii) $\overline{S}=0$ and $\overline{R}=1$. This is the *set* condition. Because $\overline{S}=0$, the upper gate must output logic-1; the inputs to the lower gate both being 1, the output is 0.

(iii) $\overline{S}=1$ and $\overline{R}=0$. This is the *reset* condition. Because $\overline{R}=0$, the lower gate must output logic-1 this time, and the two logic-1 inputs to the top gate produce an output of 0.

(iv) $\overline{S}=1$ and $\overline{R}=1$. In this instance the output from the flip-flop cannot be determined; the resulting state will be unpredictable and will depend on such factors as temperature and component tolerances.

The Clocked SR Flip-flop

Figure 4.41(b) shows the symbol for a clocked SR flip-flop. It has an additional input designated *clock* or *enable*. The circuit for a clocked SR flip-flop is shown in *Figure 4.43*.

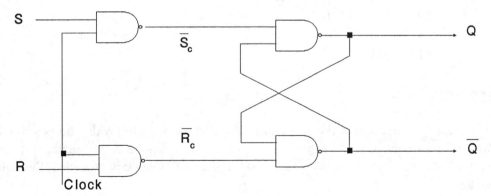

Figure 4.43

The extra input allows the operation of the flip-flop to be controlled by a timing signal which is used to synchronize the operation of the separate components of a circuit. Circuits controlled by a clock are called *synchronous* circuits; where a clock is not used the circuit is *asynchronous*. Because of the added complexity of asynchronous circuits, most circuits are of the synchronous variety.

The effect of the additional gates in the circuit is to hold the S and R inputs at the null state ($\bar{S}=\bar{Q}=1$) until a clock pulse is applied to the first two gates, at which time set and reset signals are applied to the flip-flop. In effect, the clock pulse *enables* the flip-flop to assume a new state.

Shift Registers

A four stage shift register is shown in the *Figure 4.44*.

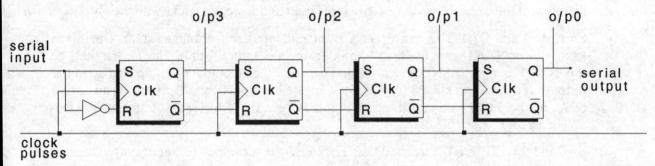

Figure 4.44

A sequence of signals representing a binary number is applied to the input. Each input is set up while the clock is at logic-0. When the clock pulse becomes logic-1, each flip-flop is enabled and assumes the value of the signal being applied to the S input. Therefore, the complete contents of the flip-flops are shifted along by one bit at every clock pulse. The current state of each flip-flop is available on the lines labelled O/P0 to O/P3. The following table illustrates the process with the binary sequence 1101, assuming that the initial contents of the shift register is 0000.

Clock pulse	Input	O/P0	O/P1	O/P2	O/P3
		0	0	0	0
1	1	1	0	0	0
2	0	0	1	0	0
3	1	1	0	1	0
4	1	1	1	0	1

Binary Counters

A binary counter consists of a collection of flip-flops each of which is associated with a bit position in the binary representation of a number. If there are n flip-flops in a binary counter, the number of possible states is 2^n and the counting sequence is from 0 to 2^n-1. If the maximum value is exceeded, the counting sequence starts at 0 again.

A simple form of a binary counter is based on an SR flip-flop connected to act as a *toggle circuit* shown in *Figure 4.45*.

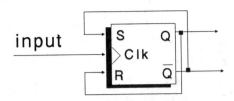

Figure 4.45

Each pulse applied to the clock input inverts the output, Q, of the circuit; in effect, this is dividing the input frequency by two by performing alternate *set* and *reset* operations. The following table shows how the output changes after each logic-1 input, assuming that the current output is logic-0:

	Input	Output(Q)
		0
1	1	1
2	0	1
3	1	0
4	0	0
5	1	1
6	0	1
	etc	

Notice that logic-0 inputs have no effect on the output.

A four-bit counter uses four toggle circuits connected in series. (See *Figure 4.46*)

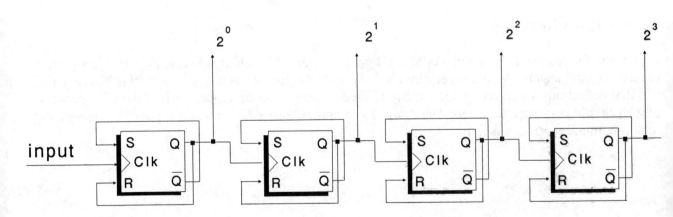

Figure 4.46

The output from the first toggle circuit alternates between 0 and 1 as shown in the previous table. Each time a logic-1 is output from the first toggle component, the second one is enabled and its output inverts; each time the output from the second component is logic-1, the third one is enabled and its output inverts, and so on. Therefore, the first component inverts after each logic-1 input, the second one inverts after two logic-1 inputs, the third after four and the fourth after eight. The following table shows how the outputs of each of the toggle circuits, A, B, C and D change for a sequence of logic-1 inputs:

Input	A	B	C	D
	0	0	0	0
1	1	0	0	0
2	0	1	0	0
3	1	1	0	0
4	0	0	1	0
5	1	0	1	0
6	0	1	1	0
7	1	1	1	0
8	0	0	0	1
9	1	0	0	1
10	0	1	0	1
11	1	1	0	1
12	0	0	1	1
13	1	0	1	1
14	0	1	1	1
15	1	1	1	1
16	0	0	0	0
17	1	0	0	0

etc.

Thus A represents the least significant bit of the 4-bit number and D the most significant bit. The counter thus counts up from 0 to 15 cyclically.

Memory Circuits

One of the fundamental characteristics of the digital computer is its ability to store data and programs in random-access memory. We have seen already that sequential circuits are capable of storing binary signals and that collections of such components may be used to store bytes or larger words of data. Large arrays of such circuits constitute the internal memory of a computer. *Figure 4.47* shows one possible arrangement for a random-access memory unit.

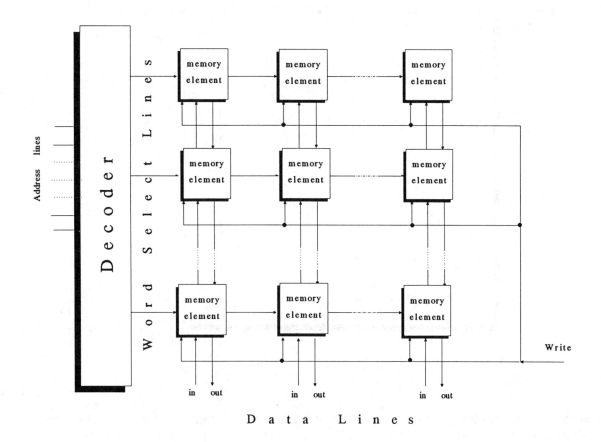

Figure 4.47

The *Address Lines*, typically 16 or 32 for a microcomputer, specify which particular memory word is to be accessed; a *Chip Enable* line (not shown) enables the chip if it is logic-1 or disables the chip if it is logic-0; when enabled, the chip may be written to by making *Write=1* and read from using *Write=0*.

Each horizontal row of memory elements represents a word of memory which may be selected by an Address Decoder. So for an 8-bit word there will be a row of eight memory elements. When an address is input to the address decoder, it selects the corresponding word. For a 16-bit address, the decoder will select one line from 2^{16} possibilities. If a read operation is required, the word, corresponding to the states of the eight memory elements, will appear on the Out lines; a write operation will cause the eight memory elements to take on the binary values on the In lines.

The construction of the memory elements, each storing a single bit, is shown in *Figure 4.48*.

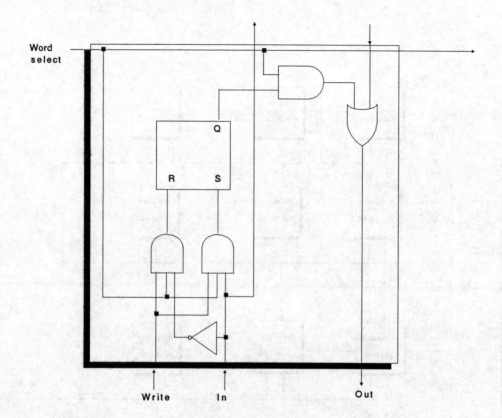

Figure 4.48

Each element comprises a flip-flop and a number of other gates to control the transfer of data between the flip-flop and the common internal data lines. Notice that the AND gates are used to control the passage of signals: only when all inputs to an AND gate are 1 will the output become 1.

Each word-select line is used to enable all elements in a row for reading or writing, and each column has two internal data lines, one for reading - data-in - and one for writing - data-out. The data-out line takes the value of the element in the currently enabled word. Thus, when *Word select*=1 the Q output from the memory element is ORed with the data-out line.

A word is written into a memory location by presenting the appropriate address to the decoder (which enables the word memory elements), the bit pattern of the word to the data-in lines and then setting *Write*=1. Two AND gates in each memory element allow its state to be changed to the value on the data-in line providing *Write* and *Word select* are both at logic-1.

Integrated Circuits

The logic elements described earlier in this chapter are fabricated using semi-conductors, transistors in particular. The speed of operation of transistors, which act as electronic switches in logic circuits, is dependent on their size; the power consumption, amount of heat generated and cost are also dependent on their size. Since size is such a critical factor, a great deal of research has been done to reduce the size of a transistor as far as possible. The result of this research has been the steady evolution of the Integrated Circuit (IC).

Though invented in 1959, integrated circuits were first used in computers in the late 1960's. The PDP-11 was one of the first commercial machines to use such devices. At that time an integrated circuit contained less than one hundred transistors; today, microprocessors can contain one million transistors on a single chip, and it is predicted that by the turn of the century there will be one hundred million transistors on a single microprocessor chip.

Electronic devices contain combinations of components such as resistors, capacitors and transistors, and at one time such devices were constructed by wiring individually manufactured components together. Microelectronic devices still use these same basic components, but now they are fabricated and interconnected in the same manufacturing process.

The most common material of microelectronic circuits is silicon, the same type that is found in ordinary sand. The silicon is first refined and made into thin discs which form the base material, the *substrate*, for a number of IC's. The manufacturing process produces several identical IC's, each perhaps only a quarter of an inch square, on one wafer of silicon. The circuit to be set into the silicon is first designed, often with the aid of a computer to minimize the number of components, before being used to prepare a series of *masks*. After being photographically reduced to the actual chip size, the masks are used in a photographic process which sequentially isolates each chip from its immediate neighbours, defines the position of the components, modifies the structure of the substrate to give it the required semiconducting characteristics and interconnects the components using etched metallic films. Further stages are required to test the circuits, separate them and package them into the familiar bug shape.

The whole process, though complex and involving a large number of delicate operations, has the tremendous advantage of allowing extremely small and complex circuits to be mass produced, thus dramatically reducing their cost.

The table below is a rough guide to the five generations of IC's in terms of chip complexity:

	No. of Components
Small Scale Integration (SSI)	2 - 64
Medium Scale Integration (MSI)	64 - 2000
Large Scale Integration (LSI)	2000 - 64,000
Very Large Scale Integration (VLSI)	64,000 - 2,000,000
Ultra Large Scale Integration (ULSI)	2,000,000 - 100,000,000

Since its invention in 1959, the IC has undergone rapid growth, its complexity following a progression known as Moore's Law which states that the maximum number of components on a microprocessor chip doubles every one and a half years. This is illustrated by the graph in *Figure 4.49*.

The graph shows how the number of components on an Intel Microprocessor IC has increased since 1967, and an estimate of how the trend might continue in the near future.

Currently, the maximum dimension, the *feature size*, of a transistor on a one-million transistor microprocessor is about one micrometre, that is, one millionth of a metre. Such a microprocessor is capable of processing perhaps twenty million instructions per second. It has been estimated that by the year 2000 the norm will be microprocessors containing forty million transistors of feature size 0·25 micrometers processing *one billion instructions per second*. Such a processor would be capable of handling animated graphics of photographic quality in real time. However, as the feature sizes of components approach atomic proportions, stability problems become increasingly problematic; with perhaps only a few hundred atoms separating components, their behaviour can become unusual. This behaviour is referred to as *quantum effects*. Obviously there is a limit to how small a transistor can be made, so continued micro-miniaturization depends on additional innovative research, and in fact quantum effects are providing one such possible avenue of research.

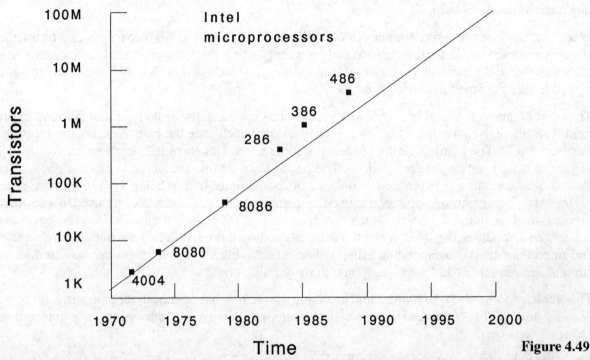

Figure 4.49

When electrons are constrained to move in less than three dimensions, their normal range of energy states is changed. When electrons are confined to two dimensions, in a very thin film of conducting material, certain electron energy states restrict the flow of current through the film, allowing it to act like an electronic switch. Furthermore, when constrained to move in less than two dimensions, in lines or even dots, other quantum effects occur, providing opportunities for multistate devices and therefore multivalued logic offering greatly enhanced speeds.

Another quantum effect device is a type of transistor whose operation is based on the charge of a single electron, and yet another invention from IBM scientists is a switch which turns on and off with the motion of a single atom.

These new devices are an order of magnitude smaller than those in current use and are capable of operating at much greater speeds, but at the moment there are serious problems to be overcome before they can be implemented in actual machines. The most serious problem is that quantum effect devices will only operate correctly at extremely low temperatures (around -450°F). However, experience tells us that apparently insurmountable technological problems remain so for only a short time and that we can expect that the near future will see a new breed of computers having capabilities greatly in excess of those in current use.

5 *Computer Systems Architecture*

Any system consists of a number of separate components working together to achieve a common aim. A car, for example, is a form of transport system comprising amongst other items, an engine, wheels and a gear box. Its aim is to transport people from one place to another. The system will only operate successfully if all these major components work. An essential additional element is the driver, without whom the car is simply a motionless piece of metal. The components of a system and the ways they interrelate constitute its architecture. The term *hardware* describes all the physical electronic and mechanical components forming part of a computer system.

Functional Components

The hardware components of a computer system can be categorized by function, as follows:

Input

To allow the computer to process data it must be in a form which the machine can handle. Before processing, data is normally in a human-readable form, for example, as it appears on an employee's time sheet or a customer's order form. Such alphabetic and numeric (decimal) data cannot be handled directly by the internal circuitry of the computer. Firstly, it has to be translated into the binary format which makes the data *machine-sensible*; this is the function of an input device. There are a wide variety of such devices, but the most common make use of a keyboard. Data is transferred from the input device to main memory.

Main Memory (RAM)

This element has two main functions:

- [ ] to temporarily store programs currently in use for processing data;

- [ ] to temporarily store data:

    entered via an input device and awaiting processing;

    currently being processed;

    which results from processing and is waiting to be output.

Central Processing Unit (CPU) or Processor

The CPU handles program instructions and data; it consists of two elements:

- [ ] *Arithmetic/Logic Unit(ALU)*. The ALU carries out arithmetic operations such as addition, multiplication, subtraction and division. It can also make logical comparisons between items of data, for example, it can determine whether one value is greater than another. Such logical operations can also be performed on non-numeric data.

☐ *Control Unit.* The control unit governs the operation of all hardware, including input and output devices and the CPU. It does this by fetching, interpreting and executing each instruction in turn, in an automatically controlled cycle; this *fetch-execute cycle* is described in detail in Chapter 3.

Output

Output devices perform the opposite function of input devices by translating machine-sensible data into a human-readable form, for example, onto a printer or the screen of a visual display unit (VDU). Sometimes, the results of computer processing may be needed for further processing, in which case, they are output to a storage medium (Chapter 6)which retains it in machine-sensible form for subsequent input.

Backing (auxiliary) Storage

Backing storage performs a *filing* function within the computer system. In this context it is important to consider a couple of important concepts.

☐ *Memory volatility.* It is not practical to store data files and programs in main memory because of its volatility. This means that the contents of the main memory can be destroyed, either by being overwritten as new data is entered for processing and new programs used, or when the machine is switched off. Such volatile memory is termed random access memory (RAM).

☐ *Retrievable data.* Backing storage media provide a more permanent store for programs (which may be used many times on different occasions) and data files (which are used for future reference or processing).

Peripherals

Those hardware devices which are external to the CPU and main memory, namely those devices used for input, output and backing storage, are called peripherals.

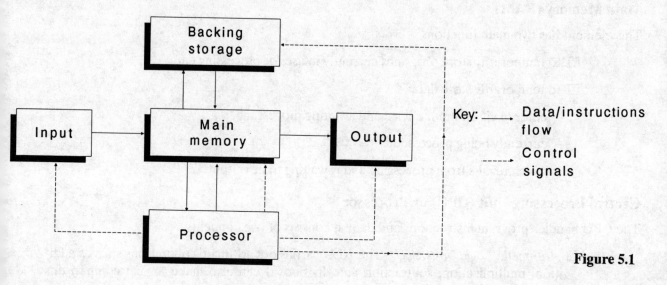

Figure 5.1

Figure 5.1 illustrates the relationships between the various hardware elements, the logical structure of the computer. It shows the data flow through the system and the flow of control signals from the control unit.

Types of Memory

RAM (Random Access Memory)

RAM serves as the *main memory* of a computer system; a full description of its characteristics is given in Chapter 10 on Microcomputer Systems Architecture.

ROM (Read Only Memory)

Firmware is used to describe programs which are hardwired into the computer using integrated circuit Read Only Memory (ROM) chips. ROM is *non-volatile*; in other words, the programs are not lost when the machine is switched off and the contents cannot be overwritten by other programs or data. ROM is normally used to store an initial set of instructions which allow the *booting* of a computer system and the subsequent loading of the rest of the operating system. There are two other types of ROM:

PROM or *programmable* ROM chips, which can be purchased content-free and used to store regularly-used pieces of software, such as word processors and spreadsheets. Plugged into vacant slots inside a computer's system casing, the software they contain can then be accessed without reference to conventional backing storage, but simply by transfer to RAM (Random Access Memory - main memory). Once recorded upon, PROM chips cannot be re-used for any other purpose;

EPROM or *eraseable programmable* ROM chips fulfil a similar function to PROM chips, except for the fact that their contents can be erased by exposure to ultra-violet light and then replaced using a special EPROM programmer device.

Associative or Content Addressable Memory

This type of memory allows its addressing according to the *contents* of locations rather than their physical addresses. Apart from Search (or Match) operations, associative memory also allows Reading and Writing according to the addressing principles used in RAM systems. For search operations, the contents of each memory word are compared with a given character string. Each memory word has an associated flag bit and if a match with the search string is found, the relevant flag is set. It is quite possible that the search string will not be unique to one memory location, so multiple matches are likely to be discovered in a single search operation.

With the use of a *mask register*, the search string does not have to be compared with the full contents of each memory word; thus, for example, it can be compared with the contents of only the first 4 bits of each 8 bit memory word. *Figure 5.2* illustrates a masked search operation.

A logical AND operation (Chapter 4) is carried out between the search register and the mask register; this ensures that only those bits in the search register which correspond with bit 1s in the mask register will be used in the search string.

Associative memory has obvious application for on-line information retrieval systems, but to be useful must make use of much longer word lengths to allow for example, search criteria involving names of people or products. To date, high cost has restricted its application.

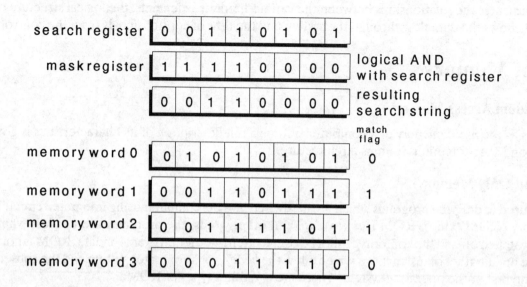

Figure 5.2

Buses

As is explained in the previous section, all computers have the same basic functional components, but the architectural details in some are far more complex than in others. A particular area of variation relates to the arrangement of the bus systems which permit communication between the various parts of the computer system. A number of features concerning buses can be identified:

☐ a bus is a group of parallel wires, one for each bit of a word, along which data can flow (as electrical signals);

☐ the *system* bus comprises a number of such communication channels, connecting a computer's processor and its associated components of memory and input/output(I/O) devices.

☐ a single bus may carry data for different functions at separate times or it may be dedicated to one function. A computer will usually have several buses, used for specific purposes, for example, the I/O bus or main memory to processor bus.

☐ some buses are *bi-directional*, that is by the enabling and inhibiting of *gates* (Chapter 4), data can flow in one direction or the other.

☐ the *width* of a bus determines the length of word which can be handled at one time. For example, a processor which used a 16-bit bus, but required a 32-bit word to address memory, would have to concatenate two 16-bit words in two separate fetch operations.

Communication is required within a processor, to allow movement of data between its various registers (Chapter 3), between the processor and memory and for I/O transfers. In a *single* bus system, both I/O and memory transfers share the same communication channel, whereas in a *two-bus* system, I/O and memory transfers are carried out independently; similarly, in small systems with few I/O devices, they may share the same bus, a larger system requiring several I/O buses to ensure efficient operation.

Each of the separately identified functions of memory, register-to-register and I/O transfers (assuming that the I/O bus is shared by a number of devices), must have the use of:

☐ a *data* bus, for the transfer of data subject to processing or manipulation in the machine;

☐ an *address* bus which carries the address of, for example, a memory word to be read (the details of memory addressing as part of the fetch-execute cycle are described in Chapters 3 and 10), or the output device to which a character is to be transmitted;

☐ a *control* bus, which as the name suggest, carries signals concerning the timing of various operations, such as memory write, memory read and I/O operations (this latter aspect of control is examined in more detail in Chapter 7).

All signals on a bus follow strict timing sequences, some operations taking longer than others. All processor operations are synchronized by a clock, the operation of which is described in Chapter 10.

I/O Ports and Interfacing

To allow an I/O device to communicate with the I/O bus, for example, to place data entered through a keyboard onto the data bus, requires the use of an I/O port. A number of I/O ports are usually available, the number and types depending on the range of devices which the system is designed to support. Each port has an *interfacing* role which must convert the data signals, as presented by the connected device, into the form required by the processor, as well as the converse for output data. Thus, for example, the *external* ASCII code used for data storage on a particular tape storage system, will probably have to be converted by the interface into the machine's particular *internal* code (Chapter 2).

Registers

Apart from the registers used in the fetch-execute cycle, most processors have a number which are *general-purpose* and as such, can be used by the low-level programmer to store intermediate results of processing. *Index* registers can be used to hold offset values to allow indexed indirect addressing methods (Chapter 3) or can be used as counters. Another register contains the *stack pointer*, which is used to store the address of the next available location in a special area of memory called the stack. The operation of the stack is described in Chapter 26 on Data Structures. A *flag* or *status* register is used for the storage of various flag bits which can be set to 1 or cleared to 0 depending on some condition, and typically include:

☐ *sign* flag (positive or negative) indicating the sign of the result of the last arithmetic operation; this would be copied from the sign bit of the result of this last operation;

☐ *carry* flag, set to 1 if the last arithmetic operation produced a carry;

☐ *zero* flag, set to 1 if the result of the last arithmetic operation was zero and to 0 if the result was non-zero;

☐ *overflow* flag to indicate the occurrence of arithmetic overflow in the last operation;

☐ *break* status, set to 1 if a break instruction has been executed;

☐ *interrupt disable* flag, set to 1 if interrupts are disabled (Chapter 7).

Register Transfer Language (RTL)

The structure of any particular computer system can be described diagrammatically, but RTL is used to define the ways in which data move within it. More particularly, RTL identifies the effects of an instruction by specifying the sequence of data transfers between registers and any arithmetic/logical operations needed for its execution.

The RTL examples used in this section assume knowledge of the fetch-execute cycle and the functions of each of the registers (Chapter 3) referred to.

RTL can be as simple or as complex as is necessary to describe the data transfers within any particular system, but for the purposes of understanding its general function, a number of *primitive* operations are identified.

The *fetch-execute cycle* can be described in RTL as follows:

Fetch phase

        PC → MAR

specifies that the contents of the *program counter* (PC) must be copied into the *memory address register* (MAR), thus ensuring that the next memory word to be fetched is a program instruction;

        PC → PC + 1

describes the incrementation of the PC to point to the next instruction;

        M [MAR] → MBR

indicates that the contents of the memory (M) location identified by the MAR are to be copied into the *memory buffer register* (MBR);

        MBR → CIR

shows that the instruction is then copied from the MBR into the *current instruction register* (CIR);

The fetching of any instruction follows this pattern, but the point at which the PC value is changed may vary, provided it occurs after its previous value has been copied to the MAR.

After the fetch phase an instruction must be *decoded* and *executed* and the nature of the instruction will determine the register transfers which are required. The first example which follows relates to a structure which uses *single address* instructions. Later, an example for *two address* instructions is provided.

Single Address Instructions

As is explained in Chapter 3, machines using this type of instruction must make use of an *accumulator* (ACC) register to perform arithmetic and logic operations and the following addition example illustrates this point; as already explained the fetch phase is common to all instructions.

fetch

```
                                        comments
              PC → MAR            {instruction address to MAR}
       M [MAR] → MBR              {copy instruction to MBR}
              PC → PC +1          {increment PC to next instruction}
             MBR → CIR            {copy instruction to CIR}
```

decode and thus identify the instruction

execute the instruction

```
       CIR<adr> → MAR            {the <adr> indicates the operand portion of the
                                    instruction word and this is copied to the MAR}
       M [MAR] → MBR             {read the operand value which is to be added to
                                    the contents of the ACC}
     ACC + MBR → ACC             {add operand value to contents of ACC and store
                                    in the ACC}
```

A complete addition process may involve the following operations (expressed in a hypothetical assembly code), assuming that two values are to be summed, that their respective memory addresses are A and B and that the result is to be stored in location C.

```
     LDA    A      {copy contents of location A into the ACC}
     ADD    B      {add the contents of B to those of the ACC, storing the result
                      there}
     STA    C      {copy contents of ACC to location C}
```

Remembering that each instruction executed is preceded by the fetch and decode phases detailed previously, it can be described in RTL thus:

execute **LDA A**

```
     CIR<adr>A → MAR            {specifies the operand A to be read}
       M [MAR] → MBR            {operand A copied to MBR}
           MBR → ACC            {operand A copied to ACC}
```

execute **ADD B**

```
     CIR <adr>B → MAR           {specifies second operand to be read}
        M [MAR] → MBR           {operand B copied to MBR}
      ACC + MBR → ACC           {add operand B to ACC giving result}
```

execute **STA C**

```
     CIR <adr>C → MAR           {specifies location C as memory location to
                                   store result}
            ACC → MBR           {copy contents of ACC to MBR}
            MBR → M [MAR]        {copy result from ACC to memory location C}
```

Two Address Instructions

As explained in Chapter 3, with two addresses available in the instruction it is implicit that the result of an operation is to be stored in one of the operands, thus overwriting its original contents. For example,

ADD A, B

would sum the contents of operand addresses A and B, and depending on the architecture, place the result in either the first or second named address.

The addition example which follows is based on the instruction set used in Chapter 28 on Assembly Language Programming. It differs from the single address addition process described earlier, not only in the number of addresses held within the instruction word, but also in the fact that the addresses refer to *registers* rather than memory locations. This means that the operands have to be moved from memory to their respective registers before the operation can be effected.

Thus,

```
LDW R1, A    {load word from memory location A into register R1}
LDW R2, B    {load word from memory location B into register R2}
ADD R1, R2   {add contents of R1 and R2, place result in R1}
STW R1, C    {store result from R1 into memory location C}
```

loads the contents of memory location with the *symbolic* address A into a register R1 and similarly, the contents of B into R2. The contents of R1 and R2 are added and the result is placed in R1, the *destination* register. The store instruction completes the process by copying the result from R1 to memory location C.

The data transfers for this operation can be specified in RTL as follows. As before, it is assumed that each instruction is preceded by the fetch and decode phases.

execute LDW R1, A

```
CIR <adr>A  → MAR       {specifies operand A to be read}
  M [MAR]   → MBR       {operand A copied to MBR}
     MBR    → R1        {operand A copied to register R1}
```

execute LDW R2, B

```
CIR< adr>B  → MAR       {specifies operand B to be read}
  M [MAR]   → MBR       {operand B copied to MBR}
     MBR    → R2        {operand B copied to register R2}
```

execute ADD R1, R2

```
  R1 + R2   → R1        {contents of R1, R2 added and result placed in
                         destination register R1}
```

execute STW R1, C

```
CIR <adr>C  → MAR       {specifies next memory write is to address C}
     R1     → MBR       {copy contents of R1 to MBR}
     MBR    → M [MAR]   {contents of MBR to memory address C, as
                         indicated by current value of MAR}
```

Parallel Processing Architectures

The potential for increasing computation speed through parallelism has long been recognized, its first real manifestation being in the change from computers which handled data serially bit by bit with a single processor to those manipulating parallel bit groupings or words, albeit still with only one processor.

Parallelism as described here is concerned with the use, in a variety of approaches, of *multiple processors* to act upon either *single* or *multiple streams* of data. A number of factors have permitted the research and development of parallel processing architectures, which previously had not been cost-effective.

Factors Encouraging Development

The development of VLSI (Very Large Scale Integration) circuits has allowed tremendous progress to be made in the miniaturization of computer components, most significantly in terms of processor and memory chips, but although users have felt the benefits of significant speed improvements, they have not been of the same order. They continue to improve, but it has been apparent for some time that the power needs of some applications go beyond single processor systems. It is also recognized that the greatest increases in speed can be obtained through changes in system architecture. The RISC (Reduced Instruction Set Computer) approach is already bringing about significant benefits and is examined in Chapter 10 on Microcomputer Systems Architecture, but parallel architectures, despite the particular difficulties they present for the design of software which can take full advantage, probably hold the greatest potential for radical performance gains. Parallel hardware is, of course, only half the solution and it must be also possible to write programs that can execute in parallel. The Occam programming language developed by Inmos, addresses the special requirements of writing code for *arrays* of *transputers* (see end section).

Architectural Approaches to Parallelism

The following sections provide information on some of the ways in which degrees of parallelism may be achieved.

Pipelining

This term refers to the activities of a 'pipeline' of processors each of which performs a mathematical operation on a *single vector stream* of data. The approach is based on the premise that any arithmetic process incorporates a number of distinct stages which can be separately allocated to individual processors.

Each processor has an associated register, isolated from the rest, and permitting parallel computation on the data. A clock pulse synchronizes the activities of all processors in the pipeline, so that the data moves through it, step by step with each clock pulse. As an illustrative example, floating point addition requires the performance of a sequence of three operations, namely to:

- □ equalize the exponents, adjusting one mantissa as necessary;

- □ add the mantissas;

- □ normalize the result.

New sets of numbers to be added can be fed into the pipeline as each set moves through it to produce the sum.

Instruction pipeline. Pipeline processing can also be applied to the instruction stream. Using the buffering principle, consecutive instructions are read from memory into the pipeline, while preceding instructions are executed by the processor. Complications arise when an instruction causes a branch out of sequence, at which point the pipe must be cleared and all instructions read from memory, but not yet processed, are discarded. The overall effect of such *queuing* is to reduce the average memory access time for reading instructions.

Although pipelining can be described as a parallel architecture, the processors are only operating on a single vector stream of data and the acronym SISD (Single Instruction Single Data-stream) is frequently used to describe its mode of operation.

A major advantage of pipeline architecture is that program code developed for von Neumann architecture, that is *serial code*, can be run without modification, whilst improvements in the performance of programs particularly suited to pipeline processing can be changed accordingly. This requires the identification of discrete processing stages and the division of particularly processor-hungry sections of code for allocation to separate processors. A number of manufacturers have produced powerful machines of this type.

Processor Arrays

Processors connected in a pipeline can be described as forming a linear array, but the following section is concerned with two and three-dimensional processor arrays, for which the Inmos transputer was specifically designed

SIMD (Single Instruction Multiple Data-stream). In a two-dimensional array, for example, 4096 processors may be connected in a 64×64 square, so that each one has 4 neighbouring elements.

Known as SIMD architecture, each program instruction is transmitted *simultaneously* to all the processors in the array, so each can then execute the instruction using its *locally* stored set of data. Because all processors are executing the same instruction at any one time, existing serial code can be used, provided the data can be conveniently divided. By the parallel processing of large numbers of data sets at one time, massive increases in job processing speed can be achieved. Of course, not all processors in the array are necessarily concerned with a particular processing stage and data may have to be passed on to the next relevant processor via a number of array elements which have no interest in the data. The length of such communications paths can have a significant effect on system performance and in efforts to reduce the number of processors handling data with which they have no concern, a number of geometrical designs (beyond the requirements of this text) are in use.

MIMD (Multiple Instruction Multiple Data-stream). This also permits the parallel processing of separate sets of data, but each processor is at a different stage in the program's execution. More complex than the SIMD approach, it requires firstly, the vectoring of the program code into separate processes, each with the potential for execution on a separate processor and secondly in some systems, the division of data into *local* (available to a particular processor) and *global* (available to all). Each processor can be viewed as dealing with a particular part of the overall program and a particular data set, as well as having access to certain data available globally to all processors. In order that they can be executed in parallel, each of the processes should be substantially independent of the rest, although in general, they need to communicate with one another. If global memory is used for such communication, co-ordination difficulties can arise. In the Cray 2 system for example, passing data from one processor to another via global memory, requires the synchronization of the write operation by the transmitting processor and the subsequent read by the receiving one.

The transputer incorporates serial links which allow communications between processors and the concept of global memory is not used.

Applications

A number of applications likely to benefit particularly from parallel processing are outlined below.

☐ *weather forecasting*, which requires 'number crunching' operations on huge volumes of data, gathered globally and from monitoring satellites, in time to produce accurate weather forecasts, rather than comments on existing weather conditions!

☐ *graphics applications*. Ray tracing, for example, where a set of descriptors of three-dimensional objects in three-dimensional space is mapped onto a flat screen complete with shadows, refraction and reflections, needs considerable computation to trace where the light on each screen pixel came from. The application is most easily implemented on pipeline architecture, where it benefits from both the faster maths and the faster communication. With about 10 million calculations to generate a single screen picture, speed is vital when generating sequences of images. A major application is in aircraft flight simulators, where the scenes to be shown are not known exactly in advance, as they depend on the pilot's actions. To be of any use they need to be generated virtually instantaneously in real-time.

☐ *simulation*. Engineering design problems benefit hugely from computer simulation. The designers of North Sea oil platforms could ill afford to build prototypes to test to destruction, so they carry out all the structural analysis on a Cray supercomputer costing around £20 million; the process only takes about 9 hours, but the time taken still makes extensive prototyping very expensive. A car body designer using a £1 million mainframe has to wait about 20 hours for a typical run to complete. These lengthy run-times mean that computer simulation tends to be used to validate designs already completed, rather than as a development tool.

☐ *image processing*. A particularly exciting example involves the use of computers to assist the plastic surgeon in the repair of facial injuries or deformities. The patient's head is scanned by cameras and the image digitized for display on a computer screen. This image can be rotated or tilted on screen by the surgeon and experimental 'cuts' made, the results of which can then be viewed on screen from any angle. In this way, a plastic surgeon can study the results of a variety of strategies before making a single mark on the patient. The complexity of such image processing requires parallel processing if rapid response to user input is to be achieved. Industrial processes frequently require robots which can recognize different shaped components and possess sufficient 'spatial aware-ness' to allow accurate assembly to take place. Artificial intelligence techniques are applied to both these areas, so that robots can 'learn' and the power of parallel processing greatly enhances the opportunity for such developments;

☐ *speech recognition* is an enormously complex process if a system is to be capable of handling a wide range of vocabulary, pronunciation and intonation, let alone the meaning of phrases and even sentences. Artificial intelligence techniques are being applied to the speech recognition process and parallel processing power greatly im-proves the opportunities for its evolution.

☐ *financial and economic system modelling*. To make realistic assessments of the effective-ness of various economic strategies requires the processing of huge volumes of raw data.

Multi-processing. Parallel processing should not be confused with multi-processing arcitectures which allow the simultaneous running of several separate programs, but with each program only having control of one processor at a time.

Transputers

The Transputer is effectively a 'building block' for parallel processing architectures; while it contains its own memory and processing elements, it also features unique serial links which allow it to communicate with other Transputers. A matrix of Transputers can be created with each one solving a small part of a complete task. The addition of extra Transputers to a system incrementally adds the full power of each unit to the overall system performance. In theory, if one Transputer operates at 10 million instructions per second (mips), then two will give a system performance of 20 mips, 10 will give 100 mips and so on. In practice, the problem still remains of splitting computer processing problems into separate parts for each of the transputers to handle.

Computer Systems Classified

Computer systems can be classified according to the following characteristics: purpose; size and complexity; generation.

Purpose

There are two categories under this heading:

General-purpose Computers

As the term suggests, general-purpose machines can carry out processing tasks for a wide variety of applications and most organizations will make use of this type of machine.

Dedicated or Special-purpose Computers

In their logical structure, these machines are fundamentally the same as the general-purpose machine except that they have been programmed for a specific application. Dedicated word processors provide one example. The advent of cheap, microprocessor-based, special-purpose systems has led to an expansion of their use in controlling machines and many household products, such as washing machines and microwave ovens, are controlled by such systems.

Size and Complexity

It should be emphasized that the following categories are only broad guidelines and changes in technology are continually blurring the differences between them. For example, there are now powerful microcomputer systems (often referred to as super-micros) which far exceed the power and flexibility of earlier generation minicomputer systems. However, the generally accepted categories of computer system are as follow:

Mainframe Computers

Such computers are commonly used by large national and multi-national organizations such as banks, airlines and oil companies. They usually support a large number and variety of peripherals and can process a number of applications concurrently *(multiprogramming)*. The mainframe's power stems from the phenomenal speeds of the processor and the large size of the main memory.

Mainframes may also play a central role in *wide area networks*. Their huge capital cost invariably places them in centralized processing roles; for the same reason, about fifty per cent of the mainframes currently in use are rented or leased from specialist companies.

Mainframe computers are generally accommodated in special-purpose, air-conditioned rooms to ensure trouble free operation.

Supercomputers with processing speeds many times those of mainframe systems are used for scientific and statistical work, being capable of completing such work in a small fraction of the time that a mainframe would require.

Minicomputers

Minicomputers are scaled-down versions of mainframe computers. The division between the two types becomes rather blurred when referring to small mainframe and supermini systems. Costing less and being robust enough to operate without a special environment, they can be used in *real-time* applications such as controlling manufacturing processes in an engineering factory. They are also used by medium sized organizations for all their processing needs or by larger organizations as part of a network system. The mini computer is technically very similar to the mainframe, with the following differences:

      ☐ it usually only has magnetic disk storage;

      ☐ the main input/output peripherals tend to be visual display units (VDUs).

Minicomputers can support a number of applications concurrently and are often used with *time-sharing* operating systems (Chapter 12) and *intelligent terminals* to provide organizations with decentralized processing facilities. Used in this way, many applications such as word processing, invoicing and customer enquiry can be carried out by users in their own departments. Generally, the volumes of input will be relatively small. This contrasts with the multiprogramming mode of operation often used in mainframe systems where, in addition to handling on-line terminals for interactive work, large volume, batch processing jobs are processed centrally and users are not directly involved.

Medium-sized organizations may use minicomputers for their main processing applications. Larger organizations may apply them to *front end* processing (FEP). Employed in this way, a minicomputer handles a mainframe's communications traffic (Chapter 8) with remote terminals or other computers, leaving the mainframe free to handle the organization's information processing tasks.

Microcomputers

The microcomputer is the smallest in the range and was first developed when the Intel Corporation succeeded in incorporating the main functional parts of a computer on a single *chip* using *integrated circuits* (IC) on silicon. Subsequently, the technique of *large scale integration* (LSI) further increased the number of electronic circuits which could be packed onto one chip. LSI has been superseded by *very large scale integration* (VLSI) which packs even more circuitry onto a single chip thus further increasing the power and storage capacity of microcomputers and computers generally. This type of computer storage is known as *metal oxide semiconductor* storage (MOS) and has completely replaced the *core store* used in earlier mainframe computers.

Originally, microcomputers were only capable of supporting a single user and a single application at any one time. The increase in processor speed and memory capacity now permits their use for *multi-tasking* (the running of several tasks concurrently by one user). *Multi-user* operation is made possible through networking; it is now extremely popular to link microcomputers into a *local area network* (LAN), to allow resource-sharing (disk, printer, programs and data files), as well as electronic communications between users (*electronic mail*). Microcomputers can now support applications packages previously restricted to mini and mainframe systems, including, for example, those used for database and *computer aided design* (CAD) work.

The range of microcomputer software is now extremely wide and the quality generally very high. There are software packages available for most business applications. One area of recent rapid growth has been in the development of graphics-based applications and most popular applications software can now be operated via a *graphical user interface*(GUI)and a *mouse*.

The low cost of microcomputers and the increase in the range of software available, makes their use possible in almost any size and type of organization. In the small firm, a microcomputer may be used for word processing, stock control, costing, and general accounting. In the larger organization they may be used as intelligent terminals. Such systems provide the user with the processing facilities of a central mini or mainframe computer and at the same time, a degree of independent processing power through the use of the microcomputer's own processor and memory store. Microcomputer architecture is examined in detail in a separate chapter of that title.

Generations

Since the first electronic computers were built in the 1940s, a number of developments in electronics have led to computer hardware being categorized by 'generation', that is, its place in the history of the computer. These generations can be simply defined as follows:

First Generation

During the 1940s, this first generation of computers used electronic components including vacuum tubes. The first computer to allow a program to be stored in memory (a stored-program computer) was EDSAC, developed at the University of Manchester. The vacuum tubes were fragile, subject to overheating and caused frequent breakdowns.

Second Generation

The introduction of low-cost and reliable transistors allowed the computer industry to develop at a tremendous rate during the late 1950s. The cost and size of the machines were radically reduced so it became possible for large commercial organizations to make use of computers. Examples of such machines include LEO III, UNIVAC and ATLAS.

Third Generation

The development of integrated circuit (IC) technology in the mid-1960s heralded the development of more powerful, reliable and compact computers, such as those of the IBM 360 series.

Fourth Generation

This generation is typified by large scale integration (LSI) of circuits which allowed the development of the microprocessor, which in turn allowed the production of the microcomputer. All computers used today make use of such silicon 'chip' technology.

Fifth Generation

At present, most computers are still of the fourth generation variety. Developments are continuing towards expanding memory size, using very large scale integration (VLSI) techniques and increasing the speed of processors. This increasing power is allowing the pursuit of new lines of development in computer systems:

☐ More human orientated input/output devices using voice recognition and speech synthesis should allow communication between computers and humans to be more flexible and 'natural'. In the future, the aim is to allow computers to be addressed in languages natural to the users. Current techniques on some microcomputers allow acceptance of some spoken commands. Others allow the selection of user options displayed as graphics on the screen via a hand-held 'mouse'.

☐ Parallel processing techniques.

Analogue Computers

Whereas digital computers store numerical information in discrete form, that is, by coded sets of electrical pulses representing digits, analogue computers use physical quantities which are proportional to the numbers involved. Examples of such physical quantities, generically referred to as analogues, include electric current, voltage, temperature, length, or the angle of a shaft. Thermometers, slide rules (obsolete since the advent of the electronic calculator), barometers, pointer instruments such as voltmeters, ammeters, speedometers and the weathervane are typical examples of analogue devices. Analogue information is in continuous form, often depicted on a graph or an oscilloscope screen. Electrical analogue computers use current or voltage as analogues.

Uses. Analogue computers are used by mathematicians and engineers to solve differential equations which occur in science and engineering, for example, in fluid flow, robotics, atomic physics and in the field of simulation. Aircraft and rocket simulation, for example, is useful for training of personnel and as a design aid, particularly where experiments might be too expensive to carry out fully, or where failure may be hazardous to life.

Advantages and disadvantages. The overriding advantage of an analogue computer, compared with a digital system, is its ability to solve differential equations extremely quickly. Therefore, it is ideally suited to real-time operation, in other words, the performance of operations in the timescale in which they actually occur. It must be said that the speed and power of modern digital machines permits their application in areas of real-time operation formerly only suited to analogue techniques. Nevertheless, there are a number of situations in control and simulation where analogue computers provide a simpler and less expensive alternative to the digital computer.

Analogue computers have a number of disadvantages:

☐ relatively inaccurate, $0 \cdot 1$ percent accuracy being typical;

☐ setting up time can be lengthy and alteration to suit another problem may be difficult;

☐ having no memory, they cannot store problems;

☐ output is only possible in graphical form;

☐ input is only acceptable in the form of dial settings;

☐ extensive maintenance is needed and the user must understand electrical engineering.

Hybrid Computers

These were developed to combine the speed of the analogue computer with the flexibility of its digital counterpart. Users must possess skills in both analogue and digital computing. The analogue section of the hybrid computer is used to give an approximate solution, which is then enhanced by the digital section. The latter generates, by table look-up, functions that the analogue part cannot easily simulate. Output from the analogue section is edited by the digital section and printed out in a convenient form. Methods are needed to convert analogue form to digital form and vice versa and these same methods are used to interface a digital computer to the real, physical world. Examples of such interfacing are found in, for example, furnace temperature control systems and image scanners.

6 *Peripherals*

As the name suggests, peripheral devices are the external elements of the computer system described in Chapter 5. They provide a means of communication between the central processor, its human operators and frequently, other computer systems. Peripheral devices can be categorized according to their general function. These functions are identified at the beginning of Chapter 5 as part of the logical computer configuration and are:

- ☐ Backing storage;
- ☐ Input and output.

There are two sections in this chapter; the first deals with backing storage devices and media and the second with *input* and *output* (I/O) peripheral devices. Descriptions of typical circumstances when each I/O device may best be used are provided and comparisons are made between storage devices, in respect of their access speeds, reliability and relative costs.

Backing Storage

All backing storage systems consist of two main elements, a *device* and a *medium*. For example, a disk drive is a device and a magnetic disk is a storage medium. Under program control, data files are generally read from and written to via the storage device which is connected on-line to the CPU. The most important kinds of backing storage devices in use today are those using *magnetic tape* and *magnetic disk*.

Magnetic Tape

Despite the continued evolution of disk storage, magnetic tape continues to be used in most large scale computer installations as a cheap and secure method of storing large volumes of data which are normally processed in a *serial* fashion. It is also useful for the storage of historic files where rapid access to individual records is not essential. An example of the former use is in the processing of an organization's payroll. An example of storing historic data on tape is provided by the Police National Computer system in Hendon, where millions of records on current criminal activities are kept *on-line* and are directly accessible from magnetic disk packs; records which are currently inactive are held *off-line* on magnetic tape, so when a record needs to be retrieved, the relevant tape has to be placed on-line and searched until the required record is found. It would be inefficient and expensive to keep all records, no matter how old, on-line all of the time.

General Features of Magnetic Tape

The tapes used on mainframe and minicomputer systems are stored on large detachable reels. Tapes are made of plastic and are covered with a coating which can be magnetized and by which means data is encoded.

A particular type of cartridge tape, which looks like a cassette tape but is slightly larger, is often used as a backup for hard disk on microcomputer systems. These *streamer* tapes have huge capacity, typically 60mb and upwards and can copy the complete contents of a hard disk in several minutes.

The rest of this section concentrates on large reel-to-reel systems.

Processing Tapes

A tape must be mounted on an on-line tape unit when it is to be used by a computer system. During processing, the tape is propelled past separate read and write heads at high speed. As is explained in Chapter 22 data is transferred between tape and main memory in physical *blocks*, each one being separated by an *inter-block gap* (IBG), to allow the tape to decelerate and stop and accelerate again to the correct speed for data transfer. Data transfer has to be carried out in block sizes which can be accommodated by main memory and provide for the quickest possible processing of a complete file.

Data Storage on Magnetic Tape

Figure 6.1 shows how data is stored on magnetic tape. The coding system used is either ASCII or EBCDIC, the latter being used on IBM equipment.

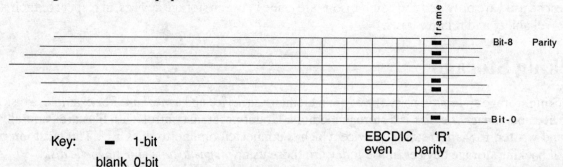

Figure 6.1

The coding systems are binary and in the case of EBCDIC, each character is represented by a group of 8 binary digits (bits), either 0 or 1, plus a parity bit (for checking transmission errors), across the width of the tape. As *Figure 6.1* shows, each 0 or 1 bit is accommodated in a single *track* and each group of bits representing one character occupies one *frame* across the tape.

The method of representing a 0 or 1 bit depends on the recording system in use but simplified examples are as follow:

 ☐ the presence of a magnetic field to represent 1 and the lack of a magnetic field to represent 0;

 ☐ the 0 and 1 bits are represented by magnetic fields of opposite polarity, say north for 1 and south for 0.

The tape unit reads across the nine tracks in a frame to identify the character represented.

Blocking Data on Magnetic Tape

As is explained in Chapter 22, a file is made up of a number of *logical* records. For example, a stock file contains a logical record for each commodity in stock. Generally, a logical record will not be large enough to constitute a physical record or block, so a number of logical records are grouped for transfer at one read or write instruction. The number of logical records in each physical record indicates the *blocking factor*. Large blocks save space (fewer inter-block gaps) and speed processing, although memory size is a limiting factor on the size of blocks.

Application of Magnetic Tape

Typically, one magnetic tape reel can store up to 40 million bytes or characters, allowing for header and trailer labels and inter-block gaps; the frequency of the latter will determine the practical capacity of any particular reel.

The *data transfer rate*, the rate at which data can be transferred between tape and main memory, is commonly in excess of half a million bytes per second.

These features, together with the media's relative cheapness when compared with magnetic disk, make it appropriate for applications requiring mass storage. However, magnetic tape does not permit direct access to records and this limits its use to applications requiring sequential access only; the most common usage of magnetic tape is for storing *back-up* files and the *archiving* of files from magnetic disk storage.

Magnetic Disks

Many computer applications require quick, direct access to individual records within a file and this facility is provided by magnetic disk. For this reason, magnetic disks are the most important backing storage media in use today.

Two popular types of magnetic disk are:

- ☐ hard disks;
- ☐ 'floppy' or flexible disks.

Hard Disks

The disk is usually made of aluminium with a coating of a magnetizable material on which data can be recorded. Records are stored in concentric rings or *tracks*. The method of encoding is fundamentally the same as that for tape, except that the magnetic states representing binary patterns are stored in single-file around the tracks. Each track is divided into a number of *sectors*, each having the same storage capacity. Each track and sector has a physical *address* which can be used by software to locate a particular record or group of records. A read/write mechanism is provided for each surface of a disk. The central area of the disk is not used, because to do so would necessitate a higher packing density than can be read or recorded by the read/write head. The number of tracks and sectors is known as the disk's *format*. The sector size can either be fixed permanently or can be altered by software. The former is known as *hard* sectoring and the latter as *soft* sectoring.

- ☐ *Hard Sectoring*. The position of each sector can be indicated by a slot or reflective marker which can be detected by sensors in the drive unit. As the smallest unit of data transfer between disk and CPU is a sector (block), this means that any application is restricted to the disk's block size. Consider, for example, an application which uses logical records of 64 bytes, stored on a disk with 512 byte hard sectors. A minimum of 8 logical records needs to be transferred to memory even if only one is required out of the sector.

☐ *Soft Sectoring.* This method allows the sectors to be set by software. All microcomputer systems use soft sectoring.

Disk Packs

To increase storage capacity, disks may be formed into a pack, with a common access mechanism. The disk pack is generally loaded from the top of the disk unit. Because the disk pack can be removed and exchanged, the heads remain in their retracted position when the pack is not in place and when the disks are not revolving at their full operating speed.

Disk Cylinders

The concept of the *cylinder* is explained in Chapter 22. Briefly, if there are ten possible recording surfaces with 200 tracks per surface, there are 200 imaginary, concentric cylinders, each consisting of ten tracks. Each vertical plane of tracks is a cylinder and as such is equivalent to a track position to which the heads on the access mechanism can move. All the read/write heads are fixed to a 'comb' so that each is in the same cylinder at any one time. Sequential files are applied to a disk pack on a cylinder-by-cylinder basis so that all records in a cylinder can be processed with the heads in one position.

Single Exchangeable Disks

Single exchangeable disks are also known as *cartridge* disks and can be inserted into the front of the disk unit, in which case, part of the disk cover automatically slides to one side to allow the read/write heads to move in, or it can be 'top loaded' and the plastic cover removed by the operator once the disk is in place. As is the case with the exchangeable disk pack, the moveable heads remain in the retracted position except when the disk is revolving at full speed.

Winchester Disks

When first introduced, Winchester disks were designed for large computer systems and are still popular on such systems. They are now used as an alternative to floppy disks on microcomputer systems. Winchester disks provide a much greater volume of on-line storage and faster access to programs and data than is possible with floppy disks.

Winchester disk systems consist of packs of hard disks, stacked in the same way as the exchangeable disk pack systems described earlier. The disks are not removable and are hermetically sealed in the storage units together with the read/write mechanism. The contamination-free environment in which the disks are stored allows very high speeds of rotation, typically, 3600 revolutions per minute. Storage capacities are increasing as technology advances, but commonly available systems for microcomputers can provide almost limitless storage, 50 to 100 megabytes being common.

Disk Access Time

Access time is the interval between the moment the command is given to transfer a data block (sector) from disk to main memory and the moment the transfer is completed; three processes can be identified.

☐ *seek time*. Suppose, for example, the read/write head unit is in cylinder 5 and that data is required from cylinder 24. To retrieve the data, the mechanism must move inwards to cylinder 24, the time taken to accomplish this movement being known as the seek time.

☐ *rotational delay*. When a read or write instruction is issued, the head is not usually positioned over the sector where the required data are stored, so there is some rotational delay while the disk rotates into the proper position. On average, the time taken is half a revolution of the disk pack. This average time is known as the *latency* of the disk.

☐ *data transfer time*. This is the time taken to read the block of data into main memory;

Two strategies can be used to reduce disk access time. The first solution is to store related records in the same cylinder so that head movement is minimized, a strategy usually adopted for sequential files where records are to be accessed sequentially. Even with random files it is sometimes possible to group related records in the same cylinder. The second solution is to use *fixed head* disks, which provide each track with its own read/write head and involve no seek time. It has to be said, however, that this second option is no longer used in disk drive systems, primarily because of their high manufacturing costs.

Application of Magnetic Disk

Exchangeable disk packs constitute the most popular form of backing storage, because despite being more expensive than magnetic tape, the provision of direct as well as sequential access, gives magnetic disk an overwhelming advantage. Its support of a variety of file and database organization methods make it appropriate for any application.

Typically, a single disk pack can store over 100 megabytes and although a single CPU can only access one surface in one disk pack at a time, a system may have a number of drive units, each containing a similar disk pack, permanently on-line. Other files may be held on additional disk packs held off-line, but these can be placed on-line as and when required, by exchanging them with those held in the drive units. A multi-processor system could, of course, access several on-line disk packs at the same time.

Direct access times will vary, depending on the amount of head movement required (this will depend on the method of file organization and the mode of access) and the performance characteristics of the disk system in use, but for the processing of a sequential file with progressive head movement through the cylinders, data transfer rates in excess of 300,000 bytes per second are typical.

Floppy Disks or Diskettes

Floppy disks are physically and operationally different from hard disks. They are flexible and encased in a square plastic protective jacket, in which the diskette revolves at approximately 360 revolutions per minute, more slowly than a conventional disk. The jacket is lined with a soft material which helps to clean the diskette as it revolves. The read/write heads make contact with the diskette surface when data transfer is in progress and withdraw at other times to reduce wear, but a diskette will eventually wear out after about 500 to 600 hours of contact. The diskette does not rotate continuously and access times are considerably inferior to those of hard disk systems.

Types of Floppy Disk

Floppy disks are available in two sizes according to diameter - 5·25 inches and 3·5 inches. Diskettes can be either 40 track or 80 track and the number of sectors can be varied (soft-sectoring is used). Suppose, for example, that a diskette has 80 tracks and that a particular computer system formats the diskettes into 9 sectors. Formatting causes it to be divided up into nine sectors 0 to 8, so an 80 track, 9 sector diskette has 720 addressable locations. Soft sectoring is used because the operating systems of different computers use different addressing formats. Thus, in principle, standard diskettes can be sold which only require formatting to be used on a particular machine. The formatting procedure also sets up a *directory* which is automatically maintained by the computer system to keep track of the contents of each location.

Double and Quad-Density Disks

Double-density disks are designed to store 48 tracks per inch (tpi) and are referred to as double density because they use double the track density available with earlier disks. The actual number of tracks available on a double density disk is 40 per side, but although the disks are designed to store data in a given number of tracks, it is the disk drive which dictates exactly how many are used. Thus, quad-density disks are designed to support 96tpi, but can be used in drives which record at 48tpi. Quad-density disks used in quad-density disk drives can store 1·2mb compared with the 360kb possible with a double-density system. The quadrupled capacity is achieved by doubling the number of sectors per track as well as doubling the track density. It is important for users to ensure that good quality quad-density disks are used in high density drives, as inferior disks will not support the required recording densities, resulting in unreliable data storage.

3·5 inch Disks

The 3·5 inch disk is stored in a rigid plastic casing which makes it more robust than its 5·25 inch counterpart. A metal sliding shutter, which covers the recording surface access slot, slides open when the disk is placed in the drive unit. The greater protection provided by this casing allows data to be recorded more densely on a 3·5 inch disk (typically 1·44mb) than is generally practicable on the 5·25 inch variety.

Application of Floppy Disk

Storage capacities are only a fraction of the Winchester hard disks available for most microcomputers and their slower revolution rate also makes access times rather slow; in microcomputer systems with twin floppy drives only, their speed is generally adequate only for the smallest of business applications. Floppy disk systems have the advantage of providing extremely cheap storage.

Alternative Backing Storage Devices and Media

Magnetic tape and disk systems account for a very large proportion of all storage systems in use, but there are a number of alternatives.

Optical Disks

The optical disk uses laser beam technology to allow data to be recorded and read using bit-densities several times greater than a typical magnetic disk. Data is recorded as bit-patterns using high-intensity laser beams to burn tiny holes into the surface of the disk. The data can then be read from the disk using a laser beam of reduced intensity. A similar technology is used for Compact Disk (CD) digitized recordings of music and film. Its application in computing is still in the early stages of development but it is likely to have a profound impact on backing storage usage.

There are two main types of optical disk system presently available.

CD-ROM (Compact Disk/Read-Only Memory) Systems

As the title suggests this type of disk only allows the computer to read data from the disk which is pre-recorded by the manufacturer. It is of no use for the storage of data which requires updating, its main application being for Interactive Video Disk systems, which can store text, images and audio signals for use in *advertising, training* and *education*. Sequences of film and sound can be retrieved under computer control.

WORM (Write Once, Read Many)

The large storage capacity of optical disks means that the writing facility can be used for a considerable period before all space is filled. Storage capacities are measured in gigabytes (thousands of millions of characters), way beyond the capacity of any magnetic disk systems. Optical disk systems which provide an erase facility are available but are still too expensive for most users.

Apart from its vast storage capacity, the optical disk is less prone to environmental hazards such as dust, largely because the read signal is more intense and the laser head can be fixed 2mm from the disk surface, allowing dust and other particles to pass underneath.

Application of Optical Disk

A single optical disk can store around 4 gigabytes of data and can transfer data at 3 megabytes per second, much faster than either magnetic tape or disk. The lack of an overwrite or erase facility is a significant drawback in respect of most common data processing systems and MIS (management information systems), but there are some specialist areas where it can be used to advantage, including databases where updating is infrequent and the prime requirement is for information retrieval. CD/ROM systems are largely used for vocational Computer Based Training (CBT). The large investment in conventional hard disk systems, both in terms of hardware and software, is likely to slow the widespread introduction of optical disk for backing storage.

Mass Storage

These storage systems provide massive storage capacity at the cost of relatively slow access times; the financial cost per record unit is low, which is an attractive feature to governments and large commercial organizations. All mass storage systems are *off-line,* with an automatic facility for placing units of storage on-line, as necessary. The unit of storage may be, for example, an optical disk or a magnetic tape cartridge. One IBM mass storage system consists of a honeycomb of locations, each containing a tape cartridge with a capacity of 50 megabytes. When a cartridge is needed, it is retrieved by a robot mechanism under program control and the contents are copied onto on-line magnetic disk, from where information can be accessed immediately; the cartridge is then automatically replaced in its proper location.

Magnetic Bubble Memory

Unlike disks and tapes, which are electro-mechanical devices, magnetic bubble memory has no moving parts at all.

Bubbles are formed in thin plates of magnetic material as tiny cylindrical 'domains'. The presence of a bubble in a location represents a 1-bit and the absence of a bubble, a 0-bit. The bubbles can be moved within the magnetic layer by tiny electrical forces, thus altering the bit patterns. Bubbles can be created and destroyed by similar forces. Because there are no moving parts, bubble memory is potentially more reliable than its electro-mechanical counterparts but as yet it has not been brought into general use for a variety of reasons.

Firstly, storage capacities and access times for magnetic disks are continually being improved. Secondly, except for very small systems, magnetic bubble memory is more expensive per bit of storage, than magnetic disk and this is likely to remain the case until increased volume of production brings down production costs. Its non-volatility makes it a possible alternative to the small disk memories used on some microcomputer systems, but currently, magnetic disk provides better access times.

The main applications of magnetic bubble memory are for memory units in terminals, microcomputers, robots and telecommunications equipment where the memory capacity required is not large. It appears that magnetic bubble memory has failed to make any real impact on storage systems.

Input and Output Devices

This section is concerned with equipment designed for input, output or both.

The most common methods of input involve the use of display devices such as the Visual Display Unit (VDU) and the first part of this section deals with such equipment. Printers are the next devices to be considered in that they provide hard copy output of the results of computer processing, sometimes at incredible speeds.

The next part examines equipment which automates input and removes the need for keyboard data entry. Equipment in this category includes, for example, OCR (Optical Character Recognition) devices and Bar Code Readers.

Finally, an examination is made of some special-purpose output devices involving microfilm and speech synthesis.

Display Devices

Visual Display Unit

The most commonly used device for communicating with a computer is the Visual Display Unit (VDU). Input of text is via a full alphanumeric keyboard and output is displayed on a viewing screen similar to a television. The term VDU terminal is normally used to describe the screen and keyboard as a combined facility for input and output, but on its own, the screen is called a *monitor*. In order that an operator can see what is being typed in via the keyboard, input is also displayed on the screen, a square of light called a *cursor* indicating where the next character to be typed by the operator will be placed.

Text and Graphics

Most display screens provide both a text and graphics facility. Text consists of letters (upper and lower case), numbers and special characters such as punctuation marks, which most applications require. Graphics output includes picture images, such as maps, charts and drawings.

Screen Resolution

A screen's resolution dictates the clarity or sharpness of the displayed text or graphics characters. The achievement of high quality graphics generally requires a higher resolution or sharper image than is required for textual display. Images are formed on the screen through the use of *pixels* (picture elements), tiny dots of light on the screen and the resolution is determined by their density on screen. The greater the density of pixels, the better the resolution.

Dot Matrix Characters

Textual characters are usually formed using a matrix of pixels and as with screen resolution, the clarity of individual characters is determined by the number of pixels used. Selected dots within the matrix are illuminated to display particular characters.

Graphics Display with Bit Mapping

To provide maximum control over the screen display, each pixel can be individually controlled by the programmer, allowing maximum flexibility in the design of individual images. Where image movement is required, for example in computer games, this is achieved in a similar manner to filmed cartoons, smooth movement being simulated by minute changes to the shape and location of successive displays of an image. This requires the high degree of precision available at the individual pixel level. Apart from movement simulation, bit mapping allows the drawing of extremely complex and life-like pictures and is therefore used in the development of, for example, application packages for Computer Aided Design (CAD).

Dumb and Intelligent Terminals

A *dumb* terminal is one which has no processing power of its own, possibly no storage, and is entirely dependent on a controlling computer. Where a terminal is connected via a telecommunications link, each character is transmitted to the central computer as soon as it is entered by the operator, making editing extremely difficult and slow; for this reason, they are not generally used for remote data entry.

An *intelligent* terminal has some memory and processing power and as such, allows the operator to store, edit and manipulate data without the support of the computer to which it is connected. The processing facility is provided by an internal processor, usually a microprocessor and storage is normally in the form of 'buffer' memory in which numerous lines of text can be held and manipulated before transmission. The facility may also include local backing storage and a printer.

A number of text editing tasks involve the use of *control codes* and these can be built into ROM (Read Only Memory) or magnetic bubble memory, both of which are non-volatile. Typical control codes are those which, via single key-presses, execute functions such as clearing the screen, moving the cursor up or down, and homing the cursor to the top-left of the screen. Function keys for these and other functions are generally specifically marked. It is also likely that the terminal is programmable thus allowing specific routines to be developed for validation of data. Microcomputer systems are often used as intelligent terminals.

Concept Keyboards

In specialist applications, the standard keyboard is not always the most convenient method of input. In a factory, for example, a limited number of functions may be necessary for the operation of a computerized lathe. These functions can be set out on a touch sensitive pad and clearly marked. This is possible because all inputs are anticipated and the range is small. The operator is saved the trouble of typing in the individual characters which form instructions.

Concept keyboards also have application in education, particularly for the mentally and physically handicapped. Instead of specific functions, interchangeable overlays, which indicate the functions of each area of the keyboard allow the user to design the keyboard to particular specifications.

Alternatives to Keyboards

Two methods of input make use of the screen display itself.

☐ *Touch screen.* Touch screen devices allow a screen to be activated by the user touching the screen with a finger. This is particularly useful where a menu of processing options is available on the screen for selection.

☐ *Light Pen.* A light pen is shaped like a pen and contains a photo-electric or light-sensitive cell in its tip. When the pen is pointed at the screen the light from the screen is detected by the cell and the computer can identify the position of the pen. By 'mapping' the screen to allocate particular functions to particular locations on the screen, the position of the pen indicates a particular function. The light pen enables specific parts of a picture on display to be selected or altered in some way, making it particularly useful for applications such as computer aided design (CAD).

Devices to control cursor movement include the joystick and the mouse.

☐ *Joystick.* The joystick is similar to a car's gear lever, except that fine variations in the angle of movement can be achieved. The cursor movement is a reflection of the movement of the joystick in terms of both direction and speed and is commonly used for computer games and CAD.

☐ *Mouse.* The mouse has a roller which dictates cursor movement. The user can move the cursor by moving the mouse across a flat surface. It is very popular with 'user friendly' software which requires the user to select from displayed screen options. Two or three select buttons are fitted on the mouse to enable the user to choose a particular screen position or function.

Printers

Printers can be categorized according to *speed* of operation and the *quality* of print, but are also identifiable as either *impact* or *non-impact* devices.

Impact Printers

Impact printing uses a print head to strike an inked ribbon which is located between the print head and the paper. Individual characters can be printed by either a dot-matrix mechanism or by print heads which contain each character as a separate font.

Dot Matrix Printers

Characters are formed from a matrix of dots produced by a column of pins in the print head (sometimes the pins may occupy two columns). Each character printed involves incremental movements of the pin column, so that a head using seven columns per character requires seven movements of the pins. The number of pins in the column is one factor determining printing quality. Thus, for example, the most basic of printers provides a nine-pin head, which is insufficient density for high quality printing but is adequate for everyday office data processing. An 18-pin head offers reasonable quality (Near Letter Quality or NLQ) at high speed and the 24-pin (arranged in two columns of 12) provides both high print quality and high speed.

The user should examine the printer specification before making a choice and may need to look at the following elements in particular:

☐ *Print quality.* Nearly all dot-matrix printers offer two speeds, one for *draft* and one for *Near Letter Quality* (NLQ), the latter producing higher quality by slowing the printing speed and by over-typing. The over-typing is achieved by shifting the location of the printer pins slightly and then reprinting the same character. In draft mode, the print head only makes one pass to print a complete line.

☐ *Print speed.* The speed at which the printer operates is measured in characters per second (cps) and varies from printer to printer and according to whether draft or NLQ mode is used. The NLQ mode usually prints at 25 to 30 per cent of the printer's draft speed. Draft mode produces legible but rough print at the highest speed.

☐ *Software package compatibility.* Most software packages support a limited number of printers. In addition, some printers have *emulation* capabilities to 'mimic' the operation of more well-known brands such as Epson. Before purchasing a printer, the user must check that the chosen software supports it.

☐ *Graphical output.* Printers which support bit-mapping (software control over individual pins in the matrix head) can produce graphical output. Without colour, pictorial effects can be achieved by double-striking to emphasize some areas of print and by moving the paper in very small increments rather than a line at a time. With a bit mapping facility and a 3-colour ribbon, a variety of colours, beyond those directly available, can be mixed by using slight paper shifts and double striking. This method makes use of software control to achieve colour output comparable with more expensive printers.

Solid Font Printing

A solid font head uses a separate font for each character and character sets have to altered by changing the head. Because they form a solid image, they have until recently provided a better quality of print than the dot-matrix type. There are a number of types, three of which are described below.

Daisy-wheel Head. As the name suggests, character fonts are attached to 'petals' on a central wheel which has to revolve to place a particular character in the print position. Inevitably, the considerable movement required between each character print means that daisy-wheel printers operate relatively slowly, about 30 to 60 characters per second. The quality of print is very high which makes it a popular device for the production of, for example, legal documents and other output where image is vital. Amongst impact printers, the daisy wheel is the noisiest. The daisy wheel's inherent disadvantages and the improvements in other printing technologies are likely to hasten its demise.

Cylinder Print Head. This type is only used on teletypewriter or teleprinter terminals and is consequently becoming uncommon. A teletypewriter has a keyboard and printer only and although largely replaced by the VDU is still used for telex communications. Only upper-case text is provided.

Golf-ball Head. The golf-ball head provides a wide range of both upper and lower case characters and has been popular with electronic typewriters.

Dot-matrix printers are much faster than solid-font printers, speeds of 100 to 300 characters per second being common for low-speed, impact models.

All the printers described above are *character* printers in that they print a single character at a time. Faster printing can be achieved by *line* and *page* printers

Line Printers

A line printer prints a complete line of characters, rather than in the serial fashion used by character printers.

Two types of line printer are described here, the barrel or drum and the chain printer.

Barrel Printer. The barrel printer has a band with a complete set of characters at each print position, of which there are generally 132. Each print position has a hammer to impact the print ribbon against the paper. The principle is illustrated in *Figure 6.2*.

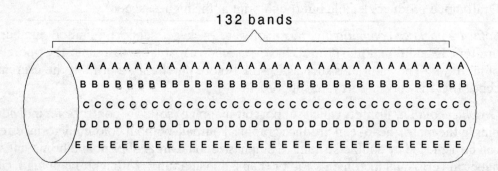

132 bands

Figure 6.2

One complete revolution of the barrel exposes all the characters to each print position, so a complete line can be printed in one revolution. The characters on the barrel are arranged so that all characters of the same type are in the same horizontal position. Thus, in a line of print, any required As can be printed, then Bs and so on, until the complete line is printed. The barrel revolves continuously during printing, the paper being fed through and the process repeated for each line of print. A printing speed of 2500 lines per minute is achievable.

Chain Printer

Several complete sets of characters are held on a continuous chain which moves horizontally across the paper. The ribbon is situated between the chain and the paper and an individual hammer is located at each of the 132 print positions. A complete line can be printed as one complete set of characters passes across the paper, so in one pass as many lines can be printed as there are sets of characters in the chain. Printing speeds are higher than is possible for barrel printers.

Line printers are expensive compared with character printers but may well be necessary where large volume output is required. Printing speeds of up to 3000 lines per minute are achieved with impact line printers, but even higher speeds are possible with non-impact types.

Non-Impact Printers

As the term suggests, non-impact printers do not involve mechanical hammers or the striking of print heads against paper. A variety of printers are available using a wide range of technologies, the most popular being as follow.

Thermal Printers

Characters are burned onto heat-sensitive thermographic paper which is white and develops colour when heated above a particular temperature. The heat is generated by rods in the dot-matrix print head and by selective heating of rods, individual characters can be formed from the matrix. Printing can be carried out serially, one character at a time or, through the use of several heads, on a line-by-line basis. Serial thermal printing is slow but speeds in excess of 1000 lines per minute are possible with line thermal printing.

Electrosensitive Printers

This type produce characters in a similar fashion to the thermal printer except that the paper used has a thin coating of aluminium which covers a layer of black, blue or red dye. Low voltage electrical discharges in the matrix rods produce sparks which selectively remove the aluminium coating to reveal the layer of dye underneath. Operated as line printers with heads at each print position, printing speeds in excess of 3000 lines per minute are achieved.

Laser Printers

Laser printers use a combination of two technologies, electro-photographic printing used in photo-copying and high intensity lasers. A photoconductive drum is initially charged and then a high intensity laser beam selectively discharges areas on the drum. As with photocopiers, toner material is spread over the surface to form an ink image, which is then transferred to the paper and made permanent through heating. Achieving print speeds of 500 pages per minute, the largest models are used in very large systems requiring exceptionally high speed output.

Effectively, complete pages are printed at one time so they come under the heading of *page* printers.

Laser Printers and Microcomputers. Laser printers used to be too costly for use in a microcomputer environment, but with rapidly falling prices, they are providing some competition for the dot matrix printers. Although still more costly than dot matrix printers, laser printers offer greater speed and quality.

☐ *Printing quality.* This is determined largely by the resolution or dot density of each character. A commonly used resolution is 300 dots per inch (dpi), which provides a printing quality superior to most dot matrix printers, but still not quite up to daisywheel standards. Machines offering 600 dpi are coming onto the market and these will produce printing quality to match the daisywheel.

☐ *Printing speed.* The printing speeds of laser printers are far beyond anything possible with any dot matrix printer and for this reason are referred to as page printers. Printing speeds range from 6 pages per minute (ppm) to 26 ppm, making the laser printer highly suitable for servicing a number of microcomputers in a network.

Ink Jet Printers

Ink jet printers spray high-speed streams of electrically charged ink droplets from individual nozzles in the matrix head onto the paper to form characters. Many will hold colour cartridges to produce excellent colour output.

Ink jet printers provide a possible alternative to the laser printer.

Case Study: The Hewlett Packard (HP) Deskjet

The HP Deskjet offers three possible print resolutions, 75, 150 and 300 dots per inch (dpi). At 300 dpi, which matches the resolution of laser printers, the Deskjet can produce near-typeset quality fonts. The noise level is extremely low but its operational speed is about 2 pages per minute (ppm) in draft mode and 1ppm in letter-quality mode. The slowest laser printer operates at about 6ppm.

The ink jet printer cannot match the laser printer for speed but it provides a possible alternative for users whose printing requirements are not satisfied by any printer in the dot matrix impact range.

Summary of Printers

Generally speaking, the smaller, low speed, character printers are of use with microcomputer systems, but the increasing popularity of such systems has demanded increased sophistication in small printers. Features which have improved printing speeds include *bi-directional printing* (in two directions) and *logic-seeking* which allows the printer to cut short a traverse across the paper if only a few characters are required on a line.

The most popular printers for microcomputers are, impact dot-matrix, daisy-wheel, electro-sensitive, ink jet and laser.

Data Capture Devices

Source data is normally collected in human-readable form. For example, customer orders are recorded on order forms and weekly pay details may be recorded on time sheets. Prior to processing, such data has to be translated into machine-sensible form and this usually involves a keying operation. There are a number of *data capture* devices available which allow data to be collected in a printed or hand-written form directly readable by a computer input device.

Optical Character Readers (OCR)

OCRs are designed to read stylized characters which are also readable by humans. There are a number of designs for such characters but any individual design is known as the *character font.*

The OCR reflects light off the characters and converts them into digital patterns for comparison with the stored character set. Originally, a highly stylized appearance was preferred to aid machine recognition but some OCRs can read the character sets of popular makes of office typewriter. Ideally, OCRs should be able to read any characters but the wider the range of styles that need to be read, the more difficult becomes the recognition process. In some applications, a restricted set of numeric and certain alphabetic characters may suffice and the reading process becomes quicker and more accurate. Nevertheless, large OCRs are capable of reading several character sets comprising more than 300 characters.

The reading of hand-printed characters presents particular problems because of the almost infinite variation of printing styles, but successful recognition can be achieved if the writer has a visual guide of the preferred style. The character set will usually be limited to numerals and a few alphabetic characters, the style of which is easy to imitate. Artificial intelligence techniques are being applied to OCRs to allow the 'learning' of new character sets.

Applications of OCR

OCR is often used to capture sales data at the *electronic point-of-sale* (EPOS). An EPOS terminal is essentially an electronic cash register linked to a computer or with storage of its own. Data captured at the terminal can, for example, be sent to update computer files. Sometimes EPOS registers have direct-access memory to hold product prices and descriptions, so that the details can be printed on the customer receipt. An OCR-character-coded price label, attached to each product, can be scanned with a wand (light pen) or laser 'gun'. OCR can also be applied to *turnaround* documents, such as advice notes and order forms.

Optical Mark Readers (OMR)

An OMR is designed to read marks placed in preset positions on a pre-printed document. Permitted values are limited as each is represented by, for example, a box in a certain position. Thus, a suitable application for OMR is a multi-choice exam paper, where the answer to each question has to be indicated by a pencil mark in one of several boxes after the question. The OMR scans the document for boxes containing pencil marks and thus identifies the values selected. Other applications include the capture of statistical data from questionnaire forms and order data from mail order forms. Optical mark readers can read up to 10,000 A4 documents per hour.

Bar Code Readers

The bar code is also an optical code which is normally read by a light pen or laser scanner. The code makes use of a series of unevenly spaced black bars of varying thickness. The bars and gaps are used to represent numeric data, the values represented often being printed beneath in decimal form.

Bar codes are commonly used to store a variety of data types, such as prices and stock codes of products in shops and supermarkets. A sticker with the relevant bar code (itself produced by computer) is attached to each product. EPOS terminals frequently have a built-in laser scanner station over which the goods pass. This is convenient if packages are of regular shape, but soft packages with creases may cause problems for the scanner. In such cases, the light pen or wand provides a more practical solution. By using the data from the code, the cash register can identify the item, look up its latest price and print the information on the customer's receipt, thus providing a fully itemized list. In addition, VAT and stock records can also be updated directly, or the information can be stored for later batch updating of the relevant files.

Another useful application is for the recording of library issues. A bar code sticker is placed inside the book cover and at the time of issue or return it can be scanned and the library stock record updated. By providing each library user with a bar coded library card, the information regarding an individual borrower can be linked with the book's details at the time of issue.

Magnetic Ink Character Reader (MICR)

This particular device is employed almost exclusively by the banking industry, where it is used for sorting and processing cheques in large volumes. As data is also input to the Electronic Funds Transfer (EFT) system, the reading speed of over 2000 documents per hour is vital. The millions of cheques which pass through the London Clearing System could not possibly be sorted and processed without the use of MICRs.

Highly stylized characters are printed along the bottom of the cheques by a special printer, using ink containing iron oxide. The MICR first magnetizes the characters as the cheque passes through and then decodes them by induced voltage signals. A high degree of reliability and accuracy is possible, partly because of the stylized font, but more importantly, because the characters are not affected by dirty marks. This is obviously important when cheques may pass through several hands before reaching their destination. Such marks may cause problems for an optical character reader.

Digitizers

Examples of digitizers in use are provided by the light pen, the mouse and the joystick, described earlier.

Another name for a digitizer is an *Analogue to Digital Converter* (ADC). Data is often not in digital format but is instead an analogue measurement, for example, of changes in temperature level or light intensity. Temperature may be measured by the movement of mercury in a thermometer and light intensity by movement of a pointer on the dial of a light meter. By reflecting these measurement changes with voltage changes, they can then be converted to the digital signals usable by the computer with an ADC or digitizer.

ADCs and Process Control

To control an industrial process, such as the temperature of a blast furnace, requires the use of a *feedback loop*; this means that data emanating from the process is used to make adjustments to its control mechanism. In the case of a blast furnace, this would mean the control of the heating mechanism. The controlling computer makes adjustments to the heating mechanism by comparing the feedback data from the furnace's temperature sensors with stored parameters. A DAC (Digital to Analogue Converter) allows any necessary conversion of the computer's output into the analogue form required by the furnace control mechanism.

Graphics Tablet

This is a particularly useful device for collecting pictorial data. A pen-like stylus enables the user to 'draw' on the tablet and reflect the results on the computer screen or store the results for future manipulation. The tablet is addressable by the computer through a matrix of thousands of tiny 'dots', each of which reflect a binary 1 or 0. When a line is drawn on the tablet, the stylus passes over these dot locations, causing the binary values in memory to change. Thus a particular drawing has a particular binary format which can be stored, manipulated or displayed.

Digitizers are used in other applications, for example, in the capturing of photographic images, via a digitizing camera and the subsequent production of a digitized image.

Voice Recognition Devices

Human speech varies in accent, personal style and pitch and the interpretation of the spoken word makes the development of voice recognition devices a difficult process. In normal conversation, humans make assumptions about the listener, often cutting sentences short or emphasizing a point with a facial expression, so voice recognition devices to deal with complete human language are likely to take some time yet to perfect.

There are however, devices which can be 'trained' to recognize a limited number of words spoken by the individual doing the training. Devices can be used to give commands for machinery control, for example, 'up', 'down', 'left', 'right', 'fast', 'slow' etc. Paralysed persons can control a wheelchair or lighting and heating through a voice recognition device controlled by a microprocessor.

Special-Purpose Output Devices

Computer Output Microform (COM) Recorders

COM recorders transfer information at high speed from computer storage onto *microfilm* or *microfiche*, by conversion of the digital information into human readable images. COM recording equipment is very expensive, but bureau organizations will generally provide a recording service. Microfilm is a continuous reel, whereas, microfiche is a sheet of film with a matrix of squares or pages. Either form can be viewed with a magnifying viewer. COM can result in large savings in paper costs, storage space and handling. For example, a 4 inch × 6 inch microfiche sheet can store the equivalent of 270 printed pages. *Computer-aided retrieval* (CAR) systems are available to automate the archiving and retrieval of microfiche frames.

COM is particularly useful for the storage of large amounts of information which do not need to be updated frequently. The information can be viewed with the use of a special magnifying projector. Large financial institutions use COM together with CAR to allow rapid retrieval of customer account statements.

Graph Plotters

A graph plotter is a device designed to produce charts, drawings, maps and other forms of graphical information on paper. There are a variety of methods for producing the image.

A *flat-bed* plotter resembles a drafting board with pens mounted on a carriage which moves along guide tracks. The paper is placed on the 'bed'. The pens can be raised or lowered as the image being created requires and different coloured pens can be brought into use at various stages of the process. Drawing movements are executed by movement of the carriage along the tracks and by the pens along the carriage. The size of paper which can be accommodated is limited by the size of the plotter 'bed', but this can be extremely large.

A *drum* plotter has a different drawing mechanism. Instead of the paper remaining still, it moves to produce one of the lateral movements whilst the pens move to execute the other movements. In order to control the paper, the drum plotter uses sprocket wheels to interlock with the paper. The main advantage of the drum plotter is its ability to handle large sheets of paper.

Their major area of use is in CAD systems for the production of complex diagrams and working drawings.

Voice Output Devices

Voice synthesis is still in its infancy, in that the complexities of human speech have yet to be mastered satisfactorily. There is a tendency for such devices to become confused between the pronunciation of words such as 'though' and 'plough'. Speech ROM 'chips' are available for many microcomputer systems and educational applications include 'speak and spell' and arithmetic. Large scale application is possible where the range of output can be anticipated, for example, stocks and share prices, railway timetables, speaking clock etc. Such services may be provided via an answerphone service.

7

Input/Output Control

Architecture

Figure 7.1 illustrates the architecture of the communication system which allows data transfers between the various elements of a computer system. This chapter examines the various methods of implementing and controlling input/output (I/O) operations. A major problem concerns the speed imbalance between the operation of the CPU and communicating peripheral devices and the various techniques used to compensate for such imbalance are also described.

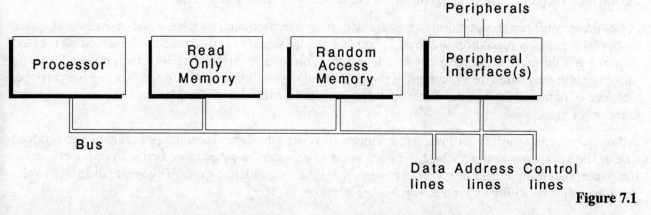

Figure 7.1

Referring to the above diagram, a number of components can be identified.

- □ *Buses or highways.* A bus consists of a number of wires, one for each bit making up the unit of data transfer. A common I/O bus connects all I/O peripherals to the CPU, so only one peripheral can use the bus at a time. This is not normally a restriction because the CPU can only handle one instruction at a time, but most computers have an I/O bus which is independent of that used for CPU/main memory transfers. Those machines using a common bus for I/O and CPU/memory data movements are referred to as *single bus* systems.

- □ *Interface.* This is a hardware device containing electronic components, which connects an I/O peripheral to the computer. The chapter on Data Representation describes the use of internal and external codes for internal computer and external peripheral operations respectively; an interface carries out the *conversion process* between the two codes, according to whether data is being transferred to or from the peripheral.

☐ *Device controller.* This device is fundamentally the same as the interface, except that it is associated with the control of data transfers to and from storage devices, such as magnetic disk and tape drives.

Programmed Input/Output

Input and output which is under program control is termed programmed I/O. The CPU instruction set contains four types of I/O instructions:

☐ input - to transfer data from peripheral to CPU;

☐ output - to transfer data from CPU to peripheral;

☐ to set individual control flags in the I/O interface unit;

☐ to test individual flags in the I/O interface unit.

A peripheral device is attached to an interface unit by a cable. The interface unit (usually inside the computer) is connected to one of a number of I/O slots. Each I/O slot has a *fixed address* by which a peripheral can be identified for input or output. There are 3 basic elements in an interface unit:

☐ a control bit or *'busy'* flag - used to signal a device to start input or output. This cannot be set by the device as it is under I/O control;

☐ a flag bit or *'done'* flag - this is set by the device when the data transfer is complete and can be tested or cleared by program instructions;

☐ a *buffer register* for the storage of data transferred into (read by) or to be transferred from (written by) the device.

When a 'start read' instruction is given, one character is transferred between the interface buffer register and the device. A single character is transferred in the opposite direction if a 'start write' instruction is given. Thus, programmed I/O is on a *character by character* basis.

Although simple to control, such a data transfer method is inefficient because it does not take advantage of the facility for many peripherals to operate *autonomously*. (See section on Direct Memory Access)

A CPU instruction commands the device to operate by setting the *busy flag* and then repeatedly tests the *done flag* to discover when the transfer is complete. Although simple to program, it is extremely inefficient in terms of CPU operation because the CPU operates at many times the speed of any peripheral device and is thus wasting much of its power waiting for each character to be transmitted. The technique is appropriate for a microcomputer system where only a few external devices are interfaced and the processor has sufficient time to continually test the devices to see if they are ready.

An instruction sequence may be as follows:

For input from a specific device:

☐ instruction to interface to set the busy flag for 'start transmit';

☐ send instruction to test done flag. If the flag indicates that the transfer is complete, skip next instruction;

□ branch to previous instruction;

□ issue instruction to transfer character from buffer register into CPU accumulator;

□ issue store instruction to transfer character from accumulator to main memory.

For output to a specific device:

□ issue instruction to transfer character from CPU accumulator into buffer register of interface device;

□ issue instruction to set busy flag to start transfer;

□ issue instruction to test done flag and if set, skip the next instruction;

□ branch to previous instruction.

The repetitive flag-test loop is necessary to ensure that a character transfer is completed before the next one is transmitted.

A more efficient method of I/O control is to use interrupts and the topic is examined in a later section.

Direct Memory Access (DMA)

Not all data transfers between peripheral devices and the CPU are carried out under continual program control. Other schemes such as DMA allow data transfer to or from high speed storage devices such as tape or disk to be effected without continual CPU control. Data is transferred in *blocks*, as opposed to character by character. DMA is possible because of the ability of some peripheral devices to operate *autonomously*, that is, after the initial input or output instruction has been given by the CPU, the peripheral is able to complete the data transfer independently. To allow the memory to be accessed directly by a peripheral, instead of via the CPU, hardware known as a DMA *controller* is needed. For transfers from main memory to peripheral, the CPU supplies the DMA controller with the *start address* in memory of the data block to be transferred and its *length*. A transfer from, for example, a disk pack to memory would require the CPU to tell the DMA controller the relevant disk address and into which memory locations the data is to be copied. The DMA controller 'steals' memory cycles from the CPU while the data transfer is taking place. Meanwhile, the CPU can continue execution of its current program, although its operation is slowed slightly by the cycle stealing. DMA is an essential component to any computer system working in *multi-programming* mode.

Off-lining

Early computer systems used punched cards as the initial form of input and to speed processing a technique of off-lining was introduced. Data would be transferred from punched cards to magnetic tape under control of a separate processor. The operator could then place the magnetic tape file on-line, from where it could be accessed and processed by the application program. The hugely superior data transfer rate of magnetic tape radically improved processing times and went some way to countering the speed imbalance between the input device and the CPU. The same technique was also applied to printed output, which could be directed to magnetic tape and then printed from there under control of a separate processor.

Buffering

Buffering is a technique which helps compensate for the speed differences between the CPU and the various input and output devices which communicate with it.

To speed processing, many computer systems contain special high-speed memory areas called buffers. An *input buffer* acts as a waiting area within memory for a block of data transferred from a peripheral; from there it can be quickly accessed and processed by the CPU. An *output buffer* stores data which has been processed by the CPU and is awaiting output. Most peripherals have the facility for autonomous operation, leaving the CPU free for other tasks; buffering and the use of autonomous peripherals allows the simultaneous operation of several of the latter.

Double Buffering

In the case of storage devices, double-buffering makes use of two buffers which work in 'tandem' to speed processing.

If the records are blocked the systems software initially places the first block into buffer 1 and the second into buffer 2. Read instructions from the applications program retrieve the data from these buffers. The CPU can retrieve logical records faster from the buffer than from tape. As soon as all logical records from buffer 1 have been processed, the reading process transfers to the logical records in buffer 2. Meanwhile, the next block on tape can be transferred into buffer 1 and so on.

The principle is also used with peripherals in general, including input and output devices, to help redress the radical imbalance between the CPU's speed and that of the device with which it is communicating. This imbalance is less significant in respect of storage devices, which have significantly faster data transfer rates than most input and output devices, particularly where direct memory access (DMA) - see earlier section, is employed.

Spooling (Simultaneous Peripheral Operation On-line)

This is a development of the off-lining technique described earlier and is used to speed data throughput. Multi-programming (Chapter 12 Operating Systems) allows data to be transferred from slow peripherals to fast backing storage devices as a background process. The process is facilitated by autonomous peripherals which can carry out data transfers independently of the CPU after it has initiated the read or write instruction.

Multiplexing

Multiplexing is a technique which enables inputs from several devices to be directed through one channel to a computer; the reverse process is known as de-multiplexing. A multiplexer normally has the facilities to carry out both operations. *Figure 7.2* illustrates its principal function.

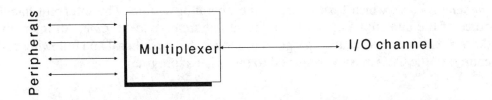

Figure 7.2

Asynchronous Terminal Multiplexer

Any multi-terminal computer system will include a *local multiplexer* to allow a number of terminals to use one interface to the computer. Apart from the benefit of removing the need for numerous separate physical interfaces, a multiplexer can support I/O devices with different data transfer rates.

A multiplexer has buffer registers for the temporary storage of characters before onward transmission, either to or from a connected device. In order to identify individual terminals, each one is given an *individual address* within the *common interface*. A multiplexer's operation is based on the realistic assumption that the data transfer rates from the various terminals will be well within the capacity of the computer's I/O interface. Typically, a single local multiplexer will support 16 terminals; even if, for example, each asynchronous (characters are sent at irregular intervals) terminal is transmitting continuously, with a transfer rate of 2400 *bits per second* (*bps*), then the resulting 38400 bps from the multiplexer to the interface would be well within the capacity of a typical minicomputer's bus transfer rate of one million bps. In practice, it is unlikely that all terminals would be transmitting continuously at that rate.

In order to give attention to each of the transmitting terminals, the multiplexer may address each terminal in a *round robin polling* sequence. Each terminal is checked to see if there is a character waiting in its buffer and if there is, the character plus the terminal's line number are removed. Once an input character from a particular terminal has been dealt with, the multiplexer checks to see if there is a character to be output to that same terminal and if so the character is fetched from memory and output. The multiplexer then directs its attention to the next terminal in the sequence and repeats the process. The scanning process is implemented by hardware and is, therefore, very quick.

Multiplexers can also operate *synchronously*, that is, transfer characters at a regularly-timed frequency.

The topic of *remote multiplexing* is dealt with in Chapter 9 on Communications.

Controlling I/O through interrupts

The simple programmed I/O described earlier requires the CPU to carry out a *cyclic testing* process to determine when a peripheral is ready for a character transfer; unfortunately, despite the CPU's spare capacity, the system's operational speed is tied to that of the peripheral and the connection of several peripherals would require a slow queuing process. The ability of peripherals to operate autonomously and the high speed of the CPU allows the latter to handle the requirements of numerous peripherals apparently simultaneously. In fact, the CPU must deal with one at a time, switching its attention from one to another under the control of some mechanism, namely the *operating system* (Chapter 12). Briefly, an operating system comprises a suite of programs which manage the resources of a computer system, including the allocation and scheduling of hardware for input and output. *Interrupts* fulfil a variety of functions in the allocation of computer resources but the following section concentrates on their role in facilitating the servicing of I/O devices (including file storage systems.)

I/O Interrupts

An interrupt causes the program which currently has control of the CPU to be *suspended* and the execution of an *interrupt handler routine*, which forms part of the operating system. The interrupt handler must establish the source of the interrupt and call the relevant *interrupt service routine*. An interrupt from a peripheral causes the computer to execute a program to service that peripheral and following completion of the service, control of the CPU must be returned to the original program.

Establishing the Source of an Interrupt

In order that the computer can enter the appropriate routine, it must be possible to identify the source of each interrupt. A simplified system is described below.

To determine when an interrupt is required, certain indicator flags are used.

☐ *Done flag.* A device sets this flag to 1 when it has completed a data transfer and is thus ready for service. The done flag is cleared to 0 if service is not required.

☐ *Enable flag.* Each peripheral device has an interrupt enable flag which can be set to 1 (permitted) or to 0 (not permitted) by an I/O control instruction from the computer.

☐ *Interrupt request flag.* If the enable flag for a device is set to 1, the computer (under program control), tests the device's done flag and if this is also set to 1 (indicating that an interrupt is required), the interrupt request flag is set to 1. An interrupt request register contains a number of flag bits, one for each device.

The 1 condition of the interrupt request flag sets the interrupt routine in progress.

Executing the Interrupt

☐ After the current instruction's execution has been completed, but before the next instruction is fetched, the CPU checks the condition of the *interrupt request register* (as part of the hardware-controlled fetch-execute cycle), to determine whether or not any devices require an interrupt. If there is more than one interrupt request, the *priority* of each device must first be checked; with simple software polling the priority of a device is pre-determined by its position in the polling sequence.

☐ Before entry to the relevant *interrupt service routine,* the contents of the Program Counter (PC) must be stored in a separate location; the contents of the PC are then replaced by the *starting address* of the interrupt service routine and the routine is executed. Once the interrupt has been serviced, control of the CPU must be returned to the appropriate point in the original program by copying its stored continuation address back into the PC.

An *interrupt-on/off flag* in the CPU must be set to *off* prior to acceptance of an interrupt and then cleared to *on* as soon as control has been returned to the original program, in order to prevent an interrupt from another device being accepted until the original program has resumed control.

Interrupt Priority

Interrupts may emanate from a variety of sources (I/O and others) and for a number of different reasons (Chapter 12 Operating Systems); the operating system can be used to allocate different *priority ratings* to particular events and devices.

In a simple interrupt handling system, entry to an interrupt servicing routine will disable the interrupt mechanism until the current one is completed and any interrupts which occur during this time are queued until the mechanism is re-enabled.

Nested Interrupts

More sophisticated systems may leave the interrupt mechanism enabled so that an interrupt service routine may itself be interrupted by a higher priority request; this may happen repeatedly, requiring the nesting of interrupts. A LIFO (Last In First Out) stack (Chapter 26 Data Structures) can be used to store the return addresses and accumulator contents relating to these nested interrupts so that they can be retrieved in reverse order.

If a higher priority interrupt occurs during I/O there is a danger of data being lost. Each peripheral is allocated a given priority rating which must be compared with that of the current process, before the interrupt routine is entered. As a general rule, *low speed devices* are given *high priority*, because frequent interruptions to relatively slow data input may result in there being insufficient data to continue processing. Where the interrupting peripheral has a priority rating lower than or equal to that of the current activity, it is kept waiting; otherwise the interrupt takes place.

Masking Device Interrupts

Where the interrupt mechanism is left enabled, it may be desirable to selectively *mask out* certain low priority devices from that facility. This can be achieved by using a register as an *interrupt mask*, with bit positions corresponding to individual devices in the interrupt request register; devices are masked out by setting the relevant bits in the mask to 0 and carrying out a logical AND operation between the *mask* and the *interrupt request register*. This is illustrated in *Figure 7.3*.

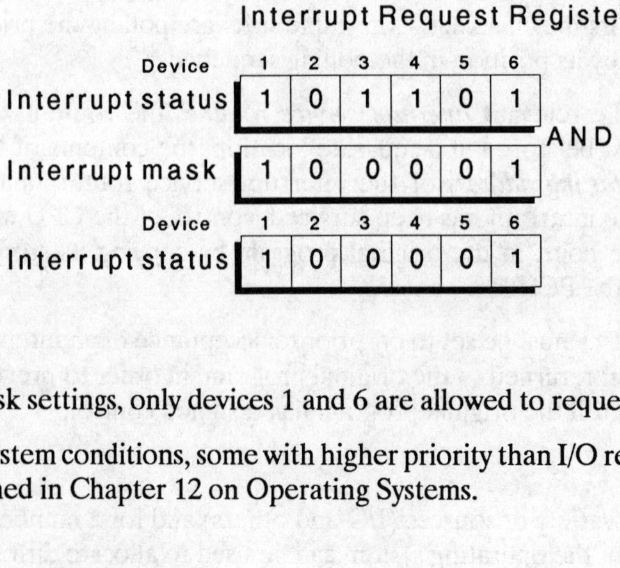

Interrupt Request Register

Device	1	2	3	4	5	6
Interrupt status	1	0	1	1	0	1

AND

Interrupt mask	1	0	0	0	0	1

Device	1	2	3	4	5	6
Interrupt status	1	0	0	0	0	1

Figure 7.3

With the current mask settings, only devices 1 and 6 are allowed to request interrupts.

A number of other system conditions, some with higher priority than I/O requests, may generate interrupts and these are examined in Chapter 12 on Operating Systems.

8 *Computer Networks and Distributed Systems*

This chapter looks at some technical aspects of computer networks and their facility for decentralizing or distributing the data processing function.

Three main factors have encouraged many organizations to adopt a decentralized policy:

☐ Many organizations already have a number of computers installed at separate sites. At first these systems tended to be used in isolation, but the need to extract and analyse information from the company as a whole has led to their connection via the telecommunications network;

☐ The cost of computers has fallen dramatically, making it cost-effective for organizations to process and analyse data at the various points of collection;

☐ The development of Local Area Networks of low-cost microcomputers with *electronic office* facilities has encouraged demand for local computer power and these networks can be readily connected to any central facility via telecommunications networks.

Data Communications and Computers

The combination of computer and telecommunications technologies has had a profound effect on the way computer systems are organized. The idea of a computer centre handling all computer processing, without any user involvement, is rapidly becoming obsolete. A computer network aims to distribute the processing work amongst a number of connected computers and to allow users direct control over processing.

Physical Components

All the external devices attached to a network may be referred to collectively as Data Terminal Equipment (DTE). Usually, the DTE belongs to the users, while the intervening connections are leased from the main telecommunications provider, which in the UK is British Telecom. The equipment which allows the DTE to be connected to and interfaced with the network is known as Data Circuit-Terminating Equipment (DCE).

Distributed Processing

Some computer networks use *intelligent* VDU or microcomputer terminals to permit some independent processing power at sites remote from the central computer. Other networks distribute even more processing power by linking together mainframe or minicomputer systems, in which case, the terminals are computer systems in themselves. Because such networks distribute some processing power to a number of different sites, they are also known as *distributed processing* systems.

Applications of Computer Networks

Networks can be configured to suit almost any application, from the provision of a world-wide airline booking service to home banking. Terminals may be only a few hundred feet apart and limited to a single building, or they may be several thousand miles apart. Some major areas of use, or potential use, are as follow:

- ☐ Computer-aided education can be supported by a network which provides Computer-Assisted Learning (CAL) packages to suit a wide range of subject and course areas;

- ☐ Public data bases can allow people to make, for example, airline, restaurant, theatre or hotel reservations from anywhere in the world, with instant confirmation. Home banking services, such as those provided by the Bank of Scotland can be accessed by Prestel subscribers. A potential area of use could be the newspaper industry. Subscribers could arrange for personalized newspapers which contained only those subjects of interest to them. Information could, of course, be completely up-to-date;

- ☐ Electronic mail has the potential to make hand-delivered communications virtually obsolete and this is discussed in Chapter 9;

- ☐ Teleconferencing allows discussion amongst individuals without their physical presence in one room. A meeting can be conducted by the typing of messages at terminals, and all contributions to a discussion are automatically recorded for later reference .

Local Area and Wide Area Networks

Computer networks can be classified according to their geographical spread. A network confined to, say, one building with workstations which are usually microcomputers distributed in different rooms, is known as a Local Area Network (LAN). One particular type, known as a *ring network*, can extend over a diameter of two or three miles. A computer network distributed nationally or even internationally makes use of telephone and sometimes, satellite links, and is referred to as a Wide Area Network (WAN). In large organizations with several branches, it is becoming popular to maintain a LAN at each branch for localized processing and to link each LAN into a WAN covering the whole organization. In this way, branches of an organization can have control over their own processing and yet have access to the organization's main database at headquarters. In addition, inter-branch communication is possible.

Network Topology

Computer networks can be categorized according to their shape or *topology*. Each terminal in a network is known as a *node*, although in a bus network a node is known as a *station*. If a central computer controls the network it is known as the *host* computer. The topology of a network is the arrangement of the nodes and the ways they are interconnected. The communication system within a network is known as the *subnet* and data can be transmitted around it either on a point-to-point basis or via a broadcast channel.

☐ If *point-to-point* transmission is used, the data passes through each device in the network. Thus, if two devices wish to communicate, they must do it indirectly, via any intervening devices. Each device must have the facility to store the entire message and forward it when the output channel is free.

☐ If a *broadcast* channel is used, a common communication channel is shared by all devices in the network. This means that any message sent by a device is received by all devices. The message contains the address of the device intended to receive it, so that the other devices can ignore it.

There are a number of recognized network topology types and some of the most common are described below.

Star Network

A star network generally has a central host computer at the hub, with the terminals or nodes connected directly to it. *Figure 8.1* illustrates one particular type of star topology.

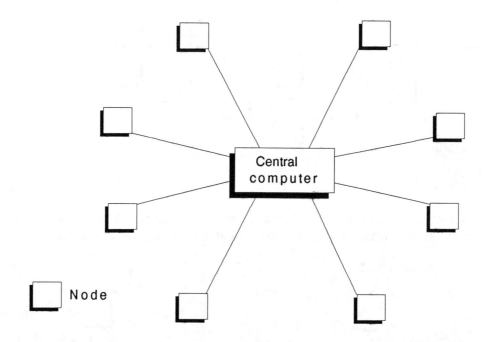

Figure 8.1

Switched Hub Star Network

In this structure, all messages pass through the host computer, which interconnects the different users on the network. Thus, in this topology the host computer at the hub has a *message switching* function and messages are transmitted point-to-point. The topology is particularly useful for communications between pairs of users on the network (via the host). The network may consist of several computer systems (the nodes), connected to a larger host computer which switches data and programs between them. The star topology is less suitable where several nodes require access to another node. In *Figure 8.1*, each node or terminal has its own physical connection to the main computer.

Where large distances are involved, such an arrangement would be extremely expensive, so the topology can be modified with the use of devices called *multiplexers* which allow several remote terminals to be channelled into a common connection to the host computer. *Figure 8.2* below illustrates such an arrangement, commonly known as *multi-drop*.

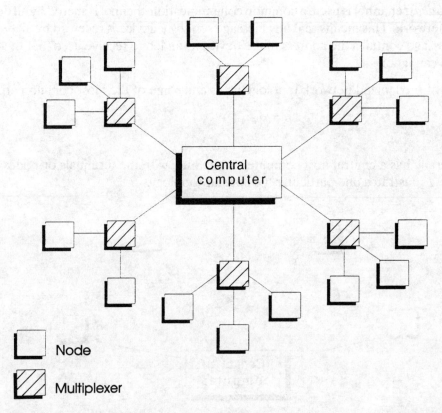

Node

Multiplexer

Figure 8.2

Figure 8.3 illustrates a popular form of network where the hub processes information fed to it via the telecommunications system. In this case, the host computer has a *processing* rather than a message switching function.

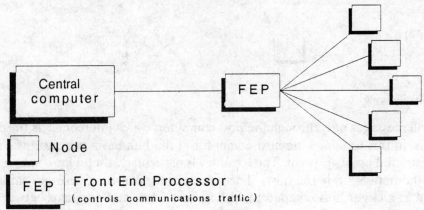

Node

FEP   Front End Processor
(controls communications traffic)

Figure 8.3

The star computer network is by far the most popular for WANS, because most large organizations start with a central computer at the head office, from which branch computer facilities are provided via the network. The main aim is to provide computer communication between the branches and head office. Most other types of network topology aim to provide communication between all devices on a network.

The advantages of a star network topology are as follow:

☐ It is suitable for WANs where organizations rely on a central computer for the bulk of processing tasks, perhaps limiting the nodes to their local processing needs and the validation of data, prior to transmission to the central computer;

☐ Centralized control of message switching allows a high degree of security control;

☐ Each spoke in the star is independent of the rest and a fault in a link or device in one spoke, can be identified by the computer at the hub;

☐ The data transmission speeds used can vary from one spoke to another. This is important if some spokes transmit using high speed devices, such as disk, whilst others transmit from low speed keyboard devices. The method of transmission may also vary. For example, one node may only require access to the network at the end of each day, in which case a *dial-u*p connection may be sufficient. A dial-up connection uses the public telephone network and the user only pays for the time taken for transmission. Alternatively, other nodes may require the link for most of the working day, in which case a permanent *leased line* is appropriate. Leased lines provide a more reliable transmission medium and also allow higher speeds of data transmission.

The main disadvantages inherent in star networks are as follow:

☐ The network is vulnerable to hub failures which affect all users. As a distributed processing system, some processing is still possible at the nodes but inter-node communication is lost when the host computer fails;

☐ The control of communications in the network requires expensive technology at the hub, probably a mini or mainframe computer. Complex operating and communications software is needed to control the network.

Ring Network

A ring network connects all the nodes in a ring, as illustrated in *Figure 8.4*.

There is no host computer and none of the nodes need have overall control of access to the network. In practice, a monitoring station is used for the control of data transmission in the network. The topology is designed for LANs and the Cambridge Ring is a popular configuration.

The ring consists of a series of *repeaters* which are joined by the physical transmission medium. Repeaters re-generate messages as they pass around the network (the number required will depend on the type of cable and the extent of the network). The user devices, fitted with *network interface cards*, are connected to the medium. Thus, a message from one node, addressed to another, is passed continually around the ring until the receiving node flags that it is ready to accept it. Data is transmitted in mini-packets of about 40 bits and contains the address of the sending node, the address of the receiving node and some control bits.

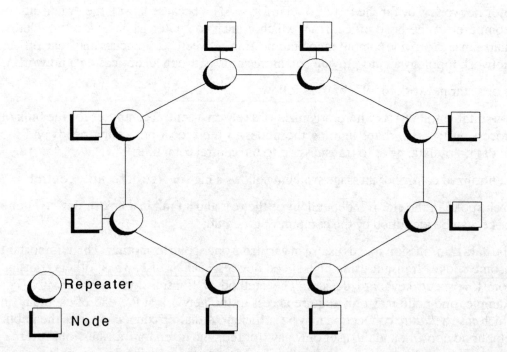

Figure 8.4

The ring network presents particular advantages:

☐ There is no dependence on a central host computer as data transmission around the network is supported by all the devices in the ring. Each node device has sufficient 'intelligence' to control the transmission of data from and to its own node;

☐ Very high transmission rates are possible;

☐ Routing between devices is relatively simple because messages normally travel in one direction only around the ring;

☐ The transmission facility is shared equally amongst the users.

The main disadvantages are as follows:

☐ The system depends on the reliability of the whole ring and the repeaters; such situations are avoidable with some token-ring systems, such as IBM's Token Ring Network;

☐ It may be difficult to extend the length of the ring because the physical installation of any new cable must ensure that the *logical* ring topology is preserved.

Bus Network

The bus or highway network can be likened to a bus route, along which traffic moves from one end to the other. To continue the analogy, the stations are like 'bus stops' and the data like 'passengers'. Data can be placed on to the route or 'picked up' as it passes. The term station is used rather than node for this type of network. The communications subnet uses a broadcast channel, so all attached nodes can 'hear' every transmission. The topology is illustrated in *Figure 8.5* and is typical of many LAN configurations.

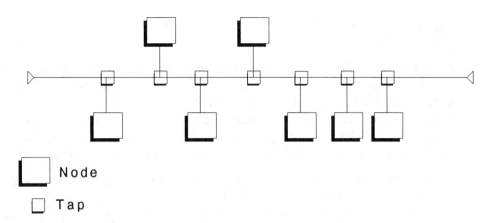

Node

Tap

Figure 8.5

As is the case in the ring network, there is no host computer and all stations have equal priority in using the network to transmit.

Physical and Logical Network Topology

A network topology can be viewed logically or physically. The latter view refers to the actual physical layout of the network cabling, whilst the logical view relates to the access *protocols* (see next section) and the way in which information travels around the physical layout. For example, IBM's Token Ring network's physical topology resembles a star shape, but the logical mode of transmission is that of a ring, data travelling from one node to another and in one direction only.

The Benefits of a LAN

The potential benefits of using a LAN relate to *resource sharing* and *communication*. A LAN allows:

- ☐ the sharing of hardware, such as printers and disk storage;

- ☐ the sharing of centrally stored information;

- ☐ communication between individual users.

Resource Sharing

It could be argued that the rapid fall in hardware costs has, to a certain extent, reduced the need for sharing peripherals and for example, it is now common for microcomputer systems, even at the cheaper end of the market, to have their own hard disk storage with capacities of 20 to 50 megabytes (mb). The prices of printers, particularly of the dot matrix type, have also fallen dramatically. However, a number of factors concerning computer usage and storage and printing technologies indicate that there are still strong arguments for resource sharing:

- ☐ *Applications.* The range of computer applications and the number of users is continually increasing;

- ☐ *Software packages.* The increasing sophistication of software means that large amounts of disk space are needed for each package. Network versions of a package are only slightly more expensive than those for stand-alone systems and obviate the need for the purchase of multiple copies;

☐ *Storage technologies.* Very high capacity disk storage devices, capable of storing hundreds of megabytes of information are still relatively expensive and optical storage devices capable of storing thousands of megabytes (gigabytes or gb) are even more so. Many individual users, each with their own hard disk-based microcomputer, are unlikely to make use of the 20 or 40 megabytes available on each machine, whereas a shared, large volume hard or optical disk can satisfy the storage needs of all users;

☐ *Printers.* Most users require only occasional use of a printer, so there is little point in providing one for each. A relatively expensive laser printer can produce the high quality output necessary for many applications and operate at speeds which allow sharing to take place, without unreasonable delay for users.

Sharing Information

Information can also be regarded as a resource, so sharing it can bring similar benefits to those available from sharing hardware. For example, a common information store supports the use of a database system, which itself reduces the need for information duplication. Traditional computer processing methods require that each application has its own files and this results in the duplication of many data items and the updating process. For example, stock control and purchasing both make use of commodity details such as Stock Codes, Descriptions and Prices so a change in the Price of a commodity requires more than one input. Even if database methods are not used, the storage of the various application files in a common disk store, means that they can be made available to all users on the LAN.

Network Security

Although LANs facilitate sharing of information, it is not always desirable to share all of it with everyone and security mechanisms must be available to exclude unauthorized users from the system and to restrict access by authorized users to the particular files and processes with which they are properly concerned. Security is also concerned with preventing data loss, so provision must exist for the backing-up of files. The separation of users' files and access control is effected through a network's *multi-user operating system.* OS/2 and Xenix operating systems for networks provide facilities for the creation and control of hierarchical *directory structures* to separate users and their files as well as *password controls* to limit access.

Locking

Another problem with sharing files is that several users may attempt to update the same data at the same time, presenting the possibility of data corruption . To combat this problem, network software usually provides a facility for locking individual records whilst they are updated. Thus, if a particular record is being altered, it is locked and made inaccessible by any other user until the updating process is complete.

User Communication

A LAN supports a number of facilities for user communication, including electronic mail and messaging, electronic diaries and calendars and electronic notice boards. These are described more fully in Chapter 9, but their general aim is to reduce the need for paper communication and to improve the efficiency of information exchange.

Local Area Network Architecture

LAN architecture comprises hardware and software, both for the control of the LAN communications and as an interface between the LAN and its users. In order that all components are compatible and operate as a coherent system, it is important that they conform to agreed standards. This means that LAN producers have to take account of generally agreed standards for linking equipment and data communications, so that as new products come onto the market, the user is not left with a system which cannot take advantage of them. Unfortunately, at the time of writing, a number of different standards exist and this means that the decision on which type of LAN to purchase is not straightforward.

Transmission Methods

There are two different ways of utilizing a LAN cable for the transmission of data; *baseband* and *broadband*.

Baseband

In a baseband network, a transmitting device uses the whole *bandwidth* (frequency range), so only one signal can be carried at any one time. Messages are transmitted as a single stream of data, which is received by every device on the network, but only those devices which recognize the destination code as their own will accept it.

Broadband

Broadband networks provide a number of frequency bands or *channels* within the total bandwidth (*frequency division multiplexing*) and thus allow simultaneous use by different devices on the network. Generally, one channel is dedicated to the user workstations, leaving others free for transmitting video pictures for the security system, voice communication, television pictures and so on.

Workstations

Workstations provide users with access to the LAN and its facilities. A workstation is a microcomputer in its own right and so provides the user with a local processing facility, in addition to providing access to shared resources.

Servers

The general function of servers is to allocate shared resources to other nodes on the network. There are a number of different types of server, which can be categorized according to the resources they control.

File Server

The file server, usually a microcomputer based on one of the more powerful processors such as the Intel 80486 or the Motorola 68000 family, handles access to shared storage, directories and files. In addition, it controls the exchange of files between network users. Some network software, such as Tapestry II (Torus Systems Ltd) provides multiple device support. This means that file servers can support several disks, allowing file storage capacity on the LAN to be increased beyond that of the file server's integral hard disk.

Print Server

The print server accepts jobs from workstations and the network software automatically *spools* (copies output to an area of disk to await printer availability) all print jobs into a queue and informs the user when their job is complete. The print server may also provide certain print management functions, for example, to attach priorities to different print jobs so that certain jobs are printed before others, no matter what their position in the spooling queue.

Communications Server

If a LAN is to have access to external networks or databases, a communications server is required. Generally, the communications server can establish a temporary link with remote computers or users on other networks. This topic is dealt with in more detail in Chapter 9 on Communications.

Local Area Network Access Methods

Token Passing Technique

This technique is used for ring networks. An imaginary 'token' is passed continuously around the ring. The token is recognized as such by the devices, as a unique character sequence. If a device is waiting to transmit, it catches the token and with it, the authority to send data. As long as one device has the token, no other device can send data. A receiving device acknowledges the receipt of a message by inverting a 1-bit field.

Carrier Sense Multiple Access with Collision Detector (CSMA/CD)

This method of access control is used on broadcast systems such as the bus network. Each device is theoretically free to transmit data to any other device at any time, but before attempting to transmit, a device 'polls' the network to ensure that the destination device is free to receive data and that the communications channel is free. A device wishing to transmit must wait until both conditions exist, generally no more than a few millionths of a second. Because of the possibility of collision through simultaneous transmission, a collision detection mechanism causes the involved devices to cease transmission and try again some time later. In order to avoid repetition of the same collision, each involved device is made to wait a different time but if a number of retries prove unsuccessful, an error will be reported to the user.

9 *Data Communications*

The benefits of Local Area Networks (LANs), in terms of resource and information sharing, are described fully in Chapter 8, but organizations may also need facilities to allow access to external systems. These external systems may be other LANs, located on separate sites of the same organization, Wide Area Networks (WANs) such as X.25 (a packet switching network described later in this chapter), or electronic mail systems such as Telecom Gold. Connection may also be required to remote minicomputers or mainframes.

From within a LAN, access to these external systems is provided by communications *gateways*. One or more of the workstations on the LAN may be designated as *communications servers* (Chapter 8), each providing a shared communications link, for LAN users, to one of the external systems mentioned above.

Apart from the requirements for linking LANs to external systems, this chapter also examines the mechanisms for linking stand-alone microcomputers to minicomputers or mainframes.

Data Transmission Modes

Communications media can be classified according to whether or not two-way transmission is supported.

- [ ] *Simplex* mode allows communication in one direction only and as such, is inappropriate for use in WANs.

- [ ] *Half-duplex* mode supports communications in both directions, but not at the same time.

- [ ] *Duplex* mode allows communication in both directions at the same time and is appropriate for interactive systems, when on-demand enquiries are needed.

Types of Signal

There are two forms of signal which can be transmitted along a medium, *analogue* and *digital*. The telephone network is designed to carry the human voice and carries signals in continuous sine wave form, whereas computers handle data in digital form. Any analogue telephone link between computer devices requires a device called a *modem* (*mo*dulation *dem*odulation) to modify the signals transmitted. A modem for the transmitter device modulates the digital signal into an appropriate analogue form for transmission along the telephone line and a modem at the receiver device fulfils the opposite function; modems normally have facilities for both sending and receiving, so that two way communications are supported.

Integrated Services Digital Network (ISDN)

The development of the Integrated Services Digital Network (ISDN) will eventually digitize all information transmissions and allow the concurrent transmission of voice, data and images. Digital networks have a number of advantages over their analogue counterparts, including higher transmission speeds, lower incidence of errors and the facility for transmitting voice, data and image on the same circuit.

Different modems provide different data transmission rates, measured in bits per second (bps or baud). Acoustic-coupler modems only allow a transmission rate of about 300 bps; the rate is also dependent on the type of line used.

Types of Telecommunications Lines

Dedicated lines. These can be leased from British Telecom and provide a permanent connection for devices in a network. They provide high transmission rates and are relatively error-free. They are only cost-effective for high volume data transmission, or when a permanent link is vital to the users. Typical transmission rates are 300, 1200, 2400, 4800 and 9600 bps. Charging is by a flat rate rather than when calls are made.

Dial-up or switched lines. These are cheaper, but support lower transmission rates than leased lines. They are more cost effective than leased lines for low-volume work and allow the operator to choose the destination of transmissions.

Communication Standards

Devices differ in the ways they communicate or 'talk' with each other. One such difference is in the number of channels they use to transmit data.

Serial Transmission

With serial transmission, the binary signals representing the data are transmitted one after another in a serial fashion, which is necessary when there is only one available channel. Serial transmission is used in all network communications other than for short distances, so all Wide Area Networks use this form. The technique is illustrated in *Figure 9.1*.

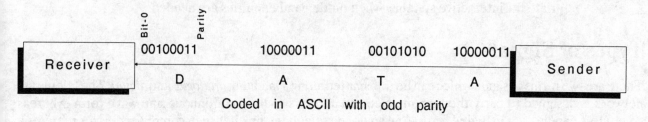

Figure 9.1

Parallel Transmission

Data bits are transmitted as groups in parallel, as *Figure 9.2* illustrates.

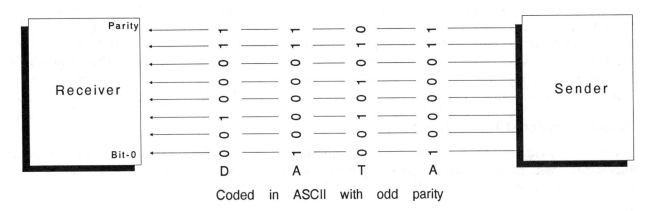

Coded in ASCII with odd parity

Figure 9.2

This is obviously faster than sending them serially, but it is only practical over short distances. Communication between a computer and its nearby peripherals can be carried out using parallel transmission, which is particularly important where high-speed devices, such as disk or tape units, are concerned. Microcomputer systems often use parallel transmission to communicate with a nearby printer.

Asynchronous Serial Transmission

When a sending device transmits characters at irregular intervals, as does for example, a keyboard device, it is said to be transmitting *asynchronously*. Although the characters are not sent at regular intervals, the bits within each character must be sent at regularly timed intervals. An example of asynchronous character format is shown in *Figure 9.3*.

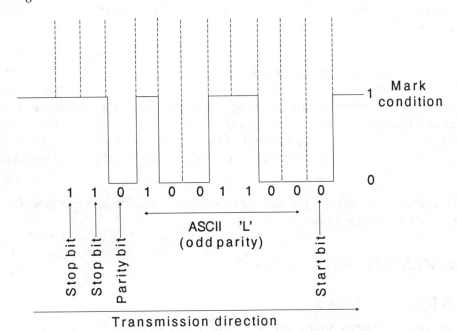

Figure 9.3

It can be seen from the *Figure 9.3* that the line has two electrical states, representing 1 and 0. Between characters, the line is in the idle state, a 1 or *mark* condition. The first or *start* bit, set to 0, indicates the start of a character, whilst a *stop* bit marks the end. The receiving machine 'listens' to the line for a start bit. When it senses this it counts off the regularly timed bits which form the character. When a stop bit is reached, the receiver switches back to its 'listening' state. The presence of start and stop bits for each character permits the time interval between characters to be irregular, or asynchronous.

Synchronous Serial Transmission

The start and stop bits used in asynchronous transmission are wasteful, in that they do not contain information. With higher speed devices or buffered low-speed devices, data can be transmitted in more efficient, timed, or *synchronous* blocks. *Figure 9.4* illustrates the technique.

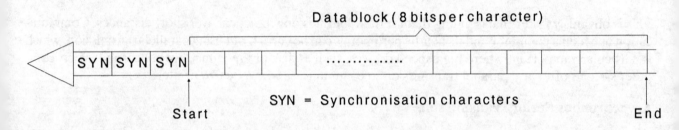

Data block (8 bits per character)

SYN = Synchronisation characters

Start

End

Figure 9.4

A variety of formats may be used, each having their own operating rules or *protocol*. Communications protocol is dealt with later in this chapter.

In synchronous transmission, a data stream may be very long, so it is vital that the timing between transmitter and receiver is synchronized and that individual characters are separated out. This is done by using a clock lead from the transmitter. Synchronization (*syn*) characters are placed at the beginning of each data block and, in case timing is lost by line disturbance, several syn characters may be situated at intervals within the data block. Thus if timing is lost, the receiver can re-time its bit groupings from the last syn character. Like the start and stop bits used in asynchronous transmission, syn characters constitute an overhead and have to be 'stripped' out by the receiver. Synchronous transmission is generally used for data speeds of 2400 bps or more.

Some VDU terminals are designed for high speed data transmission and use synchronous transmission; many others use asynchronous transmission.

Serial Transmission Controls

Block Check Characters (BCC)

The idea of even and odd parity bits for each character is introduced in Chapter 2 on Data Representation and is shown to be inadequate for the detection of even numbers of bit errors; *block check characters* (BCCs) aim to conquer this problem by checking the parity of *blocks* of characters within a data transmission stream. BCCs may carry out *longitudinal* or *cyclic redundancy* checks.

Longitudinal Redundancy Checking (LRC)

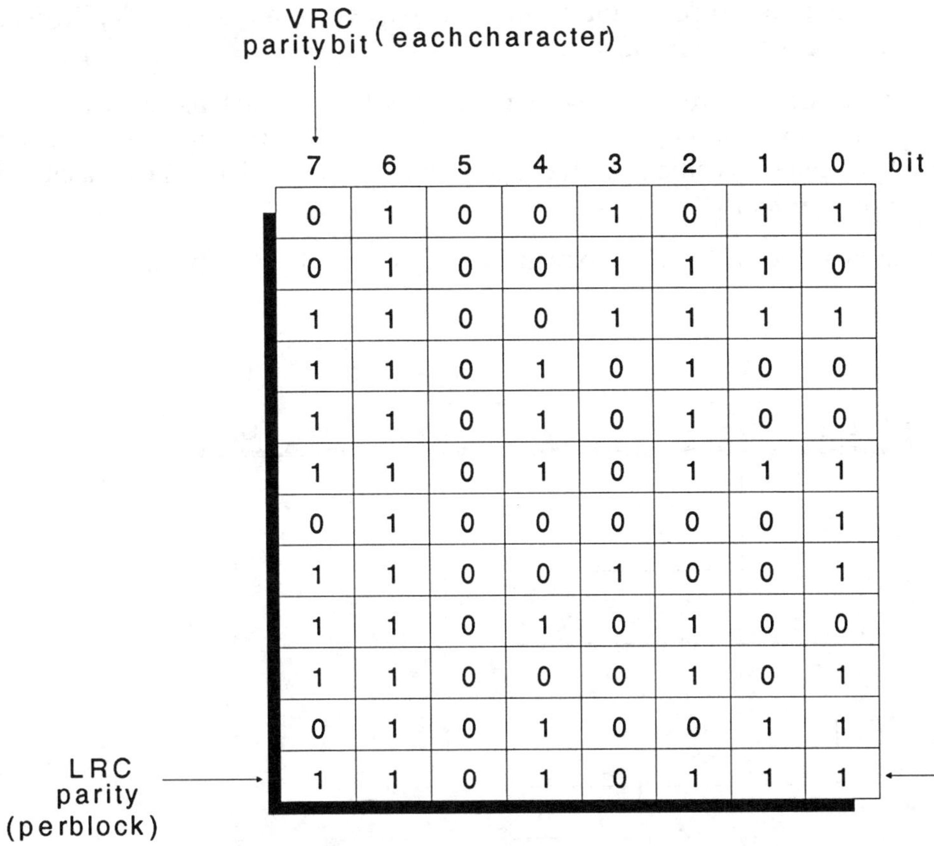

	7	6	5	4	3	2	1	0	bit
	0	1	0	0	1	0	1	1	
	0	1	0	0	1	1	1	0	
	1	1	0	0	1	1	1	1	
	1	1	0	1	0	1	0	0	
	1	1	0	1	0	1	0	0	
	1	1	0	1	0	1	1	1	
	0	1	0	0	0	0	0	1	
	1	1	0	0	1	0	0	1	
	1	1	0	1	0	1	0	0	
	1	1	0	0	0	1	0	1	
	0	1	0	1	0	0	1	1	
	1	1	0	1	0	1	1	1	

VRC parity bit (each character)

LRC parity (per block)

BCC

Figure 9.5

By reference to *Figure 9.5*, the principles of LRC can be explained as follows.

Each BCC consists of a group of parity bits which carry out LRC. However, each LRC bit is a parity check on the corresponding bits in all the characters in a block. Thus, the first parity bit in the BCC relates to the bits which occupy the first position in each character in the block, the second parity bit in the BCC relates to the second position bits in each character in the block and so on.

LRC ensures that multiple errors, whether even or odd, are likely to be discovered, so at the receiver end of the transmission, the parity of individual characters and blocks of characters is checked.

Cyclic Redundancy Checking (CRC)

The BCCs described previously treat a data block as a set of characters, whereas cyclic redundancy checking (CRC) uses a BCC which views each data block as a continuous stream of bits.

Firstly, the data block is regarded as one large binary number. That number is divided by an another agreed binary number, the quotient is discarded and the remainder is attached to the data block as a BCC. Upon receipt of the data block, the receiver repeats the calculation used to generate the BCC and compares the result with the BCC attached by the transmitter; any difference between them indicates some corruption of the block.

Hamming Code

Certain codes can be used, not only to detect the occurrence of an error, but also to identify its precise location. In addition, some errors can be rectified.

The Hamming code described here utilizes three *code* bits and four *data* bits, making seven in all, although there are circumstances when more bits may be used. *Figure 9.6* illustrates the format which positions each code bit (C_2, C_1 and C_0) in a column position which equates with its binary weight. The data bits (D_3, D_2, D_1 and D_0) occupy the other positions.

Thus, C_0 ($2^0 = 1$) is in column 1, C_1 ($2^1 = 2$) in column 2 and C_2 ($2^2 = 4$) in column 4.

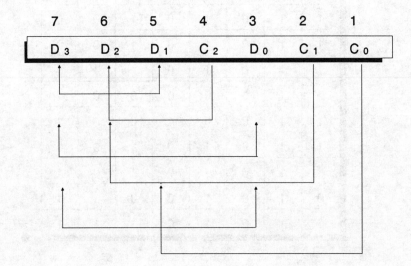

Figure 9.6

Parity is maintained in sub-groups, such that the C_0 relates to D_3, D_1 and D_0, C_1 to D_3, D_2 and D_0, and C_2 to D_3, D_2 and D_1. Thus, each sub-group of data bits has a single code bit. This is illustrated further in *Figure 9.7*.

	Column						
Group	7	6	5	4	3	2	1
0	D_3		D_1		D_0		C_0
1	D_3	D_2			D_0	C_1	
2	D_3	D_2	D_1	C_2			

Figure 9.7

The three code bits produce a unique pattern when any single bit is corrupted. A parity output of 000 would indicate the absence of any errors. To correct the word only requires the inversion of the bit position which is in error. The processes are illustrated in *Figure 9.8*.

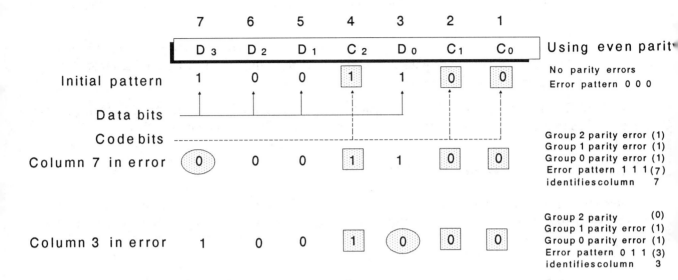

Figure 9.8

This method does not enable detection of double errors, but the limitation can be removed by the inclusion of a single parity bit across the whole word. However, double bit errors are not correctable.

Packet Switching Networks

Packet switching operates by breaking messages up into *data packets*, which are then directed through the network to their destination under computer control. In addition to a message portion, each packet contains data concerning:

- ☐ the destination address;

- ☐ the source identification;

- ☐ the sequence of the packet in the complete message;

- ☐ the detection and control of transmission errors.

The progress of a packet is monitored and controlled by *switching* computers located at each node in the network. As a packet arrives at a node, the computer checks the addressing instructions and unless it corresponds to its present location, forwards it on the most appropriate route. Each node has an *input queue*, into which all arriving packets are entered (even those which are addressed to the node itself) and a number of *output queues* to allow for the possibility of network congestion. The route on which a packet is then transmitted from a node may be determined according to one of a number of *routing strategies*;

- ☐ *hot potato*. The packet is sent as quickly as possible to the shortest output queue; such packets are not unduly delayed, although they may not be transmitted on the most direct route;

□ *pre-determined routing.* With this method, the routing details are included in the packet itself, each switching centre forwarding the packet according to the embedded instructions;

□ *directory routing.* Each switching centre has a copy of a routing table to which it refers before forwarding each packet. The appropriate output queue is determined from the table and the packet destination.

Network traffic information is continually transmitted between the various nodes, so that each switching computer has information on, for example, congested routes which can then be avoided.

Message Switching Networks

As the name suggests, this type of network deals with identifiable and complete messages, in contrast to a packet switched system where the destination user nodes are responsible for re-assembling their packets into complete messages upon receipt. A number of points can be made when comparing and contrasting packet switching and message switching networks:

□ both use a *store* and *forward* principle; each node in the network has storage facilities for the accumulation of data prior to its onward transmission and the intelligence to examine the destination data before forwarding it;

□ packet switching networks treat data *transparently.* Individual packets generally do not contain complete messages and the network does not recognize connections between packets, except from identification of their destination. The destination user nodes are left with the responsibility of re-assembling individual packets into complete messages;

□ the store and forward facilities in message switching networks need to be much larger than those for packet switching systems, because *complete messages* must be accumulated at each point of transfer in the network;

□ message switching requires increased processing time at intervening nodes while messages are accumulated before onward transmission;

□ message switching provides users with greater confidence that messages will be transmitted and received in complete form.

Value-added Networks (VAN)

As the term suggests, a value-added network (VAN) supplies users with additional facilities, including electronic mail, automatic error detection and gateways to other computer systems and networks.

Communications Protocol

The major British public packet switched network is the PSS (Packet Switching Stream). The protocols for this service are known as the X.25 standard, which is also used by a number of private wide area networks. X.25 is an asynchronous communications protocol recommended for communication through public data networks. IBM uses a synchronous communications standard in its networks. Such wide area networks can be used, either to link geographically separate LANs or to link a LAN to a remote mainframe host.

NETBIOS (networking basic input/output system) is a standard interface between a microcomputer operating system and the network. Gateway adaptor boards, such as the PC LAN to X.25, give workstations in LANs access to the X.25 protocol packet switching networks.

Closed and Open Systems

In the past, networks were designed to work with particular types of workstation and were known as *closed* networks. Unfortunately, users of such systems were unable to take advantage of improved hardware produced by other manufacturers. Neither were they able to attach any of their existing stand-alone systems to the network, unless they were compatible with it. The trend more recently has been towards *open* systems, so that workstations from different manufacturers can be attached to the same network. For example, non-IBM workstations can be attached to IBM's Token Ring network. To achieve such openness requires the setting of standards relating to hardware and software which may be used in a network. Strong standards encourage manufacturers to make products which conform to those standards, which in turn, creates a wide range of compatible products, from which users can choose.

The OSI (Open Systems Interconnection) Reference Model

The OSI model (developed by the International Standards Organization) has been used to some extent by manufacturers in a move to more open network systems, although some of the standards, initially set through commercial products, such as the Ethernet and Token Ring Networks, have been incorporated into the OSI model. The model identifies seven hierarchical layers, each of which has a specific function within a network. For example, Layer 1, the lowest in the hierarchy, is the Physical Layer and defines aspects of the hardware, such as the network connection. This may relate, for example, to the number of pins used in a network connector and the function each pin should have. It also defines standards for the electrical transmission of binary data (protocols). Layer 7, the highest in the hierarchy, defines standards, for example, concerning the transfer of information between end-users (electronic mail), applications programs and graphical data exchange. There is still much work to be done regarding the formation and acceptance of standards, particularly at the upper levels, although some LAN and communications equipment suppliers have specified their own protocols within the guidelines of the model and these have been established in many widely accepted LAN products. For example, three major standards for hardware have been established and accepted by another international standards body, the Institute of Electrical and Electronics Engineers (IEEE). They are Token Ring (IBM being the main proponent), Ethernet (DEC primarily) and Starlan (AT&T).

Special Communications Equipment

A number of different machines and devices exist to improve the efficiency of telecommunications networks. The most notable are *multiplexers* (MUX), *concentrators* and *front-end-processors* (FEP).

Multiplexers

Low speed terminals, such as those with keyboards, transmit at about 300 bps, whereas voice-grade telephone lines can support transmission speeds of up to 9600 bps. A multiplexer allows a number of low-speed devices to share a high-speed line, thus economising on the cost of leasing telephone lines. The messages from several low-speed lines are combined into one high-speed channel and then separated out at the other end by a de-multiplexer. In two-way transmissions, both these functions are carried out in one unit at each end of the higher speed channel. The operation of a multiplexer linking several remote terminals to a host computer is illustrated in *Figure 9.9*.

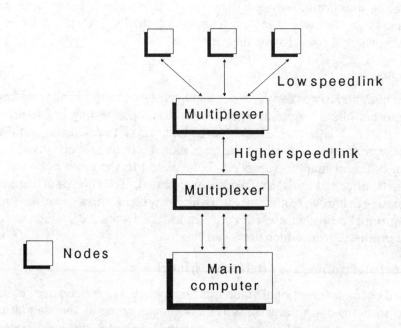

Figure 9.9

Multiplexers use different methods to combine signals and separate them out.

☐ *Frequency Division Multiplexing* (FDM) differentiates between the signals from different devices, by using a different frequency range for each. Allowing for spacing between the different ranges, a 2400 bps circuit can handle twelve 110 bps terminals.

☐ *Time Division Multiplexing* (TDM) provides a time slice on the higher-speed line for each terminal. The multiplexer has a number of registers, one per low-speed channel. Each register can store one character. The multiplexer scans each register in sequence, emptying the contents into a continuous stream of data to be transmitted and sending a null character whenever it finds an empty slot. Concentrators aim to overcome this wastage.

Concentrators

A concentrator greatly increases data throughput by increasing the number of low-speed channels and instead of transmitting a null character, empties the contents of the next full register. The data from each low-speed device is identified by extra identification bits and this constitutes an overhead.

Front-End-Processors (FEP)

A front-end-processor is the most sophisticated type of device for communications control and is usually a minicomputer held at the site of a mainframe host computer. Its main task is to handle all the communications traffic, leaving the mainframe free to concentrate on processing tasks. Its main tasks include:

☐ parity checking;

☐ 'stripping' of overhead characters from serial transmission, start/stop bits and syn characters;

    ☐ conversion from serial to parallel transmission and vice versa;

    ☐ network control;

    ☐ network accounting;

    ☐ character conversion.

Linking Microcomputers to Mainframes

In organizations with mainframe computers, it is often desirable for staff with microcomputers on their desks to be able to communicate with the mainframe via those systems. With non-IBM systems, where the host computer uses asynchronous transmission, the connection can be made via the RS232C (this refers to a standard used in most serial communications) serial transmission port, located at the back of the microcomputer's system casing. However, the most common mainframe systems, IBM and ICL in particular, use synchronous communications, so special *terminal emulation* cards are required.

Thus, microcomputer workstations can be converted to mainframe terminals using a technique called emulation. A terminal emulation card is fitted into one of the expansion slots in the microcomputer's system casing. If there are a number of terminals to be connected, the microcomputer is then connected, via a coaxial cable, to a *terminal cluster controller*. The controller is linked to a front-end processor (usually a minicomputer, dedicated to handling incoming and outgoing communications for the mainframe), which is itself connected to the mainframe computer. In this way, a microcomputer can, for example, be converted into an emulation of an IBM 3270 terminal.

The advantage of using a microcomputer as a mainframe terminal is that it can also be used on a stand-alone basis for local processing tasks, such as word processing or spreadsheet work. The terminal emulation package ensures that the mainframe responds in the same way as it would to a dedicated terminal. Security mechanisms, such as passwords, prevent users of emulated terminals from carrying out processes which are forbidden to users of dedicated terminals. However, the microcomputer's facility for local storage and processing can present serious security problems for the mainframe's data and various mechanisms have to be included to prevent unauthorized updates.

Where emulated terminals are to be linked to a mainframe via a wide area network, adaptor cards are available which combine the terminal emulation with the gateway software, to access the intervening network.

Communications Applications

Electronic Mail

Unlike telex and facsimile transmissions, which require paper for input and output, electronic mail systems based on computer networks are paper-less (except when a user requires hard copy). A major advantage is the facility for message storage if a destination terminal is busy, or has a temporary fault. When it is free, the message can be transmitted.

Certain basic features can be identified as being common to all electronic mail systems:

    ☐ a terminal for preparing, entering and storing messages. The terminal will be 'intelligent', possibly a microcomputer, mainframe terminal or dedicated word processor. In any event, it should have some word processing or text editing facilities to allow messages to be changed on screen before transmission. A printer may also be available for printing out messages received over the system;

☐ an electronic communication link with other workstations in the network and with the central computer controlling the system;

☐ a directory containing the electronic addresses of all network users;

☐ a central mailbox facility (usually the controlling computer) for the storage of messages in transit or waiting to be retrieved.

Ideally, the following facilities are available to electronic mail users:

☐ messages are automatically dated upon transmission;

☐ messages are automatically acknowledged as being received when the recipient first accesses it from the terminal;

☐ multiple addressing, that is the facility to address a message to an identified group, without addressing each member of the group individually;

☐ priority rating to allow messages to be allocated different priorities according to their importance.

Networks require two particular features in order to support electronic mail:

☐ a message storage facility to allow messages to be forwarded when the recipient is available;

☐ compatibility with a wide range of manufacturers' equipment. Devices attached to a network have to be able to 'talk' to the communications network using protocols or standards of communication.

Benefits of Electronic Mail

The following major benefits are generally claimed for electronic mail systems:

☐ Savings in stationery and telephone costs;

☐ More rapid transmission than is possible with conventional mail;

☐ Electronic mail can be integrated with other computer-based systems used in an organization;

☐ All transmissions are recorded, so costs can be carefully controlled;

☐ Electronic mail allows staff to 'telecommute', that is, to work from home via a terminal;

☐ The recipient does not have to be present when a message is sent. Messages can be retrieved from the central 'mailbox' when convenient.

The UK has several electronic mail systems, the best known being Telecom Gold, operated by British Telecom. Telecom Gold can be used by any subscriber with a modem and appropriate communications software. Communication can be established, either on a dial-up basis or via the packet switching service. Apart from facilities to send and read messages, Telecom Gold also allows message editing and storing and the setting up of personal user directories, so that they can be referred to by name, rather than by mailbox number. Telecom Gold also provides electronic diary facilities and access to a range of language processors.

LAN gateway products are available to allow any user node to access electronic mail systems such as Telecom Gold.

Telex

Conventionally, the Telex system requires the use of dedicated printer terminals (teletypes), which only allow the use of upper case characters and do not provide any editing facility. As an electronic mail system, the problem is not with Telex itself, but with the outmoded terminal equipment. However, Telex can now be accessed, from a microcomputer, through a Prestel gateway. Prestel is a public viewdata information database, with which subscribers can communicate, either via a microcomputer with a modem and appropriate software, or from a dedicated viewdata terminal.

LAN gateway products also exist to allow access to the Telex system by any user node on a LAN. Electronic mail facilities, such as those described in the previous section are not inherent in Telex, but gateway software, such as Torus's Telex Gateway, can provide them instead. For example, incoming telex messages can be stored on disk at the gateway LAN station, be sent to any shared printer on the LAN if hard copy is required, or be distributed to other nodes electronically. Personal user directories can be set up and messages can be queued or assigned a particular time for transmission.

Facsimile Transmission (FAX)

This service allows the transmission of facsimiles or exact copies of documents or pictures through a data communications network. Using a fax machine connected to a telephone line, the user simply dials the fax number of the recipient, waits for the correct signal and the document is fed though the fax machine and transmitted. The fax machine sends picture elements or *pixels* obtained by scanning the document in a series of parallel lines; a synchronized fax machine at the other end prints a facsimile from those pixels.

Viewdata Systems

A viewdata system is based on a central computer database, which provides 'pages' of information on a variety of subjects, including sport, travel and business, for access by subscribers. The major public viewdata system in the UK is Prestel.

Electronic Data Interchange (EDI)

Similar to electronic mail, EDI allows users to exchange business documents, such as invoices and orders, over the telephone network.

Bibliographic Databases

These databases provide information on specialized or widely ranging topics. For example, BLAISE, which is provided by the British Library, gives information on British book publications. Euronet Diane (Direct Information Access Network in Europe) provides information extracted from publications, research documents and so on, which may be of interest to specialists such as scientists, engineers, economists and lawyers. Each extract provides the relevant bibliographic references to allow users to access the original sources more fully.

Remote Job Entry (RJE)

RJE systems make the simplest use of data communications to transmit bulk data rapidly to a central computer; transmission is one-way, from an RJE terminal located at the remote site to the central computer, which is probably situated at the head office of the organization. In a wholesaling organization, for example, each distribution warehouse could transmit details of stock changes and requirements via an RJE terminal, at the end of each day via a simplex dial-up communications link. In the 1960s, RJE terminals commonly consisted of a card or paper tape reader and printer; more recently, transmission would be direct from a key-to-disk or key-to-tape system.

EFTPOS (Electronic Funds Transfer at Point-Of-Sale)

This service provides for the automatic debiting of customers' bank accounts at the checkout or point of sale. Many garages now have a device for reading the magnetic strip details on bank and credit cards. The system saves considerable time when contrasted with payments by cheque and as an alternative to cash, reduces the likelihood of theft. The retailer also has the assurance that the payment is authorized before the sale is made. Usually, a retailer will have a 'floor' limit, or amount above which a telephone call needs to be made to the credit card company for authorization of payment.

10 *Microcomputer Systems Architecture*

This chapter looks at a number of aspects of microcomputer systems architecture:

- ☐ the processor or CPU;
- ☐ memory (both RAM and ROM);
- ☐ system architecture;
- ☐ display screen;
- ☐ disk storage;
- ☐ expansibility.

Processor

The processor is, in fact, a CPU (Central Processing Unit) on a 'chip' and provides the central base for a machine's power. A number of processors have been produced by a range of manufacturers, including Intel, Motorola and Zilog.

The most famous, mainly because they power the IBM range of microcomputers, are those manufactured by Intel; the range includes the 8080, 8086, 8088, 80286, 80386 and 80486.

The main features which distinguish one processor from another are:

- ☐ clock speed;
- ☐ word length;
- ☐ architecture.

Clock Speed

As the initiator of all a computer's activities, the processor has a wide range of tasks to perform and to ensure that these tasks are properly sequenced and timed, a clock mechanism is used. The speed of the clock is one determinant of how quickly a computer can carry out processing tasks.

The control of program execution is exercised through the processor's automatic sequence control mechanism. The activity it controls is known as the *fetch-execute cycle* (Chapter 3) and is used here to illustrate the role of the clock.

Certain steps in the fetch-execute cycle must wait until the previous step is completed. For example, during the fetching of a program instruction from memory the instruction cannot be moved from the Memory Buffer Register (MBR) to the Current Instruction Register (CIR) until the transfer from memory to MBR has been completed. The time taken for the latter transfer is dependent on the speed of the memory read operation. Not all activities are dependent on the prior completion of another or others; for example, once the value of the Program Counter (PC) has been copied to the Memory Address Register (MAR), the PC can be incremented at any time during the fetch-execute cycle.

In order to synchronize the processor's operations, a clock generates regularly-timed 'pulses', usually at a rate of between 4 and 33 million per second. A technical specification will express this rating in MHz (Megahertz or million cycles per second) and for example, a 10 MHz processor operates with a clock running at 10 million pulses or cycles per second.

Different processor activities take different times to complete; for example, a memory read takes more time than the incrementing of an index register within the processor. Each step, however, must commence on a clock pulse and the number of clock pulses which are generated before completion of an operation will depend on the type of operation; one operation may be completed in two clock pulses, whilst another may take four clock pulses.

Wait State

A wait state is an extra clock pulse added to a processor cycle when it accesses memory. This feature will be referred to in more detail later in the section on Cache Memory.

Subject to certain limitations to be explained later, the greater the clock rate, the quicker the computer will perform, so for example, a 20 MHz processor will carry out processing more quickly than a 10 MHz processor.

Word Length

Any given processor is designed to handle a particular size of bit grouping, for example, 8 bits, 16 bits or 32 bits. This bit grouping is known as the processor's *word length*. The word length defines the number of bits normally manipulated as a unit during the execution of arithmetic, logic, data transfer or input/output instructions. Within the processor, data are transmitted along a parallel data bus; in a true 32-bit machine, for example, the data bus consists of 32 parallel lines. In addition, any working registers within the processor are also equal to the word length of the processor.

Although these basic principles may be generally applied, certain exceptions do exist. Reference is made in the previous paragraph to a 'true 32-bit machine' but not all processors have a *data bus* equal in size to their word length. Consider as an example, the range of Intel manufactured processors; this includes the 8080 (8 bits), the 8086 (16 bits), the 80286 (16 bits) and the 80386 (32 bits). The 8086 uses an 8-bit wide data bus, but handles data in groups of 16 bits. Each 16-bit word is fetched, using a 'double-fetch' operation, in two separate 8-bit bytes, so the 8086 is not a 'true' 16-bit processor. The 80286 processor, on the other hand, is a true 16-bit, in that it uses a 16-bit wide data bus.

At the time of writing, technology is concentrating on 32-bit processors because the larger the word length and accompanying data bus, the greater the amount of data which can be addressed and manipulated at one time. If, for example, a processor can perform a given operation on a 16-bit operand during the execution of one instruction, it is, all other things being equal, processing data at twice the speed of a processor that can perform the operation on only an 8-bit word.

Most processors have an associated faster processor which can be used for 'number crunching' operations such as those required for spreadsheet work. For example, associated with the Intel processors mentioned earlier are the 8087, 80287, 80387. Most technical specifications detail the *maths co-processor* as a separate 'add-on' because not all users will use software which requires its particular features.

Processor Architecture

The internal structure of a processor is generally referred to as its *architecture*. Within the integrated circuits which form the processor are a complex collection of component units: registers, counters, arithmetic and logic circuits, memory elements etc. Although the details of such architecture are mainly of concern to the programmer at machine level, one fairly recent and notable design is briefly described here.

Reduced Instruction Set Computer (RISC)

All the instructions available with a particular processor are known as its *instruction set*. A reduced instruction set processor, as the name suggests, is one which can execute only a small number of different instructions compared with the prevailing standards for contemporary processors. A RISC processor has fewer instructions available to it but can operate at many times the speed of processors with more complex instruction sets. RISC machines are effective because, as research on conventional architectures has suggested, the average processor spends most of its time executing a handful of simple instructions including add, subtract, load, store and branch. A British microcomputer manufacturer Acorn has produced a RISC machine called the ARM (Acorn Risc Machine) and the world's major computer manufacturers (including IBM) are producing their own RISC-based machines.

Memory

There are two types of internal computer memory - RAM (Random Access Memory) and ROM (Read Only Memory).

RAM

Functions

RAM constitutes the working area of the computer and is used for storage of program(s) and data currently in use. Computer memory is measured in terms of *kb*(kilobytes), where 1kb is about a 1000 bytes (more precisely 1024), though for larger memory, the unit of measurement is *mb*(megabyte) which is roughly a million bytes.

Because RAM is *volatile* (the current contents are lost when power is removed or different programs and data are entered), all programs and data files are held on a magnetic storage medium.

Many computers now make use of a CMOS (Complementary Metal Oxide Semi-conductor) RAM to store certain 'setup' instructions and also to allow the storage of, for example, the system date and time. This memory chip derives its power from an internal backup battery when the power is turned off; the battery allows the volatile CMOS RAM data to be retained between operating sessions, thus relieving the operator of re-entering the date and time whenever the system is switched on. CMOS RAM is chosen for this function because it has a lower power requirement than the RAM used for main memory.

Technical Features of RAM

RAM is directly accessible by the processor and memory/processor transfers which occur during a program's execution have to be made as quickly as possible to maximize the use of the processor's power. The previous section on processors describes the use of a 'clock' which generates regularly-timed pulses to synchronize the activities of the processor and that different activities take different numbers of clock pulses; memory/processor transfers, although extremely quick, typically 80 to 100ns (nanoseconds) for a read from RAM, constitute a penalty in terms of using the processor's power. Thus, the quicker the transfer can be carried out, the less time that the processor is left unoccupied. Predictably, the higher the speed the greater the cost.

Types of RAM

Broadly, two types of RAM are used in computers. They are:

- □ *Static* RAM (SRAM);
- □ *Dynamic* RAM (DRAM).

A number of comparisons can be drawn between the two types:

- □ DRAMs are easier to make than SRAMs;
- □ More DRAM can be packed onto a single integrated circuit or 'chip' than is possible with SRAM;
- □ DRAM consumes less power than SRAM;
- □ Static RAM, as the term suggests, retains its contents as long as power is maintained, whereas Dynamic RAM needs to be 'refreshed' (the contents of each location are rewritten) at intervals not exceeding 2 milliseconds (ms).
- □ SRAM can be written to and read from more quickly, but is more expensive than DRAM.

The most important features for comparison relate to *speed* of access and *cost*. To maximize use of a powerful processor SRAM is the obvious choice but the need for large computer memory (software packages typically require a minimum of 512kb RAM and as they become more sophisticated will require even more memory), would make computer systems based wholly on SRAM very expensive. Generally then, for economic reasons, main memory consists of DRAM chips grouped together on a memory board, for example 640kb RAM may consist of three memory chips, 2 × 256kb and 1 × 128kb. At the time of writing 1 megabyte(mb or million bytes) DRAM chips are common and as is the case with other computer technology, the limits are continually being extended; 64mb DRAM chips could be available by the mid 1990s. A conflict exists between processor speed and memory cost. Doubling the clock speed of a processor from 10 MHz to 20 MHz does not necessarily double the speed of the computer's overall operation because of other factors, including *disk access time* and *memory read time*. To help improve the speed of memory accesses and still keep down the cost of memory, a system of *cache memory* can be used.

Cache Memory

To understand the function of cache memory it is necessary to refer to a feature identified in the section on the processor, namely *wait-state*. A wait-state is an extra clock pulse added to a processor cycle when it accesses memory. The slower the memory, the more wait-states which have to be added to processor cycles to give the memory time to respond. The greater the number of wait-states, the lower the *overall* computer *system performance*. Thus, a high performance processor like the Intel 20 MHz 80386 is wasted if it is used with a slow memory system that requires many wait-states. A memory system which requires zero wait-states will allow the system (ignoring peripheral device performance) to function at the maximum performance of the processor. It must be emphasized that overall system performance depends on all components forming a computer system and that disk access time (Chapter 6) also plays a major part in determining such performance. *Disk caching* (see later section) can also radically improve system performance.

A cache memory system aims to provide the performance of fast Static RAM (SRAM) but at the lower cost of Dynamic RAM (DRAM).

A cache is a small amount of very fast SRAM located between the processor and main memory. *Figure 10.1* illustrates the relationship between main memory, the processor and the cache.

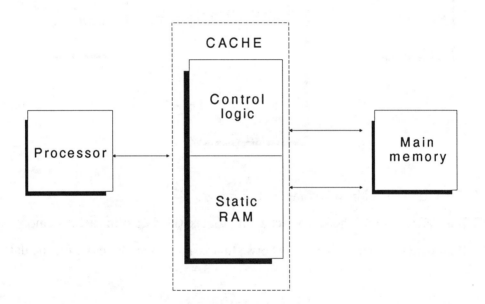

Figure 10.1

The cache size is typically 16kb to 64kb and its purpose is to hold a copy of frequently used code and data. Instead of accessing the slower main memory (consisting of DRAM) for such data, the processor can go directly to the cache memory without incurring any wait-states.

The effectiveness of cache memory is based on the principle that once a memory location has been accessed, it is likely to be accessed again in the near future. This means that after the initial access, subsequent accesses to the same memory location need go only to the cache. In view of the fact that much computer processing is repetitive, a high 'hit rate' in the cache can be anticipated. The cache hit rate is simply the ratio of cache 'hits' to the total number of memory accesses required by the processor. Systems using cache memory may achieve an 85 to 90 per cent hit rate and thus can radically improve system performance beyond that possible with other systems using the same processor but lacking a cache memory system. The Intel 80486 processor incorporates a maths co-processor and cache memory on one chip

Cache memory aims to improve memory access times and keep down memory costs. The larger the cache, the greater the hit rate but the greater the cost of the memory. For example, a cache the same size as the main memory would obviously give a 100 per cent hit rate but would defeat the object of having a cache.

The operation of the processor, cache and memory is illustrated in the *Figure 10.2*.

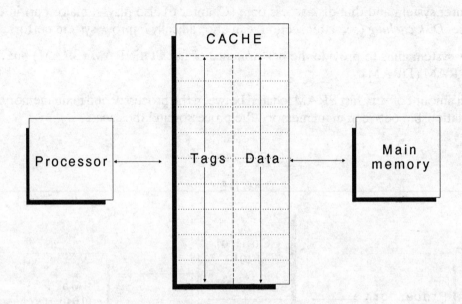

Figure 10.2

☐ The processor address is compared with tags;

☐ If a match is found there is a cache 'hit', that is, the data is in cache memory;

☐ If no match is found it's a cache 'miss', that is, go to main memory for the data.

ROM

Function

ROM (Read Only Memory) is a permanent storage area for special programs and data which have been installed during the process of computer manufacture. The contents are 'hard-wired' and cannot be altered by software.

The software contained within ROM is fairly standard for most machines and generally includes part of the BIOS (Basic Input/Output System). As the name suggests, the BIOS handles the basic hardware operations of input and output. The aim of the BIOS is to provide an interface between the user and the computer. The interface relieves the programmer of concern about the physical characteristics of the hardware devices which form the system. As such, the BIOS is machine orientated and will vary from one make of machine to another.Computer manufacturers wishing to 'clone' the IBM PC had to buy the licence to use the PC's BIOS, without which, no other machine could claim to be truly IBM compatible.

Some machines also provide expansion slots for the insertion of ROM cartridges containing applications software.

System Architecture

The internal structure of a computer, that is the ways in which the various components are connected and communicate with one another, is usually described as the system's architecture. As technological advances improve the performances of certain components, so system architectures have to change to take advantage of these improvements. A brief overview of IBM's Micro Channel Architecture is given here to provide an important example of such a change.

Micro Channel Architecture (MCA) - a Case Study

This architecture aims to overcome the limitations of the architectures used in the IBM PC (Personal Computer) and IBM PC AT (Advanced Technology) machines as well as a myriad of 'clones' produced by IBM's competitors. IBM use MCA in their 32-bit PS/2 (Personal System 2) range.

One of the many differences with the MCA approach concerns the width of the *bus*. The bus is a communication link between the processor and system components and is an essential but passive part of the system architecture. The active components, such as the processor, disk controller and other peripherals are the primary determinants of system performance. As long as the data transfer speed along the bus matches the requirements of these devices and does not create a 'bottleneck', the bus does not affect system performance. The MCA bus is 32 bits compared with the AT's 16 bits and the wider data path allows components within the system to be accessed twice as quickly and most importantly, takes advantage of the higher speed processors available. MCA is also radically different from AT architecture in many other respects. For example, the expansion slots in the PS/2 range which allow the user to insert extra features, perhaps for networking or for extra memory, are physically different from those in the AT and PC machines and their expansion cards will not fit in the PS/2 machines. The immediate problem for existing AT and PC users is that they cannot buy new PS/2 machines and still make use of their existing expansion cards.

At the time of IBM's battle to establish the new MCA standard, a consortium of IBM's competitors including Compaq, Zenith, NEC and Olivetti amongst others, are trying to establish a new architecture (EISA - Extended Industry Standard Architecture) which claims to give the benefits of MCA but also retains compatibility with existing AT and PC expansion cards.

In the longer term, whichever architecture becomes the industry standard, the main significance to users of radical changes in system architecture is that software developments, although trailing behind, tend eventually to take advantage of improved hardware design. Packages are produced with improved features which many users find are incompatible with their existing computer systems. The user is left with the choice of making do with existing software or replacing some very expensive equipment. Of course, software producers are aware of this and to maintain their markets will try, for a short time at least, to make their products compatible with both the new and existing computer systems.

Graphics Display

Graphics facilities are provided by the addition of a 'graphics adaptor card' which can be plugged into one of the expansion slots located inside a computer's system unit casing. A number of standards are available:

☐ Monochrome Graphics Adaptor (MGA);

☐ Colour Graphics Adaptor (CGA);

☐ Enhanced Graphics Adaptor (EGA);

☐ Video Graphics Array (VGA).

As the name suggests, an MGA card allows the screen to display monochrome graphics. This can mean white on black, green on black or amber on chocolate. A medium resolution card may provide a pixel density of around 320 pixels × 200 lines, compared with, say, 720 pixels × 350 lines for a high resolution card. Even for word processing, the higher resolution is advisable because the improved clarity of display reduces the likelihood of eye fatigue. Much graphical work, for example, that involved with computer-aided design (CAD), benefits from the use of colour and this is made available with CGA, EGA and VGA in varying resolutions. It must be said, however, that what ranks as high resolution today will warrant only medium resolution status in the future.

Disk Caching

Disk caching improves the rate at which data can be retrieved from a hard disk by keeping a portion of data from the hard disk in a RAM cache. As an electro-mechanical component of the computer system, the hard disk can access data at speeds measured in milliseconds (thousandths of a second), compared with purely electronic processor and RAM speeds measured in nanoseconds (thousand millionths of a second). This speed imbalance can lead to a system 'bottleneck', particularly with microcomputers using an 80286 or 80386 processor.

In general, there are two methods of caching. *Software caching* uses a portion of RAM as a cache, for example, with 640kb of RAM, 32kb may be used for the disk cache. The other method makes use of a *caching controller card* which can be slotted into an expansion slot inside the system unit. It has its own cache memory so that the full amount of RAM remains available for the user.

Expansibility

Expansion Slots

All microcomputer systems have a number of expansion slots, usually around eight in number, for the insertion of expansion boards which provide additional system features. A couple will normally be occupied by disk drive controllers and display controllers, such as the monochrome graphics adaptor (MGA) and colour graphics adaptor (CGA) mentioned in the section on screen displays. The remainder are available for the user to add extra features to the system.

Expansion boards have to be physically compatible with the expansion slots and compatible with the software to be used on the system.

Expansion Options

Expansion boards are available for a wide range of expansion options some of which are listed below:

☐ *serial/parallel adaptor*. This is a communication device that supports both serial and parallel outputs;

☐ *synchronous communications adaptor*. This can be used to link a microcomputer to a mainframe computer;

☐ *terminal emulation*. This type of board can make a microcomputer 'mimic' a mainframe or minicomputer terminal;

☐ *graphics adaptor*. A user can upgrade the graphics capability from say, CGA to EGA;

☐ *network adaptor*. This allows a microcomputer to communicate with others in a local area network;

☐ *RAM expansion*. Software improvements usually mean increased memory requirements, so a common use of expansion slots is to expand the RAM;

☐ *accelerator board*. This can be used to speed up the operation of a relatively slow microcomputer, such as the IBM XT which is based on an Intel 8088 processor (clock speed 4·77 MHz), to a speed comparable with a machine based on an Intel 80386 processor (clock speed 16 MHz).

11 *Software - an overview*

Software is the generic term which is used to describe the complete range of computer *'programs'* which will convert a general-purpose digital computer system into one capable of performing a multitude of specific functions. The term *software* implies its flexible, changeable nature, in contrast to the more permanent characteristics of the *hardware* or equipment which it controls.

The particular type, or types, of software controlling the computer system at any particular moment will determine the manner in which the system functions. For example, a certain type of software might cause the computer to behave like a wordprocessor; another might turn it into an accounting machine; another may allow it to perform a stock control function. In other words, the behaviour of the computer is entirely determined by the item of software currently controlling it.

Computer Programs

The terms *software* and *program* may be used synonymously, so what precisely is meant by the term *computer program*?

At the level at which the computer operates, a program is simply a sequence of numeric codes. Each of these codes can be directly converted by the hardware into some simple operation. Built into the central processing unit (CPU - the heart of the computer) is a set of these simple operations, combinations of which are capable of directing the computer to perform complex tasks. Computer programs, in this fundamental form, are termed *machine code*, that is code which is directly 'understandable' by the machine.

The numeric codes of the program are in binary form, or at least the electrical equivalent of binary, and are stored in the immediate access store (the 'memory') of the computer. Because this memory is *volatile* (in other words, it is temporary and can be changed), it is possible to exchange the program currently held in the memory for another when the computer is required to perform a different function. For this reason the term *stored program* is often used to describe this fundamental characteristic of the modern digital computer. This is explained in more detail in Chapter 3.

The collection of numeric codes which directs the computer to perform such simple operations as those mentioned above is called the *instruction set*. A typical computer would have some or all of the following types of instructions and, in addition, other more specialized instructions:

Data transfer. This allows data to be moved within the CPU, between the CPU and the memory of the computer system or between the CPU and external devices such as printers, VDUs and keyboards.

Arithmetic operations. Such instructions direct the computer to perform arithmetic functions such as addition, subtraction, multiplication, division, increment, decrement, comparison and logical operations such as AND, OR, NOT and EXCLUSIVE OR.

Shift operations. These move data to the left or right within a 'register' or memory location.

Transfer of control. This directs the machine to skip one or more instructions or repeat previously encountered instructions.

We explore these different types of fundamental operations in Chapter 3 and again, with reference to assembly language programming, in Chapter 27.

Programming Languages

As we saw in Chapter 3, a program, consisting of a combination of the instructions outlined above, is executed by retrieving each instruction in turn from the memory store of the computer, decoding the operation required and then performing this operation under the direction of the CPU. This sequence of events is termed the *fetch-execute cycle*.

On completion of each current instruction, the next instruction in the program's logical sequence of execution will be fetched from store automatically. This process ends, under normal circumstances, when a halt instruction in the program is recognised by the computer.

The following example illustrates the form of a machine code program:

Suppose that a computer has currently in its main store memory a simple machine code program to load two numbers into internal registers from memory, add them and store the result in memory. It could be shown as follows:

Memory Location	Contents (Hex)	Comments		
1000	220F	Load RO from..		
1001	2000	..memory	location	2000
1002	221F	Load R1 from..		
1003	2001	..memory	location	2001
1004	0901	Add R1 to RO		
1005	351F	Store RO in..		
1006	2002	..memory	location	2002
1007	1000	Halt execution		

Each instruction in turn, starting with that resident in memory location 1000, would be fetched from memory, decoded and executed. This process would continue until the halt instruction in location 1007 was decoded.

The particular binary code or combination of binary digits (0's or 1's) in the instruction (shown in hexadecimal notation in the example) causes the decoding circuitry of the CPU to transmit to other components of the hardware the sequence of control signals which is necessary to perform the required operation.

When it is considered that a typical program might contain tens of thousands of machine code instructions, it might seem that programming is a formidable task, well beyond the capabilities of all but the most determined and meticulous of computer professionals. Indeed, if machine code were the only computer language in use, it is extremely unlikely that society would today be experiencing such a widespread presence of computers in almost every aspect of industrial, commercial, domestic and social life.

Fortunately for the computer industry, programming techniques have evolved along with advances in hardware. There is now a proliferation of programming languages designed to allow the programmer to concentrate most of his attention on solving the problem rather than on the tedious task of converting the solution to machine code form.

In the history of programming languages, one of the first significant innovations was the development of *assembly languages*. A program written in an assembly language is much more readable and understandable than its equivalent in machine code; the problem arises, however, that it is no longer directly executable by the computer.

For example, a program, in some typical assembly language, equivalent to that given earlier in the chapter for the addition of two numbers, might take the following form:

Instruction	Comments
LDR R0, N1	;LoaD Register R0 with contents of location N1
LDR R1, N2	;LoaD Register R1 with contents of location N2
ADD R0, R1	;ADD R0 and R1 and store the sum in R0
STR R0, N3	;STore Register R0 in location |N3
H L T	;HaLT execution of program

Notice that the operation codes LDR, ADD, STR and HLT (representing LOAD, ADD, STORE and HALT respectively) are now easily recognizable and easy to remember; such *mnemonics*, or memory aids, are chosen for these reasons. The references, N1,N2 and N3, relate to memory locations and are called *symbolic addresses* and in many assembly languages it is possible to use meaningful names such as HRS or RATE to indicate the type of data stored there. The internal registers, R0, R1, may be two of several available within the computer for use by the programmer.

The CPU is unable to decode instructions in this form; they must first be converted into the equivalent machine code. An *assembler* is a machine code program which performs this function. It accepts an assembly language program as data, converts mnemonic operation codes to their numeric equivalents, assigns symbolic addresses to memory locations and produces as output the required machine code program. (This is represented in *Figure 11.1*).

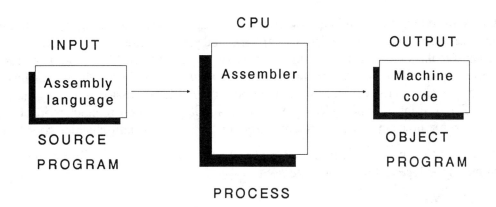

Figure 11.1

The assembly language program is termed the *source program* and the final machine code program is the *object program*. Assemblers and assembly language programming are described in Chapters 14 and 27.

Note that having an assembler means, of course, that it can be used to produce an improved version of itself! (This is illustrated in *Figure 11.2*)

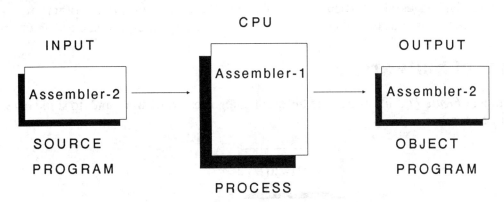

Figure 11.2

Thus there is no need to write any machine code programs at all and a considerable burden has been removed from the programming task; the computer itself now does much of the work required to produce the object program.

Though assembly languages aid the programmer considerably, they are still closely related to machine code; there is a 1:1 correspondence between a machine code instruction and one in assembly language. In other words each machine code instruction must have a matching assembly language instruction. This fundamental correspondence has led to the term *low-level* being applied to this type of programming language.

Computer scientists recognized, however, that most programs could be broken down into a collection of smaller identifiable tasks and that no matter what the program, such tasks were present in some recognizable form, though probably occurring in different logical sequences.

For instance, the majority of programs require the evaluation of arithmetic expressions such as $X + Y \times Z - P/Q$, in other words expressions involving combinations of the four arithmetic operators $+$, $-$, $\times$ and $/$ (addition, subtraction, multiplication and division respectively). Furthermore, most programs will produce some form of visible output, whether printed on paper or displayed on a screen, and most programs require data to be input for processing.

All of these tasks require lengthy, complicated sequences of instructions, but, significantly, they can all be stated in a generalized form, and can therefore be implemented using generalised machine code programs. *High-level* languages make extensive use of this characteristic. A high-level language is almost entirely constructed of these generalized sets of instructions or *statements*. A single statement, for instance, in a high-level language can specify the evaluation of a complex arithmetic expression requiring many machine code instructions. The translator required for such a source language is therefore much more complex than an assembler since each source language statement will generally generate many machine code instructions.

Taking the simple addition program introduced earlier to its conclusion, the program in a high-level language might merely reduce to the single statement

$$N3 = N1 + N2$$

meaning that the symbolic address *N3* is to store the sum of the contents of the memory locations represented by the symbolic addresses *N1* and *N2*. Notice that the programmer no longer needs to concern himself over the precise mechanics of the addition: the translator takes care of that automatically.

High-level languages are often termed *procedure orientated* or *programmer orientated* languages because they are designed for the benefit of the programmer interested in a certain type of application or procedure. For instance, some languages are particularly suitable for business applications, others for scientific programming and others for educational use. This class of languages is discussed in detail in Chapter 28.

Categories of Software

The tree diagram in *Figure 11.3* illustrates the different categories of software and, to some extent, their relationships to each other.

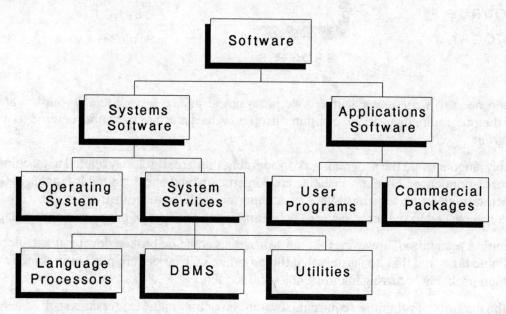

Figure 11.3

The term *systems software* covers the collection of programs usually supplied by the manufacturer of the computer. These programs protect the user from the enormous complexity of the computer system, and help him to use it to maximum effect. Without systems software a modern digital computer would be virtually impossible to use for the majority of people; as computer hardware has evolved, so systems software has been forced to become more and more complex in order to make effective use of it. The relationship between a user program and the systems software invisibly allowing its operation was once amusingly compared to an elephant riding on the back of a mouse, such is the size and complexity of systems software compared to the individual programs it supports.

Broadly speaking, systems software consists of two elements:

(i)   those programs concerned with the control and co-ordination of all aspects of the computer system, namely the *Operating System*, and

(ii) a number of other programs providing various services to users. These services include *compilers* and *interpreters* for any languages supported by the system, *database management systems* (DBMS) for the manipulation of large volumes of data, and *utility programs* such as program editors and other aids to programming.

Applications software refers to programs which have some direct value to the organization, and will normally include those programs for which the computer system was specifically purchased. For example, a mail order company might acquire a computer system initially for stock control and accounting purposes as its volume of business begins to make these functions too difficult to cope with by manual means. Applications programs would be required to record and process customers' orders, update the stock file according to goods sent or received, make appropriate entries in the various accounts ledgers, etc.

Commercial packages come in two main categories:

(i)   special-purpose packages, and

(ii) general-purpose packages.

A package consists of one or more programs on some form of file medium (such as magnetic disc). It will be accompanied by documentation explaining in detail how the programs function and how they are used. An example of a special-purpose package is a payroll program which is used to store employee details and generate details of pay for each individual employee.

A good example of a general-purpose package is a *wordprocessor*, a program which allows the computer to be used somewhat like an electronic typewriter and therefore useful in a wide variety of ways.

User programs are programs written by people within the organization for specific needs which cannot be satisfied by other sources of software. These program writers may be professional programmers employed by the organization, or other casual users with programming expertise.

These different types of software are briefly described in the following sections; a number of important topics are the subject of other chapters in the book.

Systems Software

First generation computers are normally defined in hardware terms, in that they were constructed using valve technology, but another important characteristic of this generation of computers was the equally rudimentary software support provided for programmers and other users. Modern computers perform automatically many of the tasks that programmers in those days had to handle themselves: writing routines to control peripheral devices, allocating programs to main store, executing programs, checking peripheral devices for availability, and many other routine tasks.

In subsequent generations of computers, manufacturers started addressing themselves to the problem of improving the programming environment by providing standard programs for many routine tasks. Many of these routines became linked together under the control of a single program called the *executive*, *supervisor*, or *monitor*, whose function was to supervise the running of user programs and, in general, to control and co-ordinate the functioning of the whole computer system, both hardware and software. Early programs of this type have evolved into the sophisticated programs collectively known as *Operating Systems*.

Systems software has three important functions:

(a)   to facilitate the running of user programs;

(b)   to optimize the performance of the computer system;

(c)   to provide assistance with program development.

The operating system takes care of the former two requirements, and language processors (such as compilers and interpreters), editors, diagnostic routines and other utility programs aid the third requirement.

Operating Systems

If a computer system is viewed as a set of resources, comprising elements of both hardware and software, then it is the job of the collection of programs known as the Operating System (OS) to manage these resources as efficiently as possible. In doing so, the operating system acts as a buffer between the user and the complexities of the computer itself. One way of regarding the OS is to think of it as a program which allows the user to deal with a simplified computer, but without losing any of the computational power of the machine. In this way the computer system becomes a virtual system, its enormous complexity hidden and controlled by the OS and through which the user communicates with the real system. In Chapter 12 we examine the function and operational characteristics of operating systems in more detail.

System Services

Often a manufacturer will provide a number of programs designed specifically for program or application development. Three such aids are:

(a)   Language Processors (Translators)

(b)   Database Management Systems

(c)   Utility Programs

Language Processors

Programs such as *assemblers*, *compilers* and *interpreters* fall into this category. It has already been noted that assemblers translate assembly language programs into machine code and that translators for high-level languages must perform a similar function. However, the precise mechanism by which this is accomplished for high-level languages varies considerably from language to language.

There are two main types of high-level language translators (or *language processors* as they are often known):

(a)   compilers, and

(b)   interpreters.

A compiler is essentially a sophisticated assembler, taking the source program and processing it to produce an independent object program in machine code. Note that the final object code is independent of both the source code and the compiler itself, that is neither of these two programs needs to be resident in main store when the object code is being executed. However, any alterations to the program necessitates modification and recompilation of the source code prior to executing the program again.

Examples of compiled languages are FORTRAN, COBOL and PASCAL.

The procedure used by interpreters is fundamentally different from that of compilers. With an interpreter the source code statements are translated and executed separately as they are encountered as the source code is being processed by the interpreter. The object code that is actually executed is held within the interpreter; the latter merely identifies from the source statement which piece of machine code is relevant and causes it to be executed. On completion of a statement, control returns to the interpreter which then processes the next logical statement in the program sequence.

Interpreted languages include BASIC and LISP.

Computer language translators are discussed in detail in Chapter 14.

Database Management Systems(DBMS)

The term *database* is used to describe a form of mass storage file organization where the user is not directly concerned with layout, structure, or location of files; he only defines the information that is to be stored, and the form in which any reports derived from the data are to be presented. For this method of processing to be possible, a great deal of generalised software must be provided and, since such software must be closely related to many of the routines within the operating system, manufacturers will often provide such a DBMS either with the rest of the computer system when purchased, or offer it as an additional piece of software to be purchased as and when required. Database systems are discussed in Chapter 15.

Utility Programs

As part of the systems software provided with a computer system there are a number of utility programs specifically designed to aid program development and testing. These include:

Editors - these permit the creation and modification of source programs and data files. The facilities offered by these programs usually will include such things as character, word and line insertion and deletion, automatic line numbering, line tabulation for languages which require program instructions to be spaced in a specific manner, the storage and retrieval of files from backing storage, and printing of programs or other files.

Diagnostic and Trace Routines - programs in which the appropriate translator can find no fault will often contain errors in logic, known as 'bugs', which only become apparent when the program is run and produces results which are contrary to expectations. These *run-time* errors are often very difficult to detect and may lead to long delays in the implementation of the program. Certain types of run-time errors will produce diagnostic messages to be produced by the operating system, but errors in the logic of a program must be isolated by the programmer himself.

A trace routine will allow the user to follow the path taken through the program so that it may be compared with the expected route; thus the point at which any deviation occurred can be detected. Breakpoints may be inserted at strategic points in the program such that when they are encountered program execution is halted temporarily to allow the current state of the program variables to be examined and displayed in order to check their validity. Other similar facilities can be called on from these packages to speed the debugging process. Program debugging is discussed further in Chapter 25.

File Managers - these simplify and facilitate a number of operations connected with program development and maintenance such as:

      ☐ keeping backup copies of important files;

      ☐ deleting files and creating space for new ones;

      ☐ merging files;

      ☐ listing details of current files held on backing storage;

      ☐ sorting file names into specified orders.

Without the help of such dedicated programs, operations such as these could be extremely time-consuming and consequently expensive.

Applications Software

An analysis of the uses to which companies and individuals put computers would reveal that the same types of tasks appear time and time again. Many firms use computers to facilitate payroll calculations, others to perform stock control functions, accounting procedures, management information tasks and numerous other common functions.

These types of programs are classed as *applications software*, software which is applied to practical tasks in order to make them more efficient or useful in other ways. Systems software is merely there to support the running, development and maintenance of applications software.

An organization wishing to implement one of these tasks (or any other vital to its efficient operation) on a computer has several alternatives:

      ☐ ask a software house to take on the task of writing a specific program for the organization's needs;

      ☐ use its own programming staff and produce the software 'inhouse';

      ☐ buy a commercially available program 'off the shelf' and hope that it already fulfils, or can be modified to fulfil, the organization's requirements;

      ☐ buy a general purpose program, such as a database or spreadsheet package, that has the potential to perform the required functions.

The final choice will depend on such factors as the urgency of the requirements, financial constraints, size of the company and the equipment available.

It is beyond the scope of this book to enter into a discussion regarding either the strategy for making such a decision or to investigate specific items of software available for specific applications; but, with the immense, and growing, popularity of general purpose packages, particularly for personal/business micro-computers, it is worth looking in more detail at this category of software.

General-purpose Applications Packages

Discussion of this class of software will be restricted here to the headings following, though they are not intended to represent an exhaustive list of all the categories of general purpose packages which are available:

- ☐ Wordprocessors
- ☐ Spreadsheets
- ☐ Databases
- ☐ Hypertext programs
- ☐ Graphics packages
- ☐ Expert System Shells
- ☐ Integrated packages

The main characteristic that these software types have in common is that they have been designed to be very flexible and applicable to a wide range of different applications. For instance, a spreadsheet can be used as easily for simple accountancy procedures as for stock control; a database can be used with equal facility to store information on technical papers from journals, stock item details and personnel details for payroll purposes.

The suitability of a particular general-purpose package for a specific application will be largely dependent on the characteristics of the package. For example, though the general facilities afforded by different database packages may be roughly equivalent each manufacturer will adopt its own style of presentation and will provide certain services not offered by its competitors. A prospective buyer should have a clear idea of the main uses for which the package is to be purchased right at the outset, because some packages may be much more suitable than others.

Advantages of general-purpose software compared to other forms of applications software are:

- ☐ Because large numbers of the package are sold, prices are relatively low.
- ☐ They are appropriate to a wide variety of applications.
- ☐ As they are already perfected, they allow a great reduction in the time and costs necessary for development and testing.
- ☐ They prove suitable for people with little or no computing experience.
- ☐ They are very easy to use.
- ☐ They have been thoroughly tried and tested.
- ☐ Most are provided with extensive documentation.

Some of the disadvantages are as follows:

- ☐ Sometimes the package will allow only a clumsy solution to the application.

☐ The user must still develop the application. This requires a thorough knowledge of the capabilities of the package, and how to make the best use of them.

☐ The user will need to provide his own documentation for the particular application for which the package has been tailored.

☐ Unless the software is used regularly, it is easy to forget the correct command sequences to operate the package, particularly for people inexperienced in the use of computer software of this type.

☐ The user must take responsibility for his own security measures to ensure that vital data is not lost, or to prevent unauthorized personnel gaining access to the data.

Wordprocessors

The wordprocessor performs much the same function as a typewriter, but it offers a large number of very useful additional features. Basically a wordprocessor is a computer with a keyboard for entering text, a monitor for display purposes, and a printer to provide the permanent output on paper. A wordprocessor is really nothing more than a computer system with a special piece of software to make it perform the required functions; some such systems have hardware configurations specifically for the purpose (such as special keyboards and letter-quality printers) but the majority are merely the result of obtaining an appropriate wordprocessor application package.

Wordprocessors are used for such purposes as producing

☐ letters

☐ legal documents

☐ books

☐ articles

☐ mailing lists

and in fact any type of textual material.

Some of the advantages they have over ordinary typewriters are:

☐ typing errors can corrected before printing the final version;

☐ whole document editing such as replacing every incidence of a certain combination of characters with another set of characters. For instance, replacing each occurrence of the name 'Mr. Smith' by 'Mrs. Jones';

☐ printing multiple copies, all to the same high quality;

☐ documents can be saved and printed out at some later date without any additional effort;

☐ page numbers, standard headers, appearing on the top of every page, and footers at the bottom of every page can be made to appear automatically on multi-page documents;

☐ the availability of a number of different character fonts and styles to enhance the appearance of documents;

☐ the facility to allow diagrams to be incorporated in a document.

However, wordprocessors do have some drawbacks. For instance, prolonged viewing of display monitors can produce eye strain, they are generally considerably more expensive than good typewriters, and to be used properly, a certain amount of special training is required.

Wordprocessors are now firmly established in the so-called 'electronic office' and there is no reason to suppose that their use will not continue to expand.

Spreadsheets

Just as wordprocessors are designed to manipulate text, spreadsheets are designed to do the equivalent with numerical information. A spreadsheet program presents the user with a blank grid of *cells* each of which is capable of containing one of three types of information:

☐ a label consisting of alphanumeric characters,

☐ a number,

☐ a formula, which may make reference to other cells.

These are sufficient to allow a wide range of applications to be implemented in a very convenient and easily understandable way. For example, suppose that a small business dealing in the sale of personal computer systems wishes to use such a program to record, on a monthly basis, the sales values attributable to each of its four salespersons. The spreadsheet might be set up as shown in *Figure 11.4*.

	A	B	C	D	E	F	G	H	I	J
1			| Salespersons							
2	Item		John		Jim		Joan		Janet	
3			Value(£)	Comn(£)	Value(£)	Comn(£)	Value(£)	Comn(£)	Value(£)	Comn(£)
4	Sanyo NB17 286-12				1049.00	104.90				
5	Olivetti 386-33c		2199.00	219.90						
6	Amstrad ALT 386sx						1299.00	129.90		
7	Tandon NB 386sx-20								1499.00	149.90
8	Logi 320i 386sx						1465.00	146.50		
9	Locland 386-20s		1245.00	124.50						
10	Elonex 320x								1100.00	110.00
11	Dell 320sx						1564.00	156.40		
12	Viglen Genie 3SX		1288.00	128.80						
13	Logi 320i 386sx								1465.00	146.50
14	Tandon Tower 486/33								5799.00	579.90
15	Amstrad ALT 386sx						1299.00	129.90		
16										
17										
18										
19										
20										
21										
22	Totals		4732.00	473.20	1049.00	104.90	5627.00	562.70	9863.00	986.30
23										
24	Total Sales		21271.00							
25	Total Commission		2127.10							
26										

Figure 11.4

Column A contains labels describing the systems purchased, columns C and D, E and F, G and H, and I and J show the sales and commissions for each of the four salespersons. The commission is automatically calculated using a formula established in the commission columns (D, F, H and J). *Figure 11.5* shows the formulas used for calculating John's commissions. Thus his sale of the Olivetti 386-33c costing £2199 is entered in cell C5 and the commission is calculated using the formula, = C5*10/100. This calculates 10% of the retail price. The actual value of the commission is displayed in cell D5.

The column totals, shown in cells C22 to J22 in *Figure 11.4* were calculated using a built-in function =SUM() which calculates the sum of a range of cells. For example, John's total commission, shown in cell D22 of *Figure 11.4*, was calculated using the formula =SUM (D4:D20), as shown in *Figure 11.5*. Note that empty cells, or cells containing labels, are treated as having a value of zero by formulas. Any changes made to the data supplied to the spreadsheet (changing the value of a computer sale for instance) automatically causes all formulas to be recalculated.

	A	B	C	D
1				
2	Item		John	
3			Value(£)	Comn(£)
4	Sanyo NB17 286-12			=C4*10/100
5	Olivetti 386-33c		2199	=C5*10/100
6	Amstrad ALT 386sx			=C6*10/100
7	Tandon NB 386sx-20			=C7*10/100
8	Logi 320i 386sx			=C8*10/100
9	Locland 386-20s		1245	=C9*10/100
10	Elonex 320x			=C10*10/100
11	Dell 320sx			=C11*10/100
12	Viglen Genie 3SX		1288	=C12*10/100
13	Logi 320i 386sx			=C13*10/100
14	Tandon Tower 486/33			=C14*10/100
15	Amstrad ALT 386sx			=C15*10/100
16				=C16*10/100
17				=C17*10/100
18				=C18*10/100
19				=C19*10/100
20				
21				
22	Totals		=SUM(C4:C20)	=SUM(D4:D20)
23				
24	Total Sales		=+C22+E22+G22+I22	
25	Total Commission		=+D22+F22+H22+J22	
26				

Figure 11.5

This automatic calculation facility gives rise to the expression *what if* which is often used to describe an important capability of spreadsheets. It is possible to set up complex combinations of inter-dependent factors and see *what* happens to the final result *if* one or more of the factors is changed. The spreadsheet, once set up, takes care of all the recalculations necessary for this type of exercise.

The earliest program of this form was called 'Visicalc' and it ran on an Apple Microcomputer. Many such programs now exist, having capabilities far exceeding those of Visicalc, but they still closely resemble the original concept in appearance and operation. The example shown in *Figures 11.4* and *11.5* were produced on a Microsoft Excel Spreadsheet program.

Spreadsheets have a number of attractive features compared to traditional programming solutions to processing needs:

☐ designed for laymen

☐ easy to learn and use

☐ wide range of uses

- [ ] relatively cheap

- [ ] easily modified

- [ ] well tried and tested

- [ ] provide quick development time

On the debit side, they tend to be:

- [ ] too general purpose and therefore provide satisfactory rather than ideal solutions, and

- [ ] the problem must still be analyzed and a solution method identified

Databases

At one time database programs, or Database Management Systems (DBMS) as they are often called, were restricted to mainframe computers because of the large memory requirements demanded of such applications. Currently, however, even personal business microcomputers have sufficient internal memory (2 megabytes of RAM is quite common) to make such applications not only feasible but also extremely powerful.

These programs allow files, comprising collections of records, to be created, modified, searched and printed. A good database program will offer, as a minimum, the following facilities:

- [ ] user-definable record format allowing the user to specify the fields within the record.

- [ ] user-definable input form to allow the user to define the way the data is to be entered into the computer.

- [ ] file searching capabilities for extracting records satisfying certain criteria from a file.

- [ ] file sorting capabilities so that records can be ordered according to the contents of a certain field.

- [ ] calculations on fields within records for inclusion in reports.

- [ ] user-definable report formats so that different types of reports containing different combinations of record fields may be produced.

Sometimes a database package will include a *natural language* interface to allow users to state their requirements in (almost) ordinary English. This is a very attractive feature to inexperienced users of computers. For instance, if the system has been set up for a personnel file of employees of a business, the enquirer might want to know how many of the employees are earning less than a certain salary. The question to the program could be phrased:

Print the names and departments of employees whose salaries are less than £6000

and the program would search the file and print the required details for all those records satisfying the stated criterion.

The main value of such a facility is the brevity with which quite complicated requirements may be stated; English is a very expressive and concise language compared to formal query languages or menu-driven strategies for information retrieval programs. However, natural language processing is still in its infancy, and programs offering this facility generally are able only to cope with a very limited form of English. The user, to get the most benefit from the free-form style of input, must be very much aware of the nature of these restrictions, otherwise a great deal of time will be wasted in phrasing questions in a form that the system is unable to 'understand'.

Database systems are considered in detail in Chapter 15.

Hypertext

Hypertext, also called 'linked text' and 'extended text', systems are concerned with classifying and categorizing text. Such systems allow blocks of text to be linked together in various ways for the purpose of reflecting some coherent structure and meaning. Blocks of text may be established as a connected set of nodes or subsections (called 'points' in hypertext parlance) of text nodes can be linked to other subsections or to other nodes.

A hypertext system does not rearrange the text in its database; it merely allows a user to define a method of organizing it. For example, an author engaged in researching for a book may read many papers and reference books and in the course of doing so may make notes in a notebook to summarize their contents. A hypertext notebook would, for example, allow the author to link his own annotations to references, and link references to other references. Obviously this would greatly simplify the task of collecting together material relevant to writing about a particular topic.

Hypertext systems usually allow the user to browse through a hypertext document, adding, deleting or modifying links between nodes and points. Current hypertext systems frequently allow the inclusion graphical or even sound nodes in addition to text, and the document itself may be represented graphically as a hierarchical network of icons navigated by a mouse.

HyperCard, produced by Apple computers, IBM's GUIDE and Genesis for Acorn computers are examples of hypertext systems.

Graphics Programs

These generally fall into four general categories according to main area of use:

- ☐ Business graphics
- ☐ Graphic design
- ☐ Computer-aided design(CAD)
- ☐ Desktop publishing

Business graphics packages allow the production of such things as Bar Charts, Line Graphs and Pie Diagrams, diagrams of a statistical nature likely to be included in business reports. Examples of these are shown in *Figure 11.6*.

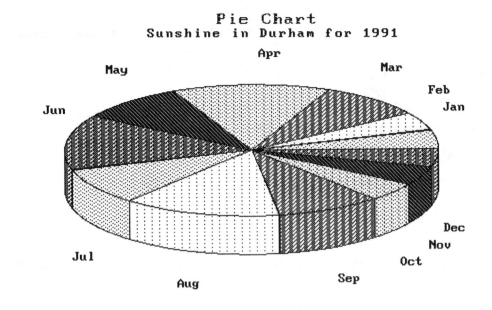

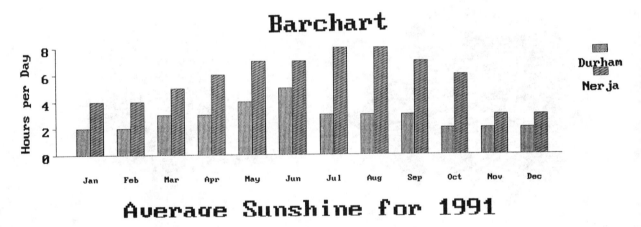

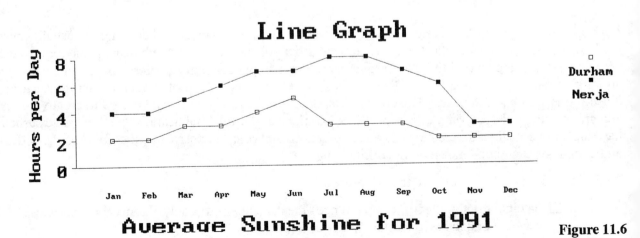

Figure 11.6

Packages for graphic design consist of a collection of special functions aimed at aiding the graphic designer. The artist uses the screen as his canvas and a light-pen (or equivalent device such as a mouse) as his brush.

They generally allow work of professional quality to be produced in a relatively short amount of time, and include such facilities as

☐ large colour palette

☐ geometric figure drawing, e.g. lines, rectangles, circles

☐ filling areas with colour or patterns

☐ undoing mistakes

☐ moving/copying/deleting/saving areas of the screen display

☐ printing the finished design

☐ choice of a variety of text styles and fonts

Figure 11.7 shows the sort of illustration that such packages are capable of producing (but also in colour):

Figure 11.7

Desktop publishing (DTP) programs are designed to facilitate the production of documents (usually called *publications*) such as posters, illustrated articles and other documents which combine large amounts of text with illustrations, the type of thing we frequently see in newspapers. Some professional quality packages are also capable of handling books. The emphasis in DTP is the layout of text and diagrams; text and illustrations are imported rather than created. In general, a wordprocessor will be used to create the text and graphic art packages will be used for the illustrations in the final publication. DTP packages usually have fairly basic facilities for creating text and illustrations, but comprehensive facilities for organizing them and enhancing their appearance on the printed page.

Typically, a DTP package will have these features:

☐ facilities for improving the appearance of text, including a variety of fonts and text styles, such as bold, italics, underlined, shadowed;

☐ allow text and graphics in a number of different formats to be loaded and placed in the publication;

☐ allow graphics to be scaled and cropped (cropping involves selecting a rectangular area of a graphic and hiding unwanted areas);

☐ copy, move and delete text and graphics;

☐ create additional pages of the publication;

☐ establish the structure of master pages so that new pages have a standard appearance. This is like an extension of headers and footers in wordprocessing by allowing graphics and text automatically to be placed anywhere on every page rather than just at the top and bottom;

☐ rudimentary graphics facilities such as line, box and circle drawing, with the option of filling boxes and circles with patterns or colours, or shades of grey.

Figure 11.8 is an example of a poster produced using a DTP package for an IBM PC:

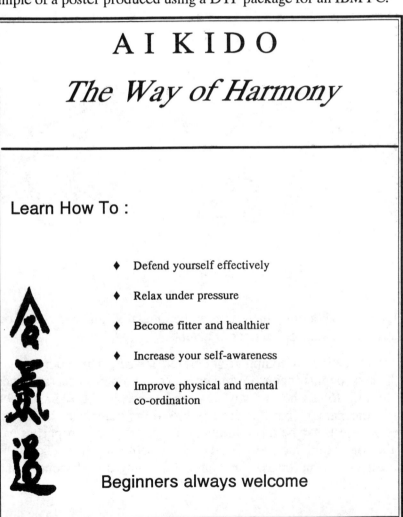

Figure 11.8

Computer-aided design constitutes the most widely used commercial application of computer graphics. Here the user simulates real-world geometrical objects using various software tools. Often, selection of the tools is by means of a WIMP style user interface. Sometimes a graphics tablet is used in conjunction with a pressure operated stylus, or a light pen might be used to draw electronically on the VDU screen. Whatever the physical method of using the system, the type of tools and facilities available are fairly standard: the user can draw two-dimensional geometrical objects, such as lines, arcs, circles, ellipses, squares, rectangles etc., and subsequently edit them by copying, moving or resizing operations.

As a minimum, the facilities provided allow the user to draw and subsequently edit any type of engineering drawing that could be produced in the traditional drawing office; but many CAD packages go a great deal further. For example, it is frequently possible to create three-dimensional representations of objects and view them from various angles, as if the user was able to walk around the object. Furthermore, these objects may be shown in wire-frame form, or even rendered to appear solid and textured. Some examples of such drawings are shown in *Figure 11.9* (courtesy of Silicon Vision Ltd).

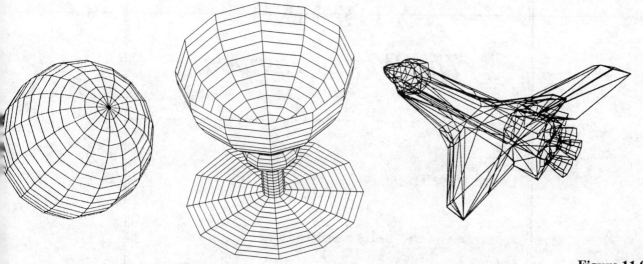

Figure 11.9

Materials such as glass or wood or other materials can be simulated, and even light sources and reflections can be shown in drawings containing a number of objects.

In the search for visual realism in computer-generated images, a number of techniques have been developed, one of the most popular being *ray tracing*. Once the multi-object scene has been created using three-dimensional drawing tools, the visibility of each surface in the scene is determined by tracing imaginary rays of light emanating from the viewer's eye to the objects in the scene. The reflective and refractive properties of objects can be taken into account by assigning properties to each of their visible surfaces. Similarly, the colour and intensity of one or more light sources can be simulated. The quality of such images can be extremely impressive. An example of a ray traced scene is shown in *Figure 11.10* (courtesy of Silicon Vision Ltd).

Figure 11.10

Applications of CAD programs include:

- [ ] engineering drawing
- [ ] architectural design
- [ ] interior design
- [ ] printed-circuit board design
- [ ] the design of integrated circuits
- [ ] advertising material
- [ ] computer animation for t.v. advertising
- [ ] special effects in films

Expert System Shells

Pure research in the field of artificial intelligence has had a number of practical spin-offs. One such spin-off has been the development of programs known as 'Expert Systems'. These are programs designed to be able to give the same sort of help or advice, or make decisions, as a human expert in some narrow field of expertise. For instance, a program called PROSPECTOR is capable of predicting the existence of mineral ores given various pieces of information gathered from physical locations. In the same way that, given certain evidence, an expert might say that a particular site looked favourable for containing ore, PROS-PECTOR indicates the probability of the existence of the ore. PROSPECTOR is in fact attributed with the discovery of an extremely valuable quantity of molybdenum which had previously been overlooked by human experts.

Expert systems have been developed in all kinds of areas which have traditionally been the responsibility of human experts, including medical diagnosis; decisions in areas such as this are so important, however, that it would be foolish to blindly accept the pronouncement of a computer. For this reason, expert systems have built-in the ability to 'explain' the reasoning behind any conclusion so that this chain of reasoning can be checked and verified (or rejected) by a human.

A typical expert system has three main components:

- [ ] a *knowledge base* consisting of facts, and rules by which facts can lead to conclusions.

☐ an *inference engine* which processes the knowledge base, and

☐ a *user interface* to facilitate communication with the user.

The term *Shell* is given to expert systems which have been given no specific knowledge base, only the inference engine and user interface; the knowledge base has to be provided by the user. An expert system shell can thus be used to provide advice or help in a number of areas of expertise, providing it is given the appropriate knowledge base for each area.

For example, an expert system shell could be used to give advice on the procedures and sequence of steps necessary for selling a house (what solicitors call 'conveyancing'), or to give advice about possible causes and cures of diseases in houseplants, or diagnosing faults in cars. Not only could these applications be of practical use, but they could also be instructive because the user could ask for and obtain the reasons behind any conclusions.

One of the problems of using such shells is the determination of the rules which represent the wisdom of a human expert; many experts are not consciously aware of the precise reasoning processes they themselves use in order to come to some conclusion, yet in order to produce an expert program, these processes must be defined in a form that is usable. The process of determining the knowledge base rules is known as *knowledge elicitation* or *knowledge acquisition* and is performed by *knowledge engineers*.

Expert systems are discussed further in Chapter 28.

Integrated Packages

Once it became evident that packages such as those described above were going to become more and more in demand, software houses started producing packages which offered integrated combinations of word-processors, databases, spreadsheets, graphics and even expert system shells. In fact one integrated package called Lotus 123, offering spreadsheet, database and business-type graphics, became the most successful ever general purpose applications package for microcomputers. Its huge success can be attributed to several important factors typifying the many variations of the program which have since appeared on the market:

☐ The extremely 'user-friendly' presentation - facilities are selected by choosing options from menus, which call up further menus until the actual operation required is displayed and performed, and there are on-line help facilities which the user can have displayed at any time.

☐ The same data can be used for each of the three main applications: for calculations, information retrieval or to provide data for the production of diagrams such as bar charts or pie diagrams.

☐ The large number of special functions by which almost every need can be met.

☐ The same command sequence and menu structures are used for each of the three functions, making the package very easy to learn.

☐ Relatively cheap considering the number of functions supplied in the one package.

Software Trends

The trend for the development of commercial software has always been towards ease of use. As computers continue to become more and more powerful in terms of memory capacity and speed of operation, software has the potential of becoming more 'user friendly'. This potential is currently being realised in a number of ways:

☐ By simplifying the interface between the user and the program, using for instance, a WIMP environment (Windows, Icons, Mice, Pointers)

☐ By providing much more assistance in the development of new applications, reducing development time and simplifying the whole process (Fourth Generation Languages - 4GL's)

☐ By incorporating some of the techniques developed by researchers in the field of Artificial Intelligence.

These ideas are explored in the following three sections.

WIMPs

The term 'WIMP' refers to a computer software environment designed to be particularly easy to use. Characteristic of this type of system is the use of a combination of Windows, Icons, Mice, Pointers and Pull-down menus. The idea was pioneered by Apple Computers when they put their Macintosh computer on the market in the early eighties. Though fairly slow to emulate this innovative approach, an increasing number of computer manufacturers are providing similar systems as standard features. Most systems use a mouse to control the operation of the software. A mouse is a small, hand-held device connected to the computer by a flexible lead and incorporating one or more buttons. The mouse is moved over the surface of the desk on which the computer is situated and, by means of an electronically monitored roller, it is linked to a screen pointer which mirrors its movement on the monitor.

A typical WIMP environment is shown in *Figure 11.11*.

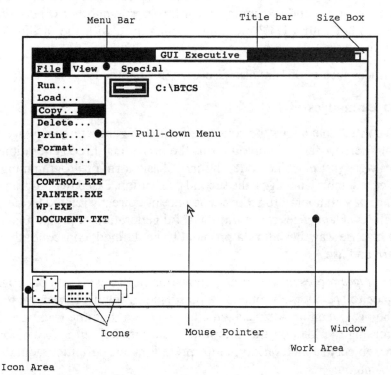

Figure 11.11

The system window shown has a number of common features:

☐ a mouse-controlled pointer. As the mouse is moved forward and backward and side to side, the pointer follows the movement on the screen; this allows the user to 'point' at special areas of the screen and click a button on the mouse to indicate selection of an item;

☐ a title bar which declares the current application;

☐ a size box allowing the window to be contracted or expanded;

☐ a menu bar of menu titles indicating the presence of pull-down menus which are selected using the mouse pointer;

☐ an icon area showing the existence of any utilities which can be 'clicked';

☐ a list of items, in this case file names, which can be selected by pointing and clicking. These item may be data files, program files or command files depending on the nature of the current application.

Just as an operating system is a simplified interface to the complexities of the computer system, so the WIMP environment, when used in the manner described above, is a convenient interface to the operating system. As such it can be used to perform file management functions such as creating, copying, renaming and deleting files, formatting and verifying disks or running applications. Moreover, the application programs themselves will run under the same style of environment, thus bringing a uniformity to the presentation and operation of applications.

An example of a commonly used WIMP environment is Microsoft Windows for IBM personal computers. The latest version of this program allows a number of applications to be running at the same time. So, for example, a user could have one window running a wordprocessor, another window containing a graphics design program and another with a DTP program running in it, with the facility for transferring work between the three applications.

Graphical User Interfaces such as this are also discussed in Chapter 19.

Fourth Generation Languages(4GLs)

In order to provide a context that allows the concept of a fourth generation language to be appreciated, it is perhaps appropriate here to define in broad terms the preceding three generations of languages. First generation languages were just machine code, the most basic form of programming language. Evolving from this original form, assembly languages, the second generation, eased the programming task by making the computer take care of a number of functions that were not directly related to the processing problems being addressed. High-level languages represent the third generation of programming languages and are characterised by the concise way they allow a problem to be defined; consequently, these languages are relatively easy to learn and use.

Fourth generation languages represent the latest innovation in the evolution of programming languages, allowing a programmer to specify the problem to be solved in relatively general terms and leaving the computer to fill in the programming details. Such languages continue the tradition of reducing the work of the user and increasing the load on the computer. The terms *Fourth Generation Language*, and its contraction, *4GL*, are subject to a wide variety of interpretations and definitions, but they all have a number of characteristics in common:

☐ easier to use than existing high-level languages, particularly by non-specialists;

☐ more concise than existing high-level languages;

☐ the language is closer to natural language;

☐ user-friendly;

☐ non-procedural.

With the possible exception of the last one, these points are self-explanatory. The terms *non-procedural* and *declarative* refer to languages which allow the user to define a goal and leave the computer to determine (within bounds) how to achieve it. To illustrate the difference, compare the following two sets of instructions for making a cup of tea:

(1) Boil the kettle
     Put tea in the teapot
     When the kettle has boiled, pour boiling water into the teapot
     Wait for the tea to infuse
     Put small amount of milk in a teacup
     Pour tea into the cup

(2) Make a cup of tea

The first list defines the procedure, step by step, for making a cup of tea. The instructions imply that the procedure is not familiar to the tea maker; this is not the case in (2) where the implication is that the tea maker already has the required knowledge and merely needs to be told to get started on the task. The person issuing the command in (2) is not interested in the precise way that the task is accomplished as long as the tea that arrives tastes good and does not take an unreasonable length of time. (1) represents procedural programming and (2) the declarative approach. Declarative high-level languages are also discussed in Chapter 28.

Two examples of current software systems which fit this loose definition of a 4GL are *Structured Query Languages (SQL's)* and *Program Generators*.

Structured Query Languages (SQLs)

Developed by IBM, SQL's operate on relational databases and are becoming the recognised standard for this type of application. Briefly, a relational database is one in which the database is considered to be a table(relation) of rows, which are equivalent to records, and columns, which are related to fields within records. New relations can be created in response to user queries. An SQL simplifies the task of specifying queries by allowing the user to use a series of key-words. The resulting query, while not being in natural language, is easily understandable to the non specialist and certainly more user friendly than many other query languages. SQLs are dealt with in more detail in Chapter 15.

Program Generators

One such system accepts a type of pseudocode as the source/specification language and uses it to generate the appropriate COBOL program. Pseudocode allows expression of processing requirements in very high-level, well structured terms which are not specific to a particular programming language. This is comparable to the way a compiler operates, accepting a high-level language as source code to generate a machine code program. In this case the output from the 4GL is the source code for a high-level language (ie COBOL). The specification language may be related to a system design technique such as Jackson Structured Design.

Fifth Generation Computers

At about the beginning of the 1980's, the Japanese announced their intention to produce the next or *Fifth Generation* computers- machines exhibiting *artificial intelligence* and operating enormously faster than current computers. These were to be based on new principles of operation, closer to the way that human beings are thought to perform processing tasks. Not only would new and faster hardware need to be designed to achieve these aims, but the software to drive it would need to be correspondingly much more sophisticated.

The Japanese identified a large number of goals to be achieved within a decade, one of which, the widespread use and support of knowledge-based systems, is of particular relevance in the present context.

Knowledge-based systems (see also Chapter 28) can be applied to a variety of applications including knowledge-based management, problem solving, inference and human interaction. An expert system is an example of a knowledge-based system for making logical inferences. 'Intelligent Assistants' for management and 'Intelligent Tutors' are further examples of such systems.

An expert system uses a knowledge-base of rules, that can be applied to data, as one component of its structure; such sets of rules serve to guide intelligently the directions that computations should take. This is particularly important when data is to be extracted from very large databases quickly. However, another important component of an expert system, and many other software applications, is the human/computer interface. The language used for this interaction between user and computer should be comfortable for the user and thus a great deal of research is being done on natural language interfaces. This research encompasses voice recognition and synthesis as well as written communication.

Whether the Japanese achieve their targets or not, in the near future we will see in the market place the fruits of the enormous research commitment undertaken by them and their competitors; the HAL computer in Arthur C. Clarke's '2001' may well be a reality by that very date, but by then it will probably be small enough to stand in a small corner of your desk!

12 *Operating Systems*

If a computer system is viewed as a set of resources, comprising elements of both hardware and software, then it is the job of the collection of programs known as the *operating system* to manage these resources as efficiently as possible. In so doing, the operating system acts as a buffer between the user and the complexities of the computer itself. One way of regarding the operating system is to think of it as software which allows the user to deal with a simplified computer, but without losing any of the computational power of the machine. In this way, the computer system becomes a *virtual* system, its enormous complexity hidden and controlled by the operating system and through which the user communicates with the real system.

The central core of an operating system, which remains in memory permanently when the computer is running, is the *executive* (also known as the *supervisor* or *kernel*); as the terms suggest, it has a controlling function, its major function being to carry out system requests from applications programs in such a way that conflicts between them are avoided. The remainder of the operating system is normally held on a direct access medium, from where parts of it can be called as and when required.

Main Functions of Operating Systems

The introduction states that the function of an operating system is to manage the *resources* of the computer system. These resources generally fall into several categories.

Central Processing Unit (CPU) or Processor

Since only one program can be executed at any one time, computer systems which allow several users simultaneous access (*multi-user*) must carefully control and monitor use of the CPU. In a *timesharing* multi-user system each user receives a small *time-slice* from the processor before it passes on to the next user in a continually repeating sequence. Another common scheme is to assign priorities to users so that the system is able to determine which user should next have control of the CPU.

Memory

Programs (or parts of programs) must be loaded into the memory before they can be executed, and moved out of the memory when no longer required there. Storage space must be provided for data generated by programs, and provision must be made for the temporary storage of data, caused by data transfer operations involving devices such as printers and disk drives.

Input/Output (I/O) Devices

Programs will request the use of these devices during the course of their execution and in a multi-user system, conflicts are bound to arise when a device being utilised by one program is requested by another.

The operating system controls the allocation of I/O devices and attempts to resolve any conflicts which arise. It also monitors the state of each I/O device and signals any faults detected.

Backing Storage

Programs and data files are usually held on mass storage devices such as magnetic disk and tape drives. The operating system supervises data transfers between these devices and memory and deals with requests from programs for space on them.

Files

These may be regarded as a limited resource in the sense that several users may wish to share the same data file at the same time. The operating system facilitates access to files and ensures that only one updating program can retrieve any particular record at any one time; the topic of file *locking* is dealt with in Chapter 15.

The above is by no means an exhaustive list of the functions of an operating system. Other functions include:

☐ interpretation of the command language by which operators can communicate with it;

☐ error handling, for example, detecting and reporting inoperative or malfunctioning peripherals;

☐ protection of data files and programs from corruption by other users;

☐ protection of data files and programs from unauthorized use;

☐ accounting and logging of the use of the computer resources.

Single-stream Systems

As the term suggests, single-stream operating systems are designed to handle only one job at a time. Today, the only operating systems which fall into this category are those designed for microcomputer systems, for example MS/DOS, but in the late 1950s the then 'state of the art' mainframe systems could only handle one job at a time. These early systems automated the running of their jobs under customized *control programs* (initially punched onto cards), which were the forerunners of operating systems.

Batch Processing Systems

The concept of batch processing is explained in detail in Chapter 23. A major advance on these early systems is made through the use of an executive which *queues* a number of separate jobs, *schedules* them according to allocated *priorities* and executes them, one after another. Some jobs will be required more urgently than others and will be allocated priority accordingly; jobs are loaded and executed according to their priority rating, not their position in the queue, so additional jobs can be added to the queue at any time.

Such systems are very inefficient for various reasons. Each job must be completed before commencement of the next; the fact that most jobs comprise a great deal of I/O and very little processing means that the processor is idling for much of the time. This feature is exacerbated by the imbalance between the operating speed of the processor and the data transfer rate of disk and tape drives; the imbalance is even greater where printed output is required. Thus, when the overall system's speed is dictated by the speed of the I/O peripheral, rather than the CPU, the system is described as being *I/O bound*. The technique of *off-lining* (Chapter 7) was introduced in the late 1950s to help deal with the problem of very slow peripherals, such as card readers and printers.

Batch Multi-programming Systems

Optimization of resource usage

Multi-programming describes the running of several jobs in main memory, apparently simultaneously, although in reality, the CPU's attention is being repeatedly switched from one to another under the control of the executive. This makes much better use of the CPU's time than the single stream batch processing described previously.

Thus, the objective of a batch multi-programming operating system is to *optimize the use of processor time and the rate of system throughput.*

Dynamic resource allocation

With single-stream processing, computer resources (CPU time, main memory space, file storage and peripherals) can be allocated to each job and remain fixed for the duration of each job. In contrast, the concurrent processing of several jobs inherent in a multi-programming environment, with the likelihood that the mix of jobs will change as some are completed and new ones are initiated, requires an executive capable of allocating resources *dynamically* to each job.

Job priority

Jobs will vary according to:

- ☐ the amount of I/O involved;
- ☐ the types and speeds of I/O devices used;
- ☐ the amount of processor time needed.

After consideration of these factors, each job is given a *priority rating*, which will determine how frequently and for how long it receives processor time. The allocation of priorities can be a complex process but simplistically:

- ☐ high priority will be given to a job requiring a large amount of I/O and a relatively small amount of CPU time. When I/O operations are being carried out, CPU attention is not required after the initial I/O command is given. Conversely, when it does require attention, a high priority will ensure that its small processing requirements are attended to promptly and fully, following which it can return to I/O;

- ☐ a low priority job will tend to be one which requires a large amount of processor time; a high priority would result in it 'hogging' the processor and preventing largely I/O jobs from receiving what little attention they require.

Scheduling

High-level scheduler. It is a function of this part of the operating system to determine which programs in the *job queue* should next be loaded into main memory. Before loading a job, the following criteria must be satisfied:

☐ there is sufficient room for it in main memory;

☐ all associated input files are on-line;

☐ the necessary peripherals are also on-line;

If priorities are allocated, then subject to fulfilment of the above criteria, these will be used by the high level scheduler to decide the order in which jobs are removed from the job queue.

Dispatcher or low-level scheduler. The dispatcher allocates the processor amongst the various *processes* in the system. To understand the operation of the dispatcher, it is useful to differentiate between the concept of a *program* and a *process*. A process is a sequence of actions produced through the execution of program instructions. Processes carried out within the system include, for example, interrupt handling, error handling, I/O control and so on; each process may involve one or more programs.

To do this the dispatcher must record the current *status* of each process selecting from the following possibilities:

☐ it is runnable, that is, free to run;

☐ it is running; in other words, it has the attention of the processor;

☐ it is unrunnable or suspended, perhaps because it is awaiting completion of an I/O operation.

A *process descriptor table* records the status of each process in the *processor queue*. The dispatcher must refer to it before deciding on re-allocation of the processor to a process in the queue; such a decision needs to be made each time there is an *interrupt* (see Chapter 7 and later in this chapter). The dispatcher will choose the process with the highest priority, from those which are runnable, unless the process which was running at the time of the interrupt still outranks them.

The dispatcher is invoked under the following circumstances:

☐ whenever the current process cannot continue; this may result, for example, from a programming error or a switch to I/O;

or

☐ when an external interrupt changes the status of a process, for example, following completion of data transfer; it thus becomes runnable.

Batch processing systems collect all input data in a file, from where it is loaded and processed to completion by the relevant application program, storing any output data in another on-line file; the executive then directs the printing program to print any hard copy results from the output file. Prominent features of such systems are:

☐ lack of any communication or interaction with the user;

☐ the delay in producing results of processing.

The following categories of operating system allow results of processing to be obtained, frequently on a VDU screen, directly after their entry. They are categorized according to the techniques used to manage the computer resources; the ways in which the systems are used are described in the Chapter on Processing Methods.

- ☐ time-sharing;
- ☐ multi-tasking;
- ☐ multi-user;
- ☐ real-time.

Time-sharing

The term time-sharing refers to the allocation of CPU *time slices* to a number of user programs in a multi-programming environment. The aim of a time-sharing operating system is to *keep the users busy*; this contrasts with the batch multi-programming system which aims to keep the *processor occupied*. The time slices are controlled and synchronized by a real-time clock which generates frequent, regularly timed pulses; each time-slice is extremely short, say 100 milliseconds.

Round robin system

With this method, the operating system works sequentially through the list of programs being run, giving each process an equal slice of processor time.

If all current programs can be accommodated in main memory at one time, users should not experience poor response times. Unfortunately, the total main memory requirements of all current users may well exceed the capacity of main memory, making it necessary to swap programs or program *segments* in and out from backing storage as the processor switches its attention from one to another. The number of such data transfers can be reduced by extending the length of each time slice, but at the cost of reducing the frequency with which the processor transfers its attention from one process to another. Optimizing system performance requires a balance to be struck between these two objectives.

Unless the processor is overloaded, perhaps because there are too many users or because the applications require a large amount of processor time (for example, program compilation), each user should feel that he or she is the sole user of the system.

Priority system

Instead of giving single time-slices on a round robin basis, they are allocated according to a system of priorities. This means that some programs will receive a number of time slices in succession before another is attended to. The priority rating of each program will not normally remain static but will be adjusted in relation to the relative amount of processing time it receives in comparison with the other programs in operation.

Time-sharing systems are used *interactively* in that users communicate directly with the computer via VDU terminals. A common use of a time-sharing operating system is to provide *multi-access* to one or more programming languages for the purposes of program development; interpretive languages such as multi-user BASIC are ideally suited to time-sharing. Other systems may provide users with access to various applications programs which can be run apparently simultaneously.

Multi-tasking

Multi-tasking is a technique which allows a computer to carry out tasks in a similar fashion to a human worker. For example, the Financial Director of a business may be composing a financial report which requires the use of a dictaphone, occasional reference to various financial summaries and telephone calls to other executive staff in the business. Although these tasks are not carried on at exactly the same time, the director is rapidly switching from one to another, as they all contribute to the completion of the financial report. At certain times, an unrelated task may have to be completed, for example, the answering of a brief query from a member of staff. This does not require complete abandonment of the other tasks in hand and the main work continues from the point at which it was left.

Computer multi-tasking requires that the system can accommodate *several tasks* in memory at one time and that these tasks can be run *concurrently* by rapidly switching the processor's attention between them. The principles of resource management are similar to those employed in multi-programming, except that they relate to a *single user*, are controlled interactively and must be executed in ways which maintain response times acceptable to the user.

IBM's OS/2 operating system provides full multi-tasking facilities and two important features which can be modified through its configuration commands MEMMAN and MAXWAIT are outlined below.

Memory Management

MEMMAN = MOVE (MOVE, NOMOVE). This relates to the operating system's facility for relocating programs to maximize use of memory. For example, when one application is replaced by another, the memory needed is likely to be different, so after a series of swaps, the available memory space becomes *fragmented*. The MOVE option allows OS/2 to *relocate* sections of program code or data to optimize memory usage. Without this facility, there may be insufficient contiguous memory for an incoming application. The swapping process takes time, so the NOMOVE option, which prevents relocation, can be selected if response time for certain applications is crucial;

Foreground/background Processing

MAXWAIT = 3 (1-255). During multi-tasking, some tasks can be selected to run in the *foreground* and are given more processor time than other tasks, running in the *background*. The operating system allocates short periods of processor time to each task. There may be occasions when a 'processor hungry' application, which is running in the foreground, takes more than its fair share of processor time and leaves other tasks with too little. The MAXWAIT option, which has a default value of 3 seconds, sets the maximum time that a task can be kept waiting before it receives some attention from the processor.

Multi-user

A multi-user system is invariably *multi-access* (although it is possible to provide multi-user facilities within a single stand-alone microcomputer, but only one user at a time) in that it provides a number of users with concurrent access to centralized computing resources, which may be part of a computer network or may comprise a centralized computer with multiplexed terminals. Additionally however, the multi-user operating system must protect each user's (or user group's) files from access and/or corruption by other users, either within memory or on backing storage. This is achieved through *dynamic memory partitioning* and directory-based *file management* respectively. The XENIX multi-user operating system illustrates the features of file management and user control.

The XENIX Operating System

File Management Facilities

Files are organized into a hierarchy of directories and files in a similar fashion to the multi-level structure used by MS/DOS (Chapter 22).

The XENIX directory structure is shown in *Figure 12.1*.

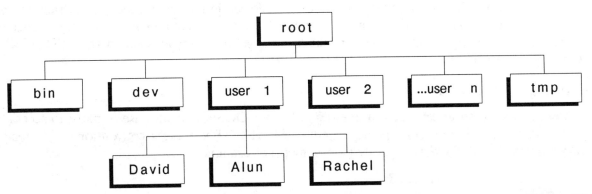

Figure 12.1

The *root directory* contains software which has overall control of the XENIX system and as such, is only accessible by a user with the *super-user* password. The topic of user access is dealt with later. The second level in the hierarchy (bin, dev etc) is for files concerned with system operations. Their functions are as follow:

bin. This contains the library of XENIX utilities, for example, sorting, copying and other file maintenance programs;

dev. This is for the storage of system routines relating to the use of various makes of hardware such as printers, which may be attached to the system. Installation involves the selection of routines appropriate to the hardware configuration in use;

usr, usr1 ... usr n. A home directory of files is set up for each user registered with the XENIX system;

tmp. Used for the temporary storage of programs.

Each of the user (usr) directories may contain sub-directories, for example, (usr1) may be identified as SALES, within which there are three sub-directories for David, Alun and Rachel respectively (these sub-directories may be further sub-divided). Although a sub-directory exists for each of these individuals, they are all members of the (usr1) group and each have access to each other's files. If it is necessary to keep, for example, Rachel's files secure from access by either David or Alun, she would have to be registered at the second level as a separate XENIX user (usr). The third level in the hierarchy is for the storage of user files.

File Ownership

Files are assigned to user-owners and each user has a separate directory which contains the names of files owned by the user. The allocation of ownership means that files are automatically protected against overwriting or access by other users. This protection can be varied to allow access to another user or group of users. Only the current owner or the super-user can transfer ownership of a file. The XENIX command for carrying out such a change is *chown*, or *chgrp* for group ownership changes.

Filenames

A filename can be 14 characters long but there is no space left for file extensions. Unlike MS/DOS, XENIX differentiates between lower and upper case, so that, for example, the filenames 'test1' and TEST1 are treated as separate files. No duplicate filenames are allowed in the same directory but they can exist in separate directories. The XENIX equivalent of the MS/DOS command *dir*, to view the filenames in a directory is *cat* (catalogue). Other file commands, amongst the many available with XENIX, include *cp* (copy) and *rm* (remove).

Accessing Files via Paths

Reference to a file requires specification of a *path*. MS/DOS also makes use of paths to access files in different directories, but the concept originated from UNIX. XENIX uses a conventional '/', instead of the backslash used by MS/DOS, to separate path-names. For example,

> *usr/sales/alun/doc3*

identifies the file 'doc3' as being located in sub-directory 'alun' which belongs to the 'sales' directory. As long as the path is unique, different users can use the same filenames. Thus,

> *usr/stock/rachel/doc3*

is valid. There is no need for any user to worry about using the same filenames as another user, because the files are made unique by the path.

User Identification

The Super-User

Each user has a password to log into the XENIX-controlled system, but overall control has to be assigned with a super-user password. Creation of the super-user password requires the following command:

> *passwd root*

This super-user password allows access to the root directory which controls all XENIX operations and is allocated during initial installation of XENIX onto the hard disk. For security reasons, the characters are not echoed on screen as the password is entered. The super-user password can be changed, but should never be lost or forgotten because the existing password is required before a change can be made. If the password is lost, then the whole XENIX system has to be re-installed.

General Users

XENIX operates in two modes, operational and system maintenance. The creation of user accounts has to be carried out with the super-user password in system maintenance mode, during which time normal operation is closed to other users. To create a user account, the super-user enters the command:

mkuser

The super-user is then prompted to enter the name chosen to identify the user. To log in to XENIX requires entry of the user-name which is used by XENIX to identify file ownership. Access control is provided with the use of passwords for each user.

User Groups

It is quite likely that several people involved in the same area of work will all want access to the same files. For this reason, XENIX allows the creation of user groups. For example, a user group account for the Purchasing Department may be known to XENIX by the user-name 'PURCHASE'. Several staff in the Purchasing Department may need to create and maintain their own files but leave them accessible to others in the department. To achieve this, a sub-directory can be allocated to each individual within the 'PURCHASE' user group, although all files remain accessible to all members.

The password for a new user or user group is entered by the super-user (system administrator) and acts as an initial authority for the user when first logging into XENIX. The user can change the assigned password when logging on for the first time and because passwords tend not to remain secret for long, should change it regularly after that, to reduce the chances of unauthorized persons gaining access to the system.

Real-time

A real-time system is one which reacts to inputs sufficiently rapidly to permit tight control of its environment. A computer system's environment can be defined as the application or activity it is controlling. Real-time operation is essential for computerized *process control*, for example, in chemical production. Such activities require continual control so that parameters of, say pressure and temperature, are adhered to. Inputs from the process, collected via *transducers*, are digitized, input and processed, to provide immediate feedback to the system's controllers, which for the previous example may be a heating mechanism and air pressure control. Chapter 31 examines process control systems in more detail.

Some business information systems also require real-time control. Typical examples include airline booking and some stock control systems where rapid turnover is the norm.

The mechanisms used by a real-time operating system to control the system resources are beyond the scope of this text.

Further Functions and Facilities of Operating Systems

Command Language Interpretation

An important function of the operating system is to interpret the command language which allows the user/operator to communicate with it. Two types of language are generally recognized:

   ☐ command language;

   ☐ job control language;

Command language

A *command line interpreter* (CLI) accepts command lines, checks them for syntax errors and passes on the relevant requests to the operating system. Such requests may be, for example, to display directory contents on screen, delete files from disk, or copy them from one disk to another. Simple, ad hoc requests will generally be made via a keyboard but lengthy, regularly used sequences of commands may be stored in a *command* or *batch file*. The MS/DOS operating system provides such a facility.

Graphical User Interface (GUI). IBM's OS/2 operating system provides a GUI called Presentation Manager, which allows the user to communicate with the operating system in a WIMP environment (Chapter 19). Operating system utilities are selected, via a mouse, from representative icons on the screen; the GUI communicates these requests in the system's command language and the CLI interprets and passes them on to the operating system in the normal way. The GUI is just another level of interface between the user and the CLI.

Job Control Language (JCL)

Associated with batch processing operating systems, JCLs allow details of job requirements to be specified to the operating system. An example JCL sequence is given below.

    BEGIN

    JOB 3367

    COMPILE payroll.cob (disk 1)

    LOAD payroll.obj (disk 1)

    RUN

    END

This sequence of commands identifies the job, compiles a COBOL (cob) source program, loads the resultant object program and executes it.

I/O Handling

The *executive* part of the operating system controls data transfers to and from peripherals, normally through a system of interrupts. The topic of I/O is dealt with in Chapter 7. Other causes of interrupts are dealt with in the following section.

Interrupt Handling

Apart from I/O operations, interrupts are necessary to notify the operating system of a variety of other system events, including:

  □ hardware failure, for example, through power loss or a memory parity error;

  □ program termination;

  □ peripheral data transfer failure, for example, because a printer is out of paper or the directory on a disk has been damaged;

  □ an attempt to access a non-existent memory address;

  □ in a time-sharing or real-time system, a clock pulse indicates completion of time slices;

  □ program instruction error, for example, an attempted division by zero or an attempt to communicate with a non-existent device;

☐ an externally generated command from the operator.

As is explained in Chapter 7, when such events occur, the *interrupt handler* routine must establish the cause/source of the interrupt and call the appropriate *interrupt service* routine. The procedures for interrupt handling are described in Chapter 7.

Error Handling/Trapping

It is important that events which would ordinarily upset or 'crash' the computer system, are *trapped* and handled in an orderly way. Thus, for example, upon encountering an illegal application program instruction, an interrupt is generated, followed by entry to an appropriate interrupt service routine in the executive. The application program is aborted and the service routine displays an error message on screen, detailing the nature of the error. Arithmetic errors, such as an attempt to divide by zero, and I/O errors should also be trapped and treated in a similar fashion. Although data lost as a result of programming errors may not be recoverable by the operating system, any loss caused by abnormal operational interrupt of an I/O activity (Chapter) should be preventable by an appropriate routine to restore the data.

Of course, applications software should, wherever possible, anticipate possible system errors such as disk read errors and other peripheral faults, and protect the user from contact with the operating system by producing its own user friendly messages. Further, in the same way that the operating system prevents system crashes, applications software should, if the fault can be corrected, be robust enough to allow its continuance without loss of data.

File Management and Security

The major facilities provided by an operating system for file management relate to:

☐ creating and deleting files;

☐ allocating space on storage media;

☐ identifying and keeping track of files on storage media;

☐ editing the contents of files;

☐ protecting files from hardware malfunction;

☐ protecting files from those of other applications or users;

☐ protecting files against unauthorized access.

More details of file management and security are illustrated by reference to the MS/DOS operating system in the Chapter on Computer Files.

Accounting and Logging

An important part of system control is that the operator should have a record of all operator communications, error conditions and applications which have been run; the operating system keeps a *log* of such events and either outputs the relevant messages to the operator's console printer or records them on backing storage for later printing.

Multi-access operating systems normally provide an accounting facility which identifies and records terminal usage, including basic details such as user-id, time logged on and off and processor time used; in this way, users or departments of an organization can be charged for computer time.

Memory Management

Single user operating systems such as MS/DOS do not provide particularly sophisticated memory facilities, as only one application is *resident* at on time. There is one special case, that of the graphical user interface (GUI, for example, Gem Desktop), which stays resident in memory; it must advise the operating system of its storage needs, in order that it is not corrupted by subsequent loading of applications.

Multi-programming and multi-tasking systems require quite complex memory management facilities in order to accommodate and maintain the *integrity* of the several programs and associated data which may be resident at any one time. Memory requirements do not remain static because the mix of programs being run may vary from moment to moment; the space left by a program swapped out of memory may not be large enough to accommodate an incoming program, requiring the *relocation* of programs already there.

Memory Partitions and Relocatable Code

To fulfil these requirements, the operating system must be able to *partition memory dynamically* and adjust those partitions as programs and data are relocated. This latter point means that all software should be capable of relocation and not be tied to *absolute* addresses in memory. This is effected with the use of *relative* addressing instructions which are examined in more detail in the Chapter on Instructions and Memory Addressing. The relocatable code is allocated to the absolute memory addresses by the executive, the relative addresses of each instruction being added to the *base* address of the relevant memory partition. Subsequent relocations can be carried out by re-specification of the base address.

Segmenting and Interleaving

Where large programs are concerned, it may be possible to divide them into *segments*, which can be rolled in and out of memory from direct access storage as required. As only one segment of a particular program need be resident in memory at any one time, any replacement segment will simply *overlay* it. In a multi-programming environment, segments from different programs are in memory at one time and are said to be *interleaved*.

Virtual Memory

Although main memory and direct access backing storage are physically separate, it is possible to present their joint capacity as being available to run programs. Such *virtual* memory can be used to accommodate much larger programs, as well as expand the level of multi-programming. A programmer can regard the addressable memory space as being beyond the physical capacity of main memory. Programs are automatically divided into *pages* (a fixed unit of virtual storage) and when one is loaded, its virtual memory addresses are mapped to the absolute memory addresses by the executive. The addresses of each page are held in main memory and during program execution, they are paged-in and paged-out as required.

13 *The Definition of Computer Languages*

Fundamental to the design of a computer language is the idea of a *grammar* which precisely defines the syntax of program statements. The chapter describes two notations commonly employed to specify such grammars; they are *Backus-Naur Form* and *Syntax Diagrams*.

All languages, whether computer languages such as Pascal or Prolog, or natural languages such as English or Japanese, have a number of rules governing the syntax of well-formed statements or sentences. The collection of these syntax rules is called the grammar of a language. The grammar of a natural language is very difficult to state precisely, and might require several hundred syntax rules to define it even approximately, but, because computer languages are relatively simple and unambiguous, they can be defined exactly using a relatively small set of rules.

Two common methods of describing the grammar of languages are

- ☐ Backus-Naur Form(BNF), named after the two men that developed this notation for defining Algol
- ☐ Syntax diagrams

These are examples of *meta-languages*, that is, languages which are used to describe other languages.

Such formal definitions of computer languages are useful for a number of reasons:

- ☐ they provide the means to determine whether a given sequence of characters constitutes a valid statement in the language
- ☐ they allow us to break down a statement into its constituent parts, that is, *parse* the statement, so that it can be converted into a machine-sensible form
- ☐ they can be used to generate well-formed statements.

Backus-Naur Form

As a simple example of the use of BNF notation, consider a grammar which defines the form of integers of any length:

<integer> ::= <digit> | <integer> <digit>

<digit> ::= 0 | 1 | 2 | 3 | 4 | 5 | 6 | 7 | 8 | 9

<integer> and <digit>, are called *non-terminals* because they are defined in terms of other non-terminals or elementary symbols called *terminal* symbols. Thus the symbols 0-9 are terminal symbols. The ::= notation is read as 'is defined as' and the symbol | means 'or'. So the first rule reads

> '*integer* is defined as a *digit* or an *integer* followed by a *digit*'.

The second rule reads

> '*digit* is defined as the symbol 0 or 1 or 2 ... or 9'.

integer and *digit* are termed *syntactic entities* since they each define a separate part of the grammar.

We can use these rules to generate integers by repeatedly replacing the left-hand syntactic entities by the right-hand terminals and non-terminals. For example, replacing *digit* by 5 produces

> <integer> ::= 5 (from the rule, <integer> ::= <digit >)

This is one instance of an integer, according to our grammar. But the grammar also states that <integer> ::= <integer><digit>, so we can replace <integer> on the right-hand side by 5 and <digit> by, say, 2 to give

> <integer> ::= 52

By repeating this procedure we can produce any integer value; for this reason, rules are also called *productions*.

Notice that the *recursive* nature of the first rule enables this simple grammar to generate an infinite number of integers. Not all grammars are recursive, but those that are describe infinite languages. (See Chapter 28 for a discussion of recursion).

A (simplified) recursive grammar for an arithmetic expression in a high-level language such as C could be expressed as:

```
<expr>          ::= <term>   |   <expr><expr operator><term>
<term>          ::= <factor>   |   <term><term operator><factor>
<factor>        ::= <variable>   |   <integer>   |   (<expression>)   | – <factor>
<variable>      ::= A   |B   |   ......   |   Z
<integer>       ::= <digit> | <integer><digit>
<digit>         ::= 0 | 1 | 2 | 3 | 4 | 5 | 6 | 7 | 8 | 9
<expr operator> ::= + | –
<term operator> ::= * | /
```

Using this grammar, examples of valid arithmetic expressions are:

```
A + B
P – Q/2
X + Y*(Z+1) – W
L*M + 3*(A*A – B/4)
```

A compiler could use this grammar to determine the syntactic validity of an expression within a program statement by attempting to establish that the expression conforms to the rules of the grammar. *Parsing*, this process of analysing a string of symbols using the production rules of the grammar, is discussed later in the section devoted to the structure and function of compilers.

Syntax Diagrams

A more graphical approach to language definition is the use of *syntax diagrams*. For example, the BNF definition of an unsigned integer given in the previous section is equivalent to the syntax diagram shown in *Figure 13.1*. The different paths that may be taken through the diagram are indicated by the arrows.

Figure 13.1

Here, *digit* represents one of the symbols 0-9 as before; shown in *Figure 13.2*.

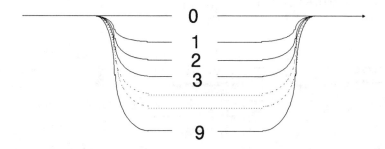

Figure 13.2

The first diagram shows that, by following a single left-to-right path, an integer can be a single digit; by following the loop path two or more times, an integer can contain two or more digits.

The arrows in the second diagram indicate that only one of the digits 0-9 may be selected in going from left to right, meaning that a digit is one of the symbols 0,1,2...9.

Syntax diagrams are read by following the routes indicated by arrows, adding the symbols indicated in the circles or oval boxes to build up strings representing valid syntactic structures. So, in the example above, we could select '8' as the first digit, and by following the loop back around once more, and this time choosing '5', we would have generated the integer 85.

Figure 13.3 defines the rules for the formation of the Roman numerals for 1-10:

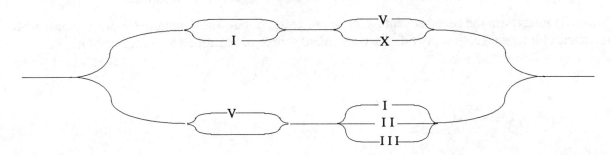

Figure 13.3

The ten possible different routes through the diagram generate the numerals

I, II, III, IV, V, VI, VII, VIII, IX, X

As a final example, the syntax diagram, *Figure 13.4*, shows the overall structure of a Pascal program. When used for this purpose, three different symbols are used:

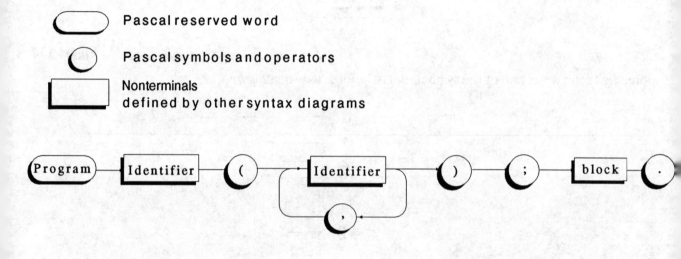

Pascal reserved word

Pascal symbols and operators

Nonterminals
defined by other syntax diagrams

Figure 13.4

Examples of valid program identifiers, according to this definition, are

program example1(input,output);<block>.

where *example1, input* and *output* are identifiers and <*block* >is a non-terminal which is defined by its own syntax diagram.

program eg2(file1,file2,file3);<block>.

Here *eg2, file1, file2* and *file3* are identifiers and <*block*> is again a non-terminal.

Syntax diagrams have the added advantage of succinctly describing the complete set of syntactic constructs of a computer language, thus providing a convenient source of reference for programmers.

14 *Computer Language Translators*

The general function of *translators* (or *language processors*) is to convert program statements written in one programming language into another, most commonly into machine code. This chapter examines the function and operational characteristics of the three main types of translators, namely *assemblers*, *compilers* and *interpreters*.

Assemblers

In the history of programming languages, one of the first significant innovations was the development of assembly languages. A program written in an assembly language is much more readable and understandable than its equivalent in machine code; the problem arises, however, that it is no longer directly executable by the computer. An *assembler* is a computer program which carries out the necessary translation.

The assembler accepts an assembly language program as data, converts *mnemonic* operation codes (op-codes) to their numeric equivalents, assigns *symbolic addresses* to memory locations and produces as output the required machine code program.

The assembly language program is termed the *source program* and the final machine code program is the *object program*. (See also Chapter 11).

Though it is true that by far the majority of computer programming today is in high-level languages such as Pascal, C or COBOL, programming in assembly languages is still essential for certain tasks. The reason for this, despite continual improvements in compiler design, is simply that the programmer, having total control over the structure of the machine code generated by the assembler, is able to write much faster and more efficient code than that produced by a compiler. The very nature of high-level languages, allowing us to deal with a greatly simplified, virtual machine, often precludes the programmer from being able to fine-tune code according to particular circumstances.

For example, a commonly used method of increasing the speed of a machine-code program is to utilize internal registers as much as possible in preference to memory locations, in order to minimize relatively slow memory accesses. While this type of code optimization is perfectly feasible in any assembly language, most high-level languages do not allow the programmer this degree of control (C is a notable exception, allowing identifiers to be specifically allocated to general purpose registers).

A consequence of the one-to-one correspondence between an assembly language instruction and its equivalent machine-code instruction is that assemblers are machine dependent, producing machine code for a specific type of processor. For instance, the machine code generated by an Intel 8086/88 assembler could not be used directly by a computer with a Motorola 68000 processor. For this reason, there is no single, archetypal assembler; rather, each assembler is related to the architecture of the processor for which it has been designed. Thus, if the processor supports two-address machine-code instructions, this will be reflected in the format of the assembly language instructions.

In the following sections we introduce a number of fundamental characteristics common to most assemblers. Assembly language programming is discussed in Chapter 27 using a hypothetical microprocessor and associated assembly language to illustrate simple programs, including an example program to illustrate the assembly process described in this chapter.

Assembler Tasks

Early assemblers did little more than convert instruction mnemonics to their equivalent numeric machine codes, but current assemblers do much more. Some of the most common assembler tasks are described below:

☐ *Op-code translation.* Numeric operation codes replace the mnemonic op-codes used in the source program.

☐ *Absolute address allocation.* Each instruction or data word in the source program must be allocated an *absolute* machine address (its physical location). The assembler maintains a *location counter* (sometimes referred to as a *load pointer*) which, having been set to an initial base address, is incremented by the length of each data or instruction word as it is assembled.

☐ *Symbolic operand conversion.* This refers to the assembly process of substituting any symbolic addresses, that is, user identifiers used in place of memory locations, with numeric machine addresses. A symbol table records each symbolic operand together with its corresponding absolute address; a similar table logs labels and their machine addresses. If relative addressing is used, labels and symbolic addresses are converted to offsets from the location counter; this enables a program to be relocatable (See Chapter 3);

☐ *Converting constants to their internal forms.* This will involve conversion from textual (ASCII, for example) representations of decimal, hexadecimal, octal or binary to pure binary.

☐ *Replacing identifiers by user-defined macros.* If the assembly language supports the use of *macro* instructions (a shorthand used by a programmer to express sequences of regularly used instructions by a macro name), any such macro must be expanded by the assembler and inserted into the source program prior to assembling it.

☐ *Obeying directives.* Many assemblers support the use of *pseudo-operations*, or *directives* which are instructions not directly translatable into machine instructions. These involve such things as reserving space for data, defining the values of identifiers used in the program and defining where the program is to be located in memory.

☐ *Generating error messages.* If the assembler detects any syntax errors in the source program, it must be able to issue a message indicating the source and nature of the problem.

☐ *Producing source-code listings.* These may take various forms including listings of the source-code, object-code and symbol table.

Assembly

The assembly process usually involves the assembler in executing several passes of the program's source code, each one carrying out certain of the tasks described above. The problem of forward referencing (an instruction uses a symbolic operand which is not defined until later in the program, so its address has not been allocated at that point and cannot be included in the instruction) means that assemblers usually carry out a minimum of two passes.

Two-pass assembly

*Pass 1.*Any macro instructions are expanded as part of the pass or as a separate initial pass, making three in all. All instructions are examined and checked for syntactical correctness; any errors are recorded in a table. After each instruction has been dealt with, the location counter is incremented, and a symbol table is constructed to link any symbolic operands and labels with their corresponding absolute addresses.

*Pass 2.*By reference to the symbol tables, the assembler generates and outputs the object code.

In Chapter 27 we illustrate three-pass assembly with a simple program, showing how the object program is generated at each stage in the assembly process.

Cross Assembler

This is an assembler which carries out the translation of an assembly program on one machine to produce object code for execution on another. For example, a certain cross assembler running on an IBM PC might assemble a source program to produce Motorola 68000 machine code for use on an Apple computer.

Compilers and Interpreters

There are two main types of high-level language *translators* (or *language processors* as they are often known):

(i)   compilers;

(ii) interpreters.

Since the choice of translator has implications regarding program development time, debugging and testing, memory requirements, execution speed and program security, it is important from a programming point of view to be quite clear about the difference between the two types.

As explained in Chapter 11, a compiler accepts a *source program*, that is, a program written in some high-level language, Pascal for instance, checks that it is correctly formed and, if so, generates the equivalent *object program* in a low-level language. The translated program may be in the form of an assembly language, in which case it must first be assembled before it is executed, or it may be in machine code, allowing it to be executed directly without further modification. If any errors are detected during compilation, they will be reported and, if serious enough, may prevent the compiler from completing the translation process.

A compiler will often have access to a library of standard routines and special routines appropriate to the application area for which the source language was designed; this collection of subroutines is called the *run-time library*. Included in this library of machine code subprograms will be routines for performing arithmetic operations, input/output operations, backing storage data transfers and other commonly used functions. Whenever the source code refers to one of these routines specifically, or needs one to perform the operation specified, the compiler will ensure that the routine is added to the object program.

Note that the final object code is independent of both the source code and the compiler itself. That is, neither of these two programs needs to be resident in main store when the object code is being executed. However, any alterations to the program subsequent to its compilation will necessitate modification and re-compilation of the source code prior to executing the program again.

An interpreter uses a different method to translate a source program into a machine-sensible form. An object program is not generated in this form of translation, rather the source program, or an intermediate form of it, is scanned statement by statement, each in turn immediately being converted into the actions specified. (See Chapter 11).

The source code statements are translated and executed separately, as they are encountered, while the source code is being processed by the interpreter. The object code actually executed is held within the interpreter; the latter merely identifies from the source statement which piece of machine code is relevant and causes it to be performed. On completion of a statement, control returns to the interpreter which then processes the next logical statement in the program sequence.

It might seem, therefore, that an interpreter has a big advantage over a compiler. In terms of the amount of effort required in obtaining an executable program, this is certainly true, but there are a number of other factors which favour the use of a compiler. For example, an interpreter must do a considerable amount of work before it can even begin to cause a source statement to be executed (error checking, for instance); on the other hand, a compiler has already done this work during compilation. Moreover, should a section of source code be repeated one or more times, an interpreter must re-interpret the section each time. Consequently, interpreted programs tend to run significantly slower than equivalent compiled programs, and for time-critical applications this might be a major concern. Furthermore, because the translation and execution phases are interwoven, the interpreter must be resident in memory at the same time as the source code. If memory space is at a premium, this can be a severe limitation of an interpreted language.

Languages designed for use by children or for teaching purposes are often interpreted. Logo, for example, originally designed as a language for children, is interpreted to facilitate its interactive nature. Similarly, BASIC is interpreted in order to simplify its use for programming novices.

A possible compromise is to provide both an interpreter and a compiler for the same language; this allows rapid development time using the interpreter, and fast execution obtained by compiling the code.

Compilers

The compilation process can be broken down into a number of stages:

(i)   lexical analysis - the source code is scanned and converted into a form more convenient for subsequent processing, and a symbol table is partially constructed;

(ii) syntax analysis and semantic analysis - the output from the lexical analyser is analysed for grammatical correctness, the symbol table is completed, error messages are generated if errors have been detected, and the program is further transformed ready for the next stages;

(iii) intermediate code generation - the output from the parser is put into an internal form permitting easier conversion into object code;

(iv) code optimization - the intermediate code is made more time or space efficient using a number of different techniques;

(v) code generation - the object code, which may be either machine code or assembly language, is generated.

These stages are discussed in more detail in the following sections.

Lexical Analysis

Most programming languages allow a certain amount of redundancy in the preparation of the program. For example, spaces can often be inserted to aid readability of the source code, and comments are used to explain the function of the program and sections of code. A section of the compiler, called the *lexical analyser* or *scanner*, removes such redundancies and performs other modifications of the source code prior to passing it to the next stage of compilation.

The lexical analyser takes the source code and translates it into a string of characters, which is to be passed to the *syntax analyser*, or *parser*. The process of *lexical analysis* identifies *lexemes,* that is, the basic lexical units of the source language, such as reserved words, operators, identifiers, constants and literals, and associates them with specific integer values or *tokens*. For example, each reserved word would be represented by a unique integer, say in the range 256-511, all identifiers would have a certain code such as 512, constants perhaps 513, and special symbols such as '(' or '*' would probably retain their ascii values. Additionally, each identifier would be replaced by a pointer to its position in a *symbol table* containing details of its characteristics.

The lexical analyser thus preprocesses the source code to facilitate subsequent stages in the compilation process. In addition, it provides an interface between the programmer and the computer, allowing some limited flexibility in the layout of the source code.

Syntax and Semantic Analysis

These analysers do the actual hard work of breaking the source program into its constituent parts. The complete source program is analysed into blocks, which are then broken down into statements, which are further analysed into instruction words, variables and constants. Each variable used in the source program is placed in a *symbol table*, together with a declaration of its attributes - type (numeric, string etc.), where it is to be located in memory (its object program address) and any other information required for object code generation.

The *syntax analyser*, or *parser*, takes the output from the lexical analyser and determines syntactic correctness of the program using the grammatical rules for the language.

The *syntax* or grammar of a programming language consists of a set of rules which define a legal program statement, as opposed to a meaningless string of characters. The rules determine correct sentence structure; the process of checking the validity of sentence structure is known as *parsing*. In English, for example, the sentence

> *the monkey ate the banana*

can be determined as *grammatically* correct by reference to the rules of English grammar. Conversely, the rules can be used to determine that

> *monkey the ate banana the*

is grammatically incorrect.

Similarly, the grammar or syntax of the Pascal programming language can be used to determine that the program statement

> *net := gross - deductions;*

is correct, and that

> *gross - deductions := net;*

is not.

However, even the first statement, though syntactically correct, might still be invalid on *semantic* grounds. For instance, if any of the variables *net, gross* or *deductions* had not been previously declared, or if any of them had been declared as having *type char* (character), the statement would be meaningless. Returning to our English example, the sentence

> *The banana ate the monkey.*

is still grammatically correct but semantically very suspect because we are aware that one of the attributes of an ordinary banana is that it is a non-carnivorous fruit.

Semantic analysis is therefore concerned with checking the meaning or interpretation to be placed on words in the particular context of their use. Once the parser has confirmed the grammatical validity of a program construct, the semantic analyser can use the symbol table to check that an operation is semantically valid. In addition, the semantic analyser may supplement the work of the parser by using the symbol table to guide the generation of intermediate code. For example, a number of languages use different routines for arithmetic, depending on whether the arithmetic expression involves integer or real values, or a mixture of the two. The semantic analyser will examine the data types of the variables in the expression and determine the appropriate routines to use.

Sometimes the parser contains semantic routines which are invoked as the parsing process progresses, sometimes semantic analysis forms a distinct stage after the parser has completed its analysis, but frequently the two methods are combined.

During the course of this stage in the compilation process, a number of data structures may be created to facilitate code optimization and generation. The symbol table has already been mentioned, but in addition a *parse tree* will be created, representing the structure of the complete program split into a hierarchy of its components, and arithmetic expressions may be converted into a more convenient internal form such as *postfix*, also known as *Reverse Polish*, notation.

The next few sections examine these data structures in more detail.

Parsing Techniques

Suppose that we are trying to determine whether a string of symbols such as

> P − Q/2

represents a valid expression in a simplified version of the grammar defined in the section on BNF:

```
<expr>        ::= <term>    |   <expr><expr operator><term>
<term>        ::= <factor>  |   <term><term operator><factor>
<factor>      ::= variable  |   integer  |  (<expr>)  | –<factor>
<expr operator>   ::= + | –
<term operator>   ::= * | /
```

Here *variable* and *integer* are named terminals, so called because they are identifiers which represent actual terminals.

The analysis could proceed as shown below, repeatedly scanning the string from left to right, replacing (at appropriate points) terminals and non-terminals by higher level non-terminals:

1. P – Q/2

2. variable <expr operator> variable <term operator> integer

3. <factor><expr operator><factor><term operator><factor>

4. <factor><expr operator><term><term operator><factor>

5. <factor><expr operator><term>

6. <term><expr operator><term>

7. <expr><expr operator><term>

8. <expression>

This process of *bottom-up parsing* repeatedly examines the string of symbols and at each pass determines whether a group of syntactic entities may be combined to form another syntactic entity. Thus the group

<term><term operator><factor>

can be replaced by <term> which is a higher level syntactic entity. Since, at stage 8, we arrive at the highest level, that is, *expr*, an expression, the string must be a well-formed arithmetic expression in this grammar.

Here is another example, this time illustrating the recursive nature of the grammar: the string to be parsed is

X*(Y + Z)

1. X*(Y + Z)

2. variable <term operator> (variable <expr operator> variable)

3. <factor><term operator>(factor><expr operator><factor>)

4. <factor><term operator>(<term><expr operator><factor>)

5. <factor><term operator>(<expr><expr operator><term>)

6. <factor><term operator>(<expr >)

7. <factor><term operator><factor >

8. <term><term operator><factor>

9. <term>

10. <expr>

Though we have used an intuitive method to determine at what point in the parse to make substitutions for syntactic entities, in practice the process is based on precedence relations between adjacent symbols which precisely determine the order in which the components of the input string are processed. However, the precise details of the process are quite complex and they are beyond the scope of this text.

An alternative approach is to use a *top-down* parser such as that employed in *recursive descent parsing*. Such a parser uses a set of recursive functions to represent the syntactic structure of the source program.

The outline pseudocode for such a recursive descent parser might take the form shown in *Listing 14.1*:

```
define function expression()
     token := function term()
     while token = expression_operator do
          case token of
          when "+": token := function term()
                    procedure addition()
          when "-": token := function term()
                    procedure subtraction()
          endcase
     endwhile
     return(token)
endfunction expression

define function term()
     token := function factor()
     while token = term_operator do
          case token of
          when "*": token := function factor()
                    procedure multiplication()
          when "/": token := function factor()
                    procedure division()
          endcase
     endwhile
     return(token)
endfunction term

define function factor()
     token := function get_next_token()
     case token of
     when variable: procedure variable_found()
                    token := function get_next_token()
     when integer : procedure integer_found()
                    token := function get_next_token()
     when "(      : token := function expression()
                    if token < >")" then
                         token := brackets_err
                         procedure error(token)
                    endif
     endcase
     return(token)
endfunction factor
```

Listing 14.1

The parser assumes that the expression to be parsed is in token form, and that the function *get_next_token*() takes care of keeping track of the next token to be processed and returns this token when called.

Each of the three functions, *expression*, *term* and *factor* corresponds to the appropriate syntax diagram, and each returns a value corresponding to the next token available. The process terminates when a NULL (terminating) token is encountered, or when an error arises during the parse.

The first function, *expression*(), immediately calls *term*(), which immediately calls *factor*() which identifies the current token as being either a variable, an integer or an expression enclosed in parentheses. Appropriate procedures (not detailed here) deal with each of these cases, storing the identified item in a parse tree. Function *factor*() then returns the next token available, or an error code if an invalid token has been detected. Function *term*() then looks for a term operator, '*' or '/' and calls *factor*() again to provide the next operand. This repeats until there are no more factors in the term being processed. A term having been identified, control returns to *expression*() which looks for an expression operator, '+' or '−', to be returned from *term*(). If this is the case, expression calls *term*() again to identify the next term in the expression; the process terminates if a NULL token is returned, or some other token signifying an error condition.

In recursive descent parsing, control continually descends through the function nesting to obtain operands, and ascends through the functions in reverse order. The recursive nature of the parse results from the definition of a factor which may be a parenthesized expression, thus causing *expression*() to call itself. These parsers are relatively simple to implement, being based directly on the language definition. BASIC interpreters frequently use recursive descent to evaluate arithmetic expressions, since such interpreters need to do no preprocessing of expressions (see the case study in the section on interpreters following).

Parse Trees

The following Pascal program calculates the area of a rectangle, given its length and width:

```
program pteg (input, output);
var area, len, wid :integer;
begin
readln (len, wid);
area := len*wid;
writeln ('The area is', area)
end.
```

When the program above is processed, the parser builds up a parse tree which identifies all the grammatical categories it encounters. The leaves of the tree are the tokens, that is the smallest grammatical entities, and the interior nodes represent non-terminals. As each non-terminal and token is identified, it is added to the parse tree being constructed until, finally, the whole program has been transformed into an intermediate representation. The parse tree is shown in *Figure 14.1*.

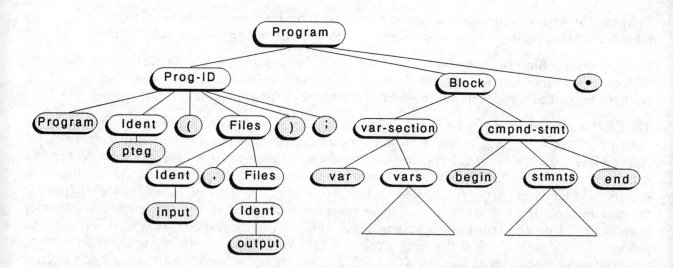

Figure 14.1

The parts of the tree shown as shaded triangles are expanded in *Figures 14.2* and *14.3*.

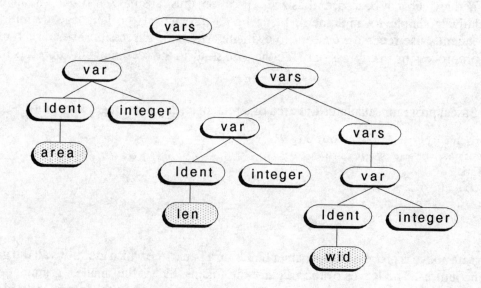

Figure 14.2

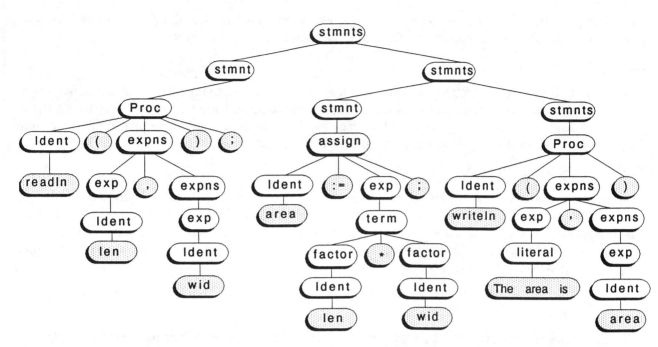

Figure 14.3

Notice that the parse tree has the same form as the syntax diagrams for the same structures, but it is specific to this program rather than being a generalized specification of Pascal. The parse tree could be conveniently implemented as a tree data structure (see Chapter 26) with each node identifying the appropriate grammatical structure and with pointers to other nodes identifying substructures. In this form, the source program is much easier to handle in the code generation phase of the compilation process.

Symbol Tables

Checking for semantic correctness and generating code requires knowledge of the attributes of the identifiers used in the source program. This information is stored in a data structure known as a *symbol table* which plays a central role in the translation process. For each occurrence of an identifier in a source program, the table will be searched for its symbol table entry, new identifiers will be inserted into the data structure, and new information regarding known identifiers will be added.

Typically, the information stored in the symbol table for each variable will comprise:

☐ name

☐ type eg integer, real, character etc.

☐ memory location allocated

Subprograms will require additional information related to parameters to be stored.

Because of its importance to the translation process, the symbol table needs to be structured in a manner which allows efficient insertion and extraction of information. Numerous strategies for structuring the symbol table are possible. One commonly used method is to use a *binary tree* organized alphabetically to facilitate access to identifiers and insertion of new nodes. Another method uses *hashing* to speed access to symbol table entries. Yet another approach is to use a combination of hashing and linked lists. The principles of these three techniques are discussed in Chapter 26:Data Structures.

Reverse Polish Notation

In Reverse Polish Notation (RPN), arithmetic or logical expressions are represented in a manner which specifies simply and exactly the order in which operations are to be performed. All operators are given the same precedence, thus removing the need for brackets. This has the advantage of providing a relatively simple way of both evaluating an arithmetic expression and of generating code.

Evaluating Expressions in RPN

Operators come after operands in RPN. For example, the infix expression A+B*C translates to ABC*+ in RPN, and (A-B)/C+D becomes AB-C/D+. Arithmetic expressions in RPN can be evaluated by a single left-to-right scan utilizing a stack. The stack is used to hold all of the operands which have been scanned or have been produced as the result of some operation, but which have not yet been used. The algorithm for processing an expression in RPN is as follows:

(i)   If the scanned symbol is a variable or constant, push its value to the stack and scan the next symbol.

(ii)   If the scanned symbol is a binary operator, pop the two topmost values on the stack, apply the operation to them and then push the result to the stack.

(iii) If the scanned symbol is a unary operator, pop the top of the stack, apply the operation to this item and then push the result to the stack.

[Note that the term *binary operator* refers to an arithmetic or logical operator which requires two operands, such as * in the expression $a+b*c$; the two operands are b and c. The term *unary operator* refers to an arithmetic or logical operator which requires a single operand, such as $-$ in the expression $-b+c*d$; the single operand is b in this case.]

For example, suppose that we wish to evaluate the RPN expression

   ab~cd*++

equivalent to $a+(-b+c*d)$ in usual infix notation, where ~ represents unary $-$. The following table illustrates how the evaluation would be handled with values a=2, b=3, c=-4 and d=5,

scanned symbol	old stack contents	operation	new stack contents
a̲b~cd*++		push a	[2]
ab̲~cd*++	[2]	push b	[2,3]
ab~̲cd*++	[2,3]	−b	[2,−3]
ab~c̲d*++	[2,−3]	push c	[2,−3,−4]
ab~cd̲*++	[2,−3,−4]	push d	[2,−3,−4,5]
ab~cd*̲++	[2,−3,−4,5]	c*d	[2,−3,−20]
ab~cd*+̲+	[2,−3,−20]	−b+c*d	[2,−23]
ab~cd*+±̲	[2,−23]	a+(−b+c*d)	[−21]

The table shows the symbol being scanned (underlined), the stack contents prior to this symbol being processed, the operation performed on the appropriate operands and, lastly, the contents of the stack after processing the scanned symbol.

Converting Arithmetic Expressions from Infix to RPN

An algorithm for converting from infix to RPN is as follows. Firstly, we associate numerical values with the relative precedences of arithmetic operators according to the following table:

Operator	Precedence level
unary + and −	4
^ (exponentiation)	3
*,/	2
+,−	1

The method also uses a stack, this time for the temporary storage of operators while processing the infix input string. The output from the algorithm is the equivalent string in RPN. The algorithm is based on the following rules which are applied as each symbol in the input string is scanned in turn:

(i)   If the incoming symbol is a variable or a constant, copy it to the output string directly.

(ii) If the incoming symbol is an operator, and it is of higher numerical precedence than the operator currently on top of the stack, or if the stack is empty, push it to the stack.

(iii) If the incoming symbol is an operator of equal or lower precedence than the current top of the stack, pop the top of the stack to the output string and go to step (ii) using the current symbol.

(iv) Left parenthesis, (, goes on top of the operator stack regardless of the current contents of the the stack, and remains on the stack until released by right parenthesis,).

(v)   Right parenthesis,), releases all operators on the stack to the output string until a) is encountered, at which point the) is removed from the stack.

(vi) When the end of the input string is reached, any operators remaining on the stack are released to the output string, and the process terminates.

The following table traces the conversion of the expression a*(b+c)−d/g to RPN.

Scanned symbol	Stack current	new	Output string
<u>a</u>*(b+c)−d/g	[]	[]	a
a<u>*</u>(b+c)−d/g	[]	[*]	a
a*<u>(</u>b+c)−d/g	[*]	[*,(]	a
a*(<u>b</u>+c)−d/g	[*,(]	[*,(]	ab
a*(b<u>+</u>c)−d/g	[*,(]	[*,(,+]	ab
a*(b+<u>c</u>)−d/g	[*,(,+]	[*,(,+]	abc
a*(b+c<u>)</u>−d/g	[*,(,+]	[*]	abc+
a*(b+c)<u>−</u>d/g	[*]	[−]	abc+*
a*(b+c)−<u>d</u>/g	[−]	[−]	abc+*d

a*(b+c)−d/g	[-]	[-,/]	abc+*d
a*(b+c)−d/g	[-,/]	[-,/]	abc+*dg
a*(b+c)−d/g_	[-,/]	[]	abc+*dg/−

Intermediate Languages

Having completed the parsing phase, it is quite common for a compiler to produce an intermediate language prior to generating code. One reason for doing this is to facilitate code optimization by tailoring the intermediate code to the needs of the optimization phase. Another reason is that it allows compilers for different target machines to use the same 'front end' stages and machine specific 'back end' stages for code optimization and generation, the intermediate code being the interface between the two ends.

One type of intermediate language consists of a set of *three-address statements*. For example, the C fragment

```
if ( a > max +1 ) a = max + 1;
b = b + 1;
```

might be transformed into

```
    T1 := max + 1
    if a < T1 goto L1
    T2 := max + 1
    a := T2
L1:T3 := b + 1
    b := T3
```

where T1, T2, T3 are temporary variables which are added to the symbol table.

Code Optimization

The example of intermediate code shown in the preceding section provides a number of opportunities for optimization. If, for instance, one or more of the variables referenced were allocated to internal CPU registers, the code would become more time efficient since fewer memory accesses would be required. In fact some high-level languages (C for instance) allow the programmer to explicitly allocate variables to registers with declarations such as

```
register int i;
```

Another opportunity for optimization is to use increment/decrement operations rather than addition/subtraction operations. For example, it is faster to increment b in the statement b := b + 1 rather than perform the addition if the target language contains an increment instruction.

Other common optimization techniques include

☐ *Constant folding* - where arithmetic operations can be executed at compile time rather than run time. For example, if the term 20*3 appears in an arithmetic expression, it can be replaced by 60 by the compiler, thus removing the need for the multiplication when the program is executed.

☐ *Algebraic identities* - code can be simplified by taking advantage of a number of algebraic identities such as

$$x + 0 = x$$
$$0 + x = x$$
$$x*0 = 0$$
$$x*1 = x$$
$$0/x = 0$$
$$x - 0 = x$$

□ *Dead code elimination* - the compiler detects code that can never be reached during execution.

□ *Loop-invariant expressions* - an expression within a loop may be exactly the same each time through the loop, so evaluating it only once outside of the loop will reduce execution time. For example,

```
for i := 1 to m*4 do procX;
```

could be compiled as if it had been written

```
T1 := m*4;
for i := 1 to T1 do procX;
```

Machine-specific compilers may use other techniques which are dependent on the target language, but, though optimization is desirable, care must be taken that optimization does not alter the original intention of the programmer; most compilers are therefore conservative with optimization, and several give the user the option of what optimizations the compiler is to attempt at compile time. As a final note, probably the best optimizations are those produced by careful algorithm design on the part of the programmer, rather than those of the compiler.

Code Generation

The final phase of the compilation process translates the optimized intermediate code to either machine code or to assembly language, depending on the particular compiler. Here the actual sequences of code necessary to, for example, call subprograms, add two floating-point numbers, and multiply two integers are emitted.

Because the intermediate form of the source program will be only slightly more abstract than assembly language, a table lookup process can be used to replace each three-address instruction by the equivalent assembly language code. At this time the compiler must determine whether a variable is to be allocated to a register or to main memory, and also take into account the context in which variables are referenced; the symbol table will contain information regarding the nature of each variable, whether it is global or local for instance.

Types of Compilers

It is possible to write a compiler that works its way through the source code once only and produces the object code at the end of the pass. This is called a *single-pass compiler*, for obvious reasons. The main problem with this approach is the necessity to deal with *forward references*. For example, the compiler may have to compile an instruction such as

goto L1

without yet knowing the location of the label L1. The solution is to leave a gap for the address of the label, note that the information is missing by adding an entry to a special list reserved for this eventuality, and then when the information becomes available, filling in the gap after consulting the list.

However, it is generally more convenient to process the source program using a multi-pass compiler in which there are number of passes, each pass performing certain functions and producing a modified version of the program to be used in the next pass. Such compilers have two major advantages over the single-pass compilers:

☐ The compiler can be written in a modular manner rather than as a monolithic program.

☐ Decreased memory requirements, since the code for the current pass is all that needs to be memory resident.

The chief disadvantage of the multi-pass compiler is the probable necessity to make frequent disk accesses to read and write the intermediate files required to allow the separate phases to communicate with each other.

Linking

Frequently, the object code produced by the compiler comprises separate modules of machine code which are related to each other via call and return addresses; the separate modules may also share common data. The object code may also make reference to library routines, held externally from the main program block. The function of the linker program, or *linkage editor*, is to incorporate the absolute call and return addresses of any external routines (*closed subroutines*) which are to be used by the program, as well as those needed to link the various modules of machine code produced by the compiler. Sometimes, linking is carried out as part of the compilation process.

Interpreters

Because interpreters do not produce stand-alone object code, they use a number of special processing techniques to optimize the speed at which a program executes. For example, before starting to execute a source statement, an interpreter might first convert it into a more convenient internal form by tokenizing keywords as they are entered so that they are more readily recognizable at run time. Rapid methods of accessing variables must be devised since this will be a major task of the interpreter.

These and other issues are addressed in the following sections using interpreted BASIC as a case study.

A Case study - BASIC

The interpreter described here is based on one of Acorn's early BASIC interpreters. It consists of a number of functional components:

☐ *Command Handler*

☐ *Tokenizer*

☐ *Statement Interpreter*

☐ *Expression Evaluator*

☐ *Heap/Stack Handler*

These are described in the following sections.

Program statements in BASIC start with a line number and contain one or more keywords such as PRINT or INPUT. These statements are tokenized before being inserted into the current program at the position determined by the line number. The program is executed when the command RUN is entered. However, if a statement is entered without an initial line number, BASIC assumes that the statement is to be treated as a command and executed immediately. Thus the line

> PRINT 'Hello there'

would be treated as a command causing the computer to display 'Hello there' on the monitor, whereas

> 100 PRINT 'Hello there'

would cause this line to be inserted at the appropriate point in the current program.

Heaps and Stacks

As well as the space required for the program, a BASIC interpreter must also be able to allocate dynamic storage for variables and other needs that arise during the running of a program. BASIC uses two data structures, a *heap* and a *stack* for such purposes.

The BASIC heap is explained in Chapter 26, Data Structures, as an application of a linked list. Briefly, the heap consists of an interwoven set of linked lists, one list for each set of variables starting with the same letter. The heap is located in the memory area just above the program storage area, and it increases in size each time a variable is allocated a value for the first time. A special pointer keeps track of the next free location available for the storage of a *variable information block* which contains the details of a variable. A variable information block contains a pointer to the location in the heap of the next variable with the same initial letter, the name of the variable (except for its initial letter which does not need to be stored) and its value. Locating an established variable involves accessing each node of the appropriate linked list until the required variable information block is located.

Two additional linked lists are included in the heap: one for procedures and the other for functions. The value field in this instance contains a pointer to the location of the start of the procedure or function definition.

The main BASIC stack is used for three main purposes:

(i)   As a temporary storage area for storing intermediate values while the expression evaluator is processing an expression.

(ii) To store the processor stack when procedures or functions are called. This is necessary if the processor's stack is limited in size because recursive subprograms might cause it to overflow very quickly.

(iii) As a temporary storage area for parameters and local variables associated with procedures and functions so that they may be restored to their original values when calls are completed.

Two other smaller stacks are used for REPEAT..UNTIL and FOR..NEXT loops. These are used to store the locations of the first statements in such loops so that control can repeatedly return to them while loops are in operation.

Tokens and Links

When a line has been typed at the keyboard, the command handler sends the line to the *tokenizer* so that keywords can be *tokenized*. This involves replacing the keyword by a single byte containing a unique value. Tokens serve the dual function of reducing the size of a program by replacing multi-character keywords with a single character, and of speeding up program execution by proving an efficient method of invoking the appropriate keyword handler.

When a keyword token is recognized, it is used as an offset to the start address of a table of pointers to keyword-handling routines. For example, assuming 16-bit addresses, suppose that the keyword FOR had a token value of 5 and the keyword address table started at address 1000:

Address	Keyword handler address(hex)	Keyword
1000	BF50	ABS
1001	AEEF	COS
1002	AEE3	DEG
1003	AF32	EVAL
1004	BF78	FN
1005	BF47	FOR
1006	AD45	GET

Then, in order to access the subprogram that deals with FOR statements, the interpreter needs only to add 5 to the base address of 1000 to obtain the starting address (BF47) of the FOR handler.

The tokenizer will also tokenize initial line numbers, again to save space but also, more importantly, to speed up the location of destination line numbers in statements such as

200 GOTO 4560

which will entail searching each line number in the program in turn from the start until 4560 is located; tokenized line numbers significantly reduce the amount of time spent in comparing line numbers with the one required, particularly when a large number of statements are involved.

Another device for speeding up searching for particular lines is by using links inserted into program lines. These links are offsets to the start of the next instruction. Thus a program line might have the following format:

Tokenized line number
Length of line
First character of statement
Second character of statement
etc
End of line character

Start of next line

The length of line item allows the line to be skipped by adding if to the address of the start of the line - this gives the start of the next line. Thus the body of unwanted lines may be ignored, saving a relatively large amount of time when searching for a particular line.

Statement Interpreter

When a program is executed, after it has been entered and tokenized, the *statement interpreter* then decides how to handle the line. If it finds a keyword, then it will call the appropriate keyword handler, if it finds a variable name, it calls the assignment handler which in turn calls an *expression evaluator* to provide a value to be assigned to the variable. Failing it finding any valid construct, the statement interpreter will generate an error message to indicate that an unrecognizable instruction has been located at this current line.

Most of the keyword handlers will also call the expression evaluator to obtain the values they require in order to perform their functions; it is therefore one of the major sections of the interpreter.

Expression Evaluation

In the earlier section on *parsing,* a technique called *recursive descent parsing* was described. It was described as being used by a compiler to analyse a source statement and to convert it into an intermediate form. The same method is often used by interpreters to evaluate expressions. The *expression evaluator* divides the expression into several processing levels according to the priorities of the operators it encounters as it scans the expression. Low priority operations are dealt with by the top levels which call lower levels to deal with higher priority operations. High priority results are passed back to the top levels for low priority operations to be completed. So, for example, in the calculation 5 − 8/2, the subtraction is a lower level operation than the division, so the division would be performed first and the result would be passed back to the subtraction routine to complete the evaluation of the expression.

This is exactly the same process as *recursive descent parsing,* but the interpreter *evaluates* the expression as it is analysing the expression rather than using it as a compiler would to produce a data structure for use later.

Tracing the expression above, (that is, 5 − 8/2), and using a simplified scheme, would produce the following steps:

(i)   the *expression* evaluator calls a routine *term* to obtain a value corresponding to a term in the expression;

(ii)   *term* calls *factor* to obtain a value;

(iii) *factor* gets the value 5 which it pushes to a stack before returning to *term*;

(iv)   since there are no more factors in the first term, *term* has completed its task and returns control to *expression*;

(v)   *expression* then finds a '-' so it calls *term* again;

(vi)   *term* calls *factor* to provide a value;

(vii) *factor* obtains the 8 and then pushes it to the BASIC stack;

(viii) *term* needs another factor because of the '/' it finds, so it calls *factor* again;

(ix)   *factor* gets the 2 which it stacks and then returns to *term*;

(x)   *term* performs the division 8/2 and stacks the result, 4, before returning to *expression*;

(xi)   *expression* then pops the 4 and the 2 from the stack and completes the subtraction to give an answer of 1.

The section on recursive descent parsing earlier in this chapter contains an algorithm for the process outlined above.

It is worth mentioning at this point that although interpreters and compilers are the main types of translators used for high-level languages, there are several variations on this theme, two of which are described below.

Threaded Interpretive Languages (TIL's) allow the programmer to define operations in terms of sequences of predefined, primitive operations, called *words* in TIL parlance, such as *add*, *subtract*, *multiply*, *divide* and many of the operations found in other languages. Words may refer to other user-defined (secondary) words which then become new commands extending the language. In fact, typical TIL programs consist of short, progressively defined new words. You enter the final word of the program to perform the required task.

In one variation of this type of language, the words are linked together using pointers to the location of either a primitive word or a secondary word, depending on how the word has been defined. When executed, an interpreter controls this process by getting the next pointer, jumping to the location pointed to and either executing the machine code found there if the routine is a primitive or repeats the process if it finds another secondary word. Usually there is no theoretical limit to the depth to which these secondary levels may be nested.

Because the interpreter must perform this function at run-time, it must be co-resident with the program in memory, taking up space and slowing down execution time. Other TIL variations overcome the speed restriction to some degree but still operate in much the same way.

An example of a TIL is Forth.

Some languages are processed using a combination of compiler and interpreter. The compiler operates in the normal way, but instead of producing machine code it produces *p-code* (pseudo-code) which is a refined form of the source code. The interpreter must then be used to actually execute the program by interpreting the p-code at run-time. Because the compiler has already performed most of the analysis and error checking of the source code, the interpreter has much less work to do than in a conventional system and can execute the p-code very efficiently.

One of the main advantages of this system is that the language is easier to implement on a variety of different computer systems since the relatively simple interpreter can be tailored to the particular machine.

Again, however, the penalty in using an interpreter is loss of speed; machine code will execute faster than p-code.

Some versions of Pascal produce interpreted p-code and BCPL also works on this principle.

15 *Databases*

General Features

The term database is often used to describe any large collection of related data, but to understand the concepts which follow, it is necessary to establish a more precise definition. More specifically a database is *a collection of data, generally related to some subject or topic area and structured so as to allow relationships to be established between separate data items according to the various needs of users.*

From this definition it is possible to identify specific features of a database:

- ☐ A database contains data of use in a *variety* of applications.

- ☐ The data is *structured* to allow separate data items to be connected, to form different *logical* records according to the requirements of users and hence, to applications programs.

- ☐ A database will normally be used for different applications, but those applications must have some *common interests* concerning the data items they use. For example, sales, purchasing, stock control and production control applications are likely to use common data in respect of raw materials or finished goods. On the other hand, a database containing data on both materials and personnel may be difficult to justify; even then connections between the separate databases can be facilitated if the information requirements so justify.

Controlled Redundancy

One feature which is not specifically referred to in the definition is that of *controlled redundancy*. Effectively, this means reducing to a minimum the number of data items which are duplicated in a database. In traditional computerized filing systems, each department in an organization may keep its own files, which results in a massive amount of duplication in the data that are stored. Although the removal of duplicated items is a desirable aim in terms of keeping database volume to a minimum, there are occasions when duplication is necessary to provide efficient access to the database. The topic of controlled redundancy is discussed more fully in a later section.

Physical Storage and Data Independence

In order that the *physical* database can be changed as necessary to accommodate user requirements, without the need to alter all applications programs (as is necessary with, for example, a COBOL program - if a file is changed, then any program accessing the file needs to be changed), the way the data is *physically* stored on the storage medium should be *independent* of the *logical* record structures required by applications programs. In a database, records can be stored essentially in two different ways.

☐ Independently - the primary key is used to decide the physical location of a record; frequently this is effected through a *randomizing* process to distribute records efficiently on the storage medium.

☐ In association - records are stored according to their relationship with other records and connections may be made between them with the use of *pointers* (Chapter 26 on Data Structures). A *physical pointer* gives the address where a record is stored and can be used to relate records anywhere in the database; a *logical pointer* is a value from which the physical address can be calculated.

The Physical and Logical Database

A database has to satisfy many users' differing information needs, generally through specially written applications programs, so it is often necessary to add further data items to satisfy changes in users' needs. The software which controls the database must relate to the data at a *data item* level rather than at *record* level because one programmer's logical record requirements may contain some data items which are also required for another programmer's logical record description. The physical database must allow for both. It must be possible for data items to be connected into a variety of *logical record forms*.

Creating the Database

A special language called a *Data Description Language* (DDL) allows the database to be created and changed and the logical data structures to be defined.

Manipulating the Database

A *Data Manipulation Language* (DML) enables the contents of the database to be altered by adding, updating or deleting records. The language is used by programmers to develop applications programs for users of the database.

The functions of both these languages are combined, together with a query language facility in *Structured Query Language* (SQL), which is dealt with later in the chapter.

Database Storage

Because the database must allow for various user applications programs accessing it at the same time, direct access storage must be used. There are many ways of physically organizing the data which are dealt with in the chapter on Data Structures, but whatever method is used it must allow for the variety of logical record forms needed by applications programs.

The applications programmer does not need to know how the data is *physically* stored. The programmer's knowledge of the data held in the database is restricted to the *logical view* required for the program.

The complete or global logical database is termed the *schema*.

The restricted or local logical views provided for different applications programs are termed *subschemas*.

Database Management Systems (DBMS)

In order that each application program may only access the data which it needs for processing or retrieval (that data which is defined in its subschema), a suite of programs referred to as the Database Management System (DBMS) controls the database and prevents accidental or deliberate corruption of data by other applications programs.

An application program cannot access the database without the DBMS. *Figure 15.1* illustrates the relationship between users, application programs, the DBMS and the database:

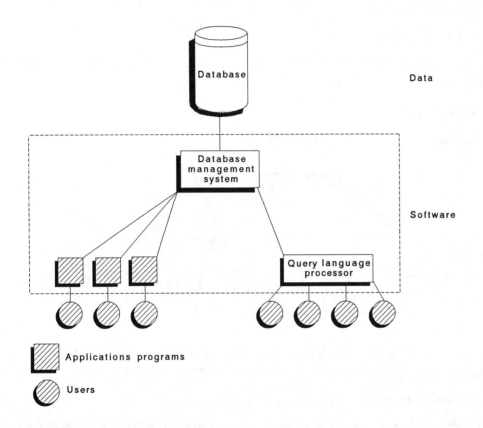

Figure 15.1

A DBMS has the following functions:

- [ ] It is the common link between all applications programs and the database.

- [ ] It facilitates the use and organization of a database and protects the database from accidental or deliberate corruption.

- [ ] It restricts a programmer's logical view of the database to those items of data which are to be used in the applications program being written.

Types of Database

The logical structure of a database can be based upon one of a number of natural data structures which the Database Management System (DBMS) uses to establish links between separate data items. Physical pointers inform the DBMS where the next logical record is to be found. In certain types of database the logical organization of the database is constrained by whatever data structure is used and can therefore be described as *formatted*. Two main categories of data structure are used in such databases:

☐ hierarchical or tree structure;

☐ complex and simple plex structure
(often called network structures).

To avoid the restrictions established by using a particular structure, another increasingly popular method of database management is to use a

☐ relational approach.

To provide a basis for comparison with relational databases it is useful first to examine the data structures used in formatted databases.

Hierarchical or Tree Structure

A hierarchical or tree structure is illustrated in *Figure 15.2*.

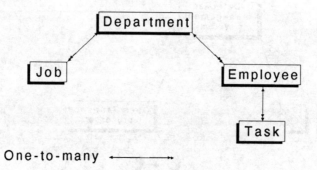

Figure 15.2

Each element is called a *node* and the only node which is not a *member* in any relationship is the *root* at the top of the tree. Three features of this structure need to be identified:

☐ only *one-to-many* relationships are supported.

For example, in the previous Figure, each Department can have many Employees, but each Employee can only belong to one Department. Similarly, each Employee may have more than one Task but each Task can only be carried out by one Employee.

☐ the highest level in the hierarchy has only one node called the *root*.

☐ each node is a member in exactly one *relationship* with a node on a level higher than itself, except for the root node at the top of the tree.

For example, Job and Employee each relate to only a single *parent* node (Department); the root node, Department, is not a member in any relationship.

The main problem with the hierarchical structure is that not all databases fit naturally into it; a record type may require more than one parent. For example, a library database may require a book to be a 'member' in more than one book category, say, Geology and Geography.

Network Data Structures

There are two types of network or plex data structures; complex and simple:

Complex Plex Structure

A complex plex structure is illustrated in *Figure 15.3*.

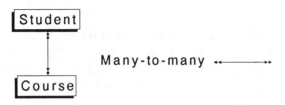

Many-to-many

Figure 15.3

This structure supports many-to-many (complex) relationships.

Thus, in *Figure 15.3*, a Student may be enrolled on one or more Courses and each Course may have many Students.

Whether or not such data structures can be used depends on the Data Description Language (DDL) being used. IBM's DDL called DL/I supports any plex structure but the Codasyl DDL (described later) does not and cannot therefore, be used to describe complex plex structures.

Simple Plex Structure

A simple plex structure is illustrated in *Figure 15.4*.

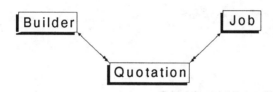

Figure 15.4

This structure supports one-to-many or simple relationships and unlike the tree structure, a node can have more than one parent.

Thus, for example, a Quotation record may be 'owned' by both one Builder and one Job record, but each Builder and Job record could own many Quotation records.

A complex plex structure can be reconstructed if the available software does not support such a structure. For example, the complex plex structure in *Figure 15.3* can be converted to a hierarchical structure or to a simple plex structure. These reconstructions are shown in the *Figures 15.5* and *15.6* respectively.

Complex Plex to Hierarchical

The structure can be converted to two hierarchical or tree structures by duplicating COURSE and STUDENT as follows in *Figure 15.5*; the course and student data will only be duplicated *logically*.

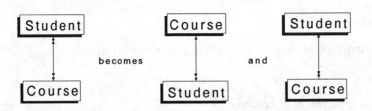

Figure 15.5

Complex Plex to Simple Plex

The simple plex structure in *Figure 15.6* is achieved through the creation of another record, which avoids the need to duplicate the Student and Course data. The relationships are now one-to-many rather than many-to-many. The new record ENROLMENT must contain the information necessary to establish the relationship between the original COURSE and STUDENT records; as in this example, the record identifiers are generally used for this purpose.

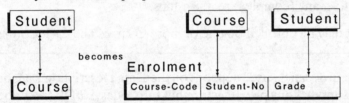

Figure 15.6

An example of a DBMS which supports *simple plex* structures is the CODASYL Database Management System.

The Codasyl logical schema in *Figure 15.7* serves to illustrate this method of database organization.

Codasyl Database Schema for Large Company

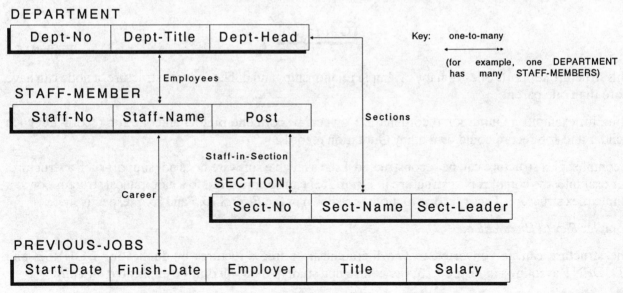

Figure 15.7

The schema can be explained in terms of sets as follows:

There are 4 record types:

1. *Department*

2. *Staff-member*

3. *Section*

4. *Previous-jobs*

Each of 1, 2 and 3 can be retrieved directly by its *record key*, Dept-No, Staff-No and Sect-No respectively. Record type 4 is only accessible via the Staff-member type record. This is reasonable as it would be unusual to search for a Previous-Jobs record without first knowing the identity of the Staff-Member.

There are 4 sets, each of which has an *owner* record and one or more *member* records. For example, one Department will have a number of Staff-Members (a one-to-many relationship). The sets are:

Employees (*owner*, Department/ *member*, Staff-member)

Sections (*owner*, Department/ *member*, Section)

Staff-in-Section (*owner*, Section/ *member*, Staff-member)

Career (*owner*, Staff-member/ *member*, Previous-jobs)

Diagrammatically, a set can be pictured as shown in *Figure 15.8*.

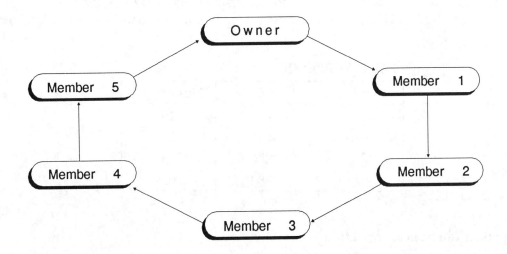

Figure 15.8

For example, referring to *Figure 15.7*, *Department 4* as an owner record may have a number of *Section* member records.

Data Manipulation Language statements could be used to retrieve a Section record directly using its Sect-No or via its Sections Set (owned by Department Record). For example, if the section is in Department No 12:

1   *move 12 to Dept_no*

2   *find any Department*

3   *show Section*

4   *find next Section*

5   *show Section*

Steps 4 and 5 are repeated until the correct Section record is found or the end of set is reached. It should be noticed that a Previous-Jobs record can *only* be found via the Career set and the appropriate Staff-member record.

As with any database, a Codasyl DBMS organizes and accesses the logical database via the *schema* description.

In all formatted databases, the structure defines the route which can be taken through the database, but the programmer/user must know what linkages have been established to be aware of how and what data can be accessed.

Relational DBMS

A fair amount of jargon is associated with this concept but the ideas are simple to understand when related to the more commonly known terms used in traditional filing systems. A *relational* DBMS is designed to handle data organized in two-dimensional table form and a single database is likely to contain a number of such tables. This tabular view of data is easy to understand; everyday examples include telephone directories, train timetables and business reports. An example of tabular data is illustrated in *Figure 15.9*.

PART_SUPPLIER

Part Code	Price	Supplier_No
012	3.25	14
015	0.76	07
016	1.26	14
018	7.84	05

Figure 15.9

A number of points can be made from this:

☐ Each table or 'flat' file is called a *relation* and each entry in the table is a single *data item value*. For example, Part Code 012 is a data item value consisting of 3 characters.

☐ Each column in the relation contains values for a given *data item type*. (The term is used here to be consistent with database jargon; the term *field* is used elsewhere in the book) The set of values for a given data item type is called its *domain*. A domain is identified by its description, that is, the name for the data item type. For example, in *Figure 15.9* the set of values in the second column is called the PRICE domain.

☐ Each row in the relation is a record occurrence and is called a *tuple*.

Establishing Relationships

The power of a relational DBMS lies in its facility to allow separate relations to be manipulated and combined in a variety of ways to establish new relations. Thus, for example, a relation containing details such as the names and addresses of a firm's employees can be combined with a relation detailing the make and registration numbers of cars owned by the employees, to produce a new relation containing the names of employees owning, say, Ford cars. In a formatted database using a simple plex structure, for example, connections between such data would have to be established when the database is constructed; a relational database can leave this task to the programmer or the Database Administrator (DBA), whose role is described later. Consider the example relations shown in *Figure 15.10*.

DEPARTMENT

Dept_No	Dept_Name
A4	Sales
A7	Personnel

EMPLOYEE

Emp_No	Name	Dept	Salary
124	Brown	A4	13000
138	Parks	A7	9500
139	Rodd	A4	14000

Figure 15.10

The important thing to realise is that the existence of a relationship depends on the presence in both relations of a given data item value or values; they may not necessarily have the same data name. Tables in a relational database are related *dynamically* through the values of the information found within them, as in Dept and Dept_No in *Figure 15.10*, rather than via inbuilt physical links. In the simplest types of relational DBMS, that is those used on small business systems, it is the responsibility of the programmer or user to be aware of the existence of common values to link relations together. In a mini or mainframe system owned by a larger organization, this responsibility may lie with a *Database Administrator*, whose task is to control database usage by programmers and users.

The need for common values to establish relationships requires some duplication of data (in the *Figure 15.10* values are duplicated in Dept and Dept_No) and thus some *controlled redundancy*.

Benefits of a Relational DBMS

The attraction of the relational approach is that logical record structures and connections between them are not constrained by pointers using rigid formats such as those provided by the tree and plex structures described earlier. Instead, with some duplication of data or controlled redundancy, a programmer can establish any relationships that need to be made for output specified by users. New relations can be added or existing relations modified as user requirements change.

Relational Database Operation

To illustrate the functioning of a relational database, consider the example relations for a motoring organization, shown in *Figure 15.11*.

CAR

Reg_No	Make	Model	Colour	Owner
A405HPJ	Ford	Fiesta	Red	512
A763YTN	Austin	Montego	White	362
B362XTN	Ford	Sierra	Blue	379
C706LTM	Volvo	360GLT	Silver	516
D198YFT	Austin	Metro	Red	514
F362LTM	Volvo	340GL	White	516

MEMBER

Member_No	Name	Address	Tel_No
362	Williams,C	3 Elm Road	362147
379	Todd,W	6 View Terrace	317653
512	Bone,F	3 Cliff Park	368973
514	Brown,C	12 Dene Road	352168
516	Downes,E	14 Main Street	374615

Figure 15.11

The following Data Manipulation Language (DML) commands may be used to manipulate the relations:

1.   GET CAR

2.   SELECT Reg_No = C706 LTM

3.   JOIN MEMBER (Owner = Member_No.)

4.   PROJECT Reg_No, Name, Address

The commands have the following effects:

1.   Copies the relation CAR into the memory workspace.

2.   Replaces the CAR relation in the workspace with a new relation containing a single tuple from that relation which matches the specified condition, that is, (Reg_No = C706 LTM). Hence the workspace now contains:

   C706 LTM   Volvo 360GLT   Silver   516

3. The relation MEMBER is 'joined' with the single tuple relation to produce a new relation with data items from both. This new relation only contains tuples where the Owner value equals the Member_No value. Thus the workspace now contains:

> **C706 LTM   Volvo   360GLT   Silver   516   Downes, E.**
> **14 Main St   374615**

4. The final command replaces the relation with one containing only the specified or PROJECTED data items; thus the workspace now contains:

> **C706 LTM   Downes, E.   14 Main St**

The production of different outputs from a variety of relations is really a 'cutting and pasting' exercise; it is up to the programmer to establish relationships between different relations in order to establish new ones. GET, SELECT, JOIN and PROJECT are all examples of *relational algebra* commands which are used in a DML for a relational database. Relational algebraic commands are explained in more detail in a later section.

Tuple Identification

To ensure the uniqueness of each tuple, one of the data items should be chosen as a *primary key*. Sometimes it is necessary to use more than one data item to ensure unique identification; this is referred to as a *composite primary key*.

A relational DBMS does not allow duplicate tuples to exist in a relation but this can occur when new relations are formed from operations on other relations.

Referring again to the motoring organization example in *Figure 15.11*, suppose that a programmer used the PROJECT command to extract information from the CAR relation on car makes and their owners.

PROJECT CAR (Make, Owner) gives the relation shown in the *Figure 15.12*; it is invalid because the 4th and 6th tuples are duplicates.

CAR

Make	Owner
Ford	512
Austin	362
Ford	379
Volvo	516*
Austin	514
Volvo	516*

* duplicates

Figure 15.12

The relational DBMS would remove the duplicate to produce the relation in *Figure 15.13* .

CAR

Make	Owner
Ford	512
Austin	362
Ford	379
Volvo	516
Austin	514

Figure 15.13

This is now valid, but note that to uniquely identify a tuple (for example, one Owner may have several cars of the same Make) requires the use of both data items as a composite key.

Data Manipulation

Relations are, in essence, two dimensional flat files and individual tuple manipulation can be carried out using the conventional file handling techniques such as those for COBOL; although there are many occasions when this is appropriate, such techniques do not explore the full power and uniqueness of a relational database. The programmer should regard a relation as a single unit for manipulation and thus be performing operations on groups of tuples, not single tuple occurrences.Operations on relations constitute 'cutting and pasting' exercises to produce new relations as required. A range of relational operators, based on relational algebra, are available for such operations, although not all relational DBMS will provide all of them.

Relational Operators

The most frequently available operators are as follow:

☐ PROJECT

☐ JOIN

☐ SELECT

The PROJECT command specifies that particular data items from a given relation are to be 'projected' or copied to form a new relation; *Figure 15.14* illustrates such a projection. Any resulting duplicated tuples are removed by the DBMS.

COMPUTING_COURSES

Course_No	Course_Title	Location_No	Location_Name
3261	BA Data Proc.	1	Bristol
3275	HND Computing	2	Newcastle
3283	BSc Comp. Science	1	Bristol
3291	BA Data Proc.	3	Leeds
3296	HND Computing	1	Bristol
3301	BSc Comp. Science	4	Dundee
3305	BA Data Proc.	2	Newcastle

Figure 15.14

PROJECT LOCATION(Location_No, Location_Name)

produces the relation in *Figure 15.15*:

LOCATION

Location_No	Location_Name
1	Bristol
2	Newcastle
3	Leeds
4	Dundee

Figure 15.15

Thus, a new relation named LOCATION, consisting of two data items, Location_No and Location_Name has been copied into the workspace. The existing relation COMPUTING_COURSES remains intact. Note that duplicated tuples which would have resulted from the projection have been removed from the new relation.

PROJECT COURSES(Course_No, Course_Title)

produces the relation in *Figure 15.16*:

COURSES

Course_No	Course_Title
3261	BA Data Proc.
3275	HND Computing
3283	BSc Comp. Science
3291	BA Data Proc.
3296	HND Computing
3301	BSc Comp. Science
3305	BA Data Proc.

Figure 15.16

JOINing two relations results in the linking of tuples from each relation to give a new relation with data items from both. For example, the JOIN operation can be used to produce a list of criminals, their former legitimate occupation (if any), and crime from two separate relations.

Consider the relations in *Figure 15.17*.

CRIMINAL

Inmate_No	Crime
1341	Burglary
1432	Robbery
1439	Burglary
1533	Fraud
1544	GBH

FORMER_JOB

Inmate_No	Name	Age	Occupation
1341	Williams, F	35	Plumber
1432	Tomkins,S	42	Unemployed
1439	Rushton,C	26	Van Driver
1533	Perkins,M	23	Bank Clerk
1544	Baker,K	53	Unemployed

Figure 15.17

Using the symbol * to represent the JOIN operator, the expression:

FULL-DETAILS = CRIMINAL * FORMER-JOB

produces the relation in *Figure 15.18*:

FULL-DETAILS

Inmate_No	Name	Age	Occupation	Crime
1341	Williams, F	35	Plumber	Burglary
1432	Tomkins,S	42	Unemployed	Robbery
1439	Rushton,C	26	Van Driver	Burglary
1533	Perkins,M	23	Bank Clerk	Fraud
1544	Baker,K	53	Unemployed	GBH

Figure 15.18

The PROJECT operation can be used to select certain data items, as shown in *Figure 15.19*;

PROJECT PART-DETAILS (Inmate-No, Name, Crime)

PART_DETAILS

Inmate_No	Name	Crime
1341	Williams, F	Burglary
1432	Tomkins,S	Robbery
1439	Rushton,C	Burglary
1533	Perkins,M	Fraud
1544	Baker,K	GBH

Figure 15.19

The PROJECT and JOIN operations apply to all tuples in the effected relations; to allow the selection of individual or groups of tuples, (known as set processing) the SELECT operation can be used.

For example, the statement CRIMINAL (Crime = Burglary) would result in the selection of two tuples (the 'Burglary set') from the relation CRIMINAL in *Figure 15.17*, to produce the relation in *Figure 15.20*.

Inmate_No	Crime
1341	Burglary
1432	Burglary

Figure 15.20

Complex Expressions

By using multiple conditions, including AND, OR, < (less than), > (greater than) and =, complex selections can be made. For example referring to *Figure 15.18*, the expression;

SELECT FULL-DETAILS (Crime = Burglary OR Crime = Robbery)

would result in the selection of criminal records of those serving sentences for either burglary or robbery.

Similarly, for example, to determine the names of criminals over 30 years of age and convicted of burglary, the expression;

PROJECT BURGLAR:Crime = Burglar yAND Age >30 (Name)

would produce the Name value (*Figure 15.21*) in the only tuple satisfying these conditions:

BURGLAR

Name
Williams,F

Figure 15.21

Structured Query Language (SQL)

Many new database packages are providing a Structured Query Language (SQL). SQL (developed by IBM) is a *non-procedural* language and as such belongs to the group of programming languages known as 4th Generation Languages(4GLs); this means that programmers and trained users can specify what they want from a database without having to specify how to do it. *Procedural* languages such as COBOL require the programmer to detail explicitly how a program must 'navigate' through a file or database to obtain the necessary output. The programmer must, for example, code procedures such as 'read the first master record, process it, read the next, process it and so on until the end of the file is reached'. As is explained below, SQL is an attempt to provide a language which includes the facilities normally provided separately by a Data Description Language, a Data Manipulation Language and a query language (to allow 'on-demand' queries by users).

Features of SQL

The following example illustrates the features of SQL by showing how a programmer or trained user could use SQL to access a database without specifying procedures.

An Extract from a Company Database

EMPLOYEE

Emp_Num	Name	Dept	Salary
123	Johnson,W	A5	10000
124	King,H	A6	12000
125	Thompson,R	A5	9000

DEPARTMENT

Dept_Code	Dept_Name
A5	Sales
A6	Accounts

Figure 15.22

Selection by Criteria

Referring to *Figure 15.22*, if the Name and Salary of EMPLOYEE 124 is required, the SQL statements may take the following form:

> SELECT Name, Salary
>
> FROM EMPLOYEE
>
> WHERE Emp_Num = 124

The output would be as shown in *Figure 15.23*.

Name	Salary
H.King	12000

Figure 15.23

SQL supports all the functions expected of a relational language including the operators, JOIN and PROJECT, for example, described earlier.

Updating the Database

SQL can also change values in a database; for example referring to *Figure 15.22*, to give all employees in the A5 (Sales) department a 6 per cent pay increase, the following statements may be used:

> UPDATE EMPLOYEE
>
> SET Salary = Salary * 1.06
>
> WHERE Dept-Code = A5

SQL has built-in functions and arithmetic operators to allow the grouping or sorting of data and the calculation of, for example, average, minimum and maximum values in a particular column or domain.

Defining the Database

As a multi-purpose database language, SQL can be used to define as well as manipulate and retrieve data. This definition function is traditionally carried out using a separate Data Description Language (DDL) but SQL incorporates this facility for implementing the logical schema for a database. For example, to create a new relation or 'table' called QUALIFICATIONS the following statements may be entered:

> CREATE TABLE QUALIFICATION
>
> (Emp-Num CHAR (3)
>
> Qual VARCHAR (20));

The table or relation would contain two data item types, namely, Emp_Num with a fixed length of three characters and Qual with a variable number of characters up to twenty.

Following creation of the relation, data can be entered immediately if required.

Modifying the Database Definition

Relations can be modified to allow for the removal or addition of new data items, according to changes in user requirements. Existing data does not have to be reorganized and applications programs unaffected by data changes do not have to be rewritten. The independence of the logical database from the applications programs is known as *logical data independence* and constitutes one of the features of databases described earlier in this chapter.

Two major aims are inherent in the design of SQL. Firstly, as a non-procedural language it is expected to increase programmer productivity and reduce the time and costs involved in application development; secondly SQL allows easier access to data for the purposes of on-demand or ad hoc queries.

Benefits and Drawbacks of Databases in General

☐ Apart from controlled redundancy, there is no unnecessary duplication of data as occurs in traditional filing systems. Apart from the economic advantage, this means that transactions can update all effected areas of the database through a single input.

☐ Because of the single input principle, there is less chance of inconsistency as may occur if the same transaction is keyed in several times to different files. Equally, of course, an incorrect entry will mean that all applications programs using the data will be working with the wrong data value.

☐ The opportunities for obtaining comprehensive information are greatly improved with a central pool of data.

☐ On-demand or ad hoc enquiries are possible through the use of a query language.

☐ Security opportunities are enhanced because access to a single database can be more readily controlled than is possible with a system based on numerous separate files. On the other hand, database design and creation is a complex process and the failure of a database affects all applications which make use of it.

Database Design

Design is an important pre-requisite for database construction; for example, a common misuse of a relational database is to define one huge relation containing all the data items required by the applications programs. Thus, for example, a database constructed for the maintenance of student academic records may contain a single relation consisting of twenty or thirty data items ranging from student name, address, and date of entry to all assignment and exam grades for all subjects studied within a given course. Clearly, such a database is unwieldy when, for example, a list of student names and addresses is all that is required by a user. The following sections describe some of the more important concepts and techniques relating to proper database design.

Entities

A relational database should contain a number of logically separate relations, each corresponding to a given subject or part-subject. *Entities* are the objects of the real world that are relevant to a particular information system. The term entity is normally used to refer to each separately identified subject or part-subject; for example, in an Academic database, the following entities may be identified:

STUDENT; COURSE; TUTOR; EDUCATION_HISTORY; EXAM_GRADES

A separate relation would be established for each of these entities.

Relationships

Any particular database contains a variety of entities, which by virtue of the fact that they form part of the data requirements for that database, are related in some way to one another. Entities do not exist in isolation, but are associated with one another by *relationships* which may be classified as:

☐ *one-to-many*. For example, a particular purchase order can only be sent to one supplier; however each supplier is sent many purchase orders;

☐ *many-to-many*. For example, a stock item may be contained in many separate orders and each order may contain many stock items.

These relationships are illustrated diagrammatically in the earlier section on hierarchical and network data structures.

Attributes

An entity has a number of properties or *attributes* relating to it and which are of interest to the users; for example, an entity, Personnel, may have the attributes of Employee#, Surname, Initials and Department#. These attributes determine the data items required and how they are to be stored as records in the database. It is not always necessary to have all the attributes for an entity stored in the same record in the database, but it is essential to be able to associate with each entity all its attributes, so that the information is properly presented. Thus, one entity does not necessarily correspond to one record - a programmer's logical record view is unlikely to correspond to the physical make-up and arrangement of records.

Some attributes, for example, Surname and Initials, are descriptive, whilst one (in this case, Employee#) forms a *unique identifier*. Attributes can be classified, therefore, as being either *identifying* or *non-identifying*. These forms are illustrated below, the unique identifier being underlined.

PERSONNEL(__Employee#__, Surname, Initials, Department#)

Sometimes, more than one attribute is needed to identify entity occurrences uniquely; such attributes form a *composite identifier*. An example of such a key is given below.

ORDER-LINE(__Order#__, __Item#__, Description, Price, Quantity)

Both Order# and Item# are needed to identify a particular order line on an order form.

Data Analysis

This process is concerned with establishing what the entities, attributes and relationships, for any given database, should be. In order to make such an analysis, it is obviously necessary to have knowledge of the organization to which the information relates, because there will be certain items of information which will only have significance to that particular organization.

Normalization

Normalization is a technique established by E.F. Codd to simplify the structure of data as it is *logically* viewed by the programmer or user. The data is systematically analysed to establish whether a particular data item type should be an entity in its own right or simply an attribute of some other entity. Once entities and attributes have been established, relationships between them must be established. Normalization is a step-by-step process for analysing data into its constituent *entities* and *attributes*. There are three stages of normalization described here, though there are others which are beyond the scope of this text.

To illustrate the process of normalization, consider the student registration forms shown in *Figure 15.24.* (a and b)

Student Number	F135654		
Name	James Sanderson		
Address	3 Beech Close, Warrington, WR3 2BH		
Course Code	**Course Code**	**Tutor Name**	**Tutor Code**
4PDCS1	Computing	R. Watkin	124
4PDNE1	Electronics	T. Parks	133
4PDMA1	Mathematics	L. Williams	146

Figure 15.24(a)

Student Number Name Address	G234563 Paul Harrison 123 Newcastle Road, Sunderland, SR3 2RJ		
Course Code	**Course Code**	**Tutor Name**	**Tutor Code**
4PDCS1	Computing	R. Watkin	124
4PDNE1	Electronics	T. Thomas	133
4PDFR1	French	J. Teneur	118
4PDGE1	German	K. Roberts	166

Figure 15.24(b)

Notice that the course titles are repeated on each form.

First Normal Form (1NF)

Treated as a single entity, the structure could be described as follows.

STUDENT (Stud#, Stud-Name, Stud-Address, [Crse-Code, Crse-Title, Tut#, Tut-Name])

The unique identifier (primary key), Stud#, is underlined. Each student registration form (*Figure 15.24*) may show enrolment on several courses and the attribute types, Crse-Code, Crse-Title, Tut# and Tut-Name can be identified as *repeating groups*.

The first stage of normalization demands the removal of any repeating groups. This is achieved by creating a new entity, ENROLMENT, to store details of individual enrolments, the uniqueness of each being established with a composite identifier comprising Stud# and Crse-Code. The entities are now in first normal form (1NF) and this is indicated by suffixing each entity name with a 1.

> **STUDENT-1(Stud#, Stud-Name, Stud-Address)**
>
> **ENROLMENT-1(Stud#, Crse-Code, Crse-Title, Tut#, Tut-Name)**

The two entities and their attributes are now in 1NF, that is, there are no repeating groups. To relate an ENROLMENT tuple to the relevant STUDENT tuple requires that Stud# is duplicated in both relations. A composite key consisting of Stud# and Crse-Code allows unique identification of each ENROLMENT tuple.

Thus, to ensure that entities and attributes are in first normal form requires the removal of repeating groups of attributes, rewriting them as new entities. The identifier of the original entity is always included as an attribute of any such new entity, although it is not essential for it to form part of the identifier of the new entity.

Some necessary *data redundancy* is created by including Stud# in both entities, to allow a given student to be connected with a particular enrolment. Such duplication of data does not necessarily mean an increased use of storage because normalization is concerned with the *logical structure* of the data and not with the ways in which the data is physically organized.

Second Normal Form

The second stage of normalization ensures that all non-identifying attributes are *functionally dependent* on the identifying attribute (the primary key); if the identifier is composite (comprising more that one attribute), then non-identifying attributes must be functionally dependent on the whole of the identifier. Functional dependence indicates, for example, that the value of p determines the value of q and can be illustrated diagrammatically as follows.

Thus, from the entities

STUDENT-1(<u>Stud#</u>, Stud-Name, Stud-Address)

ENROLMENT-1(<u>Stud#</u>, <u>Crse-Code</u>, Crse-Title, Tut#, Tut-Name)

it can be seen that Tut# and Tut-Name each depend on both parts of the composite identifier (<u>Stud#</u>, <u>Crse-Code</u>); *Figure 15.25* shows an arrowed line connecting the box which surrounds both attributes to Tut# and Tut-Name. However, Crse-Title is not functionally dependent on the whole of the composite identifier, only on Crse-Code; accordingly an arrowed line only connects the Crse-Code and Crse-Title boxes.

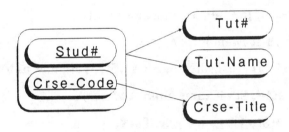

Figure 15.25

The second stage of normalization is achieved by the creation of a new entity, COURSE-2, with the attributes Crse-Code (identifier) and Crse-Title. The entities now become

STUDENT-2(<u>Stud#</u>, Stud-Name, Stud-Address)

ENROLMENT-2(<u>Stud#</u>, <u>Crse-Code</u>, Tut#, Tut-Name)

COURSE-2(<u>Crse-Code</u>, Crse-Title)

with the suffix 2 to indicate that all entities and attributes are now in second normal form.

Conversion of entities and attributes to second normal form brings advantages apart from the avoidance of some duplication. The entry of new data into the database is also facilitated. Suppose, for example, that a new course is to be added to the database and that the data is stored as arranged after the first stage of normalization; the entry could not be made until the first enrolment for that particular course. Additionally, if an enrolment for that course does not happen to exist, then no information concerning the course, can be extracted from the database.

To summarize, this second stage of normalization requires the identification and separation into new entities, of non-identifying attributes which are *not* functionally dependent on their identifying attribute, or in the case of a composite identifier, the *whole* of the identifier.

Third Normal Form

This stage is concerned with finding any functional dependencies between non-identifying attributes. Continuing with the example of student enrolments and with the entities and attributes in second normal form,

> **STUDENT-2(<u>Stud#</u>, Stud-Name, Stud-Address)**
>
> **ENROLMENT-2(<u>Stud#</u>, <u>Crse-Code</u>, Tut#, Tut-Name)**
>
> **COURSE-2(<u>Crse-Code</u>, Crse-Title)**

the functional dependencies can be illustrated as shown in *Figure 15.26*:

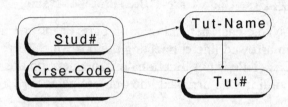

Figure 15.26

Again, the problem is solved by the creation of a new entity,

> **TUTOR-3(<u>Tut#</u>, Tut-Name)**

The entities in third normal form (indicated by the suffix, 3) are now as follow:

> **STUDENT-3(<u>Stud#</u>, Stud-Name, Stud-Address)**
>
> **ENROLMENT-3(<u>Stud#</u>, <u>Crse-Code</u>, Tut#,)**
>
> **COURSE-3(<u>Crse-Code</u>, Crse-Title)**
>
> **TUTOR-3(<u>Tut#</u>, Tut-Name)**

To summarize, data is in *third normal form* when there are no functional dependencies between non-identifying attributes. The attributes are now *mutually independent*.

Database Administrator (DBA)

A database administrator (DBA) appointed with a corporate function has special responsibility for:

> ☐ database design and development;
>
> ☐ selection of database software;
>
> ☐ database maintenance;
>
> ☐ database accuracy and security.

A DBA should have a working knowledge of both the DBMS and the organization. A DBA will supervise the addition of new data items to the database (changes to the schema). Supervision of the *data dictionary* is also the DBA's responsibility (see next paragraph).

Techniques for Database Administration

Data Dictionaries

A data dictionary system is a data processing department's own information system, with the database administrator, systems analysts and programmers as the main users; it should contain information *about the data* in the database, including descriptions of entities (record types) and attributes (data item types), the applications programs which use them, together with associated validation controls. The dictionary's main role is to ensure consistent data usage; frequently, synonyms are used (different data names are often used by different functional areas of an organization to refer to the same data item type) and the dictionary must record their use accordingly to prevent duplication.

Database Recovery

Recovery techniques can be used in certain circumstances to recover lost data when a database is corrupted. Most recovery techniques depend on making a *dump* (copy) of the whole (or a selected part) of the data in the database. Recovery of a database requires:

☐ that the cause of the failure be diagnosed and remedied;

☐ replacement of the corrupted database with the most recent dump of the database;

☐ updating of the database with all the transactions and amendments which occurred since the last dump until the time of the database's failure.

Difficulties are apparent in this procedure; re-processing may take a long time and all updating transactions which have taken place since the last dump must be recorded, together with their sequence of entry, since the order of processing can determine the eventual state of the database. To allow for this, a DBMS will record each entry in a sequential file or transaction log; re-processing can then take place in the correct sequence, without the need for any re-keying of data.

Data Sharing and Data Integrity

Sharing of data by different users is fundamental to the database concept and the DBMS has to allow for it, whilst at the same time protecting the *integrity* of the database. Such access may be through different applications programs or through the same one. Database integrity is not affected by accesses which only read data; no matter how many users are reading the same data, its integrity will not be affected. *Concurrent updates* present the possibility of updates being lost.

Consider, for example a database schema which held the following stock record type.

STOCK(Item#, Item-Description, Quantity-held)

Two applications programs PR1 and PR2 are updating the Quantity-held for Item# 3254; following the delivery of units of that item, PR1 is to increase the balance by 200, whilst PR2 is to reduce it by 150 in respect of stock issues. If the initial value of Quantity-held is 200, then the following sequence of events could occur:

(i)   PR1 reads Stock record, Item# 3254;

(ii) PR2 reads Stock record, Item# 3254;

(iii) PR1 increases Quantity-held by 200 and re-writes the record to the database;

(iv) PR2 decreases Quantity-held by 150 and re-writes the record to the database.

At this stage, Stock record, Item#3254, would show a Quantity-held value of 50, when it should be 250. This error has occurred because PR2 read the record before PR1 had re-written its updated version to the database.

With the use of *integrity locks*, a DBMS can ensure that any program which reads a record for the purpose of updating, must result in the *locking* of that record against access by any other updating program, until the updated version has been re-written to the database. Programs accessing the record for *reading purposes only*, are not prevented access by an integrity lock.

Integrity locks can be implemented through the use of an additional data item within a record, the value of which can be set to *on*, as and when required. Integrity locks can present their own problems, but they are not of concern in this text.

Database Security

Security is concerned with controlling access to data, both to prevent its accidental or deliberate corruption and, in the case of confidential data concerning individuals or organizations, to maintain appropriate *privacy*.

Access Control Mechanisms

Identification, Authentication and Authorization. Before being granted access to a database, users must *identify* themselves, normally with an assigned account number or identification code. *Authentication* of a user's identity normally requires provision of a *password*, known only to the system and its legitimate users; the Chapter on System Controls examines the topic of passwords in more detail. The system holds information, supplied initially by the database administrator (DBA), on each user or category of user. This information is held to allow the system to carry out its identification and authentication procedures and to determine the level of authorization - the kinds of access any particular user is permitted.

Another mechanism for controlling access uses *access control locks* and *access control keys*. Consider the following example of how a very simple access lock could work; the extracts of a schema description and application program are coded in the Codasyl Data Description Language and Data Manipulation Language.

```
Schema Extract


RECORD NAME IS CLIENT
   CLIENT-NUM     PICTURE 9 (8)
   DATE-OF-BIRTH PICTURE 9 (6)
   BALANCE        PICTURE 9 (6) V99
      ACCESS CONTROL LOCK FOR GET IS 'ZEBRA'

Program Extract


MOVE 'ZEBRA' TO KEY-CHECK
USE FOR ACCESS CONTROL ON GET FOR CLIENT
```

The character string 'ZEBRA' is declared as being the access control lock on the command GET for the data item BALANCE, only. Thus, the Balance data cannot be used by an application program unless the access control key 'ZEBRA' is provided and transferred to the location called KEY-CHECK, where it is compared by the DBMS with the access control lock. If the values do not agree then access is prevented to the Balance data. This is a fairly trivial example and not particularly secure, as a glance at the schema listing would reveal the access control lock's value; more sophisticated ways of assigning the access control lock are generally used.

Levels of Authorization. A fundamental principle of security is that access is limited to those persons who require it and a degree of access necessary to their jobs. For example, authorization to alter schema or sub-schema descriptions may be limited to the DBA; user A may be given access to particular data for enquiry, but not for alteration purposes, whilst User B may be the only person authorized to change prices in the Stock File.

16 *Systems Analysis - an overview*

Systems analysis can be defined as *a disciplined process which begins with the establishment of user requirements for a given application and concludes with the implementation of a fully operational system.* The work of systems analysis has been carried out by trained professionals since the introduction of early mainframe computers but its processes are equally appropriate to the task of computerizing small business applications. Many businesses will not employ specialist staff capable of carrying out an analysis of their computer requirements and may employ the services of an outside consultant. The main stages of systems analysis - the *system life cycle* - are given in *Figure 16.1*.

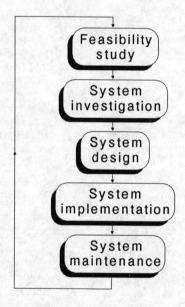

Figure 16.1

The following sections give a brief overview of their functions within the systems analysis process.

Feasibility Study

The aim of this stage is to establish whether or not a proposal for the computerization of a particular application is worthwhile or feasible. In simple terms, the feasibility study has to answer questions such as follow:

- ☐ Will computerization achieve the users' objectives?

- ☐ What type of system will be most suitable?

- ☐ Will it be financially worthwhile?

System Investigation and Design

Assuming that the feasibility study produces a recommendation to proceed with computerization of an application (there may, of course, be several), then before any system specification is produced, an analysis has to be made of the processes and procedures involved in the application under consideration. For example, an analysis of Sales Order Processing should identify how orders are received, the order forms used and the procedures necessary to fulfil orders. Analysis is not simply the recording of an application as it currently operates. Through a variety of information gathering methods such as interviewing and observation, the requirements of a new system should be identified. Although the needs of the organization will be of paramount importance, employees are more likely to be concerned with matters of job satisfaction and working conditions. Successful implementation of a computerized system requires a great deal of work, involvement and willingness to co-operate by everyone concerned. If staff feel that their views have been considered such cooperation is more likely. Although users' views are important an outside observer can often identify problems with current practice which have never been questioned. A systems analyst from outside the firm needs therefore, to possess qualities of tact and diplomacy if his or her views are to be considered.

The process of design should produce a complete picture of the input, processing, storage and output requirements of the new system. The picture will include narrative descriptions, as well as flowcharts illustrating clerical procedures, data flows and the role of the computer in broad outline. The design of a computerized system should include as many improvements suggested in the investigation stage as is practicable and it will almost certainly be necessary to question users further when, for example, problems arise in the implementation of particular system requirements. Compromises will have to be made between what is desirable and what is practicable. Management and users may have specified requirements during the investigation stage which prove either too expensive or extremely difficult to satisfy.

System Implementation

System implementation or 'going live' involves a range of preparatory activities, although the importance of each will depend on the type and size of the project and the number of people involved. The main activities are as follow:

- [ ] *development and/or testing of software.* If an 'off the shelf' system is chosen, then no development time is necessary, but testing is still vital;

- [ ] *file conversion.* This is probably the most time-consuming activity in that all data relating to the application, which is currently held in manual files, has to be encoded onto the chosen magnetic storage medium. Although a laborious task, accuracy is obviously vital and both software and clerical checking procedures should be employed;

- [ ] *staff training and education.* This may take a variety of forms but may be part of the proposals put forward by the chosen supplier. It is an extremely important activity if the system's effectiveness is to be maximized and if staff are to feel happy and confident in its operation;

- [ ] *introduction of new clerical procedures.* The computer software which has been developed or purchased forms only part of the whole information processing system and if the whole system is to function correctly, the computer processing aspect has to be supported by the clerical procedures designed to work with it. Part of staff training, therefore, has to be dedicated to purely clerical tasks such as the preparation of input data or source documents;

☐ *choice of a changeover or 'going live' plan.* A number of alternatives are available and each has costs and benefits associated with it. Parallel running, for example, requires that the old and new systems are operated alongside one another until the new system is fully tested. Although this minimizes the risks consequent upon system failure, it is an expensive option in that it involves a great deal of staff time. A 'once and for all' changeover is obviously less expensive if the new system works but failure could mean catastrophe for the business. The plan used will depend on a number of factors, for example, the importance of the system to the success of the business.

System Maintenance

After its initial introduction a system should be flexible to the changing needs of the business. An allowance for the business's expansion should be made in the original system specification and the supplier should be able to satisfy those expansion needs as and when necessary. Equally, advances in hardware technology and the sophistication of software mean that a system soon becomes outdated. Even if a business chooses not to take advantage of improved software, hardware is likely to become less reliable and will need replacement after about five years of business use. Agreements on software and hardware maintenance should be established with the supplier and formalized in the contract signed by purchaser and supplier.

17 *The Feasibility Study*

The traditional purpose of a feasibility study is to determine whether or not the purchase of a computer system can be justified. The study has to answer two fundamental questions:

- ☐ Can the envisaged applications be carried out by a computer system more efficiently than with existing facilities?

- ☐ Will a computer system be economically viable?

Since the early 1970s, prices of all types of computer system have fallen dramatically and their power has increased to such a degree that, for example, microcomputers challenge the minicomputer in their range of applications. This may be part of the reason why many organizations find it difficult to justify undertaking a detailed feasibility study and argue that no matter how limited their needs there is a computer system to satisfy them at a cost-effective price; it is only necessary to decide on its best application(s). Although this is an understandable view, it should be remembered that any item of equipment should be justified in terms of its costs and benefits to the business and that a computer system should be no exception. Although there are few businesses which cannot benefit from computerization at all, the process of carrying out a feasibility study disciplines the purchaser to think carefully about how it is to be used. In modifying the purpose of a feasibility study, the previous questions can be replaced by the following:

- ☐ Which applications can be computerized to give most benefit to the organization?

- ☐ What type of computer will be required?

- ☐ What are the likely acquisition and running costs?

- ☐ What are the likely implications, especially those concerning personnel and organizational procedures?

Pressures for Computerization

There are many and various pressures which can 'trigger' the thought of using a computer, either for the first time or, where a computer is already installed, for other applications still operated manually. Some examples are as follows:

(i)   business is expanding and to cope with the increased workload it appears that the only the alternative to computerization is increased staffing;

(ii) a business is growing at such a rate that more information is needed to manage it properly. To obtain the information manually is too time-consuming and by the time it has been gathered is probably out-of-date;

(iii)   staff are being asked to work regular and increasing amounts of overtime and backlogs of work are building up.

(iv)   customers are complaining about the speed and quality of the service provided;

(v)   where stock is involved, it is difficult to keep track of stock levels and while some customer orders cannot be filled because of stock shortages, other stock is 'gathering dust' on the shelves.

(vi)   a great deal of advertising literature is constantly reminding business management that they are out-of-date and at a disadvantage with their competitors;

(vii)   other businesses providing a similar service use a computer;

Examples (i), (ii) and (iii) suggest that the business is operating successfully and needs to take on extra staff or streamline its systems. Examples (iv) and (v) may be symptomatic of generally poor business management and in such cases, computerization alone may not solve the problems. Examples (vi) and (vii) may tempt the management to computerize simply 'to keep up with the Jones's'. Although a computerization programme resulting directly from one or more such pressures may be completely successful and worthwhile, the pressure itself should not be the reason for computerization. Instead, management should establish the organizational objectives they wish to achieve through computerization.

Establishing Objectives for Computerization

It is important for management to establish what they are trying to achieve in terms of the overall objectives of the business and in the light of this, the objectives of the systems which contribute to their achievement. For example, two major business objectives may be to improve the delivery of customers' orders and to minimize the stock levels which tie up valuable cash resources. The achievement of these objectives may involve contributions from several different information processing systems and the list may include:

☐ Stock Control - records stock movements and controls stock levels;

☐ Purchasing - responsible for the ordering of new supplies from suppliers;

☐ Sales Order Processing - receives customers' orders and initiates the process of order fulfilment;

☐ Purchase Ledger - the accounting record of amounts owed and paid to suppliers of stock;

☐ Invoicing - the production of invoices requesting payment from customers for goods supplied;

☐ Sales Ledger - the accounting record of amounts owing by and received from customers for goods supplied;

These and other applications within a business are interconnected by the information which flows between them. Such connections can be illustrated with the use of data flow diagrams (DFD), which are described in Chapter 21.

Establishing Priorities for Computerization

It is not generally advisable or even practicable to attempt the computerization of more than one or two applications at the same time, even if they are closely linked. In any case, it is likely that some applications make a greater contribution to the achievement of the required business objectives than do others. Thus, the applications which are going to bring greatest benefit to the business should be computerized first.

Establishing Individual System Objectives

Before any single application can be computerized, it is necessary to establish its objectives clearly because users may have become so used to its procedures that they no longer question their purpose. It is self-evident that before any informed judgements can be made on the design of a computerized system, the objectives of the relevant application must first be clearly understood.

The following list for stock control serves to illustrate the definition of such objectives.

- ☐ to maintain levels of stock which will be sufficient to meet customer orders promptly;

- ☐ to provide a mechanism which removes the need for excessively high safety margins of stock to cover customer orders. This is usually effected by setting minimum stock levels which the computer can use to report variations below these levels;

- ☐ to provide automatic re-ordering of stock items which fall below minimum levels;

- ☐ to provide management with up-to-date information on stock levels and values of stocks held.

The Feasibility Report

The Feasibility Report should contain the following sections:

Terms of Reference

These should set out the original purpose of the study, as agreed by management and detail the business objectives to be achieved, for example:

- ☐ the improvement of customer service, such that orders are delivered within 24 hours of order receipt;

- ☐ the provision of more up-to-date management information on current stock levels and projected customer demand;

- ☐ a tighter control of the business's cash resources, primarily through better stock management.

Applications Considered for Computerization

The applications which may assist the achievement of the business objectives set out in the Terms of Reference are listed, for example:

- ☐ stock control;

- [ ] purchasing;
- [ ] sales order processing;
- [ ] invoicing;
- [ ] accounts.

System Investigations

For each application under consideration there should be:

- [ ] a description of the existing system;
- [ ] an assessment of its good and bad points. For example, the sales order processing system may be slow to process customer orders and this results in poor delivery times, which in turn causes customers to take away their business;
- [ ] an estimate of the costs of the existing system. For example, apart from the cost of staffing, an estimate has to be made of the cost of lost business, which could be avoided with an improved system.

Envisaged System Requirements

This section should detail, in general terms, those aspects of each application which need to be improved and a broad outline of how each system may operate following computerization. Of course, it is still possible that not all applications will benefit from computerization but can be improved by other methods.

Costs of Development and Implementation

These will include both capital costs and revenue or running costs. Capital costs are likely to be incurred for the following:

- [ ] computer hardware;
- [ ] systems software and software packages (either 'off-the-shelf' or 'tailor-made');
- [ ] installation charges for hardware and software;
- [ ] staff training.

Revenue costs include those for the maintenance and insurance of the system. In addition, unless there are existing computer specialists in the organization, additional suitable staff may need to be recruited.

Timescale for Implementation

This will depend on the scale of the operation, the type of application and whether or not packaged software is to be used.

Expected Benefits

These are more difficult to quantify than the costs but may include, for example:

- [ ] estimated savings in capital expenditure on typewriters and photocopiers;

☐ more efficient stock management allows customer service to be maintained whilst keeping stock levels lower. This releases valuable cash resources and reduces possible interest charges on borrowed capital;

☐ expansion in business turnover, without the need for extra staff and reduced overtime requirements.

Other Considerations

The staff have to support any development for it to be properly successful and this usually means consultation at an early stage in the feasibility study and the provision of a proper staff training programme. Customers must also be considered. For example, when a customer receives a computer-produced invoice it should be at least as easy to understand as the type it replaced.

Assuming that the feasibility study concludes that the proposed computerization is worthwhile, according to the criteria set out in the report, then more detailed investigation and design can follow.

18 *System Investigation and Design*

If the feasibility report gives the go-ahead to the computerization project, then a more detailed investigation of each candidate system begins. The facts gathered about each system will be analysed in terms of their bearing on the design and implementation of a computerized version. The objectives of the analysis are to gain a thorough knowledge of the operational characteristics of the current system and to settle, in a fair amount of detail, the way in which a computerized system will operate. It is extremely important that the new system does not simply computerize existing procedures. The design should, as far as possible, ignore existing departmental structures which may inhibit the introduction of different and improved procedures.

For example, it may be that customer credit limits are fixed by the Accounts Department and that Sales staff have to refer to the Accounts Department before accepting a customer order. A computerized system may allow Sales staff to access credit limits directly without reference to the Accounts Department. This method could be used in most cases and the computer could indicate any customer accounts which needed to be specially referred to the Accounts staff.

The aim of the investigation and design process is to produce a specification of users' requirements in documented form. This is referred to as the Statement of User Requirements and will be used to tender for supply of hardware and software.

Fact-finding Methods

There are several methods which can be used to gather facts about a system:

- ☐ Interviewing;
- ☐ Questionnaires;
- ☐ Examination of records and procedure manuals;
- ☐ Examination of documents;
- ☐ Observation.

Each method has its own particular advantages and disadvantages and the method or methods chosen will depend on the specific circumstances surrounding the investigation, for example, the size of the business, the number of staff employed and their location and distribution.

Interviewing

This method has much to recommend it, in that the facts can be gathered directly from the person or persons who have experience of the system under investigation. On the other hand, a business with a number of geographically distributed branches makes the process of extensive interviewing expensive and time-consuming. Further, interviewing skills need to be acquired if the process is to be effective. The interviewer needs to know how to gain the confidence of the interviewee and ensure that the information which is given will be of value in the design of the new system. Questions need to be phrased unambiguously in order that the interviewee supplies the information actually required and a checklist of points will help to ensure that all relevant questions are asked. Of course, the interview may need to 'stray' from the points in the checklist, if it becomes apparent that the interviewee is able to provide relevant information not previously considered. For example, clerical procedures may be designed quite satisfactorily but may be made less effective because of personality conflicts between staff. Such tensions may only be revealed through personal interview.

The interviewer also needs to detect any unsatisfactory responses to questions and possibly use alternative methods to glean the required information. Some possible unsatisfactory responses are given below:

refusal to answer. Such refusal may indicate, for example, that set procedures are not being followed and that the member of staff does not wish to be 'incriminated';

answer with irrelevant information. It may be that the question is ambiguous and has to be re-phrased in order to elicit the required information;

answer with insufficient information. If a system is to be designed which covers all foreseeable user requirements and operational circumstances, it is important that the analyst has all relevant information;

inaccurate answer. The interviewer may or may not be aware that an inaccurate answer has been given but it is important that other sources of information are used to cross-check answers.

Questionnaires

Questionnaires are useful when only a small amount of information is required from a large number of people, but to provide accurate responses, questions need to be unambiguous and precise. The questionnaire has a number of advantages over the interview:

☐ each respondent is asked exactly the same questions, so responses can be analysed according to the pre-defined categories of information;

☐ the lack of personal contact allows the respondent to feel completely at ease when providing information, particularly if responses are to be anonymous;

☐ questionnaires are particularly suited to the gathering of factual information, for example, the number of customer orders received in one week;

☐ it is cheap, particularly if users are scattered over a wide geographical area.

A number of disadvantages attach to the use of questionnaires:

☐ questions have to be simple and their meaning completely unambiguous to the respondents;

☐ if the responses indicate that the wrong questions were asked, or that they were phrased badly, it may be difficult to clarify the information, particularly if the respondents were anonymous;

☐ without direct observation it is difficult to obtain a realistic view of a system's operation. The questionnaire often provides only statistical information on, for example, volumes of sales transactions or customer enquiries.

Examination of Records and Procedure Manuals

If existing procedures are already well documented, then the procedure manuals can provide a ready-made source of information on the way procedures should be carried out. It is less likely, however, that procedures will be documented in the smaller organization. In any event, it is important to realise that procedures detailed in manuals may not accord entirely with what actually happens. The examination of current records and the tracing of particular transactions can be a useful method of discovering what procedures are carried out.

Special purpose records which may involve, for example, the ticking of a box when an activity has been completed, can be used to analyse procedures which are causing delays or are not functioning efficiently. The use of special purpose records imposes extra burdens on staff who have to record procedures as they happen and the technique should only be used when strictly necessary.

Examination of Documents

It is important that the analyst examines all documents used in a system, to ensure that each:

☐ fulfils some purpose, that is, it records or transmits information which is actually used at some stage. Systems are subject to some inertia, for example, there may have been a 'one-off' requirement to record and analyse the geographical distribution of customers over a single month and yet the summary document is still completed because no-one told the staff it was no longer necessary;

☐ is clear and satisfies its purpose, for example, a form may not indicate clearly the type of data to be entered under each heading. In any case, it may well require re-designing for any new system which is introduced.

The documents, which should include, for example, source documents, report summaries, customer invoices and delivery notes, help to build a picture of the information flows which take place from input to output.

Observation

It is most important to observe a procedure in action, so that irregularities and exceptional procedures are noticed. Observation should always be carried out with tact and staff under observation should be made fully aware of its purpose, to avoid suspicions of 'snooping'.

The following list details some of the features of office procedures and conditions which may usefully be observed during the investigation:

☐ office layout - this may determine whether the positioning of desks, filing cabinets and other office equipment is convenient for staff and conducive to efficient working;

- [ ] work load - this should indicate whether the volume of documents awaiting processing is fairly constant or if there are peak periods of activity;

- [ ] delays - these could show that there are some procedures which are constantly behind schedule;

- [ ] methods of working - a trained observer can, through experience, recognize a slow, reasonable or quick pace of working and decide whether or not the method of working is efficient. It is important that such observations should be followed up by an interview to obtain the cooperation of the person under observation;

- [ ] office conditions - these should be examined, as poor ventilation, inadequate or excessive temperatures, or poor lighting can adversely affect staff efficiency.

Often the observation will be carried out in an informal way but it may be useful on occasion to, for example, work at a user's desk, so as to observe directly the way that customer orders are dealt with. It is important to realise that a user may 'put on a performance' whilst under observation and that this reduces the value of the information gathered.

Documenting the Results of Analysis

A number of standard approaches, apart from narrative description, can be used to document the result of the system analysis, including:

- [ ] data flow diagrams (DFDs);

- [ ] organization charts;

- [ ] systems flowcharts.

Their applications are illustrated in the following section, which examines the categories of information which need to be gathered and recorded during a system investigation; data flow diagrams are further examined in the Chapter on Structured Analysis and Design Techniques.

Categories of System Information

The major categories of information which need to be gathered involve:

- [ ] Functional relationships and data flows;

- [ ] Personnel and jobs;

- [ ] Inputs;

- [ ] Processes;

- [ ] Outputs;

- [ ] Storage.

Functional Relationships and Data Flows

A business has a number of functional areas, such as Sales, Accounts, Stock Control and Purchasing, each having its own information system. However, the computerization of a system in one functional area cannot be carried out without considering its effects on the rest of the business. Information systems within a business interact with and affect one another. The business, as an entity, also interacts with and is influenced by individuals and organizations in the surrounding 'environment' and the business's individual information systems should be co-ordinated to allow the achievement of overall business objectives.

The relationships between individual functional areas can be illustrated with the use of a Data Flow Diagram (Chapter 21).

Personnel and Jobs

It is possible to design a computerized system without involving staff, but it is likely to be less successful, partly because users can provide valuable insights into the practical aspects of system operation and partly because they will feel less motivated if they have had little or no influence on the final design. A formal organization chart can be used to gain an overall picture of staff relationships and responsibilities but it should be borne in mind that designated and actual job responsibilities can differ radically. For example, it may turn out that a junior sales clerk is carrying out the checking of orders, which should be the responsibility of the sales supervisor.

Thus, it may be necessary for the analyst to draw an alternative informal organization chart to show the actual working relationships of staff.

Apart from identifying working relationships between staff, it is useful to draw up brief job descriptions so that consultation on individual system procedures can take place with the appropriate staff. For example, a job description for a sales clerk may include the following activities:

- □ completion of standard order forms;
- □ checking stock availability;
- □ notification of orders to accounts.

Therefore, although the sales departmental manager may have knowledge of such procedures, the sales clerk will have practical experience of their operation and should be consulted.

System Inputs

A number of details concerning the data inputs to a system need to be established:

- □ *source.* It may, for example, originate from a customer, a supplier, or another department in the business;
- □ *form.* The data may arrive, for example, by telephone, letter, or a standard form such as an order form or supplier's invoice;
- □ *volume and frequency.* For example, the number of orders received each day or week;

□ *contents.* For example, the individual items of data which appear on a supplier's invoice.

Such information will allow the analyst to make recommendations on the most appropriate methods of computer input. The design of appropriate input methods also has to take account of several tasks involved with the collection and entry of data to a system:

□ *recording.* For example, the completion of a customer order form following receipt of a customer order by telephone;

□ *transmission.* For example, the order details may need to be transferred to another department or branch of the business for encoding and computer processing or they may be keyed in directly at the point of collection;

□ *visual checking.* It may be, for example, that a customer order has no quantities entered;

□ *encoding.* Verification procedures need to be designed to prevent transcription errors when data is encoded onto a computer storage medium for processing;

□ *validation.* Data is checked by a data validation program against set limits of validity, for example, account numbers may have to fall between a particular range of values.

Thus, decisions need to be made concerning:

□ data collection procedures;

□ methods for the transmission of data to the place of processing;

□ data entry, data verification and data validation procedures.

Data Collection

The designer needs to be aware of the available input technologies. These can be divided into two categories, keyboard entry and data capture technologies such as bar code reading, optical character reading (OCR) and optical mark reading (OMR), which allow direct input to the computer from specially designed input forms.

Keyboard Entry

This is the most common method of input and requires the transcription of data from source documents. These can be designed to minimize the possibility of transcription errors at the data collection stage.

Direct Input

Bar codes are pre-encoded and are thus immune from errors of transcription (assuming that the bar code is correct in the first place). Optical mark reading requires that pencil marks are used to indicate particular values from a limited set on a pre-designed form. Although no keyboard entry is required, mistakes may be made by the originator of the document and good design is therefore important.

Data Transmission

It may be that no data transmission is necessary because the data is processed at the point of collection. For example, customer orders may be recorded on order forms at the sales desk and then taken into the next room for keying into the computer. Alternatively, the data may have to be transmitted some distance, perhaps to another floor of the building or to another building some miles away. A fundamental decision has to be made, whether to localize processing at the points of collection, or to use a central facility with data communications links from each location.

Data Entry

The data entry method chosen will depend on the data collection methods used and may involve keyboard transcription from source documents or data may be captured directly from bar codes, OCR or OMR type documents. Where keyboard transcription is used, verification and validation procedures are likely to be interactive, in that the data entry operator has to respond to prompts on screen and make corrections as and when the system indicates. Most small business computer systems will be used for on-line processing, where transactions are processed immediately with master files at the data entry stage. Consequently, validation and verification have to be carried out immediately prior to the processing of each transaction.

On-screen Verification

At the end of each transaction entry, the operator is given the opportunity to scan the data on the screen and to re-enter any incorrect entries detected. This usually takes the form of a message at the bottom of the screen which is phrased in a way such as "Verify (yes or no)".

On-screen Validation

Character, data item and record checks, such as range and mode checks, can be made each time the RETURN key is pressed during data entry. For example, the screen may prompt for the entry of an account number, which must be 6 digits long and be within the range 000001 to 500000. Any entry which does not conform with these parameters is erased and the prompt re-displayed for another attempt.

Appropriate screen dialogue to allow the data entry operator to enter into a 'conversation' with the computer is a crucial part of the input design process and is dealt with as a separate topic in Chapter 19.

Batch Data Entry

The type of keyboard transcription used will be affected by the type of input data. Where, for example, files only need to be updated weekly, transaction data may be batched and entered onto magnetic disk for processing at a later stage in one update program run.

System Processes

All the clerical and machine-assisted processes, which are necessary to achieve the desired output from the given inputs, need to be identified. This will allow the systems analyst to determine the role of the computer in the new system, the programs necessary to take over the processing stages and the changes needed to clerical procedures, before and after computer processing. There are many instances when the processing requires not only the input data but also data retrieved from files. For example, to generate a customer invoice requires:

- ☐ input data concerning commodity codes and quantities ordered;
- ☐ data from the stock master file concerning prices of items ordered by reference to the input commodity codes;
- ☐ customer details from the customer master file.

The above processes can be completely computerized but other processes may require human intervention. For example, before a customer order is processed, the customer's credit status may need to be checked and referred to a supervisor before authorization.

Non-Standard Procedures

Most processes will follow standards suitable for their particular circumstances. For example, before an order is processed, stock items ordered are checked for availability. It is important, however, that the investigation identifies and notes any non-standard procedures. For example, what procedure is followed when there is an insufficient quantity of an ordered item to completely fulfil a customer order? It may be that some customers will take part-orders, whilst others require the full quantity of an item or none at all. If non-standard procedures are needed, it is important to know their complexity, how often they are used and what extra information is required. Ideally, a system should be designed to cope with all possible circumstances, but cost sometimes forces a compromise. If cost prohibits the inclusion of certain system features, for example, the ability to deal with part-orders, then it is important that the business is aware of such limitations so that it can modify its business objectives.

Document Flow

Most processes involve the use of documents to allow the transmission of information from one stage to another. System flowcharts can be used to model the movement and interaction of documents and the data they record, as well as the processes involved, as they pass from one functional area or department of the business to another. In order that the involvement of each section, department or personnel grouping in the processes can be identified, the system flowchart is divided into columns representing these divisions of responsibility.

A system flowchart may use a range of standard symbols which are illustrated in *Figure 18.1*.

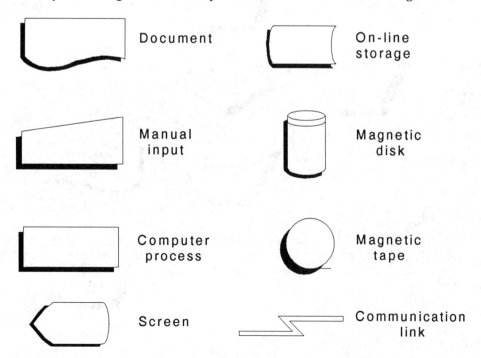

Figure 18.1

A number of standards exist for the drawing of system flowcharts and the range of symbols used depends on which stage of the investigation and design process has been reached. For example, in the early stages of investigation of an existing manual system, there will be no representation of computer methods of input, processing, output or storage. At a later stage, when computer methods are being considered, it will be necessary to use suitable symbols in the flowchart.

Figures 18.2 and *18.3* show respectively, a system flowchart without any specification of computer involvement and one with computer involvement.

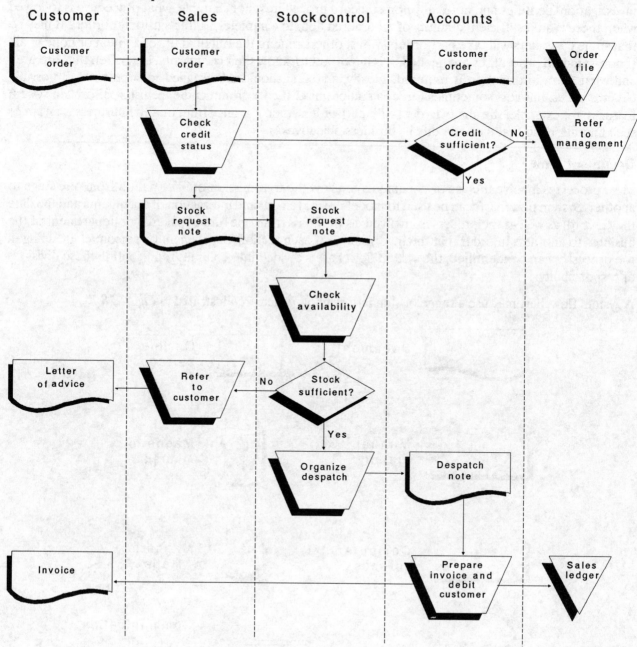

Figure 18.2

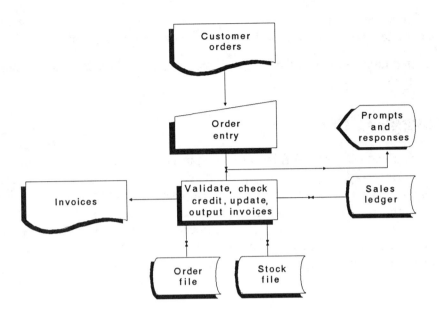

Figure 18.3

Most business systems require alternative actions to be taken dependent upon some variable condition or circumstance. For example, 15 per cent customer discount may be allowed if the invoiced amount is paid within, say, 14 days of the invoice date, after which time all discount is lost. In order that computerized and non-computerized processes can be properly designed, the investigation must identify:

☐ all decisions made during system operation;

☐ all conditions and circumstances which lead to alternative decisions;

☐ all actions to be taken following a decision.

Some decisions and consequent actions will need to be documented for clerical procedure guidelines, whilst others which involve computer processing will form part of program specifications used in program writing or as bases for choice of packaged software.

System Outputs

Output design first requires identification of the following:

☐ *contents.* Some may be revealed in the existing system, whilst others may be requested by users as being desirable in any new system;

☐ *form,* for example, whether or not printed copy is required;

☐ *volume and frequency.* This information assists decisions on the type and number of output devices required.

Based on the above information, the following tasks can be carried out:

- ☐ selection of an appropriate output device to display or communicate the outputs. Available technologies are described in Chapter 6 on Peripherals;

- ☐ designing output screen and document layouts. This topic is examined in more detail in Chapter 19.

System Storage (Files)

The storage of historic and current information is a vital part of any business system. For example, to produce a payslip not only requires transient input data concerning hours worked and sickness days but also data on rate of pay, tax code, deductions of tax and superannuation to date etc., which are held in the payroll master file stored on magnetic disk. Information on the contents of files will be gathered from existing manual files, together with responses from users regarding the output requirements of any new system. If packaged software is to be used then the contents of files will be dictated by the package, in which case some data item types may be surplus to requirements, whilst others which are required may not be available.

File Contents

Each file consists of a number of logical records, each of which has a number of associated data items. For example, each stock record in a stock master file may include:

- ☐ Stock Code
- ☐ Description
- ☐ Unit Price
- ☐ Minimum Stock Level
- ☐ Re-order Quantity
- ☐ Quantity in Stock

File Organization and Access

This concerns the logical ordering of records within a file. The available file organization and access methods are described in Chapter 22.

Database Management Systems (DBMS)

An increasingly popular alternative to traditional file processing systems is to construct databases controlled by a DBMS. The design process requires that data is analysed according to subject area, for example, raw materials or staffing, rather than by department or functional area. The tools and techniques for database design are examined in the Chapter on Databases; the structured analysis and design techniques examined in Chapter 21 are relevant to both database and non-database systems.

Choice of Storage Device

Choice is concerned with storage capacity, mode and speed of access. A full description of the various storage technologies is given in Chapter 6.

19 *User Interface Design*

The movement from centralized to distributed systems and the expansion in microcomputer usage has spawned the need for a variety of approaches to the design of user interfaces (UI)which fulfil the requirements of an increasing population of computer users, the majority of whom are not computer specialists. When all computer processing was controlled by small numbers of experts, in centralized data processing departments, there was little pressure for UI design to be particularly 'friendly'. This is probably a major reason why many people used to regard computers with some suspicion and apprehension. UIs are also variously known as *human-computer* and *man-machine interfaces*.

UI design is now recognized as being of critical importance and is usually the yardstick by which a system is judged; poor UI design can seriously affect a user's view of a system's functionality.

Several design principles can be identified:

- □ it should be a product of collaboration between the designer and the users;

- □ user, not designer, convenience should be paramount;

- □ the interface should be of consistent design throughout the system;

- □ built-in help and advice should be accessible at different levels, depending on the degree of assistance required.

Interface Metaphors

Through the use of metaphors, an interface can present a system's facilities in a form familiar to the user. A number of metaphors are commonly employed.

Desktop Metaphor

As the term indicates, the UI relates everyday desktop or office facilities to routine computer tasks such as loading, saving or deleting files. The following representations are usual:

- □ filing cabinets for disc drives;

- □ documents for files;

- □ folders for directories;

- □ waste paper baskets for the deletion of files from backing storage.

Control Panel Metaphor

A screen control panel may include a variety of elements, such as:

- ☐ *buttons* for initiating actions, for example, print;

- ☐ *switches* for setting options on and off, for example, a grid on a spreadsheet;

- ☐ *radio buttons* for choosing from ESGs (exclusive selection groups), for example, A5/A4/A3 documents sizes;

- ☐ *sub-panel menu* of buttons or switches to select, for example, system default settings;

- ☐ *lights* to indicate some active event, for example, printing;

- ☐ *signs* displaying, for example, which file is currently active;

- ☐ *sliders*, to vary for example, RGB (red green blue) colour mixes.

WIMP Interfaces

An acronym for Windows, Icons, Menus, Pointing (alternatively, Windows, Icons, Mice and Pull-down menus), the WIMP concept stems from original work by Xerox PARC Laboratories in the mid-1970s and was first employed on Apple Lisa and Macintosh computer systems. Since then a number of WIMP orientated UIs have been developed, notably, GEM, MS-Windows, ARC and Sun.

Such interfaces have a number of characteristics and features:

- ☐ the necessary skills are easy to grasp and the systems are easy to use;

- ☐ multiple windows for switching between tasks (multi-tasking);

- ☐ full-screen interaction allows quicker command execution than is usually possible through a command line interpreter (Chapter 12);

- ☐ control panels (see previous section).

However, as a relatively new concept, there are no standards for the design of WIMP-based products. Certain difficulties in their design may be experienced:

- ☐ although multiple windows are useful for task switching, too numerous windows can be confusing;

- ☐ designing icons which unambiguously tell the user of specific functions can be difficult and some may need to be augmented with text support, perhaps in a help window.

Menu Systems

A menu of options is displayed, from which a user can make a selection. Menus are only appropriate where a limited range of options is available at any one time, although the selection of an item may cause the display of a further sub-menu. Commonly, each option is identified by a single letter or number which has to be keyed to select the option.

Some packages, for example, Lotus 123 use a menu system which allows selection of an option either by highlighting the option with the cursor and pressing the 'enter' or 'return' key or simply by keying the first letter of the option (without the need for 'return' confirmation). The problem for all such systems is to design each menu such that the first letter of each option is unique in that menu.

The use of main menus which give access to sub-menus, each of which in turn may provide access to further sub-menus, follows a *hierarchical* structure.

A number of design principles may be employed:

☐ provided a simple mechanism is available for the user to return to the main menu, then several levels of menu can be used without the user becoming 'lost'. Commonly, the Esc key allows the user to work backwards from lower level menus to the main menu. Alternatively, each sub-menu may include an option "Return to Main Menu";

☐ the designer of a menu structure should limit the number of options displayed in a menu to a maximum of about eight, at which point, a sub-menu should be considered for further options. An excessive number of options on screen at one time looks untidy and may be rather intimidating to the user;

Pull-down Menus

This method generally displays the main menu along the top of the screen and is popularly associated with WIMP orientated systems. When an option is selected with the cursor or mouse pointer, the range of sub-options associated with it are 'pulled down' and displayed.

Menu systems provide a number of benefits:

☐ all possibilities are presented as a command list;

☐ minimal typing is required;

☐ error trapping is simple;

☐ inappropriate choices can be withheld from the user;

☐ context sensitive help can be provided

and drawbacks:

☐ they can be tedious for experienced users;

☐ an extended hierarchy of menus can be difficult for the user to follow;

☐ a large number of choices may require the use of several screens, as is the case, for example, with viewdata systems.

Form-fill Dialogue

This type of dialogue requires that the screen layout matches the associated input document as closely as possible. The operator is then able to make the entries in the same logical progression as the hand-filled form.

A number of features are usually evident:

☐ boxed in areas indicate fields for data entry;

☐ form headings are protected and cannot be overwritten by the user;

☐ cursor movement is restricted to the variable data entry points adjacent to each heading;

A number of design features can be applied to the data entry process:

☐ with fixed length data items, for example, a 6-digit account number, the cursor skips automatically to the next field as soon as the last character is entered.

☐ with variable length data items, the TAB key is pressed by the user when an entry is complete. This causes the cursor to skip to the next field;

☐ when all entries have been made, the user scans the screen to ensure all entries appear correct and the confirms them by pressing 'return';

☐ if errors are discovered before the 'return' key is pressed, a mechanism is available to enable corrections to be made.

The form-fill method is inappropriate when system responses are displayed which may obscure the screen headings or entries. Thus, if an invalid entry is made, the system should 'bleep' to indicate that a correction is required, without displaying an error message or display the message in a status line at the bottom of the screen; users should be well trained and aware of the valid data formats, so the need for help messages should be minimal.

Instruction and Response

This design of dialogue is particularly appropriate for inexperienced users, where the main task is to input data. An example is given in *Figure 19.1*.

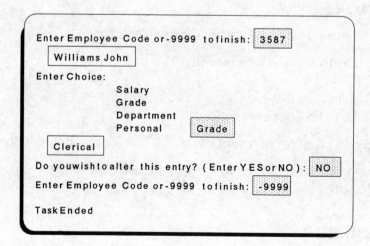

Figure 19.1

For more experienced users, such a dialogue would seem laboured and extremely frustrating, in which case it could be modified to omit many of the prompts. A modified example is shown *Figure 19.2*.

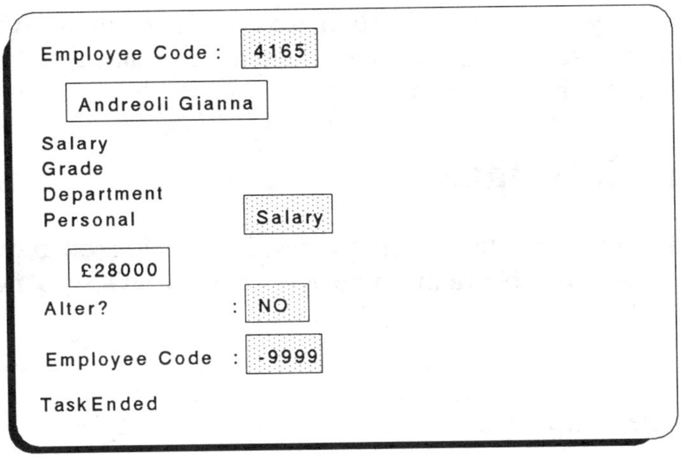

Figure 19.2

Natural Language Dialogue

This type of dialogue is frequently used in database systems to allow users to specify their requirements in a 'natural' language style. The construction of the language is a complex process and many systems only allow the use of strictly limited syntax and sentence construction. Thus although the language can be described as 'natural', there is limited flexibility to allow different users to form requests in a way which is natural to each. As a result, the casual user may become frustrated by having to rephrase requests in attempts to resolve ambiguities. Queries tend to be verbose and speech recognition may provide useful support in the future.

Mnemonic Driven Dialogue

This design is suitable for highly trained users carrying out specialized tasks. Virtually no explanatory prompts are provided. A typical example can be found in airline reservation systems. The operator can carry out a variety of tasks relating to seat reservations using only brief mnemonic (memory aid) representations for the input. For example, in response to a customer enquiry, the operator requests a list of flights which may satisfy the customer's requirements. These may be:

> Departure Date: 23rd June
> Departure Time: 2.30pm
> Departure From: London
> Destination City: New York, USA

The operator's screen entry may appear as follows:

> ? A23JUNLHRNYCJFK1430

The string of characters is in strict sequence according to function. Thus:

> A = Available
> 23JUN = 23rd June
> LHR = London, Heathrow Airport
> NYCJFK = New York City, John F. Kennedy Airport
> 1430 = 2.30pm or up to one hour earlier or later.

The system then displays any flights which satisfy these criteria, together with details of seats available, arrival times, type of aircraft etc. The operator can, if requested, immediately make a reservation for the customer with a similar mnemonic command.

Command Line Interface

The user enters a command to initiate action, to access information, or to call up a sequence of other commands. Commonly used with operating systems such as MS/DOS, a number of advantages and disadvantages are evident.

Advantages

- [ ] easy to implement with low resolution alphanumeric displays;

- [ ] the language processing techniques used with the command line interpreter (CLI) are well developed in the related area of compiler design and CLI's are thus cheap to produce;

- [ ] the power of the interface can be extended with macro commands;

- [ ] the brevity of commands, although not particularly user friendly, is ideally suited for rapid expert use.

Disadvantages

- [ ] unsuitable for inexperienced users;

- [ ] the command language must be learned and remembered;

- [ ] system interaction is restricted to the keyboard.

Some Design Considerations

- [ ] when designing command mnemonics, trying to achieve clarity of meaning tends to conflict with the aim of making them brief enough for rapid use;

- [ ] it may be helpful to use a two-tier system, providing menus for novices, leaving the 'hot key' facilities for experiences users;

Communication of Errors

Where data validation is to be performed at the time of data entry, it is important that the interface facilitates error detection and correction. Before designing error dialogues, the following points should be noted:

- [ ] a screen which leaves error messages on screen and re-displays the prompt beneath is untidy and confusing to the user;

- [ ] repeated rejection of data without any explanation can be extremely frustrating. Such systems are only suitable for properly trained users who know the forms of input expected;

☐ validation alone cannot ensure accuracy. Proper input document design, staff training and clerical checking are also vital. Users should be made aware of what validation is and its limitations, otherwise they may come to think of the system as infallible;

☐ it can save considerable frustration if the system is 'transparent' in terms of upper and lower case characters. In other words, entries are not made invalid simply because they are upper or lower case. Even if characters are to be output in only one case, the conversion can be carried out by the software;

☐ where inexperienced users are involved, it may be useful if the system produces appropriate help messages from a file on disk. This facility is provided with many general-purpose packages.

☐ error messages should be concise but detailed enough to allow the user to correct the error;

☐ whilst using an application program, the user should not be presented with an error message directly from the operating system; as far as possible, all errors should be capable of being handled by the application and communicated via it to the user.

Other Design Considerations

It is important that the interface presents screen prompts and responses in a way which aids interpretation and to this end,

☐ any dialogue should follow a logical progression appropriate to the user, the activity and in the case of data entry, to the input document;

☐ spacing is important. Full use should be made of the screen space available;

☐ the interface should, as far as possible, be consistent across all applications in a given user area. This is particularly desirable when several packages are being used in a general application area such as accounts. The dialogue for sales ledger, purchase ledger, stock control and so on, should follow a similar structure. Many integrated packages allow the user to learn basic dialogue structure which allows rapid transfer of skills from one part of the package to another;

☐ techniques of highlighting such as brightness variation, blinking and colour coding should be used sparingly. Brightness variation should be limited to two levels, bold and normal as other variations will be difficult to detect. The blinking of a field on screen to attract the user's attention can be useful provided it does not continue once appropriate action has been taken. Continual blinking can be extremely annoying;

☐ colour coding can be very useful provided colour combinations are chosen with care. Users may find some colours garish and thus irritating, whilst colour blind users will be unable to distinguish red from green.

Whatever design is chosen (it may be a combination of some of the approaches outlined in this chapter), it is vital that it is tested 'to destruction'. Users should be allowed to enter any values they please to test its effectiveness.

20 *System Implementation, Maintenance and Review*

System Implementation

There are several clearly identifiable areas which require attention in the implementation of a new system, including:

- ☐ File conversion;
- ☐ System testing;
- ☐ Staff training;
- ☐ Changeover plan - 'going live'.

File Conversion

All records to which the computer requires access must be transferred to the appropriate backing storage medium. Records may include those concerning, for example, customer accounting and stock control. The encoding of large files is a time-consuming process and because 'live' transaction data will be continually changing the values in the master files, they may need to be phased into the computer system in stages. In a stock control system, for example, records for certain categories of stock item may be encoded and computer processed, leaving the remainder to be processed by existing methods and encoded at a later stage. If a business has inadequate staffing to cope with the encoding exercise, a computer bureau may be used. Where possible, the bureau's staff should carry out the work on site because the records will be needed for the continued operation of the business. In favourable circumstances, a large scale encoding exercise may be undertaken to initially create the file and then, through an application program, transactions which have occurred since the encoding began can be used to update the file to reflect the correct values. Users will have to be made aware of which records have already been encoded into the system, so that they can properly update them as transactions occur.

An additional problem is that records in their existing state may not conform with the file layouts designed for the new system and the data may have to be copied onto special-purpose input forms to assist with accurate encoding.

System Testing

Before a system is made fully operational it should be thoroughly tested, generally in stages. If reputable and popular packaged software is being used, then provided it is being used with a wholly compatible hardware configuration, its reliability can probably be assumed. It is essential, however, that the user tests the system with real data from the business. With tailor-made systems, the testing needs to be more complex and lengthy.

Once the reliability of the system has been tested, the user should run it with historical data, for which the results of processing are already known. The computerized results can then be checked for accuracy and consistency against the known manual results; software testing is examined in detail in the Chapter on Program Design.

Staff Training

The education and training of the users of a system is vital if it is to be operated correctly and the full benefits are to be obtained.

Generally, although managerial staff will not carry out routine data entry, except in the event of staff sickness, they should possess some basic skill in the operation of a terminal or desk-top microcomputer, to allow them, for example, to make database enquiries.

The supplier should provide training for everyone connected with the computer system, so that they are aware of its functions and are confident in its use. In the main, this will consist of computer operating skills for data entry staff, but those receiving computer output need to know what to expect and to be able to interpret it readily.

Deciding when to carry out the training can be difficult. If too early, some staff will have forgotten what they have been taught by the time the system is introduced. If too late, staff may feel panicked because they have not been properly prepared.

Going 'Live'

Switching from the old to the new system can be carried out in stages or all at once. There are three generally recognized approaches to going 'live':

- ☐ parallel running;
- ☐ pilot running;
- ☐ direct changeover.

Parallel Running

With this approach, the old and new systems are run concurrently and the results of each are compared with the other for accuracy and consistency. The old system is not abandoned until the user has complete confidence in the reliability and accuracy of the new one.

Obviously, parallel running places a great administrative strain on the business, in that staff are effectively doing many of the jobs twice. Any inconsistencies in results have to be cross-checked and the source of errors located (they may result from the old or the new system).

The major advantage of parallel running is that the old system can be used whenever the computer system 'crashes' or fails to function as it should. However, the two systems cannot operate together indefinitely and 'Murphy's Law' will probably ensure that some errors only become apparent after the old system has been abandoned.

In conclusion, it can be said that parallel running provides a safe, but expensive and time consuming, method of going 'live'. It is unlikely that many businesses will use it for any extended period, except where system failure would be completely catastrophic.

Pilot Running

This strategy requires that only a portion of 'live' transactions go through the new computerized system, the rest being processed by the old method. Thus, for example, the transactions for one section of the business, or a sample of transactions from the whole business, could be used to test the system. This is a reasonably safe strategy but again, Murphy's Law may dictate that the transactions which cause errors will be amongst those which do not pass through the computer system.

Direct Changeover

This is the riskiest option in that the new system completely replaces the old, without any interim parallel or pilot running. Its major benefit is the lack of administrative costs experienced with the other two methods. The potential costs can be severe, in that system failure could mean complete loss of data access and business failure.

To minimize these risks, changeover should be preceded by careful system testing and thorough staff training. It is also helpful if the changeover is carried out during a slack period so that staff are not under pressure. The considerable cost of parallel and pilot running mean that this, the riskiest strategy, is often used in small businesses.

System Maintenance and Review

Maintenance

Following its initial introduction, a system will not remain static and dealing with the necessary changes is termed *system maintenance*. Problems will probably become apparent as the system is operated but even if they do not, the information needs of the business will probably change after a time. Some changes will come from within the business, as staff and management identify new possibilities for the system, whilst others may be forced upon the organization because of changes in the strategies of competitors or government legislation.

The most important catalyst for change is probably the desire for better and more timely information by management, to assist their decision-making and planning.

Maintenance may concern updating of hardware or amendment of software. The hardware purchased should be expansible and the software should, ideally, be flexible enough to allow amendments to be made. Often, where packaged software is used the manufacturer provides, either free or more usually for an additional payment, upgraded versions of the software with extra features (this can be a supplier-led method of system maintenance).

Review

Three to six months after system implementation, a review should be undertaken to assess the performance of the system against the supplier's specification. This should be agreed with the supplier beforehand to help avoid dispute. Following the review, the user can agree deficiencies with the supplier and hopefully have them remedied.

21 *Structured Systems Development Techniques*

Current Trends

The value of structure and methodology in programming is well recognized. Jackson's Structured Programming (JSP), described in Chapter 25 on Program Design is one such methodology which defines the structure of the data to be processed, determines the programming processes based on those structures and then defines the necessary tasks to be performed in more detail.

The task of analysing and designing a complete system comes within the framework of the *system life cycle*, described in Chapter 16 Systems Analysis - an Overview. The main drawback of the traditional analysis and design approaches, is that progress tends to be incremental and problems discovered at one stage frequently necessitate a return to an earlier stage to deal with them.

The *data modelling* techniques described in this chapter and in Chapter 15 on Databases seek to improve on the traditional approach and like JSP, the approach described here is *data-driven* and typified by Entity-Relationship Modelling (ERM), which forms part of the *data analysis* technique developed by Chen in 1976. Methodologies developed since then have adopted the data driven approach or used ERM as a basis for another, such as the SSADM (Structured Systems Analysis and Design Methodology). The following sections describe the main tools and techniques used in data-driven methodologies.

Data Modelling Tools and Techniques

Data Analysis

Data analysis is a technique primarily concerned with determining the *structure* of the data, its *properties* and the *processes* needed to make use of it. Its objective is to produce a model which represents the information needs of a particular information system or sub-system and it should be understandable by users as well as analysts, in order to provide a basis for discussion and agreement. The main tool used within data analysis is the Entity-Relationship Model (ERM), which classifies information into:

- ☐ entities;
- ☐ attributes;
- ☐ relationships.

Entities are objects which are of interest or relevance to the organization, for example, SUPPLIER, CUSTOMER, STOCK. An entity will normally equate with a file; an *entity occurrence* will normally be synonymous with a *record* within that file.

Attributes comprise those properties of an entity which are identified as being of interest to users. It may be helpful to equate attributes with *fields* in a conventional record, but it is important to note that in database systems (where the term *data item type* is used), it is not always necessary to have all the attributes for an entity stored in the relevant record in the database; it is necessary, however, to ensure that all attributes relevant to a particular entity can be associated with it. This point is explained further in Chapter 15 on Databases.

Relationships exist between entities; for example, an EMPLOYEE works for a particular DEPARTMENT and a PURCHASE ORDER is sent to one particular SUPPLIER. The degree of the relationship may be:

one-to-one

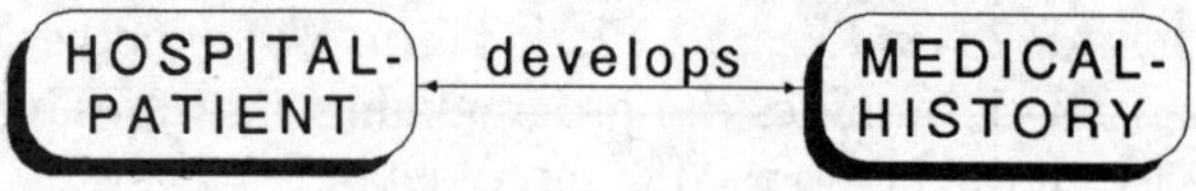

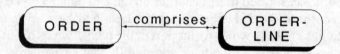

Figure 21.1

Each hospital patient develops a unique medical history and each medical history can only relate to one hospital patient.

one-to-many

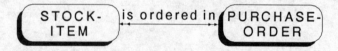

Figure 21.2

Each order may comprise one or many order lines, but each order line will be unique to a particular order.

many-to-many

STOCK-ITEM — is ordered in — PURCHASE-ORDER

Figure 21.3

Thus, a stock item may be ordered in a number of purchase orders and a single purchase order may include a number of stock items.

An ERM for a given information system or sub-system may consist of a number of entities, the attributes associated with each and the *relationships* between those entities. The modelling process requires that any given model is continually refined until its efficiency in satisfying users' needs is optimized and its structure is in a form dictated by the requirements of the Database Management System (DBMS) in use. This form will comply with one of a number of natural data structures, such as the tree and network structures (described in Chapter 15 on Databases).

Functional Analysis

This activity is concerned with identifying the data requirements, processes and activities relevant to each business function which is to use the data model established in the data analysis stage.

Data Flow Diagrams (DFDs)

DFDs are used to illustrate, in a diagrammatic form, the *logical data flows* between entities, accompanying *processes* and any file storage or *data stores*. DFDs can be used at various stages in the analysis and design process. In the early stages, they will be at a high level and may, for example, show little detail except for a department's general function, such as sales accounting or stock control; later, DFDs may be drawn at a lower, more detailed level, to show for example, the checking of a customer's account before sending an invoice reminder or statement of account. Standard symbols are generally used, typically as shown in Figure 21.4.

MILL HILL COUNTY
HIGH SCHOOL
WORCESTER CRESCENT
MILL HILL NW7 4LL

Figure 21.4

Figures 21.5 and *21.6* show two DFDs, each having a different level of detail.

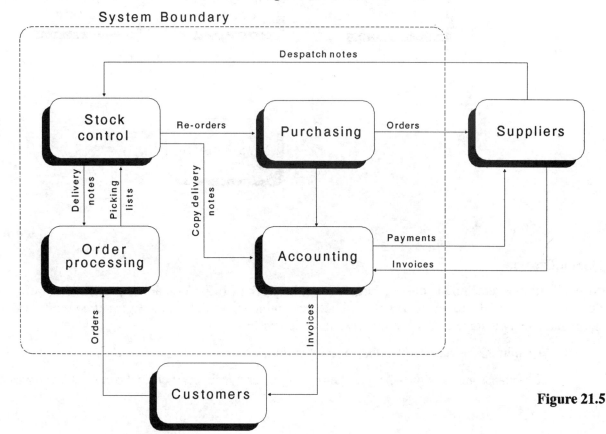

Figure 21.5

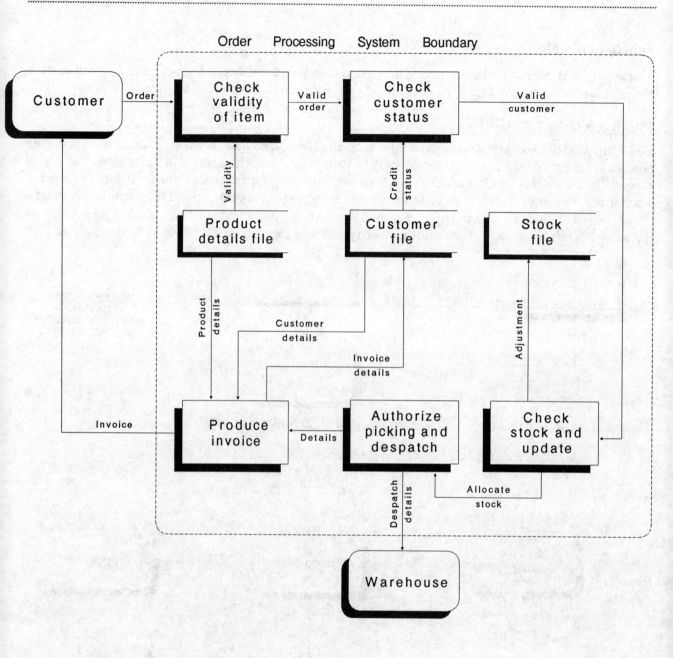

Figure 21.6

Normalization

Normalization is a technique derived largely from the work of E.F. Codd and is particularly useful in the design of relational database models. It is used to determine the validity of the *logical data model* produced in the data analysis stage and is particularly concerned with:

☐ minimizing *data redundancy* or duplication;

☐ establishing dependencies between data items and grouping them in the most efficient way;

    ☐ obtaining a measure of *data independence*, such that a database can be supplemented with new data without changing the existing logical structure and thus the applications programs.

The topic of normalization is examined more fully in Chapter 15 on Databases.

Prototyping

A prototype is, in effect, a first try at manufacturing a newly designed product; it is not expected to be perfect, but will form a basis for future development and design improvements. Car manufacturers do this when trying to incorporate revolutionary features and technologies into a new car. A prototype of an information system allows users to test it for achievement of their desired objectives. Prototyping can take place at various stages of the system development cycle, but its use must be planned and anticipated to ensure maximum feedback is obtained from users. In the early stages, a prototype may be developed to test the appropriateness of screen dialogues, without constructing the main files, whilst later it may include a section of database and some applications software. Prototyping is expensive, in terms of time and resources and is unlikely to be used where user requirements are well established or the system is fairly standard.

CASE (Computer-aided Software Engineering) Tools

Software engineering is a concept which recognises the fact that the principles of engineering normally applied to other disciplines, can be highly relevant to the 'engineering' of information systems; the parameters for the effectiveness and quality of an information system have to be set at the design stage, if users' needs are to be properly met.

A CASE tool can loosely refer to any software tool used in the development of information systems, for example:

    ☐ language processors (compilers and interpreters);

    ☐ fourth generation languages (4GLs - see Chapter 13);

    ☐ graphics programs to allow analysts to draw DFDs or ERMs.

A more precise definition of the term requires reference to the typical features of CASE proprietary software; complete CASE packages or *toolkits* are commercially available to aid the systems analyst and/or programmer in system development. A CASE toolkit would normally contain components for:

    ☐ diagram construction;

    ☐ data dictionary development and control;

    ☐ interface generation;

    ☐ source code generation;

    ☐ project management.

Diagram construction. This tool is essential for the support of a structured systems methodology. The graphical facilities allow the drawing, storage and modification of diagrams and charts, such as data flow diagrams (DFDs), entity-relationship models (ERMs) and data structure diagrams (for program development).

Data dictionary. Being particularly important in the development of database systems for the control and consistency of data, the function of data dictionaries is described in Chapter 15 on Databases.

Interface generation. Interface generators support the preparation of prototypes of user interfaces, such as screen dialogues, menus and reports.

Source code generation. These tools allow the automated preparation of computer software, in other words, the conversion of a system specification into the source code of a chosen programming language, which can then be compiled into executable object or machine code. CASE tools for code generation are general purpose and are, as a consequence less efficient in the production of source code than specialized applications generators; most code generators will only produce, say, 75% of the code automatically, leaving the rest to be hand-coded by a programmer.

Project management. Such tools support the scheduling of analysis and design activities and the allocation of resources to the various project activities.

Integrated CASE Tools

CASE tools can be used as separate, discrete elements or as a complete system. The integrated use of CASE tools can best be managed through windowing software, which allows, for example, the simultaneous viewing of data flow diagrams and data dictionary entries on screen. Integration also has the benefit of allowing data from one component of the toolkit to be transferred to another, for example, data dictionary entries to entity-relationship diagrams.

22 *Computer Files*

This chapter deals with the ways in which information is stored, organized and processed by computer.

Files, Records and Fields

In data processing, it is necessary to store information on particular subjects, for example, customers, suppliers or personnel and such information needs to be structured so that it is readily controllable and accessible to the user.

In traditional data processing systems, each of these 'topics' of information is allocated a *file*. *Figure 22.1* illustrates the structure of a typical Personnel file.

Works Number	Surname	Initial	Department	Grade	D.O.B.	Salary
357638	Watkins	P.	Sales	3	100755	9500
367462	Groves	L.	Marketing	4	170748	12800
388864	Harrison	F.	Sales	2	121066	6500
344772	Williams	J.L.	Productions	4	010837	14700

Figure 22.1

A file consists of a collection of related *records*. The Personnel file which shown in *Figure 22.1* has a record for each employee. For example, the row containing information on P. Watkins is one individual record. The complete file would be made up of a number of such records, each one relating to a different employee.

Each record contains specific items of information relating to each employee and each item occupies a *field*. In the example, there are seven such fields, Works Number, Surname and so on, each field containing values for a given category of information. Thus, the field value of record 388864 for Department is 'Sales'.

Types of File

Files can be categorized by the ways in which they are used and there are generally recognized to be four such categories.

Master Files

They are used for the storage of *permanent* data which is used in applications such as stock, sales or payroll. Some of the fields tend to contain data which is fairly static, for example, customer name and address, whilst data in some fields is continually changing, for example, customer balance, as transactions are applied to the file. Such *updating* is carried out, either through the direct entry (on-line) of individual transactions, or from an accumulated set of entries stored on a *transaction file*.

Transaction Files

These are transient and only exist to allow the updating of master files. Each transaction record contains the *key field value* of the master record it is to update (to allow correct matching with its relevant master record), together with data gathered from source documents, for example, invoice amounts which update the balance field in customer accounts.

Reference Files

These contain data used for reference or look-up purposes, such as price catalogue and customer name and address files.

Archive or Historic Files

These contain data which, for legal or organizational reasons, must be kept and tend to be used on an ad hoc basis and may be referred to only occasionally.

Fixed and Variable Length Records

The extent to which the information in a particular file can be standardized and categorized will determine whether each record in the file can be fixed or variable in length. The *length* of the record is the number of *character positions* allocated to it within the file. In *Figure 22.1* the file would probably contain *fixed length* records because:

- ☐ the number and types of data items required in this case are likely to be the same for each employee;

- ☐ the number of character positions for each field can be fixed or at least set to a maximum. For example, the Works Number is fixed at 6 character positions and Surname could be set to a maximum of 20, provided that no surnames exceeded this length.

Variable length records may be used in files which have storage requirements markedly different from those referred to above, for instance:

- ☐ Some records could have more fields than others. In a personnel file, for example, each record may contain details of previous jobs held and as the number of previous jobs may vary considerably from one employee to another, so the number of fields would be similarly varied;

  or

- ☐ the number of character positions used for individual values within a field is variable. For example, in a library system each record may contain a field for data which describes the subject of the book and the amount of text needed to adequately describe this may vary from book to book.

Listed below are some of the advantages of *fixed length* records:

☐ Fixed length records are simpler to process, in that the start and end points of each record can be readily identified by the number of character positions. For instance, if a record has a fixed length of 80 character positions, a program reading the file from the start will assume that the second record starts at the 81st character position, the third at the 161st character position and so on, making easier the programming of file handling operations;

☐ Fixed length records allow an accurate estimation of file storage requirements. For example, a file containing 1000 records, each of fixed 80 characters length, will take approximately 80000 characters of storage;

☐ Where direct access files are being used, fixed length records can be readily updated 'in situ' (in other words the updated record overwrites the old version in the same position on the storage medium). As the new version will have the same number of characters as the old, any changes to a record will not change its physical length. On the other hand, a variable length record may increase in length after updating, preventing its return to its home location.

There are some instances when variable length records are more appropriate. For example:

☐ Where records in a file contain highly variable quantities of information, variable length records may be more economical of storage space;

☐ When the saving in storage space makes the introduction of more complex file handling techniques worthwhile.

The Identification of Records - Primary and Secondary Keys

In most organisations, when an information system is operational it will be necessary to identify each record uniquely. In the Personnel File example given above, it might be thought that it is possible to identify each individual record simply by the employee's Surname and this would be satisfactory as long as no two employees had the same surname. In reality, most organizations will of course have several employees with the same surnames, so to ensure uniqueness, each employee is assigned a unique Works Number. The works number field is then used as the *primary key* in the filing system, each individual having his or her own unique Works Number and so a unique primary key.

There are certain circumstances when the primary key may be a *composite key*, that is, one made up of more than one field and the following example shows how a pair of fields, which individually may not be unique, can be combined to provide a unique identifier.

Figure 22.2 shows an extract from a file which details suppliers' quotations for a number of different products. There is a need for a composite key because there may be a number of quotations from one supplier (in this case, supplier 41192) and a number of quotations for the same part (in this instance, part number A112).

Supplier-No	Part-No	Price	Delivery-Date
23783	A361	2.59	31/01/86
37643	B452	1.50	29/01/86
40923	A112	3.29	30/01/86
41192	A112	3.29	28/01/86
41192	C345	2.15	30/01/86

Figure 22.2

It is necessary, therefore, to use both Supplier-No and Part-No to identify one quotation record uniquely.

Uniqueness is not always necessary. For example, if it is required to retrieve records which fulfil a criterion, or several criteria, *secondary keys* may be used. Thus, for example, in an information retrieval system on Personnel, the secondary key Department may be used to retrieve the records of all employees who work in, say, the Sales Department.

File Storage Media

File storage media may be classified according to the kind of access they provide

   ☐ serial access;

   ☐ direct access.

Serial Access Media

Serial access means that in order to identify and retrieve a particular record, it is necessary to 'read' all the records which precede it in the relevant file. An example of such a storage medium is a normal cassette tape. One of the difficulties with such a storage medium is that there are no readily identifiable physical areas on the medium which can be addressed. In other words, it is not possible to give a name or code and refer this to a particular location. It is said to be *non-addressable*. To look for an individual record stored on such a medium requires the software to examine each record's *key field* in sequence from the beginning of the file until the required record is found.

Direct Access Media

Storage media such as floppy or hard disks allow *direct access* to individual records, without reference to the rest of the relevant file. They have physical divisions which can be identified by computer software (and sometimes hardware) and are *addressable*, so that particular locations can be referred to by a name or code to retrieve a record which is stored at that location. Retrieval of an individual record stored on such a medium is achieved (depending on the way the file is organized) by specifying the relevant *primary key field value*, thus providing the software with a means of finding and retrieving the specific individual record directly.

File Organization Methods

Another function of the *primary key* is to provide a value which can be used by computer software to assign a record to a particular position within a file. The file organization method chosen will dictate how individual records are assigned to particular *logical* positions within a file.

File Storage Media and File Organization Methods

Serial access media are limited in the file organization methods they permit because they are *non-addressable*. Direct access media are more versatile in that they allow a variety of file organization methods in addition to those allowed by serial access media. The different types of file storage media are discussed in some detail in the next section.

Magnetic Tape - a Serial Access Medium

Physical and Logical Records

Because of the physical characteristics of magnetic tape it is necessary, when processing a file, that the tape unit (the device onto which a tape is loaded for processing) starts to read the tape at the beginning of the reel. The takeup spool receives the tape from the feed spool via a read/write head in the unit which can either record information onto or read information from the tape as it passes. As there are no specific physical locations on the tape which can be identified and referred to by the computer (except of course the beginning and end), the only way it can find a particular record is by reading the whole file. Unless the whole tape is to be processed, it may only be necessary to read up to the point where the specific record it is seeking is found. There may well be more than one logical file on a tape but these will have to be read in the sequence that they appear on the tape. As the tape is read, the computer will compare the key field value of each record which it comes to, with the specified key value, until the required record is found. *Figure 22.3* illustrates the way in which a file is arranged on tape both *logically* and *physically*.

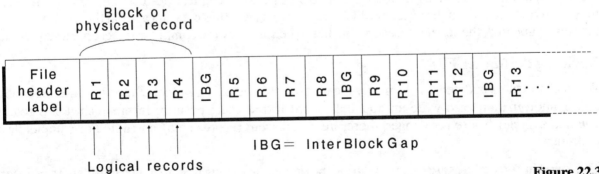

Figure 22.3

You should note from *Figure 22.3* that records R1, R2, R3 etc are *logical* records. For example, if this were a stock file, each logical record would relate to one commodity held in stock. On the other hand each logical or physical record consists, in this illustration, of 4 logical records. The reason for making the distinction between *logical* and *physical* records stems from the fact that data is transferred between the computer's internal memory and the tape storage medium in manageable *blocks*, the optimum size of each depending on factors such as the size of the computer's internal memory.

Each block of data is referred to as a physical record. Between each block transfer, the tape has to stop while the previous block is processed by the computer. In order to give the tape time to stop and then restart for the next block, there is an *Inter Block Gap*(IBG), a blank area of tape between each block. It is unlikely that the optimum block size will coincide with the actual length of a single logical record, so it is necessary to transfer a number of logical records between tape and internal memory at one time. Thus, a *physical* record or *block* will often consist of a number of *logical* records.

The example of a stock file is used again to illustrate this point further. Assume that each block contains 3 logical stock records (in other words three individual commodities). If the first record to be processed is stored in the fifth block, then the first four blocks have to be read in sequence into memory and each logical stock record examined for its key field value, without any records actually being used. When the fifth block is eventually read into memory each of the three logical stock records is then examined for its key field value until the required key and thus logical record, is identified.

File Organization Methods on Magnetic Tape

There are two ways in which a file can be organized on tape:

- ☐ serially;

- ☐ sequentially.

This restriction stems from the fact that magnetic tape is a *serial* access medium. As is noted earlier, this means that it has no addressable locations, so records have to be traced by reading the file from beginning to end.

The processing of tape files can only be carried out satisfactorily if they are organized in the sequence of their primary keys. This restriction applies to both master and transaction files. Serial files, which are out of sequence, are only useful as an interim measure, prior to processing.

Generally, when a transaction file is being created on tape, for example, when customer orders are received, they are written to tape in the order in which they are received, thus creating a serial file. Before the master file can be updated, the serial transaction file has to be sorted by the computer to become a sequential file.

Updating the Master File

When a tape file is updated, a new master file must be created on a new reel of tape because the tape drive unit cannot guarantee to write an updated record to the exact position from which it was read (it is *non-addressable*). There is a danger, therefore, of adjacent records being corrupted or completely over-written.

The following procedures are followed during the update (assuming that no new records are to be inserted). For the sake of clarity, some complexities are not mentioned.

- ☐ A transaction is read into memory.

- ☐ A master record is read into memory. If the record keys do not match, the master record is written, unchanged, to the new reel. Master records continue to be read, examined and written in the original sequence to the new reel until a match for the transaction is found.

☐ Once the match is found, the master record is updated in main memory and then written to the new reel.

These steps are repeated until all transactions have been processed and the complete updated master file has been written to the new reel. If the transaction files were not sorted into the same sequence as the master file, it would be necessary to rewind the master file whenever a transaction required a master record which had already passed through the system; clearly, this would be both inefficient and impractical. The process is illustrated in the chapter on System Controls.

Magnetic Disk - a Direct Access Medium

Addressing Magnetic Disk

Magnetic disk provides file storage facilities which are more flexible and powerful than those provided by magnetic tape. As an *addressable* medium, the surface of the disk is divided into physical locations which are illustrated in *Figure 22.4*.

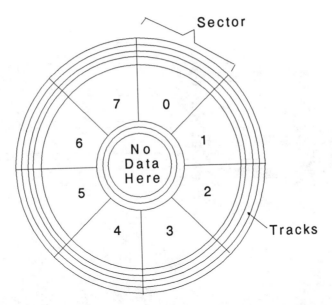

Figure 22.4

The address of any one physical location on a single disk incorporates a *track* number, and within that track, a *sector* number. A sector is the smallest physical area on the disk which can be addressed, each addressable unit being referred to as a *block* or *physical record*. The size of the blocks is normally determined by the systems designer through the use of systems software, although some disk storage systems use *hard sectoring* (the block size cannot be altered). The number of logical records which can be accommodated in a particular block obviously depends upon the physical size of the block and the length of each logical record. The maximum number of logical records which can be fitted into a block is known as the *blocking factor*. Considerations regarding the determination of block size are beyond the scope of this text, but some of the design factors can be readily explained by the following example:

Example

If a disk's block size approximates to the storage of 500 characters and a stock file has logical records, each with a fixed length of 110 characters, then the maximum number of records which can be stored in a block is 4. To retrieve one logical stock record requires the software to address the relevant block and retrieve the physical record. This means that it will retrieve all the logical stock records in the block. Therefore, the larger the number of logical records stored in any specific block, the less selective the software can be in retrieving them but the faster the complete file is processed.

Operational Features of Magnetic Disk

Although there are many variations in the capacities and sizes of disk that are available, there are certain physical characteristics which are common to all.

On smaller computer systems disks tend to be handled singly on individual disk drive units. On larger systems a number of disks may be mounted on a central spindle. This is shown in *Figure 22.5*. To transfer data to or from the disk pack it is necessary to mount it on a disk drive unit which rotates the pack at high speed. Data is recorded magnetically on disk in a similar fashion to the recording on magnetic tape. Special read/write heads are mounted on moveable arms within the disk drive unit in such a way that they move in synchronization across the disk surface. The software positions the heads for the writing or retrieval of records.

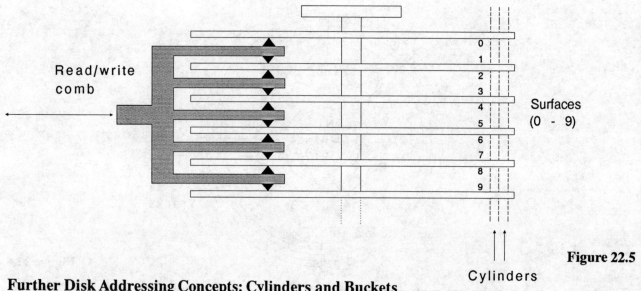

Read/write comb

Surfaces (0 - 9)

Cylinders

Figure 22.5

Further Disk Addressing Concepts: Cylinders and Buckets

Cylinders

If the *Figures 22.4* and *22.5* are considered together it can be seen that, in a disk pack, a specified track on one disk (track 0) is vertically above other tracks on lower disks which are also specified as track 0. In other words, all the track 0s are in the same vertical plane. Such a grouping is known as a *cylinder* or *seek area*. Similarly, all track 1s form another cylinder, as do track 2s and so on. It can be seen therefore, that there are as many cylinders as there are tracks on each disk surface.

The fastest way of reading or writing records on disks is achieved by minimizing the movement of the read/write arms. This is achieved by positioning associated records, which are likely to needed as a group (they may form a complete file), into sequence (as a sequential file) on tracks in the same cylinder. Records are written to the disk pack, such that track 0 on surface 1 is filled first, followed by track 0 on surface 2 and so on, until all number 0 tracks are filled (the first cylinder). Then, if the file requires more than one cylinder, adjacent tracks are filled to form further cylinders, until the file is complete.

When access is required to the file it is quickest, in terms of keeping read/write head movement to a minimum, to deal with a cylinder of records at a time. Thus, a complete cylinder of records is processed before any head movement is required. A cylinder is also known as a seek area, because all records in a cylinder can be accessed by the read/write heads whilst they are positioned in that cylinder.

Buckets

The minimum amount of data which can be transferred between the backing store of the computer and its internal store is the *block*. However, there are occasions when a larger unit of transfer is required and on such occasions the concept of the *bucket* is used; a number of blocks (up to the maximum of one track) is given the same disk address (this is usually the address of the first block in the bucket) and any logical records held within such a bucket are retrieved when that disk address is used.

File Organization Methods using Magnetic Disk

Magnetic disk supports the following file organization methods:

Serial

As is the case for a serial tape file, records are placed onto disk one after another in no particular sequence;

Sequential

As for a sequential tape file, records are stored on disk ordered by each record's primary key;

Indexed Sequential

Records are stored in sequence according to their primary keys and an *index* is produced when the file is created, allowing direct retrieval of individual records. The software searches different levels of the index (a *multi-level index*) - the cylinder index, track index and the bucket or block index- before positioning the read/write heads to retrieve the block containing the required record.

The indexes may be structured as shown in *Figure 22.6*, using a five-digit primary key in the range 00001 to 50000. The table represents an extract only.

Cylinder Index		Track Index for Cylinder 55		Sector/block Index for Track 3	
Cylinder	Highest Key	Track	Highest Key	Sector	Highest Key
1	00452	1	26000	1	26071
2	00940	2	26063	2	26076
3	01650	3	*26120*	3	26080
.	.	4	26185	4	26087
55	*26500*	5	26242	5	26095
56	27015	6	26320	6	26104
.	.	7	26426	7	26112
115	50000	8	*26500*	8	*26120*

Figure 22.6

The indexes are constructed as the records are written sequentially (according to the primary key) to the disk pack. As each sector is filled, the primary key of the last record to be placed in the sector (the highest key) is recorded in the *sector index* and once all sectors in a track have been filled, the last key to be entered is added to the *track index*, the completion of a cylinder causing the highest key field in it to be recorded in the *cylinder index*. This process is repeated with subsequent cylinders until the file is complete.

The retrieval of records requires a *serial search* to be made of the cylinder, track and sector indexes respectively, unless a complete track is to be read, in which case the sector index is not used. Referring to the *Figure 22.6*, suppose that the record with primary key 26085 is required; the indexes may be used as follows:

☐ a serial search of the cylinder index is made until a highest key entry is found which is equal to or greater than the required key. The entry which meets this requirement is 26500, indicating that a search of the track index for cylinder 55 is needed;

☐ a serial search of that track index, again looking for an entry greater than or equal to record key 26085, reveals that the record is to be found in track 3, where the highest key field is 26120;

☐ searching the sector index for track 3 returns the entry of 26087, the highest key field entry for sector 4.

Unless record 26085 has been placed in an *overflow area*, owing to a full sector, it can be retrieved by reading in the block of data occupying the address - sector 4, track 3, cylinder 55.

The cylinder index for a given file will normally be read into main memory when the file is first opened and held there until processing is complete. Each track index is normally held in the cylinder to which it relates and will be read into main memory as required. Similarly, the sector index is usually held within its relevant track.

The preceding procedures and mechanisms only illustrate the main principles of index construction and usage, as the detail is likely to vary considerably from one system to another. To facilitate updating, space will normally be left in sectors, tracks and cylinders to allow for the insertion of new records.

This method allows the efficient sequential processing of the file as well as direct retrieval of records using the indexes. Indexes can become quite large and the file may need to be re-organized periodically so that new records can be inserted in the correct sequence. Records which are marked for deletion need to be removed from the file and the indexes then have to be reconstructed. The frequency with which such re-organization is necessary depends on the level of file activity and the number of insertions and deletions. File re-organization is a *house-keeping* activity.

Overflow

Where new records, or variable length records which have been extended by updating, cannot be inserted into their correct sequenced positions, they are assigned to *overflow areas*.

Local overflow areas include any located within the same cylinder as their associated home locations; thus, local overflow areas may be located within each track or sector of a cylinder, or at the end of the cylinder. These overflow areas have the advantage that access to them requires no head movement and therefore, no increase in *seek time*.

Global overflow areas may be formed from a separate cylinder or cylinders and will tend to be used when local overflow areas are full. The main disadvantage is that access to an overflow record requires additional head movement.

A file may use either local or global overflow areas, or a combination of the two; the use of global overflow only, tends to be less wasteful of space but with the disadvantage that the retrieval of any overflow record will require additional head movement.

If frequent reference is required to overflow records, *performance degradation* (a worsening of the system's response times) is likely to be noted by users and file re-organization will be beneficial.

Random Organization

This is a method which is impractical in any non-computerized situation. However, in a computerized system it is feasible to place records onto disk at random. The procedure for placing specific records in a particular position on disk may simply relate the primary key *directly* to its disk address, for example,

$$disk\ address = primary\ key$$

$$disk\ address = primary\ key + index\ value$$

With *absolute* and *indexed addressing*, each record has a unique address and can be retrieved directly with its own primary key. A major disadvantage of this method is its orientation towards the needs of the computer; the values needed for disk addressing may well be inappropriate for use as meaningful (to the user) primary keys for logical records. Further, the unique link between a disk address and a particular logical record means that any vacated space cannot be used by another record unless it adopts the same key as the previous occupant record.

Hashing Algorithms

A more usual method of addressing uses a mathematical formula called a *hashing algorithm*, which generates a disk address from the record's primary key.

The hashing algorithm operates on the primary keys within a given range to produce pseudo-random numbers which may then be used as bucket addresses, to which the logical records are allocated. Each pseudo-random number could refer to an address where a single record is stored, but it is more economical for it to refer to an area where a group of records is stored; thus a *bucket address* will normally contain a number of logical records.

Overflow

An uneven distribution of records means that some buckets overflow and cannot accommodate all the logical records allocated to them, whilst others remain empty or are seriously under-used. Excessive overflow slows the access time for any record which cannot be allocated to its home address.

To achieve a reasonably even spread, the selection of a particular algorithm requires consideration of the following factors:

- [ ] the pattern and range of the primary keys within the file;

- [ ] the size of each bucket and the number available;

- [ ] the *packing density* required (number of records, divided by, the total record capacity of the available buckets).

The topics of bucket size and packing density are dealt with in more detail in the section on overflow handling.

Example Algorithm

Prime Number Division. The primary key is divided by the largest prime number which is less than the number of available buckets. The remainder of this calculation is taken as the *relative* bucket number, that is, the number of buckets after the first. For example:

> *available buckets* 2000
>
> *prime number*   1999
>
> *primary key*   22316
>
> *22316/1999 = 11 remainder 327*

The relative bucket number is thus 327.

The same mathematical formula is used to subsequently retrieve records, which is ideal in situations where random enquiries are the norm and there is little need for sequential processing. Randomly organized files can be processed sequentially but with less efficiency than sequentially organized files. An advantage of this method is the lack of large indexes which tend to take up considerable storage space on the disk.

The aim of any randomizing or *hashing algorithm* is to achieve an even distribution of records over the disk space allocated to a file. Most random files allow more than one logical record to occupy a single bucket, as any given algorithm will normally generate the same disk address from several different primary keys; conversely, any hashing algorithm is likely to leave some buckets with no allocated records. Any record which is stored in the address allocated to it by an algorithm is referred to as a *home record.*

Synonyms and Collisions

If an address can only hold one record, the first one to be allocated to it, then subsequent records have to be stored elsewhere; such records are referred to as *synonyms* and the circumstances causing their re-allocation, as *collisions*. Synonyms increase access times for affected records, so one aim of an algorithm is to minimize their occurrence. Other factors to be considered by the file designer include, *bucket size* and *packing density* (see previous section). A large bucket size (the maximum is one track) will obviously reduce the number of synonyms, but at the cost of reduced precision in the retrieval of individual logical records. It is fairly unlikely that, in a random file, more than one logical record from the same bucket will be required at the same time, so a number of records are read unnecessarily. In deciding on the packing density (the percentage of the file space occupied) for any particular file, the designer has to consider the *volatility* or activity of the file. It is generally recognized that 50 per cent is probably the minimum packing density and is appropriate only for highly volatile files where a large number of record additions is likely; most files are designed to be 75 to 80 per cent packed when they are set up. A low packing density will further reduce the likelihood of synonyms, but at a cost of increased storage space.

Overflow Handling Techniques

As can be seen from the previous sections, overflow is a problem encountered with both indexed sequential and random files. There are three methods of tracking the location of overflow records:

Progressive Overflow

This is the most simplistic method, in that synonyms are placed in the next available bucket following their home bucket; there are no pointers from home buckets to the appropriate overflow locations. Retrieval of an overflow record requires a serial search of buckets following the home bucket, such simplicity bringing the disadvantage that a request for a non-existent record would not be rejected until the whole file had been searched. Further, if a record is deleted from its home area, a search has to be made to discover if any synonyms of that record exist and if one is found, it must be placed in the vacant home area; if this is not done, and the area is left vacant, it will appear that no synonyms for that address exist.

Chaining

A chain is a data structure which enables items to be accessed by a series of *pointers* leading from the first in the chain, to the second, to the third and so on until the last one is reached. A *link* field in each chained record provides the necessary pointer. Thus, once a bucket is full, the last record to be placed in it is chained to the next record to be assigned to that bucket - the first synonym; each subsequent synonym is linked to its predecessor. Chained overflow records may be held in a separate overflow area, or more efficiently, in the next available bucket. This method combines the benefits of progressive overflow with those of chaining. The main disadvantages of progressive overflow, described in the previous paragraph, are thus removed. Greater efficiency can be obtained by ensuring that chain lengths are kept to a minimum; this can be effected by moving synonyms into home buckets as and when vacancies occur through deletions. *Figure 22.7* illustrates the chaining technique. Removing and adding synonyms to a chain requires the adjustment of pointers, a process described in Chapter 26 on Data Structures.

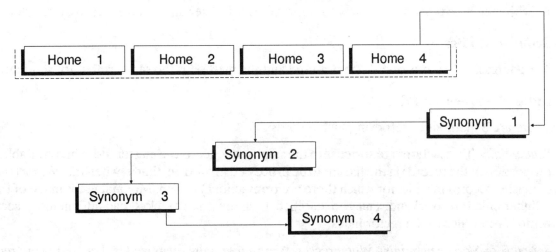

Figure 22.7

Tagging

This method ensures that each synonym can be accessed directly after reference to its home bucket, the address of each overflow record being directly referenced or tagged from its home bucket. The technique is illustrated in the *Figure 22.8*.

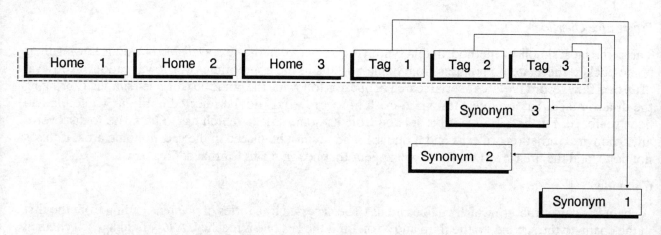

Figure 22.8

The maintenance of tags in home buckets takes up space, so the number of synonyms should be kept to a minimum. Performance degradation is likely to be minimized with tagging, the most effective of the overflow tracing techniques.

Accessing Disk Files

Serial Files

As with magnetic tape, the only way to retrieve records is serially, in other words, one after another.

Sequential Files

The addressing features of disk are not used and the method is the same as that for sequential tape files.

Indexed Sequential Files

There are 3 methods of retrieving such records:

Sequentially. Transactions are sorted into the same sequence as the master file. This is suitable when a large proportion of the records in the file are to be processed in one run, that is, when the *hit rate* (the percentage of master records in a file, for which there are transactions) is high. Minimal use is made of the index. The cylinder index and track index may be searched, then the whole track is read into memory, sector by sector, without reference to the sector index;

Selective or Skip Sequentially. When records are sequentially organized by key, not every record need be read when scanning the file. The transactions are sorted into master file sequence and the indexes are used, so that only those blocks containing master records for which there is a transaction are read into memory. This is suitable when the hit rate is low;

Randomly. Transactions are not sorted. They are processed in the order in which they occur, the indexes being used to find the relevant master records as they are required. The read/write heads have to move back and forth through the file and so head movement is greater than with sequential methods of processing. This method is appropriate when records are updated immediately after the transaction occurs or, for example, when there is a need for random enquiries of a stock file.

Random Files

Transactions or enquiries need not be in any logical sequence. Records are retrieved by generating the physical address from the record key. The software uses the same hashing algorithm it used to assign the record to its address in the first place.

Choice of File Organization Method and Storage Medium

Choice should be based on the type and purpose of the system to be used. For example, an on-line enquiry system or stock control system needing frequent, rapid, direct access to individual records within large files will best be served by a randomly organized file, using hash addressing. Very large files, of an archival nature are probably best held off-line on magnetic tape; the medium's lack of an addressing facility would necessitate such files being maintained sequentially. It may be reasonable to hold sections of such archival data, those which are most in demand, on magnetic disk and organized indexed sequentially. An illustration of this is provided by the Police National Computer system, which holds more recent data on magnetic disk, with older files held on magnetic tape. Systems which do not require direct access, for example, monthly payroll files, can be efficiently stored and processed on magnetic tape and even if the computer system only has disk storage, sequential organization is still likely to be the chosen method. Applications which require both sequential and direct access are generally best served by indexed sequential files.

Typically, the only files which are held serially, are temporary files, such as transaction files prior to sorting for a sequential update run.

Case Study - MS/DOS Operating System

The MS/DOS operating system is used as a case study to illustrate the concepts of file management.

File Management Facilities

Each filename is held in a *directory*, together with its size (expressed in bytes) and the date it was created or last accessed. Directories can be used to divide disk space into a number of user or application areas. A floppy disk with 360kb (kilobytes) capacity may contain, say, 30 or 40 files at most, so that it is fairly easy for a user to scan a single directory in the search for a particular file name. Hard disks, on the other hand, with capacities of 20 mb (megabytes) to 100 mb and more, may contain hundreds or even thousands of files, which makes management in a single directory extremely difficult. For this reason, all operating systems which support hard disk-based machines allow the creation of *sub-directories* to which groups of files can be assigned. When the operating system's attention is directed to a particular directory, it is known as the current or working directory. MS/DOS keeps track of files on disk with the use of a *File Allocation Table* (FAT) and when a disk is formatted, MS/DOS initially sets up two system areas, one for the FAT and the other for the main or *root directory*. The FAT has an entry for each *cluster* (on a 360kb diskette one cluster equals two sectors). Clusters containing part of a file have a FAT entry which points to the next cluster relating to that file, or, if it is the last part of a file, a special indicator. Thus, MS/DOS can find a complete file by reference to the pointers in each cluster containing part of it. Empty clusters have a zero entry in the FAT.

File Management Techniques

Directories and Sub-directories

If a computer is used by more than one user, or a single user is working on a number of different projects, it is advisable to organize files accordingly into different directories. This is similar to separating manual files by placing them in different drawers or sections of a filing cabinet. Although it may be common practice to maintain all files in the root directory of a floppy disk, it is virtually essential, if any proper control is to be maintained, to organize files on hard disk into different directories. A user has to decide what logical divisions can be made to divide files into groups. For example, there may be one directory for a spreadsheet program, another for the word processing program and another for the accounts programs. Each of these directories may contain further sub-directories for the data files associated with each of the applications programs. Organizing files in this way makes use of what is termed a *multi-level directory structure*. *Figure 22.9* following figure provides an illustration of such a structure.

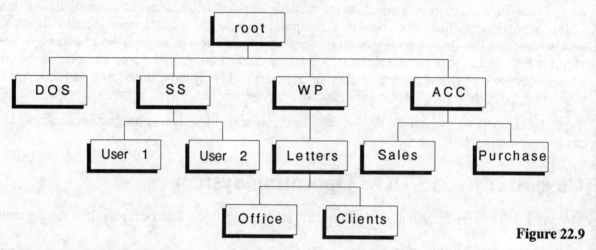

Figure 22.9

Each of the directories and sub-directories may contain a number of files.

A multi-level directory structure looks rather like an up-turned tree with a single *root* at the top and *branches* growing downwards. The root directory is created when the disk is formatted but any other directories have to be created by the user. Any directory with sub-directories beneath it is called a *parent directory*. Once directories have been created, any file can be directed to its relevant directory, either directly with the use of MS/DOS commands or through the applications software. For example, referring to *Figure 22.9*, when the spreadsheet program is used by User Carole, she has to use the appropriate package option to direct the operating system's attention to the required disk drive and the User Carole directory. Similarly, when User James operates the spreadsheet package, the User James directory should be selected. Each file stored within a single directory or sub-directory must have a unique filename, or if the filename is the same, the extension must differ. However, files in different directories can have the same name.

Directory Commands

Creating Directories - MKDIR (or MD)

MKDIR stands for 'make directory' and is used for the creation of directories from the root directory. Referring to the directory structure in the *Figure 22.9*, the following procedure may be used to create it.

1. *md\lotus*. This command creates a directory called 'lotus' for the spreadsheet program. The directory name relates to the name of the package - Lotus 123.

2.   *md\lotus\james*. This creates a sub-directory of the 'lotus' directory for the user called James.

3.   *md\lotus\carole*. A similar sub-directory is set up for the user called Carole.

4.   *md\word*. A directory is created for the word processing package.

5.   *md\word\documents*. This creates a sub-directory called 'documents', accessible via the 'word' directory.

6.   *md\word\documents\office*. In this way 'office' is a sub-directory of the sub-directory 'documents', which is itself a sub-directory of the 'word' directory.

7.   *md\word\documents\customer*. This creates a sub-directory called 'customer' at the same level as the 'office' sub-directory in the multi-level structure.

Similar commands can be entered to create the directories for the accounts package and associated files. The backslash (\) symbol is used to separate directory names, the first backslash indicating separation from the root directory which is inferred within the command. The series of directory names and backslashes indicates the PATH to be taken by the operating system to access particular files.

Once files have been entered to the structure, the DIR command can be used as follows to view them. For example,

> *dir\lotus\carole*

lists the files stored in Carole's spreadsheet directory.

Changing the Working Directory - CHDIR (or CD)

Assuming that the root directory is currently the working directory, then the command

> *cd\word\customer*

would make the 'customer' sub-directory the working directory. The command

> *cd\word\office*

would switch the attention of the operating system to the sub-directory called 'office'. The command

> *cd*

always returns control to the root directory from any point in the structure.

Removing Directories - RMDIR (or RD)

A directory can only be deleted when it is empty. Suppose, for example, that the sub-directory called 'carole' is to be removed, but that it still contains some files. The sequence of commands could be as follows.

1.   *erase\lotus\carole*

MS/DOS displays a prompt 'Are you sure (Y/N)?' which allows the user to confirm or abort the command. If 'Y' is entered, all files in the 'carole' sub-directory are deleted.

2.   *rd\lotus\carole*

The sub-directory 'carole' is removed from the directory structure.

23 *Processing Methods*

There are a number of types of information processing system, categorized according to the ways in which data is controlled, stored and passed through the system; four are identified here:

- ☐ batch processing;
- ☐ on-line processing;
- ☐ distributed processing;
- ☐ database systems.

A separate chapter is devoted to the topic of database systems.

Batch Processing Systems

Such systems process 'batches' of data at regular intervals. The data is usually in large volumes and of identical type. Examples of such data are customer orders, current weekly payroll details and stock issues or receipts.

The procedure can be illustrated with the example of payroll, which is a typical application for batch processing. Each pay date, whether it is every week or every month, the payroll details, such as hours worked, overtime earned or sickness days claimed, are gathered for each employee and processed in batches against the payroll master file. The computer then produces payslips for all employees in the company.

A major feature of this and similar applications is that a large percentage (known as the *hit rate*) of the payroll records in the master file are processed during the payroll run. In general high hit rate processing is suitable for batch processing and if, as is usual, the master file is organized sequentially, then the transaction file will be sorted into the same sequence. In the chapter on Computer Files, it is explained that the sorting of transactions is essential if the master file does not allow direct access (as is the case for magnetic tape files).

Batch processing closely resembles manual methods of data processing, in that data on transactions is collected together into batches, sent to the computer centre, sorted into the order of the master file and processed. Such systems are known as 'traditional' data processing systems. There is normally an intermediate stage in the process when the data must be encoded *off-line*, which means that the data is transferred onto tape or disk. Such encoding may be carried out using another computer, such as in *key-to-disk* systems, but the operation is carried out without the use of the main computer system.

A disadvantage of batch processing is the delay, often of hours or days, between collecting the transactions and receiving the results of processing and this has to be borne in mind when an organization is considering whether or not batch processing is suitable for a particular application.

Conversely, batch processing has the advantage of providing many opportunities for controlling the accuracy of data and thus is commonly used when the immediate updating of files is not crucial.

The accuracy controls used in batch and other processing methods are explained in detail in the chapter on System Controls.

On-Line Processing Systems

If a peripheral, such as a Visual Display Unit or keyboard, is on-line, it is under the control of the Central Processing Unit (CPU) of the computer. On-line processing systems, therefore, are those where all peripherals in use are connected to the CPU of the main computer. Transactions can be keyed in directly.

The main advantage of an on-line system is the reduction in time between the collection and processing of data.

There are two main methods of on-line processing:

- □ real-time processing;
- □ time-share processing.

Real-time Processing

Process Control in Real-time

Real-time processing originally referred only to process control systems where, for example, the temperature of a gas furnace is monitored and controlled by a computer. The computer, via an appropriate sensing device, responds immediately to the boiler's variations outside pre-set temperature limits, by switching the boiler on and off to keep the temperature within those limits.

Real-time processing is now used in everyday consumer goods, such as video cameras, because of the development of 'the computer on a chip', more properly called the microprocessor. An important example of the use of the microprocessor is the engine management system, which is now standard on an increasing range of cars. A car's engine performance can be monitored and controlled, by sensing and immediately responding to changes in such factors as air temperature, ignition timing or engine load. Microprocessors dedicated to such functions cannot be used for other purposes and as such are referred to as *embedded systems*. Further examples of the use of microprocessors can be found on the automated production lines of engineering works and car plants where operations requiring fine engineering control can be carried out by Computer Numerical Controlled (CNC) machines.

The important feature common to all these applications is that the speed of the computer allows almost immediate response to external changes.

Information Processing in Real-time

To be acceptable as a real-time information processing system, the *response-time* (that is the time between the entry of a transaction or enquiry at a VDU terminal, the processing of the data and the computer's response) must meet the needs of the user. The delay or response time may vary from a fraction of a second to 2-3 seconds depending on the nature of the transaction and the size of the computer. Any delay beyond these times would generally be unacceptable and would indicate the need for the system to be updated.

There are two types of information processing systems which can be operated in real-time. These are:

☐ transaction processing;

☐ information storage/retrieval.

Transaction Processing. This type of system handles clearly defined transactions one at a time, each transaction being processed completely, including the updating of files, before the next transaction is dealt with. The amount of data input for each transaction is small and is usually entered on an *interactive* basis via a VDU. Interactive means that the user's communication with the computer is carried out by question and answer. In this way, the user can enter queries via the keyboard and receive a response, or the computer can display a prompt on the screen to which the user responds. Such 'conversations' are usually heavily structured and in a fixed format and so do not allow users to ask any questions they wish.

A typical example of transaction processing is provided by an airline booking system and the following procedures describe a client's enquiry for a seat reservation:

(i)   A prospective passenger provides the booking clerk with information regarding his/her flight requirements;

(ii) Following prompts on the screen, the clerk keys the details into the system so that a check can be made on the availability of seats;

(iii) Vacancies appear on the screen and the client can confirm the booking;

(iv) Confirmation of the reservation is keyed into the system, usually by a single key press and the flight seating records are immediately updated;

(v)   Passenger details (such as name, address etc) can now be entered.

Such a system needs to be real-time to avoid the possibility of two clients booking the same seat, on the same flight and at the same time, at different booking offices.

Information Storage/Retrieval. This type of system differs from transaction processing in that, although the information is updated in real-time, the number of updates and the number of sources of updating is relatively small.

Consider, for example, the medical records system in a hospital. A record is maintained for each patient currently undergoing treatment in the hospital. Medical staff require the patient's medical history to be available at any time and the system must also have a facility for entering new information as the patient undergoes treatment in hospital. Sources of information are likely to include a doctor, nurses and perhaps, a surgeon and new entries probably do not number more than one or two per day.

This is an entirely different situation from an airline booking system where the number of entries for one flight record may be 200-300 and entries could be made from many different booking offices throughout the world.

Time-Share Processing

The term time-sharing refers to the activity of the CPU in allocating *time-slices* to a number of users who are given access to centralized computer resources. The technique is described more fully in the Chapter on Operating Systems. In a *multi-user* system, the various users will be engaged with a variety of different applications at the same time.

The aim of a multi-user, time-sharing system is to give each user a good response-time - no more than 2 seconds. The CPU is able to operate at such speed that, provided the system is not overloaded by too many users, each has the impression of being the sole user of the system.

A particular computer system will be designed to support a maximum number of user terminals, so if the number is exceeded or the applications being run on the system are 'heavy' on CPU time, the response time will become lengthy and unacceptable. Time-share systems are possible because of the extreme speed of the CPU in comparison with peripheral devices such as keyboards, VDU screens and printers. Most information processing tasks consist largely of input and output operations which do not occupy the CPU, leaving it free to do any processing required on other users' tasks.

Distributed Processing

As the term suggests, a distributed processing system is one which spreads the processing tasks of an organization across several computer systems; frequently, these systems are connected and *share resources,* (this may relate to common access to files or programs, or even the processing of a single task) through a data communications system. Each computer system in the network must have the ability to process independently, so a central computer with a number of remote intelligent terminals cannot be classified as distributed, even though some limited validation on data may be carried out separately from the host computer. Examples of distributed processing include, mini or mainframe computers interconnected via wide area networks, or a number of local area networks similarly linked. Distributed processing systems may also share resources.

Reasons for Distributed Systems

☐ *Economy.* The transmission of data over telecommunications systems can be costly and local database storage and processing facilities can reduce costs. The radical reduction in computer hardware costs has favoured the expansion of distributed systems against centralized systems.

☐ *Minicomputers and microcomputers.* The availability of minicomputer and microcomputer systems with data transmission facilities has made distributed processing economically viable. An increasingly popular option in large, multi-sited organizations, is to set up local area networks of microcomputers at each site and connect them via communications networks to each other and/or to a central mainframe computer at the Head Office. This provides each site with the advantages of local processing power, local and inter-site communications through Electronic Mail (Chapter 9 Communications) and access to a central mainframe for the main filing and database systems.

☐ *Local Management Control.* It is not always convenient, particularly where an organization controls diverse activities, to have all information processing centralized. Local management control means that the information systems used will be developed by people with direct knowledge of their own information needs. Responsibility for the success or otherwise of their section of the organization may well be placed with local management, so it is desirable that they have control over the accuracy and reliability of the data they use.

24 *System Controls*

Computerized information systems present particular problems for the control of data entering the system, because for much of the time this data is not in human-readable form and even when it is stored, the information remains invisible unless it is printed out or displayed on a VDU screen. If proper system controls are not used, inaccurate data may reach the master files or unauthorized changes to data may be made, resulting in decision-making which may be based on incorrect information.

System controls can be divided into three main types, according to the purposes they serve:

- ☐ Data Control;
- ☐ Auditing;
- ☐ Data Security.

Data Control

A number of data control mechanisms, including for example, the validation of input data, can be employed. Controls should be exerted at all stages in the data processing cycle, which commonly recognizes the following stages:

- ☐ data collection;
- ☐ input;
- ☐ processing, including file processing;
- ☐ output.

Controls can be implemented by:

- ☐ clerical procedures;
- ☐ software procedures.

It is only through the combined application of both clerical and software controls that errors can be minimized, although their entire exclusion can never be guaranteed.

Data Collection and Input Controls

Before describing the controls it is necessary to outline the activities which may be involved in the collection and input of data.

Depending on the application these may include one or more of the following:

- ☐ *Source document preparation.* To ensure standardization of practice and to facilitate checking, data collected for input, for example, customer orders, are clerically transcribed onto source documents specially designed for the purpose;

- ☐ *Data transmission.* If the computer centre is geographically remote from the data collection point, the source documents may be physically transported there, or be keyed and transmitted via a terminal and telecommunications link to the computer;

- ☐ *Data encoding and verification.* This involves the transcription, usually via a keyboard device, of the data onto a storage medium such as magnetic tape or disk; a process of machine verification accompanied by a repeated keying operation assists the checking of keying accuracy. *Key-to-disk* and *key-to-tape* systems are used for encoding, commonly making use of diskette and cassette tape storage, from which media the data is then merged onto a large reel of magnetic tape or a disk pack for subsequent rapid input;

- ☐ *Data input and validation.* Data validation is a computer controlled process which checks the data for its validity according to certain pre-defined parameters, so it must be input to the computer first. The topic of validation is examined in more detail later;

- ☐ *Sorting.* In order to improve the efficiency of processing, input data is sorted into a sequence determined by the *primary key* of each record in the relevant master file (Chapter 22 Computer Files); this is always necessary for efficient sequential file processing, but direct access files allow records to be processed by transactions "as they come".

Possible Controls

Transcription of data from one medium to another, for example, from telephone notepad to customer order form, or from source document to magnetic disk, provides the greatest opportunity for error. A number of strategies can be adopted to help limit data collection input errors, including:

- ☐ minimizing transcription. This may involve the use of automated input methods such as bar code reading (Chapter 6 Peripherals). Another solution is to use *turnaround documents*, which are originally produced by the computer and later become input documents, for example, remittance advices which, having been sent to customers, are then returned with their payments. Because these remittance advices already show customers' details, including account numbers, only the amounts remitted need to be entered for them to become complete input documents;

- ☐ designing data collection and input documents in ways which encourage accurate completion.

- ☐ using clerical checking procedures such as the re-calculation of totals or the visual comparison of document entries with the original sources of information;

- ☐ using codes with a restricted format, for example, customer account numbers consisting of two alphabetic characters, followed by six digits, permits easy validation;

- ☐ employing *batch* methods of input which allow the accumulation and checking of batch control totals, both by clerical and computerized methods;

☐ using screen verification before input data is processed and applied to computer files. Screen dialogue (the form of conversation between the computer and the user) techniques, which allow data verification and correction at the time of entry, can be used to provide this facility;

☐ checking input data with the use of *batch* or *interactive screen* validation techniques;

☐ ensuring that staff are well trained and that clerical procedure manuals are available for newly trained staff;

☐ controlling access to input documents. This is particularly important where documents are used for sensitive applications such as payroll. For example, input documents for changing pay rates should only be available to, say, the Personnel Manager.

File Processing Controls

Once validated data has entered the computer system, checks have to be made to ensure that it is;

☐ applied to the correct files;

☐ consistent with the filed data.

Header Records

Files can have header records which detail the *function*, for example, Sales Ledger, *version number* and *purge date*. The purge date indicates the date after which the file is no longer required and can be overwritten. Thus, a file with a purge date after the current date should not be overwritten. Such details can be checked by the application program to ensure that the correct file is used and that a current file is not accidentally destroyed.

File Validation Checks

Some validation checks can only be made after data input when reference can be made to the relevant master file data. These are described in the later section on data control in batch processing systems.

Data Integrity

The printing of all master file changes allows the user department and auditors to check that all such changes are *authorized* and *consistent* with transaction documents. All data used by applications for reference purposes should be printed periodically; price lists, for example, may be held as permanent data on master files or in table form within computer programs.

Output Controls

It might reasonably be supposed that input and file processing controls are sufficient to ensure accurate output. Nevertheless, a number of simple controls at the output stage can help to ensure that it is complete and is distributed to the relevant users on time. They include:

☐ the comparison of *filed* control totals with *run* control totals. For example, when an entire sequential file is processed, the computer counts all processed records and compares the total with a stored record total held in a *trailer record* at the end of the file;

☐ the *conciliation* of control totals specific to the application, with totals obtained from a related application. For example, the sales transactions total posted to the Sales Ledger for one day should agree with the total sales transactions recorded in the Sales Day Book or Journal;

☐ the following of set procedures for the treatment of error reports;

☐ the proper checking and re-submission of rejected transactions.

Data Control in a Batch Processing System

It is extremely important that all relevant data is processed and that accuracy is maintained throughout the data processing cycle. The controls which are used will depend on the type of processing method in operation, but batch processing provides the greatest opportunity for exerting control over the data, from the input stage through to the output stage. Amongst the control methods outlined above, there are two which are particularly important - *verification* and *validation*. These control methods can be used to maximum advantage in a batch processing system and typical procedures are described below.

The stages involved in a batch processing *system cycle* are illustrated in *Figure 24.1* with a systems flowchart for a payroll run.

The following controls can be used at certain stages within the cycle:

Clerical Controls

These can be used at any stage in the cycle when the data is in a human-readable form. The types of check include:

☐ visual checking of source documents to detect missing, illegible or unlikely data values, an example of the latter being a total of 100 in the weekly overtime hours entry for an individual worker;

☐ the verification of entries by checking them against another source, for example, the price catalogue for the price of a stock item on an invoice;

☐ the re-working of calculations on a source document, for example, the checking of additions which make up the total quantity for an item on an order form.

Verification

Before processing, data has to be transcribed from the source documents onto a computer input medium, usually involving a keying operation to encode the data onto magnetic tape or magnetic disk. This stage can be prone to error, particularly if large volumes of data are involved and verification, which is usually a machine-assisted process, can ensure that data is encoded accurately. Magnetic tape encoders (*key-to-tape* systems), for example, can operate in two modes, *record* and *verify*. The operation involves one person keying the data in the record mode, after which a second person re-keys the data with the machine in verify mode. In effect the machine reads the data from the first keying operation and then checks it against the second keying as it occurs. The machine signals if characters do not agree, thus indicating a possible transcription error. *Key-to-disk* systems operate on a similar principle, either with stand-alone workstations or via terminals linked to a minicomputer and usually incorporate some facility for *validation* of data.

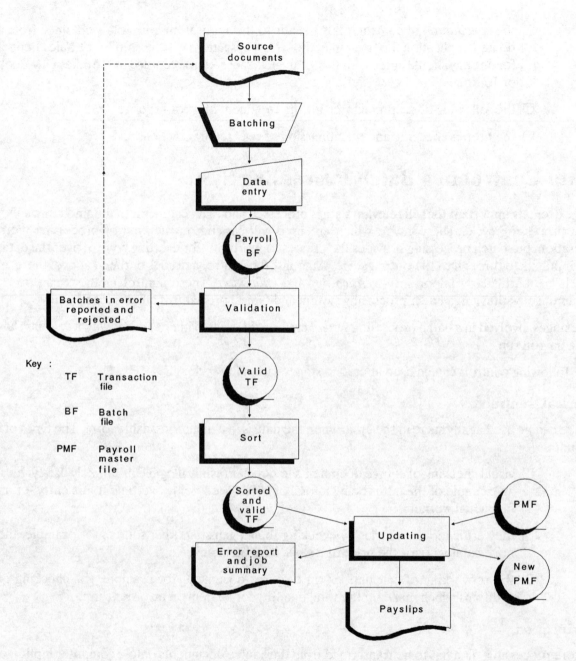

Figure 24.1

Validation

This process is carried out after the data has been encoded onto the input medium and involves a program called the *data vet* or *validation* program. Its purpose is to check that the data falls within certain parameters defined by the systems analyst. A judgement as to whether or not data is valid is made possible by the validation program, but it cannot ensure absolute accuracy. That can only be achieved by the use of all the clerical and computer controls built into the system at the design stage. The difference between *validity* and *accuracy* can be illustrated by the following example.

A company has established a Personnel file. Each record in the file may contain a field for the Job Grade. The permitted values of job grade are A, B, C or D. An entry in an individual's record may be *valid* and accepted by the system if it is recorded as A,B,C or D, but of course this may not be the *correct* grade for the individual worker concerned. Whether or not the grade is correct can only be established by the clerical checks discussed earlier.

Types of Validation Check

Character, Field and Record Checks

☐ *Size*. The number of characters in a field is checked. For example, an account number may require 6 characters and if there are more or less than this, then the item is rejected.

☐ *Mode*. It may be that particular fields must contain particular types of character, for example alphabetic or numeric. If the system is programmed to accept only numbers then letters would be rejected.

☐ *Format*. This refers to the way characters within a field are organized. For example, an Item Code may consist of 2 alphabetic characters followed by 6 numeric characters, so the system would reject any entry which did not correspond to this format.

☐ *Reasonableness*. Quantities can be checked for unusually high or low values. For example, a gas consumer with one small appliance may have a meter reading appropriate to a consumer with a large central heating system and a reasonableness test could be used to reject or highlight it.

☐ *Presence*. If a field must always have a value then it can be checked for existence. For example, the field 'Sex' in a Personnel record would always have to have an M(ale) or F(emale) entry.

☐ *Range*. Values are checked for certain upper and lower limits, for example, account numbers may have to be between 00001 and 10000.

☐ *Check Digits*. An extra digit calculated on an account number can be used as a self checking device. When the number is input to the computer, the validation program carries out a calculation similar to that used to generate the check digit originally and thus checks its validity. This kind of check will highlight transposition errors caused by, for instance, keying digits in the wrong order.

The following example serves to illustrate the operation of one such check digit method.

Example: Modulus 11 Check Digit

Consider a stock code consisting of six digits, for example 462137.

The check digit is calculated as follows:

Firstly, each digit of the stock code is multiplied by its own *weight*. Each digit has a weight relative to its position, assuming the presence of a check digit in the rightmost position. Beginning from the check digit position (x) the digits are weighted 1,2,3,4,5,6 and 7 respectively.

Stock Code	4	6	2	1	3	7	(x)
Multiplied by Weight	7	6	5	4	3	2	(1)
Product	28	36	10	4	9	14	

Secondly, the products are totalled. In this example, the sum produces 101.

Thirdly, divide the sum by modulus 11. This produces 9, remainder 2.

Finally, the check digit is produced by subtracting the remainder 2 from 11, giving 9.

Whenever a code is entered with the relevant check digit, the validation software carries out the same algorithm, including the check digit in the calculation. Provided that the fourth stage produces a *remainder* of *zero* the code is accepted as valid. This can be proved using the same example as above.

Stock code	4	6	2	1	3	7	9
Multiplied by Weight	7	6	5	4	3	2	1
Product	28	36	10	4	9	14	9

Sum of Products 110

Divide sum by 11 giving 10 remainder 0.

If some of the digits are transposed the check digit is no longer applicable to the code and is rejected by the validation program because the results of the algorithm will not leave a remainder of zero. This is shown below.

Stock Code	6	4	1	2	3	7	9
Multiplied by Weight	7	6	5	4	3	2	1
Product	42	24	5	8	9	14	9

Sum of Products 111

Divide sum by 11 giving 10 remainder 1.

All the above checks can be carried out prior to the master file updating stage. Further checks on data can be made through the use of a validation program at the *update* stage, by comparison with the master file. They are as follow:

- [ ] *New records.* When a new record is to be added to the master file, a check can be made to ensure that a record does not already use the entered record key .

- [ ] *Deleted records.* It may be that a transaction is entered for which there is no longer a matching master record.

- [ ] *Consistency.* A check is made that the transaction values are consistent with the values held on the master record which is to be updated. For instance a deduction for pension contributions by an employee who is not old enough to be in a pension scheme would obviously be inconsistent.

Validation using Batch Controls

These checks are only possible in a batch processing system.

Batch Totals

The purpose of batch totals is to allow a conciliation of manually produced totals for a batch with comparable computer-produced totals. Differences are signalled and the batch is rejected for checking and re-submission.

Preparation of Batch Totals. Following the arrangement of source documents into batches of say 30 in each batch, totals are calculated on add-listing machines for each value it is required to control. On an order form, for example, quantities and prices may be separately totalled to provide two control totals. Totals may also be produced for each account number or item code simply for purposes of control although they are otherwise meaningless. For this reason such totals are called *hash* or *nonsense* totals. The totals are recorded on a batch control slip *Figure 24.2* attached to the batch, together with a value for the number of documents in the batch and a batch number. The batch number is kept in a register held by the originating department so that missing or delayed batches can be traced.

```
DeptRef: Sales            Date: 30/06/92
DataType: Orders          BatchNo: 37

Number in Batch: 40

Quantity Total: 30450

Price Total: 13223.66
                          Prepared by: N W
Item-code Total: 576216   Checked by: G K
                          Entered by: A K
```

Figure 24.2

It should be noted that hash totals may produce a figure which has a large number of digits, so extra digits over and above the original length of the data item are truncated.

Reconciliation of Batch Totals. The details from each batch control slip are entered with each batch of transactions at the encoding stage. The serial transaction file which results may be arranged as in *Figure 24.3*

```
BT1 TR TR TR TR TR BT2 TR TR TR TR TR BT3 TR TR TR TR ....
```

Key: TR Transaction
          record

      BT Batch
         total

Figure 24.3

The serial transaction file is processed from beginning to end by the validation program. The sum of the transaction records relating to each batch should match the batch total. If any validation error is detected, either by differences in batch totals or through the character of field checks described earlier, the offending batch is rejected to be checked and re-submitted. The rejected batches are reported on a computer printout.

Validation During Updating

Checks can be made in the manner described earlier, on transactions for deleted or new records, or on data which is inconsistent with the relevant record on the master file.

The above controls can be used in conjunction with proper clerical procedures to ensure that as far as possible, the information stored on the master files is accurate.

File Controls

In addition to controlling the accuracy of data entering the system it is essential to check both that the data is complete and that all relevant data is processed. This can be done through the use of file controls on the transaction file.

Following the validation of the batches of transactions, correct batches are written to another file to be sorted and used for updating the relevant master file. During validation, the validation program accumulates totals for all the correct batches. These can be used during the update run to ensure that the whole transaction file is processed.

Validation in On-Line Systems

On-line systems as described in the Chapter on Processing Methods tend to be interactive and transactions are processed immediately with the master files at the data entry stage. The main controls which can be introduced to such systems include:

☐ the character, field and record validation checks described earlier. Error messages are displayed on the screen at the time data is entered and require immediate correction at that time;

☐ visual verification. At the end of each transaction entry, the operator is given the opportunity to scan the data on the screen and to re-enter any incorrect entries detected. This usually takes the form of a message at the bottom of the screen which is phrased in a way such as "Verify (yes or no)";

☐ the use of well-trained data entry operators. They should have sufficient knowledge of the data being entered and the application it serves, to respond to error messages and make corrections to data accordingly.

Auditing

There are two main techniques available for computer system auditing. One technique involves the use of *test data* and the other of *audit enquiry programs*.

The Test Data Method

With this method, the auditor runs the target application with test data, the expected processing results of which are already known. In this way, the computation of for example, payroll figures, can be tested for accuracy in a variety of circumstances. The logical outputs of the program can also be verified. In fact, the method is similar to that used by systems designers prior to a system's implementation. The test data may be recorded on a batch of source documents, in which case, the input will not only test the application's computerized processing and controls, but also the suitability of the source document design for input purposes. The auditing process may also include the testing of batch preparation and input data verification procedures. Software validation checks should be subjected to testing with *normal* and *exceptional* data. Normal data includes the most general data which the software is designed to handle. Exceptional data includes any which the software is not designed to accept. The software should demonstrate that it can reject all such data and continue its normal operation. Test data runs may take one of the following forms.

Live Data Testing

The auditor selects examples of live data from the system which fulfil the conditions to be tested. The results are calculated manually and checked against the computer-produced outputs. It is essential that manual calculations are made, as a casual assessment of the accuracy of processing can often lead to errors being overlooked. A severe disadvantage of this approach is that the auditor may be unable to find examples of all conditions to be tested in the available live data. It is also quite possible that examples of exceptional or nonsensical data will not be found at the time of the audit and it is important that such conditions are tested. 'Murphy's law' will probably ensure that such exceptional data appears the day after the audit. The testing can only give a 'snapshot' of the system's performance which may be radically different on other occasions.

Historical Data Testing

Sampling of transactions which have already passed through the system is an important part of internal auditing. It is important that the original transaction documents are made available for inspection to allow the auditor to check their *validity, authorization* and *consistency* with associated results. Results can be calculated manually and then compared with any printed results. If results were not printed at the time, then use may be made of a *file dump utility* to access the appropriate historic file.

Dummy Data Testing

With this method, the auditor constructs fictitious or dummy data which contains the conditions to be tested. To ensure that such test data is not applied to the application's operational files, it is also usual to set up dummy files, for example, customer or supplier files, specifically for audit purposes. If such data is used in an actual processing run, and the entries are not reversed out in time, there is a danger that the results will be taken as real by users. There are a number of apocryphal stories concerning lorries which delivered goods to non-existent addresses as a result of such fictitious entries. For this reason, it is always advisable to make use of specially created audit files or copies of the master files.

In summary, the test data method is useful for the audit of:

- ☐ data preparation procedures, such as batching;
- ☐ data verification and validation controls;
- ☐ an application's computational and logical processes.

A number of drawbacks and limitations of the test data method of auditing can also be identified:

- ☐ it only provides a snapshot view of the system at the time of the audit. On the other hand, it may be used repeatedly in order to cover a more extended period of assessment;
- ☐ it may involve the setting up of dummy files if fictitious data is to be used;

□ source documents and batch totals have to be prepared for fictitious data which is not of operational use to the business;

□ the computer system has to be made available to the auditor for the period of the test. During this time it is not available for operational use.

Audit Enquiry Programs

These programs overcome many of the disadvantages inherent in the test data method and are an essential audit tool, particularly for external auditing which requires the examination of live data already processed. Audit enquiry programs vary in sophistication but generally provide facilities to:

□ examine the contents of computer files;

□ retrieve data from computer files;

□ compare the contents of files. Thus, for example, two versions of identical files may be compared to ensure that the structure has not been altered, perhaps to include an extra field or record type;

□ produce formatted reports according to the auditor's requirements.

A major benefit to the auditor is that any data stored on computer file can be retrieved. Many financial packages update files 'in situ', so that each updating transaction causes the *overwriting* of the relevant master record with new values. Thus, there may be circumstances when the results of processing individual transactions can only be established in terms of the cumulative effect of a group of transactions on a particular record. For example, during one day, a stock record may be updated by several transactions but the values held in the stock record at the end will not show their individual effects. However, provided that the source documents are retained or the transactions are logged onto a separate file (see Transaction Logging in the next section on Security), the auditor can still reconcile their expected effect on the master file with the actual values held there.

Audit Trails

An audit trail should allow the tracing of a transaction's history as it progresses from input through to output. Computerized systems present particular difficulties in that the trail disappears as it enters the computer system. The auditor may ignore the computer system and pick up the trail at the output stage (auditing around the computer). This has obvious limitations in that the auditor cannot trace a transaction which does not result in printed output. Although audit enquiry programs allow the auditor to examine the contents of files, not every transaction effect is recorded permanently on computer file. Audit trails have to be designed into the system in such a way that intermediate stages of a transaction's progress are recorded for audit purposes.

Data Security

□ The controls used have several main functions:

□ to prevent loss of data files caused by software or procedural errors, or physical by hazards;

☐ to protect data from accidental or deliberate disclosure to unauthorized individuals or groups;

☐ to protect the data from accidental or deliberate corruption or modification. This is known as maintaining *data integrity*;

☐ to protect the rights of individuals and organizations to restrict access to information which relates to them and is of a private nature, to those entitled or authorized to receive it. This is known as *data privacy*.

Security Against Data Loss

The loss of master files can be an extremely serious occurrence for any organization so properly organized security procedures need to be employed. Among commercial organizations that have lost the major part of their information store, a large percentage subsequently go out of business.

Master Files

The main causes of data loss are as follow:

☐ Environmental hazards such as fire, flood and other natural accidents;

☐ Mechanical problems, for example the danger of disk or tape damage caused by a drive unit malfunction;

☐ Software errors resulting from programming error;

☐ Human error. A wrong file may be loaded, the wrong program version used, a tape or disk mislaid, or physical damage caused to tape or disk;

☐ Malicious damage. It is not unknown for staff to intentionally damage storage media or to misuse programs at a terminal.

The standard solution to such problems is to take regular copies of master files and to store the copies in a separate secure location. It is also necessary to maintain a record of transactions affecting a file since the last copy was taken, so that if necessary they can be used to reconstruct the latest version of the file.

Magnetic Tape Files

When a tape master file is updated by a tape transaction file the physical nature of the medium makes it necessary for a new tape file to be produced. As the systems flowchart in *Figure 24.4* illustrates, the updating procedure provides a built-in security system referred to as the Grandfather, Father and Son (generation) System.

In the first run, Master 1 is updated by the transactions file to produce Master File 2 as its *son*. Master File 1 is the *father*. Should the *son* file be damaged and the data lost, it can be re-created from the *father* master file and the relevant transactions. At the end of the second run, Master File 1 becomes the *grandfather*, Master File 2 becomes the *father* and Master File 3, the *son*.

Each generation provides security for subsequent files. The number of generations used will depend on the policy of the organization. Three generations are usually regarded as providing sufficient security and the oldest files are re-used by being overwritten as each cycle of generations is completed.

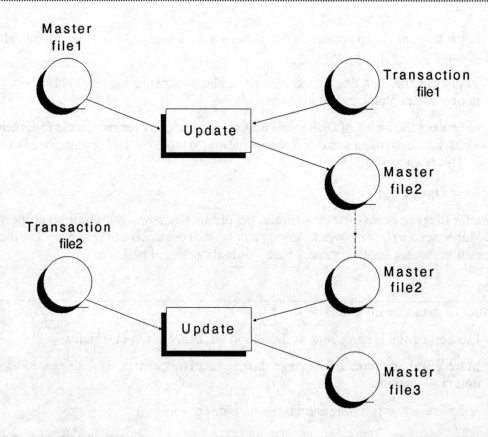

Figure 24.4

Internal Header Labels

Internal header labels are designed to deal with two major areas of concern:

☐ It is important that the correct file is used in a file processing operation to ensure correct results. Thus, the *subject* of the file and the *version* must be identifiable. For example, it is no good producing monthly payslips using information from a payroll master file three months out of date.

☐ A tape file must be protected against accidental erasure. This may occur because tapes are re-usable and when a file is no longer required it can be overwritten by new information.

To ensure that the correct file is used for any particular job, a tape file usually has an internal header label. The label appears at the beginning of the tape and identifies it. The identifying information in the label is usually recorded under program control or by a data encoding device.

A tape header label usually contains the following items of information:

☐ File name e.g. PAYROLL, STOCK, SALES;

☐ Date created;

☐ Purge date - the date from which the tape is no longer required and may be re-used.

The label is checked by the program, before the file is processed, to ensure that the correct tape is being used.

File Protection Ring

A device called a file protection ring can be used to prevent accidental erasure. When tapes are stored off-line, the rings are not fitted. To *write* to a tape, the ring must first be fitted to the centre of the reel. A tape can be *read* by the computer whether or not a ring is fitted. The simple rule to remember is 'no ring, no write'.

Magnetic Disk Files

Security Backups

Disk files can be treated in the same way as tape files in that the updating procedure may produce a new master file leaving the original file intact. On the other hand, if the file is updated *in-situ* (which in so doing overwrites the existing data), then it will be necessary to take regular back-up copies as processing proceeds. The frequency with which copies are taken will depend on the volume of transactions affecting the master file. If the latest version of the master file is corrupted or lost, then it can be re-created using the previous back-up together with the transaction data received since the back-up.

Transaction Logging

In an on-line system, transactions may enter the system from a number of terminals in different locations, thus making it difficult to re-enter transactions for the re-creation of a damaged master file. One solution is to log all the transactions onto a serial transaction file at the same time as the master file is updated. Thus, the re-creation process can be carried out without the need for keying in the transactions again.

The systems flowchart in *Figure 24.5* illustrates this procedure.

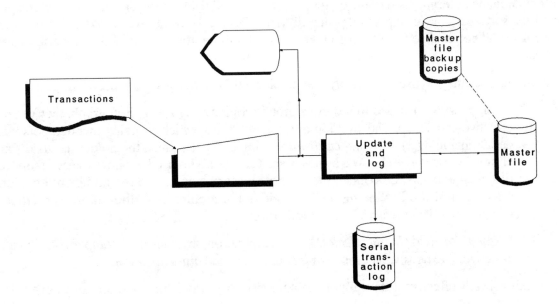

Figure 24.5

Access Controls

Unauthorized access to a system may: provide vital information to competitors; result in the deliberate or accidental corruption of data; allow fraudulent changes to be made to data; result in loss of privacy for individuals or organizations.

To avoid such hazards an information system should be protected *physically*, by *administrative procedures* and *software*.

To detect any unauthorized access or changes to the information system:

☐ users should require *authorization* (with different levels of authority depending on the purpose of access);

☐ the computer should *log* all successful and attempted accesses;

☐ users should be *identifiable* and their identity *authenticated*;

☐ the files should be capable of being *audited*;

☐ the actions of *programmers* should be carefully controlled to prevent fraud through changes to software.

Physical Protection

These include the use of security staff, mechanical devices, such as locks and keys and electronic alarm/identification systems.

Computer systems with terminals at remote sites present a weak link in any system and they must be properly protected and software plays an important protection role. Disk and tape libraries also need to be protected, otherwise it would be possible for a thief to take file media to another centre with compatible hardware and software.

A variety of methods may be used to *identify* and possibly *authenticate* a system user. They include:

☐ *Identity Cards*. Provided that they cannot be copied and have a photograph, they can be effective and cheap. The addition of a magnetic strip which contains encoded personal details including a *personal identification number* (PIN), which the holder has to key in, allows the user to be checked by machine. This method is used to allow access to service tills outside banks. Of course, the user of the card may not be the authorized holder, possession of the PIN being the only additional requirement; the following methods allow authentication as well as identification;

☐ *Personal Physical Characteristics*. Voice recognition or fingerprint comparison provide effective, if expensive, methods of *identification* and *authentication*.

Such methods are only effective if the supporting administrative procedures are properly adhered to.

Software Protection

Ideally, before a user is given access to a system, the log-in procedures should check for:

☐ authorization;

☐ identification;

☐ authentication.

Authorization is usually provided by an account code, which must be keyed in response to a computer prompt; similar prompts may appear for a user-id (*identification*) and a password (*authentication*).

Further control can be exerted with *fixed terminal identifiers*, whereby each terminal and its location is physically identifiable by the controlling computer, thus preventing access from additional unauthorized locations. Such controls can also be used to restrict particular terminals to particular forms and levels of access.

Password Controls

Access to files can be controlled at different levels by a series of passwords, which have to be keyed into the terminal in response to a series of questions displayed on the screen. For example, a clerk in a Personnel Department may be given authority to display information regarding an employee's career record but only the Personnel Manager is authorized to change the information held on file.

Passwords should be carefully chosen, kept secure (memorized and not divulged) and changed frequently. Using people's names, for example, may allow entry by trial and error. Characters should not be echoed on screen as the password is entered.

Handshaking. This technique requires more than a simple password and may be used between two computers or a computer and a user, as a means of access control. In the latter case, the user would be given a pseudo-random number by the computer and the expected response would be a transform, of that random number. The transform may be to multiply the first and last digits of the number and add the product to a value equal to the day of the month plus 1. Provided the transform is kept secret, handshaking provides more security than simple passwords.

One-time passwords. With this method, the computer will only accept a password for *one access occasion*; subsequently, it will expect the user to provide a different password for each additional access, in a pre-defined sequence. Provided the password list and their expected sequence list are kept separate, then possession of one list only will not be of any assistance.

The number of attempts at logging-on should be controlled, so, for example, after three unsuccessful attempts, the user should be locked out and a record kept of the time and nature of the attempt.

Authorization Tables

These are held with the relevant files and detail the kinds of access permitted by particular users or groups of users - read only, read and write or delete. Control may also be exerted at a record or field level.

Data Encryption

If data signals being transmitted along the telecommunication links are not properly protected, *hackers* can pick up the signals and display them on their own machines. To prevent such intrusion, data encryption methods are used to protect important financial, legal and other confidential information during transmission from one centre to another. Encryption scrambles the data to make it unintelligible during transmission. As the power and speed of computers has increased, so the breaking of codes has been made easier.

Code designers have produced methods of encryption which are currently unbreakable in any reasonable time period, even by the largest and most powerful computers available. An example of such an elaborate coding system is illustrated by the operation of the Electronic Funds Transfer (EFT) system. This is used by banks and other financial institutions to transfer vast sums of money so these transmissions are protected by the latest data encryption techniques. The Data Encryption Standard (DES) was approved by the American National Bureau of Standards in 1977, but as costs of powerful computers have fallen and come within the reach of criminal organization, EFT makes use of the DES standard, plus additional encryption techniques.

Security to Maintain Data Integrity

Data integrity refers to the accuracy and consistency of the information stored and is thus covered by the security methods outlined above.

Security to Maintain Privacy of Data

The rights of individuals and organizations concerning their confidential records are similarly protected by the security controls outlined earlier. In addition, legislation by parliament (the Data Protection Act 1984) attempts to exert some control by requiring persons or organizations holding personal information on computer files to register with the Data Protection Registrar. Some countries have 'Freedom of Information Acts' which allow the individual to see any personal information stored their own files, except where national security is thought to be threatened. It is generally accepted that the Data Protection Act falls far short of complete freedom of information.

25 *Program Design*

The task of programming may be broken down into a number of stages:

(i)   Definition of the problem. This is often provided in the form of a program specification which states the function of the program in terms of the data to be processed and the output to be produced.

(ii)   Designing the logical solution to the problem. Program design is a crucial stage in which the programmer identifies the processing tasks required, and the precise order in which they are to be carried out. The design process takes no account of the programming language to be used in the final product; the emphasis is on defining program logic rather than syntax. Many techniques have been developed to assist the programmer to design programs effectively, and a number of these techniques are described in later sections of this chapter.

(iii)   Coding the program. Having spent time in thinking about and designing the logical structure of the program, the programmer's next task is to convert the design specification into actual computer instructions in the implementation language. If sufficient care has been taken on the design stage, coding should be an almost mechanical process for an experienced programmer.

(iv)   Program debugging. This is the term used for detecting and correcting 'bugs' or errors in a program. Three types of errors can occur in a program: syntax errors, runtime errors and logic errors.

The first result from using the programming language incorrectly by, for example, making punctuation errors, or typing errors or by forming programming instructions incorrectly. The computer will be able to detect these because the rules for the correct formation of the program statements are stored in the computer.

Runtime errors occur as a result of the program attempting to perform some operation which is not possible. For example, a division calculation would generate a runtime error if the denominator was zero, division by zero not being permissible. Similarly, an error condition might arise if the program required a file to be read from backing storage and the file was not present.

Finally, logic errors, the most difficult type to find, are often the result of incorrect program design. The program, either all of the time or under certain conditions, does not behave as required. For instance, a logic error in a payroll program might lead to an employee being given too much or too little money, either situation being unacceptable. Thorough program testing is the only way to ensure the elimination of such errors.

(v)   Program testing. As mentioned above, the only way to be completely confident that a program will behave as expected, under all circumstances that can conceivably arise, is to test the program thoroughly before it is put into commission.

(vi)   Documentation. Having written, tested and debugged a program, it must be documented. Program documentation is the reference source providing essential information for anyone concerned with the program. As such it could be consulted by systems analysts, programmers, computer operators, users or other interested parties.

The stages outlined above are treated in more depth in the sections following.

Program Design

In the early days of programming using high-level languages, *monolithic* programs were the norm, programs which effectively comprised a single unstructured sequence of statements. Such programs were generally difficult to understand, debug and modify.

Modular programming seemed to offer a solution to these problems by breaking down a programming task into a number of components or *modules*. Essentially modular programming was based on three ideas:

☐ A program should be split into a number of modules which could be separately compiled.

☐ Modules should be small (no more than 50 lines of code for example).

☐ Modules should be separately tested before being integrated into the final program.

In principle these ideas seemed to have a number of benefits over previous programming practices:

☐ General-purpose modules could be re-used in other applications.

☐ The independence of modules would aid program maintenance, updating and testing.

☐ Programs would be more reliable.

Unfortunately these benefits frequently failed to materialize: many users were unable to create or take advantage of libraries of modules; integration of modules often proved to be difficult; modifying a program could necessitate having to modify and recompile several modules rather than just a single program as before; some compilers introduced very large overheads for small modules; it was frequently difficult to determine the most appropriate way to split a program into convenient modules.

Top-down, Structured programming allowed a single program to retain the advantages of modular programming, and at the same time remove many of its disadvantages.

When professor Edsger Dijkstra of the University of Eindhoven in the Netherlands, a pioneer of structured programming, first presented his ideas in about 1965 they had relatively little impact. At that time programming, using languages such as Fortran and PL/1, relied heavily on the use of GOTO statements; professor Dijkstra maintained that this encouraged bad programming habits and such statements could in fact be completely eliminated from programming languages, and that doing so would lead to programs of much greater quality. He also advocated the adoption of top-down program design.

Today his ideas are widely accepted, and we realise the importance of combining top-down design with structured programming principles in developing clear programs which are relatively easy to test and maintain. Top-down design provides us with a methodical approach to analysing a problem and deriving a solution to it in terms of a hierarchical organization of program components; structured programming additionally provides simple rules for implementing these components clearly and efficiently.

In this chapter we first examine the ideas behind top-down design before considering structured programming, and in particular Jackson Structured Programming which takes structured programming a stage further in the search for efficient and reliable program design techniques.

Note that another design technique continuing to attract great interest is object-orientated design and this is discussed in Chapter 28 in relation to programming languages.

Top-down Design

In top-down design the skeleton framework, or mainline program, is designed first, showing the main components of the program, and the order in which they are to be executed. Each main component is then decomposed into smaller, more manageable components; this process continues, at each level of component definition, until the program designer judges that there is sufficient detail in the design to allow the coding stage to commence. This approach is the complete opposite of *bottom-up* programming in which primitive components are combined to form larger components which are themselves combined with others until the complete program has been synthesized.

The process of decomposing components into sequences of smaller components is often termed *stepwise refinement*. Top-down design allows a program to be designed methodically by providing a complete definition of the program at each level of complexity. To illustrate the process in a simple case, consider the following problem:

> The sales details for a number of company salesmen are held on a computer file. Each record in the file contains the following data:
>
> > *Salesman name*
> > *District code*
> > *Item sold*
> > *Number of units sold*
> > *Value of sale*
>
> There may be any number of records for each salesman, each record detailing one sale. There are three districts each having two salesmen. The records in the file are ordered according to salesman within district code, that is, all the records for a particular salesman are together, and the salesmen in a certain district are grouped together.
>
> A report is to be produced giving the total sales value for each salesman, the total sales value for each district, and a grand total for the company.

The structure of the report might be as follows:

ACME COMPUTER SERVICES
SALES REPORT : January 1988

Salesman	District	Sales Value	District	Total
J. Smith	North	213.55		
R. Moray	North	334.90		
			548.45	
R. Winns	Mid	476.50		
P. Scott	Mid	254.60		
			731.10	
A. Williams	South	515.40		
T. Tyson	South	668.80		
			1184.20	
		GRAND TOTAL		2463.75

Adopting the top-down approach, the report program can be described at the highest level as a sequence of three components as shown in *Figure 25.1*.

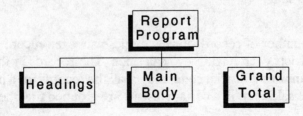

Figure 25.1

Report Program structure:

1. The report starts with the page headings identifying the company and nature of the report, and these lines are followed by the column headings.

2. Next is the body of the report summarising salesmen totals and district totals.

3. Then follows the final grand total line.

These three components are then decomposed into the smaller components shown in *Figures 25.2, 25.3* and *25.5.*

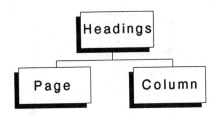

Figure 25.2

Headings structure:

1. Page headings.

2. Column headings.

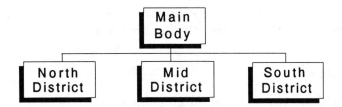

Figure 25.3

Main Body structure:

1. North District details giving sales figures for each salesman and the district total.

2. Mid District (as above).

3. South District (as above).

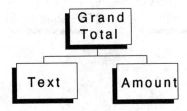

Figure 25.4

Grand Total structure:

1. Text : 'GRAND TOTAL'.

2. The sum of the district totals.

The first and last components, that is, *Headings* and *Grand Total* have now been defined in as much detail as necessary but the processing for the three districts can be further decomposed (for example, *Figure 25.5* showing structure of *North District*):

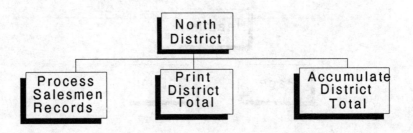

Figure 25.5

North District structure:

1.   Read the records for each salesman, accumulate the sales value and print the salesmen details. Accumulate the sales value for the district by adding the sales totals for the salesmen.

2.   Print the district total.

3.   Accumulate the district total so that the grand total can be printed.

Mid and *South* districts would be treated identically.

The component 'Process Salesmen Records' can be expandedas shown in *Figure 25.6*.

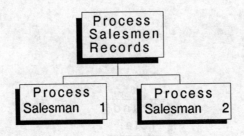

Figure 25.6

Process Salesmen Records structure:

1.   Process Salesman 1 involves reading each record for that salesman, accumulating his sales values, printing the total and accumulating the total to form a district total.

2.   Salesman 2 is treated identically.

Thus, after reaching a point where further decomposition of components is unnecessary, the final program design would be as shown in *Figure 25.7*.

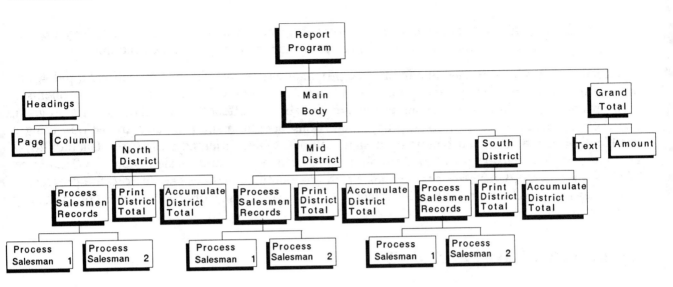

Figure 25.7

Guidelines for Top-down Design

Here are a number of suggestions for successfully adopting top-down design:

☐ Initially, the structure of a program should be expressed diagrammatically (using a structure chart or equivalent representation, for example) for clarity. Later, if necessary, it can be converted to a more appropriate form (pseudocode, for example) in preparation for coding.

☐ The diagrammatic specification of the internal structure of a component should not occupy more than a single page of paper. If this is not the case then decompose the component into two or more parts which comply with this rule. The function of each component should be easy to comprehend; the larger the component, the harder it is to understand how it achieves its purpose.

☐ Pay careful attention to the way in which components interface with each other in the program. Components are often subprograms which may have parameters and may return values; be careful to specify precisely the nature of each of these.

☐ Having identified a component, its function and interface, do not immediately concern yourself with how it is to be implemented. Concentrate on the structure of the design level by level without becoming distracted by trivial details.

Advantages of Top-down Design

☐ It provides a systematic method of analysing a programming task, by breaking down complex problems into small understandable components.

☐ It is generally accepted that it is more likely to produce readable and reliable programs than bottom-up approaches.

☐ Coding the program can follow the same procedure used in its design, that is, top-down, stepwise refinement, and this facilitates the use of subprograms.

☐ Program testing is simplified by allowing program components to be tested as they are defined in a top-down manner. This is explained more fully in a later section.

As a final note, it should be said that in practice programs are rarely written in an entirely top-down or bottom-up fashion. For example, programmers will frequently use pre-written and tested components in their programs; knowing that such components are available can affect the overall design of a program, and their use amounts to a bottom-up approach. Consequently many programs are written using a combination of top-down and bottom-up design methods. Object-oriented design (see Chapter 28) is another example which does not fit comfortably into top-down or bottom-up design categories. The *objects* of object-oriented programs are components which are identified and designed before the program in which they are to be used, and indeed Smalltalk, a language specifically for object-oriented programming provides an extensive library of object classes for the programmer to use.

Structured Programming

Structured programming is closely connected to the previous section on top-down design. Structured programming also uses the principle of designing a program in terms of a hierarchy of components, but in addition imposes a number of restrictions on the way that these components are written:

(i)   Programs should use combinations of components chosen exclusively from three simple types of program constructs, namely, *sequences* (two or more operations, one after the other), *selections* (choosing one component from two or more possibilities) and *iterations* (repeating one or more operations until some condition is satisfied). The implication of this statement is that GOTO instructions are not necessary. In fact, structured programming is sometimes referred to as GOTO-less programming.

(ii)   Program modules should be small and clear enough to be easily comprehensible.

(iii) Program modules should have only one entry point at the beginning of the module, and one exit point at the end of the module.

The first restriction regarding permissible program constructs derives from theoretical studies which have shown that any proper program can be written using only these control structures, in appropriate combinations, and such programs tend to be easy to understand, test and debug. The three structures are usually available in one form or another in most common high-level languages. Pascal, designed to teach good programming habits, is an ideal language for structured programming.

The other two principles outlined above encourage programmers to pay close attention to the readability of their programs; simply constructed programs, easy to read, with clear paths through modules result in shorter development and testing times. Such programs are also easier to maintain by a programmer schooled in structured programming techniques, other than the author of the program.

Structured programming techniques are receiving an increasing amount of attention as their benefits are becoming recognised. In particular, structured programs are easier to write, understand, modify and debug than other types of programs. This leads to greater programmer productivity and cheaper software.

Most procedural computer languages now embody the basic constructs required for structured programming. However, no matter to what degree a programming language supports structured programming, it is the programmer who determines whether a program is structured, not the language. In other words, programmers are 'structured', not languages. The implication is that even if a language explicitly supports structured programming, a program written in that language may not be structured; and the converse, that a language (assembler for example) which does not explicitly support structured programming could be used to write structured programs, is also true.

The notion that in structured programming GOTO instructions must be avoided at all costs needs to be qualified also. The work done by professor Dijkstra on the avoidance of GOTO statements related to the high-level languages commonly used at that time, notably Fortran, COBOL and PL/1. Fortran, in particular, being a first generation high-level language, embodied control structures related to the instruction sets of the computers in existence when it was developed. Consequently branching instructions were used unreservedly in Fortran programs. However, professor Dijkstra was mainly concerned that when these branch instructions were used in an unrestricted manner, it frequently led to 'spaghetti' programs in which the flow of control was far from obvious. He argued that if the structured programming constructs outlined above were available in a language, then the use of branching instructions would be obviated, and program structure could be clarified enormously.

However, as we have implied earlier, structured programs could still be written in Fortran (in its original form, that is - it has changed considerably since those early days) even though these programs might still contain a significant number of branch statements, *providing such statements are used exclusively to simulate the control structures necessary for structured programming*. This is the reason why it is perfectly feasible to write structured programs in assembly languages. For example, to simulate a while..do loop we could write (in pseudocode):

```
label_1:if flag = 1 then goto label_2
           {statement block to be repeated}
           goto label_1
label_2: {exit loop}
```

This would be easy to implement in Fortran or assembler, and it is equivalent to writing in structured form:

```
while flag = 1 do
   {statement block to be repeated}
endwhile
```

A form of structured programming, now well established, is *Jackson Structured Programming* (JSP) developed by M.A.Jackson, and described in his book *Principles of Program Design* (Academic Press 1975). JSP is a structured design process particularly relevant to data processing problems, mainly as a result of its emphasis on the early consideration of data structures. The design technique in its entirety consists of a number of distinct stages eventually culminating in a detailed specification from which a program can be written very easily. Jackson argues that it is not sufficient to mechanically apply the principles of structured programming - they must be applied in a manner appropriate to the problem being addressed. He points out that a poorly structured program will not be saved by the quality of its individual components. He stresses that the structure of a program must be determined by the *structure of the data* that it uses, and he provides a systematic method of ensuring this.

The first stage of the JSP process is to identify the logical data structures used or produced by the program. These data structures lead to the derivation of a program structure which is then refined and augmented until it forms a detailed program specification. Though the full process is particularly suited to data processing tasks involving easily identified data structures, because it has as its basis the principles of structured programming, it is a design technique which can be adapted to a wide variety of problems. The graphical notation it employs facilitates the clear top-down definition of program logic independently of implementation languages.

We describe the full JSP design process in the next section.

Jackson Structured Programming

One of the major problems which confronts the beginner faced with the task of writing a computer program, is where to start. How is it possible to organize program instructions to perform the required task, and how can the programmer be sure that the finished program will always perform as desired? The aim of this section is to answer these questions by introducing a program design technique which replaces inspiration with a simple logical sequence of steps which are easy to learn, understand and apply.

The technique is called *Jackson Structured Programming*, or *JSP*. It has the following characteristics:

(a) it depends on the application of a small number of simple, clearly defined steps;

(b) it can be taught because of (a);

(c) it is practical, resulting in programs which are easy to write, understand, test and maintain.

JSP is a 'Top-down' programming technique in which the programmer, starting from the premise that the complete program will be too difficult to comprehend in its entirety, breaks the problem down into a sequence of manageable components. Each such component is then broken down into smaller components, and so on until a level is reached which cannot easily be further simplified. Without this technique, a programming problem can be too large and complex in its complete form. This process produces a hierarchical program structure resembling a tree diagram as shown in *Figure 25.8*.

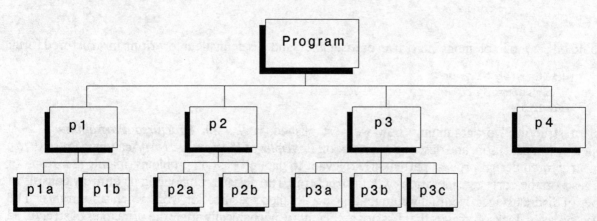

Figure 25.8

Each level lists the procedures (*p1, p2* etc) which provide a complete description of the program. The amount of detail increases as the level number increases. Thus the program consists of the sequence

>   *p1..p2..p3..p4*

or equivalently

>   *p1a..p1b..p2a..p2b..p3a..p3b..p3c..p4*

since both sequences describe the same program but at differing levels of detail.

p1a and *p1b*, for example, provide a more detailed picture of *p1*.

The Basic Components of JSP Design

There are only four basic components:

☐ ELEMENTARY COMPONENTs which are not further subdivided into constituent components;

☐ SEQUENCE of two or more components occurring in order;

☐ SELECTION of one component from a number of alternatives;

☐ ITERATION in which a single component is repeated zero or more times.

Each separate component of a sequence, selection or iteration may be a sequence, a selection or an iteration, so there is no limit to the complexity of structure which can be formed.

The structures developed using combinations of these four component types are as equally useful for describing data structures as for describing program structures. This property forms the basis of JSP design, which uses descriptions of data structures to define the fundamental structure of the program. The next sections illustrate the idea of data structures and how they can be described through the use of the four basic components identified above.

Sequences

A sequence has two or more components occurring in order. It would be represented as shown in *Figure 25.9*, for a sequence of three components:

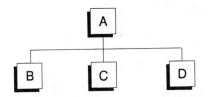

Figure 25.9

If we wish to describe a pack of cards which has been sorted into suits, we might consider it as being a sequence of four suits (*Figure 25.10*).

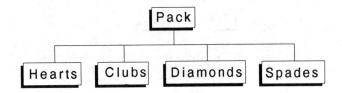

Figure 25.10

A meal might be considered to be a sequence of *starter*, *main course* and *dessert* (*Figure 25.11*)

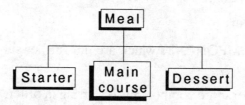

Figure 25.11

A file consisting of a *header record* (describing certain characteristics of the file, for instance) followed by a set of data records can be regarded as a sequence of two components (*Figure 25.12*).

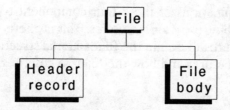

Figure 25.12

A computer-generated report of a sales file might consist of a list of *transaction* details followed by a *grand total* of sales value (*Figure 25.13*).

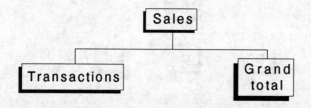

Figure 25.13

Each transaction could itself be regarded as a sequence of three components: *item description*, *number sold*, and *sales value*. In fact the item description might also be recognised as a sequence of *code number* and *name*.

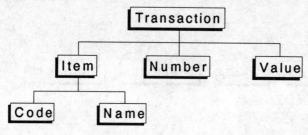

Figure 25.14

In this instance, the elementary components of *Transaction* would be *code number, name, number*, and *value*, since none of these is further defined. This hierarchical type of description illustrates the way in which a simple concept such as sequence can give rise to quite complicated structures.

As a final example of a sequence, a COBOL program which consists of four divisions could be represented as the sequence as shown in *Figure 25.15*.

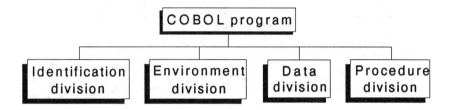

Figure 25.15

The examples illustrate that it is just as easy to describe a data structure as it is to describe a sequence of processes.

Selections

The selection component indicates what choices are available when one single component is to be selected from several alternatives (*Figure 25.16*).

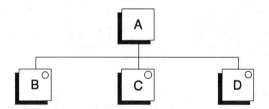

Figure 25.16

The small circles in the three boxes show that *A* is a selection and that only one of the three items shown is to be selected.

Suppose that we wish to represent the possible results when two people cut a pack of cards in order to see who has the higher card. The process could be represented as a sequence of two actions, the second of which can have one of two possible outcomes as shown in *Figure 25.17*.

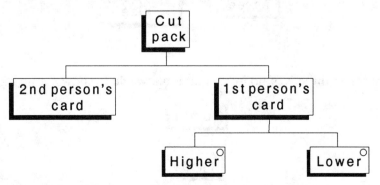

Figure 25.17

We could use this notation to describe a menu having a number of alternatives for each course (*Figure 25.18*).

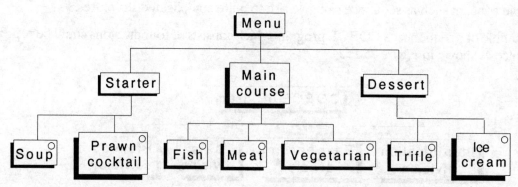

Figure 25.18

Similarly, in the sales file report described earlier, we might wish to differentiate between cash sales and credit sales for each transaction (*Figure 25.19*).

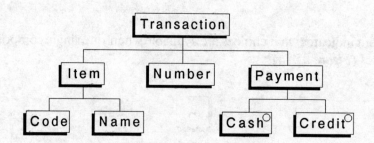

Figure 25.19

Sometimes a selection will consist of only one component which will be of interest while any other possibility is of no interest. For example, if we wished to count the number of times that three shows when a die is thrown, it could be represented as shown in *Figure 25.20(a)*.

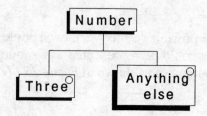

Figure 25.20(a)

But as anything other than three is of no interest, it is allowable to show it as in *Figure 25.20(b)*.

Figure 25.20(b)

Iterations

An iteration consists of one component which is repeated zero or more times. Diagrammatically, an iteration A with iterated component *B*, could be shown as in *Figure 25.21*.

Figure 25.21

The asterisk indicates that *B* is repeated zero or more times, and *A* represents the complete process.

A shuffled pack of cards can be represented as in *Figure 25.22*.

Figure 25.22

and the pack organised into suits would be (*Figure 25.23*)

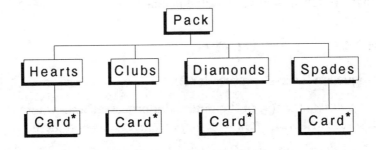

Figure 25.23

A file consisting of a header record followed by a set of data records becomes (*Figure 25.24*)

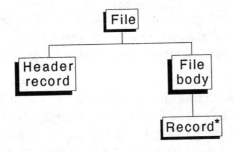

Figure 25.24

and our sales report can now show that the report consists of a number of lines, each showing the details of one transaction (*Figure 25.25*)

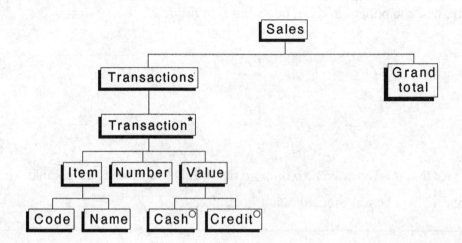

Figure 25.25

The iterated component for a process continues until some terminating condition is encountered, or only while some condition holds true. For example, the condition to terminate the processing of a file could be the physical end of the file, that is the process continues UNTIL the end of file is encountered; alternatively, this could be regarded as the continuance of processing WHILE the end of file has *not* been detected. Both conditions amount to the same thing. However, there are occasions when one form of the conditions may be more suitable than the other. The conditions for terminating iterations or for making choices, are specified as part of the design process after the various structure diagrams have been created, and this aspect of program design is dealt with in more detail in a later section.

Principal Stages of JSP Design

The basic design technique is a three-step procedure:

(a) define the *logical* structure(s) of the data to be processed and, where there is more than one data structure involved, identify *correspondences* between them;

(b) determine the program structure from the data structures. This, in effect, identifies the main processing tasks needed to process the data. The program structure thus formed will generally need filling out when step (c) is performed;

(c) define the tasks to be performed in more detail by allocating elementary operations available to appropriate components of the program structure. Such elementary operations represent single (or at least small numbers) of programming statements.

The first step is to define the *logical* data structures. The form in which the data is to be supplied to the program must be clearly stated, and the form of the data to be output from the program must also be defined. Normally these specifications will be descriptions of *physical* data structures, that is, statements about the data structures which ignore the task to be performed by the program; logical data structures are physical data structures modified according to the function of the program.

The distinction between physical and logical data structures being crucial to JSP design, we will discuss a number of examples to clarify the point.

Physical vs Logical Data Structures

Suppose that a large estate agency uses a computer system to store details of its properties, and that the property file has been sorted into ascending order of price. A program is required to extract the details of all detached houses costing less than £80,000. *Physically* the file merely consists of an iteration of records each containing the details of a house for sale. This is shown in *Figure 25.26(a)*.

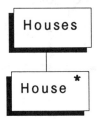

Figure 25.26(a)

The *logical* description of this file shown in *Figure 25.26(b)* is somewhat different, however.

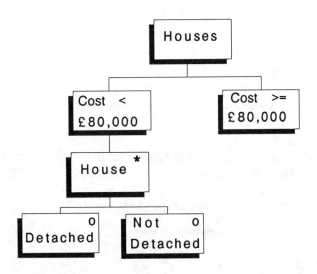

Figure 25.26(b)

Based on the function of the program and our knowledge of the property file, we have described the file in a much more informative manner, emphasizing the characteristics in which we are most interested.

If we were interested only in four-bedroomed houses costing between £70,000 and £120,000 then our logical view of the data structure would be as shown in *Figure 25.26(c)*.

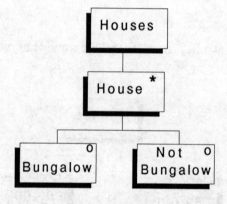

Figure 25.26(c)

Finally, a program to extract all the bungalows in the file would use the logical data structure shown in *Figure 25.26(d)*.

Figure 25.26(d)

As a further example of the description of logical data structures, consider a college personnel file sorted by grade within department. The physical data structure is shown in *Figure 25.27(a)*.

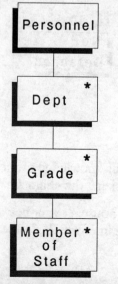

Figure 25.27(a)

If we were interested in the number of staff within five years of retirement age, then the logical data structure would be as in *Figure 25.27(b)*.

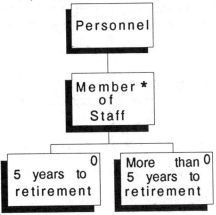

Figure 25.27(b)

To count the number of members of staff in each department we would use *Figure 25.27(c)*.

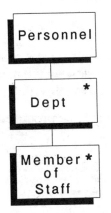

Figure 25.27(c)

and to extract the number of members of staff in each department of grade SL, the appropriate logical data structure is shown in *Figure 25.27(d)*.

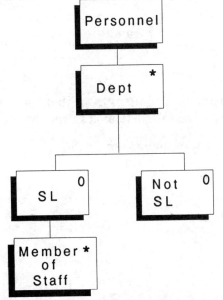

Figure 25.27(d)

All of these examples illustrate the point that the same physical data structure may be viewed in as many different logical ways as there are processing requirements. Choosing the most appropriate logical data structures directly affects the structure of the program which will process them, and can have significant consequences in terms of program clarity, efficiency and error-free operation.

Correspondences

In addition to identifying the appropriate logical data structures, it is necessary to identify *correspondences* between them in order to combine them to form the program structure. For a correspondence to exist, three conditions must be satisfied:

(i)   the components occur the same number of times,

(ii)   the components occur in the same order, and

(iii)   the components occur in the same context.

The correspondences identify the common components of two or more data structures. The following diagrams illustrate the process of identifying correspondences.

Example 1

Suppose that a certain company employs a number of sales representatives, and every month a file of their sales is produced. The file is sorted such that following the name of each salesperson in turn there is a list of his or her sales. A report must be produced from this file showing the total sales value for each person.

To begin, the data file from which the report is to be produced is defined (*see Figure 25.28(a)*).

Figure 25.28(a)

This indicates that the *sales file* is an iteration of *salesperson* (there are a number of salespersons records), and *salesperson* is an iteration of *sale* (each salesperson has a number of sales figures).

The summary report that is required is shown in *Figure 25.28(b)*.

Microphile	Computers		
Sales Summary	December 1991		
Sales Person	Total Sales (£)	Commission (£)	
J. Smith	3275.62	263.56	
H. Morgan	4456.40	345.22	
P. Sheridan	3986.80	286.45	
....	....	....	
....	....	....	
A. Morrow	2269.50	200.34	
TOTALS	52986.28	5032.66	

Figure 25.28(b)

Our data structure for the report would have the representation shown in *Figure 25.28(c)*.

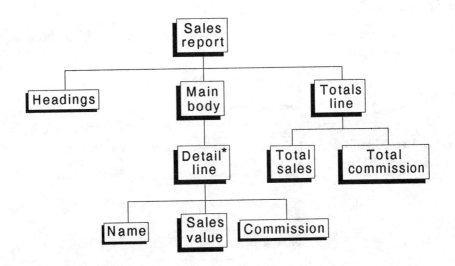

Figure 25.28(c)

The Sales Report is a sequence of *Headings, Main Body* and *Totals Line. Main Body* is an iteration of *Detail Line* which is to contain three items of information: *Name, Sales Value* and *Commission. Totals Line* is a sequence of *Total Sales* and *Total Commission*.

The correspondences are shown in the *Figure 25.28(d)*.

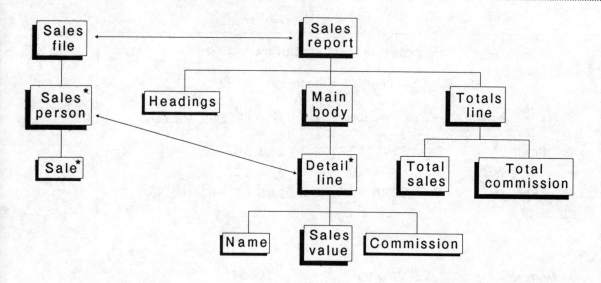

Figure 25.28(d)

The first correspondence is quite obvious since it is the sales file which is used to produce the sales report.

The second correspondence results from the fact that for each salesperson a single line is required which is the sales summary for that person.

It is usual to draw the data structures side-by-side with arrowed lines indicating the correspondence as illustrated in *Figure 25.28(d)*.

The two structures are now combined into a program structure in which the components represent processing operations. (*Figure 25.28(e)*)

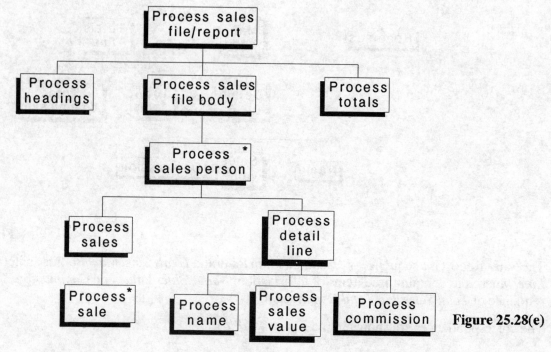

Figure 25.28(e)

The program structure thus reflects both of the data structures used in its design. The correspondence between *Salesperson* and *Detail Line* is shown in the program structure as a sequence since the complete set of sales for each person must be processed before the summary line can be produced.

Example 2

A sequential file consists of records containing details of magazine articles about computer-related subjects, such as hardware, software, programming. A program is required to print out the titles and authors of all articles about programming. Titles and authors relating to other subjects are to be ignored.

(i) Consider first the case where the articles are in random order of subject. The data structure is shown in *Figure 25.29(a)*.

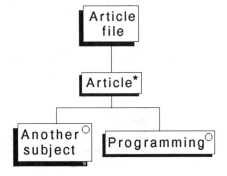

Figure 25.29(a)

The output structure is of the form shown in *Figure 25.29(b)*.

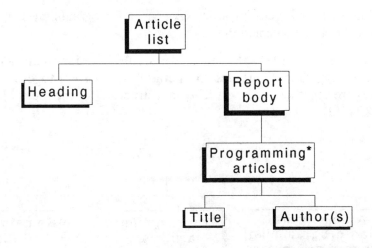

Figure 25.29(b)

The correspondences in this case are

> *Article File* <————> *Article List*

> *Programming* <————> *Programming Articles*

The second correspondence is between the *Programming* component of *Articles* in the *Article File* and the *Programming Articles* component of the selection in the *Article List* report. Because the file is not sequenced according to subject, it is necessary for the whole *Article File* to be processed to allow the extraction of *Programming* articles as and when they are reached.

The program structure is then as shown in *Figure 25.29(c)*.

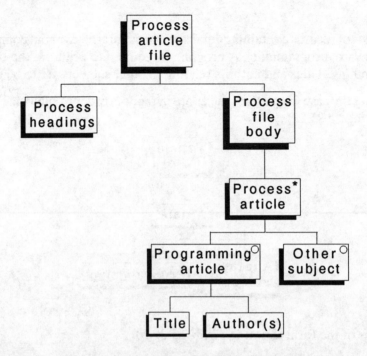

Figure 25.29(c)

Since we are only interested in processing articles concerning programming, it is not necessary to show the other alternative for the selection component.

(ii)   Suppose now that the file has been sorted into subject order, so that all articles on software are grouped together, all articles on operating systems are together, all articles on programming are together and so on. The data structure for the input file is now as shown in Figure 25.29(d).

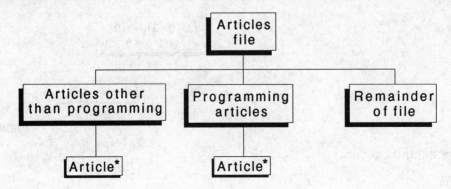

Figure 25.29(d)

where the file now may be considered to consist of three components:

(i)   A number of articles not relating to programming;

(ii)　A number of articles on programming;

(iii)　The rest of the file, which is of no interest.

Notice that in this instance the selection component is missing, and it is replaced by two iterations, one of unwanted records and the other of records of interest. The report structure is still the same, but the correspondence is now between *Programming Articles* in the *Articles File* and *Report Body* in the report file. The sorting of the file into subject order means that the records on programming are grouped together and therefore correspond directly to the data required in the report. The outline program design is shown in *Figure 25.29(e)*.

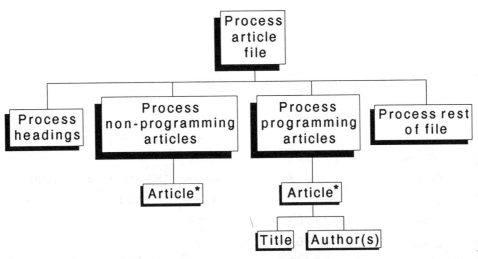

Figure 25.29(e)

Notice that the final procedure, *Process Rest of File*, does not involve an iteration; once the subject changes from programming to something else, the processing is finished and the program in effect stops.

Example 3

The previous examples deal with the process of combining a single input file with a single output file to produce a program structure. However there is an important class of processing problems which involve two input files whose records need to be *matched* or *collated*.

The process might, for example, require the matching of a *Master File* of items of stock and a *Transaction File* containing details of items received from suppliers or sold to customers. If both of these files are in some particular order (for instance in ascending order of stock reference number) then updating the *Master File* involves reading a transaction record and then attempting to find a stock record in the *Master File* with the same key value (in this case the stock reference number). If it is assumed that there should be a stock record for every transaction then, in the process of comparing a transaction record key value with a stock record key value, a number of situations can arise:

(i)　The transaction record key has a value which is greater than the stock record key. In this instance the stock record does not have a matching transaction and does not require updating. The stock record merely needs to be copied to the file holding the updated stock records. We will call this new file the *Updated Master File*.

(ii) The transaction record key is the same as the stock record key. Here it is necessary to determine the nature of the transaction, whether a sale or receipt, before processing the stock record. The updated record will then be written to the *Updated Master File*.

(iii) The transaction record key has a value which is less than the stock record key. This situation should not arise in this example and therefore indicates that an error has occurred, possibly as a result of the transaction file being out of sequence. To help clarify the nature of the processing tasks, consider the table in *Figure 25.30(a)* showing a list of transaction record keys, type of transaction and keys of records in the Master File to be updated.

Trans	Type	Master file	Action			
123001	Receipt	122500	Copy			
123001	Sale	122570	Copy			
123001	Sale	122595	Copy			
123067	Sale	123001	Update	(3 trans)	and	Write
123189	Receipt	123048	Copy			
123189	Sale	123067	Update	(1 trans)	and	Write
123345	Sale	123189	Update	(2 trans)	and	Write
123345	Sale	123224	Copy			
123345	Sale	123297	Copy			
		123445	Update	(3 trans)	and	Write
		123890	Copy			

etc

Figure 25.30(a)

Notice that it is possible to have several transactions for the same stock record in the *Master File*. The first three records of the *Master File* do not have any matching transaction records and therefore are copied to the *Updated Master File* without modification. All stock records occurring after the end of the *Transaction File* are also written to the new *Updated Master File*.

The data structures and correspondences for this example are therefore as shown in *Figure 25.30(b)*.

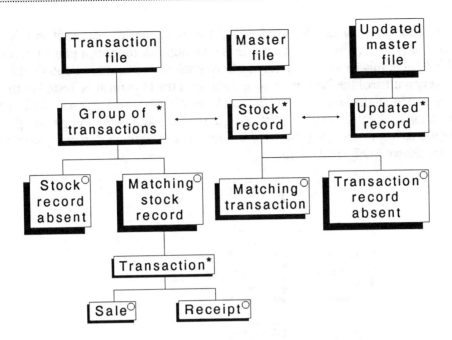

Figure 25.30(b)

The *Transaction File* is considered to contain a number of groups of transactions, each group containing records with the same key value (stock reference number); each record in the group is used to update a single stock record from the *Master File*. In the table described earlier (*Figure 25.30(a)*), the stock item with key value 123001 has a group of three transactions comprising a receipt and two sales transactions, whereas stock item 122570 has no transactions associated with it (that is, the transaction record is absent).

The outline program structure is shown in *Figure 25.30(c)*.

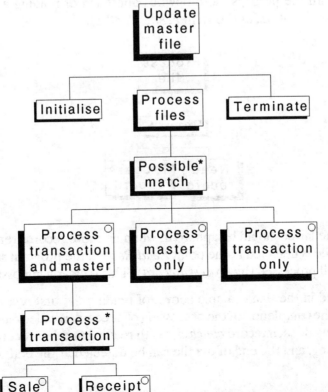

Figure 25.30(c)

Before describing the final stage of the design process, it is important to note that in this example it is assumed that before the iteration *Process Master File* is commenced, there is a pair of records ready for testing for a *Possible Match*; this means that a record from each of the files has been read in preparation for processing. The very nature of the iteration necessitates that the keys must be tested at the commencement of the iteration, and in this instance the end of the *Master File* and the *Transaction File* is the required condition for termination of the iteration. Reading a sequential file and performing some processing until there are no more records left to process (that is, when the end of the file is detected) would thus require the program structure shown in *Figure 25.30(d)*.

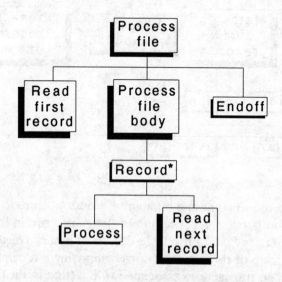

Figure 25.30(d)

Compare this scheme with the perhaps more obvious approach of reading a record at the start of the iterated component of the iteration, as shown in *Figure 25.30(e)*.

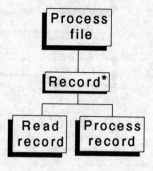

Figure 25.30(e)

and the inadequacy of the latter should be apparent: when no more records remain to be processed, that is, when the end of the file is detected at the point *Read Record*, the program structure requires that this non-existent record is still processed (by *Process Record*)! This is clearly impossible.

The technique, illustrated in the first example above, of reading the first record as soon as possible and subsequently reading at the completion of the processing of a record, is called *reading ahead*. It is important to note that the processing of each record *concludes* with reading another record, so that there is always a record ready for processing, and the end of the file can be detected at the end of each iteration.

Allocation of Elementary Operations

The final stage in the design technique is to allocate elementary operations to the program structure. The elementary operations include the following types :

> *Opening files ready for reading or writing,*
> *Closing files after processing,*
> *Reading records,*
> *Writing records,*
> *Displaying information,*
> *Printing information,*
> *Incrementing counts,*
> *Making calculations,*
> *Specifying conditions for the termination (or continuance) of iterations,*
> *Specifying criteria for selections.*

To illustrate the process we will list and allocate the elementary operations required for Example 3.

Initialization operations:

1. Open *Master File* for Input
2. Open *Updated Stock File* for Output
3. Open *Transaction File* for Input

Program Termination operations:

4. Close *Master File*
5. Close *Updated Stock File*
6. Close *Transaction File*
7. Stop

Input/Output operations:

8. Read *Master File*
9. Read *Transaction File*
10. Write *Updated Stock Record*

Processing operations:

11. Subtract number of sales from stock level
12. Add receipts to stock level
13. Display error message: "No stock record for this transaction"
14. Store transaction record key

Iteration conditions:

> C1. Until End of *Master File* and *Transaction File*.

C2. Until change of transaction record key.

Selection conditions:

C3. Transaction record key matches stock record key

C4. Transaction record key > stock record key

C5. Transaction record key < stock record key

C6. Transaction type = Sale

C7. Transaction type = Receipt

It is now possible to add some detail to the program structure diagram. (See *Figure 25.20(f)*)

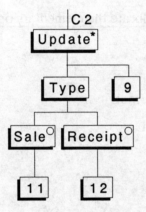

Figure 25.30(f)

Examination of the program structure above might suggest the possibility of 'improving' its efficiency by combining such operations as '9. Read Transaction File' or '8. Read Master File', both of which appear to be repeated unnecessarily. For example, operation 9 could be extracted from the *Sale* and *Receipt* operations and it could become a separate operation following the selection. (See *Figure 25.30(g)*)

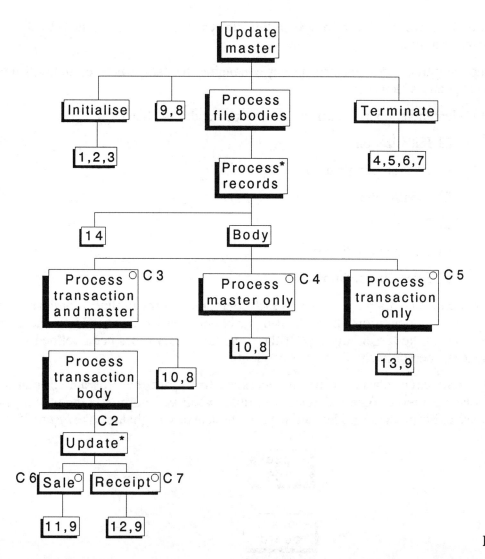

Figure 25.30(g)

Though this simplified program structure would still be correct, the danger is that should it be necessary to modify the program at some later date, unnecessary complications might result. In his book *Principles of Program Design*, M.A. Jackson, talking about this process of program optimization, provides two rules:

> Rule 1: *Don't do it*
> Rule 2: *Don't do it yet*

meaning that it is best, in the interests of program clarity, not to optimize the structure at all, but if you must do it, first begin within an unoptimized program that works and then optimize it later.

To summarise, the steps by which the final program structure is defined are as follows:

(i) Define the structure of the data to be processed. In many data processing applications these will be files.

(ii) Define the structure of the desired result of the processing. This output could be in the form of files or printed reports, for instance.

(iii) Identify the correspondences between the data structures in order to help to clarify the program structure.

(iv) Define the outline program structure by combining the data structures and utilizing the correspondences identified.

(v) List the elementary operations available grouped under the headings:

☐ Initialization

☐ Program termination

☐ Input/Output

☐ Processing

☐ Iteration conditions

☐ Selection conditions

(vi) Assign these elementary operations to each component of the outline program structure. The elementary operations should be capable of being easily converted into one or more instructions in the target language. If the program structure has been defined well, the elementary operations should be easy to identify.

(vii) Under some circumstances it may be necessary to fill out the program structure with additional operations. A typical example of this is when we incorporate the reading ahead approach to file processing. The outline program structure might look like *Figure 25.31(a)*.

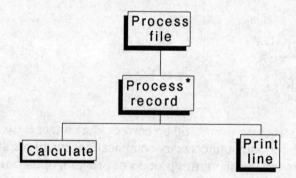

Figure 25.31(a)

When more detail is added, it might then become as shown in *Figure 25.31(b)*.

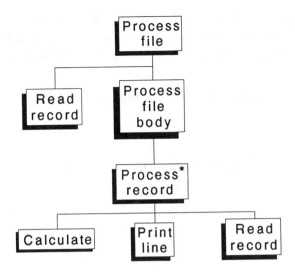

Figure 25.31(b)

Program Design Aids

The previous section dealt with strategies for designing programs; here we consider a number of established techniques which aid the programmer to convert designs to code by defining the logic of the program in detail. We describe *pseudocode, flowcharts, decision tables, state transition diagrams* and *state tables*, and *data-flow diagrams*.

Pseudocode can be used as an intermediate step between a diagrammatic program design specification and the implementation language, or it can be used directly to describe processing algorithms in a language-independent manner.

Flowcharts describe diagrammatically the flow of control within a program, and can be a useful in helping a programmer to understand the coding requirements of a programming task in detail.

Decision tables are used to define under what circumstances each of the possible program actions are to be taken, given every combination of conditions which can arise during the execution of a program.

State transition diagrams and *state tables* are alternatives to decision tables, but have the additional advantage of providing a convenient method of implementing a wide range of problems using a single algorithm.

Finally, *data-flow diagrams* are used to describe a system in terms of how input data is transformed into output data. They do so without reference to control structures and have the advantage of being easy to understand without special training.

Pseudocode

In the process of developing a computer program, *pseudocode*, sometimes called *schematic logic*, offers a transition stage between an initial program design, which may be in the form of a structure diagram, and the final program coded in the target language. Converting a program design expressed in pseudocode to a high-level language such as Pascal or C or COBOL is a relatively straightforward matter.

Another use of pseudocode is in the documentation of a program, to describe its logic using a formal notation independent of the implementation language. Pseudocode is also used to present algorithms, that is, it is used as a formal method of expressing the logic of processing techniques such as sorting data and searching data structures.

The purpose of this section is to explain the syntax of the pseudocode used in this book and to illustrate its use by means of examples.

Comments

These follow the Pascal convention of being enclosed between braces. Comments may extend over several lines.

Examples:

```
{This is a comment}
{So
   is
this}
```

Typestyle Conventions

The following conventions regarding the use of normal, **bold** and *italic* typestyles are used throughout:

1.   Normal type: standard HLL keywords/reserved words.

   Examples:print, input, readfile, writefile, declare

   These are the kind of operations that appear in the majority of commonly used languages.

2.   *Italics:* identifiers for variables, algorithms, procedures and functions.

   Examples: *count, total, ptr, i, number_of_values, find_word(ptr), calculate_cost(code,no_of_items,unit_cost).*

3.   **Bold type**:

   (i)   algorithm declarations.

   Example:

```
algorithm bubble_sort
 . . . . . . . .
   {body of algorithm}
 . . . . . . . .
end bubble_sort
```

   (ii)   Procedure/function declarations.

   Examples:

```
define procedure exchange(x,y)
 . . . . . . .
   {body of procedure}
 . . . . . . .
endprocedure exchange
```

```
define function calc_value(a,b,c)
    .......
    {body of function}
    .......
    return(value)
endfunction calc_value
```

(iii) Procedure/function calls.

Examples:

```
procedure get_word(i)
x := function find_word(i)
```

(iv) Control structures.

Examples:

```
if {condition}
    then {statements}
    else {statements}
endif

while {condition} do
  {statements}
  endwhile
```

(v) Logical operators **and, or, not.**

Variables

Simple variables such as integers, reals and single characters are not declared unless necessary to the operation of the process being defined. Their type may be inferred from the context in which they are used. More complex data structures such as arrays are declared in order to establish their dimension. For example, a 2-dimensional array, *table*, of size 10x3 is declared as follows:

declare array *table*$_{10,3}$

The element of the array corresponding to row *i* and column *j* would be shown as *table*$_{i,j}$.

Assignment Operations

When variables are assigned values, the following syntax is used:

variable_name := <expression>

meaning that the value resulting from the evaluation of <expression> is to be assigned to *variable_name*.

Examples:

sum := *sum* + value
total := 0
p := **function** *find_word*(*p*)

In the last example, the value returned from the function *find_word* is to be assigned to variable *p*.

The symbols used for addition, subtraction, multiplication and division are +, −, * and / respectively.

Conditional Expressions

Conditional expressions evaluate to logical *TRUE* or *FALSE*. *TRUE* relates to any non-zero arithmetic value and *FALSE* relates to zero.

Relational operators used in comparison operations are :

> = *equal to*
> <> *not equal to*
> \> *greater than*
> >= *greater than or equal to*
> < *less than*
> <= *less than or equal to*

Simple conditional expressions can be combined using the operators **and/or**, and can be logically inverted using **not**.

Examples:

char >= 'A'
This is a simple conditional expression.

> *char* >= 'A' **and** *char* <= 'Z'

This is a compound conditional expression.

> **not** *end_of_file*

Here, the variable *end-of-file* is being used as a boolean variable with two possible values: zero meaning *FALSE* and non-zero meaning *TRUE*.

Control Structures

In accordance with the rules of structured programming, pseudocode control structures are restricted to the following types:

Selection:

(i)
```
if {conditional expression}
    then {statement block}
endif
```

(ii)
```
if {conditional expression}
    then {statement block}
    else {statement block}
endif
```

Examples:

```
if   type = 'A'
     then A_count = A_count + 1
endif

if code = 3
  then procedure proc1
       procedure proc2
```

```
                    value := function get_value(code)
                    total := total + value
              else  procedure proc5(code)
          endif
```

(iii) **case** {variable name} **of**
       when value 1: {statement block}
       when value 2: {statement block}
       etc
       otherwise : {statement block}
   endcase

This is used when there exist a number of possible actions which depend on the value of a simple variable. In the example below, variable *type* is assumed to have the value 1 or 2 or 3 only.

Example:

```
          case type of
           when 1: procedure proc_type_1
           when 2: procedure proc_type_2
           when 3: procedure proc_type 3
           otherwise: procedure error_message
          endcase
```

Iteration:

(i) **while** {conditional expression} **do**
   {statement block}
   endwhile

The statements in the statement block are executed while the conditional expression is true. The conditional expression is of the same form as that in the **if** statement. If the conditional expression evaluates to true initially, the statement block will not be executed at all. In other words, the **while** construct allows zero or more iterations of the statement block.

(ii) **repeat**
   {statement block}
   until {conditional expression}

The statement block is repeated until the conditional expression is true. Note that, unlike the **while** statement, the **repeat** will execute the statement block at least once.

(iii) **for** {variable name} := {start value} **to** {end value}
   {statement block}
   endfor

The specified control variable is given the specified initial value and the statement block is executed while the variable is less than or equal to the specified end value. The control variable is incremented by 1 after each iteration.

Example:

```
for i := 1 to 10
  print i
endfor
```

The control variable, *i*, is initially given the value 1. The statement block is merely a single statement to print the current value of the control variable. The loop terminator, **endfor**, causes *i* to be incremented and the print statement to be executed as long as *i* is less than or equal to 10.

Flowcharts

Although, in general, a flowchart can be used to represent any sequence of definable activities, in the current context it is specifically used to convey, in diagrammatic form, the logic, processing operations and flow of control required of a computer program. The flowchart is independent of programming languages, using a small number of standard symbols to represent common types of computer operations. These symbols are shown in the *Figure 25.32*.

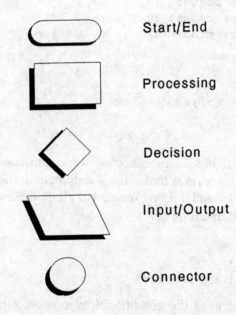

Figure 25.32

The first symbol is used to indicate the start or end of a process. The rectangle represents a calculation, the nature of which is written inside the box. The diamond shape shows that a decision is to be made between two alternatives, and the criteria for making the decision is shown inside the symbol. Any input or output operations are shown by the parallelogram. Finally, a small circle containing a number or letter is used to split a large flowchart into smaller parts.

To illustrate the form of a flowchart consider the following task:

Read three numbers and calculate their average value.

The flowchart might be as shown in the *Figure 25.33*.

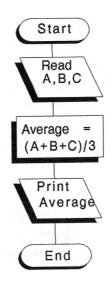

Figure 25.33

This is a trivial example, so now suppose that the requirement is to read one thousand numbers. If the previous flowchart is used as a model for this problem, then it would become prohibitively long, and would also contain a great deal of redundant information. The *process* of adding 1000 numbers is the same as that of adding three numbers; all that is different is the *number* of numbers.

Figure 25.34 illustrates how a flowchart can summarise a lengthy process by using a loop.

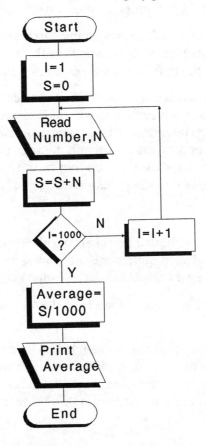

Figure 25.34

Notice that the arrows on the lines joining the symbols show the direction to follow when reading the flowchart, and that the decision box provides the means by which a loop can be introduced.

Decision boxes can also show how to cope with different situations that might occur during some processing activity. For instance, suppose that a program is required to calculate the selling price for some item which may or may not be VAT rated. The flowchart fragment in the *Figure 25.35* shows how this situation could be represented.

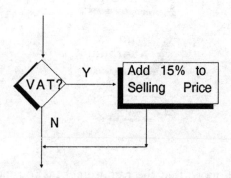

Figure 25.35

Flowcharts are used by programmers in two main ways:

(i)   To plan the structure of a program before it is written.

(ii)   To describe the structure of a program after it has been written.

The first use is primarily for the benefit of the programmer, to aid the process of program design; the second use documents the program structure so that anyone with an interest in the program will be able to understand its structure, even if the person has little or no programming expertise.

As a programming aid, the flowchart is sometimes criticized as encouraging program designers to become involved in programming details at too early a stage, which clearly conflicts with the tenets of top-down design. In addition, flowcharts are intended, as their name suggests, to specify the flow of control inside a computer, but this is not the aim of program design; program design establishes the structure of a program, how its components fit together and what functions they perform. For these reasons, other diagrammatic forms such as JSP diagrams or data-flow diagrams are often used in preference to flowcharts.

Decision Tables

As an alternative, or even supplement, to a flowchart or other design aid a program designer might use a *decision table* to define the logical requirements of a program. A decision table identifies possible combinations of conditions that might arise, and defines what action must be taken in each case.

Suppose that a bank uses the following procedure for determining charges on transactions for its deposit account customers:

There is a charge of 50p for each cash withdrawal unless the account is in credit by at least £100, in which case there is no charge. If the customer would become overdrawn as a result of the cash withdrawal, the transaction is not allowed and no charge is made. The maximum cash withdrawal allowed at any one time is £50. If the transaction is a deposit, no charge is made.

A decision table for the logic might look like this:

```
                                       1
                         1 2 3 4 5 6 7 8 9 0 1 2 3 4 5 6

Cash    withdrawal?      Y Y Y Y Y Y Y Y Y N N N N N N N N
Withdrawal  >  £50?      Y Y Y Y N N N N Y Y Y Y N N N N
Balance  <  £100?        Y Y N N Y Y N N Y Y N N Y Y N N
Withrawal  >  Balance?   Y N Y N Y N Y N Y N Y N Y N Y N
_____

Charge 50p                             X
No charge                                      X X X X X X X X X
Refuse withdrawal        X X X X X   X
```

Conditions are phrased as questions and appear in the top left-hand stub of the table. All possible combinations of the answers (Yes or No) are listed in the top right-hand stub. All possible actions are listed in the bottom left-hand stub. An X in the final stub indicates under what combinations of conditions the action is to be performed.

Taking, for example, the sixth column of Y/N combinations, it shows that

IF	it is a cash withdrawal
AND	the withdrawal is not greater than £50
AND	the balance is less than £100
AND	the amount of the withdrawal is not greater than the current balance
THEN	make a charge of 50p

Notice that some combinations of conditions are not relevant. For example, if a cash withdrawal is greater than £50, then the final two conditions are irrelevant. Irrelevant conditions are indicated by dashes:

```
                                       1
                         1 2 3 4 5 6 7 8 9 0 1 2 3 4 5 6

Cash    withdrawal?      Y Y Y Y Y Y Y Y Y N N N N N N N N
Withdrawal  >  £50?      Y Y Y Y N N N N - - - - - - - -
Balance  <  £100?        - - - - Y Y N N - - - - - - - -
Withrawal  >  Balance?   - - - - Y N - - - - - - - - - -
_____

Charge 50p                             X
No charge                                      X X X X X X X X X
Refuse withdrawal        X X X X X   X
```

Notice also that several combinations are now repeated so that the table could be summarised as:

	1 1 2 3 4 5 6 7 8 9 0 1 2 3 4 5 6
Cash withdrawal?	Y Y YY Y N
Withdrawal > £50?	Y N NN N-
Balance < £100?	- N YN N-
Withrawal > Balance?	- N YY N-
Charge 50p	X
No charge	XX
Refuse withdrawal	XX X

When drawing decision tables it is important to ensure that all combinations of conditions have been included. The maximum number of combinations is calculated as follows:

No. of Conditions	Combinations	
2	2 x 2	= 4
3	2 x 2 x 2	= 8
4	2 x 2 x 2 x 2	= 16
5	2 x 2 x 2 x 2 x 2	= 32
etc		

There is also a certain way of writing these combinations so that all of them are covered:

(i)   Determine the maximum number of combinations;

(ii)   Halve this number;

(iii) Along the first condition line write this number of Y's followed by the same number of N's until the line is complete;

(iv)   Halve this number;

(v)   Repeat steps (iii) and (iv) until the final condition line consisting of alternate Y's and N's has been completed.

For example, suppose there are 3 conditions, then the number of combinations is $2 \times 2 \times 2 = 8$. Half of this is 4. Therefore the first line is

Y Y Y Y N N N N

The second line will consist of two Y's followed by two N's alternating to the end of the line:

   Y Y N N Y Y N N

The last line has one Y and one N alternating:

   Y N Y N Y N Y N

Thus the decision table will have the form

		1 2 3 4 5 6 7 8
Condition	1	Y Y Y Y N N N N
Condition	2	Y Y N N Y Y N N
Condition	3	Y N Y N Y N Y N
Actions		

State Transition Diagrams and State Tables

State diagrams and state tables offer a further means of defining the logic of a program containing a number of combinations of conditions and consequent actions.

Suppose that we are required to write a program to validate a string of characters representing a signed real number, assuming that the rules for their construction are as follows:

   ☐ there may be a number of leading and trailing spaces

   ☐ there may be a single + or − sign preceding the first digit

   ☐ there may be a number of spaces between the sign and the first digit

   ☐ there may be an optional decimal point embedded in the number

Examples of valid numbers: 12.4   − 31.36   +15.   − 16   .44   − .1

Examples of invalid numbers:
1,000	("," not allowed)
12E06	(no alphabetic characters allowed)
6. 32	(embedded space)
+−3	(only one sign allowed)
+.	(no digits)

We will assume that there will always be a unique character terminating the string (indicated by *null* in *Figure 25.36*), and that the string is to be processed character by character from left to right.

The approach is to imagine that the scanning process can have a number of different states, and that each character scanned can either cause the scanner to enter a new state or remain in its existing state. A diagram consisting of circles, representing all possible states, connected by arcs labelled with the reason for a *transition* to a new state, is called a *state transition diagram*. The state transition diagram appropriate to our problem is shown in *Figure 25.36*.

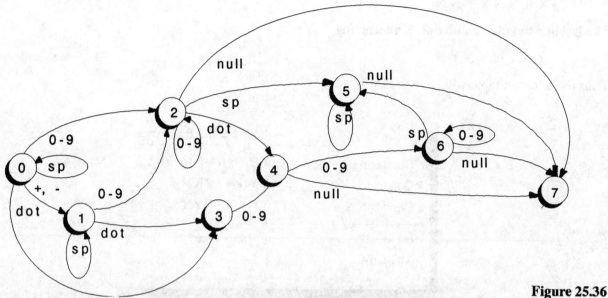

Figure 25.36

In this particular state transition diagram, any symbols other than those specified at any state are assumed to be 'illegal' characters which lead to an error state (8) (not shown for reasons of clarity) which is a terminating state.

In this diagram, achieving state (9) represents a valid number. The following table traces the diagram for the valid number '+ 31.6':

current state	next character	new state
1	+	2
2	space	2
2	space	2
2	3	3
3	1	3
3	.	5
5	6	7
7	null	9

The diagram, though fairly complex has two important benefits to the programmer:

☐ it encourages all possible combinations of characters to be considered and understood

☐ it can be converted into a *state table* which is easy to implement as a program

The equivalent state table is shown below.

state	scanned character					
	space	+ or -	digit	.	null	other
1	1	2	3	4	8	8
2	2	8	3	4	8	8
3	6	8	3	5	9	8
4	8	8	5	8	8	8
5	8	8	7	8	9	8
6	6	8	8	8	9	8
7	6	8	7	8	9	8
8	i n v a l i d n u m b e r					
9	v a l i d n u m b e r					

So, for initial state 1, a space causes no transition, a + or − causes a transition to state 2, a digit to state 3, a decimal point (.) to state 4, and any other characters result in the invalid state 8. Each row of the table shows the transitions appropriate to every possible character scanned while in the state indicated. Thus the table encapsulates the complete logic of the state transition diagram.

The algorithm in *Listing 25.1* below for implementing the validation routine assumes that a two-dimensional table, $TT_{i,j}$ has been initialized to contain the transition table in the form shown above, that is with nine rows (i going from 0 to 8), each having six elements (j going from 0 to 5).

```
algorithm validate_num
    state := 0
    while state < 8 do
        ch := getchar          {get the next character}
        state := function get_new_state(ch,state)
    endwhile

    if state = 9
        then {number is valid}
        else {number is invalid}
    endif
end validate-num

define function get_new_state(ch,state)
    case ch of
        when space    : column := 0
        when + or -   : column := 1
        when digit    : column := 2
        when .        : column := 3
        when null     : column := 4
        otherwise     : column := 5
    endcase
    new_state := TTstate,column
    return (new_state)
endfunction get_new_state
```

Listing 25.1

The variable *state* is initialized to 0, and then, while *state* is less than 8, that is a state which is not an end state, the next character (*ch*) is obtained from the string before calling a function which uses *ch* to determine the next transition.

The function *get_new_state()* checks the category of the incoming character and returns the corresponding new state after accessing the transition table.

Notice that this same algorithm could easily be adapted for a different state table and is therefore appropriate to a wide variety of problems.

Data-flow Diagrams

Data-flow diagrams document the flow of data between functions, showing how data is transformed from input to output. They provide a useful way of planning or describing a system or program. Data-flow diagrams have several important features related to program design:

☐ they are easy to understand without special training

☐ they make no assumptions about the manner in which the data is transformed by a function

☐ they make no assumptions about the form of the functions represented in the diagram: they could be separate programs or part of the same program.

Data-flow diagrams are frequently used for systems analysis and are therefore described in more detail in Chapter 21.

Program Testing and Debugging

Once the program has been written, it must go through two stages in order to remove errors which almost inevitably will be present. No matter how much care has been taken in the design and coding of a program, it is very likely to contain errors in syntax, that is incorrectly formed statements, and almost as likely to contain errors in logic as well. *Debugging* is the term given to the process of detecting and correcting these errors or bugs.

The first stage in the removal of errors is the correction of syntax errors and obvious errors in logic. Fortunately for the programmer, modern interpreters and compilers provide considerable assistance in the detection of syntax errors in the source code. Malformed statements will be reported by a compiler after it has attempted to compile the source code; an interpreter will report illegal statements as it attempts to execute them. Logic errors, however, are largely undetectable by the translating program. These are errors which cause the program to behave in a manner contrary to expectations. The individual statements in the program are correctly formed and it runs, but the program does not work as it should; it may give incorrect answers, or terminate prematurely, or not terminate at all.

Hopefully, even the most puzzling logic errors, once detected, can eventually be removed. But how can the programmer be confident that the program will continue to behave properly when it is in use? The answer is that one never can be absolutely certain that a program will not fail, but by the careful choice of test data in the second stage of the debugging process, the programmer can test the program under the sort of conditions that are most likely to occur in practice. Test data is designed to determine the robustness of the program, how well it can cope with unexpected or spurious inputs as well as those for which it has been designed specifically to process.

The purpose of program testing being to establish the presence of faults, it can never show that a program is correct; it can only demonstrate the presence of errors in a program, not their absence. Since testing is a destructive process, aimed at causing a program to behave in a way that was not intended by its designer, a *successful* test is regarded as one which establishes the presence of an error.

At some point the programmer must decide that the program has had sufficient testing. He or she will be confident that the program will operate according to specification and without 'crashing' or 'hanging up' under extreme or unexpected circumstances; the reputation of a professional programmer relies on this. However, programmers tend to be reluctant (consciously or unconsciously) to find faults in their programs, so it is important that independent tests are conducted in addition to those performed by the programmer or system developer. Consequently, prior to release, customers or end users should be involved in final testing. This is termed validation. The programmer may have overlooked something because it is often difficult to view a program objectively or entirely from the point of view of the user. If this is the case then the program will be modified and retested until all user requirements are met.

Types of Errors in Programs

There are four distinct types of errors which programs can contain:

☐ *syntax* errors caused by malformed statements;

☐ *semantic* errors due to violating rules governing the use of programming entities;

☐ *run-time* errors which cause the program to terminate prematurely;

☐ *logic* errors which manifest themselves as incorrect program operation.

Because translation programs such as compilers must contain detailed rules concerning allowable statement structures and the use of identifiers in the language, they are generally able to provide the programmer with quite detailed information on the cause and location of syntax and semantic infringements. Such errors result from such things as:

☐ accidental spelling mistakes;

☐ keywords being used out of context;

☐ incomplete knowledge of the language;

☐ using data types in the wrong contexts;

A COBOL compiler for example, having attempted to compile a source program, might produce an error report of the following form:

```
Keyed      C Seq   Error Lvl Messages
Line #       #    Col #
GASH                        <=PROGRAM NAME and Compiled DATE => 04\07\92
C-BAL               055   W Warning Two RECORDS in a file have
                            different sizes.
TRANSACTION         055   W Warning Two RECORDS in a file have
                            different sizes.
001000    0098 31 181   F Must have 'AT END' or 'INVALID KEY'.
                            'USE PROCEDURE' not supported.
          0164 15 032     Last line read by the Compiler.
                          F=>`FATAL'.  OBJ file won't run.
                                    Try again!
                          Correct errors and recompile.
```

Each line of the report gives the following information:

☐ the position in the source code at which the error was located;

☐ the degree of severity of the error, that is to what extent it has prevented the production of the object code;

☐ a description of the error;

☐ the offending part of the statement if this can be isolated.

After correcting the source code, the program must be recompiled. Further errors may then be revealed and the process repeated.

Only after the program has been compiled successfully, with no errors reported, should the object code be run. At this stage the operating system may report difficulties in attempting to execute the object code. For instance, if the program attempts to read a file which has not been opened prior to the read instruction, the operating system might halt execution of the program and report the detection of this run-time error. This constitutes an error in logic which the compiler is unable to detect; the error only becomes apparent when the program is run. Generally, the nature of the run-time error and perhaps its location in the source code will be reported, again with an error code through which further information might be obtained.

With a compiled programming language the programmer can be confident that all syntax errors have been removed from the program; the compiler itself will report this fact. However, since an interpreter only processes instructions as they are encountered, a syntax error in a statement will only be detected if that statement is executed. As a result, a complex program written in BASIC for instance, might hide a number of syntax errors which may only reveal themselves after the program has been run several times. For example, the following program statement contains a syntax error which might not reveal itself immediately:

```
. . . . . . . . . . . .
. . . . . . . . . . . .
100 IF code = 89 THEN GOTO SUB 2000
. . . . . . . . . . . .
```

The fact that the instruction should have read

```
100 IF code =   89 THEN GOSUB 2000
```

would only become apparent when the variable *code* actually had the value 89. Any other value would cause the coding following the condition in the statement to be ignored and allow the syntax error to remain hidden.

This same instruction could also hide a run-time error. If, for example, line 2000 did not exist then it would be impossible to execute the subroutine starting at this point. Again the error might not become apparent immediately.

A run-time error could also arise from unanticipated inputs from a user. For example, the algorithm shown below for calculates the roots of a quadratic equation, given the values of the three coefficients a, b and c supplied by the user:

```
algorithm roots
      print "Enter the three coefficients"
      input a, b, c
      x1 := -b + sqrt((b*b  -  4*a*c)/2*a))
      x2 := -b - sqrt((b*b  -  4*a*c)/2*a))
      print "The roots are :", x1, "and", x2
end roots
```

If the user entered the values *0,1,2* for a, b and c respectively then the program would report a divide overflow error caused by attempting to divide by zero, the value of a.

Logic errors result in the program failing to perform as required, but without causing the program to terminate prematurely. Such errors may arise from the use of an erroneous formula for example. In the algorithm above, if the line

```
x1 := -b + sqrt((b*b  -  4*a*c)/2*a))
```

had been incorrectly written as

```
x1 := -b + sqrt((b  - 4*a*c)/2*a))
```

then *x1* would be assigned an incorrect value. Logic errors in large, complex programs may be much less obvious.

These examples illustrate the importance of testing a program thoroughly using data which will exercise every part of the program.

Program Debugging

As we have illustrated in the preceding section, logic errors may not prevent the program from executing, rather they cause some sort of processing error. The symptoms of the error may be obvious, but the cause might not be so apparent. Every programmer comes up against the logic error which 'cannot' exist; the coding appears to be perfectly correct and yet the program behaves incorrectly. No matter how many times the coding is scrutinized, there seems to be no reason for the problem. The mistake that many beginners at programming make is to spend an inordinate amount of time looking at program listings in order to find the error; though intuitively this seems to be the obvious approach, in practice it is a sort of 'gumption trap' which can waste a great deal of time and result in a great deal of frustration. It seems easier to stare at a listing in the belief that the error must eventually reveal itself rather than having the 'gumption' to adopt some positive and systematic approach which might appear to involve more unnecessary work.

The formal name for this approach to program debugging is *static verification*, the examination and analysis of source code without executing the program.

If, after examining a program listing for a reasonable amount of time, the cause of the error remains elusive, there are a number of courses of action which will probably be much more productive than continuing to pore over the listing:

☐ Ask a fellow programmer to listen critically while you explain the operation of the program and the way it is behaving. Quite often you will see the cause of the error as you are making the explanation. Alternatively, your helper might recognise the type of error and its probable cause from his/her own experience, or might ask a question which makes you reconsider some aspect of the program which you have assumed to be correct or had no direct bearing on the problem. It is surprising how often this technique works.

☐ Examine the values of key variables while the program is running. Install temporary lines of coding throughout the program to display the value of variables and to pause until you press a key. For example, in COBOL you might insert the statements

```
DISPLAY "AT PARAGRAPH /PROC-REC/ ", inrec.
ACCEPT dummy.
```

The *DISPLAY* statement indicates the current position in the program, and the contents of the variable *inrec*. The *ACCEPT* statement causes the program to wait until *dummy* (defined in the *WORKING-STORAGE SECTION* as *PIC X*) is given a value (pressing the RETURN /ENTER key is sufficient). In BASIC, *PRINT* and *INPUT* instructions can be used to perform the equivalent operations.

Comparison of the values actually displayed with expected values will normally indicate the likely source of the error.

☐ Use debugging utilities provided in the language itself or separately in the system software. Several versions of BASIC have a trace facility which, when turned on, displays the line number of statements prior to their execution. Sometimes a particular implementation of a language will provide more sophisticated debugging facilities which will display the values of particular variables as they are encountered during program execution. Good examples of this are Borland's Turbo Pascal and Turbo C, both of which provide a number of powerful debugging facilities. Minicomputer systems and mainframes usually will have special debugging software which can be used with any of the languages supported by the system. It is up to the programmer to investigate the debugging aids available and make good use of them.

Finding an error in a program presupposes that it has initially been detected; this is the purpose of program testing described in the next few sections of the chapter.

Program Testing

With large programs, attempting to test the finished product is unlikely to reveal all of its errors. The combinations of test cases required to test each of its constituent parts increases exponentially with its size, resulting in a prohibitively large number of them if the program is to be tested thoroughly. Furthermore, the identification of an error does not automatically ensure its isolation; it may be a long and expensive task to find an error that could have its roots anywhere in the program. The only feasible way to test a large program is to divide the task into manageable pieces and test each piece separately before integrating it with the others.

The components of a large program often form a hierarchical structure such as that shown in *Figure 25.37*.

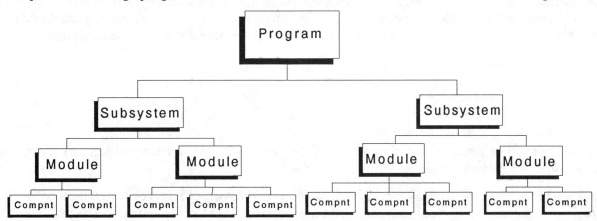

Figure 25.37

At the top level, the program consists of a number of subsystems, each comprising one or more independent modules which themselves are collections of interdependent components. Components are equivalent to subprograms which we regard as the smallest testable entities.

Testing is performed at each of these levels: subprograms are tested to ensure that they operate correctly according to their specifications; when combined to form a module, these components must not interact in unexpected ways and therefore the operation of the integrated module requires careful testing;

subsystems, perhaps developed by different programmers, or even different companies, must interface correctly, again requiring confirmation by rigorous testing.

Integration is carried out next; subsystems are integrated to make up the entire system. At this stage, testing is concerned with finding errors which normally result from unanticipated interactions between subsystems and components.

It is sometimes appropriate to devise stress tests to supplement the testing procedures described above. These tests are designed to place an unnatural load on a system and confirm that when overloaded it will fail 'gracefully', that is, in a manner that can be anticipated and catered for.

Acceptance testing is the process of testing the system with real data - sometimes called *alpha testing* in which the developer tests the system in the presence of the customer until there is agreement that the system performs as it should.

Beta testing is the process of delivering the system to a number of customers who have agreed to use the system and report any problems that arise in the course of normal use.

There are two important ways in which system testing usually proceeds, namely *top-down* and *bottom-up* testing and these are described in the next section.

Top-down and Bottom-up Testing

Top-down program design techniques, such as those discussed earlier in this chapter lend themselves to methodical testing. In top-down design, the program is constructed by defining the main sections of the program first. These sections are then defined in terms of sub-sections which themselves may be further defined. *Top-down testing* proceeds in parallel with the top-down development of the program. As a component of the program is coded, it can be tested by using program *stubs* for components as yet uncoded. A stub has the same interface as the component it is representing but is 'empty' or a very simplified version of it. For example, in C a program stub could be a function merely returning a constant value:

```
int area(a,b) int a,b;
 {
  int value = 44;
  return(value);
 }
```

At the appropriate time, the function *area*() will be fully coded but, for the moment, to allow another component to be tested, it merely returns a typical value.

In this way the program need not exist in its final form before parts of it can be tested thoroughly. As the program skeleton is fleshed out, more test data is generated. Thus the test data grows in parallel with the production of the program coding. Furthermore, the logic of the program can be tested right at the outset, and can continue to be tested as more coding is added.

When combined with top-down programming, top-down testing has the additional advantage of providing a complete and working (if limited) version of the program at an early stage of its development cycle.

On the debit side, provision of stubs involves additional labour and in some instances may in fact prove to be difficult to provide if they are required to simulate complex components.

Bottom-up testing involves testing bottom level components before they are integrated into higher level modules which are themselves tested, the process gradually working up the component hierarchy until the complete program has been tested.

One major problem with this method is that some mechanism must be devised for driving the component being tested. For example, if the component is a Pascal procedure, it must be part of a program before it can be executed, and since the final program does not yet exist, a suitable simplified version of it must be provided. Another problem is that it could easily be a considerable time before a working version of the program can be demonstrated to interested parties such as customers.

However, it has the attraction that testing is simplified, since it can be performed without the possibility of unwanted interaction with other components of the program.

Testing Techniques

In principle, testing of a program should be exhaustive, every possible combination of routes being exercised. In practice, this is impossible in a program which contains loops as the number of possible combinations will often be extremely large. As a minimum aim, the test programme should cause every statement to be executed at least once.

Test cases should be selected using the following guidelines:

- ☐ Test cases should be chosen to identify faults which will prevent users from doing their jobs, for example programs which 'hang up' or corrupt data.

- ☐ Testing old capabilities is more important than testing new ones. Existing functions should continue to work when new, and possibly less important, ones are added.

- ☐ Testing typical situations is more important than testing boundary cases. If it is necessary (and it usually is) to restrict the number of test cases, then it is preferable to reduce atypical test cases rather than normal test cases.

When the programmer feels that the gross program errors have been detected and removed, the next stage is to test the program using carefully selected data. The nature of the test data should be such that:

- ☐ every statement in the program is executed at least once;

- ☐ the effectiveness of every section of coding devoted to detecting erroneous input is verified;

- ☐ every route through the program is tried;

- ☐ the accuracy of the processing is verified;

- ☐ the program operates according to its original design specification.

In order to achieve these aims, the programmer must be inventive in the design of the test data. Each test case must check something not tested by previous runs; there is no point in proving that a program which can add successfully a certain set of numbers can also add another similar set of numbers. The goal is to strain the program to its limit, and this is particularly important when the program is to be used frequently by a number of different people.

There are three general categories of test data:

(a) *Normal data*. This includes the most general data for which the program was designed to handle.

(b) *Extreme values*. These test the behaviour of the program when valid data at the upper and lower limits of acceptability are used. The process of using extreme values is called *boundary testing* and is often a fruitful place to look for errors. For numeric data this could be the use of very large or very small values. Text could be the shortest or longest sequence of characters permitted. A program for file processing could be tested with a file containing no records, or just a single record. The cases where zero or null values are used are very important test cases, frequently highlighting programming oversights.

(c) *Exceptional data*. Programs are usually designed to accept a certain range or class of inputs. If 'illegal' data is used, (that is data which the program is not designed to handle), the program should be capable of rejecting it rather than attempting to process it. This is particularly important when the program is to be used by people other than the programmer, since they may be unaware of what constitutes illegal data. From the outset a programmer should assume that incorrect data will be used with the program; this may save a great deal of time looking for program errors which may actually be data errors.

In the next two sections we look at two specific methods for testing programs: *equivalence partitioning* and *structural testing*. The first treats the program as a 'black box' where we know what output it should provide for specific inputs, but we have no knowledge of its internal construction; the second method, also known as 'white box testing', uses the detailed knowledge of a program's structure to determine appropriate test cases.

Equivalence Partitioning

This is a method of determining which classes of input data have common properties. Classes that represent sets of expected, valid inputs and also invalid inputs are identified. The idea is that if a program does not fail for one member of a certain class, then it should not do so for any other members of the same class. Determination of equivalence classes most likely to produce errors is by means of a combination of system specification, user documentation and experience.

When equivalence classes have been determined, the next step is to choose values from each class which are most likely to lead to a successful test.

Example

To test a procedure written in a high-level language to read a file from a disk using MS-DOS (see Chapter 12). The procedure is expected to intercept any invalid filenames.

The filename is subject to the following constraints:

☐ the filename is allowed to comprise combinations of the following characters only

A-Z a-z 0-9 $ &
% ' ( ) - @
^ { } ~ ! #

☐ invalid characters are

blank   ? * + = " , \

☐ the following names are recognised by MS-DOS as having special meanings and must not be used as filenames:

AUX CON PRN NUL

☐ the filename is allowed to contain a maximum of 8 characters; extra characters are ignored

☐ the filename may have an additional optional extension consisting of three characters preceded by a period (.)

☐ the filename may be preceded by an optional drive identifier (*a:, b:, c:, d:* or *e:*) followed by zero or more directory names.

☐ the full pathname, consisting of a sequence of directory names followed by the filename, must not exceed 63 characters

☐ a directory name uses the same characters as a filename, but is not allowed an extension or more than eight characters

☐ leading and trailing spaces are ignored

☐ the only valid file extension is .ASC, and if the file extension is not provided, .ASC is to be assumed

Equivalence classes are as follows:

Class Name	Type	Class
C1	Valid	filename consisting of 1 - 8 non-blank characters without an extension
C2	Valid	filename consisting of 1 - 8 non-blank characters with valid extension
C3	Valid	drive name + filename excl. extension
C4	Valid	drive name + filename incl. extension
C5	Valid	one directory name + filename
C6	Valid	several directory names + filename
C7	Valid	drive name + pathname
C8	Valid	blanks + drive name + pathname
C9	Valid	drive name + pathname + blanks
C10	Valid	single character filename
C11	Valid	maximum length pathname
C12	Valid	too many characters in filename
C13	Valid	too many characters in pathname
C14	Syntax	illegal characters in pathname
C15	Syntax	pathname without filename
C16	Syntax	illegal drivename
C17	Logic	file nonexistent
C18	Logic	incorrect path
C19	Logic	incorrect drive

The heading *Type* in the table above refers to whether the input should be acceptable (Valid), should be recognised as being syntactically incorrect (Syntax) or should produce an error message owing to a runtime condition occurring (Logic).

Examples of test cases derived from the classes are shown below. Note that they assume appropriate files and directories have been created previously.

Test	Input	Expected result	Classes tested
1	abc	file loaded	C1
2	abcd.asc	"	C2
3	A:test1	"	C1,C3
4	B:#1.ASC	"	C2,C4
5	DIR1\test1	"	C5,C1
6	DIR2\dir1\abcd.asc	"	C6,C2
7	c:\dir1\abc.ASC	"	C7,C2
8	bbbD:dir2\test1	"	C8,C5
9	d:abcd.ASCbbbbb	"	C9,C2
10	x	"	C10,C1
11	\dir1\dir2\dir3\dir4\.. ..dir5\dir6\dir7\dir8\.. ..dir9\dir10\dir11\test1	"	C11,C6
12	123456789abc	12345678 loaded	C12,C1
13	\dir1\dir2\dir3\dir4\.. ..dir5\dir6\dir7\dir8\.. ..dir9\dir10\dir11\.. ..12345678abc	file not found	C13,C6,C12
14	B:btest1	invalid filename	C14
15	ab>c	"	C14
16	?abcd	"	C14
17	abcd.*	"	C14
18	etc....		

Test cases should be devised to check each class at least once; in the above example, the procedure should be tested with every invalid character and with filenames AUX, CON, PRN and NUL to make sure that the procedure does in fact intercept them.

It is important that the result of each test is carefully noted, particularly, of course, if the test is successful and requires the program to be modified. After modification, the same tests should be repeated to ensure that any changes to the procedure have had no unexpected side effects.

Structural Testing

Black box testing is where the tester is presented with the specification of a component to be tested and uses this to derive the test cases. This has the advantage that the testers need no information about the code used in the component and need not understand its internal structure. This is also a disadvantage in that knowledge of the code can aid in devising tests which will thoroughly exercise the program.

An alternative approach is *structural testing* (also known as *glass-box* or *white-box testing*), which relies on the tester having access to the component's code and structure to devise test cases.

An exhaustive structural test involves testing all combinations of routes through the program, generally impractical for all but the most trivial programs. A compromise is to test all independent routes, that is, all possible paths through the program. This is given by a metric (a measure of the product, for example lines of code, man days to write) called the *cyclomatic complexity* which is calculated by determining the number of simple conditions in the program. For example, if there are 5 *if* statements and one *while* loop, the cyclomatic complexity is 6. Compound conditions of N predicates count as N rather than 1.

As an example, consider the simple BASIC program in Listing 25.2. The program is designed to calculate the charge that a tool hire firm makes for its power tools. The hire charge depends on two factors : (1) the type of tool, A or B or C, depending on its value, and (2) the hire period. Tools hired for 7 days or more qualify for a 25% discount. A deposit, related to the tool type, is also required. The following table summarises the hire charges:

TYPE	DAILY RATE	DEPOSIT
A	£3.00	£10.00
B	£4.50	£15.00
C	£7.00	£20.00

The program first accepts the two items of data required for the calculation - *type* and *period* -, determines the appropriate daily rate and deposit, and then calculates the total charge, applying a discount if the number of days is seven or more. The results are printed out and the process is repeated if required.

```
10  REM ——————————————————————————-
20  REM Example program to calculate tool hire charges
30  REM ——————————————————————————-
40  REM
42  REPEAT
45  REM **** Get input data ***
50    INPUT "ENTER TOOL TYPE (A/B/C) ",type$
60    INPUT "ENTER HIRE PERIOD (NO. OF DAYS) ",days
70    REM *** Calculate rate per day and deposit required ***
80    IF type$ = "A" THEN rate = 3    :deposit = 10
90    IF type$ = "B" THEN rate = 4.5 :deposit = 15
100   IF type$ = "C" THEN rate = 7    :deposit = 20
200   REM ***Calculate hire charge ***
210   charge = rate * days
220   IF days = 7 THEN charge = charge * 0.75
230   REM *** Display the appropriate results ***
240   PRINT
250   PRINT "Tool is  type "; type$
260   PRINT
270   PRINT "Period of hire is "; days ; " days"
280   PRINT "Hire charge is £"; charge
290   PRINT "Deposit required is £"; deposit
300   REM *** If required repeat for another customer ***
310   INPUT "REPEAT FOR ANOTHER CUSTOMER (Y/N) ? ",answer$
320 UNTIL  answer$ = "N" OR answer$ = "n"
330 END
```

Listing 25.2

Here the cyclomatic complexity is 6 since there are four *IF* statements and a *REPEAT..UNTIL* loop containing a compound condition.

However, this metric must be used with discretion as certain program constructs will disguise a program's actual complexity. For example, compare the following two equivalent C fragments which assign a value between 0 and 4 to a vowel entered by the user:

```
(1)  int n;
     char ch;
     ch=getchar();
     switch (ch)
          {
              case 'a':n=0;break;
              case 'e':n=1;break;
              case 'i':n=2;break;
              case 'o':n=3;break;
              case 'u':n=4;break;
          }
```

cyclomatic complexity 5

```
(2)  char ch, vowel[5]={"aeiou"};
     int n=0;
     ch=getchar();
     while ( ch != vowel[n] ) n++;
```

cyclomatic complexity 1

Both fragments would require the same amount of testing even though the metric suggests otherwise.

Program Documentation

The purpose of documentation is to provide the user with all the information necessary to fully understand the purpose of the program and how that purpose has been achieved. The precise form that the documentation takes will be determined by a number of factors:

☐ The type of program.

☐ Who is likely to use the program.

☐ Whether it will be necessary to modify the program coding after it has been finally tested and accepted.

This section will explore documentation requirements and provide general guidelines for the contents of the documentation, but because of the wide variety of opinion regarding its format, no particular documentation standard will be advocated. The section concludes with an example of how a C function might be documented.

Documentation Requirements

A program which validates a temporary file prior to creating it permanently will probably require a minimum of user interaction and only a small number of instructions for the benefit of the person who will run the program. However, at some later date, it might be necessary for the author of the program, or a different programmer, to modify it. This possibility means that the structure of the program will have to be explained in great detail, and test procedures to ensure its correct operation will have to be provided.

A general purpose program such as a spreadsheet, designed for naive users, will entail the provision of extremely detailed instructions regarding its function and use. Such programs are generally accompanied by extremely detailed user manuals and tutorials. On the other hand, users would not be expected (and definitely not encouraged) to modify the program coding; thus no details would be provided regarding the way the program has been written. This latter type of documentation would only be required for the people responsible for producing the program.

In addition to the documentation requirements of users and programmers, there is a third category of person to be catered for. These are people such as managers who are neither likely to use programs extensively nor want to attempt to modify them. They merely need to have an overview of the program - its function, capabilities, hardware requirements etc.

Thus there are many factors governing the coverage of documentation, and for this reason, in the next section, it is only possible to provide a checklist of items which might reasonably be included.

Checklist

The documentation for a simple program generally falls into four sections:

1. Identification
2. General specification
3. User information
4. Program specification.

Most users will need access to the first three sections; in general the fourth section will only be needed if the program is to be modified. The amount of detail in each section will depend entirely on the particular application and, to some extent, the implementation language. COBOL, for example, is largely self-documenting: it contains an identification division containing all the information listed in the first section below; the Data Division of a COBOL program contains precise details regarding all of the files used by the program and which devices are required; the Procedure Division is written in 'English-like' sentences which are generally easy to understand, even by a non-programmer. Consequently, a program written in COBOL will generally require less documentation than one written in C.

The following checklist is a guide to what might reasonably be included in the documentation for a program.

1. Identification.

☐ title of program;

☐ short statement of its function;

☐ author;

☐ date written;

☐ language used and version if relevant;

☐ hardware requirements.

2. General specification.

☐ description of the main action(s) of the program under normal circumstances;

☐ data-flow diagrams;

☐ description of data structures, including data structure diagrams and file specifications;

☐ restrictions and/or limitations of the program;

☐ equations used or references to texts explaining any complex procedures/techniques involved.

3. User information.

☐ format of input required, for example, source document or screen mask;

☐ output produced, for example, typical printout or screen display;

☐ detailed instructions for initially running the program;

☐ medium on which program located, for example, $3\frac{1}{2}$ inch floppy disk(s).

4. Program specification.

☐ structure charts;

☐ pseudocode;

☐ annotated listing;

☐ data dictionary describing, in table form and alphabetically ordered, the purpose and structure of all identifiers used in the program;

☐ testing procedure including test data and expected output.

Documentation Example

A simple string validation routine will be used to illustrate the depth of detail appropriate to the documentation and testing of a small subprogram. The subprogram, in this instance a C function, reads a sequence of characters representing the notation for a chess move, rejecting invalid characters and stripping blanks in the process. The function stores the move in a specified character array.

Identification

Program ID	: get_move.
Author	: Nick Waites.
Purpose	: To read a chess move, perform preprocessing by stripping blanks from the input, and store a syntactically valid move.
Date written	: December 1991.
Language	: Turbo C.
Hardware	: IBM PC compatible.
Operating system	: MS-DOS 3.3 or later.

General Specification

The purpose of the function is to read a chess move, written in algebraic notation, reject invalid characters, strip any spaces, and store the move in a character array whose address is supplied as a parameter to the function. The notation used for the function is as follows:

The chessboard consists of north-south files labelled a-h from left to right, and east-west ranks labelled 1-8 from white's side to black's side, as shown in *Figure 25.38*.

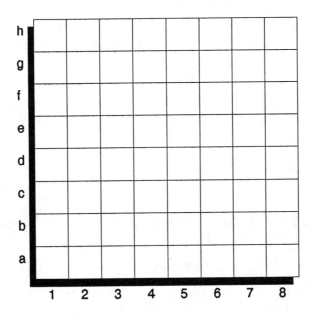

Figure 25.38

The notation for a move consists of a source square co-ordinate followed by a destination square co-ordinate separated by a '−' meaning 'to' or a '×' meaning 'takes'. For example, *d2 - d4* means 'move the piece on d2 to d4', and *c4 × d6* means 'the piece on c4 takes the piece on d6'.

Castling uses the notation O-O for the king side and O-O-O for the queen side.

The routine is required to:

- ☐ inform the user audibly if an invalid character is entered
- ☐ convert any upper case letters to lower case, except for castling moves in which upper case 'O' is allowed and lower case 'o' is converted to upper case if necessary
- ☐ allow spaces anywhere in the input but not to store them
- ☐ allow the move to be aborted by pressing the 'Esc' key
- ☐ ignore any characters following a valid move
- ☐ return the move in a character array whose address is passed as a parameter to the function

□ return a null string if the current input is aborted by the user pressing 'Esc'

User Information

When invoked, the function accepts a string of characters entered at the keyboard.

The function will issue an audible tone if the user attempts to enter a syntactically invalid move.

At the completion of entering a valid move, the routine will confirm its acceptance by displaying 'OK'; the user does not need to press the 'Enter' or 'Return' key.

At any point before a valid move has been entered, the 'Esc' key may be pressed to abort the current input, and the function will report this occurrence by displaying the message 'MOVE ABORTED'.

Restrictions/limitations

The function is used as a preprocessor, similar in some ways to the scanner component of a compiler, for a user move validation routine. As such it makes no attempt to determine the legality of the move input, only its syntactic correctness.

Detailed Function Specification

Operation of Function

The function performs a rudimentary form of parsing by identifying the separate components of a valid move. These separate components consist of

□ a board position specifier such as d4 or g7

□ a 'move to' symbol, '–'

□ a take symbol, '×'

□ a castling symbol, 'O'

The function uses a transition state table (shown later) to determine the order in which these components may appear and to reject symbols which are inappropriate at every stage of the move input. Valid characters are echoed to the screen and stored, spaces are also echoed but not stored, and invalid characters, neither echoed nor stored, cause the function to issue a warning tone.

Upper or lower case characters are accepted, though the function converts the letters *A* to *H* to lower case and the letter *o* to upper case irrespective of how they are entered.

At any stage of the input the input may be aborted by pressing the Escape key. This action results in the function returning a null string.

The function automatically returns a valid move as soon as one is detected; there is no need for the user to indicate the end of the input by pressing Enter, for instance. The function acknowledges a valid move by displaying 'OK' and an aborted move with 'MOVE ABORTED'.

Structure Diagram for Chess Move

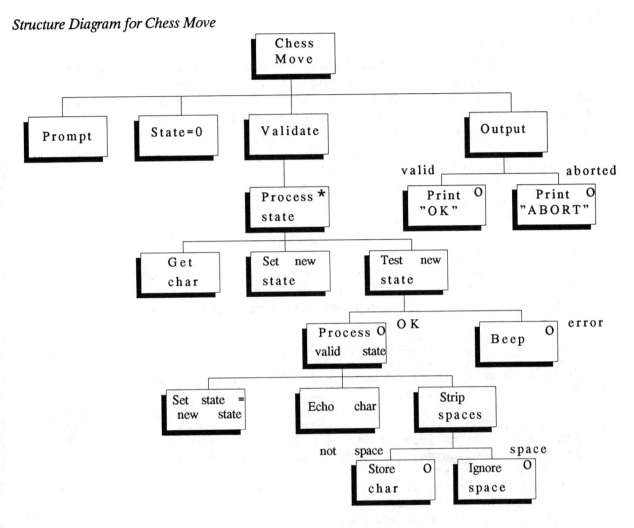

Transition State Diagram for Chess Move

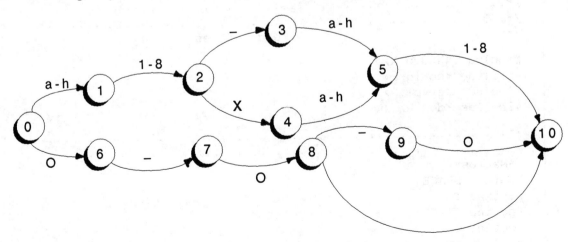

Data Dictionary

Name	Type	Use
column	integer	Stores column in state table appropriate to current symbol
delay()	TC function	Delays execution for specified number of millisecs
getch()	TC function	Accepts character from keyboard without echo to screen
get_move()	function	Validates, preprocesses and returns valid move
move	string pointer	Copy of *str*
new_state	integer	Holds new state
nosound()	TC function	Turns sound off
putchar()	TC function	Displays single character
sound()	TC function	Emits tone of specified frequency
state	integer	Holds current state
str	string pointer	Pointer to string containing validated move
sym	character	Copy of *symbol*
symbol	character	Holds the current character being processed
t[][]	integer array	Stores the state transition table
tolower()	TC function	Converts upper case character to lower case

Function Code

```
/*..............................................................*/
/*Function to accept a chess move in algebraic notation         */
/*..............................................................*/
/*..............................................................*/
/*                    Summary                                   */
/*Moves are of the form d2-d4, e4 x f5, 0-0, 0-0-0.             */
/*The function stores a valid move in a string array            */
/*after removing spaces.                                        */
/*Invalid characters are beeped. Extra characters at the        */
/*end of a valid move are ignored.                              */
/*Input is aborted with escape key                              */
/*A valid move is returned in function parameter                */
/*..............................................................*/
/*..............................................................*/
/*                    Header files                              */

#include <stdio.h>
#include <conio.h>
#include <ctype.h>
#include <dos.h>

/*..............................................................*/
/*..............................................................*/
/*Macros*/
#define SPACE          32
#define TO             '-'
#define TAKES          'x'
#define O              'O'
#define o              'o'
#define LETTER(_A)     _A >= 'a' && _A< = 'h'
#define DIGIT(_N)      _N> = '1'  && _N< = '8'
```

```
#define FILE                    'F'
#define RANK                    'R'
#define STATES                  10
#define COLUMNS                  8
#define OK                      10
#define ERR                     11
#define EXIT                    12
#define ESC                     27
/*.........................................................*/
/*.........................................................*/
/                       *Function code*/
void   get_move(char *str)
{
/*                      State transition table*/
static int t[STATES][COLUMNS] = { {1,ERR,6,ERR,ERR,0,EXIT,ERR},
                                  {ERR,2,ERR,ERR,ERR,1,EXIT,ERR},
                                  {ERR,ERR,ERR,3,4,2,EXIT,ERR},
                                  {5,ERR,ERR,ERR,ERR,3,EXIT,ERR},
                                  {5,ERR,ERR,ERR,ERR,4,EXIT,ERR},
                                  {ERR,OK,ERR,ERR,ERR,5,EXIT,ERR},
                                  {ERR,ERR,ERR,7,ERR,6,EXIT,ERR},
                                  {ERR,ERR,8,ERR,ERR,7,EXIT,ERR},
                                  {OK,OK,OK,9,OK,OK,EXIT,OK},
                                  {ERR,ERR,OK,ERR,ERR,9,EXIT,ERR}
                                };
           int   state, new_state;
           char  symbol;
           char     *move = str;
 puts("Enter move\n");
 state = 0;
 /*                     Loop until valid move is entered..
                        .. or esc pressed*/
 while(state < OK)
   {
        int column;
        char sym;
        symbol = getch();
        symbol = tolower(symbol);        /*convert to lower case */
        if(symbol == o ) symbol = O;     /*check for castling    */
        sym = symbol;                    /*make copy of char     */
        if(LETTER(symbol)) sym = FILE;   /*check for letter      */
        if(DIGIT(symbol))  sym = RANK;   /*check for number      */
/* Now test type of symbol and set corresponding column
   of state table                                               */
switch (sym)
 {
        case FILE  : column = 0;break;
        case RANK  : column = 1;break;
        case O     : column = 2;break;
        case TO    : column = 3;break;
```

```
            case TAKES : column = 4;break;
            case SPACE : column = 5;break;
            case ESC   : column = 6;break;
            default    : column = 7;break;
   }
 /* Get new state, print current symbol, store symbol
    if not a space. Beep if invalid character detected       */
 new_state = t[state][column];
 if(new_state != ERR)
        { state = new_state;
          putchar(symbol);
          if(symbol != SPACE) *move++ = symbol; }
 else
   { sound(1000);delay(100);nosound();        }
   }
   /* Print confirmation if move ok, terminate output string..
   .. else clear string if escape pressed to abort input      */
   if(state == OK) {puts("\nOK\n"); *move = '\0';}
   else            {puts("\MOVE ABORTED\n"); *str='\0';}
 }
/*..............................................................*/
/*                     Driver to test function                  */
/*..............................................................*/
 void main()

{
  char move[5] = {"     "};/* valid moves are stored here..   */
  /* ..or empty if move is aborted                            */
  int i = 0;

  for(i=0;move[0] != '\0';i++){
        get_move(move);
        printf("[Output from function: %s]\n", move);
  }
}
/*..............................................................*/
```

Testing Procedure

Test Classes

Class Name	Type	Class
C1	Valid	lower case, no spaces
C2	Valid	upper case, no spaces
C3	Valid	mixed case, no spaces
C4	Valid	leading spaces
C5	Valid	embedded spaces
C6	Valid	king side castling
C7	Valid	queen side castling
C8	Valid	escape pressed immediately
C9	Valid	escape pressed during input

C10	Invalid	Illegal character(s)	
C11	Invalid	legal character, invalid position	

Test Cases and Results

The following table shows the output produced for 16 test cases. The output consists of the string returned by the function followed by the message that it displays to the user, that is, 'OK' or 'MOVE ABORTED'. At which point a warning note was emitted is designated by < *beep*>. The input shows blanks as *b* and invalid characters, which were not echoed to the screen, are shown as strike-through characters such as s̶.

Test	Input	Output	Classes Tested
1	c3-g5	c3-c5 :OK	C1
2	D4-F2	d4-f2 :OK	C2
3	b8-B1	b8-b1 :OK	C3
4	a1xa2	a1xa2 :OK	C1
5	E4XG7	e4xg7 :OK	C2
6	*bbb*H6-J2	h6-j2 :OK	C4, C2
7	f*bb*6*bb-bAbb*5	f6-a5 :OK	C5, C1
8	*bb*D4*bx*c*bbbb*2	d4xc2 :OK	C5, C3
9	0-0*b*	O-O :OK	C6
10	0*b-bbb*0x	O-O :OK	C7, C5
11	<Esc>	null:MOVE ABORTED	C8
12	F3x<Esc>	null:MOVE ABORTED	C9
13	d7Xa9̶8	d7xa<beep>8 :OK	C10, C1
14	s̶f1*bb*-g0̶3	<*beep*>f1-g<*beep*>3:OK	C10, C1, C5
15	A2—dx̶2	a2-<*beep*>d<*beep*>2:OK	C11, C3
16	bf4*̶xc-3	f4<*beep*>xc<*beep*>3:OK	C11, C6, C1

26 *Data Structures*

A sound knowledge of basic data structures is essential for any computer programmer. A programming task will almost invariably involve the manipulation of a set of data which normally will be organized according to some coherent structure. It could be that the data is to be read in and processed, in which case a detailed knowledge of its structure is obviously essential. Furthermore, processing the data might involve organizing it in a way that facilitates its subsequent retrieval, as in information retrieval applications. Output from the program might require that the data is presented in yet another form. So a single program might be required to handle a number of data structures; only by having a thorough knowledge of basic data structures can the programmer choose, or design, the structures most appropriate to the problems being addressed.

From a programming viewpoint, the study of data structures involves two aspects, namely, the theoretical principles upon which the structures are founded, and the practicalities of implementing them using a computer. This chapter addresses both of these considerations by describing a number of important data structures and their applications to programming tasks.

A data structure is essentially a number of data *items,* also called *elements* or *nodes*, with some relationship linking them together. Each item consists of one or more named parts called *fields* occupying one or more memory locations in the computer. In its simplest form, an element can be a single field occupying a single word of memory.

A list of numbers occupying consecutive memory locations in a computer is a simple data structure called an *array*:

Memory Location	Contents
1000	56
1001	34
1002	123
1003	11
1004	77

The relationship linking the individual elements is merely the order in which they are stored in memory. In order to access the next element in the list (that is, an element's *successor*) it is necessary only to increment the memory address; the previous element at any point in the list (that is an element's *predecessor*) is found by decrementing the current memory address. This simple structural relationship allows the list to be accessed in sequential order.

Data structures such as *linked lists* provide *pointers* linking elements together. So, for example, to access the above numeric list in ascending order of magnitude, an extra field could be added to each element to point to the next element in the sequence:

Memory Location	Contents	
	Link	Value
1000	1004	56
1001	1000	34
1002	0000	123
1003	1001	11
1004	1002	77

Now, starting with location 1003 and following the links, the list can be accessed in ascending order: the link contained in location 1003 indicates that the number succeeding 11 is in location 1001; location 1001 contains the number 34 plus a pointer showing that the next number in the sequence is to be found at location 1000; the list terminates at location 1002 which contains the final number, 123, and a zero link indicating that there are no more elements in the list.

Linked lists make it easier to insert or delete elements at any position in the sequence of items, at the cost of increased complexity and increased memory demands.

Other data structures such as *stacks* and *queues* restrict access to elements to certain points of a sequential data structure, normally the start or end. With stacks, elements may only be added or deleted at one end of the list; queues allow items to be added at one end and deleted at the other.

The attraction of using a simple array data structure is that a data item may be accessed by means of a simple key which specifies its position within the array. So, for example, if we used an array to store details of a collection of 30 videos, and we assigned to each of them a different code number in the range 1 to 30, searching the array for the details of a particular video would merely entail entering the code number; the required details would be obtained in a fixed length of time by using the code number as an index value.

However, if for a video hire shop we also wanted to use an array to store its videos, so that any one could be accessed in the shortest possible time, the amount of storage space required would be prohibitive. For instance, using a six-digit key would require 1,000,000 digits to be stored for the keys alone, and then the video details would be in addition. If the key was to be used to encode information concerning the video - how many duplicates, children's or adult's for example - then we would expect that out of these 1,000,000 possible keys only a relatively small proportion of them would be used. Suppose that this proportion is 10%, that is, the system is only intended to cope with a maximum of 1,000 videos. Then 90% of the space allocated to the storage of video details would be wasted.

What is required is a method of mapping the 1,000,000 keys to a table containing only 1,000 keys. Hashing allows us to do this by applying a *hash function* to the key to produce an integer, in a much smaller range, which is used as the actual index to the table containing the records. The chief disadvantage of this scheme is that the hashing function will most probably generate non-unique index values, that is, two different keys could easily produce exactly the same index. This is termed a *collision*, and any hashing process must allow for this occurrence and cope with it using a *collision resolution strategy*.

Where a data structure is to be searched using an alphabetic key such as a surname, which could be incorrectly spelled, a useful method of coping with this problem is to use *Soundex Coding*. This allows words which sound alike, though spelled differently, to be given an identical code. Because of its usefulness in many application areas, the chapter concludes with a description of soundex coding and a soundex algorithm.

Arrays

Storage of Arrays

High-level procedural languages such as BASIC, COBOL and Pascal allow programmers to manipulate tabular data stored in *arrays*. The programmer merely declares the name, size and dimension of the array and the language processor takes care of allocating memory for it.

The immediate access store (memory) of a computer consists of a large number of memory locations, each with its own unique address (see Chapter 3). Memory locations have addresses ranging from 0 to $n-1$, where n represents the total number of memory locations available in the computer. For example, in a computer which has 640K bytes of user memory, byte addresses will range from 0 to $(640 \times 1024) - 1$, that is, 0 to 655359.

If a programmer defines a one-dimensional array of, say, twenty integers each occupying a single word, then the language processor must assign sufficient storage space for the array in user RAM and be able to find any array element as quickly as possible. Locating an array element requires a small calculation involving the starting address of the array, which is termed the *base address,* and the number of bytes per array element.

For example, suppose we have a one-dimensional array A_k of single byte words, where k is over the range 0 to 20, with base address b. Then element A_0 will have address

$$b + 0 = b$$

Element A_1 will have address

$$b + 1$$

and, in general, element A_k will have address

$$b + k.$$

Figure 26.1 shows the relationship between array elements and memory locations:

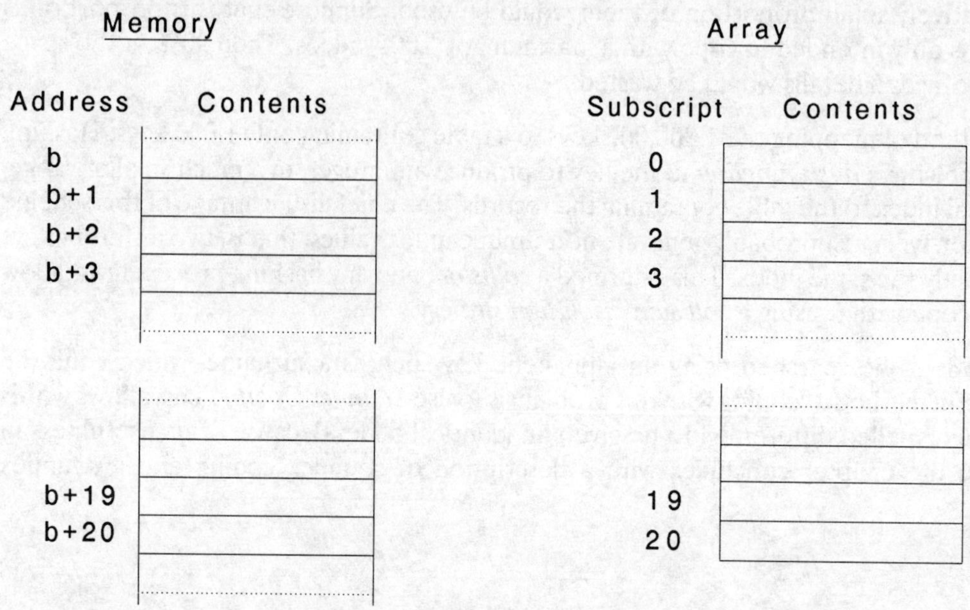

Memory			Array		
Address	Contents		Subscript	Contents	
b			0		
b+1			1		
b+2			2		
b+3			3		
b+19			19		
b+20			20		

Figure 26.1

Because the memory of a computer is essentially a one-dimensional array of memory locations, when it is required to represent a two-dimensional table, a slightly more complicated calculation is necessary: the language processor must convert the subscripts of two-dimensional array element into a one-dimensional physical memory address.

Suppose now that we are considering the storage requirements of a two-dimensional array, $T_{j,k}$, single word integers and size 10 × 6 that is, a table with 10 rows (j=0 to 9) and 6 columns (k=0 to 5) as shown in *Figure 26.2*.

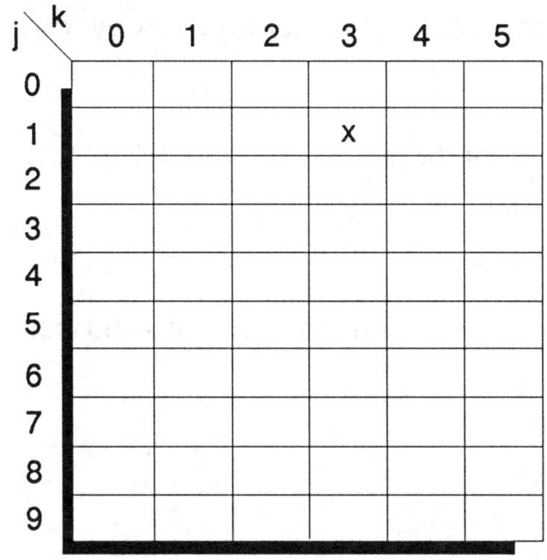

Figure 26.2

If the base address is at location b, and the array is stored row by row, then the elements of the array might be stored in memory as shown in *Figure 26.3*.

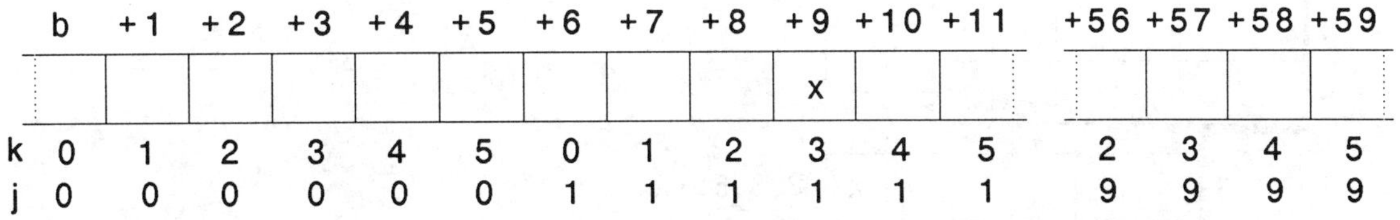

Figure 26.3

The positions marked by an '×' in *Figures 26.2* and *26.3* show the correspondence between a two-dimensional array element and the same element's memory address.

The calculation required to convert the position of a two-dimensional array element $T_{j,k}$ to a memory location, M, is

$$M = b + j \times 6 + k$$

For example, element $T_{0,3}$ would occupy the location

$$M = b + 0 \times 6 + 3 = b + 3,$$

and element $T_{3,2}$ would be at location

$$M = b + 3 \times 6 + 2 = b + 20$$

The calculations above assume that the array is of size 10×6. In general, if the array is of size $m \times n$, then an element $T_{j,k}$ would translate to the location

$$M = b + j \times n + k$$

This is called a *mapping function,* a formula which uses the array size and the element subscripts to calculate the memory address at which that element is located.

Note that if the array is stored column by column rather than row by row, the mapping function becomes

$$M = b + k \times m + j$$

Extending this scheme to an array, $D_{i,j,k}$, of three dimensions and size $l \times m \times n$, the conversion calculation becomes,

$$M = b + i \times m \times n + j \times n + k$$

Figure 26.4 illustrates the correspondence between array elements and memory locations for a three-dimensional table of size $3 \times 5 \times 6$.

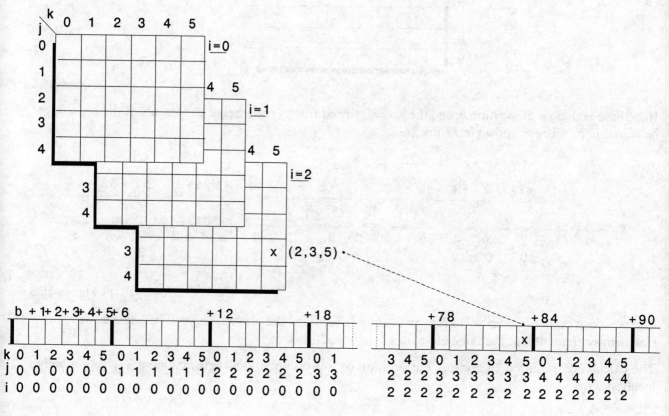

Figure 26.4

Here, i can be considered to be the subscript which specifies a number of tables, each of size $j \times k$. Thus, $D_{2,3,5}$ references element (3,5) of the third table (for which $i=2$). This corresponds to the location

$$M = b + 2 \times 5 \times 6 + 3 \times 6 + 5 = b + 83$$

Further application of the principles explained above allow arrays of any number of dimensions to be handled.

Iliffe Vectors

When speed has a higher priority than memory requirements, a table look-up scheme is sometimes adopted for accessing array elements. The main drawback of using a mapping function is the time taken to perform the address calculation, which will generally involve one or more relatively slow multiplication operations. The number of calculations can be significantly reduced by pre-calculating row or column addresses and storing them in another table.

For example, suppose that we have a 3×5 array as illustrated in *Figure 26.5*.

j \ k	0	1	2	3	4
0	b	b+1	b+2	b+3	b+4
1	b+5	b+6	b+7	b+8	b+9
2	b+10	b+11	b+12	b+13	b+14

Figure 26.5

We first calculate, and then store in three consecutive memory locations, the starting address for each of the three rows. This is called an Iliffe vector (see *Figure 26.6*).

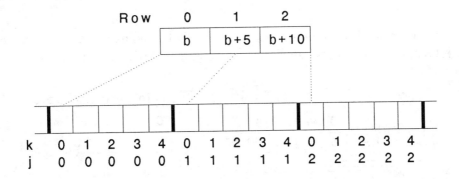

Figure 26.6

So, given the row subscript for the array element to be accessed, the Iliffe vector is consulted for the starting address of that row, and the location of the required element is found by using the column subscript as an offset to be added to this row address. When implemented in assembly language or machine code using appropriate addressing modes, this scheme virtually eliminates the necessity for any address calculations.

Access Tables

The principle of using a table containing the starting addresses of data items is particularly useful for accessing elements of string arrays. *Figure 26.7* shows how an access table is used to point to the starting locations of string array elements stored in memory.

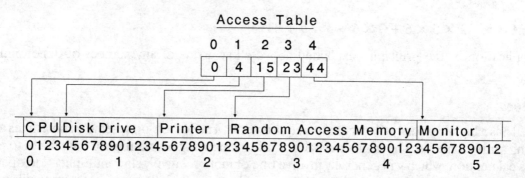

Figure 26.7

The array S_k (k = 0 to 4) to be represented consists of a number of string elements of variable sizes, each terminated by a special character indicating the end of the string. In this instance, the strings, with their subscripts, are:

0   CPU

1   Disk Drive

2   Printer

3   Random Access Memory

4   Monitor

The access table contains entries which point to the starting locations of each of the strings in order. For example, if the element S_3 was to be accessed, the entry in the access table corresponding to this element (that is, the element with subscript 3) provides the starting address for S_3 which has a value 'Random Access Memory'.

Sometimes, rather than indicating the end of a string element by means of a special character such as an ASCII carriage return code, the access table is used in conjunction with another table giving the length of the string (*Figure 26.8*).

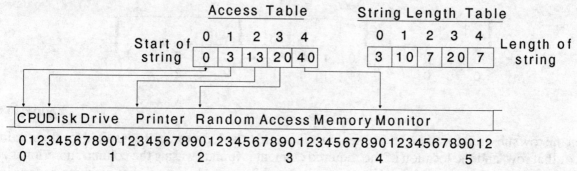

Figure 26.8

This scheme improves access speed but at the expense of additional storage requirements.

Search Strategies

Having stored a number of data items in an array, it is more than likely that it will be necessary at some time to search the data structure for the occurrence of specific items of data. For example, suppose that an array A_k ($k=0$ to 9999) is being used to store stolen credit card numbers, and it is to be searched in order to ascertain whether a shop customer is using a stolen credit card. The search algorithm might be as follows:

```
algorithm search_array
k:= 0
pos:= -1
card_found: = FALSE
while k < array_size and not card_found
        if S(k) = Card_number
                then card_found:= TRUE;
        pos:= k
      endif
      k:= k + 1
endwhile
if card_found
        then card number is located in S(pos)
else card number is not in stolen cards list
endif
end search_array
```

Each element in the list is compared with the number of the customer's card; if a match is found, the iteration is terminated by setting the boolean variable *card_found* to *TRUE*, and the position of the value in the array is stored in the variable *pos*; if the loop ends and the variable *card_found* still has a value of *FALSE*, then the customer's card is not in the list of stolen credit cards. This technique is called a *sequential search*.

Though very straightforward, a sequential search can be very time consuming, since it could necessitate the complete list of 10,000 elements being searched. A faster method is possible if the list of card numbers is in ascending or descending numerical order. This alternative method is called *binary search*, or sometimes *binary chop*.

For example, suppose that the list of stolen card numbers is in ascending numerical order, then a binary search proceeds as follows:

1.   Set the array subscript to *mid*, middle value. In this case *mid* is 9999/2, which is 5000 to the nearest integer.

2.   Compare required *card_number* with S(*mid*).

3.   (a) If *card_number* < S(*mid*) then *card_number* can only be in the first half of the array.
     (b) If *card_number* > S(*mid*) then *card_number* can only be somewhere in the latter half of the array.
     (c) If *card_number* = S(*mid*) then the card number has been found.

4.   If the card number has not yet been found, repeat from step 1 using *mid* as the size of the array.

The procedure successively reduces the size of the array to be searched by a factor of two. For an array of size 10,000, this means that only a maximum of 14 elements need to be examined in order to determine whether a particular element is a member of the list. Thus, for 10,000 elements, the search size reduces as follows:

Number of comparisons	Array size to be searched
0	10,000
1	5,000
2	2,500
3	1,250
4	625
5	313
6	157
7	79
8	40
9	20
10	10
11	5
12	3
13	2
14	1

Notice that 2^{14} is the smallest power of 2 which exceeds the maximum array size of 10,000:

$2^{13} = 8,192$ which is less than 10,000;

$2^{14} = 16,384$ which is greater than 10,000.

This is how the maximum figure of 14 comparisons has been derived.

A more formal version of the binary search algorithm can be stated as follows:

```
algorithm binary
low:= 0
high:= array_size - 1
pos:= -1
card_found:= FALSE
while low < high and not card_found
        mid:= int((low + high))/2
        case TRUE of
        when S(mid) = card_number : card_found:= TRUE
                                     pos:= mid
        when S(mid) > card_number : high:= mid - 1
        when S(mid) < card_number : low:= mid + 1
        endcase
endwhile
if card_found
        then stolen card number is located in S(pos)
else card number is not in list
endif
end binary
```

In order to select the appropriate part of the array to be searched, the algorithm uses two variables, *low* and *high*, to store the lower and upper bounds of that part of the array. They are used to calculate the mid point, *mid*, (rounded to the nearest integer value using the *int* function), so that the value stored there can be compared with the value required (the card number, in this example). Each time the comparison fails, the lower or upper bound is adjusted and the procedure is repeated. The process continues until either the value is located or the lower and upper bounds coincide, in which case the value does not exist in the array. The variable *pos* is used to store the position of the value if it exists in the array; a negative value for *pos* indicates that the search was unsuccessful.

The binary search method will usually be employed when the array size is large, otherwise the processing overheads caused by the algorithm's increased complexity make it unsuitable.

The Stack

A *stack* is a data structure characterized by the expression 'Last In First Out' (LIFO), meaning that the most recent item added to the stack is the first one which can be removed from the stack. A *stack pointer* is used to keep track of the last item added to the stack, that is, the current top of the stack.

Suppose that we wish to implement a stack using a one-dimensional array, S_i where $i=1$ to 5. A special register, *sp*, must be reserved as the stack pointer, and this will have an initial value of 0 indicating that the stack is empty.

To add, or *push*, an item to the stack, the following steps are required:

1. Check that there is room in the stack to add another item. In this case, the stack is full when *sp* has a value of 5, that is, when all of the elements in the array S_i have been used to store items. When the stack pointer is at its maximum value, and another item is required to be stored on the stack, a *stack overflow* condition has occurred, and it will not be possible to push the item onto the stack.

2. If an overflow condition does not exist, the stack pointer is incremented and the item is transferred to the array element pointed to by the stack pointer.

For example, suppose that the number 15 is to be pushed to the stack. After completing the operation the stack will look like this:

i	S_i	
1	15	$\longleftarrow$ —————$sp=1$
2	-	
3	-	
4	-	
5	-	

After adding two more numbers the stack will contain three elements and the stack pointer will have a value of 3:

i	S_i	
1	15	
2	6	
3	21	$\longleftarrow$ —————$sp=3$
4	-	
5	-	

The algorithm for pushing a value to a stack can be summarized as follows:

```
    algorithm push      {add item to top of stack}
      if sp < maximum size of stack        {test for overflow}
         then sp := sp + 1;                {increment stack ptr}
              Ssp := item                  {push item}
         else     Stack overflow
    endif
    end
```

To remove an item from the stack, often called *pulling* or *popping* a value, requires the reverse procedure:

1.   Check that the stack is not empty, that is, *sp* is greater than zero. If the stack is empty, an attempt to pull a non-existent value causes a *stack underflow* condition to arise.

2.   If the stack is not empty, the item on the top of the stack, as shown by the stack pointer, is transferred to its destination and the stack pointer is decremented.

Thus, after pulling a value from the stack S_i, it would be in the state shown below:

i	S_i
1	15
2	6 <—— sp=2
3	21
4	-
5	-

Notice that the value pulled from the stack, 21 in this instance, still exists in the stack: it is not necessary to actually remove a value from the stack since, by decrementing the stack pointer, this is effectively what has happened. Pulling a value from a stack is effected by copying the value to its destination before decrementing the stack pointer. The top of the stack is now the second element of the array which contains the value 6.

To summarize, the algorithm for pulling a value from a stack is:

```
    algorithm pop      {remove item from top of stack}
      if sp > 0                {that is, stack is not empty}
         then item := Ssp;     {transfer item to destination}
              sp := sp - 1     {decrement stack pointer}
         else stack underflow
    endif
    end
```

Application of Stacks

The stack is used frequently in programming languages for control structures. In Acorn's BASIC, for example, GOSUB, FOR...NEXT, REPEAT...UNTIL and procedure/function calls all use stacks in their implementation.

The GOSUB instruction causes control to be transferred to the line specified in the instruction. Subroutine instructions are executed as normal until a RETURN instruction is encountered, whereupon control returns to the instruction following the last GOSUB instruction executed. Thus, with the fragments of

BASIC code illustrated in *Listing 26.1*, the subroutine starting at line 1000 is called at line 100 by the GOSUB 1000 instruction. The BASIC interpreter must store its current position in the program so that after executing the subroutine it can return control to this same position when a RETURN instruction is encountered. This is accomplished by pushing the return address to a stack prior to jumping to the start of the subroutine.

```
   10 REM        *** Mainline program ***
  . . . . . . . . . . . .
  . . . . . . . . . . . .
   90 REM      Call subroutine at line 1000
  100 GOSUB 1000
  105 REM      Program contines here after completing subroutine
  110 LET a = x + 1
  120
  . . . . . . . . . . . .
  990 STOP
  999 REM        *** End of Mainline program ***
 1000 REM        *** Subroutine code goes here ***
 1010
  . . . . . . . . . . . .
 etc
  . . . . . . . . . . . .
 1490 RETURN
```

Listing 26.1

When a RETURN instruction is executed, the top of the stack is pulled and the interpreter continues from that address. In this way the same subroutine can be called from different parts of the program and control will always return to the instruction following the GOSUB instruction.

Another reason for using a stack is that it facilitates the use of nested control structures. In the example shown in *Listing 26.1* it is possible to have another GOSUB instruction in the subroutine at line 1100. (See *Listing 26.2*).

```
     10 REM          *** Mainline program ***
.............
.............
     90 REM       Call subroutine at line 1000
    100 GOSUB 1000
    105 REM      Program contines here after completing subroutine
    110 LET a = x + 1
    120
.............
    etc
.............
    990 STOP
    999 REM               *** End of Mainline program ***
   1000 REM                  *** Subroutine code goes here ***
   1010
.............
   1100 GOSUB 2000
   1200
.............
   1490 RETURN
   2000 REM               *** Code for second subroutine goes here ***
   2010
.............
   etc
   2490 RETURN
```

Listing 26.2

In this instance the stack is used twice: the return address appropriate to the subroutine call at line 100 is pushed to the stack, then the return address for the second, nested, subroutine call is pushed to the stack during execution of the first subroutine at line 1100.

When the RETURN statement at line 2490 is executed, BASIC pulls the top of the GOSUB stack causing control to return to line 1200, the line following the most recent GOSUB instruction. The RETURN statement at line 1490 causes BASIC to pull the new top of the stack which provides the return address for the first GOSUB call at line 100. This technique allows subroutines to be nested to any depth, subject to the size of the GOSUB stack.

The same principle applies to the management of FOR..NEXT loops in BASIC. A separate stack is used to store information regarding the FOR..NEXT control variables. The BASIC interpreter stores on the stack five pieces of information when it encounters a FOR statement:

☐ the address of the control variable

☐ the type of the control variable

☐ STEP size

☐ TO limit

☐ the address of the next statement following FOR

The stack pointer is incremented by the number of words occupied by this information, and then the statement following the FOR instruction is executed.

A NEXT instruction will cause BASIC to use the information on the top of the stack to either repeat the statements between the FOR and NEXT instructions, or to exit the loop if the control variable has exceeded its maximum value. If the latter is the case, the FOR..NEXT stack pointer will be decremented to remove the top of the stack thus terminating this loop.

The use of a stack again allows nesting of FOR..NEXT loops, subject to a depth governed by the size of the FOR..NEXT stack.

A REPEAT..UNTIL stack is used in a similar way to that of the FOR..NEXT stack, though the procedures for managing REPEAT..UNTIL loops are simpler.

Procedures and functions in BASIC are handled in a similar manner to the GOSUB structure, but the BASIC interpreter has to cope with additional problems associated with passing parameters and saving the values of local variables so that they can be subsequently restored. These extra problems are once again overcome by the use of stacks.

The Queue

The data structure known as a *queue* has the same characteristics as the queues we encounter in everyday life. For instance, a queue at the checkout counter of a supermarket increases at its rear as customers join the queue to have their purchases totalled, and only reduces in size when a customer is served at the head of the queue, the checkout counter. A queue of cars at traffic lights behaves in a similar manner, with cars exiting the queue only at its head and joining the queue only at its rear.

A *queue* is a data structure in which elements are added only at the rear of a linear list and removed only from the front, or head, of the list. A queue is often given the name FIFO list, from the initial letters of the words in the phrase 'First In First Out' which describes the order of processing the elements of the list.

Suppose that an array, Q_k ($k=0$ to 31), is to be used as a queue. *Head* will be used to keep track of the front of the queue and *Rear*, the end of the queue as shown in *Figure 26.9*.

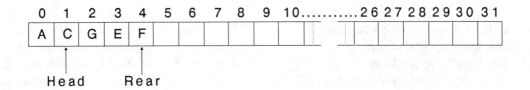

Figure 26.9

Initially, the queue is empty so that *Head* = *Rear* = 0. When an item is added to the queue, *Rear* is incremented; when an item is removed from the list, *Head* is incremented. Assuming that the queue is simply storing single alphabetic characters, the table below illustrates the operation of the queue for ten queue operations:

Operation	Item	Head	Rear	State of queue
		0	0	Empty
1. Add item	A	0	1	A
2. Add item	C	0	2	AC
3. Add item	G	0	3	ACG
4. Add item	E	0	4	ACGE
5. Remove item	A	1	4	CGE
6. Add item	F	1	5	CGEF
7. Remove item	C	2	5	GEF
8. Remove item	G	3	5	EF
9. Remove item	E	4	5	F
10. Remove item	F	5	5	Empty

The following algorithms show how items are added to a queue and removed from a queue, assuming *array_size* is the maximum size of the array *Q* used for storing the queue.

```
algorithm queue        {Add item to queue}
  if  Rear <= array_size - 1
    then  Q(Rear) := item
          Rear := Rear + 1
    else Queue is full
  endif
end
```

```
algorithm queue            {Remove item from queue}
  if Rear <> Head
    then item := Q(Head)
         Head := Head + 1
    else Queue is empty
  endif
end
```

Notice that the queue is empty when the head pointer has the same value as the rear pointer. Notice also that, unlike a queue in real life, as items are added and removed, the queue moves through the array since both the head and rear pointers are incremented. This means that eventually the queue will run out of space, at which time an overflow condition will occur. One solution to this problem is to implement a circular queue which re-uses array elements that are empty.

Circular Queues

Figure 26.10 illustrates the principles of a circular queue:

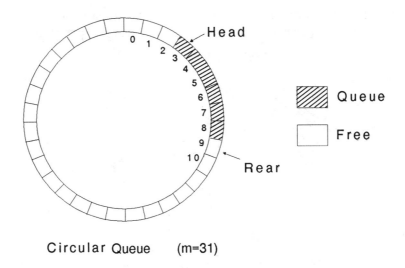

Circular Queue   (m=31)

Figure 26.10

The circular arrangement of the array elements is merely a means of illustrating the principles of operation of a circular queue; the data structure used to store the queue is physically the same as before, that is, a one-dimensional array.

Head and *Rear* are again used, but this time when either of them reach a value equal to m, the upper bound of the array, they start again at the beginning, using up elements which previously have been removed from the queue. The diagram shows the queue in a state where ten items have been added to the queue and three items have been removed. *Figure 26.11* shows that the queue has completely traversed the array such that *Rear* is equal to m, and there are five items in the queue.

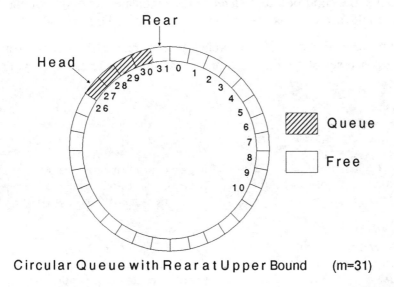

Circular Queue with Rear at Upper Bound   (m=31)

Figure 26.11

The next item to be added to the queue will be inserted at position 1, so that *Rear* has a value of 0 rather than $m + 1$. In other words, when *Rear* exceeds the upper bound reserved for the queue, it takes the value of the lower bound. The same thing applies to the *Head* of the queue. *Figure 26.12* shows the queue, having traversed all the elements of the array, starting to re-use unoccupied positions at the beginning of the array.

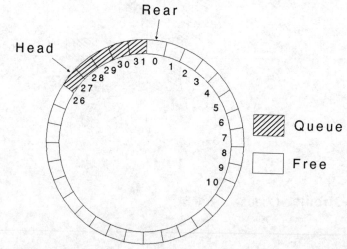

Circular Queue Re-using Deleted Elements   (m=31)   **Figure 26.12**

A slight difficulty with a circular queue is being able to differentiate between an empty queue and a full queue; the condition for a non-empty queue can no longer be that *Rear < Head* since, depending how many items have been added and removed, it is possible for a non-empty queue to be such that *Rear* has larger value than *Head*. *Figures 26.11* and *26.12* illustrate both queue states, the first where *Head < Rear* and the second where *Head > Rear*.

One solution to this problem is to adopt the convention that *Head* always points to the array element immediately preceding the first item in the queue rather pointing to the first item itself; since *Rear* points to the last item in the queue, the condition that *Head = Rear* indicates an empty queue. *Head* and *Rear* are initialized to be equal to the array's upper bound rather than zero. Thus, initially, the queue is empty.

The queue becomes full only when the rear pointer catches up with the head pointer. The algorithms shown in *Listing 26.3* define the processes of adding an item to a circular queue and removing an item from a circular queue:

```
algorith c_queue     {Add item to circular queue}
  temp:= Rear                      {Copy Rear Pointer}
  if Rear = Upper_bound            {check for upper limit}
     then Rear := Lower_bound      {start at beginning or..
     else Rear := Rear + 1          .. increment rear pointer}
  endif
  if Rear <>Head                   {check for queue full}
     then Q(Rear) := item          {add item to queue}
     else Queue is full            {overflow condition}
          Rear := temp             {restore Rear pointer}
  endif
end
```

```
algorithm c_dequeue   {Remove item from circular queue}
   if Head <>Rear                {check for queue not empty}
    then if Head = Upper_bound    {check for upper limit}
           then Head := Lower_bound  {start at beginning or..
           else Head := Head + 1     .. increment head pointer}
         endif
         item := Q(Head)          {remove item from queue}
    else Queue is empty           {underflow condition}
   endif
end
```

Listing 26.3

Applications of Queues

Most printers in common use today contain a quantity of RAM for the purpose of temporarily storing (or *buffering*) data transmitted from a computer. The buffer allows the computer to transmit, for example, a few kilobytes of data to the printer very quickly and allow the printer to print it autonomously, (that is, without further intervention from the computer). This allows the computer to continue processing other tasks while the relatively slow printer deals with the data it has received.

The printer buffer must operate as a queue, because the data must be printed in the same order as it was transmitted from the computer. As data is received by the printer, it is added to the buffer queue until either the computer stops transmitting data or the queue is full. The printer then commences to process the data in the queue, starting at the head of the queue and ending when the queue is empty. This process of filling up the buffer quickly and then emptying it at the speed of the printer continues until the computer ceases to transmit data. Buffers may range in size from a few kilobytes to several megabytes of RAM. A microprocessor in the printer itself deals with the way the data queue is processed.

Circular queues are frequently used by operating systems for spooling operations. For example, in a multi-user system in which a printer is shared between a number of users, print jobs may be spooled to a disk drive. The queue thus formed on the disk will be processed by the printer in the order the jobs were received (unless a priority system is in operation). As one job is printed, room will be available on the disk area allocated to the printer for another job; the circular queue principle applied to spooling will allow optimum use of the disk area allocated to print jobs. The operating system keeps track of the appropriate queue head and rear pointers required to operate the circular queue.

Linked Lists

Suppose that we are using an array to store a number of alphabetic items in alphabetical order as shown:

Element	Data
0	Aaron
1	Abelson
2	Bateman
3	Craddock
4	Dunfy
5	Eastman
6	
7	
8	
9	

Adding a new item such as 'Gregory', while maintaining the alphabetic ordering, is easy:

Element	Data
0	Aaron
1	Abelson
2	Bateman
3	Craddock
4	Dunfy
5	Eastman
6	Gregory
7	
8	
9	

The item is merely added to the end of the list. However, to insert 'Crawford' requires rather more effort: all of those entries after 'Craddock' must be moved down the array so that 'Crawford' may be inserted immediately after 'Craddock'. The list becomes:

Element	Data
0	Aaron
1	Abelson
2	Bateman
3	Craddock
4	Crawford
5	Dunfy
6	Eastman
7	Gregory
8	
9	

For a list containing hundreds or thousands of entries, this process could be considerably time-consuming.

An alternative approach is to introduce a second array containing pointers which link the elements together in the required order. Now an element, or *node,* contains a pointer in addition to the data. So, returning to the original list, it would be represented as follows:

Node	Data Pointer		
Start———>0	Aaron	1
1	Abelson	2
2	Bateman	3
3	Craddock	4
4	Dunfy	5
5	Eastman	− 1
Free———> 6
7
8
9

The original list is now in *linked list* form. Given the start position of the list, stored in *Start*, the pointers link the items together in the correct alphabetical order. The end of the list is indicated by a *null pointer*, in this case −1. Another pointer, *Free*, keeps track of the next free location for storing new items, and it is incremented whenever a new item is inserted or added to the list. Adding 'Gregory' to the list would entail changing the 'Eastman' pointer from −1 to 6 (that is, the value currently given by *Free*) and putting 'Gregory' at the position indicated by *Free*:

Node	Data	Pointer
Start———>0	Aaron	1
1	Abelson	2
2	Bateman	3
3	Craddock	4
4	Dunfy	5
5	Eastman	6
6	Gregory	− 1
Free———> 7		
8		
9		

'Gregory' is given a null pointer to indicate that it is the last item in the list, and *Free* is incremented.

In pseudocode form, the steps illustrated above to add an item to the end of a linked list are as shown in *Listing 26.4*.

```
algorithm add_node
    i := Start;                {copy start pointer}
    while ptr(i)<>null         {follow pointers until null pointer found}
        i := ptr(i)
    endwhile
    ptr(i) := Free             {link new item to current last node}
    data(Free) := item         {store new data in next free node}
    ptr(Free) := null          {store null pointer in next free node}
    Free := Free + 1           {increment next free ptr}
end
```

Listing 26.4

The notation *ptr(i)* is used for the pointer located at node *i*, and *data(i)* represents the data at node *i*. For example, in the alphabetical list above, *ptr(2)* = 3 and *data(2)* = 'Bateman'.

Now, to add 'Crawford' only one pointer is altered, rather than re-arranging the items in the array, and the new node is added to the end of the list:

	Node	**Data**	**Pointer**
Start——>	0	Aaron	1
	1	Abelson	2
	2	Bateman	3
	3	Craddock	7
	4	Dunfy	5
	5	Eastman	6
	6	Gregory	−1
	7	Crawford	4 <——————— inserted node
Free——>	8		
	9		

Thus, the order of accessing the array in alphabetical order is

0 - 1 - 2 - 3 - 7 - 4 - 5 - 6

In pseudocode, the algorithm for inserting a node to maintain the alphabetic ordering, is shown in *Listing 26.5*.

```
algorithm insert_node
  i := Start                          {copy start pointer}
  found := FALSE
    repeat
      if data(i) > item               {ie alphabetically}
             or Start = null          {allow for empty list}
        then found := TRUE            {insertion position found}
        else p := i                   {save current node}
             i := ptr(p)              {next node in list}
      endif
    until found                       {insertion position located}
             or i = null              {reached end of list}
    if i = start
      then data(Free) := item         {insert at head of list}
           ptr(Free) := Start
           Start := Free
      else ptr(p) = Free;             {insert in body of list}
           data(Free) := item
           ptr(Free) := i
    endif
    Free := Free + 1                  {increment next-free pointer}
  end
```

Listing 26.5

The increased complexity of this algorithm arises partially from the necessity to allow for the list being initially empty, this state being recognised by *Start* containing a null pointer. If the list is empty initially, then *Start* is set equal to *Free* which contains a pointer to the first available node, and the new data together with a null pointer are stored in this node. To delete a node merely entails ensuring that its predecessor's pointer links the node following it. For example, to delete 'Bateman', the pointers would be adjusted as follows:

	Node	Data	Pointer	
Start——>	0	Aaron	1	
	1	Abelson	3	
	2	*Bateman*	3<——————— deleted node	
	3	Craddock	7	
	4	Dunfy	5	
	5	Eastman	6	
	6	Gregory	−1	
	7	Crawford	4	
Free——>	8			
	9			

The pointer order is now

0 - 1 - 3 - 7 - 4 - 5 - 6

which misses out the third item in the array containing 'Bateman'.

The pseudocode algorithm is shown in *Listing 26.6*.

```
algorithm delete_node
i := Start                              {copy start pointer}
found := FALSE
repeat
    if data(i) = item or Start = null   {ie found node or empty list}
        then found := TRUE              {deletion position found}
        else p := i                     {save current node}
            i := ptr(p)                 {next node in list}
    endif
until found or i = null                 {deletion position located
                                         or reached end of list}

if Start = null or i = null             {ie empty list or reached
                                         end of list without finding
                                         node}

    then  node does not exist!          {not possible to delete node}
    else if i = start
        then  Start := ptr(i)           {delete head of list}
        else  ptr(p) := ptr(i)          {skip node in body of list}
        endif
endif
end
```

Listing 26.6

The algorithm allows for three special cases:

(i)   The list is empty - this means that it is not possible to delete an element.

(ii)   The item to be deleted is not in the list - again, it is not possible to delete this item.

(iii) The item to be deleted is the first one in the list - this requires that *Start* must be set to point to the second node in the linked list.

With a linked list it is possible to locate any element by following the pointers, irrespective of the physical location of the item. Rather than storing the list in consecutive elements of an array, confined to a certain range of memory locations, it is perfectly feasible to store the elements of the linked list anywhere in the memory space allocated to a user program. For this reason, an alternative, and more general, diagrammatic form is often used for linked lists, in which each node contains one or more pointers and one or more words of data. For example, the linked list immediately above might be represented as shown in *Figure 26.13*.

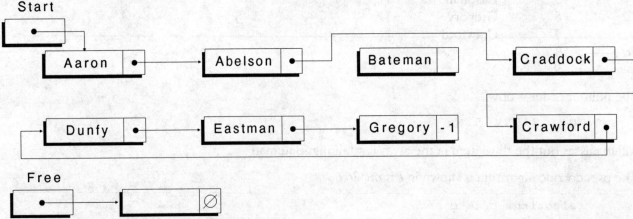

Figure 26.13

Arrowed lines are used to show the order in which nodes are linked together, and special nodes indicate the start point of the list and the next free node.

Linked lists have a number of advantages over arrays :

☐ Greater flexibility for the location of nodes in memory (it is even possible for nodes to be located on auxiliary storage, such as magnetic disks, rather than in main memory).

☐ The ease with which nodes may be added or deleted from the list.

☐ By adding more pointers, the list may be traversed in a number of different orders.

On the debit side for linked lists:

☐ Locating specific items necessitates searching the list from the start node, whereas arrays allow direct access to elements.

☐ Linked lists require more memory because of the need for pointers.

☐ Linked lists involve more 'housekeeping' operations because of the necessity to change pointers when adding or deleting nodes.

Applications of Linked Lists

With an interpreted language such as BASIC, variables must be accessed as quickly as possible so that program processing speed is acceptably fast. One method of ensuring this is by the use of linked lists.

In one such scheme, used by Acorn BASIC, variables starting with the same character are given their own linked list, so that there is a linked list for each possible starting character. Though the lists are quite separate, each with its own start pointer, they occupy a common area of memory and link around each other. Each node in the linked lists contains the name and value of the variable, plus a pointer to the next variable with the same starting letter. *Figure 26.14* illustrates this scheme at the stage where a number of variables with starting letters *A*, *B* or *C* have been created.

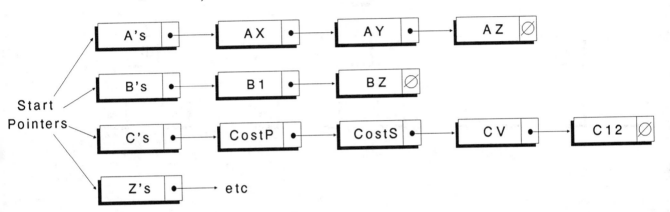

Figure 26.14

The start pointers for the linked lists are stored in a table in a specific area of memory. The first pointer in the table contains the address of the node for the first variable starting with the letter *A* to be created in the current program, in this case *AX*. This node contains a pointer to the second variable created, *AY*, and its node contains a pointer to *AZ*, the last variable created starting with the letter *A*. Similar lists occur for the variables starting with *B* (*B1* and *B2*) and *C* (*CostP*, *CostS*, *CV* and *C12*). Because the lists link around each other, there is a common free-space pointer for all the lists.

To find a particular variable's node, the starting letter of the variable is converted into an address giving the start pointer for its linked list, and the nodes of this list are traversed in pointer order until the variable is located. For example, suppose that the table of start pointers was at memory location 1000, and the variable *BZ* is to be accessed. The letter *B* is first converted into a number indicating its position in the alphabet, that is 2, and this is added to the start address of the table.

Thus, 1000 + 2 = 1002 is the location of the start pointer for the linked list of variables beginning with *B*. The first node in the list is for variable *B1*, which is not the one required, so its pointer is used to access the next node in the list. This time the variable found is *BZ* as required.

For a program containing many variables, this scheme can dramatically reduce the time required to locate a certain variable, provided variable names are chosen with different starting letters. It is worth noting that in this instance, a knowledge of the internal organization of an interpreter can help the programmer to write more efficient programs.

Linked lists are also used for procedures and functions so that they can be located as quickly as possible no matter where in the program they are referenced. Otherwise, a program would have to be searched sequentially from the beginning every time a procedure or function was invoked.

The Tree

The term *tree* refers to a non-linear data structure in which nodes have two or more pointers to other nodes, forming a hierarchical structure as illustrated in *Figure 26.15*.

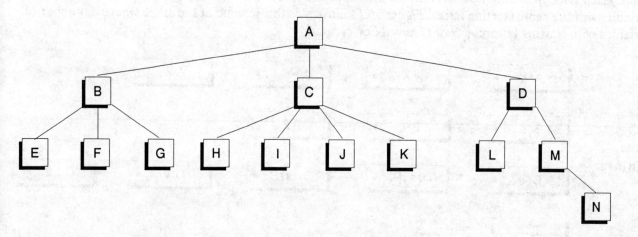

Figure 26.15

Node *A* is the *root* node of the entire tree with pointers to three *subtrees*. *B, C* and *D* are known as *children* of the *parent* node *A*. Similarly, *E, F* and *G* are children of *B*. Nodes *B* to *N* are all *descendants* of *A*, just as nodes *L* to *N* are all descendants of *D*. Nodes such as *H, I* and *L*, which have no children, are known as *leaves* or *terminal nodes*.

Trees are useful for representing hierarchical relationships between data items, such as those found in databases. For example, a record in an employee file might have the structure shown in *Figure 26.16*.

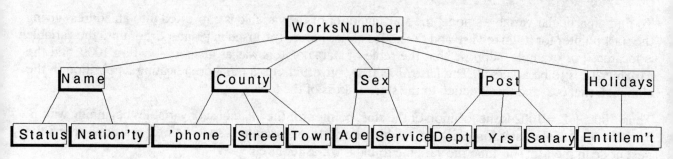

Figure 26.16

Stored as a tree, the data can be accessed in a number of ways. For example, extracting the first level of the tree provides a summary of the employee, giving Name, Home county, Sex, Post and Holidays taken; accessing only the fourth subtree provides details of the employees current position; accessing the tree in order of the five subtrees provides all the employees details.

A binary tree is a particular type of tree which has more uses than a general tree as described above, and is also much easier to implement. Binary trees are described in the following two sections.

Binary Trees

A binary tree is a special type of tree in which each parent has a maximum of two children which are linked to the parent node using a left pointer and a right pointer. The general form of a binary tree is shown in *Figure 26.17*.

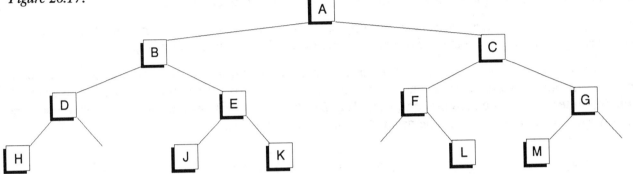

Figure 26.17

Binary trees have many important applications, a number of which are described in the next section. This section explores the nature of binary trees, how they are created, modified and accessed.

In the previous section we saw that in order to locate a specific node in a linked list it is necessary to search the list from the beginning, following the pointers linking the nodes together in the appropriate order. For a list containing a large number of elements, this process could be very time consuming. The solution to the same problem with an array structure was to use the binary search technique (see section on Search Strategies); the same principle can be applied to a linked list if the list is in the form of a *Binary Tree*. Consider the alphabetically ordered linked list described earlier in the section on linked lists and shown in *Figure 26.18*.

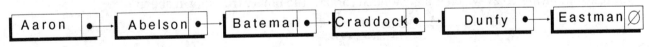

Figure 26.18

Now suppose that the same list is represented as a binary tree with two pointers in each node, one pointing to an element alphabetically less than the node data (a *left pointer*) and the other pointing to an element alphabetically greater than the node data (a *right pointer*). (See *Figure 26.19*).

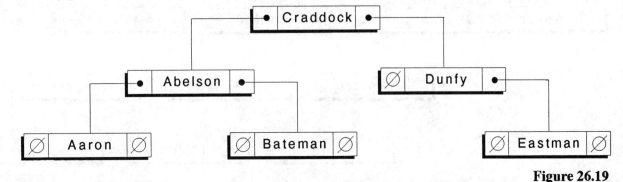

Figure 26.19

If we were looking for *Eastman*, the procedure would be as follows:

(i)   Compare *Eastman* with the *root node*, *Craddock*.

(ii)   Because *Craddock* is alphabetically less than *Eastman*, follow the right pointer to *Dunfy*.

(iii) Compare *Eastman* with *Dunfy*.

(iv)   *Dunfy* is alphabetically less than *Eastman* so again follow the right pointer to *Eastman*.

(v)   The next comparison shows that the required node has been located.

Each comparison confines the search to either the upper or lower part of the alphabetic list, thus significantly reducing the number of comparisons needed to locate the element required.

To add an element, *Crawford* for example, to the configuration shown above, whilst retaining the alphabetic ordering, is merely a matter of searching for the new item until a null pointer is encountered. In this example, a null pointer occurs when attempting to go left at *Dunfy*. *Crawford* is installed in the next free node and *Dunfy's* left pointer points to it. The new tree is shown in *Figure 26.20*.

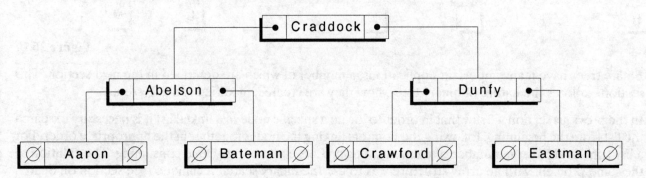

Figure 26.20

Unfortunately, deleting a node is not quite so simple. Three cases can arise, and these are described with reference to *Figure 26.21* which is an extended form of the binary tree shown above.

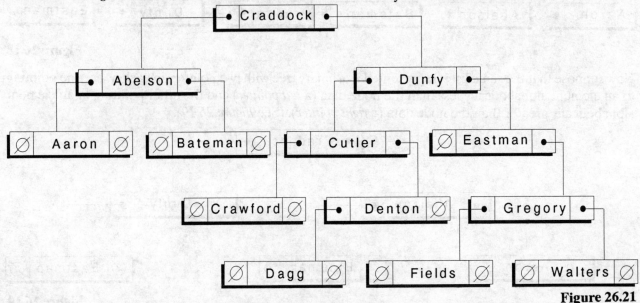

Figure 26.21

(i) The node to be deleted is a terminal node, or leaf, having null left and right pointers. *Bateman* is an example of such a node. Deleting it is simply a matter of setting *Abelson's* right pointer to the null pointer: (*Figure 26.22*)

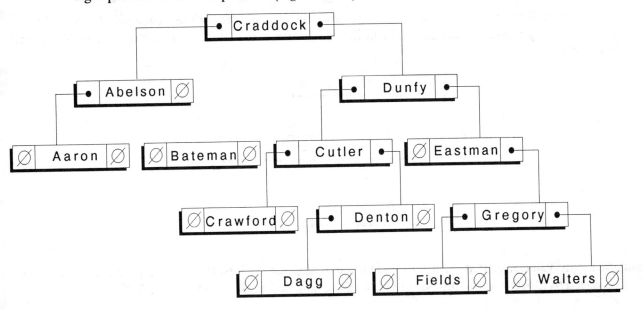

Figure 26.22

(ii) The node to be deleted contains one null pointer. *Eastman* is an example of this type of node. This case is handled in the same way as deleting a node from a linked list - *Dunfy's* right pointer is replaced by *Eastman's* right pointer: (*Figure 26.23*)

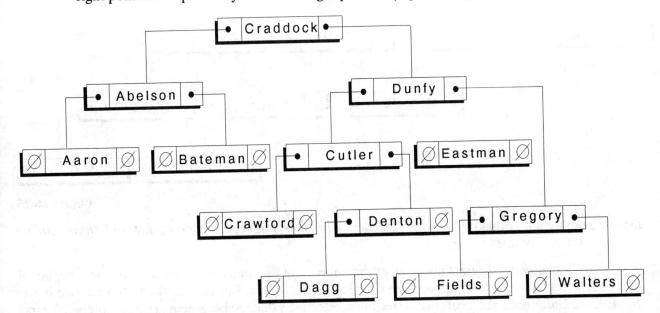

Figure 26.23

(iii) The node to be deleted contains no null pointers. There are two possibilities here: replace the deleted entry with an entry from its right subtree, or an entry from its left subtree. We will consider both of these using *Dunfy* as the item to be deleted from the original tree.

Taking the left subtree first, the procedure is to search the left subtree for the alphabetically largest entry by following the right pointers at each node until a null pointer is found. The left subtree of *Dunfy* is shown in *Figure 26.24*.

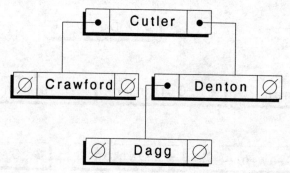

Figure 26.24

and the largest value is *Denton*. In order that *Dunfy* can be deleted whilst still retaining the correct ordering, it is replaced by *Denton* and a number of pointers are adjusted as shown in *Figure 26.25*.

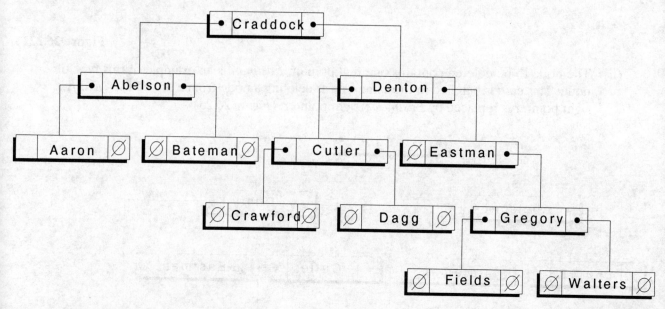

Figure 26.25

Denton's pointers are replaced by *Dunfy's* pointers; *Craddock's* right pointer now points to *Denton*; *Cutler's* right pointer now points to *Dagg*.

Note that for clarity the diagram above gives the impression that nodes have been moved around, but all that occurs in practice is that pointers are changed to alter the nodes that are to be linked together or deleted; the *Dunfy* node still exists in the tree but is effectively deleted because no node pointers reference it.

This is made clear when the tree is represented in tabular form. The table following shows the structure of the original tree.

Node	Left	Data	Right
0	1	Craddock	4
1	2	Abelson	3
2	−1	Aaron	−1
3	−1	Bateman	−1
4	5	Dunfy	9
5	6	Cutler	7
6	−1	Crawford	−1
7	8	Denton	−1
8	−1	Dagg	−1
9	−1	Eastman	10
10	11	Gregory	12
11	−1	Fields	−1
12	−1	Walters	−1

With the node *Dunfy* deleted, the table becomes

Node	Left	Data	Right	
0	1	Craddock	7	
1	2	Abelson	3	
2	−1	Aaron	−1	
3	−1	Bateman	−1	
4	5	Dunfy	9<	———— deleted node
5	6	Cutler	18	
6	−1	Crawford	−1	
7	5	Denton	9	
8	−1	Dagg	−1	
9	−1	Eastman	10	
10	11	Gregory	12	
11	−1	Fields	−1	
12	−1	Walters	−1	

If the right subtree of *Dunfy* is selected rather than the left subtree to search for a replacement, then the procedure is very similar: this time the left pointers are followed in order to find the alphabetically smallest item, which then replaces *Dunfy*. In this case the smallest item is *Eastman* and the tree becomes as shown in *Figure 26.26*.

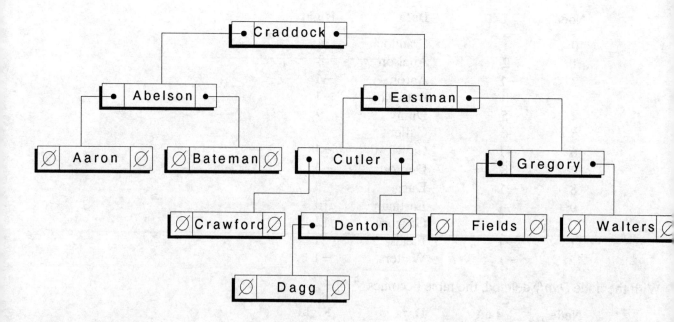

Figure 26.26

Methods of Tree Traversal

Having created a binary tree, it is likely that it will need to be accessed in some particular order, alphabetically for example. The algorithm for visiting the data items of a binary tree in alphabetical order is an example of *in-order* traversal and can be stated quite simply:

> **In-order traversal:**
>
> ```
> visit the left subtree in in-order then
> visit the root node then
> visit the right subtree in in-order.
> ```

Notice that the algorithm makes reference to itself. In other words, the algorithm for visiting a subtree is exactly the same as that for visiting a tree. The seemingly endless process of visiting trees within trees within trees etc. continues until a null pointer is encountered, allowing the process to terminate, or *bottom out*. The operation of the algorithm is best illustrated by means of an example. Consider the tree shown in *Figure 26.27*.

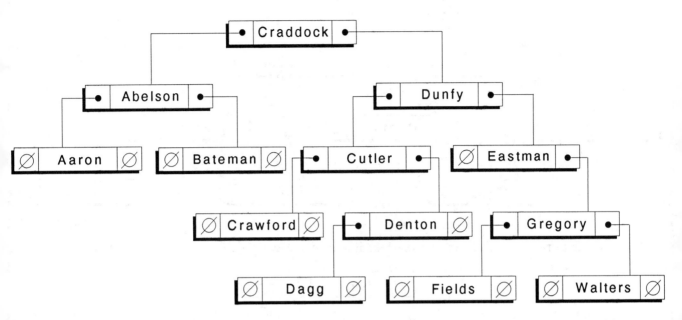

Figure 26.27

Suppose that we wish to print this tree in alphabetical order, that is perform an in-order traversal. Then the procedure would be as follows.

The left subtree of the *root node, Craddock* is shown in *Figure 26.28*.

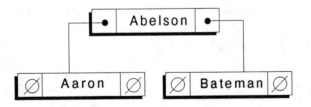

Figure 26.28

To print this subtree, we must first print its left subtree, which is just the entry *Aaron* which has no descendants. We therefore print 'Aaron'. Now we can print the node data, 'Abelson' and turn to the right subtree of *Abelson*. This right subtree is simply *Bateman*, which is then printed.

This completes the printing of the left subtree of *Craddock*, so now 'Craddock' can be printed. Now the right subtree of *Craddock* is to be printed. The right subtree of *Craddock* has as its root node *Dunfy* (*Figure 26.29*).

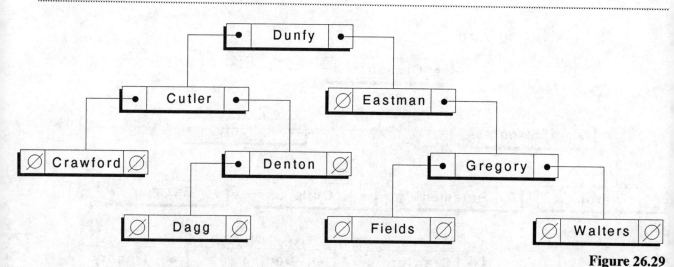

Figure 26.29

We must first print Dunfy's left subtree, which is shown in *Figure 26.30*.

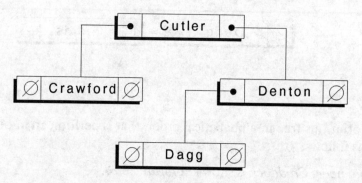

Figure 26.30

Cutler's left subtree is *Crawford* which is a terminal node and is therefore printed. 'Cutler' is then printed, followed by 'Dagg' then 'Denton'. This completes the printing of *Dunfy's* left subtree, so 'Dunfy' is printed followed by its right subtree. (Shown in *Figure 26.31*).

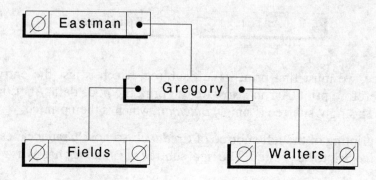

Figure 26.31

In order, this subtree would be printed:

      'Eastman' - 'Fields' - 'Gregory' - 'Walters'

which completes the process.

The simplicity of this method is also reflected in the pseudocode version of the algorithm. We begin by defining a procedure called 'Tree' which prints a tree starting at a specified node (*Listing 26.7*).

```
define procedure Tree(node)
   l := lptr(node)        {get this node's left pointer}
   if l <> null           {if there is a left subtree, print it}
       then Tree(l)
   endif
   print(node)            {print the data at this node}
   r := rptr(node)        {get this node's right pointer}
   if r <>null            {if there is a right subtree, print it}
      then Tree(r)
   endif
endprocedure Tree
```

Listing 26.7

Notice that this procedure calls itself; this is termed *recursion*, a very useful programming device. The procedure *Tree* is invoked to print the left subtree at a particlar node by passing the left pointer as a procedure *parameter*, or to print the right subtree by passing the right pointer as a procedure parameter. A procedure parameter allows values to be transmitted to the procedure which are local to the procedure, having no existence outside the procedure.

In *Listing 26.7, node* is a parameter which initially points to the root node. By making the procedure call, *Tree(root)*, the procedure is invoked with the value of *root* passed to the parameter *node*. In the procedure, *node* is used to get the value of the left pointer using *l = lptr(node)*. If it is not a null pointer, *l* is now passed to the procedure recursively using *Tree(l),* and now node has the value of the pointer for the left subtree. In this way, the procedure *Tree* is used recursively to process subtrees, only printing a node and going on to the right subtree when a null pointer is encountered.

To illustrate the operation of the pseudocode, consider the binary tree shown in *Figure 26.32* which is to be processed in alphabetical order.

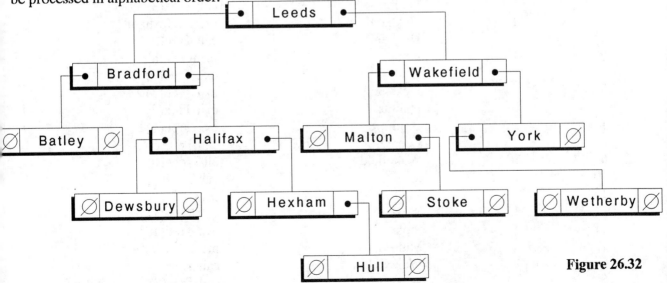

Figure 26.32

The equivalent table is as follows:

Node	Left	Data	Right
0	1	Leeds	6
1	4	Bradford	2
2	5	Halifax	3
3	−1	Hexham	9
4	−1	Batley	−1
5	−1	Dewsbury	−1
6	10	Wakefield	7
7	8	York	−1
8	−1	Wetherby	−1
9	−1	Hull	−1
10	−1	Malton	11
11	−1	Stoke	−1

The next table traces the pseuedocode, indicating the action taken at each invocation of *Tree*. Only the pointer currently relevant is indicated in the two pointer columns. The process is started by the call *Tree(0)*.

Node	Left	Data	Right	Action
0	1	Leeds		call Tree(1)
1	4	Bradford		call Tree(4)
4	-1	Batley		print "Batley"
4		Batley	-1	exit Tree(4)
1		Bradford		print "Bradford"
1		Bradford	2	call Tree(2)
2	5	Halifax		call Tree(5)
5	-1	Dewsbury		print "Dewsbury"
5		Dewsbury	-1	exit Tree(5)
2		Halifax		print "Halifax"
2		Halifax	3	call Tree(3)
3	-1	Hexham		print "Hexham"
3		Hexham	9	call Tree(9)
9	-1	Hull		print "Hull"
9		Hull	-1	exit Tree(9)
3		Hexham		exit Tree(3)
2		Halifax		exit Tree(2)
1		Bradford		exit Tree(1)
0		Leeds	6	call Tree(6)
6	10	Wakefield		all Tree(10)
10	-1	Malton		call Tree(11)
10		Malton	11	print "Stoke"
11	-1	Stoke		exit Tree(11)
11		Stoke	-1	exit Tree(10)
10		Malton		print "Wakefield"
6		Wakefield		call Tree(7)
6		Wakefield	7	call Tree(8)

7	8	York		print "Wetherby"
8	-1	Wetherby		exit Tree(8)
8		Wetherby	-1	print "York"
7		York		exit Tree(7)
7		York	-1	exit Tree(6)
6		Wakefield		exit Tree(0)
0		Leeds		

As each invocation of *Tree* is completed, control is returned to the point where the procedure was called. For example, if currently the root node of a subtree is node 7, *York*, then *exit Tree(7)* returns control to the instruction following *call Tree(7)* which happens to be the end of *Tree(6)*, *Wakefield*; similarly, exit *Tree(6)* returns control to the point where *Tree(6)* was called, the end of *Tree(0)*. Successively returning to parent nodes is the bottoming out process referred to above, and it relies heavily on the use of a stack (see the section on applications of stacks earlier).

Using the recursive procedure, *Tree,* hides the use of the stack because of the way that procedure parameters are handled. On entering a procedure, the current values of its parameters are pushed to a stack and are replaced by the values passed to the procedure; the original values of the parameters are restored only when the procedure is exited. For example, the procedure call *Tree(2)* passes the value 2 to the parameter *node*. At this point, *Tree(1)* is being processed with *node* having a value of 1. So before *node* takes the value 2, its current value, that is 1, is pushed onto the stack. Then *node* is given the value 2 and the procedure is executed. When control returns to the point following the call *Tree(2)*, the top of the stack, the value 1, is pulled and copied to *node* thus restoring it to its local value.

The tree traversal algorithm given above is called in-order tree traversal, one of three main method of accessing trees. The other two methods are called *pre-order* and *post-order* traversal. These are defined as follows:

```
Pre-order traversal:
visit the root node, then
visit all the nodes in the left subtree in pre-order, then
visit all the nodes in the right subtree in pre-order
```

With reference to the tree above, pre-order traversal would produce the list

Leeds Bradford Batley Halifax Dewsbury Hexham Hull Wakefield Malton Stoke York Wetherby

```
Post-order traversal:
visit all the nodes of the left subtree in post-order, then
visit all the nodes in the right subtree in post-order, then
visit the root node
```

This would produce the list

Batley Dewsbury Hull Hexham Halifax Bradford Stoke Malton Wetherby York Wakefield Leeds

Notice that the definitions of pre-order and post-order traversals again are recursive, allowing them to be handled in the same way as the in-order traversal.

Applications of Binary Trees

Sorting

A binary tree can be used to order a set of integers using the algorithm given in *Listing 26.8*.

```
    algorithm tree_sort
      repeat
        read num                    {get next number}
        addnode(0)                  {call procedure}
      until no_more_numbers         {continue until all  numbers read}
    end


    define procedure addnode(node)
     if  data(node) >num
        then if  lptr(node) = null
              then createnode(num)
              else addnode(lptr(node))    {recurse using lptr}
            endif
        else if rptr(node) = null
              then createnode(num)
              else addnode(rptr(node))       {recurse using rptr}
            endif
      endif
    endprocedure addnode
```

Listing 26.8

Initially, the first number in the list is stored in the root node. Then, in turn, each of the remaining numbers is compared with the current root node (ie *data(node)*) to determine whether the number should be in the left subtree or the right subtree. If the number is greater, then it must go somewhere in the right subtree, otherwise it must go somewhere in the left subtree. If the appropriate subtree pointer is null, a new node is created containing the number and the subtree pointer links it to the tree; when the subtree pointer is not null, the process calls itself (recurses) using the pointer as the new root node. The procedure *createnode(num)*, referred to in the algorithm merely allocates space for new nodes, stores the number in the new node and links it to the tree by adjusting the parent's left or right pointer.

As an example, suppose the following list of numbers is to be used to created an ordered tree as described above:

57   10   26   13   85   2   30   63   120

The tree would assume the form shown in *Figure 26.33*.

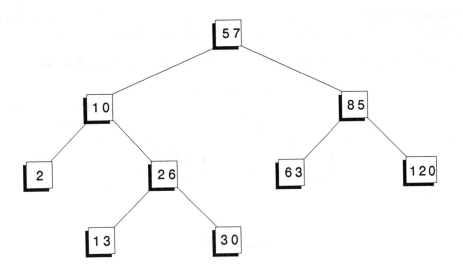

Figure 26.33

The numbers could be visited in ascending order using in-order traversal, as described in the previous section, to give the list

     2   10   13   26   30   57   63   85   120

Representing Arithmetic Expressions

Compilers often transform arithmetic expressions into more manageable forms prior to generating object code. A binary tree representation of an arithmetic expression is one such transformation. Consider the expression

     B + C*D

The equivalent binary tree representation is shown in *Figure 26.34.*

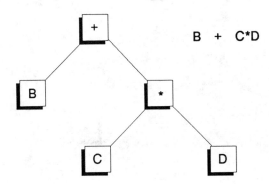

Figure 26.34

An in-order traversal of the tree produces the original expression. This type of representation is relatively easy to handle by a compiler: if a node contains an operator, the left subtree is evaluated, the right subtree is evaluated and the two values obtained are the operands for the operator at that node. If a subtree also contains an operator node, the same procedure is used recursively to produce the intermediate result. In the example above, + at the root node causes the left subtree to be evaluated, resulting in the value assigned to *B*; however, the right subtree contains the operator node * (multiplication) causing a recursive call to its left and right subtrees before the multiplication, *C*D*, can be evaluated.

Figures 26.35 to *26.37* provide some further examples of expressions represented as binary trees:

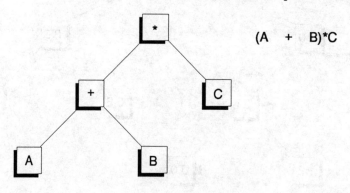

(A + B)*C

Figure 26.35

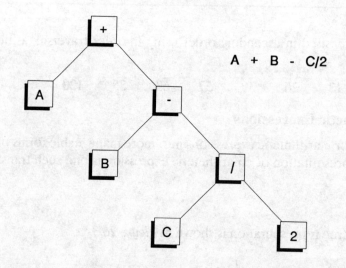

A + B - C/2

Figure 26.36

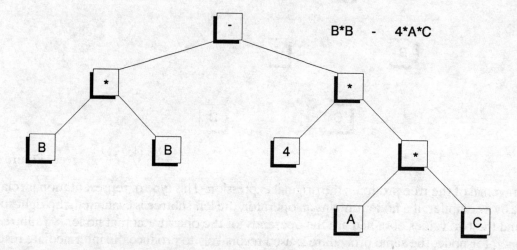

B*B - 4*A*C

Figure 26.37

All of the expressions provided above are in *infix notation*, that is, with the arithmetic operators positioned between the operands. Thus, to add two numbers, A and B, using infix notation we would write A + B. There are two other standard notations for arithmetic expressions, namely, *postfix* and *prefix* notations. In postfix notation, A + B is written AB+ and in prefix, +AB. By traversing the binary tree in in-order we saw that the infix expression resulted. Perhaps unsurprisingly, traversing the tree in post-order gives the postfix expression, and traversing the tree in pre-order gives the prefix expression. The table below shows the same expressions in the three different forms:

Infix	Postfix	Prefix
B+C*D	BCD*+	+B*CD
(A+B)*C	AB+C*	*+ABC
A+B−C/2	ABC2/−+	+A−B/C2
B*B−4*A*C	BB*4AC**−	−*BB*4*AC

Postfix notation is also known by the name Reverse Polish notation, extensively used in the programming language Forth and of general importance in computing.

Hash Functions

A hash function takes a numeric key lying within a certain range of values and transforms it into a table index which is within a smaller range of values. For example, if we have, say, under 200 data items with keys in the range 135246 to 791824 which are to be stored in a table of size 200, the mapping function will need to perform some mathematical operation on any given key to convert it to a number in the range 0 to 198. This number produced by the hash function is an index to the table. Furthermore, it is desirable to use a hash function which evenly maps key values to table index values in order to avoid two keys producing the same hash value.

A commonly used method of producing this even spread of hash values is to use the MOD function. This is simply a function which returns the integer remainder after one integer is divided by another. For instance,

$$MOD(11,4) = 3, \text{ since } 11/4 = 2 \text{ remainder } 3.$$

In the example above we could use 199 (prime numbers give a more random spread than non-primes) as the modulus, that is the number used as the divisor, in order to generate an index value in the range 0 to 198. Here are some examples of keys and corresponding table index values:

key	index
123456	76
232345	112
232324	91
436170	161
660912	33
376888	181
234023	198
456000	91
345999	137

Having used a hash function to establish the position of a data item within a table, and having stored it there, it is simply a matter of applying the same hash function again to the item's key in order to locate it at some future time. This allows almost direct access to items stored in this manner.

Notice that the third and the eighth keys both give an index value of 91. This is termed a *collision* and some method of coping with this eventuality must be devised; *collision resolution strategies* are discussed in the next section.

As another example of hash functions, suppose that this time the keys of the data items are alphanumeric, containing up to eight characters, and that there are no more than, say, 50 items to be stored in a table of size 60. The first step is to convert the key to an integer; an easy way to do this is to sum the ascii values of the characters in the key. The following table illustrates this procedure:

Key	ASCII values							Sum	MOD 59
williams	119	105	108	108	105	97	109 115	866	40
knott	107	110	111	116	116			679	30
smith	115	109	105	116	104			668	19
jones	106	111	110	101	115			662	13
waites	119	97	105	116	101	115		772	5
craven	99	114	97	118	101	110		758	50
gold	103	111	108	100				541	10
collins	99	111	108	108	105	110	115	875	49
bates	98	97	116	101	115			646	56

The ascii values are then summed, and finally they are expressed as a MOD 59 number which is, as before, the index of the data item in the storage table.

Collision Resolution Strategies

When a hash function produces the same value from two different keys, a *collision* is said to have occurred. Two common methods of coping with collisions are:

☐ direct chaining

☐ open addressing

In *direct chaining* each data item is extended to include a pointer to another item. Initially this pointer is a null pointer, but if a collision occurs, it is used to record the location of a collision item in some overflow area. Thus each element in the storage table is either empty, or contains the first item of a linked list of items all having the same hash value. Where collisions have not occurred, these linked lists contain only one item. *Figure 26.38* illustrates this data structure.

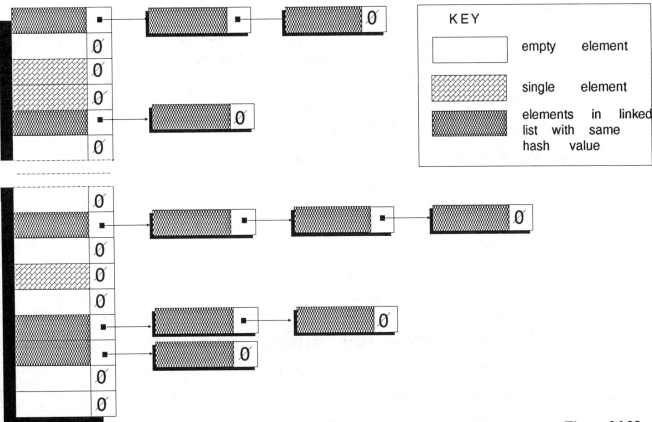

Figure 26.38

With *open addressing,* collision items are stored in the next available location in the storage table. Thus, if the table element for a particular item is already occupied, the remaining table is searched sequentially until a vacant slot is found for it. The table is searched circularly. That is, if the end of the table is reached before a vacant slot is found, the search continues at the beginning of the table.

Applications of Hash Tables

Earlier in this chapter we saw that linked lists could be used for dynamic allocation of variables by an interpreter. In fact, this particular application of linked lists also incorporates an elementary form of hashing using direct chaining: the first letter of an identifier is used as an index to a table of pointers to linked lists of all identifiers starting wih the same letter.

Another application of hash functions is described in Chapter 22. In address generation a hash function is used to determine the disk block address for a record to allow the record to be accessed as quickly as possible.

A third application of hash functions is in the production of symbol tables by compilers (see Chapter 14). In this instance, as identifiers are encountered in the source code, a table containing details of their type and value must be consulted. If an identifier does not have an entry in the symbol table, one must be inserted; if it does have an entry already, further information may need to be added. Because of the frequency with which the symbol table needs to be consulted, and because of its central role in the compilation process, it is important that accessing it is made to be as efficient as possible; the use of hash functions is a possible solution.

Soundex Coding

If the user of a personnel records system were to be asked to locate a record having the key 'Waites', then it is unlikely that the record would be retrieved if the user typed in 'Whaites' or 'Waits'. A possible solution is to convert the name to a *Soundex Code* defined as follows:

☐ the first letter of the name is the first letter of the code

☐ all vowels and the letters H, W and Y are ignored

☐ double letters are replaced by a single instance of the letter

☐ the remaining letters are replaced by values according to the table below:

Letter	Code
B F P V	1
C G J K Q S X Z	2
D T	3
L	4
M N	5
R	6

☐ the code is restricted to four characters in length

☐ if the code contains less than four characters, it is padded with trailing zeros.

Here are some examples of names converted to soundex codes:

Name	Soundex Code
Waites	W320
Whaites	W320
Waits	W320
Williams	W452
Johnson	J525
Jonson	J525
Johnsen	J525
Morton	M635
Morten	M635
Summerville	S561
Sommerset	S562

Soundex coding techniques are used extensively by the police force for searching criminal records. It is important to find all similar sounding names from their files because of the high probability of a name being reported incorrectly.

Soundex coding is also very useful for helping to make interactive information retrieval systems more user friendly. For example, rather than the computer saying, "There are no personnel records with the name JOHNSON" it reported, "There are no personnel records with the name JOHNSON, but here is a list of records closely matching this name: A. JONSON, B. JOHNSEN... etc", this would be much more useful to the user.

27 *Assembly Language Programming*

In this section we describe the instruction set and assembly language for a hypothetical 16-bit microprocessor, the BEP/16. The instruction set has been designed to allow us to present a representative sample of typical microprocessor instructions, and to illustrate some simple programming tasks.

The chapter concludes with a number of small assembly language programs to illustrate how some common programming tasks may be implemented, and a final program is used to illustrate the way that an assembler produces a machine code program.

A Typical Microprocessor: The BEP/16

The BEP/16 is a simple, hypothetical 16-bit microprocessor loosely based on the Intel 8086/88. The BEP/16 processor contains the following 16-bit registers:

- ☐ 11 general-purpose registers, *R0-R10*
- ☐ a 16-bit Program Counter, *PC*
- ☐ a 16-bit Stack Pointer, *SP*
- ☐ a 16-bit Flag Register, *FR*
- ☐ a 16-bit Overflow Register, *VR*

Addressable RAM is limited to 64K bytes, though an additional 16K bytes are used for the stack. Memory is accessed in 16-bit words.

The flag register contains the following flags:

- ☐ the carry flag (*C*)-bit0
- ☐ the zero flag (*Z*)-bit1
- ☐ the sign flag (*S*)-bit2
- ☐ the overflow flag (*V*)-bit3
- ☐ the trap flag (*T*)-bit4

Carry flag: the *C* flag is *set* (*C*=1) if there is a carry out from the most significant bit (m.s.b.) as a result of an arithmetic operation. The *C* flag is *cleared* (*C*=0) if there is no carry out.

Zero flag: the *Z* flag is set if the result of an operation is zero. It is cleared if the result is non-zero.

Sign flag: the S flag reflects the state of the m.s.b. after an arithmetic operation. $S = 0$ represents a positive value and $S = 1$ represents a negative value.

Overflow flag: the V flag is set when an arithmetic overflow occurs, that is when as a result of a signed arithmetic operation the most significant bit of the result is lost.

Trap flag: when set, the T flag puts the processor into single-step mode. Each instruction generates an internal interrupt which executes a program to display the contents of all the internal registers. The interrupt routine waits for a key depression before returning to the next program instruction.

Instruction opcodes are all 16-bit words with the following format:

2	6	4	4	bits
Mode	Operation	Reg1	Reg2	

The *Operation field* is a numeric code which specifies the type of instruction: *ADD, MOV, JGT* etc.

Reg1 and *Reg2* are codes, as defined below, for instructions which use one or two registers:

Register	Code
R0	0000
R1	0001
R2	0010
R3	0011
R4	0100
R5	0101
R6	0110
R7	0111
R8	1000
R9	1001
R10	1010
VR	1011
PC	1100
FR	1101
SP	1110

Where two registers are not necessary in an instruction, for example in *MOV R3, @10,* the code 1111 (hexadecimal F) is inserted into the unused register slot or slots in the instruction.

Examples of instructions using two registers are

        MOV R1,R2   ; Register transfer

        ADD R2,R4   ; Arithmetic operations

        LDR R0,&8000+R1   ; Indexed addressing

The *Mode* field contains a 2-bit code indicating the addressing mode to be used. The following codes are used:

Addressing Mode	Code
Immediate	00
Direct	01
Indexed	10
Indirect	11

The last three modes are appropriate to the *LDR* and *STR* instructions only.

Immediate operands are restricted to signed integers in the range −32768 to +32767. Instructions containing immediate operands or memory addresses require an extra 16-bit word.

The instruction set is first summarized and then described in more detail in the next sections. In the summary, the flags that are affected (if any) are indicated by a 1 (flag set), a 0 (flag reset) or * (depends on the result of the instruction).

Summary

The instruction set is summarized in the following table.

reg refers to any one of the registers.

addr is an address which may be a number or a symbolic address.

immed is an immediate operand which may be a single character enclosed in single quotes, or a number or an identifier preceded by the @ symbol. Immediate numeric constants may also be preceded by the & symbol for hexadecimal constants or the % symbol for binary constants.

offset is used in indexed addressing to indicate an offset from a base address.

Mnemonic	Operation	Formats	Words	Flags T V S Z C
ADC: Add with carry	Adds reg2 to reg1 then adds carry to reg1	ADC reg1,reg2 ADC reg,immed	1 2	- * * * *
ADD: Add	Adds reg2 to reg1	ADD reg1,reg2 ADD reg,immed	1	- * * * *
AND: Logical AND	Ands reg1 with reg2	AND reg1,reg2 AND reg,immed	1	- - * * -
CLC: Clear carry flag	C = 0	CLC	1	- - - - 0
CLT: Clear trap flag	T = 0	CLT	1	0 - - - -
CMP: Compare	Compares reg1 and reg2 and sets flags	CMP reg1,reg2 CMP reg,immed	1 2	- - * * *
DEC: Decrement	Subtracts 1 from operand	DEC reg DEC addr	1	- * * * * - * * * *

Mnemonic	Operation	Formats	Words	Flags T V S Z C
DIV: Divide	Divides reg1 by reg2 Unsigned integer division	DIV reg1,reg2 DIV reg,immed	1 2	- - - - *
HLT: Halt	Halts execution of the program	HLT	1	- - - - -
INC: Increment	Adds 1 to operand	INC reg INC addr	1 2	- * * * *
Jcondition	Conditional jump		2	- - - - -
	Jump if equal Jump if not equal	JEQ label JNE label		
	Jump if overflow set Jump if overflow clear	JVS label JVC label		
	Jump if higher Jump if lower or same	JHI label JLS label		
	Jump if plus Jump if minus	JPL label JMI label		
	Jump if carry set Jump if carry clear	JCS label JCC label		
	Jump if greater or equal Jump if less than	JGE label JLT label		
	Jump if greater than Jump if less or equal	JGT label JLE label		
JMP: Unconditional jump		JMP label	2	- - - - -
JSR: Jump to subroutine	Pushes the PC to stack then jumps to label	JSR label	2	- - - - -
LDR: Load register	Copies contents of memory address to register	LDR reg,addr LDR reg,addr+offset LDR reg,[addr]	2 2 2	- - * * -
MOV: Move	Copies reg2 to reg1	MOV reg1,reg2 MOV reg,immed	1 2	- - * * -
MUL: Unsigned multiply	Multiplies reg1 by reg2	MUL reg1,reg2 MUL reg,immed	1 2	- - - - *
NOP: No operation		NOP	1	- - - - -
NOT: Logical NOT	Inverts operand	NOT reg	1	- - * * -

Mnemonic	Operation	Formats	Words	Flags T V S Z C
OR: Logical OR	Ors reg1 with reg2	OR reg1,reg2 OR reg,immed	1 2	- - * * -
POP: Pop from stack	Top of stack is copied to operand and the stack pointer is decremented	POP reg	1	- - * * -
PUSH: Push on stack	Increments the stack and copies operand to top of stack	PUSH reg	1	- - * * -
ROL: Rotate left	Rotates operand specified number of places left	ROL reg1,reg2 ROL reg,immed	1 2	- - * * *
ROR: Rotate right	Rotates operand specified number of places right	ROR reg1,reg2 ROR reg,immed	1 2	- - * * *
RRX: Rotate right extend	Rotates operand through the carry flag	RRX reg1,reg2 RRX reg,immed	1 2	- - * * *
RTS: Return from subroutine	Copies the top of the stack to PC	RTS	1	- - - - -
SAR: Arithmetic shift right	Shifts operand specified number of places right retaining sign of operand	SAR reg1,reg2 SAR reg,immed	1 2	- - * * *
SBB: Subtract with borrow	Subtracts reg2 from reg1 then subtracts carry from reg1	SBB reg1,reg2 SBB reg,immed	1 2	- * * * *
SEC: Set carry flag	C = 1	SEC	1	- - - - 1
SET: Set trap flag	T = 1	SET	1	1 - - - -
SHL: Shift left	Shifts operand specified number of places left	SHL reg1,reg2 SHL reg,immed	1 2	- - * * *
SHR: Shift right	Shifts operand specified number of places right	SHR reg1,reg2 SHR reg,immed	1 2	- - * * *
STR: Store register	Copies contents of register to memory	STR reg,addr STR reg,addr+offset STR reg,[addr]	2 2 2	- - * * -

Mnemonic	Operation	Formats	Words	Flags T V S Z C
SUB: Subtract	Subtracts reg2 from reg1	SUB reg1,reg2 SUB reg,immed	1 2	_ * * * *
SWI: Software interrupt	Invokes an operating system routine	SWI addr	2	_ _ _ _ _
XOR: Logical exclusive or	Exclusively ors reg1 with reg2	XOR reg1,reg2 XOR reg,immed	1 2	_ _ * * _

Data Transfer Instructions: MOV, LDR, STR

This set of instructions deals with transferring data to and from memory, and between internal registers.

MOV: Copies a word from from a source operand to a destination operand. The source operand may be an immediate constant or a register, but the destination must be a register.

LDR: Copies the contents of a memory location to a specified register. Three memory addressing modes are supported:
direct, as in *LDR R1, &1234* or *LDR R3*, cost, where cost is a symbolic memory address;
indexed, as in *LDR R4, table+R1*, where table is a memory address and *R1* contains a value to be added to table before the contents of the resulting address are loaded into *R4*;
indirect, as in *LDR R2,[vector]*, where *vector* contains an address, the contents of which are loaded into *R2*.

STR: Copies the contents of a specified register to a memory location. Uses the same addressing modes as *Load Register*.

Arithmetic Instructions: ADD, ADC, SUB, SBB, MUL, DIV, CMP, INC, DEC

This set of instructions allows simple arithmetic operations to be performed on the contents of registers. The multiply and divide instructions use the overflow register (*VR*) to hold part of the result of the operations.

ADD: Performs addition on two words, putting the sum in the first operand. For example, the instruction *ADD R10, @3* would add 3 to the contents of *R10*. Note that, since any register is allowed to be used in this instruction, unconditional jumps may be performed using instructions of the form *ADD PC, R2*. This would add the contents of *R2* to the contents of the *PC*, thus causing a relative jump to the resulting address. An absolute jump would result from *MOV PC, R4*, assuming that *R4* contained a valid address to which to branch.

ADC: Similar to *ADD*, the difference being that the current contents of the carry flag are also added to the first operand. This facilitates multiple-precision addition.

SUB: Subtracts the second operand from the first operand, putting the difference in the first operand. For example, *SUB R5, R3* subtracts the contents of *R3* from

R5 and stores the difference in *R5*. In a similar way to that described for *ADD*, this instruction could also be used to manipulate the *PC*.

SBB: Similar to *SUB*, but subtracts the carry flag, the equivalent of a borrow, from the first operand. Again, this is used for multiple precision arithmetic.

CMP: Performs the same operation as *SUB*, but does not store the difference in the first operand. It is used to compare two values and set appropriate flags (*V*, *C* and *Z*) according to the result so that a conditional branch instruction may follow it.

MUL: Multiplies two 16-bit unsigned numbers to produce a 32-bit product. The carry flag is set if the product exceeds the size of a 16-bit register; in this instance, the overflow (the most significant word) is stored in *VR*, the overflow register, which is reserved for this purpose, though it may also be used as a general-purpose register.

DIV: Divides the first unsigned operand by the second and stores the integer quotient in the first. The remainder after division is stored in *VR*.

INC: Adds 1 to the specified register or memory location.

DEC: Subtracts 1 from the specified register or memory location.

Transfer of Control Instructions: JMP, Jcond, JSR, RTS, SWI

This set of instructions allows the normal sequential flow of instructions to be modified. Normally, the *PC* is incremented after every fetch cycle so that each instruction is performed in the order in which it is stored in memory; this set of instructions allows the contents of the *PC* to be changed to any value in the memory space so that program instructions may be executed in orders other than sequential. This allows, for instance, sections of code to be repeated in a loop, and it facilitates decomposing a single complex program into smaller more manageable subprograms.

JMP: Causes an unconditional jump by adding a signed offset to the *PC*. That is, it performs a relative jump forwards or backwards. The assembler automatically converts label addresses to the appropriate offsets.

JEQ: Performs the transfer of control only if $Z=1$, that is, if the result of an arithmetic operation was zero.

JNE: Performs the transfer of control only if $Z=0$, that is, if the result of an arithmetic operation was not zero.

JVS: Performs the transfer of control only if $V=1$, that is, if the result of an arithmetic operation produces a value which cannot be represented in the 16-bit destination register.

JVC: Performs the transfer of control only if $V=0$.

JHI: Performs the transfer of control assuming that a previous comparison was between two unsigned numbers and that the first was greater than the second, that is $C=0$ and $Z=0$.

JLS: Performs the transfer of control assuming that a previous comparison was between two unsigned numbers and that the first was less than or equal to the second, that is $C=1$ or $Z=1$.

JPL: Performs the transfer of control only if $S=0$, that is, the last operation produced a positive number with a sign bit of 0.

JMI: Performs the transfer of control only if $S=1$, that is, the last operation produced a negative number with a sign bit of 1.

JCS: Performs the transfer of control only if $C=1$. If this occurs then it means that the result of an operation could not be represented in 16 bits, and the carry flag represents the 17th bit of the destination register.

JCC: Performs the transfer of control only if $C=0$.

JGE: This assumes that the previous operation used signed integers in two's complement representation. The branch is performed if the first operand was greater or equal to the second operand, that is, ($S=1$ and $V=1$) or ($S=0$ and $V=0$).

JLT: This assumes that the previous operation used signed integers in two's complement representation. The branch is performed if the first operand was less than the second operand, that is, ($S=1$ and $V=0$) or ($S=0$ and $V=1$).

JGT: This again assumes signed arithmetic with the first operand greater than the second, that is, $Z=0$ and (($S=1$ and $V=1$) or ($S=0$ and $V=0$)).

JLE: Again assuming signed arithmetic with the first operand less than or equal to the second, that is, $Z=1$ or (($S=1$ and $V=0$) or ($S=0$ and $V=1$)).

JSR: Jumps to a subroutine after pushing the *PC* to the stack.

RTS: Returns from a subroutine by popping the top of the stack (assuming it contains the required return address) to the *PC*.

SWI: This instruction performs an indirect call to an operating system subroutine. It allows access to pre-written routines for standard tasks such as keyboard input and displaying text on the screen. Some of the possible calls are described in a later section in this chapter.

Shift and Rotate Instructions: SHR, SHL, SAR, ROL, ROR, RRX

This set of instructions is used for manipulating the contents of registers by shifting them left or right. They are often used for performing multiplication or division by powers of two.

SHR: Shifts the contents of the first operand a number of places right. The number of places is specified by the second operand which is either a register or an immediate numeric operand. For example,
SHR R5, @4 would shift the contents of *R5* four places right. Zeroes are moved into the most significant bit positions and the bits that are shifted out go into the carry flag. This instruction divides the first operand by a power of two; in the example above, *R5* would be divided by 16 ($=2^4$)

SHL:	As above, but shifts left. This time the most significant bit is moved into the carry flag after each bit shift, and zeroes are introduced at the least significant end of the word.
SAR:	As *SHR*, but the sign (in the most significant bit) is retained. Thus two's complement numbers retain the appropriate sign.
ROR:	Rotates the first operand a specified number of bits right. The number of bits rotated is determined by the second operand. At each bit shift, the bits are moved right one position and the least significant bit is rotated to the most significant bit position.
ROL:	As *ROR* but the rotation is to the left.
RRX:	As *ROR* but the carry register is included in the rotation. That is, it is a 17-bit rotation.

Logical operations: AND, OR, NOT, XOR

Logical instructions perform bit operations on the contents of a register. They are frequently used for performing masking operations on a binary word, to change certain bits without affecting the other bits in the word.

AND:	Performs a logical *AND* operation with the two operands, storing the result in the first operand. For example, the instruction *AND R4, %0111111101111111* would set bits 7 and 15 of *R4* to 0 whilst leaving the rest of the bits unchanged.
OR:	Performs a logical *OR* operation between the two operands, storing the result in the first operand. For example, the instruction *OR R3, %0000000011111111* would set bits 0-7 of *R3* to 1 and leave the remaining bits unchanged.
NOT:	Inverts the operand, changing 1's to 0's and 0's to 1's. Thus the instruction *NOT R1* followed by *INC R1* would take the two's complement of *R1*.
XOR:	Performs a logical exclusive *OR* operation with the two operands, storing the result in the first operand. For example, the instruction *XOR R2,R2* clears the *R2* register. This is faster than *MOV R2, @0* because it uses only one word.

Stack Operations: PUSH, POP

Stack operations are frequently used to preserve the contents of registers when subroutines are called. For example, if a subroutine uses registers *R0*, *R3* and *R4*, then the first three instructions of the subroutine might be

```
PUSH R0
PUSH R3
PUSH R4
```
and the last instructions might be

```
        POP R4
        POP R3
        POP R0
        RTS
```

so that initially the three registers are copied to the stack, and at the end of the subroutine they are restored to their initial values ready for returning to the calling program. This ensures that subroutines do not corrupt the contents of registers required by the calling program.

> *PUSH*:   Copies the contents of the specified register to the top of the stack and increments the stack pointer.
>
> *POP*:   Decrements the stack pointer and transfers the top of the stack to the specified register.

Flag Operations: CLC, CLT, SEC, SET

These instructions allow the carry and the trap flags to be set or cleared. When the trap flag is set the processor operates in single-step mode for debugging purposes. After each instruction is executed, an interrupt is generated which calls an operating system routine to display or allow the user to change the contents of all the registers. The routine also allows memory locations to be displayed or changed.

> *CLC*:   Clears the carry flag, that is, $C=0$.
>
> *SEC*:   Sets the carry flag, that is, $C=1$.
>
> *CLT*:   Clears the trap flag, that is, $T=0$ and returns the processor to normal execution mode.
>
> *SET*:   Sets the trap flag, that is, $T=1$ and puts the processor into single-step, trace mode.

Other Instructions: HLT, NOP

> *HLT*:   Terminates program execution, returning control to the operating system.
>
> *NOP*:   This instruction does not perform any function. Possible uses are in setting up timed delays in which one or more *NOP*s are included in a loop, or for modifying an assembled program without the need to re-assemble it. For example, in single-step mode, memory locations containing the program being executed could be replaced by *NOP*s to prevent the execution of certain instructions, *JSR*s perhaps.

The following table shows the numeric equivalents of the instruction mnemonic codes recognized by the assembler. The assembler uses these when converting the source program into machine code.

Mnemonic	Operation code	Mnemonic	Operation code
ADC	08	JSR	21
ADD	09	LDR	22
AND	0A		
CLC	0B	MOV	24
CLT	0C	MUL	25

CMP	0D	NOP	26
DEC	0E	NOT	27
DIV	0F	OR	28
HLT	10	POP	29
INC	11	PUSH	2A
JCC	12	ROL	2B
JCS	13	ROR	2C
JLT	14		
JEQ	15	RRX	2D
JGE	16	RTS	2E
JGT	17	SAR	2F
JHI	18	SBB	30
JLE	19	SEC	31
JLS	1A	SET	32
JMI	1B	SHL	33
JNE	1C	SHR	34
JPL	1D	STR	35
JVC	1E	SUB	36
JVS	1F	SWI	37
JMP	20	XOR	38

The BEP/16 Macro Assembler

The BEP/16 assembler facilitates low-level programming by offering the following facilities:

- ☐ the use of mnemonics for operation codes
- ☐ the use of labels for branching instructions
- ☐ the use of comments for annotating programs
- ☐ symbolic addresses
- ☐ convenient notations for the various addressing modes available
- ☐ a number of pseudo-ops (directives) for controlling various assembler functions
- ☐ the use of macros

BEP/16 Assembly Language Instruction Format

Assembly language instructions, or *statements*, are divided into a number of fields:

(i) *Operation code field.* This contains the instruction mnemonic and therefore must always be present in the instruction.

(ii) *Operand(s) field.* The composition of this field depends on the operation and the addressing mode. It may contain zero or more operands which may be registers, addresses or immediate operands.

(iii) *Label field.* This optional field allows the programmer to establish a point of reference in the program. Certain other instructions, such as branch instructions, use these labels in their operand field.

(iv) *Comment field*. This is another optional field, ignored by the assembler, to allow the programmer to annotate the program.

Assemblers provide varying degrees of flexibility in how these fields may be combined in program statements. Fields are separated from one another by means of *delimiters*, which are special characters (such as spaces, semi-colons or colons) recognised by the assembler as serving this function.

Below is a short assembly language subroutine illustrating the concepts explained above. Internal registers are designated *R0, R1, R2* etc. The subroutine adds the numbers 5 to 14 inclusive, that is, the 10 consecutive numbers starting with 5, by accumulating them in register *R2*.

Label	Opcode	Operand(s)	Comments
start:	MOV	R0, @10	;init loop counter
	MOV	R1, @5	;start value, R1=5
	MOV	R2, @0	;clear running total, R2=0
loop:	ADD	R2, R1	;accumulate total, R2=R2+R1
	INC	R1	;add 1 to R1
	DEC	R0	;decrement R0
	JGT	loop	;branch to label if R0>0
	RTS		;return from subroutine

The labels *start* and *loop* are identified by the use of the colon delimiter. *MOV, ADD, INC, DEC,* and *JGT* are opcode mnemonics as defined in the table on pages 423-425. Opcodes are followed by a space delimiter. Where there are two operands, they are separated by the comma delimiter. Immediate operands are preceded by the @ sign. Comments always start with a semi-colon and continue to the end of the line.

Labels and comments are usually allowed to be on separate lines:

```
;
;This is a comment on a separate line
;
;The label below is also on a separate line
;
start:
        MOV   R0, @10      ;init loop counter
        MOV   R1, @5       ;start value, R1=5
    etc.
```

Semi-colons by themselves, as illustrated above, provide a convenient way of making the program easier to read.

Software Interrupt Routines (SWI's)

It is often possible to use operating system subroutines from within an assembly language. The BEP/16 provides the SWI instruction for this purpose. The opcode, *SWI*, is followed by either the address of a pointer to the operating system routine or an identifier representing the address of the pointer. Some of the identifiers recognised by the BEP/16 assembler and used in the example programs at the end of the chapter are as follows:

OS routine	Address	Function
getInt	&F000	Read a 16-bit integer in denary form from the keyboard. Value returned in *R0*.
putInt	&F004	Display the contents of *R0* on the VDU as a denary integer.
getChar	&F008	Read a character from the keyboard. Ascii value returned in *R0*. Character is echoed to VDU.
putChar	&F00C	Display ascii character in *R0* on VDU.

These addresses form a table of addresses of the actual routines. The *SWI* instruction uses the operand provided in the instruction as a pointer to the appropriate routine. This allows for the operating system routines to be located in different areas in different machines while still retaining the same *SWI* call.

Other *SWI* calls allow graphics operations to be performed and input/output devices to be used.

Addressing modes

The BEP/16 offers seven addressing modes:

- ☐ Immediate
- ☐ Register
- ☐ Implied
- ☐ Direct
- ☐ Indexed
- ☐ Indirect
- ☐ Relative

Three of these modes, namely Direct, Indexed and Indirect are exclusively used in conjunction with *STR* and *LDR* for accessing memory.

The functions of the addressing modes are explained below.

Immediate

In this mode, the operand is contained within the instruction itself, that is, the operand is a constant numeric value stored in a location immediately following the operation code. For example,

    MOV R0, @100

contains the immediate value 100 which is stored immediately after the opcode *MOV R0*. The instruction, when executed, would transfer the immediate operand 100 from memory to the *R0* register.

Examples:

SAR R5, @3	;Arithmetic shift right 3 places
ADC R3, @&30	;Add with carry hex 30 (ie 48)
SUB R1, @num	;Subtract the value stored in num from R1

Register

Here, the operand is one of the internal registers.

Examples:

MOV R2, R3	;Transfer contents of R3 to R2
ADD R2, R2	;Add contents of R2 to itself
MOV PC, R7	;Transfer contents of R7 to PC ie jump to
	; address in R7

Implied

Sometimes termed inherent addressing, this is where the operand is implied in the operation code. For example, the instruction *NOP* requires no operand because the opcode itself specifies the action to be performed (which is nothing in this case).

Direct

Here the instruction refers to an address in memory which is to be accessed. Only the operation codes *LDR* and *STR* use this mode. For example,

LDR R5, &1E00

transfers the contents of location &1E00 to *R5*.

Examples:

LDR R0, base	;Load R0 with the contents of the address
	; stored in the label base
STR R1, value	;Store the contents of R1 in address value

Indexed

In this mode an offset is added to a direct address to produce an effective address to be accessed. The offset may be an immediate operand or the contents of a register. Again, this addressing mode is restricted to the *LDR* and *STR* instructions. For example, the indexed instruction

LDR R1, base + R0

loads *R1* with the contents of address base plus the contents of register *R0*. So if the label base contained the address 5000, and *R0* contained the number 6, *R1* would be loaded with the contents of the word at location 5006.

Examples:

LDR R4, base + @2	;Add 2 to base and load R4 with
	; the contents of this address
STR R1, &FF00 + R0	;Add R0 to hex FF00 and load R1 with
	; the contents of this address

Indirect

Here the second operand, in square brackets, contains the *address* of the value to be accessed; this is an indirect reference to a memory address. Square brackets are used to indicate indirection. For example, suppose that location &1000 contained the number 65 and location &3000 contained the number &1000, then the instruction

        LDR R4,[&3000]

would first access location &3000 to retrieve the actual address of the operand, that is location &1000, and then load the number in location &1000 into register *R4*. Thus *R4* would contain the number 65 after execution of this instruction.

Examples:

LDR R6,[pointers]	;Load R6 with the contents of the address stored in the ;location represented by *pointers*
STR R7,[table]	;Store the value in R7 in the word ; pointed to by the contents ;of *table*

Relative

This mode is used in conjunction with transfer of control instructions such as *JGT, JEQ* etc. The label following the instruction is converted by the assembler into an offset (from the position of the current instruction) which is to be added to the program counter at runtime in order to effect a jump. Using an offset to the program counter(*PC*), rather than an absolute value to be transferred to the *PC*, allows programs to be made relocatable, since branch references are always relative to the current value of the *PC*. The offset may be positive for a forward branch, or negative to branch back to a previous instruction.

As an example, consider the short program described in the previous section. It is assumed the the subprogram starts at location 1000, so that the numbers at the left-hand side represent the start locations of each instruction.

```
1000      start:   MOV   R0,    @10    ;init loop counter
1002               MOV   R1,    @5     ;start value, R1=5
1006               MOV   R2,    @0     ;clear running total, R2=0
1008      loop:    ADD   R2,    R1     ;accumulate total, R2=R2+R1
1009               INC   R1            ;add 1 to R1
100A               DEC   R0            ;decrement R0
100B               JGT   loop          ;branch to label if R0>0
100D               RTS                 ;return from subroutine
```

The label in the instruction *JGT loop* is converted to a word offset of -5 by the assembler since the *PC* would be pointing to the next instruction following it at location 100E after the *JGT* instruction had been fetched and loop is at address 1008.

Assembler Directives

Assembler directives, or pseudo-operations, are instructions to the assembler to perform functions which are not directly translatable into machine code. They perform such functions as reserving blocks of memory for use by the program, or for assigning values to identifiers.

The BEP/16 supports the use of the following directives:

        ☐ DATA

☐ EQU

☐ ORG

☐ RES

☐ ON

☐ OFF

The DATA Directive

This directive allows data to be stored in memory and assign an optional symbolic address to the starting location of the data. For example, the directive

flag   DATA   0

stores the value 0 at the current address being allocated by the assembler and gives it the symbolic name *flag*. Thus, an instruction such as

LDR R6, flag

will load the value stored in address flag into register *R6*, that is, *R6* will contain the value 0. Similarly,

STR R0, flag

will transfer the contents of register *R0* to the location represented by *flag*.

A set of values can be stored using

list   DATA   1,2,4,8,16

such that the numbers are stored in consecutive words of memory starting at address *list*.

The DATA directive can also be used to allocate memory space for strings:

text   DATA   "This is a string"

This would store the ASCII values of the characters in the string in consecutive locations starting at address *text*. The string is terminated with a null value (0).

Long strings or lists of integers may be spread over several lines:

lines   DATA   "121 Hope Street"
           DATA   "Bilsworth"
           DATA   "Lancashire"

values   DATA   43,−15,35,0
           DATA   5,67,222,−9,1
           DATA   −1

The EQUate Directive

The EQU directive merely assigns a value to an identifier and enters it into the assembler's symbol table. Examples:

end	EQU	−1	; end = −1
CR	EQU	&0D	; CR = 13. The & means hexadecimal
base	EQU	'A'	; base = 65. The ASCII value of the ; letter A is stored in the identifier ; base

The ORiGin directive

As the assembler is translating the program into machine-code, it maintains a location counter containing the address of the next instruction to be assembled. The *ORG* directive allows the programmer to determine the starting value of this counter, which determines where in memory the machine-code is to be loaded before it is executed. The *ORG* directive can be used more than once to cause different parts of the program to be loaded into different parts of memory. *ORG* directives are typically used for the following purposes:

☐ Interrupt routines

☐ User stack allocation

☐ Subroutines

☐ Lookup tables

Examples:

ORG 1000	; Set location counter to 1000
ORG &8000	; Set location counter to hexadecimal 8000
ORG INTRTNS	; Set location counter to value stored in INTRTNS

The REServe directive

This directive allows memory space to be reserved, similarly to the *DATA* directive, but without assigning any values to the reserved locations. This allows the programmer to reserve RAM for such purposes as lookup tables, indirection addresses, temporary buffers, stacks etc.

Examples:

table RES 100	; Reserve 100 locations starting at address table
heap RES &FF	; Reserve hexadecimal FF (255) locations
buf RES maxlen	; Reserve maxlen locations. maxlen could be a macro name or ;have been defined by an EQU directive.

The ON/OFF Directives

These are used to put the program into single step, debug mode when it is executed. The *ON* directive has the effect of setting the Trap flag(T) and *OFF* resets the flag. This results in an operating system debug routine being invoked after the execution of every instruction, allowing the contents of registers and memory locations to be displayed.

Macros

The BEP/16 assembler supports the use of multi-line macros. A macro allows you to give a name to a sequence of instructions so that you can merely refer to this name whenever you want that particular sequence of instructions inserted into your source program. The assembler will take care of actually replacing the macro name with the appropriate sequence of instructions. The macro may also contain up to eight dummy operands. A macro is declared with *#MACRO* followed by the macro name with a list of (optional) dummy operand names, comma delimited, in parentheses. The actual macro is then listed using the dummy operands where necessary. The macro is terminated with *#ENDM*.

Macros must be defined before they appear in the source program because the assembler first inserts macros into the source program before assembling it.

Examples

1.   Use meaningful names for registers:

> #MACRO counter
> R1
> #ENDM

or equivalently,

> #MACRO counter R1 #ENDM

This macro allows you to use the identifier *counter* instead of a register name. The assembler would replace every incidence of *counter* with *R1*. Thus, an instruction such as

> INC counter

would become

> INC R1

2.   Exchange the contents of any two registers (excluding *R0*):

> #MACRO swap(a,b)
> MOV R0, a
> MOV a, b
> MOV b, R0
> #ENDM

The macro name is *swap* and it has two dummy operands, *a* and *b*.

Suppose that within the program a line contained the macro reference

> ....
> swap(R2,R6)
> ....

etc

The assembler would replace the macro by

```
.........
MOV R0, R2
MOV R2, R6
MOV R6, R0
.........
```

etc

Macros have a number of advantages, including:

(i) Reducing the size of the source program.

(ii) The assembler automatically handles any changes to the macro definition by making the corresponding changes to the source code wherever the macro appears.

(iii) Once a macro has been debugged, it can be used with confidence every time it is subsequently used.

(iv) Macros can be used to clarify and simplify the source code, as illustrated in Example 1 above.

Programming Examples

The following examples illustrate a number of commonly encountered programming tasks. We also take the opportunity to introduce appropriate assembler directives and macros as illustrations of their usefulness in aiding program writing and program clarity.

Arithmetic

```
; Program to illustrate 16-bit integer arithmetic. There are no checks for
; overflow. The two numbers, a and b are input from the keyboard and the
; program calculates a^2 - b^2 using (a+b)(a-b).

        ;
        ORG 0                   ; Origin at 0
        ;
        SWI getInt              ; Operating system call to get a
                                ; 16-bit integer from the keyboard.
                                ; Value is returned in R0
        MOV R1, R0              ; Store the first value in R1
        SWI getInt              ; Get the second value
        MOV R2, R0              ; Store in R2
        MOV R3, R1              ; R3=a
        ADD R3, R2              ; R3=a+b
        MOV R4, R1              ; R4=a
        SUB R4, R2              ; R4=a-b
        MUL R3, R4              ; R3=(a+b)(a-b)
        MOV R0, R3              ; Copy answer to R0
        SWI putInt              ; Operating system call to output a
                                ; 16-bit integer in R0 to the VDU.

        HLT                     ; Terminate program.
```

Listing 27.1

Memory Transfer

```
; This program reads a string of characters terminated by a carriage
; return character (ASCII value 13) and stores the string in
; consecutive words in memory using indexed addressing. Each word
; contains a single character.
        ;
        maxlen EQU 100                 ; Set max string length
        CR     EQU 13                  ; Ascii value of carriage return
        ;
               ORG 0
        String RES maxlen              ; Reserve space for string
        ;
               ORG 1000                ; Start of program
        Start:
               MOV R1, @0              ; R1=0
        Loop:
               SWI getChar             ; Read character
               STR R0, String + R1     ; R1 is offset from string base address
               CMP R0, @CR             ; Look for end of string
               JEQ End                 ; Stop if CR
               INC R1                  ; Add 1 to index
               JMP Loop                ; Repeat
        End:
               HLT
```

Listing 27.2

```
; Program to transfer a block of data from one part of memory to another.
; The address of the block to be moved, its destination start address
; and the number of words in the block are supplied to the program.
; The two blocks are not allowed to overlap.

        ;
        ORG100
source  RES  1                  ; Start address of block
dest    RES  1                  ; Start address of destination
len     RES  1                  ; No. of words in block
        ;
        LDR R0, len             ; Get no. of words to be copied
Loop:   CMP R0, @0              ; Check for all words copied
        JLE Finish              ; If so finish
        LDR R1, [source]        ; Get word
        STR R1, [dest]          ; Store in destination
        DEC R0                  ; Decrement count
        INC source              ; Point to next word for transfer
        INC dest                ; Point to destination of next word
        JMP Loop
Finish:
        HLT
```

Listing 27.3

Logical and Shift Operations

```
; Program to separate and display 2 ascii characters in a 16-bit word.
; The character in the most significant byte of the word is printed
; first.

        ;
mask    EQU &00FF               ; Used to mask off most significant char
        ORG 100
char    RES 1                   ; Reserve one word
        ;
        LDR R2, char            ; Load word into R2
        MOV R0, R2              ; Make copy in R0
        SHR R0, @8              ; Shift right 8 places to move most
                                ; significant byte to the right of the word

        SWI putChar             ; Display single character in R0 on VDU
        MOV R0, R2              ; Copy original word into R0 again
        AND R0, @mask           ; Mask off most significant byte
        SWI putChar             ; Display single character in R0 on VDU
        HLT
```

Listing 27.4

```
; Program to pack two characters held in separate words into a single
; word.

        ;
    mask   EQU &00FF           ; Used to mask of most significant char
           ORG 100
    char1  RES 1               ; Reserve one word for first character
    char2  RES 1               ; Reserve one word for second character
    pack   RES 1               ; Reserve one word for packed characters
    ;
           LDR R1, char1       ; Load first character into R1
           SHL R1, @8          ; Shift left one byte
           LDR R2, char2       ; Load second character into R2
           OR  R1, R2          ; Combine the two characters in R1
           STR R1, pack        ; Write packed word
           HLT
```

Listing 27.5

Bubble Sort

```
; Program to perform a bubble sort on a list of 16-bit integers held in a table
; in memory. The first element of the table contains the number of values
; to be sorted (maximum 500). The stack is used for swapping two elements of
; the array. The two numbers to be swapped are held in R5 and R6.

        ;
        ;
        #MACRO SWAP(A,B)
            PUSH A
            PUSH B
            POP A
            POP B
        #ENDM
            ORG 0
table   RES 500
        ;
            ORG 600
            MOV R1, @0          ; R1 = 0
            MOV R3, @1          ; R3 = 1
            LDR R9, table       ; Get number of values
L1:     CMP R3, @0          ; List is sorted when R3 = 0
            JEQ End             ; Finish
            MOV R3, @0          ; Set flag = 0
            MOV R1, @0          ; Index to table of values
L2:     LDR R5, table + R1  ; First of two numbers to be compared
            INC R1
            LDR R6, table + R1  ; Second of the two numbers
            CMP R5, R6          ; Compare numbers
            JLE L3              ; Skip if R5 <= R6
            SWAP(R5,R6)         ; Macro to swap R5 and R6
            MOV R3, @1          ; Set flag
L3:     CMP R1, R9          ; At end of table?
            JLT L2              ; No: get next pair of numbers
            JMP L1              ; Yes: repeat pass if necessary
End:    HLT
```

Listing 27.6

The Assembly Process

The BEP/16 assembler performs three passes of the source code:

Pass 1:   Comments are removed and macros are inserted where required.

Pass 2:   A symbol table is constructed, assembler directives are obeyed and instructions are converted into machine code where possible.

Pass 3:   Any forward referenced addresses are inserted with the aid of the symbol table.

These processes are illustrated by means of a program designed to display a box on the VDU using text characters. The original source program and the stages through which it goes in order to produce the object program are described in the following sections.

The example program is shown in *Listing 27.7*.

```
;    ***************************************************
;    *                                                 *
;    *        Program to draw a box like this          *
;    *                                                 *
;    *        Width = 47     Ht = 7                     *
;    *                                                 *
;    ***************************************************


#MACRO      WIDTH       47          #ENDM
#MACRO      HT          7           #ENDM
#MACRO      CHAR1       '*'         #ENDM
#MACRO      CHAR2       ' '         #ENDM
;

cr    EQU    &0D
;
            ORG         1000


;
;
Box:        MOV         R1, @WIDTH          ; Width of box
            MOV         R2, CHAR1           ; Solid line character, eg '*'
            MOV         R3, CHAR1           ; Box 'inside' character, eg space
            JSR         Line                ; Call subroutine to draw top line
            MOV         R3, CHAR2           ; Change middle of line character
            MOV         R4, @HT             ; Height of box
            SUB         R4, @2              ; Remove top and bottom lines
Middle:     JEQ         Bline               ; Test for any more middle lines
            JSR         Line                ; If yes draw a middle line
            DEC         R4                  ; Decrement count
            JMP         Middle              ; Repeat if necessary
Bline:      MOV         R3, CHAR1           ; Restore middle of line character
```

```
            JSR         Line                    ; Draw bottom line
            HLT

;
;————————————————————————————————— -
;Subroutine to display a line of the form:
;************************         or,
;*                          *
;————————————————————————————————— -
;
Line:       PUSH        R1                      ; Save R1
            PUSH        R0                      ; Save R2
            MOV         R0, R2                  ; First character of line
            SWI         putChar
            MOV         R0, R3                  ; Middle character ready for displaying
            SUB         R1, @2                  ; Remove first and last characters
Loop:       JEQ         Last                    ; Check for more characters
            SWI         putChar                 ; Draw middle character, eg space
            DEC         R1                      ; Decrement count
            JMP         Loop                    ; Repeat if necessary
Last:       MOV         R0, R2                  ; Draw last character, eg '*'
            SWI         putChar
            MOV         R0, @cr                 ; Carriage return control character
            SWI         putChar
            POP         R0                      ; Restore registers
            POP         R1
            RTS                                 ; Return from subroutine
```

Listing 27.7

The program displays a line consisting of a single character repeated a number of times determined by the value specified in the macro *WIDTH*. The character displayed is the macro *CHAR1*. The subroutine Line is called to display the line. The body of the box is displayed using two characters: one, the same as that for the first line, is used for the start and end of the line; the other character, *CHAR2*, is used for characters in between these two. This second type of line is repeated a number of times determined by the value specified by the macro *HT*. The program then completes the box by displaying another line identical to the first. This is illustrated below with *CHAR1* a "*" and *CHAR2* a space:

```
*******************************************    } First line
*                                         *    } Repeated lines
*                                         *    }
*                                         *    }
*                                         *    }
*                                         *    }
*******************************************    } Last line
```

The subroutine, Line, displays a line by printing *CHAR1* once, a number of *CHAR2* and terminated by *CHAR1*. The subroutine also prints a carriage return character (ascii value 13) so that each line starts on a new line. By making the two characters the same, a line of a single character may be displayed.

The output from the first pass is shown in *Listing 27.8*.

First Pass Output

```
                ORG      1000
        Box:    MOV      R1, @20
                MOV      R2, '*'
                MOV      R3, '*'
                JSR      Line
                MOV      R3, ' '
                MOV      R4, @10
                SUB      R4, @2
        Middle: JEQ      Bline
                JSR      Line
                DEC      R4
                JMP      Middle
        Bline:  MOV      R3, '*'
                JSR      Line
                HLT
        Line:   PUSH     R1
                PUSH     R0
                MOV      R0, R2
                SWI      putChar
                MOV      R0, R3
                SUB      R1, @2
        Loop:   JEQ      Last
                SWI      putChar
                DEC      R1
                JMP      Loop
        Last:   MOV      R0, R2
                SWI      putChar
                MOV      R0, @cr
                SWI      putChar
                POP      R0
                POP      R1
                RTS
```

Listing 27.8

The first pass substitutes all the macros defined at the beginning of the program wherever the macro names are encountered in the source program. In addition, comments and any blank lines are removed. This constitutes the assembler's preprocessing phase.

In the second pass shown in *Listing 27.9*, the assembler obeys any embedded directives, such as *ORG* and *EQU*, and as far as it is able, converts the instructions into machine code, storing the program in the area of memory specified in the *ORG* directive or starting at location 0 if no origin is given. The starting memory location of each instruction, occupying one or two 16-bit words, is shown in *Listing 27.9*

Second Pass Output

Loc	Word1	Word2			
1000	241F	0014	Box:	MOV	R1, @20
1002	242F	002A		MOV	R2, '*'
1004	243F	002A		MOV	R3, '*'
1006	21FF	****		JSR	Line
1008	243F	0020		MOV	R3, ' '
100A	244F	000A		MOV	R4, @10
100C	364F	0002		SUB	R4, @2
100E	15FF	****	Middle:	JEQ	Bline
1010	21FF	****		JSR	Line
1012	0E4F			DEC	R4
1013	20FF	FFF9		JMP	Middle
1015	243F	002A	Bline:	MOV	R3, '*'
1017	21FF	****		JSR	Line
1019	10FF			HLT	
101A	2A1F		Line:	PUSH	R1
101B	2A0F			PUSH	R0
101C	2402			MOV	R0, R2
101D	37FF	F00C		SWI	putChar
101F	2403			MOV	R0, R3
1020	361F	0002		SUB	R1, @2
1022	15FF	****	Loop:	JEQ	Last
1024	37FF	F00C		SWI	putChar
1026	0E1F			DEC	R1
1027	20FF	FFF9		JMP	Loop
1029	2402		Last:	MOV	R0, R2
102A	37FF	F00C		SWI	putChar
102C	240F	000D		MOV	R0, @cr
102E	37FF	F00C		SWI	putChar
1031	290F			POP	R0
1032	291F			POP	R1
1033	2EFF			RTS	

Listing 27.9

As the program is scanned, any labels or other symbolic addresses are added to a symbol table which stores the name of the identifier and its address; where the assembler is unable to provide an address for a label, it puts a special marker (shown as asterisks in the listing above) and adds the identifier name to the symbol table. At the end of this pass, the assembler will have all the information it needs to complete the assembly process in the final pass.

At the end of the second pass, the symbol table would contain the following information:

Identifier	Type	Location/Value(Hex)
cr	value	0D
Box	label	1000
Middle	label	100E
Bline	label	1015
Line	label	101A
Loop	label	1022

Notice that transfer of control instructions, that is, conditional and unconditional branches and jumps to subroutines, are converted into offsets relative to the position of the instruction. For example, at location 1013, the instruction *JMP* middle specifies a jump address of FFF9, which is the two's complement representation of -7. Forward references translate to positive offsets. Remember that the offset is relative to the address of the instruction following the transfer of control, since this is the contents of the **PC** after the current instruction has been fetched. Relative offsets allow relocatable code to be written so that programs will be able to execute correctly wherever they are installed in memory.

Finally, in the third pass, shown in *Listing 27.10* the missing jump offsets are inserted into the object program:

Third Pass Output

Loc	Word1	Word2			
1000	241F	0014	Box:	MOV	R1, @20
1002	242F	002A		MOV	R2, '*'
1004	243F	002A		MOV	R3, '*'
1006	21FF	0012		JSR	Line
1008	243F	0020		MOV	R3, ' '
100A	244F	000A		MOV	R4, @10
100C	364F	0002		SUB	R4, @2
100E	15FF	0005	Middle:	JEQ	Bline
1010	21FF	0008		JSR	Line
1012	0E4F			DEC	R4
1013	20FF	FFF9		JMP	Middle
1015	243F	002A	Bline:	MOV	R3, '*'
1017	21FF	0001		JSR	Line
1019	10FF			HLT	
101A	2A1F		Line:	PUSH	R1
101B	2A0F			PUSH	R0
101C	2402			MOV	R0, R2
101D	37FF	F00C		SWI	putChar
101F	2403			MOV	R0, R3
1020	361F	0002		SUB	R1, @2
1022	15FF	0005	Loop:	JEQ	Last
1024	37FF	F00C		SWI	putChar
1026	0E1F			DEC	R1
1027	20FF	FFF9		JMP	Loop

```
1029    2402              Last:    MOV    R0, R2
102A    37FF    F00C               SWI    putChar
102C    240F    000D               MOV    R0, @13
102E    37FF    F00C               SWI    putChar
1031    290F                       POP    R0
1032    291F                       POP    R1
1033    2EFF                       RTS
```

Listing 27.10

28 *Programming in High-level Languages*

General Characteristics of High-level Languages

The general characteristics of high-level languages (HLLs) are discussed briefly in Chapter 11. Here we consider the common characteristics of HLLs in more detail before examining a number of languages in depth.

Like computer hardware, computer languages can be categorized according to generations, from the first to the latest fifth generation languages. The five generations may be summarized as follows:

First Generation

Appearing in the 1960s, these languages were based on the architectures of the current computers. Control structures were very basic, closely related to the instruction set of machines such as the IBM 704. Data structures were similarly based on the internal representations used for numbers and characters. The rather rigid syntactic structure of first generation languages was influenced by the constraints arising from the use of punched cards as the main input medium for programs. Fortran is typical of this generation of languages.

Second Generation

These elaborated on the structure of first generation languages in a number of important ways. Firstly, block structuring (see later) was introduced, facilitating program design. Secondly, there was a move towards structured programming by the introduction of more structured control constructs. Thirdly, the syntax of the languages became more flexible, allowing statements to be expressed in a freer format. Algol-60 is typical of this generation.

Third Generation

User-defined data structures became available, allowing a more application orientated approach to programming to be adopted. Control structures were modified to make them simpler and more efficient than those of the previous generation, and new, application oriented control structures such as the *case* statement, were added. These changes resulted in third generation languages becoming much more independent of computer hardware. Pascal is a good example of third generation languages.

Fourth Generation

Such languages continue the tradition of reducing the work of the user and increasing the load on the computer. The terms *Fourth Generation Language*, and its contraction, *4GL*, are subject to a wide variety of interpretations and definitions, but they all have a number of characteristics in common:

☐ easier to use than existing high-level languages, particularly by non-specialists;

☐ allow quick solutions to data processing tasks;

☐ more concise than existing high-level languages;

☐ the language is closer to natural language;

☐ user-friendly;

☐ non-procedural.

Two examples of current software systems which fit this loose definition of a 4GL are Structured Query Languages (SQL's) and Program Generators. (See Chapters 11 and 15)

Fifth Generation

These languages break away from the conventional imperative language format in ways which facilitate implementation on alternative computer architectures. For example, the declarative nature of the fifth generation language PROLOG allows programs to be implemented using parallel processing techniques. Object oriented languages and functional languages also allow this possibility, while still usable on conventional computers. LISP and Smalltalk are two further examples of fifth generation languages.

Though all HLLs can be applied to a wide variety of programming tasks, and are in that sense general-purpose languages, most high-level languages have been designed specifically for particular application areas. For example, Fortran's syntax facilitates modelling mathematical problems, COBOL allows data processing and file handling applications to be coded in a convenient manner, and LOGO was written to encourage children to approach problem solving logically and to explore mathematical concepts.

The table below summarizes the characteristics of a number of well-known languages. All of the languages below are to a greater or lesser extent general-purpose, so only special application areas are mentioned. The code *c* means 'Compiled', *i* means 'Interpreted' and *t* means 'Threaded Interpretive Language'.

Language	Date	Type	Application areas
Ada	1979	c	Real-time systems programming; embedded systems for military vehicles.
ALGOL	1960	c	General-purpose.
APL	1966	i	Scientific/mathematical problems involving vectors and matrices.
BASIC	1963	i,c	Teaching programming; for casual users rather than serious professional programmers.
C	1972	c	Systems programming.
COBOL	1960	c	Data processing.
Forth	1969	t	Control of servo-driven devices.
FORTRAN	1954	c	Mathematical/scientific problems.
LISP	1960	i	Artificial intelligence.
Logo	1967	i	Helping children with problem solving;artificial intelligence.
Modula-2	1979	c	Systems programming.
Pascal	1970	c	Teaching program/algorithm design.
PL/1	1965	c	General-purpose.
PROLOG	1972	i	Artificial intelligence.

| Smalltalk | 1972 | c | Object oriented programming. |
| SNOBOL | 1966 | i | Text processing. |

All of these languages, and many others, have a considerable number of similarities; most programming problems require data to be stored, calculations to be performed, values to be read from some external source or displayed in some form, alternative sets of operations to be executed depending on some condition arising, sections of programs to be repeated a specified number of times, and so on. For convenience, we can group these similarities under a number of headings:

- ☐ Reserved words and keywords
- ☐ Identifiers
- ☐ Data structures
- ☐ Operations on data
- ☐ Input/output operations
- ☐ Control structures
- ☐ File handling
- ☐ Functions and procedures

Reserved Words and Keywords

All high-level languages contain a number of words having special meanings. For example, in Pascal *begin*, *end* and *while* are such words. These are called *reserved* words because the programmer is not allowed to use them as identifiers; they are used only in specific contexts and their meanings are recognised by the language compiler. In languages such as COBOL, having over 300 reserved words, this constitutes something of a problem for programmers.

An alternative approach, one used by some early HLLs, notably Fortran, is to use *keywords* which are only recognised by the compiler as being special words if they are used in prescribed circumstances; used in any other contexts they are assumed by the compiler to be identifiers.

Most modern HLLs use reserved words as this method is less prone to ambiguity.

Identifiers

In addition to reserved words or keywords, programs contain names created by the programmer. Names are given to program *variables* or *constants*; names are assigned to *subprograms* or program *modules;* names are given to user-defined *data structures*. These names are collectively called *Identifiers*. They comprise groups of alphanumeric characters, typically beginning with a letter, which allow programmers to give convenient names to program items.

Data items whose values are allowed to change during the execution of a program are called *variables*; *constant* data items retain their values throughout the execution of the program. In some HLLs, *variables*, *constants*, *procedures* and *functions* have to be *declared* before they can be used, usually at the start of the program or subprogram in which they appear. Declarations are used to define the form or *type* of identifiers.

Scope of Variables

The term *scope* refers to the degree of accessibility of a variable. For example, variables declared within the main program are often accessible to any part of the whole program, whereas the accessibility of variables defined within a subprogram (see later) is restricted to that subprogram only. The former are termed *global variables*, and the latter *local variables*. The precise rules governing scope vary according to the particular language.

Data Structures

The commonest data types are:

- [ ] *Numerics*, either *Integers* (e.g. 255) or *Reals* (e.g. 1.45),

- [ ] *Characters* (e.g. 'a') and *Character Strings* (e.g. 'Freddy'),

- [ ] *Booleans*, which can take only one of two values (e.g. TRUE or FALSE),

- [ ] *Pointers*, which contain the location of other data items.

These primitive data types can be combined to form *data structures*, the commonest of which are:

Arrays or lists of data of one specific type, with individual elements referenced by means of one or more subscripts;

Records, which allow collective names to be assigned to groups of variables of different types;

Files, which are collections of identically structured records;

A number of HLLs, notably Pascal and C, allow new user-defined data types to be constructed from primitives or other (previously declared) user-defined data types, in order to create data structures of almost any complexity.

Operations on Data

The operations available in a HLL normally include:

- [ ] *Arithmetic operations* involving addition, subtraction, multiplication and division,

- [ ] *Logical operations*, usually the operations 'AND', 'OR', 'NOT' and 'EOR'(exclusive OR).

Results of such operations may be stored in variables by means of *assignment* statements taking the form of mathematical identities. For example, an assignment statement in Fortran looks like this:

$$Sum = A + B$$

The variable *Sum* would be assigned the value corresponding to the sum of the values of the variables A and B. The normal rules of precedence normally apply, and brackets may be used freely as in ordinary algebra.

Input and Output Operations

Most HLLs provide special input statements for capturing data from a standard input device such as a keyboard for allocation to a specified variable, and special output statements for displaying data on a standard output device such as a VDU.

Control Structures

Control structures are the means by which the normal top to bottom execution order of statements may be modified. The basic control constructs are:

> *Selections*, such as IF..THEN..ELSE, CASE, ON X..GOSUB, allowing the current states of specified variables to determine the next action to be taken by the program; in other words, the means by which alternative courses of action may be taken.

> *Iterations*, such as FOR..NEXT, REPEAT..UNTIL, WHILE..DO, allowing blocks of instructions to be repeated.

Note that certain HLLs, for example Prolog, do not explicitly have the above types of control structures; the reason for this is explained later in the section on Logic Programming.

File Handling

High-level languages invariably provide a set of instructions for manipulating files held on backing storage devices such as magnetic disks. By means of these types of instructions, blocks of data may be transferred to and from backing storage. A typical set of file-handling instructions might include instructions for:

- ☐ opening files ready for use
- ☐ closing files
- ☐ reading records from a sequential file
- ☐ writing records to a sequential file
- ☐ reading records from a random file
- ☐ writing records to a random file

Other languages, COBOL for example, provide facilities for processing indexed-sequential files. Sometimes a language will provide low-level file-handling instructions for reading/writing single bytes, single numbers or strings from backing-storage. C is such a language.

Functions and Procedures

Languages such as Pascal and C allow the programmer to create *subprograms* (also called *subroutines* or *modules*) which may be referenced by name in the main program. Broadly speaking, a subprogram is a self-contained section of program code which performs some identifiable task. This facility is invaluable when designing large programs because it allows the programmer to split a large, complex task into a collection of smaller, simpler tasks.

Subprograms are usually allowed to contain local variables, which are declared within the subprogram, and whose scopes are restricted to the extent of the subprogram. These variables are usually dynamically created when the subprogram is invoked and are destroyed, that is, their memory areas are released, on completion of the subprogram.

Subprograms, are frequently called *procedures* or *functions*. Simply speaking, a procedure is a subprogram which when invoked, or *called*, from the main program (or another subprogram) performs some task and then returns control to the place where it was called; a function does much the same thing but, in addition, returns a value to the calling program or subprogram.

The difference between procedures and functions is best illustrated by means of an example. Suppose, as part of a large program which has been produced as an aid in the design of buildings, a subprogram is required to display a rectangle, of given dimensions, on the VDU. Then this would probably be written as a procedure invoked by a statement such as

```
procedure draw_rectangle(10, 5)
```

where the numbers in the brackets are *parameters* specifying the dimensions of the rectangle to be drawn. The code for the procedure *draw_rectangle* would exist either within the program or on some backing storage medium, such as a magnetic disk, accessible to the language compiler. The code would be executed, causing a rectangle of the required dimensions to be drawn, and the program would continue with the next instruction following the call.

Suppose now that another subprogram is required to calculate the area of building material required to produce a rectangular shape of the same dimensions. This task would most probably be implemented as a function of the form

```
area = function calc_area(10, 5)
```

Again two parameters are passed to the function, but this time it is expected to calculate and, on completion, return a value which is to be stored in the variable *area*.

This is a rather simplistic view of procedures and functions; in practice there are many variations and enhancements of these basic ideas. Pascal and C both make extensive use of subprograms assuming a variety of different forms.

Block Structuring

Earlier it was mentioned that some languages require that variables are defined prior to their use by means of declarations. When such declarations are made in subprograms, the declared variables are usually termed *local* variables. This means that their values are defined only when the subprogram is being executed, and otherwise, as far as the main program is concerned, they do not exist. The *scope* of these variables, depends on the language. In C, the scope of such variables, that is the area of the program able to recognise them, is restricted to the subprogram only; in Pascal it is restricted to that subprogram and any other subprograms defined within it. Variables which are defined in the main program have global scope, that is they are accessible to the whole program, including its subprograms. Such variables are called *global* variables.

A number of languages allow the use of compound statements, where a number of statements can be grouped together to form a block. For example, in C a block starts with the delimiter { and ends with the delimiter }. Within these block delimiters it is possible to declare variables whose scope is restricted to the block, as if they had been defined as local variables within a subprogram. Indeed, a block in this context is a kind of open subroutine, that is a subprogram which is inserted where it is required rather than being referenced by name, with the actual code appearing elsewhere in the program. Blocks may be nested to any depth.

Languages which exhibit these types of structures, that is nested subprograms or compound statements containing declarations of variables in addition to program statements, are called *block-structured* languages. In Pascal, Modula-2 and Ada the block-structuring is implemented by means of nested procedure definitions, whereas in C nested compound statements, with similar scoping rules, are used.

Parameters

An important characteristic of procedures and functions is the ability to pass parameters to and from them. Parameters are frequently shown as variables enclosed within brackets after the name of the procedure/function, as illustrated in an earlier section. Parameters allow the programmer to use the same subprogram to process different values, without the necessity of repeating the code for the subprogram wherever it is needed. Two types of parameters are in common use: *value* parameters and *variable* parameters.

With value parameters, the transfer of data is one way only - from the calling program to the subprogram. A copy of the value to be passed to the subprogram is made before transfer takes place, and therefore the original is unchanged by whatever processing occurs within the subprogram. This is often termed a *call by value*.

In the case of variable parameters, the subprogram uses an alias (ie a different name) for the variable passed as a parameter; this means that the subprogram can alter the value of the variable even though it may use a different name for the variable. This is often termed a *call by value-result*.

Pascal supports both of these systems of parameter passing.

Summary of High-Level Languages

In the following sections we give a brief introduction to a number of well-known high-level languages. A number of other languages, PROLOG as an example, are dealt with elsewhere because of their special natures. All of the languages in this section are conventional high-level languages in the sense that they were designed for use on computers based on Von Neumann's model of a digital computer. A growing number of other high-level languages, regarded as being fourth or fifth generation, have been developed with other computer architectures in mind. Languages such as PROLOG, Ada, and Modula-2 fall into this category.

BASIC

BASIC was developed at Dartmouth College, in the USA, in 1963 and was intended to be easy to learn and appropriate for a wide variety of applications. Its popularity has been largely the result of its ease of implementation on microcomputers, and it is frequently supplied with them. There is a standard for BASIC, just as there are standards for Fortran and COBOL, and most versions of BASIC adhere to this standard, but each version usually has additional features, many of which are specific to the particular version. Fortunately, however, having learnt one version makes it easy to adapt to a different one.

In the past, BASIC has been heavily criticised for its tendency to encourage bad programming habits. Initially, few versions of BASIC had control structures to encourage or facilitate the use of structured programming techniques, and consequently large programs tended to be difficult to understand and modify. Some recent versions, however, have rectified this deficiency to greater or lesser extents by incorporating Pascal-like facilities.

Originally BASIC was an interpreted language, a feature which contributed to its suitability for novices, but over the past few years, such has been its popularity, that a significant number of software houses have produced BASIC compilers which allow programs to be run independently of an interpreter and with the usual speed and security benefits provided by compiled languages.

C

C is a programming language developed by Bell Laboratories of the USA around 1972. It was designed and written by Dennis Ritchie who was at the time working on the development of the UNIX operating system. UNIX was designed to be particularly useful to the software engineer by providing a wide variety of software tools. In fact, the UNIX operating system was written in C, and even the C compiler is now written in C.

It was designed to be easy to learn and use, powerful and reliable and it has many characteristics of structured languages such as Pascal. Its roots are based in the language Algol, and C retains many of its features, but C's strength lies in its simplicity, the facility with which complex programs may be built from simple building blocks.

Because Dennis Ritchie worked in the field of systems software, C is orientated to such applications as operating systems, computer language development and text processing. Its suitability for these areas is largely attributable to the fact that it is a relatively low-level language which facilitates very efficient programming, yet at the same time it retains the advantage of high-level languages to hide the details of the computer's architecture.

COBOL

On the whole, data processing applications involve a great deal of input and output operations with a relatively minor amount of calculation in between. The data operated upon generally consists of files comprising a large number of records. For example, a computerized stock control system for a wholefood warehouse would contain details of each item held: description of item, sale price, unit size, number currently in stock etc. This collection of data is termed a record, and together all these records form the stock file. Each time an item of stock is sold, the record for that item would need to be changed by reducing the stock level for that item. In terms of the data processing requirements of this type of operation, it would be necessary for the computer to read the details of the sales, find the appropriate stock records, subtract the appropriate amounts from the current stock levels and store the modified records. This sequence would be necessary for each sale recorded on a sales file.

COBOL is ideally suited to this type of application; it was designed to facilitate the manipulation of large amounts of data requiring fairly simple processing operations. Programs written in COBOL tend to be lengthy compared to other languages capable of performing similar processing tasks, the reason being that it requires the programmer to identify the purpose of the program, the computing equipment to be used, and the format of the files to be processed, as well as the procedure to be adopted for processing the files. All this information must be contained within the program itself. Subsequently, COBOL is often criticised for being very cumbersome, but on the credit side, all this detail helps to make a COBOL program easy to read and understand.

A COBOL program is divided into four areas termed DIVISIONS which appear in the order IDENTIFI-CATION division, ENVIRONMENT division, DATA division and PROCEDURE division. Each division comprises a number of SECTIONS and these are further divided into SENTENCES.

The IDENTIFICATION DIVISION allows the programmer to describe the whole program in general terms by supplying, under appropriate headings, such information as the name of the program, its author, when it was written and what it does. Some of this information is optional and none of it has a direct effect on the program's operation.

In the CONFIGURATION SECTION of the ENVIRONMENT DIVISION are details of the computers on which the program was developed and is intended to be run, and the INFUT-OUTPUT SECTION specifies the peripheral devices to be used for reading or writing the files which will be defined later in the program.

The DATA DIVISION contains a FILE SECTION in which each file named in the INPUT-OUTPUT SECTION is given a File Description (FD). The FD contains the file name and one or more record names. The structure of a record is defined hierarchically using LEVEL numbers starting at 01 and getting progressively bigger for finer definitions. The WORKING-STORAGE SECTION of the DATA DIVISION contains definitions of other data items specifically referenced in the PROCEDURE DIVISION of the program but which are not part of any file.

Finally, the PROCEDURE DIVISION defines precisely how the processing is to be performed. The programmer may give PARAGRAPH names to groups of SENTENCES to which reference may be made from other parts of the program, and these paragraphs may be grouped together into SECTIONS.

Each SENTENCE, terminated with a full stop, defines one or more basic operations to be performed on data; in keeping with the general philosophy of making a COBOL program easily readable, the instructions often read like ordinary English sentences as, for example, the SENTENCE

```
ADD vat TO cost GIVING total
```

FORTH

Forth was developed around 1969 by Charles H. Moore who, dissatisfied with the traditional languages available to him, designed Forth as an interface between himself and the computers he was programming at the time. He developed the final version of the language while working on an IBM 1130 regarded, at the time of its introduction, to be an advanced 'third generation' computer. The resulting language seemed to him to be so powerful that he regarded it as a 'fourth-generation language'. He therefore would have liked to call it 'Fourth' but the 1130 would only allow five-character identifiers, so he settled for 'Forth'.

Because Forth is a threaded interpretive language, as described in Chapter 14, it offers a combination of fast execution time and interactive program development. Forth is an extensible language in the sense that the programmer is allowed to add new facilities to the language by defining them in terms of the basic operations that are originally supplied. These new facilities may be temporary or permanent features depending on how they are defined by the programmer.

The language makes extensive use of a data structure called a *stack* (see Chapter 26) and arithmetic operations are defined in *Reverse Polish Notation*. (In this form of notation an expression such as $A \times (B+C)$ would be written as $ABC+\times$, where the arithmetic operators $+, -, \times$ and $/$ follow their arguments rather than separate them).

A program is defined in a modular fashion in which sections , called *words*, of a program are defined in terms of basic operations; further *words* can make reference to *words* defined previously in a hierarchical structure.

FORTRAN

FORTRAN was designed by John Backus of IBM in 1953 for the science and engineering field. A compiler for the language first appeared in 1955 for an IBM machine, and since that time it has enjoyed widespread popularity as a powerful software tool. Since its introduction, FORTRAN has steadily evolved, giving rise to such versions as WATFOR (developed at the university of WATerloo, Canada) and WATFIV as well as FORTRAN IV.

Mainly orientated towards scientific / mathematical / engineering applications, many of its statements resemble and provide for numerical calculations. A FORTRAN program may be defined as a subroutine (subprogram) which may be referred to (*called*) by other programs in order to perform some standard or common operation. By forming libraries of these subroutines a programmer is able to reduce the amount of work required to write a new program; where possible, his program will make reference to these prewritten modules which will be combined with his code when the program is compiled. The language has many standard mathematical functions, such as SIN, COS, and SQRT, built in.

PASCAL

Devised by Professor Niklaus Wirth in 1970 and named after the gifted 17th century mathematician and philosopher Blaise Pascal, Pascal is a general-purpose language based on Algol-60.

Because Pascal, like BASIC, was designed as a teaching language, it is a very easy language to learn. Moreover, being orientated towards structured programming, it encourages the clear expression of the logical structure of the program. This makes Pascal a very easy language to write programs in, and is particularly suitable for the development of large programs. For these reasons it is widely used in teaching, and is being adopted by more and more establishments of further and higher education as the main programming language for computing courses. Many people believe Pascal to be superior to any other general-purpose programming language in use today, and its expanding use in all sectors of industry is evidence in support of this claim.

Each Pascal program consists of a *declarations* section in which the structure of the data to be processed and produced is defined, a section for the definition of *functions* and *procedures* which are referenced in the *program body* section. The program body defines the operation of the program in a precise series of steps. Functions and procedures may be *called* from the program body whenever required.

A Comparison of BASIC, Pascal and C

A Text Processing Problem

As an illustration of the different ways that the features of HLLs are actually implemented, the same text processing task has been coded in BASIC, Pascal and C. The three programs are structurally identical to facilitate comparison, and the pseudocode in *Listing 28.1* shows the outline program structure adopted.

```
        algorithm separate_words
        declare array word_ptr_20,2
        word_count := 0
        ptr := 0
        procedure get_sentence              {get the sentence}
        len := length(sentence)             {determine its length}
        more_words := function find_word(ptr) {find the start of a word}
        while more_words do                 {loop to process words}
            word_count := word_count + 1
            procedure get_word(ptr)         {find the start of a word}
        endwhile
        print "Here are the separated words:"
        for i := 1 to word_count            {loop to print words}
            procedure print_word(i)
        endfor
        end separate_words
```

Listing 28.1

The task is to read a text string and identify the start position and end position of each word relative to the beginning of the string. The start and end positions of the words are to be stored in a two-dimensional array, and the words are to be printed on separate lines.

The solution involves four principal stages:

1. Capture the sentence from the keyboard and store it in an appropriate data structure. A procedure called *get_sentence* is used for this purpose.

2. Determine the starting position of the first word. This involves skipping any leading blanks. This is a boolean function called *find_word(ptr)* which will locate the first non-blank character in a text string starting at a specified position in the string. It will return a logical value of TRUE if a word is located, and FALSE otherwise. It will also update a pointer, *ptr,* which keeps track of how many characters of the string have currently been processed.

3. While there are more words to locate, determine and store the start and end positions of each word. This requires a procedure, called *get_word(ptr)* to locate the position of the first blank character after a specified position in the string. That is, it is required to find the end position of a word. The function *find_word(ptr)* described above in note 2 is then used to locate another word before repeating the process for the remaining characters of the string.

4. Finally, the words are printed out on separate lines in the same order as they appear in the sentence. The procedure *print_word(i)* prints the ith word of the sentence.

The pseudocode for the four subprograms is as follows:

(i)   **define procedure** *get_sentence*
      print "Type sentence followed by <Enter>:
      input *sentence*
   endprocedure *get_sentence*

This procedure merely displays a message on the monitor and then stores the text typed in at the keyboard in a data structure such as a string variable or character array, depending on the target language.

(ii)
```
define function find_word(variable p)
    while sentence_p = blank and p <= len do
        p := p + 1
    endwhile
    if p <= len then
        return(TRUE)
    else
        return(FALSE)
    endif
endfunction find_word
```

This function uses a loop to examine each character of a string, starting from the pth character, looking for a non-blank. Each time a blank character is found, p is incremented. The notation $sentence_p$ means the pth character from the start of the string stored in *sentence*. The loop is exited when either a non-blank is found or there are no more characters left, that is when p is equal to the length of the string being searched.

If a non-blank character is found, the function returns logical value TRUE, otherwise it returns FALSE. Thus TRUE indicates that there is still another word in the sentence, and FALSE means that the sentence has been completely processed.

In addition, because p is a variable parameter (shown by the word "variable" in the first line of the function), its new value will be copied into the parameter used in the function call, that is the variable, *ptr*.

(iii)
```
define procedure get_word(variable p)
    word_ptr_word_count,1 := p
    while sentence_p <> blank and p <= len do
        p := p + 1
    endwhile
    word_ptr_word_count,2 := p - 1
endprocedure get_word
```

The current value of p is stored in a 2-dimensional array, *word_ptr*. This is the start position of the current word being processed. Then a loop examines each subsequent character in the string, incrementing p for every non-blank character found. On exiting the loop, p points to the next character *after* the end of the current word, so $p-1$ is the actual end position stored in *word_ptr*.

Again, p is a variable parameter (shown by the word "variable" in the first line of the procedure), so its new value will be copied into the parameter used in the function call, that is the variable, *ptr*.

(iv)
```
define procedure print_word(i)
    for j := word_ptr_i,1 to word_ptr_i,2
        print sentence_j
    endfor
endprocedure print_word
```

A single word is printed by printing all the characters between the start position, $word\_ptr_{i,1}$ and the end position, $word\_ptr_{i,2}$, of the word specified by the value of the parameter i.

Because the following three programs are structurally so similar to the pseudocode presented above, comments on the programs will be reserved for emphasizing the different syntactic requirements of implementing them in the target languages.

BASIC

```
 10  REM****************************************************
 20  REM                                                  *
 30  REM    Program to separate and print the words in a sentence  *
 40  REM                                                  *
 50  REM****************************************************
 60
 70
 80  REM************ Global variables are declared here *********
 90
100  DIM word_ptr%(20,1)
110  sentence$=""
120  blank$=" "
130  len%=0
140  ptr%=0
150  word_count%=0
160
170  REM*********** Mainline program starts here ***************
180
190  PROCget_sentence                    :REM get the sentence
200
210  len%=LEN(sentence$)
220  more_words%=FNfind_word(ptr%)        :REM find the first word
230  WHILE more_words%                     :REM loop to process words
240       word_count%=word_count%+1
250       PROCget_word(ptr%)              :REM get the word
260       more_words%=FNfind_word(ptr%)   :REM find the next word
270  ENDWHILE
280
290  PRINT "Here are the separated words:"
300  FOR i%=1 TO word_count%              :REM loop to print the words
310       PROCprint_word(i%)
320  NEXT i%
330  STOP
340
350  REM******** Procedures and functions are defined here *********
360
370  REM...........................................................
380  REM                   get_sentence
390  REM                                                          .
400  REM    This procedure captures the sentence and stores it in a .
410  REM    string called sentence$                               .
420  REM...........................................................
430
440  DEF PROCget_sentence
450  PRINT "Type sentence followed by   <ENTER>:"
460  INPUT sentence$
470  ENDPROC
480
```

Listing 28.2

```
490 REM...............................................
500 REM            find_word
510 REM
520 REM    Function to locate the start of the next word (if there
530 REM    is one). Returns TRUE if a word has been found, FALSE
540 REM    otherwise. On exit, variable parameter, p%, points to
550 REM    the start of the word or to the end of the sentence
560 REM...............................................
570
580 DEF FNfind_word(RETURN p%)
600 WHILE (MID$(sentence$,p%,1) = blank$) AND (p% <= len%)
610      p%=p%+1
620 ENDWHILE
630 IF p% <= len% THEN =TRUE ELSE =FALSE
650
660 REM...............................................
670 REM            get_word
680 REM
690 REM    Procedure to store the start and end positions of a
700 REM    word in word_ptr%(word_count%,0) and
710 REM    word_ptr%(word_count%,1) resp. On exit, variable
720 REM    parameter, p%, points to the end of the word
730 REM...............................................
740
750 DEF PROCget_word(RETURN p%)
760 word_ptr%(word_count%,0)=p%
770 WHILE (MID$(sentence$,p%,1)  blank$) AND (p% <= len%)
780      p%=p%+1
790 ENDWHILE
800 word_ptr%(word_count%,1)=p%-1
810 ENDPROC
820
830
840 REM...............................................
850 REM            print_word
860 REM
870 REM    This procedure prints a single word of the sentence.
871 REM    The parameter, i%, specifies which word is to be printed.
890 REM...............................................
891
900 DEF PROCprint_word(i%)
910 LOCAL p1%,p2%
920 p1%=word_ptr%(i%,0)
930 p2%=word_ptr%(i%,1)
940 PRINT MID$(sentence$,p1%,p2%-p1%+1)
950 ENDPROC
```

Listing 28.2 continued

The dialect of BASIC used for this example was developed by Acorn Computers for use on their Archimedes range of computers. It incorporates many features supporting structured programming, not the least important of which being the facility to use multi-line functions and procedures with value or variable parameters (or combinations of both).

The main program, lines 100-330, follows the structure of the pseudocode described earlier. BASIC is usually an interpreted language in which variables are allocated storage space in memory dynamically, that is, as they are encountered. The only data structure which needs to be declared in advance of its use is the array. However, for the sake of conformity with the Pascal and C programs following, in which all variables must be declared before they are used, we have initialized (and thus in effect declared) all global variables in lines 100 to 150.

The keyword REM indicates that the line is to be treated as a comment.

The program uses four subprograms which are defined after the mainline program. The keyword DEF signals a subprogram definition, DEF PROC being used for procedures and DEF FN for functions. On the first call to a subprogram, the interpreter searches the program for its definition and stores its location in a linked list of subprogram names; subsequent calls to the subprogram are much faster since its address is now known and can be located by searching the linked list rather than the complete program.

The first subprogram, PROCget_sentence, is a procedure to read the text into a string variable sentence$. A trailing $ sign identifies a variable as a string variable which can store up to 255 alphanumeric characters. Special functions are available to manipulate character strings. Integer variable names have a trailing % sign; variables without either a % or $ sign are assumed to be floating point (that is, *real*) variables.

The second subprogram, FNfind_word(), starting at line 580, has a single *variable* parameter p%. Variable parameters are identified by the preceding RETURN keyword. Strings, such as sentence$ are manipulated in BASIC using string functions such as MID$(sentence$,p%,1) which extracts and returns a single character from sentence$ starting at position p%. If four characters were to be extracted from the string, the function would read MID$(sentence$,p%,4).

Functions are terminated using the "=" sign followed by the value to be returned. Thus the line

```
     630   IF p%< = len% THEN =TRUE ELSE =FALSE
```

means "return TRUE if p% <= len%, else return FALSE"

In the third subprogram, the procedure PROCget_word(), reference is made to the 2-dimensional array, word_ptrs%(). This was defined in the main program using the DIM declaration which reserves space for an integer array of the specified dimensions. Array elements are referenced using the appropriate number of subscripts, separated by commas, within brackets.

Notice that in the final procedure, PROCprint_word(i%), i% is a *value parameter* in which a value is transferred to i% but not back again as with variable parameters. The keyword LOCAL precedes any variable names that are to be local to the procedure.

PASCAL

In Pascal, comments are enclosed between (* and *) or { and }. Comments may extend over several lines, as illustrated in the program shown in *Listing 28.3*.

A pascal program is block structured, allowing procedure and function definitions to be nested, as shown in *Figure 28.1*. *Scope* rules govern the visibility of variables in blocks. For example, all the procedures in `main()` have access to the integer variables a and b. However, variables defined in the inner-most procedure, `p_1_1()` are local to that procedure only, and are not visible to any other procedures. Furthermore, the real variable p in `p_1_1()` takes precedence over the integer variable with the same name in `p_1()`, so that within `p_1_1()` the variable p is of type real and is completely independent of the variable with the same name in the parent procedure `p_1()`.

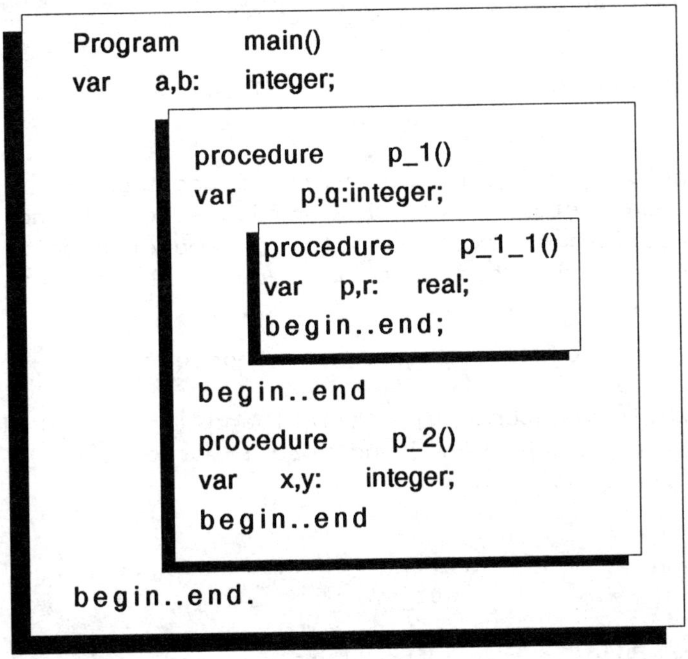

```
Program     main()
var    a,b:    integer;

    procedure      p_1()
    var      p,q:integer;

        procedure      p_1_1()
        var    p,r:    real;
        begin..end;

    begin..end
    procedure      p_2()
    var    x,y:    integer;
    begin..end

begin..end.
```

Figure 28.1

Thus all variables declared at the start of a program are global variables, and similarly, variables defined in a subprogram are global to subprograms defined within it.

```
(*****************************************************************
 *                                                            *
 *     Program to separate and print the words in a sentence  *
 *                                                            *
 *****************************************************************)
program sepsen(input, output);                          {1}
(********** Global variables are declared here ***************)
const blank = ' ';                                      {2}
var ptr, len, word_count, i: integer;                   {3}
    word_ptr: array[1..20,0..1] of integer;
    sentence: string;
    more_words: boolean;
(************** Functions and procedures are defined here ******)
(*.....................................................
 .                    get_sentence.                      .
```

Listing 28.3

```
.           This procedure captures the sentence and stores it in     .
.           a string/character array called sentence                   .
..........................................................................*)
procedure get_sentence;                                              {4}
    begin
      writeln('Type sentence followed by <Enter>:');
      readln(sentence)
    end;

(*........................................................................
.                           find_word                                 .
.                                                                     .
.      Function to locate the start of the next word (if there        .
.      is one. Returns TRUE if a word has been found, FALSE           .
.      otherwise. On exit, variable parameter p points to the         .
.      start of the word or to the end of the sentence.               .
..........................................................................*)
function find_word(var p: integer) :boolean;                        {5}
    begin
        while (sentence[p] = blank) and (p <= len) do p := p + 1;
        if p <= len then  find_word := true
        else find_word := false
    end;

(*........................................................................
.                           get_word                                  .
.                                                                     .
.      Procedure to store the start and end positions of a word       .
. in word_ptr[word_count,0] and word_ptr[word_count,1] resp.          .
. On exit, variable parameter p points to the end of the              .
. word..                                                              .
..........................................................................*)
procedure get_word(var p: integer);
    begin
        word_ptr[word_count,0]  := p;                              {6}
        while (sentence[p] <> blank) and (p <= len) do  p := p + 1;
        word_ptr[word_count,1]  := p-1
    end;

(*........................................................................
.                           print_word                                .
.                                                                     .
.      This function prints a single word of the sentence.            .
. The parameter, i, specifies which word is to be printed.            .
..........................................................................*)
procedure print_word(i:integer);
var j: integer;                                                    {7}
```

Listing 28.3 continued

```
       begin
           for j:= word_ptr[i,0] to word_ptr[i,1] do write(sentence[j]);
           writeln
       end;

   (************** This is the mainline program *******************)

   begin
     ptr := 1;
     word_count := 0;
     get_sentence;                          {get the sentence}
     len := length(sentence);
     more_words := find_word(ptr);          {find the first word}
     while more_words do                    {loop to find words}
        begin
          word_count := word_count + 1;
          get_word(ptr);
          more_words := find_word(ptr)      {find the next word}
        end;
     writeln('Here are the separated words:');
     for i := 1 to word_count do            {loop to print words}
     print_word(i)
   end.
```

Listing 28.3 continued

The following numbered notes correspond to the lines with comments {1}, {2}, {3} etc. in the program *Listing 28.3*.

{1}. Every Pascal program must be declared and given a name followed by any files used in the program in parentheses. sepsen(input,output) means that program sepsen uses the standard keyboard as an input file and the VDU as an output file.

{2}. Identifiers whose values are not intended to be changed during execution of the program are declared as const. Any subsequent attempt in the program to change such values will result in the compiler generating an error message.

{3}. Global variables are declared at the beginning of the program before any subprograms are defined.

{4}. Procedures definitions are declared using the keyword procedure. The body of the procedure is enclosed between begin and end.

{5}. Function definitions are declared using the keyword function. Parameters are enclosed in parentheses after the function name. Variable parameters are preceded by var. The type of value returned by the function must also be declared at this point. In this case the function returns a boolean value of true or false. The value to be returned from a function is assigned to the name of the function (in this instance, find_word).

{6}. Array elements are enclosed in square brackets, [], with commas between each dimension. Here, the integer array `word_ptr[ , ]` is a two-dimensional array. It is also permissible in Pascal to use the notation `word_ptr[][]` to mean the same thing.

{7}. Variables defined at this point in a procedure or function are local variables, taking precedence over any global variables with the same name defined elsewhere.

The main program body appears between `begin` and `end` after the subprogram definitions. Note also that `begin` and `end` are used to enclose a compound statement (that is, a statement block) in control structures such as `if..then` or `while..do`. This is illustrated in the while loop to process the words in the main program.

C

In C, comments are enclosed between * and *\ as illustrated in the program below.

C is also a block structured language, but in a different way from Pascal. C uses { and } to enclose compound statements, that is a group of statements which are to be executed as a single unit; any variables declared within these are *local* to that compound statement and *global* to any nested compound statements. The outline program in *Figure 28.2* illustrates this point.

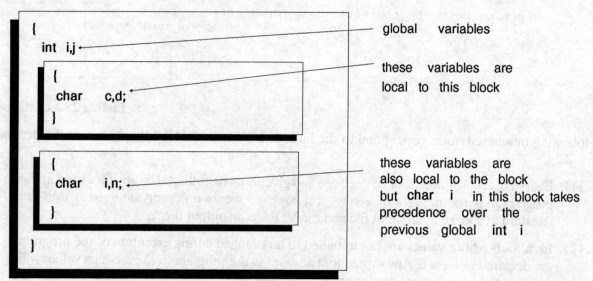

Figure 28.2

Variables which are declared before any function declarations at the beginning of the program are global variables, accessible from any part of the complete program.

```
    \********************************************************************\
    \*                                                                  *\
    \*      Program to separate and print the words in a sentence       *\
    \*                                                                  *\
    \********************************************************************\
```

Listing 28.4

```
#include <stdio.h>                                       \*1*\
#define TRUE 1                                           \*2*\
#define FALSE 0

\********** Global variables are declared here ***************\

char blank = ' ';                                        \*3*\
int len, word_count, word_ptr[20][2];
char sentence[256];

\************** Functions are defined here *********************\

\*...............................................................
.                        get_sentence                          .
.                                                               .
.    This procedure captures the sentence and stores it in      .
.    a string/character array called sentence                   .
...............................................................*\

void get_sentence()                                      \*4*\
{
puts("Type sentence followed by <Enter>:\n ");
gets(sentence);
}

\*...................................................
.                                                               .
.                        find_word                              .
.                                                               .
.    Function to locate the start of the next word (if there    .
.    is one. Returns TRUE if a word has been found, FALSE       .
.    otherwise. On exit, variable parameter p points to the     .
.    start of the word or to the end of the sentence.           .
...............................................................*\

int find_word(p)                                         \*5*\
int *p;                                                  \*6*\
{
 int word_found, p1 = *p;
 while (sentence[p1] == blank && p1 <= len)  p1++;
 if (p1 <= len) word_found = TRUE;
 else           word_found = FALSE;
 *p=p1;
 return(word_found);
}
```

Listing 28.4 continued

```
\*..........................................................................
.                       get_word()                                          .
.                                                                           .
.       Procedure to store the start and end positions of a                 .
.       word in word_ptr[word_count][0] and word_ptr[word_count][1]         .
.       resp.                                                               .
.                                                                           .
L
.       On exit, variable parameter p points to the end of the             .
.       word.                            (                                   .
...........................................................................*\

void get_word(p)
int *p;
{
 int p1=*p;
 word_ptr[word_count][0] = p1;
 while (sentence[p1] != blank && p1 <= len)  p1++;
 word_ptr[word_count][1] = p1 - 1;
 *p = p1;
}

\*...........................................................................
.                       print_word                                          .
.                                                                           .
.       This function prints a single word of the sentence.                 .
.       The parameter, i, specifies which word is to be printed.            .
...........................................................................*\
 void print_word(i)
 int i;
{
int j;
for (j = word_ptr[i][0]; j <= word_ptr[i][1]; j++)
          putchar(sentence[j]);
putchar('\n');
}

\*************** This is the mainline program *******************\
void main()
{
int ptr, i, more_words;
ptr = 0;
word_count = 0;
get_sentence();                                 \* get the sentence *\
len = strlen(sentence) - 1;
more_words = find_word(&ptr);                    \* find the first word  *\
```

Listing 28.4 continued

```
      while (more_words)                        \* loop to process words *\
       {
         word_count++;
         get_word(&ptr);                        \* get the word *\
         more_words = find_word(&ptr);          \* find the next word   *\
       }
     puts ("Here are the separate words:\n");
     for (i = 1; i <= word_count; i++)          \* loop to print words *\
        print_word(i);
     }.
```

Listing 28.4 continued

The following numbered notes correspond to the lines with comments *1*\, *2*\, *3*\etc. in the program given in *Listing 28.4*.

1\   The facility to include the contents of other C files at compile time is a very powerful feature of C. It allows code previously written and tested to be used in a program, thus keeping it more manageable and less error prone. #include files are loaded and compiled with the current file automatically. The # symbol is used for preprocessor directives which control how the source code is modified before it is compiled. The preprocessor is the first component of the complete C compiler.

2\   #define is another preprocessor directive, this time to define a macro. The compiler replaces the identifier with everything following it up to the end of the line. Thus, everywhere the identifier TRUE occurred in the program, it would be replaced by 1.

3\   Global variables are declared at this point.

4\   This is the first subprogram. In C there is no difference between defining a procedure and defining a function: all subprograms are functions in C. The return type is declared first; void means that the function is being used as a procedure, not returning a value. The brackets after the function name are mandatory, even if the function does not take any parameters.

5\   The second function, find_word returns an integer value (hence int), and takes a single parameter which is defined on the next line. The notation p1++ in the body of the function means "add 1 to p1". C contains a number of such shorthand notations for commonly used operations.

6\   The declaration int *p is read as "integer pointer, p", the * indicating that p is a pointer variable. This is the means by which p can be used as a variable parameter in C. p actually represents the memory location at which the parameter is stored.

          The notation *p used in the line
                    p1 = *p;
          has a different interpretation from that in the declaration; it now means "the contents of the memory location pointed to by p", that is, a value rather than an address. The * is being used as an indirection operator in this context. So this line gets the value of

the character pointer `ptr` defined in the main program and transfers it to `p1`. Towards the end of the function, the line

```
*p = p1;
```

copies the new value into `ptr`. Note that when the function is called from `main()` using

```
word_found = find_word(&ptr);
```

the notation `&ptr` means "the address of the variable `ptr`", so that the parameter being sent to the function is also a pointer to a variable rather than its value.

Pointers are also regarded as a very powerful feature of C.

Finally, note that the value to be returned from the function is preceded by the keyword `return`.

Recursive Programming

The term *recursion* is used to refer to the process of subprograms calling themselves. This is best explained by means of an example. The pseudocode program in *Listing 28.5* uses a recursive call to print integers starting at 1 up to a given value:

```
algorithm recurse_eg
  input number
  if number < 1 then
     print "error: negative number"
  else
     procedure print_back(number)
  endif
end recurse_eg

define procedure print_back(N)
  if N > 1 then
     procedure print_back(N-1)
  endif
  print N
endprocedure  print_back
```

Listing 28.5

The recursive procedure is called `print_back(number)` taking, as a parameter, the integer variable `number` which is read at the start of the program. `number` is the upper limit for the integers to be printed.

Notice that, in the procedure `print_back(N)`, the parameter `N` enclosed in brackets is automatically *local* to the procedure; this property of procedures, vital to recursive programming, is illustrated by the program trace which follows (the value of `number` is taken to be 3):

Step	Active statement	Depth of Recursion
1	call print_back(3)	
2	if N(=3) > 1 then call print_back(3-1)	0
3	if N(=2) > 1 then call print_back(2-1)	1
	print 1	
4	if N(=1) > 1 then	2
5	endprocedure	2
6	print 2	1
7	endprocedure	1
8	print 3	0
9	endprocedure	0
10	endprogram	

Step 1 : the procedure is called from the main program passing as a parameter the value of *number* (taken to be 3 in this example).

Step 2 : the first line of the procedure tests the value of the parameter (called N in the procedure) and, because it is greater than 1, calls itself, this time passing a parameter value of N-1, that is 2. Because the procedure has not yet been completed, local variables (in this case just N) are saved to a stack so that when control eventually returns, the values of the local variables can be restored.

Step 3 : the process is now at a recursion depth of 1 because the procedure has called itself once. The parameter N now has a value of 2, which is still greater than 1. Because the condition tested is true, the procedure *calls* itself once more. The current value of N (ie 2) is saved to a stack before the procedure is called.

Step 4 : the process is now at a recursion depth of 2 because the procedure has called itself twice. The parameter N now has a value of 1, which is not greater than 1. Because the condition tested is not true this time, the procedure ignores the *call* statement and goes on to the next statement in the procedure which prints the current value of N (ie 1).

Step 5 : the endprocedure statement causes local variables to be discarded and their memory space reclaimed before program control is returned to the calling (sub)program. This process of returning back through recursive calls is often termed *bottoming out*.

Step 6 : the process resumes at recursion depth of 1 having returned from the *call* statement invoked in Step 3. The values of all local variables are restored from the stack. The print statement prints the value of local variable N (ie 2).

Step 7 : this is identical to step 5.

Step 8 : the process arrives at the first invocation of the procedure having returned from the *call* statement in Step 2. The values of all local variables are restored from the stack. The print statement prints the value of local variable N (ie 3).

Step 9 : this is identical to steps 5 and 7.

Step 10: finally, the program terminates.

Problems that lend themselves to recursion are often definable in terms of simpler versions of themselves as illustrated above: printing the numbers 1, 2, 3, 4 is just a simpler version of the problem of printing the numbers 1, 2, 3, 4, 5; printing 1, 2, 3 is just a simpler version of the problem of printing 1, 2, 3, 4, and so on. A number of data structures, including trees and linked lists, lend themselves to recursive processing techniques for this reason (see Chapter 26). The next examples further illustrate the point.

Two Simple Examples of Recursive Algorithms

The algorithm in *Listing 28.6* calculates the value of an integer number, base, raised to certain positive integer power, *exp*:

```
algorithm calc_power
  input base, exp
  print function power(base,exp)
end
define function power(b,e)
local v
 if e = 0 then
    v = 1
 else
    v = b * function power(b,e-1)
endif
 return(v)
endfunction power
```

Listing 28.6

Here are some of examples of the values returned by the algorithm:

base	exp	result	
10	0	1	$=10^0$
10	3	1000	$=10^3$
2	0	1	$= 2^0$
2	5	32	$= 2^5$

The example in *Listing 28.7* uses a very similar method to calculate the factorial of a positive integer:

```
algorithm calc_factorial
   input fac
   print function factorial(fac)
end calc_factorial

define function factorial(f)
local v
 if f = 0 then
    v = 1
 else
    v = f * function factorial(f-1)
endif
 return(v)
endfunction factorial
```

Listing 28.7

Here are some factorials calculated by the algorithm:

factorial	result		
0	1		
1	1		
2	2	=	2× 1
3	6	=	3 × 2 × 1
4	24	=	4 × 3 × 2 × 1
5	120	=	5 × 4 × 3 × 2 × 1

Tracing through these algorithms in the same way as illustrated for the first example in this section should help to clarify the mechanisms used to obtain the desired results.

A Text Processing Example Revisited

In the previous section we considered a simple text processing problem which involved identifying the first and last character positions of words in a sentence. The problem was solved using an iterative approach in which a loop was used to process the text string character by character. The algorithm sepsenR, shown in *Listing 28.8*, uses recursion to solve the same problem.

Here the approach recognises that, having found the first word in a string, the remaining text is of exactly the same *form* as the original text, though of course it is shorter by one word. This means that we can apply exactly the same process to the second, shorter, text as we did to the original; we can continue doing this until there are no more words left and the process terminates.

The new algorithm is very similar to the previous one; subprograms get_sentence, find_word(), get_word() and print_word() are all exactly as before. The difference between the two algorithms occurs at line { 1 } where a new procedure process_text(ptr) is invoked with the parameter ptr pointing to the first character of the global string variable sentence.

Line { 2 } is the start of the definition of new procedure process_text(ptr). The function find_word(p) first looks for a word starting at position p in the text. It returns a value of TRUE if a word is found, or FALSE if no more words are left. In addition it updates p to point to the start of the word if one has been located. Next, if there is a word to be processed, word_count is incremented and the procedure get_word(p) is called to locate and store the end points of the word. get_word(p) also updates p to point to the character following the end of the word just processed.

Finally, a recursive call is made to process_text(p). In effect this is repeating the whole process of locating and processing a new word, but starting at the end of the word just located, given by parameter p. The process bottoms out when there are no more words left to process, that is when word_found is FALSE.

Advantages and Disadvantages of Recursive Programming

Recursive solutions to programming tasks are often elegant and concise. They tend to be most effective when the solution to a problem may be expressed in terms of a simpler version of itself.

When a subprogram is executed, its data area is stored on a stack, so that if a subprogram calls itself a number of times, there will be a number of similar data areas on the stack at the same time, one for each recursive call. Therefore there is always the possibility of running out of stack space when executing recursive programs.

Another not insignificant problem with recursive programming is understanding how it works sufficiently well to be able to write programs which use recursion; being able to appreciate a recursive solution to a programming task is often very much easier than originating such a solution. Furthermore, detecting and correcting bugs in recursive programs may not be as straightforward as debugging more traditional, iteration-based programs.

Recursion is one of the central features of logic and functional programming languages both of which are discussed in later sections.

Declarative vs Imperative Languages

The languages discussed so far are often classified as *imperative* or *procedural* languages. These terms are used to describe high-level languages which require the programmer to show explicitly the order in which program statements are to be executed, and precisely how the programming solution is to be reached. The sequence of commands in a program is a key feature of imperative languages such as Pascal, FORTRAN and COBOL, since they are based on the Von Neumann computer model in which a stored program is executed by sequentially stepping through instructions stored in the immediate access store of a computer. Store locations are modified as a direct result of the action of the program. Similarly, imperative languages achieve their objectives by modifying program variables using assignment statements, and by causing sequential execution of program statements. Because imperative languages are so closely related to the operation of conventional computers, they are relatively efficient.

However, other computer architectures, such as those using parallel processing, give rise to different types of programming languages.

Declarative languages rely on a different mechanism for solving programming problems. In these languages the emphasis is on defining the problem to be solved, not on the detailed sequence of instructions that are required in order to achieve the desired solution. It can be argued that a language such as Pascal is less procedural, and therefore more declarative, than an assembly language because there is less need for the programmer to define precisely how to do standard processing tasks such as input/output or arithmetic operations. For example, in an assembly language, it would require quite a complex sequence of instructions to perform the Pascal floating point calculation

```
x := (-b + sqrt(det))/(2.0*a);
```

Yet in Pascal it is merely a matter of specifying the calculation to be performed and allowing the compiler to determine how to organize the instructions required to do it. Thus languages that are predominantly procedural have elements of non-procedural characteristics. Declarative languages take this a stage further, allowing the language translator to do much more of the work, so that the programmer can concentrate on specifying *what* the problem is rather than *how* to solve it.

Because declarative languages do not rely on the programmer specifying precisely in which order instructions are to be executed, it is often possible to process a number of instructions in parallel if the mechanism exists to allow this. In the next section we examine the logic programming language PROLOG which is generally regarded as a good example of a predominantly declarative, or non-procedural, language. Functional languages, LISP for example, also essentially declarative, are described in a later section. Both PROLOG and LISP have features which allow them to take advantage of alternative computer architectures.

```
         algorithm sepsenR
         declare word_ptr_{20,2}, sentence_{255}
             ptr := 1
             word_count := 0
             procedure get_sentence
             len := length(sentence)
             procedure process_text(ptr)              { 1 }
             print "Here are the separated words:"
             for i := 1 to word_count
                 procedure print_word(i)
             endfor
         end SepsenR

         define procedure get_sentence
           print "Type sentence followed by :"
           input sentence
         endprocedure get_sentence

         define procedure process_text(p)            { 2 }
             word_found := function find_word(p)
             if word_found then
                 word_count := word_count + 1
                 procedure get_word(p)
                 procedure process_words(p)
             endif
         endprocedure process_words

         define function find_word(variable p)
           while sentence_p = blank and p <= len do
             p := p + 1
           endwhile
           if p <= len then
             return(TRUE)
           else
             return(FALSE)
           endif
         endfunction find_word

         define procedure get_word(variable p)
           word_ptr_{word_count,1} := p
           while sentence_p <> blank and p < len do
             p := p + 1
           endwhile
           word_ptr_{word_count,2} := p - 1
         endprocedure get_word

         define procedure print_word(i)
           for j := word_ptr_{i,1} to word_ptr_{i,2}
             print sentence_j
           endfor
         endprocedure print_word
```

Listing 28.8

Logic Programming

PROLOG, PROgramming in LOGic

Invented by Alain Colmerauer in the early 1970's, PROLOG was first implemented in Marseilles in 1972. It provided a means of allowing the programmer to specify a problem in terms related to formal logic rather than procedures.

The language has been adopted as the basis of software development for the Japanese fifth-generation project because of its relevance to research in artificial intelligence. It has been used extensively in the development of expert systems because it includes facilities ideal for this type of application.

PROLOG is said to be *goal oriented*, that is to say the programmer specifies the problem to be solved in terms of a *goal*, and is not expected to provide detailed instructions regarding the achievement of the goal. A goal is defined in terms of subgoals, the achievement of which will lead to the final solution. A subgoal may be a simple statement which evaluates to logical true or false, or may depend on its own subgoals which PROLOG will try to evaluate. Since there may be alternative sets of subgoals for a particular goal, PROLOG may, having failed to successfully resolve one combination, *backtrack* and try another combination. It will continue to try different combinations until either a solution is reached or there are no further combinations of subgoals to try. The power of PROLOG lies in its built-in ability to select goal combinations and to backtrack; in other languages this would have to be programmed explicitly.

Programming in PROLOG involves defining *objects* to be manipulated and relationships between them. A program consists of *facts* and *rules* (or *clauses*): *facts* are taken to be true statements about *objects* and *rules* declare that statements about *objects* are true if certain conditions (*subgoals*) are true. Executing a PROLOG program involves stating *a goal* to be achieved and allowing PROLOG to determine whether the *goal* can be achieved with the current *facts* and *rules*.

As an example, suppose that we wish to represent the relationships between the members of a family spanning three generations as illustrated by the family tree shown in *Figure 28.3*.

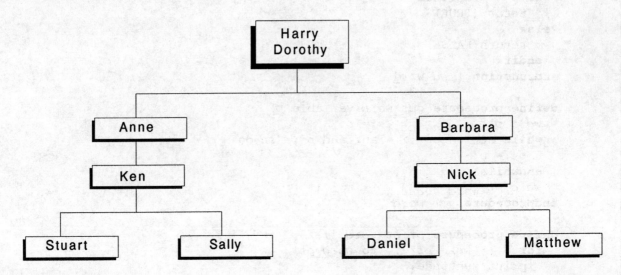

Figure 28.3

This shows that Harry and Dorothy had two daughters, Anne who married Ken, and Barbara who married Nick. Anne and Ken had a son, Stuart, and a daughter, Sally. Barabara and Nick had two sons, Daniel and Matthew. Not shown on the diagram are Nick's parents, Raymond and Margaret.

These facts could be represented as follows in PROLOG:

```
male(raymond).
female(margaret).
male(harry).
female(dorothy).

male(nick).
female(barbara).
male(ken).
female(anne).

female(sally).
male(stuart).
male(matthew).
male(daniel).

parent(raymond,nick).
parent(margaret,nick).

parent(harry,barbara).
parent(dorothy,barbara).
parent(harry,anne).
parent(dorothy,anne).

parent(nick,daniel).
parent(nick,matthew).
parent(barbara,daniel).
parent(barbara,matthew).

parent(anne,sally).
parent(anne,stuart).
parent(ken,sally).
parent(ken,stuart).
```

The first type of fact concerns the sex of each member of the family:

```
male(raymond).
```

This asserts that raymond belongs to the set male. Similarly, barbara belongs to the set female.

The other type of fact, parent, asserts that, for example, nick is a parent of daniel.

At this point we could ask PROLOG questions, in the form of simple goals, about this small database. For example, at the PROLOG prompt, '?-', we could type

```
?- parent(X,barbara).
```

PROLOG would search its collection of facts and respond

```
X = harry
More(y/n)?
```

Having found one value of variable X satisfying the goal, PROLOG displays this and asks if the search is to continue for another fact satisfying the goal. If we answered 'y', PROLOG would respond

```
X = dorothy
More(y/n)?
```

This is the only other solution to the goal and if we responded 'y' again, PROLOG would answer with 'No', indicating that there were no more solutions to the goal.

The goal

```
?- parent(anne,X).
```

would return values 'X = stuart' and 'X = sally', that is, the children of Anne.

Moreover, the goal

```
?- parent(X,Y).
```

would return all of the parent/child pairs in the database in the form

```
X = nick, Y = daniel
```

Rules could be added to the database in order to establish connections between facts. For example, the rule

```
childof(Y,X) :- parent(X,Y).
```

says that Y is a childof X if X is a parent of Y.

If we wanted to find out from the collection of facts all the children of Dorothy, at the PROLOG prompt (?-) we would type

```
?- childof(y,dorothy).
```

PROLOG would regard this as a goal to be achieved and would try to find a fact or rule satisfying this goal. Because childof is a rule consisting of one subgoal, parent, PROLOG tries to find a value of X such that parent(X,dorothy) succeeds. It therefore produces 'Y = anne' and 'Y = barbara' as solutions to the goal.

The slightly more complex rule

```
mother(X,Y) :- parent(X,Y), female(X).
```

establishes that X is the mother of Y if X is the parent of Y and X is also female.

Suppose we wished to establish whether Barbara is the mother of Matthew. We would pose the question

```
?- mother(barbara,matthew).
```

Substituting for X and Y, PROLOG would generate the two subgoals

```
parent(barbara,matthew),
female(barbara).
```

Since both of these facts exist in the database, both goals could be achieved and PROLOG would answer 'Yes'.

Posing the question

```
?- mother(X,sally).
```

would again generate two subgoals, this time of the form

```
parent(X,sally),
female(X).
```

Now PROLOG would first find a solution to the first subgoal in the form `parent(ken,sally)`, and then attempt to satisfy the second subgoal, `female(ken)` which would fail. PROLOG would then backtrack to search for another solution to `parent(X,sally)`. It would find `parent(anne,sally)` as a solution and then search for `female(anne)`, this time succeeding. Finally, PROLOG would respond with 'X = anne'.

As a further example, the rule

```
grandparent(X,Z) :- parent(X,Y), parent(Y,Z).
```

establishes the condition for X to be the grandparent of Y.

Recursion plays a prominent role in PROLOG programs. Consider, for example, a rule which generalizes the previous rule for a grandparent:

```
predecessor(X,Z) :- parent(X,Z).
predecessor(X,Z) :- parent(X,Y), predecessor(Y,Z).
```

This time there are two clauses associated with the same definition: the first is necessary to halt the recursion exhibited in the second. To understand how this works, suppose that we posed the question

```
?- predecessor(X,daniel).
```

We would expect the solutions to be X = nick, X = barbara (these are parents), X= raymond, X = margaret, X = harry and X = dorothy (grandparents).

PROLOG would start by finding solutions to the first rule and simply find X = nick and X = barbara. The second rule would also be used as a goal, generating the subgoals

```
parent(X,Y),
predecessor(Y,daniel).
```

One solution to `parent(X,Y)` is `parent(raymond, nick)`, so PROLOG would try to find `predecessor(nick,daniel)`. This recursively generates the subgoal `parent(nick,daniel)` from the first rule for `predecessor`, and this succeeds producing in effect

```
parent(raymond,nick), parent(nick,daniel)
```

allowing PROLOG to exit from the recursion. PROLOG would therefore announce 'X = raymond' as another solution.

PROLOG has been used extensively as a database language and in AI for natural language processing, expert systems and applications requiring knowledge representation.

PROLOG's suitability as a database language can be attributed to three main characteristics:

☐ A database defined in Prolog can be extended readily without any special provision for this growth needing to be made. This is in contrast to languages such as BASIC and COBOL where new information or requirements might necessitate a complete software revision.

☐ Databases can be merged or pooled with great ease; systems can be extended without the necessity for extensive forward planning.

☐ The language has, built in, the facility for drawing logical conclusions from a user's inputs, and for extracting information embedded in complex sequences of rules. This obviates the need for a special database query language.

Since natural language has a large number of rules regarding the composition of sentences, PROLOG is well suited to natural language processing where it is necessary to reduce sentences into their constituent parts. For example, in BNF notation (see Chapter 13) a simple sentence can be represented by

```
<sentence> ::=<noun  phrase><verb phrase>
<noun  phrase> ::= <determiner><noun>
<verb phrase> ::= <verb><noun phrase>
<determiner> ::= the|a|an
<noun> ::= dog|man
<verb> ::= bit|fed
```

This is sufficient to successfully parse the sentences

```
The dog bit the man,
A man fed the dog
```

Notice the close similarity with PROLOG: the *facts* are <determiner>, <noun> and <verb>, and the *rules* are <sentence>, <noun phrase> and <verb phrase>. Natural language is of course much more complex than shown by this example, but PROLOG's suitability for this type of problem should be quite obvious.

Expert systems and other *knowledge-based systems* also require collections of facts combined with rules for establishing connections between them, again just what PROLOG is designed to handle.

Knowledge-based Systems

A *knowledge-based system* embodies human knowledge in a form amenable to processing by a computer program. Such a system will store facts about a certain subject area, and relationships, often in the form of rules, which will allow conclusions to be drawn from the facts. A PROLOG program such as that provided in the previous section is a good example of a knowledge base, and a PROLOG translator executing such a program could be classed as a knowledge-based system.

The most common type of knowledge-based system is the *expert system*, and this is discussed in some detail in the following section.

Expert Systems

Pure research in the field of artificial intelligence has had a number of practical spin-offs. One such spin-off has been the development of programs known as *Expert Systems*, or *Intelligent Knowledge Based Systems*. These are programs designed to be able to give the same sort of help or advice, or make decisions, as a human expert in some narrow field of expertise. For instance, a program called PROSPECTOR is capable of predicting the existence of mineral ores given various pieces of information gathered from physical locations. In the same way that, given certain evidence, an expert might say that a particular site looked favourable for containing ore, PROSPECTOR indicates the probability of the existence of the ore. PROSPECTOR is in fact attributed with the discovery of an extremely valuable quantity of molybdenum which had previously been overlooked by human experts.

Expert systems have been developed in numerous areas which traditionally have been the province of human experts. For example, several expert systems have been developed to aid medical diagnosis and treatment. However, decisions in areas such as this are often so critical that it would be foolish to blindly accept the pronouncement of a computer. For this reason, expert systems have the built-in ability to justify the chain of logical reasoning leading to any conclusion, so that it can be checked and verified (or rejected) by a human.

Another characteristic of many expert systems is the use of *fuzzy logic* which allows degrees of uncertainty to be built in to logical deduction processes. Such expert systems are able to state conclusions which are qualified by a probability value indicating the probability of the conclusion being correct.

Other successful expert systems include:

- [ ] MYCIN - diagnosis of infections
- [ ] HEURISTIC DENDRAL - identifies organic compounds
- [ ] XCON - for configuring (VAX) computer systems
- [ ] SACON - for advice on structural analysis

An expert system has three main components:

(a) A knowledge base consisting of rules which use facts supplied by some external source, typically a user.

(b) An inference engine which processes the knowledge base.

(c) A user interface to facilitate communication with the user.

As an example, the following knowledge base is for a simple botanical expert system to identify whether a particular plant is a shrub, tree, herb or vine.

Four rules are to be used:

```
1      IF        STEM IS GREEN
       THEN      TYPE IS HERB.

2      IF        STEM IS WOODY
       AND       ATTITUDE IS CREEPING
       THEN      TYPE IS VINE.

3      IF        STEM IS WOODY
       AND       ATTITUDE IS UPRIGHT
       AND       ONE MAIN TRUNK IS TRUE
       THEN      TYPE IS TREE.
```

```
4        IF      STEM IS WOODY
         AND     ATTITUDE IS UPRIGHT
         AND     ONE MAIN TRUNK IS FALSE
         THEN    TYPE IS SHRUB.
```

This forms the knowledge base.

The inference engine starts by attempting to satisfy a primary goal, in this instance to determine the TYPE of the plant. To this end, it searches its knowledge base for the goal by looking for a rule containing the word TYPE in the conclusion part of the rule (after the THEN part of a rule). This process of examining conclusions to rules while attempting to resolve goals is called *backward chaining* (or *goal-driven inference*).

Rule 1 satisfies this requirement, but in order to establish if the plant is a HERB, the system must obtain information regarding the STEM. Initially this information will not be available and must be supplied by the user. Consequently, obtaining the STEM information is added to a list of subgoals to be evaluated, along with rule 1, and the system looks for another rule containing the goal in its conclusion. The subgoal list also notes the rule which generated the subgoal in question.

After the remaining rules have been processed in a similar fashion, the system must then attempt to satisfy the subgoal list. Consequently, the user interface is invoked. This generates a question of the form

```
IS THE STEM OF THE PLANT GREEN?
```

Let us suppose that the plant is a SHRUB (which has a woody stem, grows upright, and has more than one main trunk). The user answers 'NO' which is stored as a fact relating to the stem of the plant.

Having succeeded with a subgoal, the inference engine again searches for a rule conclusion containing TYPE. It can attempt to evaluate the first rule now that it has all the necessary information. The rule does not produce a conclusion since the STEM is not green. This rule is therefore discarded since it can never cause the primary goal to succeed in this particular consultation.

Examination of the second rule reveals to the inference engine that it cannot be resolved until the ATTITUDE of the plant is in its list of facts, so this is added to its list of subgoals.

Eventually, all the necessary facts are available and the inference engine is able to discard all rules except rule 4 which establishes that the plant is a SHRUB.

In the course of a consultation the user might wish to know why the system is asking a certain question. The information required to answer this question is easy to find: the subgoal generating the question being asked was stored along with the rule from which it came, and this contains all the necessary information. For example, if the inference engine was attempting to resolve rule 4 by asking about the number of TRUNKS, the user interface might respond,

```
    "I am trying to determine the TYPE.
 I know that the STEM is woody.
 I know that the ATTITUDE is upright.
 If ONE MAIN TRUNK is false
 Then I will know that the TYPE is SHRUB".
```

Expert System Shells

The term 'Shell' is given to expert systems which have been given no specific knowledge base, only the inference engine and user interface; the knowledge base has to be provided by the user. A single expert system shell can thus be used to provide advice or help in a number of areas of expertise, providing it is given the appropriate knowledge base for each area.

For example, an expert system shell could be used to give advice on the procedures and sequence of steps necessary for selling a house (what solicitors call 'conveyancing'), or to give advice about possible causes and cures of diseases in houseplants, or diagnosing faults in cars. Not only could these applications be of practical use, but they could also be instructive because the user could ask for and obtain the reasons behind any conclusions.

One of the problems of using such shells is the determination of the rules which represent the wisdom of a human expert; many experts are not consciously aware of the precise reasoning processes they themselves use in order to come to some conclusion, yet in order to produce an expert program, these processes must be defined in a form that is usable. The process of determining the knowledge base rules is known as 'knowledge elicitation' or 'knowledge acquisition' and is performed by 'knowledge engineers'.

Functional Languages

The pseudocode function, *range*, shown in *Listing 28.9* determines the range of three numbers by finding the difference between the largest number and the smallest number:

```
define function range(x, y, z)
    a = function max(x, y)
    b = function max(a, z)
    c = function min(x, y)
    d = function min(c, z)
    r = b - d
    return(r)
endfunction range

define function max(m, n)
    if m > n then
    return(m)
    else return(n)
    endif
endfunction max

define function min(m, n)
    if m < n then
    return(m)
    else return(n)
    endif
endfunction min
```

Listing 28.9

Notice that function *range* uses a number of assignment operations for intermediate calculations, and that these calculations must be executed in the order specified because they occur on consecutive lines. In fact, all of these assignment statements can be eliminated by writing the *range* function in the following way (the word "function" has been omitted from functions *max* and *min* for the sake of clarity);

```
define function range(x, y, z)
    return(max(max(x, y), z) - min(min(x, y), z))
endfunction range
```

This is the function-based version which eliminates all assignment statements and no longer specifies the order in which intermediate calculations are to be executed. Moreover, the *max* and *min* functions may be executed in parallel since neither depends on the other.

Functional languages such as LISP and, to a lesser degree, LOGO use this nested function approach, thereby allowing more flexibility in the implementation of programs. However, these languages take the use of functions a stage further than that shown in the example.

In LISP, for instance, the same program might appear thus:

```
(defun max(m n)
     (cond((greaterp m n) m)
          (t             ) n)
]
(defun min(m n)
     (cond((lessp m n) m)
          (t           ) n)
]
(defun range(x y z)
     (- (max (max x y) z) (min (min x y) z)
]
```

All functions, which are defined using `defun`, are enclosed in brackets and return a value. Thus the built-in function `greaterp` returns `t` (true) if `m` is greater than `n`.

The selection function, `cond`, takes the form

```
(cond (exp₁ val₁)
      (exp₂ val₂)
      .
      .
      (expₙ valₙ))
```

and it returns the value (`val`) corresponding to the first true expression (`exp`) in the list of value/expression pairs. So, for example, the pseudocode

```
if exp then return(val₁)
else return(val₂)
endif
```

translates in LISP to

```
(cond (exp val₁)
      (t   val₂))
```

where `t` is boolean `true`. Thus if `exp` is true, val_1 is returned from `cond`, else val_2 is returned since `t` is always true.

The subtraction function is merely the '−' sign. So, to subtract the two values `a` and `b` we would write

```
(- a b)
```

where a and b could be numbers or functions returning values.

As a final note of explanation, the terminating square bracket, ']', is used to represent any number of close parentheses, ')'; with complex nested expressions it is quite difficult sometimes to determine the correct number of ')', and easy to get it wrong, so the ']' is provided to prevent this occurring.

The following two sections describe in very general terms the main characteristics of LISP and LOGO as examples of functional languages.

LISP

Though LISP is one of the oldest computer languages (nearly as old as FORTRAN) it is used extensively in one of the most innovative of today's research areas: artificial intelligence. As its popularity increases it is becoming available on more and more machines; most main-frames and an increasing number of micros support a version of the language.

LISP was designed as a purely functional language. By this we mean that statements in LISP look like functions. For instance, the function which adds numbers in LISP is called PLUS and is written

(PLUS 2 3)

The function PLUS operates on the 'arguments' 2 and 3. All statements are written in this way.

However, LISP is primarily a language for manipulating symbols rather than performing complex numeric calculations. It treats all forms of data as being elements of lists and has facilities for conveniently manipulating these lists in various ways. Moreover, the language is extensible in that the user is able to create his own functions to be used like any of those supplied.

Programs in LISP are developed interactively. Typing the name of a function, followed by its arguments, causes the function to be performed and the result displayed. In the addition example above, LISP would return the number 5 as soon as the function had been entered. This characteristic is one of the strengths of the language in that programs are written in small, easily testable steps, the effects of which can be seen immediately.

LOGO

Designed as a language to provide a very early and easy route into programming, LOGO is probably best known as the first language to use 'turtle graphics'. When running LOGO, the turtle appears as a graphics cursor which can be instructed to move across the screen using commands such as FORWARD 20 or RIGHT 30. Remotely controllable devices can also be connected to the computer and controlled by the same commands.

The 'turtle' commands have been designed to be appealing and to motivate children to write programs to make the turtle perform visually pleasing manoeuvres. Seymour Papert, the American mathematician who designed the language, was largely influenced by Piaget's well-known ideas on intellectual development in children. Consequently LOGO is emerging as an important educational tool. Unlike much educational software currently available in which the computer is the teacher, and the child reacts to it, LOGO offers a completely different approach to computer assisted learning. With LOGO the roles are reversed, the child teaching the computer what to do.

In his book,'Mindstorms', Seymour Papert explains the philosophy of LOGO, how it was developed and how it works.

LOGO, however, is more than a language just for children. It is based on LISP and shares many of its features. Like LISP it is extensible, based on list processing, and allows recursion. Because it is interpreted, it is easy to use and allows programs to be edited without difficulty. In fact it is a surprisingly powerful language, as well as being easy to learn. It is by no means a 'toy' language and is attracting much interest in all kinds of areas, including artificial intelligence applications.

Here are two simple subprograms in LOGO to enable the turtle to draw a box of side L screen units:

```
TO SIDE :L
        FORWARD :L
        RIGHT 90
END
TO SQUARE :L
        REPEAT 4 [SIDE :L]
END
```

The first subprogram, SIDE, instructs the turtle to move forward L units and then turn right by 90 degrees.

The second subprogram, SQUARE, draws a square of side L by repeatedly calling SIDE.

The turtle would be instructed to draw a square of side 100 units with the command

```
SQUARE 100
```

The functional nature of the language is illustrated by the manner in which arithmetic is performed. For example, to add two numbers and store them in the variable, S, we would write:

```
MAKE "S SUM :A :B
```

where SUM is the function taking two arguments, in this case the values of variables A and B.

As a second example, the calculation

```
x = a + b*c
```

would become

```
MAKE "X SUM :A PROD :B :C
```

Object Oriented Programming (OOP)

Object oriented programming attempts to simulate the real world by means of objects which have characteristics and functions. Object oriented languages are classed as fifth generation languages.

As its name suggests, *object oriented* programming is based on the idea of an *object*. An object is a combination of local variables and procedures, called *methods*, together forming a self-contained programming entity. The term *encapsulation* is sometimes used to describe the combination of a data structure and the methods which manipulate it in an object. Invoking a method is called passing a *message* to an object.

The individual variables in an object together form a data structure which exists intact throughout program runtime. This is not the case with similar structures such as subprograms whose variables are in effect destroyed on completion of the subprogram. An object can retain state information even while it is inactive.

Information hiding is another characteristic of object oriented programming. The idea is that the programmer needs to know only *what* an object does, *not how* it does it, in order to use it in a program.

By means of *inheritance*, new objects may be derived that inherit data and methods from one or more defined objects. Further data structures and methods may be redefined or added to the derived objects, hence forming a hierarchy of structures and reducing the code required to define a new object.

These ideas need to be clarified by means of an example. Borland's Turbo C++, an object oriented extension of C, will be used as the vehicle for the example which involves part of an interactive drawing program. Suppose that we wish to provide a facility for drawing a dot of a certain colour. The dot object could be defined as

```
class point
    {
    private:
     int X,Y;
     int colour;
    public:
     int getX() {return X;}
     int getY() {return Y;}
     int getcolour() {return colour;}
     void setcolour(int c) {colour=c;}
     void plot() {putpixel(X,Y,colour);}
    }dot;
```

The declarative `class` allows objects to be defined. In addition, `class` allows the use of the word `private`, which restricts access to the variables (`X`, `Y` and `colour` in this case) exclusively to the object's methods, and `public` which allows access to variables and methods by functions external to the object being defined.

Five methods are defined: the first three allow external functions to obtain the position of the point and its colour, the fourth allows the point's colour to be set at some integer value, and the final one displays the dot using a predefined function, `putpixel()`. Notice that the methods are defined within the object, that is in-line, though C++ also allows them to be defined elsewhere if required.

In order to obtain `dot's` X co-ordinate we would invoke method `getX()` using a statement such as

```
x_coord = dot.getX();
```

To change its colour to 1 would require

```
dot.setcolour(1);
```

and it could be displayed using

```
dot.plot();
```

It is important to note that the only way to use the `dot` object is by means of the appropriate method; this means that if any of the methods are changed, there will be no need to alter any other part of the program which makes use of the object. This is a very important characteristic of object oriented programming. Furthermore, there is no possibility of an object's variables being corrupted inadvertently elsewhere in the program since, having been declared as `private`, the only functions allowed to access them are the object's methods. Together, these two features characterize *information hiding* mentioned earlier.

Notice also that the `dot` object's state information, that is, its co-ordinates and colour, is retained throughout the execution of the program, unlike local variables within a subprogram.

Object oriented programming languages usually allow defined objects to be the basis of derived objects, in which variables and methods may be *inherited*. For example, we could use the `point` object as the basis of a more general dot which would allow its co-ordinates to be changed. This would involve defining the new dot in terms of `point` and adding two more methods, one to set X and the other to set Y.

This type of situation, where a base object may be used to derive a special object, occurs frequently in programming tasks. A car object, for instance, could be the basis of a number of different types of cars, such as sports, saloon, hatchback, and so on, each inheriting the basic car characteristics and adding to or modifying them according to special data/functional requirements.

A convenient way to start when using object oriented design is to state the system requirements in narrative form and identify key nouns which relate to object classes, and key verbs which correspond to object methods. For example, consider the outline system specification below:

> The temperature control system regulates the temperature of a number of <u>rooms</u> in the building. Each room has a <u>minimum temperature</u> and <u>maximum temperature</u> and the system **keeps** the temperature of the room between these two limits. The limits may be **changed** by means of the <u>system console</u>, which also **shows** the <u>current temperature</u> of each room in the form of a <u>dynamic display</u>.

Nouns are shown underlined and verbs in bold.

Thus the nouns identify a room object which requires temperature regulation, and a system console object for data input and display purposes. As a preliminary step we might therefore identify the following object classes and associated operations:

Object class:	Room
Operations:	Detect temperature
	Increase temperature
	Decrease temperature

Object class:	System Console Keyboard
Operations:	Get new/initial temperature limits
	Communicate with user

Object class:	System Console Display
Operations:	Update room temperatures
	Display room temperatures

This would provide a reasonable starting point for the detailed design which would follow.

Implementation Languages

A number of computer languages have features which facilitate object oriented design without having been specifically written for this purpose. These languages include Simula, Ada, Modula-2, C++ and some versions of Pascal. Smalltalk on the other hand was designed specifically as a language which could be used to implement an object oriented design directly.

Smalltalk was developed by the Xerox Corporation following an idea by Alan Kay regarding the development of personal computers. The original research in the 1970s involved the development of a notebook computer called a'Dynabook'. To this end, a windows-based, graphical user environment was developed, with the underlying control of the system being achieved by Smalltalk. The system was highly interactive, having been influenced by the type of user interface employed by Logo.

Since object oriented design encourages software re-usability, Smalltalk provides a large library of basic object classes which may be used directly or tailored to specific needs. Since it was originally designed to be used with powerful personal computers supporting WIMP environments, its use is likely to increase, particularly with the increasing speed and memory size of personal computers we are currently experiencing.

Advantages of Object Oriented Programming

We have already seen that communication between objects is via messages, eliminating the need for shared data areas such as sets of global variables, and removing the possibility of accidental modification to data shared by a number of functions or programs. This is particularly important when a large programming project is being developed by a team of programmers simultaneously working on different aspects of the job, because it ensures that the work of one programmer will not interact in unforeseen ways with that of any other.

Furthermore, access to an object's methods are exclusively by means of a well-defined, unchanging interface. The way that an object performs its characteristic functions is of no interest to users of the object, and any internal changes to its structure will be invisible. This ensures that modification of an object, being independent of other objects, will have no effect whatsoever on any other part of the program.

The inheritance property of object oriented programming languages allows the hierarchical structuring of objects, reducing coding effort and simplifying the program structure.

Because objects are self-contained entities which may be used sequentially or in parallel, an object oriented design offers substantial flexibility in its implementation; decisions regarding the use of processing method, whether serial or parallel, need not be made immediately, and programs may be converted to a different processing method without the necessity for a complete rewrite.

Disadvantages of Object Oriented Programming

Object inheritance can produce significant run-time overheads, reducing the execution speed of a program. A complex hierarchical object structure might involve a substantial number of cross-referenced objects, giving the program extra work to do.

An object oriented design is not always the most appropriate solution. Sometimes a more functional approach can simplify the programming task, particularly where system state information does not need to be retained by a program. Remember that an object can retain state information during the execution of a program, unlike the values of variables in subprograms which are lost as soon as the subprogram is exited;

in certain applications this may not be required. For example, the common cash dispenser comprises a screen, a numeric keypad and a number of function keys such as 'Withdraw cash', 'Obtain balance', 'Proceed', 'Cancel request'. The customer, having entered his or her PIN (personal identification number), selects a function by pressing the appropriate function key.

A natural program design would be to assign a subprogram to process each function. Since each function operates independently of the others, there is no need to retain any sort of state information. An object oriented approach could of course still be used, but there would be no particular advantage in doing so.

29 *Sorting Techniques*

For computing purposes, a distinction has to be made between *internal* and *external* sorting. Where large volumes of data have to be sorted, such as entire files held on magnetic tape or disk, an external sort is used; this involves repeated transfers of data between memory and backing storage media.

The basis of all such external sorting is *merging*, a process of forming one single sorted sequence from two previously sorted sequences.

Merging

The following pseudocode algorithm describes the process of merging two files, *file_1* and *file_2*, into a new file, *file_3*. If the files were held on magnetic tape, then three tape drives would be needed to effect the merge.

```
algorithm merge
open file1, file2, file 3          {Initialize}
    read file_1
    read file_2
                                   {start of main processing loop}
  while not eof(file_1) and not eof(file_2)
    if record-key(file_1) < record-key(file_2) then
        write record(file_1) to file_3, read file_1
      else write record(file_2) to file_3, read file_2
    endif
  endwhile
                                   {one of files is now empty}
  while not eof(file_n)
    write to file_3, read file_n
  endwhile
end
```

Listing 29.1

Merge Sort

The merge algorithm assumes that the two files to be merged are already sorted, but the same process, used repeatedly, can be used to sort a completely unsorted file. The following example presupposes the use of three files, *file_1*, *file_2* and *file_3*, and a set of record keys with no repeated values.

Stage 1

```
file_3 contains the sequence
(18 26)(3 9 34)(5 21)(14)(6)
```

The brackets denote that there are already groups of values in ascending sequence, referred to as *runs*.

Place alternate runs into file_1 and file_2, thus

```
file_1:  (18 26)(5 21)(6)
file_2:  (3 9 34)(14)
```

Stage 2

Using the following procedure, file_1 and file_2 onto file_3.

Compare the leading values from file_1 and file_2 and write to file_3 the smallest of the two which is also greater than the immediately preceding value written to file_3. If both are smaller than the latter, write the smaller of the two.

Thus, proceeding with the values currently in file_1 and file_2,

The first pair for file_1 and file_2 are 18 and 3, respectively; 3 is the smaller value and since file_3 is, at present, empty, 3 is selected.

```
file_1:  (18 26)(5 21)(6)
file_2:  (9 34)(14)
file_3:  3
```

Next, 18 and 9 are compared and 9 is selected because it is smallest and also greater than 3, the last value written to file_3.

```
file_1:  (18 26)(5 21)(6)
file_2:  (34)(14)
file_3:  3 9
```

Of the next pairs 18 and 34, 18 is smaller but greater than the trailing value, 9, in file_3.

```
file_1:  (26)(5 21)(6)
file_2:  (34)(14)
file_3:  3 9 18
```

Comparing the next pair, 26 and 34, the former is selected.

```
file_1:  (5 21)(6)
file_2:  (34)(14)
file_3:  3 9 18 26
```

Comparison of 5 and 34 results in the selection of 34, because 5 is less than 26, the trailing value in file_3.

```
file_1: (5 21)(6)
file_2: (14)
file_3: 3 9 18 26 34
```

The next comparison reveals that 5 and 14 are both less than 34, so 5 is selected.

```
file_1: (21)(6)
file_2: (14)
file_3: 3 9 18 26 34 5
```

14 is the next chosen value.

```
file_1: (21)(6)
file_2:
file_3: 3 9 18 26 34 5 14
```

file_2 is now empty and the remaining values in file_1 are transferred to file_3.

```
file_3: (3 9 18 26 34)(5 14 21)(6)
```

Stage 1 is repeated.

The runs have increased in length and are directed alternately to file_1 and file_2

```
file_1: (3 9 18 26 34)(6)
file_2: (5 14 21)
```

Stage 2 is repeated, merging the runs in file_1 and file_2 back to file_3, to produce

```
file_3: (3 5 9 14 18 21 26 34)(6)
```

Stage 1 is repeated and runs are written alternately to file_1 and file_2

```
file_1: (3 5 9 14 18 21 26 34)
file_2: (6)
```

Stage 2 again merges file_1 and file_2 onto file_3, this time as a completely sorted sequence.

```
file_3: 3 5 6 9 14 18 21 26 34
```

The following pseudocode algorithm describes the process. x denotes the most recent value written to file_3, a is the smaller of the two leading values in file_1 and file_2 and b the larger.

```
algorithm mergesort
  procedure initialize                    {open file_1, file_2, file_3}
    repeat
      procedure split_and_merge
                                          {split file_3 into file_1 and
                                           file_2, putting alternate
                                           runs into alternate files}
        while not eof(file_1) and not eof(file_2)
          if eof(file_3) or (x < a) or (b < x) then
            write a to file_3
              else write b to file_3
                endif
        endwhile
                                          {one of files is now empty}
        while not eof(file_n)
          write to file_3
        endwhile
      until file_3                        {consists of only one run}
  end
```

Listing 29.2

4-File Merge Sort

The efficiency of the process can be increased with the use of four files as follows.

The following values are to be sorted

```
21 14 54 6 87 15 32 76 38 23 44 16 17
```

This time, single values are written alternately to file_1 and file_2

```
file_1: 21 54 87 32 38 44 17
file_2: 14 6 15 76 23 16
```

The values are successively merged in pairs using file_3 and file_4 alternately.

```
file_3: (14 21)(15 87)(23 38)(17)
file_4: (6 54)(32 76)(16 44)
```

These runs are now merged alternately to file_1 and file_2.

```
file_1: (6 14 21 54)(16 23 38 44)
file_2: (15 32 76 87)(17)
```

The extended runs are merged alternately to file_3 and file_4.

```
file_3: (6 14 15 21 32 54 76 87)
file_4: (16 17 23 38 44)
```

A final merge back to file_1 only, produces the final sorted sequence.

```
file_1: 6 14 15 16 17 21 23 32 38 44 54 76 87
```

Internal sorting, which is the subject of study in the following sections, involves the sorting of items entirely within memory into a strict ascending or descending order. For programming purposes, the items to be sorted are held in a one-dimensional array. The purpose of the data items will vary according to the application, but they may serve, for example, as keys to logical records. Direct access files frequently make use of indexes to identify the locations of individual records on a storage medium. Searching such an index for a particular record key value is often more efficient if the index is sorted into a particular sequence.

The study of sorting algorithms is a long standing area of research in computer science and many highly efficient but complex methods have been developed. In order that the main principles of sorting can be understood, this text provides a detailed description of three relatively simple and two more complex sorting techniques namely the:

- exchange or 'bubble' sort;
- selection sort;
- insertion sort;
- shell sort;
- quicksort.

Each narrative description is followed by:

- an outline of the main programming requirements needed to implement the sort in a high level language;
- a pseudocode algorithm with detailed annotation of the main processes;
- annotated sample programs implemented in Microsoft BASIC and Turbo Pascal.

Exchange Sort or Bubble Sort

If it is assumed, for example, that items are to be sorted into ascending sequence, then the idea of the bubble sort is that, firstly the smallest value 'bubbles' to the top or beginning of the list, followed by the second smallest into the second position, the third smallest into third position and so on. The process can best be illustrated by a practical example as follows.

Consider a one-dimensional array of 5 elements, each containing an integer value. The array is known by the symbol M and each element in the array is identified by its subscript. The array elements and their contents are shown below.

```
Array elements  M(1) M(2) M(3) M(4) M(5)
Contents         3    6    2    1    5
```

The bubble sort requires that the array of values be scanned repeatedly and that with each scan, or more properly, *pass,* adjacent pairs of numbers are compared to see if they are in the required order; if necessary they exchange positions. In the above example, the first pair, 3 and 6, are compared and found to be in the correct order; no exchange is necessary. Then the second and third items, 6 and 2, are compared, found to be in the incorrect order and are exchanged. The array now appears as follows:

```
Array elements  M(1) M(2) M(3) M(4) M(5)
Contents         3    2    6    1    5
```

The first pass continues with the comparison of the third and fourth items, 6 and 1; these require exchanging and the list becomes:

```
Array elements  M(1) M(2) M(3) M(4) M(5)
Contents         3    2    1    6    5
```

The first pass ends with a comparison of the fourth and fifth items, now 6 and 5 respectively; again, an exchange is required. At the end of this first pass, the sequence appears as:

```
Array elements  M(1) M(2) M(3) M(4) M(5)
Contents         3    2    1    5    6
```

The sort is not yet complete and further passes are needed. The complete process is illustrated below. Underlining indicates those values currently being compared and, if necessary, exchanged.

```
Array elements  M(1) M(2) M(3) M(4) M(5)

Pass 1           3    6    2    1    5
                 3    6    2    1    5    exchange
                 3    2    6    1    5    exchange
                 3    2    1    6    5    exchange

End of Pass 1    3    2    1    5    6

Pass 2           3    2    1    5    6    exchange
                 2    3    1    5    6    exchange
                 2    1    3    5    6
                 2    1    3    5    6

End of Pass 2    2    1    3    5    6

Pass 3           2    1    3    5    6    exchange
                 1    2    3    5    6
                 1    2    3    5    6
                 1    2    3    5    6

End of Pass 3    1    2    3    5    6

Pass 4           1    2    3    5    6
                 1    2    3    5    6
                 1    2    3    5    6
                 1    2    3    5    6

End of Pass 4    1    2    3    5    6
```

A number of features can be identified in the above process:

☐ with each pass, the smallest value moves one position towards the beginning (the left) of the array;

☐ after the first pass, the largest value is at the end of the array. At the end of each subsequent pass, the next largest number moves to its correct position;

☐ the sort has been completed before the final pass.

Referring to this last feature, the sort is complete by the end of Pass 3. Why then is a further pass necessary? The answer is that the first comparison in Pass 3 results in an exchange between the values 2 and 1. If it is assumed that the occurrence of an exchange indicates that the sort is not complete, then a further pass is needed to determine that the array is sorted; that is, there have been no exchanges. The maximum number of passes required is always *n-1*, *n* being the number of items in the array. Frequently, the sort is complete well before this maximum is reached and any further passes are wasted. Consider the following sequence.

```
Array elements   M(1)  M(2)  M(3)  M(4)  M(5)  M(6)

Contents          3     1     2     6     7     9

Pass 1            3     1     2     6     7     9    exchange
                  1     3     2     6     7     9    exchange
                  1     2     3     6     7     9
                  1     2     3     6     7     9
                  1     2     3     6     7     9

End of Pass 1     1     2     3     6     7     9

Pass 2            1     2     3     6     7     9
                  1     2     3     6     7     9
                  1     2     3     6     7     9
                  1     2     3     6     7     9
                  1     2     3     6     7     9

End of Pass 2     1     2     3     6     7     9
```

The maximum number of passes necessary should be *n-1*, that is, 5. Instead, the sort is completed by the end of the first pass and confirmed by the lack of exchanges in the second pass.

Program Requirements

☐ *Comparison* of adjacent values in an array. Assuming that the values are held in a one-dimensional array, reference is made to elements within the array by subscript. For example, the 4th element in an array called *list*, is addressed by *list*(4). To carry out a pass of all the elements in an array requires the use of a program loop to increment the subscript from 1 to *n*, the variable *n* being the size of the array. This can reduce by 1 after each complete pass, because the largest number 'sinks' to the bottom of the list and therefore need not be considered in subsequent passes; the efficiency of the algorithm is thus improved. For the sake of simplicity, this particular feature is not used in the illustrative algorithm or programs.

☐ *Exchanging* the positions of adjacent values. Assuming that the programming language in use does not provide an 'exchange' or 'swap' instruction, then a temporary store is required to allow the exchange to take place, For example, to exchange the contents of two variables, *first* and *second*, using a temporary store, *hold*, requires the following processes:

1.   Copy contents of *first* into *hold;*

2.   Copy contents of *second* into *first*;

3.   Copy contents of *hold* into *second*.

This can be illustrated as follows with some example values:

```
Location                 first      second      hold

Initial contents          6           3
After process 1           6           3          6
After process 2           3           3          6
After process 3           3           6          6
```

□ *Detecting* completion of the sort. A *flag* or *sentinel* variable, initialized for example, to 0 at the beginning of each pass and set to 1 if any exchanges take place during a pass, can be used to detect the completion of the sort before the maximum number of passes has been completed. For simplicity, the following algorithm does not include this feature, although it is used in the sample BASIC and Pascal programs;

A Bubble Sort Algorithm in pseudocode of array *M*, containing *n* elements

```
algorithm       bubble sort
 number:= n                          {number of values and subscript of
 passes:=1                            last item}
 while passes <= number - 1 do       {control number of passes}
  item := 1                          {initialize array subscript}
   while item <= number - 1 do       {loop for one pass}
    if M(item) > M(item + 1) then swap
                                     {swap if necessary}

    endif
    item := item + 1                 {increment subscript}
   endwhile                          {end of single pass}
  passes := passes + 1               {increment number of passes}
  endwhile                           {end of all passes}
 end
```

Listing 29.3

Bubble Sort in Microsoft BASIC of 20 numeric values in array *M*

```
10    dim M(20)                                     {declare array}
20    for item = 1 to 20
30      input M(item)                               {fill array}
40    next item
50    number = 20                                   {number of items}
60    passes = 1                                    {initialize passes}
70    exchange = 1
80    while passes <= number - 1 and exchange <> 0  {while not sorted}
90      item = 1                                    {initialize subscript}
100     exchange = 0                                {flag for swap}
```

Listing 29.4

```
110    while item <= number - 1              {n-1 comparisons}
120      if M(item) > M(item + 1) then gosub 210   {swap elements}
130      item = item + 1
140    wend                                  {single pass}
150    passes = passes + 1                   {increment passes}
160 wend                                     {completion of all passes}
170 for item = 1 to 20
180    print M(item) ;                       {print sorted items}
190 next item
200 end
210 rem subroutine to swap array element positions
220 spare = M(item)                          {temporary location}
230 M(item) = M(item + 1)                    {Item + element into
                                              Item element}
                                             {Item element from
240 M(item + 1) = spare                        temporary location into
                                               Item + 1 element}
                                             {set flag for swap}
250 exchange = 1                             {end of swap routine}
260 return
```

Listing 29.4 continued

Some versions of BASIC, including the Microsoft version, provide a *swap* command, so the subroutine in the above listing could be removed and line 120 amended to read:

```
if M(item) > M(item + 1) then swap M(item), M(item + 1)
```

Bubble sort in Turbo Pascal to sort 20 integer items in array M

```
program bubble (input, output);
const
 number = 20;                               {number of values to
                                             sort}

var
 M :array[1..number] of integer;            {declare array}
 exchange :boolean;                         {flag for swap}
 item, passes, spare :integer;
begin
 for item := 1 to number do                 {fill array M}
  begin
   writeln('number');
   readln(M[item]);
  end;
 passes := 1;                               {initialize to first
                                             pass}

 exchange := true;
        while (passes <= number - 1) and (exchange) do {control passes}
  begin
```

Listing 29.5

```
        item := 1;                              {initialize element
                                                 pointer}
        exchange := false;                      {initialize swap flag
                                                 before each pass}
        while item <= number - 1 do             {control number of
                                                 comparisons}
         begin
          if M[item] > M[item +1] then          {compare adjacent values}
           begin                                {swap elements}
            spare := M[item];
            M[item] := M[item + 1];
            M[item + 1] := spare;
               exchange := true;                {set flag to indicate  swap}
           end;
             item := item + 1;                  {move pointer to next
                                                 element}
         end;
            passes := passes + 1;               {increment pass counter}
       end;
        for item := 1 to number do              {display sorted array}
         begin
          writeln(M[item]);
         end;
       end.
```

Listing 29.5 continued

Selection Sort

This method also requires the comparison and exchange of elements in a list. It is based on the principal that the item with the lowest value is exchanged with the item at the beginning or *head* of the list and that the process is repeated with *n-1* items, *n-2* items and so on, until only the largest item is left.

Consider an array M which contains six integer values as follows:

```
M(1)  M(2)  M(3)  M(4)  M(5)  M(6)
15     8    -3    62    24    12
```

The list is to be sorted into strict ascending sequence to become:

```
M(1)  M(2)  M(3)  M(4)  M(5)  M(6)
-3     8    12    15    24    62
```

The underlined values indicate the length of the list to be examined in each scan.

```
15 8 -3 62 24 12      Starting sequence
-3  8 15 62 24 12     -3 exchanged with 15 at head of list
-3  8 15 62 24 12     no exchange needed
-3  8 12 62 24 15     12 exchanged with 15 at head of list
-3  8 12 15 24 62     15 exchanged with 62 at head of list
-3  8 12 15 24 62     no exchange needed
```

The first pass of *n* items returns the value of -3 as being the smallest value in the list; this value moves to the head of the list and the previous head, 15, is moved to the position formerly occupied by -3. The list to be scanned is now *n-1* items and has the value 8 at its head. The next pass reveals 8 as the smallest value, but no exchange is made because it already heads the shortened list. The next pass examines *n-2* items and returns 12 as the lowest value, which is exchanged with 15 at the head of the shortened list. The process continues until only two items remain, 24 at the head and 62 at the rear; no exchange is needed and the list is sorted.

Program Requirements

Certain features are similar to those of the bubble sort described earlier.

- ☐ Comparison of values in different locations in an array.

- ☐ Exchange of values in different, although not necessarily adjacent, positions in the array.

- ☐ The use of a pointer to allow element positions to be stored and incremented and also to be used as a subscript to refer to the contents of an individual location.

- ☐ The use of a temporary store to enable an exchange of element positions.

A Selection Sort Algorithm in Pseudocode of array M Containing n Elements

```
algorithm selection
 number:= n                                      {number of values to
                                                  sort}

 for head := 1 to n - 1                          {increment head}
  present_value := M(head)                        {value of current head}
  present_pointer := head                         {position of current
                                                  head}

  for next_one := present_pointer + 1 to n       {increment
                                                  search pointer}

  if M(next_one) < present_value then
   present_value := M(next_one)                   {store smaller value and
   present_pointer := next_one                    {its position in the
                                                  list}

  endif
 endfor
 if present_pointer <> head then                  {check smallest value
                                                  not already at head}
  temp := M(head)                                 {temp is a temporary
                                                  store for the swap}

  M(head) := M(present_pointer)                   {exchange smallest/head
                                                  values}

  M(present_pointer) := temp
  endif
 endfor
end
```

Listing 29.6

The use of a temporary location *temp* in the above algorithm is not strictly necessary, since the smallest value is assigned to *present_value* at the end of a pass and as the following program implementations illustrate, the swap could be implemented with:

```
M(present_pointer) := M(head);
M(head) := present_value.
```

Selection Sort in Microsoft BASIC for 20 Items in Array M

```
10   dim M(20)                                        {declare array}
20   for item = 1 to 20
30    input M(item)                                   {fill array}
40   next item
50   number = 20                                      {length of array}
60   for head = 1 to number - 1                       {increment head}
70    present.value = M(head)                          {store head value}
80    present.pointer = head                          {and its position}
90    for next.one = present.pointer + 1 to number    {step through list}
100    if M(next.one) < present.value then
           present.value = M(next.one):               {store smaller value}
           present.pointer = next.one                 {and its position}
110   next next.one
120   if present.pointer <> head then gosub 180       {check smallest value not
                                                        already at head}
130 next head
140 for item = 1 to 20
150   print M(item);
160 next item
170 end
180 rem swap routine
190 M(present.pointer) = M(head)                      {exchange smallest value
                                                        with head value}
200 M(head) = present.value
210 return
```

Listing 29.7

Turbo Pascal Selection Sort of 20 Integer Values in Array M

```
program selection (input, output);
 const
  number = 20;
 var
  M :array[1..number] of integer;              {declare array}
  head, next_one, present_value,
  present_pointer :integer;
begin
 for next_one := 1 to number do
  begin
```

Listing 29.8

```
  write ('number');
  readln (M[next_one]);                                {fill array}
 end;
for head := 1 to number - 1 do                         {increment head}
 begin
  present_value := M[head];                             {store head value}
  present_pointer := head;                              {and its position}
 for next_one := present_pointer + 1 to number do      {step through list}
  begin
   if M[next_one] < present_value then
    begin
     present_value := M[next_one];                      {store smaller value}
     present_pointer := next_one;                       {and its position}
    end;
  end;
  if present_pointer <> head then                       {check smallest value
                                                          not already at head}

   begin
    M[present_pointer] := M[head];                      {exchange smallest value}
    M[head] := present_value;                           {with head value}
   end;
 end;
 for next_one := 1 to number do
  begin
   writeln(M[next_one]);
  end;
end.
```

Listing 29.8 continued

Insertion Sort

This method can best be illustrated with the example of an unsorted pack of playing cards. Assuming that the cards are to be put into a row of ascending sequence (the least value on the left), the procedure may be as follows:

☐ take the first card from the *source* pile and begin the *destination* row;

☐ continuing with the rest of the source pile, pick one card at a time and place it in the correct sequence in the destination row.

The process of finding the correct point of insertion requires repeated comparisons and where an insertion requires it, movement of cards to make space in the sequence. Thus, the card to be inserted, x, is compared with successive cards in the destination row (beginning from the largest value at the right hand end of the destination row) and where x is less than the card under comparison, the latter is moved to the right; otherwise x is inserted in the next position to the right.

Program Requirements

☐ The procedures are fairly simple, although a practical exercise with a pack of cards should help to clarify them.

☐ As with previous sorts, reference to array subscripts is required to allow comparison with different elements in the array.

☐ Nested loops are needed; the outer one for selecting successive values to be inserted into a destination sequence and the inner for allowing the insertion value to be compared with those already in sequence.

☐ Control of the outer loop does not present a problem as it simply ensures that all values are inserted, starting with the second; the first obviously needs no comparison as it is the first to be inserted.

☐ The inner loop controls the movement of values through the destination list to allow insertion of new values at the appropriate points. This loop may be terminated under two distinct conditions:

    - a value in the destination sequence is less than the value to be inserted;

    - there are no further items to the left in the destination sequence.

To ensure termination under these conditions, a *flag* or *sentinel* is used. In the algorithm and the program implementations, array element (0) is used to store the value to be inserted, thus ensuring that when the left hand end is reached, no further comparisons are made.

The following algorithm illustrates the procedure; the analogy of a pack of cards is continued.

Insertion Sort Algorithm in Pseudocode of *n* Elements in Array M

```
algorithm   insertion
 for pick_card = 2 to num_in_pack      {pick cards singly, starting with second)
  in_hand := M(pick_card)              {store value of card to insert}
  m(0) := in_hand                      {to prevent insertion beyond left}
                                       {end of destination sequence}
  j := pick_card - 1                   {ensures comparison with first card}
  while in hand < M(j) do              {card to insert < next card to the left in}
                                       {destination sequence}
   M(j + 1) := M(j)                    {move card > card to insert, to the right}
   j := j - 1                          {pointer to next card}
                                       {compared with card to insert}
  endwhile
  M(j + 1) := in_hand                  {insert card into destination sequence}
 endfor
end
```

Listing 29.9

Insertion Sort in Microsoft BASIC of 20 Numeric Values in Array M

```
10   dim M(20)
20   for card = 1 to 20
30     input M(card)                  {fill array}
40   next card
50   num.in.pack = 20                 {number of cards to be sorted}
60   for pick.card = 2 to num.in.pack {pick cards singly, starting with second}
70    in.hand = M(pick.card)          {store value of card to insert}
80    M(0) = in.hand                  {prevent insertion beyond left end of
                                        destination sequence}
90    j = pick.card - 1               {ensures comparison with first card}
100   while in.hand < M(j)            {card to insert < next card to left in
                                        destination sequence}
110     M(j + 1) = M(j)               {move card > card to insert to the right}
120     j = j - 1                     {pointer to next card compared with card
                                        to insert}
130   wend
140   M(j + 1) = in.hand              {insert card into destination sequence}
150 next pick.card
160 for card = 1 to 20
170   print M(card);                  {display sorted card values}
180 next card
190 end
```

Listing 29.10

Turbo Pascal Insertion Sort of 20 Integer Values in Array M

```
program insertion (input, output);
 const
  num_in_pack = 20;                   {number of items to sort}
 var
  M :array[0..num_in_pack] of integer; {declare array}
  card, pick_card, in_hand, j :integer;
begin
 for card := 1 to num_in_pack do      {fill array}
  begin
   write ('number');
   readln (M[card]);
  end;
 for pick_card := 2 to num_in_pack do {pick cards singly, starting with second}
  begin
   in_hand := M[pick_card];           {store value of card to insert}
   M[0] := in_hand;                   {prevent insertion beyond left end of
                                        destination sequence}
   j := pick_card - 1;                {ensures comparison with first card}
   while in_hand < M[j] do            {card to insert < card to left in
                                        destination sequence}
```

Listing 29.11

```
    begin
     M[j + 1] := M[j];                    {move card > card to insert to right}
     j := j - 1;                          {pointer to next card compared with
                                           card to insert}

     end;
    M[j + 1] := in_hand;                  {insert card into destination sequence}
   end;
 for card := 1 to num_in_pack do
 begin
   writeln (M[card]);                     {display sorted list}
 end;
end.
```

Listing 29.11 continued

Comparative Efficiency of Sorting Methods

The sorts described so far are not the most sophisticated, and in many cases, are not very quick. They are, however, relatively simple to understand and they have been chosen for this reason. More efficient, and consequently more complex, sorting algorithms include the:

Shell Sort

Named after its designer, D.L. Shell in 1959, it is a refinement of the insertion sort and divides the list into groups which are sorted separately. For example, with an array of eight items, those which are four positions apart are sorted first; the four groups will each contain two items. A second pass groups and sorts afresh the items which are two positions apart; this involves two groups, each with 4 items. Finally, all items (only one position apart) are sorted in a final pass. With each pass, the *distance* between the keys is *halved*, effectively changing the contents of each group. Successive passes continue until the distance between the elements in a group is one. The idea of the Shell sort is that the early passes compare items which are widely separated and thus remove the main disorders in the array. Later passes may then require fewer movements of items.

The Turbo Pascal programs for the Shell sort (*Listing 29.13*) and the Quicksort (*Listing 29.15*) include routines for the generation of random numbers and the calculation of execution times. These routines were used in all the Pascal sort programs in this chapter to test the effectiveness of each on various sets of random numbers. The table in *Figure 29.1* shows the results of these test runs, which were carried out using an 8086 processor-based machine with a processor clock speed of 4.77 MHz. Even with such a slow machine the performance of the Quicksort is particularly impressive, with the Shell sort taking a close second place.

A Shell Sort Algorithm

```
algorithm shellsort
 numkeys := n
 gap := numkeys                          {set gap to full list}
 repeat
  pnt1 := 1                              {set pointer to top of list}
  gap := trunc(gap/2)                    {calculate gap between keys}
  pnt2 := pnt1 + gap                     {set pointer to 2nd key}
   repeat
    if m(pnt1) > m(pnt2) then            {compare keys}
     procedure exchange                  {call procedure exchange}
    endif
    pnt1 := pnt1 + 1                      {move pointers down the list}
     pnt2 := pnt2 + 1
    until pnt2 > numkeys                 {test for bottom of list}
 until gap =1                            {sort completed}
end

define procedure exchange
 temp := m(pnt1)                         {swap keys using temporary}
 m(pnt1) := m(pnt2)                      {location}
 m(pnt2) := temp
 pnt4 := pnt1                            {set pointers for pass}
 pnt3 := pnt1 - gap
 while (pnt3 > 0) and (m(pnt3) > m(pnt4)) do  {not top of list and}
                                              { swap needed}
  temp := m(pnt3)                        {swap keys using temporary}
  m(pnt3) := m(pnt4)                     {location}
  m(pnt4) := temp
  pnt3 := pnt3 - gap                     {move pointers up the list}
  pnt4 := pnt4 - gap
 endwhile
end procedure exchange
```

Listing 29.12

Turbo Pascal Shell Sort of 1000 Pseudo Random Numbers in Array M

```
program shell (output);
uses dos;
const
  numkeys = 1000;

var
 m :array[1..numkeys] of integer;
```

Listing 29.13

```
i, item, gap, pnt1, pnt2, pnt3, pnt4, temp :integer;
hrs, min, sec, sec100 :word;

procedure exchange;
begin
 temp := m[pnt1];                                   {swap keys using temporary}
 m[pnt1]  := m[pnt2];                               {location}
 m[pnt2] :=temp;
 pnt4 :=pnt1;                                       {set pointers for pass}
 pnt3 :=pnt1 - gap;
 while (pnt3 > 0) and (m[pnt3]  >m[pnt4]) do {not top of list and}
 begin                                              {swap needed}
  temp := m[pnt3];                                  {swap keys using temporary}
  m[pnt3]  :=m[pnt4];                               {location}
  m[pnt4]  :=temp;
  pnt3 :=pnt3 - gap;                                {move pointers up the list}
  pnt4 :=pnt4 - gap;
 end;
end;

procedure sort;
begin
 settime(0, 0, 0, 0);
 gap :=numkeys;                                     {set gap to full list}
 repeat
  pnt1 :=1;                                         {set pointer to top of list}
  gap :=trunc(gap/2) ;                              {calculate gap between keys}
  pnt2 := pnt1 + gap;                               {set pointer to 2nd key}
   repeat
    if m[pnt1] > m[pnt2] then                       {compare keys}
     exchange;                                      {execute procedure exchange}
    pnt1 :=pnt1 + 1;                                {move pointers down the list}
    pnt2 :=pnt2 + 1;
   until pnt2 > numkeys;                            {test for bottom of list}
 until gap =1;                                      {sort completed}
 gettime(hrs, min, sec, sec100);
end;

procedure showtime;
begin
 writeln(hrs:10, min:15, sec:20, sec100:25);
end;

begin
 Write('Creating', numkeys, 'random numbers...');
 Randomize;
  for i:=1 to numkeys do
   begin
    m[i]:=Random(30000);
```

Listing 29.13

```
   end;
Writeln;
Write('Sorting', numkeys, 'random numbers...');
 sort;                                          {call sort procedure}
Writeln;
  for i:=1 to numkeys do
   begin
    Write(m[i]:8);
   end;
 showtime;                                      {call procedure to}
end.                                            {display sorted array}
```

Listing 29.13 continued

Quicksort

This *partition* sort was invented by C.A.R Hoare, who called it 'Quicksort' because of its remarkable speed. It is based on the exchange principle used in the bubble sort described earlier and is one of the fastest array sorting techniques, for large numbers of items, currently available. Quicksort is based on the general principle that exchanges should preferably be made between items which are located a large *distance* apart in an array. Initially, the array is divided into two *partitions,* using the mid-point. Beginning at the left-most position in the array, the item in this position is compared with the item at the mid-point position. If the former is less than the latter, the next item in the partition is compared with the mid-point element. The comparisons with the mid-point item are repeated with successive items in the partition until one is found which is greater than or equal to the mid-point item. The same process is used on the right-hand partition until an item is found which is less than or equal to that at the mid-point position. Once items are found in both partitions which satisfy these respective conditions, they are swapped. Successive comparisons and swaps are carried out until each item in each partition has been compared with the mid-point item. The whole process continues *recursively* (it calls itself repeatedly), further sub-dividing the partitions, until each sub-partition contains only one item, when the array is sorted. The topic of recursion is dealt with in Chapter 26 on Data Structures.

A Quicksort Algorithm in Pseudocode of Array *m*, containing *n* elements

```
algorithm quicksort
 numkeys := n                         {number of keys to sort}
 lo := 1                              {store lower limit of array}
 hi := numkeys                        {store upper limit of array}
 procedure qsort(lo, hi)              {call recursive sort procedure
                                       passing initial parameters}

end

define procedure qsort(lowend, topend) {recursive sort procedure}
 leftpntr := lowend                   {set pointers to current
 rightpntr := topend                   left and right partition limits}
 midvalue := m((lowend + topend)/2)   {store value at mid point between
                                       new left and right partitions}

 repeat
  while m(leftpntr) < midvalue do     {continue pass of left partition
   leftpntr := leftpntr + 1            while mid value greater than
  endwhile                             each key examined}

  while midvalue < m(rightpntr) do    {continue pass of right partition
   rightpntr := rightpntr - 1          while mid value less than each
  endwhile                             key examined}

  if leftpntr <= rightpntr then       {provided the pointers have not
   temp := m(leftpntr)                 yet crossed, swap the smaller
   m(leftpntr) := m(rightpntr)         key from the right partition
   m(rightpntr) := temp               with the larger key in the left}
   leftpntr := leftpntr + 1           {move left pointer one right}
   rightpntr : = rightpntr - 1        {move right pointer one left}
  endif
 until leftpntr > rightpntr           {until pointers cross}
 if lowend < rightpntr then           {if left partition still has more
                                       than one element}
  procedure qsort(lowend, rightpntr) {procedure calls itself to sort
                                       left partition with new parameters}
 endif
 if leftpntr < topend then            {if right partition still has more
                                       than one element}
  procedure qsort(leftpntr, topend)  {procedure calls itself to sort
                                       right partition with new parameters}
 endif
end procedure qsort
```

Listing 29.14

Quicksort in Turbo Pascal to Sort 1000 Numbers in Array M

```
program quicksort(output);
uses dos;
const
 numkeys = 1000;
var
 m :array[1..numkeys] of integer;
 i, lo, hi :integer;
 hrs, min, sec, sec100 :word;

procedure sort(var lowend, topend :integer);
var
 leftpntr, rightpntr, midvalue, temp :integer;
begin
 leftpntr := lowend;                          {set pointers to current left}
 rightpntr := topend;                         {and right partition limits}
 midvalue := m[(lowend + topend) div 2];      {store value at midpoint}
                                              {between new left and right
                                               partitions}


 repeat
  while m[leftpntr] < midvalue do             {continue pass of left partition}
   leftpntr := leftpntr + 1;                  {while mid value greater than each
                                               key examined}

  while midvalue < m[rightpntr] do            {continue pass of right partition}
   rightpntr := rightpntr - 1;                {while mid value less than each
                                               key examined}

   if leftpntr < rightpntr then               {provided the pointers have not yet}
   begin                                   {crossed, swap the smaller key in the}
    temp := m[leftpntr];                    {right partition with the larger key}
    m[leftpntr] := m[rightpntr];            {in the left partition}
    m[rightpntr] := temp;
    leftpntr := leftpntr + 1;                 {move left pointer one right}
    rightpntr := rightpntr - 1;               {move right pointer one left}
   end;
 until leftpntr > rightpntr;                   {until pointers cross}
 if lowend < rightpntr then                    {if left partition still has more than}
   sort(lowend, rightpntr);                    {one element, procedure calls itself
                                                to sort left partition with new
                                                parameters}

 if leftpntr < topend then                     {if right partition still has more}
   sort(leftpntr, topend);                     {than one element, procedure calls
                                                itself with new parameters}

 end;

procedure showtime;
begin                                          {display time taken to complete sort}
```

Listing 29.15

```
  writeln(hrs:10, min:15, sec:20, sec100:25);
end;

begin                                   {fill array with random numbers}
  Write('Creating', numkeys, 'random numbers...');
  Randomize;
  for i:=1 to numkeys do
    begin
     m[i]:=Random(30000);
    end;
  Writeln;
  Write('Sorting', numkeys, 'random numbers...');
  settime(0,0,0,0);                     {initialize time before sort starts}
  lo := 1;                              {initialize lower and upper limits
  hi := numkeys;                        {of array}
  sort(lo, hi);                         {call recursive quicksort procedure}
  gettime(hrs, min, sec, sec100);       {store time at end of sort}
  Writeln;
   for i:=1 to numkeys do
    begin
      Write(m[i]:8);                    {display sorted array}
    end;
  Showtime;
end.
```

Listing 29.15 continued

Quicksort's speed stems from the fact that the early passes bring items close to their final sequence, leaving the last few passes to make only minor changes.

Number of Numbers Sorted	Comparison of Sort Speeds Time in Seconds				
	Bubble	Selection	Insertion	Shell	Quick
100	0.85	0.38	0.16	0.10	0.10
250	4.80	1.86	1.00	0.27	0.24
500	18.80	6.53	3.80	0.60	0.50
1000	75.00	22.00	15.40	1.60	1.10
2000	295.00	87.00	62.00	3.78	2.50
3000		195.00	142.00	6.30	4.00
4000				9.20	5.40
5000				12.00	6.90
6000				15.00	8.50
7000				17.00	10.00
8000				22.00	11.60
9000				24.00	13.00
10000				28.00	14.60
15000				42.50	23.00
20000				67.00	30.90
30000				100.00	47.50

Figure 29.1

Tree Sort

This is a *selection* sort and is described in the chapter on Data Structures. Like Quicksort, the binary tree sort uses the technique of recursion.

Comparing the efficiency of various sorting algorithms with one another requires careful use of 'bench test' data to ensure that comparisons are fair and specialists in the subject of sorting have spent a great deal of time analysing the various methods. It is beyond the scope of this text to pursue such analysis in detail, but some broad comparisons can be made of the relative efficiency of the simple sorts described so far. It must be said that where only a few items are to be sorted, little tangible benefit will be gained from using a sophisticated sort, as opposed to a simple one. With a larger number of items, the limitations of simple sorting algorithms, such as the bubble sort, soon become apparent. Another factor which may affect a sort's performance is the degree to which items are out of order to begin with.

The *bubble sort* is probably the least efficient and is rarely used by experienced programmers. It is, however, a simple sort to understand and provides a good introduction to any programmer wishing to develop their skill in this area. The *selection sort* generally performs better than the *insertion sort*, except when the items are almost in order to begin with.

30 *Organizational Aspects of Computerization*

The introduction of a computer to an organization cannot be effective if computerization simply means the transfer of manual files to computer storage and the automation of some of the existing clerical procedures. To achieve the full potential of computerization, an organization needs to implement certain changes which will affect its staff and its form of management. This chapter examines the functions of Management Information Services and the roles of its staff, the possible effects of computerization on staff in other functional areas and the implications of distributing computing power. In many organizations, a separate department has overall responsibility for computer system provision and operation.

Management Information Services

Some organizations still use the title Data Processing Department, but because of its changing role in producing management information as well as carrying out the routine data processing tasks, the title Management Information Services is used in this text.

As its title implies, this department fulfils a servicing function and in large organizations, generally has some centralized computer facility which carries out most of the computerized data processing. Smaller organizations may not have a central facility but instead have microcomputer systems in each department. In this context however, it is proposed to concentrate on the provision in larger organisations.

Functions

Management Information Services provides two principal forms of information:

- ☐ Operational;
- ☐ Management.

Operational Information

Each *functional area* has its own operational information needs. For example, payroll details and payslips are produced for Wages and Salaries and customer invoices for Sales Order Processing. Here is a typical list of such routine operations:

- ☐ Keeping stock records;
- ☐ Payment of suppliers;
- ☐ General ledger, sales and purchase accounting;

☐ Payroll;

☐ Invoicing;

☐ Production of delivery notes;

☐ Routine costing;

☐ Filing of customer orders.

This routine data processing work forms the bulk of the activity within Management Information Services, but there is an increasing demand for *management information.*

Management Information

Such information is designed to assist with operations which require management involvement and may support decision making in respect of, for example:

☐ Production planning;

☐ Short term and long term forecasting;

☐ The setting of budgets;

☐ Decision making on financial policies;

☐ Marketing decisions;

☐ Sales management;

☐ Factory maintenance and management;

☐ Price determination;

☐ The selection of suppliers.

Although Management Information Services plays a central role, the advent of microcomputers and remote terminals (those connected to the computer by a telecommunications link) has meant that some of the above operations can be carried out by executive staff, with or without the use of the centralized facility.

Example

Consider the situation of a Sales Manager who is planning a sales strategy in terms of which geographical locations to increase sales representatives' visits. With the use of a microcomputer and database software package, records could be kept of sales staff. To obtain the required results, the SalesManager may also need information stored with Management Information Services and using a telecommunications link, the information could be downloaded from the central computer, combined with the information on sales staff and the database query facilities used to extract an appropriate report. This example assumes that the organization uses a Database Management System (Chapter 15) which allows such enquiries. However, in this context it is not the particular methods of computer processing which are of interest. It is sufficient to know that such facilities exist.

The *Figure 30.1* illustrates the staffing structure of a typical Management Information Services department.

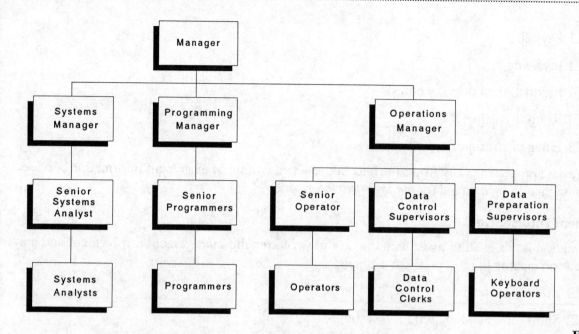

Figure 30.1

The department is normally headed by a Management Information Services Manager or Data Processing (DP) Manager whose major responsibility is for the efficient running of the department in satisfying the organization's information needs.

Beneath the control of the manager are staff involved in two specialist areas of work within the department:

☐ Systems Development and Maintenance;

☐ Operations.

Systems Development and Maintenance

The development of new computerized systems and the maintenance of existing systems involves specialist staff trained in *systems analysis* and *programming*.

Systems analysis is concerned with the design of new computerized systems according to requirements laid down by corporate management. Prior to the design stage there is an investigative stage which necessitates close consultation with potential users in the various functional areas of the organization, to discover their information needs.

The result of the design stage is a System Specification which, rather like an architect's plans for a house, details all necessary materials and procedures to fulfil the specification. The specification will detail the clerical procedures necessary, the hardware required and most importantly, what the computer has to produce for the users.

Once a system has been implemented it will require continual monitoring and modification as the information needs of the users change. These tasks are also part of the systems analyst's job.

Programming is a task which perhaps lacks the creative element present in systems analysis and design. The programmer's job is concerned with coding the necessary computer instructions in a *programming language* such as COBOL or DbaseIV, in order to implement the requirements laid down by the systems analysts, in the Program Specification (this forms part of the System Specification). Programmers involved in writing computer programs for user applications such as invoicing or payroll are known as *applications programmers.*

Operations

The Operations section is usually led by an Operations Manager who is responsible for three sub-sections:

- ☐ Data Control;
- ☐ Data Preparation;
- ☐ Computer Operations.

Data Control

The staff in this section are responsible for the co-ordination and control of data flowing through the Operations section. The data received from, for example, Wages and Salaries to enable the payroll master file to be updated and payslips to be produced, has to be controlled to ensure its accuracy at all stages of processing. Chapter 24 describes the methods of control in detail.

Data Preparation

The work in this section involves the encoding of data from source documents such as customers' orders onto a 'machine-sensible' medium. Currently, this is usually magnetic tape or disk. *Key-to-tape* systems are dedicated, off-line devices, which allow data to be encoded directly onto cassette tape, without the use of a central computer. Prior to processing by computer, the cassettes from the magnetic tape encoders (it is likely that many will be in use) are gathered together and the data is merged onto a large reel for input to the computer. This form of encoding is rather outmoded and *key-to-disk* systems are generally more popular for large volume encoding, making use of a minicomputer and a number of on-line keying stations. The processing power of the minicomputer allows much greater control, both in terms of *verification* and *validation* of the data, than is possible with key-to-tape systems. The data entered via the keying stations is stored on magnetic disk and can be input to the main computer directly from there, or after transfer to magnetic tape.

Computer Operations

The staff in this section are essentially computer operators and responsible for the day-to-day running of the hardware, including the loading and unloading of input and output media, such as disk and tape. The computer hardware is controlled by the *operating system* with which the operator communicates regarding the processing of jobs and the resolution of any error conditions which may arise. This communication is effected through a terminal dedicated to that purpose.

Storage of Magnetic Tapes and Disks

Depending on the size of the organization, the tape or disk library (the cataloguing and storage area for computer file media) may be staffed by a librarian or by the operators. In any event it is vital that information files are properly indexed and kept in a secure environment, protected from physical hazards and unauthorized access.

Staffing in Small Firms

In large organizations, computer installations are run by teams of specialists, comprising systems analysts, programmers and operators. In a small business, there may be one person with special responsibility for a number of aspects of computer usage. Even if there are other computer specialists in the business, each is likely to have a wider range of responsibilities than is the norm for large computer installations. These responsibilities may include, for example, hardware assessment, system design and implementation, software assessment and purchase, routine hardware maintenance, network management and staff training.

Effects on Staff in Other Functional Areas

These will be extremely varied and the degree of change will depend on the extent to which individual staff are involved with a computerized system.

Computerization within an organization tends not to be an instantaneous event affecting all functional areas at the same time. Rather, it tends to be progressive, sometimes planned and sometimes piecemeal.

Consider the following situation in a commercial trading organisation:

    (i)   Assume that Sales Order Processing (SOP) is computerized and that the output includes Picking Lists (these are lists of products and quantities of each that need to be retrieved from the warehouse to satisfy customer orders).

    (ii)   Assume further that Stock Control in the warehouse is not computerized but that the staff will receive computer-printed picking lists.

    (iii)   Assume finally that the Accounting function is not computerized, but that its staff will receive sales details on computer printout from SOP from which they will produce invoices to send to customers.

Clerical Staff

The staff in these three departments, SOP, Stock Control and Accounting are all affected by computerization but to varying degrees.

Least affected are staff in Stock Control and Accounting who only receive computer output. They have to become familiar with the reading and interpretation of printed computer output, which is not a difficult task, but one which requires some adjustment on the part of staff.

At a more complex level, the staff in SOP are more significantly affected and will require education and training in the various parts of the computerized process.

Preparation of Input Data

Computerization imposes a discipline on clerical and managerial procedures. To deal with data correctly it needs to be presented accurately and in a form suitable for input to the computer. Usually, prior to data entry, all source data, (in this case customer orders) have to be recorded on standard, specially designed source documents which match the order of data requested by the computer software. For example, if the first item of data required by the computer is an order number, then this should be the first data item on the source document. The second data item required should be next and so on.

Therefore, however the orders are received, by telephone, by word of mouth at the sales desk or by post, the first job is to transcribe the details onto the Source Document. Such tasks need to be documented in office procedure manuals and staff need to be instructed in their proper execution.

Data Entry

Staff involved in this task will need to develop keyboard skills and even if they are already skilled typists, some training or period of familiarization is required to use a computer terminal correctly.

Training will be needed in the day-to-day operation of the software, including 'signing on' with codes and passwords, making appropriate responses to screen prompts, dealing with simple error conditions when an incorrect key is pressed and correcting or editing keying errors during data entry.

Where the volume of data entry is such that a member of staff can be fully occupied with this task there are health and safety considerations to be examined. There are, for example, recommended guidelines concerning time limits for personnel operating VDU's, as headaches and eye strain can result from prolonged viewing of a computer screen.

Where the volume of data entry is limited, specialist staff may not be justified and a number of clerical staff with a variety of duties may have to 'take their turn' at the keyboard. Thus, more staff will need some basic training in the use of the system.

Managerial Staff

Usually, day-to-day clerical routines will not directly involve managerial staff, although the degree of their involvement will depend on the size of the organization and the hierarchical staffing structure. However, their role in the development, introduction and implementation of a computerized system and their responsibilities for the efficient running of departments mean that the consequences of computerization for the working lives of managers can be even more significant than for clerical staff.

To continue the Sales Order Processing example, the manager of that department may:

- [ ] be closely involved, in a consultative role, with systems analysts in the analysis of the old manual system and the design of the new computerized system;

- [ ] have to maintain communication with the staff in the SOP department to ensure that their views are taken into account and that envisaged changes are reported to them;

- [ ] require some computer education and training. A prerequisite of communication between staff is that the manager has developed sufficient computer 'awareness' and 'literacy' to understand the role of the computer and the necessary changes in departmental procedures .

This educational or training need has to be satisfied if the manager is to be effective in ensuring that operational procedures are being followed and that efficiency is being maintained. Without knowledge of the powers and limitations of a computerized system a manager cannot assess its effectiveness or suggest improvements.

At the managerial level of involvement, it may seem that the more mundane skills of operating a VDU are not needed. Often this is not so. A manager may wish to access files from a terminal in the office, so a minimal level of skill is required.

Other Computer Applications Involving Management

There are a number of computer applications which make use of 'content free' software. Such software is not fixed to one particular application or type of data; packages are available for spreadsheet work, and database or file management.

There is an increasing awareness that microcomputers or terminals linked to a central computer can be used by managers and executive staff (although not exclusively) to aid their decision-making with the provision of more high quality information.

An example may illustrate this point. Spreadsheet packages can be used for the preparation of cash budgets and sales forecasting with the added facility of generating 'what if' projections. So, a cash budget based on current and anticipated figures of cash due in and out of the organization over the next few months, can be quickly modified to present the results of an alternative strategy of, say, an injection of cash from a bank loan.

Database packages can be used by managers as a local information store on which they can make enquiry. Where a database is held centrally, a manager could, with appropriate training, access files through the use of a Query Language (Chapter 15).

The efficient and effective use of such packages demands a high level of knowledge and skill which will probably require some sort of training programme, perhaps with the software supplier.

Effects on Managers not yet Involved

The use of such facilities by one departmental manager or the issue of a general directive from top management within an organization will place pressure on other managers to follow suit. Of course the pressure may be in the other direction where departmental managers wish to get involved and pressurize top management for training and the introduction of new computerized systems.

Changes in Job Descriptions

It can be seen from the previous section that where computerized systems are used within an organization and new staff are to be recruited, advertised job descriptions request computer knowledge and skills which are appropriate to the demands of the job. Existing staff will have to have their job descriptions modified, in some cases necessitating upgrading of skills or professional status and a commensurate increase in salary. Disputes over re-grading can lead to delay in the introduction of computer systems. In local government, for example, some secretarial staff were prevented from using word processors because their union demanded an increase in their job grading. In other jobs it can lead to what is considered to be de-skilling. For example, in the newspaper industry the traditional skill of metal typesetting is now obsolete.

Effects on Functional Relationships

Earlier in this chapter, it is explained that computerization influences the relationships between different functions such as Sales and Accounts, in terms of how information flows between them and the activities in which each is engaged.

Without computers, the Sales and Accounting departments would maintain their own files and transaction data such as a customer's order details would be used to update each of the department's files separately. This would tend to consolidate the separation of autonomous areas within an organization and work against a corporate approach to the achievement of the organization's objectives. Although each department would tend to have its own working practices, provided information was presented to other departments in a form they could use, there may be little pressure for change.

Computerization imposes discipline and standardization. Information flows between departments may have to pass through a computer process and although the user requirements should take priority over what is convenient for the computer, some modifications will need to be made to the ways in which data is presented to the computer for processing. Earlier in this chapter, the example was used of customer order details being transcribed onto source documents designed to be compatible with the order of input to the computer.

A feature of manual systems is the separateness of related operations. For example, a customer order is used to update the customer file, the stock file and for the production of a customer invoice, in separate operations carried out in each separate functional area. A computerized system could allow these tasks to be carried out with a single data input.

Inter-departmental Conflict

Organizations are formed to allow a rational and co-ordinated approach to the achievement of certain aims which may be the provision of a service or product for which there is a profitable market. The problem is that organizations are made up of individuals who may not always be rational. Each individual has his or her own ambitions, fears and emotions, and management styles derived from such personal characteristics may lead departmental heads to compete for, rather than co-operate in, the achievement of the organization's corporate objectives.

Personal Fears

To many people, computerization is a venture into the unknown and they feel threatened because insufficient knowledge or experience reduces their power to control their own futures. Being made to look a fool, or worse, the possibility of being made redundant by computerization, can be a major obstacle to the acceptance of change.

Resistance to Change

Sometimes, because of inter-departmental rivalry or simply incompetence, a manager may keep secret certain facts which computerization may make available and thus provide another reason for resisting the introduction of computerized systems.

Managers are forced to change their style of management because of the introduction of computers and may attempt to resist the threat to their power, by doing less than they might to make the innovation work and constantly find fault, without making constructive suggestions.

'The Enthusiast'

An alternative reaction, which is usually irrational, is the whole-hearted, eager acceptance of computerization as being the ideal solution to every problem. There are many circumstances where computerization is inappropriate or where the immediately available standard package is far from ideal.

Because organizations are made up of individuals, computer systems should be designed with the full co-operation of management and staff, enlisting their help wherever possible so as to take proper account of their individual or at least departmental information needs.

Effects on Management Style

Many managers work intuitively and have confidence in their own methods which have served them well. Such 'flying by the seat of the pants' often leads to a natural derision for any system designed by 'experts' and 'theorists'. Of course such confidence is usually based on previous success and the specialist in computer systems will often be young and, as far as the experienced manager is concerned, 'wet behind the ears'. Thus, the computer specialist may have a difficult job in convincing existing management that a new computerized system will be an improvement on the old. The systems analyst will need to have the interpersonal skills to deal with such resistance.

Computerized systems usually increase the volume of information available to a manager and the speed with which it can be obtained. A resulting danger is that the manager may become too concerned with low level departmental decisions and interfere with the responsibilities of lower levels of management or supervisory staff. The problem can be more serious if it extends upwards from departmental to corporate management and information which should be the direct concern of the department manager may be viewed by the chief general manager first. Excessive or inappropriate information can be more damaging to the efficient operation of an organization than a limited degree of insufficiency.

Implications of Decentralizing Computing Power

Centralized and distributed systems are discussed in Chapters 8, 9 and 23 but broadly speaking, the combined technologies of computing and telecommunications have facilitated the decentralization of computer power through Wide and Local Area Networks and stand-alone microcomputer systems. The main benefits for an organization may be as follow:

- [ ] The delegation of some information processing control to branch level management, hopefully results in systems which respond to local requirements. The control of information processing systems are thereby the responsibility of those who use them;

- [ ] More rapid, up-to-date information at the local level, because it is processed locally;

- [ ] The rapid distribution of centrally produced information via network systems;

- [ ] Provided that the local systems are linked to a central facility, then information which is locally produced can be transmitted and stored so as to be available at a corporate level. Overall control is not lost, but enhanced.

The above benefits are not automatic and may have certain implications for an organization:

- [ ] New hardware and software needs to be purchased, which is compatible with any existing centralized facility;

- [ ] Local management and workers need to be trained in the operation of any new system introduced, if the maximum benefit is to be obtained. The use of microcomputers with, for example, database and spreadsheet packages requires extensive training and this can be expensive;

- [ ] A complete re-appraisal of specialist staffing may be necessary, including, for example, the recruitment of systems analysts already familiar with the design and implementation of distributed systems;

- [ ] Specialist personnel, including programmers and operators, may be required at the local level;

- [ ] Decentralized systems present new problems in terms of controlling the security of information (Chapter 24) and the additional risks must be considered and covered.

31 *Applications and Benefits of Computerization*

Business applications such as payroll and stock control were among the earliest to be computerized. Although increasing use is being made of computers in manufacturing industry, science and medicine, business applications still constitute the greatest usage. A number of categories of computer application can be identified:

- ☐ Accounting systems;
- ☐ Management Information Systems (MIS);
- ☐ Decision Support Systems (DSS);
- ☐ Electronic Office systems;
- ☐ Computer-aided Design and Manufacture (CAD/CAM);
- ☐ Computers in science and medicine;
- ☐ Artificial Intelligence;

Accounting Systems

Payroll

Payroll systems are concerned with the production of payslips for employees and the maintenance of records required for taxation and other deductions. In a manual system, the preparation of payroll figures and the maintenance of payroll records is a labour intensive task. Although tedious and repetitive, it is a vitally important task. Most employees naturally regard pay as being the main reason for work and resent delays in payment or incorrect payments, unless of course it is in their favour! The weekly or monthly payroll run affects almost all employee records in the payroll master file, so batch processing is normally used. This processing method allows numerous opportunities to maintain the accuracy of the information. The repetitive nature of the task makes it a popular candidate for computerization, especially with organizations which employ large numbers of people. The automatic production of reports for taxation purposes also provides a valuable benefit. Smaller organizations with only several employees probably do not regard payroll as a high priority application for computerization, because the benefits are not as great if the payroll can be processed by one or two employees who also carry out a number of other tasks.

Stock Control

Any organization which keeps stocks of raw materials or finished goods needs to operate a stock control system. Although stock constitutes an asset, it ties up cash resources which could be invested in other aspects of the business. Equally, a company must keep sufficient quantities of items to satisfy customer demand or manufacturing requirements. To maintain this balance, a stock control system should provide up-to-date information on quantities, prices, minimum stock levels, and re-order quantities, as well as warning of excessively high, or dangerously low levels of stock. In the latter case, orders may be produced automatically. A stock control system can also generate valuable management reports on, for example, sales patterns, slow-moving items, and overdue orders.

Sales Accounting

When credit sales are made to customers, a record needs to be kept of amounts owing and paid. Payment is normally requested with an invoice, which gives details of goods supplied, quantities, prices and VAT. Credit sales are usually made on for example, a 14, 21 or 28 day basis, which means that the customer has to pay within the specified period to obtain any discounts offered. Overdue payments need to be chased, so sales accounting systems normally produce reports analysing the indebtedness of different customers. Debt control is vital to business profitability and computerized systems can produce prompt and up-to-date reports as a by-product of the main application.

Purchase Accounting

These systems record the amounts owed and payments made, to suppliers of services, goods or materials used in the main business of the company. For example, a car manufacturer needs to record amounts owing to car components suppliers and sheet steel manufacturers. Delayed payments to suppliers may help cash flow, but can harm an organization's image, or even cut off a source of supply when a supplier refuses to deliver any more goods until payment is made. A computerized system will not ensure payment, but it can provide the information that payment is due.

General Ledger

The general ledger keeps control of financial summaries, including those originating from payroll, sales and purchase accounting and acts as a balance in a double entry system. Reports are generally produced at the end of financial periods, including a trading and profit and loss account and balance sheet.

For many organizations, all these systems can be satisfactorily computerized with packaged software.

Management Information Systems (MIS)

Although computers can perform routine processing tasks very efficiently, it is generally recognized that limiting a computer's use to the processing of operational information constitutes a waste of computer power. A MIS is designed to make use of the computer's power of selection and analysis to produce useful management information.

A MIS has a number of key features:

- ☐ it produces information beyond that required for routine data processing;
- ☐ timing of information production is critical;

☐ the information it produces is an aid to decision-making;

☐ it is usually based on the database concept (explained in Chapter 15).

The claims for MIS are sometimes excessive. It is rarely the complete answer to all a company's information needs, but when successfully implemented, it provides a valuable information advantage over competitors.

Decision Support Systems (DSS)

A DSS aims to provide a more flexible decision tool than that supplied by a MIS which tends to produce information in an anticipated, pre-defined form and as such, does not allow managers to make ad hoc requests for information. DSS tend to be narrower in scope than MIS, often making use of microcomputer systems and software packages. Examples of DSS include electronic spreadsheets, such as Lotus 123, file managers and relational database management systems such as Dbase IV. The main features of these and other packages are described in some detail in Chapter 11. Additionally, financial modelling and statistical packages are considered to be DSS tools. A major benefit is the independence they allow for information control by individual managers and executives. When, for example, a sales manager requires a report on sales figures for the last three months, a microcomputer with database package may provide the report more quickly than a centralized data processing department.

Electronic Office Systems

Currently, automation of office procedures tends to be rather fragmented, some staff making extensive use of computers, whilst others rely almost completely on manual methods. The Electronic Office is a concept which views the office as an integrated whole, with many automated procedures and much of the communication by electronic means. The main components of the Electronic Office are described in Chapter 9, but may include the following:

☐ Word processing;

☐ Decision Support Systems (DSS) - discussed above;

☐ Electronic messaging and electronic mail;

☐ Electronic diaries and calendars;

☐ Electronic notice boards;

☐ Telecommuting.

The last component, telecommuting has the potential to revolutionize working habits. Basically, it requires the use of a terminal or microcomputer workstation linked to a company's computer at another location. For workers such as programmers, typists and executive staff, this removes the need for regular attendance at the traditional office. A major disadvantage is the loss of personal contact between staff, which can require considerable cultural re-adjustment. Such a system also has consequences for employee supervision and security of information.

Computer-Aided Design and Manufacture (CAD/CAM)

Computer-Aided Design (CAD)

With the use of a graphics terminal and mouse, or similar device, a designer can produce and modify designs more rapidly than is possible with a conventional drawing board. Ideas can be sketched on the screen, stored, recalled and modified. The computer can also be instructed to analyse a design for comparison with some specified criteria. Drawings can be rotated and tilted on the screen to reveal different three-dimensional views. CAD is used in the design of ships, cars, buildings, microprocessor circuits, clothing and many other products. With the use of CAD a manufacturer has a distinct advantage over non-computerized competitors, in terms of speed and flexibility of design.

Computer-Aided Manufacture (CAM)

A number of areas of computer use can be identified in the manufacturing process.

- ☐ Industrial robots and process control;
- ☐ Computer numerical control (CNC) of machine tools;
- ☐ Integrated CAD/CAM;
- ☐ Automated materials handling;
- ☐ Flexible manufacturing systems (FMS);

Industrial Robots

Basically, a robot replaces the actions of a human arm and consists of 3 main elements, a mechanical arm with 'wrist' joint, power unit and microprocessor or central controlling computer. To be called a robot, it must be able to react, albeit in a limited way, to external events and alter its course of action according to a stored program. Such sensitivity to the environment is provided by sensors, for example, to recognize stylized characters and differentiate between shapes. The main areas of use are in spot welding, paint spraying, die casting and to a lesser but increasing extent, assembly.

Use of robots can provide significant benefits for industry, its employees and the population in general:

- ☐ operation in environments unsuitable for the health of workers;
- ☐ performance of tasks, particularly those which are repetitive, at a consistent level of quality, which is generally high, and without fatigue;
- ☐ lack of human weaknesses generally allows robots to be many times more productive and, apart from small specialist companies, car manufacturers could not stay in business without the use of extensive automation;
- ☐ labour costs are drastically reduced and the capital costs of robots are recoverable through increased production and a consequent fall in the unit costs of production (the cost of producing a single unit of a particular product).

Clearly, there are potential drawbacks to the use of robots, although the degree of disadvantage depends largely on how much human control is retained. For example, an aircraft can be landed virtually without pilot intervention, but it would be placing rather too much faith in a system's reliability and ability to deal with exceptional circumstances, to fly without a pilot. Thus,

> ☐ the consequences of an automated system's failure need to be taken into account when determining the level of reliance to be placed on it and the fallback procedures which need to be employed.

Social disadvantages of using robots are examined in Chapter 32 on Computers and Employment.

Computer Numerical Control (CNC)

CNC operation of machine tools has been widespread for some years because the repetitive nature of machining tasks lends itself to simple programming. However, as is the case with robots, the use of microprocessors allows the machine tool to vary its actions according to external information. The actions of the machine can be compared with a design pattern held by the computer. Any significant variations from the pattern are signalled to the machine tool which, through the microprocessor, reacts appropriately (known as Computer Aided Quality Assessment - CAQ). Other information regarding tool wear or damage can be picked up by sensors and communicated to the human supervisor who takes remedial action.

Integrated CAD/CAM

In fully integrated CAD/CAM systems, the designs produced using CAD are fed straight through to the software which controls the CNC machine tools, which can then produce the design piece. The CAD software checks the compatibility of the design with a component specification already stored in the computer.

Automated Materials Handling

There are around 80 fully automated warehouses in Britain. A fully automated materials handling system consists of a number of sub-systems:

> ☐ stock control;
>
> ☐ part or pallet co-ordination;
>
> ☐ storage and retrieval;
>
> ☐ conveyor control.

Installation generally proceeds one sub-system at a time, each being fully tested before proceeding with the next sub-system. A materials handling system, controlled by a central computer, allocates storage locations in the warehouse, automatically re-orders when a pre-determined minimum level is reached, retrieves parts as required by the factory and delivers them by conveyor belt to the waiting robots or CNC machines.

Flexible Manufacturing Systems (FMS)

Such systems are beneficial where production batches are small and necessitate frequent changes in the sequence and types of processes. The aim of FMS is to remove, as far as possible, the need for human intervention (other than a supervisor or 'machine minder') in the production process. The main elements of FMS are, CNC machine tools (with diagnostic facilities), robots, conveyor belt and central computer and controlling software. In simple terms, the computer has information on parts, machine tools and operations required. The robots serve the CNC machines by presenting them with parts to be machined and loading the correct machine tools from racks.

Process Control

Industrial processes, such as iron smelting and chemical manufacture, can be controlled by computers in a real-time environment, so that, for example, conditions of temperature, speed or pressure can be kept within prescribed limits. Industrial process control systems must include certain functional elements to ensure continual and accurate control:

☐ *sensors* to detect changes in, for example, temperature or pressure;

☐ *transducers* to convert the analogue signals (which change continually over time) from sensing devices, into analogue voltages;

☐ *analogue-to-digital converter* (ADC) to allow these analogue voltages to be presented in the digital form which the computer can accept;

☐ *comparator* to compare outputs from the process, such as temperature or pressure levels, with the parameters required by the process.

The whole system operates in what is generally referred to as a *closed loop*. The sensors provide *feedback* data which the controlling computer can compare with the parameters it has been given, before sending the appropriate signal to the *process control mechanism*, which may be, for example, gas burners in a furnace, or a pump for pressure control.

So, for example, in the computerized process control of a gas furnace, the following components can be identified:

☐ the thermometer is the *sensor*, providing *feedback* for the *comparator*;

☐ the *transducer* to convert the analogue temperature measurements to voltage equivalents;

☐ the ADC to convert the analogue signals to digital form;

☐ the computer is the *comparator,* using its controlling program and parameter data, for example, 2000°C to 2005°C, for temperature control;

☐ the gas burners which are adjusted by signals given by the computer.

Robots which adjust their operation according to feedback from sensors, are also operating in *closed loop* mode. A robot which, for example, sprays car panels regardless of whether or not a panel is in position, is operating in *open loop* mode.

Computers in Science and Medicine

Science

To predict weather conditions accurately requires vast amounts of data regarding past conditions. Large supercomputers allow such volumes of data to be stored, recalled, updated, and analysed on a national and sometimes international basis. Computer graphics and computer enhanced satellite pictures are also used to provide interesting and informative weather forecasts for television viewers. Computer simulations can allow testing of product designs without, at least in the initial stages, the expense of building the prototype product. Airline pilots are trained in computerized flight simulators which can simulate almost any event a pilot is likely to encounter.

Medicine

Computer-controlled life support systems can monitor a patient's condition via a number of sensor devices checking on, for example, pulse rate, body temperature and blood pressure. This frees nursing staff for other duties and has the benefit of providing a continuous monitoring facility. Computer-assisted diagnosis systems make use of artificial intelligence to assist a physician in diagnosing a patient's condition. This raises the question of how much reliance should be placed on computers with artificial intelligence. It seems reasonable that a doctor should use an expert system as an aid to diagnosis, but less reasonable that a treatment decision should be made on the basis of computer diagnosis alone. A particularly exciting development involves the use of computers to assist the plastic surgeon in the repair of facial injuries or deformities. The patient's face is scanned by a camera and the image digitized for display on a computer screen in three-dimensional form. This image can be rotated or tilted on screen by the surgeon and experimental 'cuts' made, the results of which can then be viewed on screen from any angle. In this way, a plastic surgeon can study the results of a variety of strategies before making a single mark on the patient.

Artificial Intelligence (AI)

Artificial intelligence is an attempt to model human thought processes and is finding application in a number of areas:

☐ Expert or Knowledge-Based Systems (Chapter 11);

☐ Robotics (described earlier in this Chapter);

☐ Natural Language (which is considered in Chapter 11).

Expert Systems

Expert systems may, in the future, pose a threat to the autonomy at present held by doctors, lawyers and other professionals. It is not inconceivable that medical diagnosis and legal advice may be provided by machine. Such systems exist already but only provide limited support. The restraint, if any, on such developments may stem from ethical and moral forces, as well as a profession's wish to protect its interests. Equally, humans may well prefer to retain personal contact with their doctor or solicitor, even if a machine is supporting the decision-making process.

32 Computers and Employment

The rapid advances in computer and micro-electronic technologies have occurred during periods of considerable change in the Western economies and although many different factors have conspired towards the generally higher levels of unemployment, computerization has undoubtedly played a major role. No attempt is made in this text to relate particular numbers of employed or unemployed to computerization and discussion will centre on the identifiable effects of computerization on employment patterns and prospects. Computerization requires consideration of a number of possible effects/implications:

☐ Retraining;

☐ Redeployment;

☐ De-skilling;

☐ Changes in working practices;

☐ Regrading and changes in career prospects;

☐ Redundancy;

☐ Changes in working conditions (health and safety).

Each of the above can be identified in different types of job.

Office Work

Computerization is common in most areas of office work, for example, word processing, electronic messaging, and accounting systems. Additionally in some specialized areas such as banking, automatic tellers are replacing humans for routine banking transactions and staffing requirements are likely to reduce quite drastically as new automated services such as telephone banking expand.

Re-training

Generally, an organization will choose to make full use of its existing staff, rather than search for new staff who already have the skills required. Depending on the nature of the job, the retraining needed may be radical or quite minor. For example, a typist has keyboard skills which are quite readily transferrable to the task of word processing and retraining needs centre on the concept of text editing, mailing lists and the use of floppy disks and printers. The aim is to give the operator the knowledge, skill and understanding to make maximum use of the facilities provided by a word processor. Word processing is a general skill which can be applied in different ways in different organizations. Similarly, the use of a software package for sales accounting or stock control needs knowledge and skills, some of which are transferrable to other packages.

Familiarity with computers in general and expertise in the use of some packages, provides an individual with the confidence to quickly pick up skills for new applications as they arise.

Redeployment
Computerization generally reduces manpower requirements but increases the opportunities for business expansion. Redeployment means moving staff from one area of work or responsibility to another, generally with retraining and is a common consequence of computerization in any area of work.

De-skilling
The judgement as to whether or not a job is de-skilled by computerization is a rather subjective one. For example, does a wages clerk using manual methods require a higher level of skill than a data entry operator? The answer is probably "yes", although a trade union may argue otherwise in the interests of improved job re-grading. On the other hand it is generally accepted that higher level skills are required to use a word processor than a typewriter.

Changes in Working Practices
Staff may be required to carry out a wider range of tasks as a result of computerization. For example, in smaller offices a clerk may be required to answer customer enquiries and carry out data entry at a terminal. Flexibility rather than specialization is often the key to the introduction of new technology. The lines of demarcation in the newspaper industry had to disappear before computerization could take place.

Regrading and Career Prospects

Sometimes, improvements in job gradings are introduced in order to encourage staff to accept computerization. At the same time, career prospects in office work are generally diminished. In the banking industry, the prospects for managerial jobs have diminished drastically in the last two decades and currently, few clerical staff who did not enter the job with a degree have prospects for managerial posts.

Redundancy
Computerization of office work inevitably reduces the manpower requirements for an existing level of work, but redundancy does not always result, usually because computers are introduced in response to an expansion in the business of an organization.

Health and Safety
Anxiety and stress frequently result from subjection to frequent and rapid change. Many staff, particularly older members, may feel anxious about the security of their jobs or possible redeployment and may become unhappy about personal contact being replaced by a computer screen.

As they get older, many people prefer continuity rather than constant change and computerization usually means radical and frequent change. Anxiety can also result from a fear of 'falling behind', a common malady amongst people working with computers, because the changes and advances are so rapid.

Ergonomics
Certain health and safety problems can result from computer usage and ergonomically designed equipment and working environments can help minimize the hazards. A number of health and safety concerns are recognized in relation to VDU screens:

- [ ] exposure to radiation;

- [ ] induction of epileptic fits;

- [ ] mental and physical fatigue;

☐ eyestrain, eye damage and visual fatigue;

☐ muscular strain.

Suitable working practices and well-designed equipment can largely avoid such dangers, for example, gentle lighting, lack of screen flicker and hourly breaks for VDU operators. Other concerns relate to the design of office furniture and the general office environment, including temperature and noise levels.

Manufacturing Industry

Most of the factors described in relation to office work apply equally to factory work, but the following additional points are worth mentioning.

☐ *Job satisfaction.* Shop floor workers who supervise and service the machines have a cleaner, less dangerous job than traditionally skilled machinists. It may be surmised that young people, without the experience of the old skills, will look more favourably on such supervisory jobs than the older workers.

☐ *New job opportunities.* If automated systems such as Flexible Manufacturing Systems (FMS) are to be successful, then the number of jobs in factories using FMS must inevitably decrease. Opportunities lie in the creation of a new range of jobs, many of which are in software engineering and in the design of automated systems. The Japanese experience is that new, highly-skilled jobs are created in the development and design fields in companies manufacturing automated equipment and commercial machinery, whereas both skilled and unskilled jobs are lost in the companies using this equipment. The Japanese experience is being mirrored in the UK.

☐ *Increased unemployment.* Many older, skilled workers have been made redundant because of the loss or de-skilling of their jobs through automation. On the other hand, the redundancies may have occurred without automation because of loss of competitiveness.

Computers and Society

There is general agreement that computers and related technologies will bring great social changes, but there are wide differences of opinion about what they will be, the rate at which they will occur and the extent to which they are beneficial. It must be emphasized that many of the following points are highly subjective and open to debate.

Benefits
The benefits include:

☐ increased productivity;

☐ higher standard of living;

☐ cleaner and safer working conditions;

☐ shorter working hours;

☐ more leisure time.

Costs

The costs include:

- polarization of people into two groups - the technologically advantaged and disadvantaged;
- increasing crime and delinquency rates;
- the threat of a totalitarian state;
- invasion of privacy.

The remainder of this section looks at an important area of concern regarding the future impact of computers on society, namely telecommuting. Some of the effects are already apparent.

Telecommuting - The Office at Home

At present, millions of office workers travel by car or public transport to their respective places of work. Nearly all organizations carry out their business from centralized offices because information needs to be exchanged, usually on paper documents and decisions need to be made, which requires consultation between individuals. Through the use of telecommunications, and centrally available computer databases, office staff of the future may work from home via a computer terminal. There are a number of advantages to be gained from home-based work.

Advantages of Telecommuting:

- savings in travel costs;
- no necessity to live within travelling distance;
- flexible hours of work;
- equality between men and women. Bringing up children can be a shared activity;
- savings for the organization in terms of expensive city-centre offices.

Disadvantages of Telecommuting:

- loss of social contact;
- need for quiet workroom at home. This can be difficult in a small flat;
- the difficulty of 'office' accommodation is compounded when two or three members of a family all work from home;
- loss of visible status for senior staff in terms of a 'plush' office and other staff to command.

33 *Personal Privacy and Computer Fraud*

Personal Privacy

Since the 1960s, there has been growing public concern about the threat that computers pose to personal privacy. Most countries, including the UK, have introduced legislation to safeguard the privacy of the individual. The Data Protection Act of 1984 was passed after a number of Government commissioned reports on the subject. The Younger Report of 1972 identified ten principles which were intended as guidelines to computer users in the private sector. A Government White Paper was published in 1975 in response to the Younger Report, but no legislation followed. The Lindop Report of 1978 was followed by a White Paper in 1982 and this resulted in the 1984 Data Protection Act. Apart from public pressure concerning the protection of personal privacy, a major incentive for the Government to introduce the Act stemmed from the need to ratify the Council of Europe Data Protection Convention. In the absence of this ratification, firms within the UK could have been considerably disadvantaged in trading terms through the Convention's provision to allow participating countries to refuse the transfer of personal information to non-participating countries. The principles detailed in the Younger Report formed the foundation for future reports and the Data Protection Act. They are listed below.

- ☐ Information should be regarded as being held for a specific purpose and should not be used, without appropriate authorization, for other purposes.

- ☐ Access to information should be confined to those authorized to have it for the purpose for which it was supplied.

- ☐ The amount of information collected and held should be the minimum necessary for the achievement of a specified purpose.

- ☐ In computerized systems handling information for statistical purposes, adequate provision should be made in their design and programs for separating identities from the rest of the data.

- ☐ There should be arrangements whereby a subject could be told about the information held concerning him or her.

- ☐ The level of security to be achieved by a system should be specified in advance by the user and should include precautions against the deliberate abuse or misuse of information.

- ☐ A monitoring system should be provided to facilitate the detection of any violation of the security system.

☐ In the design of information systems, periods should be specified beyond which information should not be retained.

☐ Data held should be accurate. There should be machinery for the correction of inaccuracy and updating of information.

☐ Care should be taken in coding value judgements.

The White Paper which followed the Younger Report identified certain features of computerized information systems which could be a threat to personal privacy:

☐ The facility for storing vast quantities of data;

☐ The speed and power of computers make it possible for data to be retrieved quickly and easily from many access points;

☐ Data can be rapidly transferred between interconnected systems;

☐ Computers make it possible for data to be combined in ways which might otherwise not be practicable;

☐ Data is often transferred in a form not directly intelligible.

The 1984 Data Protection Act sets boundaries for the gathering and use of personal data. It requires all holders of computerized personal files to register with a Registrar appointed by the Home Secretary. The holder of personal data is required to keep to both the general terms of the Act, and to the specific purposes declared in the application for registration.

Terminology

The Act uses a number of terms which require some explanation:

☐ *Data*. Information held in a form which can be processed automatically. By this definition, manual information systems are not covered by the Act;

☐ *Personal data*. That which relates to a living individual who is identifiable from the information, including any which is based on fact or opinion;

☐ *Data subject*. The living individual who is the subject of the data;

☐ *Data user*. A person who processes or intends to process the data concerning a data subject.

From the individual's point of view, the Act can be said to have a number of weaknesses:

☐ Penalties for infringement of the rules are thought to be weak and ineffective;

☐ There are a number of exemptions from the Act. Some holders do not need to register and there are exceptions to the right of access to one's own file. There are also limits to confidentiality;

☐ The Registrar is appointed by the Home Secretary and cannot therefore, be wholly independent.

Computer Fraud

Computer fraud is invariably committed for financial gain, but unlike some forms of fraud, the perpetrator(s) will make considerable efforts to prevent discovery of any loss by the victim. The rewards for such efforts may be complete freedom from prosecution, or at least a delay in discovery of the fraud and a consequent chance of escape. Unless proper controls and checks are implemented, computer systems are particularly vulnerable to fraudulent activity, because much of the time processing and its results are hidden. The following section examines some methods for committing fraud and the measures which can be taken to foil them.

To extract money from a financial accounting system requires its diversion into fictitious, but accessible accounts. To avoid detection, appropriate adjustments must be made to ensure that the accounts still balance. Sometimes, fraudulent activity may involve the misappropriation of goods rather than cash. Frequently, the collusion of several people is necessary to effect a fraud, because responsibility for different stages of the processing cycle is likely to be shared. Some common methods of fraud are given below.

☐ *bogus data entry.* This may involve entering additional, unauthorised data, modifying valid data or preventing its entry altogether. Such activity may take place during the data preparation or data entry stages.

☐ *bogus output.* Output may be destroyed or altered to prevent discovery of fraudulent data entry or processing.

☐ *alteration of files.* For example, an employee may alter his salary grading in the payroll file or adjust the amount owing in a colluding customer's account.

☐ *program patching.* This method requires access to program coding and a detailed knowledge of the functioning of the program in question, as well as the necessary programming skill. By introducing additional code, in the form of a *conditional subroutine*, certain circumstances determined by the perpetrator can trigger entry to the subroutine, which may, for example, channel funds to a fictitious account.

☐ *suspense accounts.* Rejected and unreconciled transactions tend to be allocated to suspense accounts until they can be dealt with; fraud may be effected by directing such transactions to the account of someone colluding in the crime. Transactions can be tampered with at the input stage to ensure their rejection and allocation to the suspense/personal account.

Fraud Prevention and Detection

An organization can minimize the risk of computer fraud by:

☐ *controlling access to computer hardware;* in centralized systems with a limited number of specialist staff access can be readily controlled (Chapter 24). On the other hand, if power is concentrated in the hands of few staff, then the opportunities for undetected fraud are increased. Distributed systems or centralized systems with remote access may increase the number of locations where fraud can be perpetrated;

☐ *auditing of data and procedures;* until hard copy is produced the contents of files remain invisible and a number of auditing techniques can be used to detect fraudulent entries or changes. The topic of auditing is dealt with in Chapter 24;

☐ *careful monitoring of the programming function;* program patching can be controlled by division of the programming task, so that an individual programmer does not have complete responsibility for one application program. Unauthorized alterations to existing software can be detected by auditing utilities which compare the *object code* of an operational program with an original and authorized copy.

Computer Viruses

A computer virus is program code designed to create nuisance for users, or more seriously, to effect varying degrees of damage to files stored on magnetic media. Generally, the code

☐ is introduced via portable media, such as floppy disks, particularly those storing 'pirated' or 'shareware' programs;

☐ transfers itself from the *infected* medium into the computer's main memory as soon as the medium is accessed;

☐ transfers from memory onto any integral storage device, such as a hard disk and commonly conceals itself in the boot sector (and sometimes in the partition sector where it is less likely to be traced), from where it can readily infect any other media placed on line in that computer system, whether it be stand-alone or networked. Naturally, any write-protected media cannot be infected.

Some virus codes are merely a nuisance, whilst others are developed specifically to destroy, or make inaccessible, whole filing systems. They pose a serious threat to any computer-based information system, but a number of measures can be taken to minimize the risk:

☐ only use proprietary software from a reliable source;

☐ write-protect disks being used for reading purposes only;

☐ use virus detection software, although this is only effective in respect of viruses using known storage and proliferation techniques;

☐ use diskless workstations on networks;

☐ control access to portable media and forbid employees to use their own media on the organization's computer system.

Computer Copyright

A computer program can now obtain the status of literary work and as such, retains protection for 50 years from the first publishing date. Computer software is now covered by the Copyright Designs and Patents Act 1988 and infringements include:

☐ the pirating of copyright protected software;

☐ the running of pirated software, in that a copy is created in memory;

☐ transmitting software over telecommunications links, thereby producing a copy.

The major software producers have funded an organization called FAST (Federation Against Software Theft) which successfully lobbied for the inclusion of computer software into the above-mentioned Act.

EXAM QUESTIONS

Fundamental Concepts

JMB (May 1989) Paper 2

Q1. An arithmetic processor handles floating point numbers in 12 bit registers consisting of a 4 bit exponent in bits 0-3 (bit 0 is the least significant bit) and an 8 bit normalized mantissa in bits 4−11. The binary point of the mantissa is between bits 10 and 11. Both exponent and mantissa are in two's complement notation.

The calculation $(9 \cdot 2) + (-0 \cdot 375)$ is to be performed by this arithmetic processor.

(a) Show how the two numbers, $9 \cdot 2$ and $-0 \cdot 375$, are held by the above processor. Explain any rounding used.

(10)

(b) Show how the processor would add together the representation of the two numbers, arrived at in part a. What is the decimal equivalent of your answer?

(6)

(c) The calculation $(9 \cdot 2) + (-0 \cdot 375)$ has the exact arithmetical result $8 \cdot 825$.

Explain any difference between this and your answer obtained in b.

(2)

(d) Explain the precautions that should be taken to avoid errors when using conditional statements that involve testing floating point numbers.

(2)

ULSEB (June 1990) Paper 1

Q2. A twelve-bit register in a certain computer is split up such that 8 bits are used in fractional two's complement representation to represent the mantissa and the remaining 4 bits are used as an integer two's complement representation for the exponent. Using this register, write down the bit pattern which represents the following numbers in normalized form.

(i) +1(ii) −3
(ii) +0·125(iv) −0·25

You should state any assumptions which you make.

(4)

ULSEB (June 1991) Paper 2

Q3. Biologists surveying a plot of land to assess its agricultural value are using the distribution of earthworms as one possible indicator. The region being surveyed is subdivided into a large number of squares. The land within each square is sampled systematically to provide an estimate of the earthworm population. In order to produce a schematic map of the whole area the estimated population figures are converted into one of four categories: abundant (or a), common (or c), relatively few (or f) and rare (or r). The nature of the land suggests that the earthworm population is likely to be concentrated mainly in a few squares.

The data from the first few squares can be summarized by the string ffcfrrrfrrfcacfrr ...

One technique of encoding the categories is as follows:

a as 111 ; c as 110 ; f as 10 ; r as 0

(a)   What sequence of categories would the binary string 1000111110 represent?   (1)

(b)   Could the code for c be replaced by 101? Explain your answer.   (2)

(c)   Discuss the effectiveness of the given encoding technique in *this* application.   (2)

ULSEB (June 1991) Paper 2

Q4. The continuous output of a scanning sensor is encoded prior to being displayed as a flat monochrome image. Examples of such sensors include a scanning electron microscope, a T.V. camera or a satellite radiometer. A corresponding digital image capable of being stored on a computer system can be considered as a two-dimensional array of integers in the range 0 to 255.

(a)

   (i)   What tasks need to be performed in transforming the analogue representation into a digital representation? What might the numbers 0 to 255 represent when the digital image is displayed?   (2)

   (ii) What are the advantages of storing images in digital form?   (2)

   (iii) Provide a specification for a computer system (including architecture, peripherals and software) that would be capable of taking full advantage of the stored digital images. Give reasons for your choices.   (5)

   (iv) By stating any assumptions that you make, estimate the amount of storage required for a single displayed digital image on this system.   (2)

(b)   One application of image processing is in the field of medical radiology. Some hospitals store X-ray pictures in digital form. When a mass screening is conducted each stored digital image is scanned automatically for patterns that need to be drawn to the attention of experienced medical staff. Outline some of the issues that hospitals will need to consider before installing such a system.   (4)

JMB (June 1988) Paper 2

Q5. The following *figure* shows the structure of a 16-bit central processing unit (CPU) and memory system. The register IN is an input buffer for data from the memory. The register OUT is an output buffer for the arithmetic and logic unit (ALU). An instruction comprises an 8-bit function code (F) and an 8-bit operand field (O).

(a)   Explain the use of the following registers:

   (i)   IR - Instruction Register,

   (ii) ACC - Accumulator,

   (iii) PC - Program Counter,

   (iv) MBR - Memory Buffer Register,

   (v)   MAR - Memory Address Register.   (5)

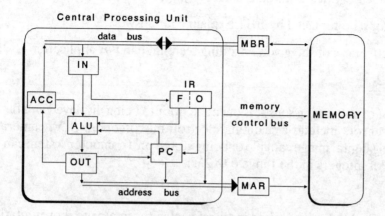

Figure 1

(b)   What signals will be required on the memory control bus.   (2)

(c)   From the diagram construct the sequence of register transfers and memory control signals that carry out the following instructions:

   (i)   Jump Relative- the program counter is to be incremented by the value in the operand field,

   (ii)   Add Direct - the address of the value to be added is contained in the operand field,

   (iii)   Load ACC Indexed - the value to be loaded has the base address of the table initially stored in the accumulator and the offset stored in the operand field.   (13)

Explain your notation.

ULSEB (June 1990) Paper 2

Q6.

(a)   A *bus* can be viewed as the circuitry used to carry data between the components of a system. The following *figure* is a simplified representation of a single bus computer. No control signals are shown and the arrows indicate the possible flow of data. The following abbreviations have been used:

ACC	- accumulator
MBR	- memory buffer register
MAR	- memory address register
ALU	- arithmetic logic unit
PC	- program counter
CIR	- current instruction register
RAM	- random access memory

The processor handles single address instructions of the form

   LOAD   ACC,   2001

where 2001 is a memory location.

An instruction comprises an operation-code followed by an address.

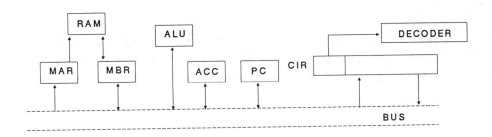

Figure 2

(i) Describe the sequence of events involved in the *fetch* process of the fetch-execute cycle. (2)

(ii) Describe carefully the sequence of events involved in the *execution* phase of each of the instructions

LOAD   ACC,   2001   ; transfer the contents of location 2001 to
                          the accumulator

JUMP   3000   ; jump to location 3000 (3)

(iii) What is the major disadvantage of having a single bus for the transfer of data? Suggest an alternative approach. (2)

Cambridge (May 1990) Paper 2

Q7.

(a) Write down an algorithm, using pseudocode or otherwise, which will store in LARGE and SMALL the largest and smallest values among a set of positive integer values stored in elements zero to MAX of an array named PLACE. (4)

(b) Your algorithm will eventually be translated into a machine-code program which uses indexed addressing. Explain why indexed addressing is used. (4)

(c) Use an example to illustrate the steps within the fetch, decode, execute cycle which perform the address calculations required for an instruction which uses indexed addressing. (4)

JMB (May 1989) Paper 1

Q8. A display device has two inputs, X and Y. The four possible combinations of inputs cause the indicated characters to be displayed:

| INPUT | | OUTPUT |
X	Y	
0	0	E
0	1	1
1	0	2
1	1	3

The figure below shows a railway terminus having three platforms numbered 1, 2 and 3. The points labelled A, B and C route the train entering the station into one of these platforms according to their setting. The points A and B have sensors indicating their orientation:

> 0 = direction set straight
> 1 = direction set switched to the right.

The 'crossover' pair of points, C, always operate together and have a sensor detecting their mutual setting:

> 0 = both set straight
> 1 = both set switched.

Note that it is dangerous for a train to be routed over the point labelled * when it is set against the direction of travel.

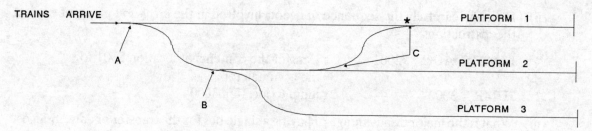

Figure 3

The settings of the points are relayed to a logic circuit having the three sensor values, A, B and C, as inputs and producing two outputs X and Y. These outputs are fed to the display device described above. The display shows the platform number to which the next train *entering* the station is routed and if the points are dangerously set it shows the character 'E'.

(a)

    (i)   Construct a truth table with column headings A, B, C, X and Y.   (5)

    (ii)   Derive minimized Boolean expressions for X and Y in terms of A, B and C.   (5)

(b)

    (i)   Rather than using a logic circuit, a microcomputer is employed to perform the same task. Give one advantage of implementing a hardware only solution and two advantages of implementing a software solution to this problem.   (3)

    (ii)   Write an algorithm which will convert the decimal value corresponding to the 3-bit input value from the sensors into the decimal value of the two bits representing X and Y.   (3)

JMB (May 1990) Paper 1

Q9. In a certain type of central heating system a single boiler is used both to heat the hot water tank and to heat the radiators. The system is controlled by the signals received from three thermostats. These thermostats are:

B   - connected to the boiler. If the water in the boiler is at or above a critical temperature a 1 is output, otherwise a 0 is output

W   - connected to the hot water tank. If the temperature of the water in the tank is below a predetermined setting a 1 is output, otherwise a 0 is output.

H   - in the hall of the house. If the temperature in the hall falls below a predetermined setting a 1 is output, otherwise a 0 is output.

The flow of water round the system is controlled by two pumps:

WP - controls the flow of water to the hot water tank and is activated if W = 1,

RP - controls the flow of water around the radiators throughout the house and is activated if H = 1.

The boiler will be switched on if the required temperature of the hot water tank or the hall has not been reached. However, the boiler must not be switched on if the temperature of the water in the boiler is at or above its critical value. The boiler cannot be switched on if both pumps off.

  (a) As one solution to the method of control of the heating system a dedicated circuit has been suggested.

     (i)   Draw up a truth table for the circuit which would use the three inputs from the thermostats and would control the boiler and each of the pumps. (4)

     (ii) Derive a simplified Boolean expression for the circuit required to control the boiler. Hence design a single logic circuit using only NOR or only NAND gates to control the boiler. (6)

  (b) An alternative solution using a microcomputer would involve the thermostats B, W and H, the water pumps WP and RP and the boiler being connected to the microcomputer. Develop an algorithm which could be used to produce a program to control the heating system. Within your algorithm you should assume a procedure GETVALUE (thermostat, state) which returns the value of the output (in the parameter 'state') from the appropriate thermostat. (6)

JMB (June 1988) Paper 2

Q10.

  (a) (i) What is meant by BCD and why is it used?
      (ii) What is the BCD code for 149? (4)

  (b) A code convertor is required to convert BCD into the code given below.

Decimal value	Code			
	b3	b2	b1	b0
0	0	0	0	0
1	0	0	0	1
2	0	0	1	1
3	0	0	1	0
4	0	1	1	0
5	0	1	1	1
6	0	1	0	1
7	0	1	0	0
8	1	1	0	0
9	1	0	0	0

The BCD codes for ten to fifteen can never be generated on the input side of the convertor, therefore the corresponding output bits can take either a 1 or 0 in the complete truth table. Using appropriate values in the output column for the input codes ten to fifteen, derive a simplified Boolean expression for the convertor circuit for *each* of the four code bits (b0 to b3) to be output.   (16)

ULSEB (June 1990) Paper 1

Q11. A mail order firm employs a number of agents who collect orders from customers and prepare the orders for input to a central computer. Each agent is provided with a portable device for encoding data on a suitable medium.

    (a)   Briefly describe a possible hardware configuration of such a portable device.   (4)

    (b)   How might errors be minimised

        (i)   as the agent inputs data,

        (ii) as the program accepts the data at the central computer?

        (4)

    (c)   Considering cost, convenience and accuracy, compare the use of a portable device with the use of an on-line terminal for this application.   (4)

    (d)   The customers' accounts file is updated in batch mode at Head Office. Describe how the data collected by the agents might be processed for this purpose.   (3)

Computer Hardware

Welsh Joint Education Committee (May 1990) Paper 1

Q12. A large supermarket has thirty check-out stations, each with a point-of-sale terminal linked to a computer in the stock room in the basement. The supermarket is one of a chain of similar supermarkets, all supplied from a large warehouse through a centralized distribution system. Once each day the supermarket's computer is connected to the computer in the warehouse to communicate requirements for the supply of stock. A different basis is used for the supply of fresh food; the supermarket orders this direct from local suppliers each day, according to demand.

(a) Discuss the functions carried out by this system and the advantages it offers:

    (i)   to the manager of the supermarket;

    (ii) to the manager of the warehouse and the distribution system.   (10)

(b) Occasional failures of equipment inevitably occur, affecting point-of-sale terminals, the supermarket computer, the communication links, or the warehouse computer. Discuss how the whole system can be designed to cope with such failures without causing serious loss of data or making it impossible for the supermarket to continue to function.   (10)

JMB (June 1988) Paper 2

Q13.

  (a)

    (i)   Briefly explain why modems are needed in data transmission and why they will become obsolete when digital telephone systems are fully implemented.   (3)

    (ii) When fully implemented, such digital telephone systems will require A-D and D-A converters in the home. Why will these be needed and where will they be located?   (2)

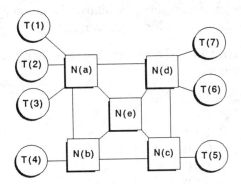

Figure 4

(b) The above *figure* represents a wide area network packet switched system consisting of seven intelligent terminals T(1) to T(7) and five nodes N(a) to N(e). Such a system sends packets of digital information between the geographically remote intelligent terminals.

    (i)   Briefly explain the transmission facilities of the nodes.   (3)

    (ii) Explain in general terms how data is routed through the network from terminal T(3) to T(5).   (3)

    (iii) Explain how the system can tell which terminal a packet is being sent to and how a terminal can tell where a packet has come from.   (2)

    (iv) Explain how packets sent from one terminal to another can arrive out of sequence.   (3)

    (v) What would be the effect to users of this system if node N(a) failed? What would be the effect of node N(e) failing?   (4)

ULSEB (June 1990) Paper 2

Q14. A financial institution has a large number of offices scattered throughout Britain. The company has invested in a substantial network of computers to monitor and control its trading activities.

(a) What is meant by *distributed data processing* in this context and what facilities would you expect to be offered?

What are the possible advantages of such a system over a centralized system?   (4)

(b) Several offices in a small town need to send information to, and receive information from, a remote mainframe which houses a copy of the company's main database. The mainframe is heavily used by a number of sites. The only transmission medium currently accessible in the town is the standard voice grade telephone network.

Briefly describe the problems of transmitting data over such a network and indicate how they can be overcome.

Suggest, with reasons, an alternative transmission medium that could be considered.   (6)

(c) The elements a[i,j] of a two-dimensional array are assigned the values 0 or 1. The maximum number of rows and columns is 8. The elements of the 8th column are chosen to make the number of ones in a row an even number. Similarly, the elements of the 8th row are chosen to make the number of ones in a column an even number.

(i) If the elements a[1,1] to a[7,7] are as given below then write down the contents of the 8th row and 8th column.   (1)

```
        1 2 3 4 5 6 7 8

1       0 1 0 1 1 1 1
2       1 1 1 0 0 0 0
3       0 1 1 1 0 0 0
4       1 0 1 0 1 0 1
5       0 0 0 0 0 1 1
6       1 1 1 0 0 0 1
7       1 0 1 0 0 0 1
8
```

(ii) If the contents of a[4,3] are changed from 1 to 0 how does this affect the 8th row and 8th column?   (1)

(iii) Explain how the results of c(i) *and* c(ii) could be used to detect *and* correct an error in the transmission of data from a terminal to a computer.

What are the drawbacks of this approach?   (3)

Computer Software

ULSEB (June 1990) Paper 2

Q15. Most database management packages allow the user to associate conditions with the fields of a record. These conditions are then activated during the data entry stage. Data entry is via the keyboard and the fields are displayed on a monitor.

Three conditions that can be placed on data entry to fields are

- ☐ the data entered must be *unique*,
- ☐ the data must be verified,
- ☐ data entry is *prohibited*.

   (a)   An application using such a package has records with fields

       ORDER_NUMBER, PART_NUMBER, UNIT_COST, QUANTITY_ORDERED, VALUE_OF_ORDER

In this context,

       (i)   give an example showing why the application would require data entry to a particular field to be unique.

       (ii)   what is meant by verification? How might verification be achieved in this case?

       (iii)   indicate why entry to a particular field might be prohibited?

       (iv)   give an example of a command line a user might enter to obtain information via a query language.   (6)

   (b)   One of the objectives of a database management system is to offer *program-data independence*. What is meant by this term?   (2)

ULSEB (June 1991) Paper 2

Q16. A company specializing in the maintenance and repair of an extensive range of industrial and office equipment has administrative centres scattered throughout Britain. Each centre offers a 24-hour call out service. The local manager is responsible for scheduling and supervising the tasks allocated to each engineer attached to the centre. Each engineer can be qualified in one or more skills and for each skill is allocated a proficiency rating of 1 to 5 depending on experience and qualifications. One of the functions of the centralized administration system is to monitor the workforce to ensure an equitable distribution of skill across all centres. The attributes of interest in this application are:

       ENGINEER_CODE, ENGINEER_NAME, SKILL_CODE, SKILL_DESCRIPTION, PROFICIENCY_RATING, CENTRE, MANAGER

This information is subdivided and stored in two distinct files. The first file contains records with fields

       (ENGINEER_CODE, ENGINEER_NAME, CENTRE, MANAGER)

whilst the second file contains records with the fields

ENGINEER_CODE, SKILL_CODE, SKILL_DESCRIPTION, PROFI-CIENCY_RATING).

(a) Assume that a package supporting these files has been produced in-house using a general purpose high level language.

    (i) Identify suitable primary keys for both records and justify why splitting the attributes over two files is useful in this case. (3)

    (ii) Discuss the possible problems that still remain with keeping the data in the two files described above. Your answer should make reference to

    ☐ the deletion of information about an engineer who has just retired after 30 years service,

    ☐ the addition of information about a skill before the necessary staff have been retrained or employed,

    ☐ amending the description of a skill with code 123. (4)

    (iii) Explain how the use of subsidiary files, or extra fields, could help in answering queries of the form

    "Find the names of all engineers with a proficiency rating of 5 in the skill with code 107."

    Explain any assumptions that you make about the file organizations involved. (3)

    (iv) How might the two files be subdivided to alleviate the problems highlighted in part (ii)? (2)

(b) To what extent would the use of a database management system, together with a built-in non-procedural query language have affected the issues raised in part (a)? (3)

Cambridge (June 1990) Special Paper

Q17. A European research project is concerned with the problem of developing software to translate text from one language to another. Studies have shown that a simple word for word translation produces hopeless results and that progress can only be made by analysing the syntactic structure of each sentence before attempting to translate it. A program development team is given the task of writing software which will accept sentences in English and will analyse and display their syntactic structure. Another team of language experts is already at work defining the rules of syntax for English sentences. There are several hundred of these rules, of which a few simplified ones are given in BNF below.

```
<sentence> :: = <noun phrase> <verb phrase> |
                <noun phrase> <verb phrase> <noun phrase> | ...
<noun phrase> :: = <noun> | <adjective> <noun phrase> |
                <article> <noun phrase> | <pronoun> | ...
<verb phrase> :: = <verb> | <adverb> <verb> | ...
```

The language experts are also creating a dictionary of words with their associated parts of speech - noun, verb, adjective and so on. A few entries in the dictionary are as follows.

a	\<article\>
bit	\<verb\>
dog	\<noun\>
examiner	\<noun\>
horrible	\<adjective\>
hungry	\<adjective\>
the	\<article\>
unkindly	\<adverb\>
weary	\<adjective\>

(a) Use the example rules and dictionary entries to show in detail the syntactic structure of the following sentence.   (7)

a horrible hungry dog unkindly bit the weary examiner

(b) Explain in general terms how you would set about designing the required software. Comment on any particular programming techniques which will be needed.   (13)

Numerous problems are likely to occur in practice. For example, some words can have different parts of speech depending on their context (such as bit), and due to the size and flexibility of the English language, the language experts will be unable to define the dictionary or the rules of syntax completely and unambiguously.

(c) Discuss how the software could be designed to recognize such problems and to interact with a language expert so as to establish the correct syntax and then be able to cope with similar problems in the future.   (13)

JMB (May 1989) Paper 2

Q18. When developing large computer programs, it is very difficult to ensure that the procedure and variable names used are unique and are not being used elsewhere in the program.

(a) Explain the features and mechanisms required in a high-level programming language to help programmers avoid the problem of conflicting variable or procedure names. Include in your answer an explanation of how conflict is avoided when passing parameters to and from procedures.   (6)

(b) When a team is working together on a project with different programmers working on different program units, what additional features and precautions are required to avoid problems of conflicting variable and procedure names when the units are linked together?   (2)

(c) In the program segment given below assume the procedure 'print' generates a new line.

```
global integer n
n := 10
reduce (n - 5)
print (n)
STOP
```

The procedure 'reduce' is given below.

```
procedure reduce (n : local integer)
begin
```

```
        if n < >1 then
            reduce (n - 1)
        endif
        print (n)
    end
```

    (i)   Using a trace table demonstrate the effect of executing the program segment clearly showing the printout.

                (8)

    (ii) How many versions of the procedure 'reduce' are stored by the computer when executing this program segment?

                (2)

    (iii) What changes would make the program segment more readable?

                (2)

JMB (May 1989) Paper 1

Q19. A subprogram is otherwise known as a subroutine, procedure or function.

    (a)   Give three reasons why previously compiled subprograms are a useful software development aid.

                (6)

    (b)   A high-level language program comprises an uncompiled main program and two previously compiled subroutines, A and B.

    (i)   Explain how a compiler, when compiling the main program, would treat the references to the subroutines. Name *two* other types of subprogram that may be referenced as a result of the compilation.

                (6)

    (ii) Describe the role of a linkage editor in consolidating the main program and the subprograms into an executable program.

                (4)

ULSEB (June 1991) Paper 1

Q20. Many high level programming languages support both

        WHILE....DO   and   REPEAT.....UNTIL loops.

    (a)   Give an example of the use of each type of loop and explain why the stage at which the test is performed in the loop is relevant to your examples.

                (4)

    (b)   What are the problems of using real variables to control loop termination? Describe how the problems can be overcome.

                (3)

JMB (June 1988) Paper 2

Q21.

    (a)   A microcomputer has a 40 character by 25 line monitor display. Each character on the screen is represented by a character code stored in an area of memory called the 'screen memory'. The first 40 locations in the screen memory represent the first line of characters, the next 40 the second line and so on. Screen memory commences at location 5000. There is a location, 'CURSOR', which holds the address of the current cursor position within screen memory. Any changes in the contents of locations within screen memory, or 'CURSOR', are instantly and automatically reflected in the screen display.

Construct algorithms to explain how the following fundamental screen handling procedures can be effected.

    (i)   Move the cursor to the home position (top left hand corner of the screen).   (1)

    (ii) Clear the screen.   (2)

    (iii) Move the cursor to the beginning of the current line.   (2)

    (iv) Delete the previous character but only if it is on the current line.   (3)

    (v)   Scroll the display up one line, losing the top line of text and producing a blank line at the bottom.   (4)

    (vi) Move the cursor to the beginning of the next line.   (4)

  (b) Describe how a screen could be scrolled up and down without any loss of text. Discuss the limitations of this facility.   (4)

AEB (June 1991) Paper 2

Q22.

  (a) Describe two of the main objectives of an operating system.   (4)

  (b) A mainframe computer appears to communicate with a number of users and execute their programs simultaneously. Describe how the operating system can handle the requirements of each of these functions. Include in your answer an explanation of:

    (i)   how it protects one program from another;

    (ii) how it shares resources amongst the programs;

    (iii) how it selects the next process to be executed.   (12)

  (c) Explain the steps needed for a user to log on to the mainframe computer. Why are these steps needed?   (4)

ULSEB (June 1991) Paper 1

Q23.

  (a) A computer software company is using a computer system with a number of terminals to develop software for its customers. During the working day a time slice system is used; at other times batch processing is employed. What priorities might the computer manager assign

    (i)   during the working day

    (ii) at other times?   (5)

  (b) Describe, by giving an example, how deadlock might occur in a multi-programming system.

    Explain

    (i)   how deadlock can be avoided

(ii)   if deadlock does occur how recovery may be effected

(iii)   why peripheral devices are usually controlled by the operating system rather than by users' programs.   (10)

JMB (May 1990) Paper 1

Q24.

(a)   Explain how a computer system is designed to handle an interrupt condition, describing both the hardware and the software provision.   (4)

(b)   For *four* of the following interrupt conditions, explain what the condition is, why the condition might have arisen and how the operating system might handle it.

(i)   arithmetic overflow;

(ii)   clock;

(iii)   instruction error;

(iv)   memory parity error;

(v)   peripheral transfer complete;

(vi)   peripheral transfer error.   (12)

Systems Analysis

ULSEB (June 1989) Paper 1

Q25. A small book-lending library has decided to install a computer system for the administration of loans. Each borrower is given a unique identification number. Each title is given a unique reference number and each copy of a book is given a unique accession number. The system keeps track of current loans and reservation requests. It immediately advises the librarian when borrowers attempt to borrow more books than they are allowed, and when reserved books have been returned. At the end of each day the system generates a recall list for newly overdue books.

The system caters for the addition, removal and amendment of records of books and borrowers.

(a)   Describe briefly the processing of a transaction when a book is returned.   (3)

(b)   List *three* other input transactions which the system must support, and describe the data items to be entered.   (6)

(c)   Design a suitable menu-driven interface for the system, providing sketches of individual menus and indicating their inter-relationship. The size of the screen limits the number of choices on an individual menu to a maximum of 6.   (6)

ULSEB (June 1991) Paper 1

Q26. A large city railway station, which has sixteen platforms, has trains arriving and departing every few minutes during the day. To keep the travelling public informed of train movements a total of forty large visual display units (VDUs) are placed in prominent places throughout the station complex. Twenty of the VDUs display the information about the next ten arrivals and the other twenty display the information about the next ten departures. All the VDUs are connected to a central computer system which is controlled by an operator. For each train, the system stores information on its origin and destination, intermediate stations at which it stops, its time-tabled arrival/departure time, its expected arrival/departure and the number of the platform it uses.

(a) What data structure could be used to store the information about the trains? Justify your answer. (3)

(b) How might data be captured

    (i) about incoming trains

    (ii) as trains depart from the station? (4)

(c) A suite of programs has been written for this application.

    (i) Design a testing strategy to be employed before such a system is fully implemented.

    (ii) Describe a suitable method of implementing the system and explain your answer. (8)

ULSEB (June 1990) Paper 2

Q27. The information centre of a large organization has a computerized loan and return system for its books, manuals, journals, tapes etc. However, the catalogue for each category still exists as a number of separate card index files. It has been decided to computerize these catalogues to provide users with a single centralized catalogue which can be queried simultaneously by a number of users. The current computer system is not powerful enough to cope with this additional task. A firm of analysts is called in to recommend the steps to be taken and to supervise the transition process.

(a) What are the likely problems involved in transferring these manual files onto disk? Suggest how these problems could be overcome. (5)

(b) Why is it important for the analysts to provide documentation for the new system even though it is running satisfactorily?

Why are professional bodies within the computing industry keen to support documentation standards?

Outline the content of the documentation that should be given to the staff who use the system at the information centre. (7)

(c) What change-over method do you think is appropriate in this case? Justify your choice. (3)

ULSEB (June 1989) Paper 1

Q28. A company manufactures and markets screws. The company is considering computerizing some of its activities. The departments listed below, with their functions, could benefit from computerization.

Department	Functions
Ordering	Maintain stock of raw materials.
Production	Arrange production of screws according to known requirements and forecasts; ensure labour and machinery are available.
Sales	Receive orders; make forecasts and market screws.
Despatch	Make up and send out orders received.
Accounts	Process company's financial transactions.
Planning	Devise possible future developments.

(a)　Describe, with the aid of a diagram, the data flow in to and out of the departments, being careful to indicate the direction of the flow.

(7)

(b)　Describe four tasks within the departments of the company in which a computer system could usefully be involved.

(8)

Data Processing

JMB (May 1989) Paper 1

Q29. Many financial institutions now issue plastic cards which can be used at cash dispensers to withdraw money and, if requested, give details of the holder's account.

These cash dispensers are available 24 hours a day, 7 days a week. When issued with a card the holder is given a PIN (Personal Identification Number). On the back of this card there is a thin strip containing magnetically encoded information relating to the holder's account. This strip has three rows on which information can be stored. The financial institutions have adopted two main ways of using the information on these strips.

Method 1

Stores the holder's account number on row 2, and on row 3 a coded version of the PIN, together with that holder's weekly cash withdrawal limit and the money removed so far that week. The system is normally on-line during the day and off-line at night.

Method 2

Stores only the holder's account number on row 2 and leaves row 3 empty. This method requires the system to be on-line at all times. The cash dispensers hold no information of the transactions which have been carried out.

To use the card it has to be inserted into the machine and the PIN entered when requested.

(a)　(i) Why must method 2 be an on-line system?
　　　(ii) Why must the PIN on the card in method 1 be held in coded form?

(2)

(b)　Give an example of a potential invasion of privacy in this application.

(1)

(c) Give an example of a potential breach of security in this application. (1)

(d) Describe how the security of each of these systems could be broken by the following people and in each case indicate what measures could be taken to prevent that breach of security.

    (i)   members of the general public,

    (ii) the bank's computer staff. (5)

(e) Describe two checks which could be held in the rows of the magnetic strip to ensure that the data has been read correctly. (4)

(f) Using method 2, when the card holder enters the PIN, what is it checked against? (1)

(g) Suggest what information could be held in row 1 of the card in both methods. (2)

ULSEB (June 1990) Paper 2

Q30. A particular microcomputer has a built-in 130Mb sealed hard-disk drive. The operating system used has a file management module that views a disk as a collection of 1Kb blocks. The disk address of each block is 32 bits long. Three tasks performed by the file management system are:

☐ maintaining a directory of files on the disk;

☐ maintaining a list of 'free' blocks that can be allocated to a new file;

☐ keeping track of the blocks allocated to each file.

(a)

    (i)   An entry in the directory contains the name of a file and a pointer to the first block allocated to that file. What other information might be found in this entry? (3)

    (ii) An entry in a directory can also point to another (sub)directory of files. The user is thus offered a tree-structured file system. Indicate one advantage of such a system. (1)

(b) A collection of blocks has been set aside for a structure to keep track of the unallocated blocks.

    (i)   Confirm that each block can store up to 256 block addresses. (1)

    (ii) Show by using a diagram how a *linked list* of blocks can be used to keep track of the unallocated blocks. Show also that when the disk is almost empty this structure occupies approximately 0.5 Mb of the disk. (4)

(c) Associated with each file is a table containing twelve entries. The first ten of these are the disk addresses of the first ten blocks of the file. The remaining two are only used if the size of the file becomes larger than 10 Kb.

If needed, the eleventh entry is the address of a *second level block* which contains up to 256 block addresses and the twelfth entry is the address of a *third level block* which contains the address of 256 *second level blocks*.

    (i)   Draw a diagram to show how blocks could be allocated to a 600Kb file. (4)

    (ii) Show that by using this technique the size of a single file could exceed 64 Mb. (2)

Q31. A company intends storing details of its products on computer. At any time the company has a maximum of 1000 products. Each product has a unique four digit code associated with it. The systems analyst has decided that the file will require 500 blocks and will be organized randomly with each block in the file capable of holding two records. The location of the record on disk is obtained by a hashing algorithm which involves the following processes:

1.   take the last three digits of the product code;

2.   divide this number by two;

3.   take the integer value of the result of this division.

Using this algorithm the record for the product with code number 1427 will generate a block address of 213. However, products with code numbers 4426 and 2427 will also generate 213 as the block address even though each block is only capable of holding 2 records. When a block is full and the algorithm generates that block address again for the record being added, the next block is tested, and so on, until a free area is found into which the record is written.

(a)   Records with the following product numbers are submitted in the sequence indicated. Into which blocks will they be written, assuming the file is initially empty?

   0462   3464   1465   1463   4462   (3)

(b)   Write an algorithm for locating a record in the file.   (4)

(c)   If product 1465 is discontinued how would the record be deleted without re-organizing the file?   (2)

(d)   Write an algorithm for adding a record to the file.   (7)

(e)   Every six months the company performs a stock check and this requires the file to be printed out in product number order. Describe an efficient method of producing a tape file which could be used for this print-out.   (4)

Q32.

(a)   Describe what is meant by an indexed sequential file organization. Why may it be necessary to maintain a *multi-level index* and *overflow areas* in the maintenance of this file structure.   (6)

(b)   A microcomputer system has been installed in a busy video hire shop. The backing storage for this system comprises a floppy disk drive, a 40 megabyte sealed hard disk drive (Winchester drive) and a high capacity magnetic tape unit.

   Two of the *many* tasks performed by this system are:

   ☐ to monitor the loan and return of the videos; there are, on average, 400 transactions per day;

   ☐ to provide a weekly listing of the popularity of all the films in stock over the previous 7 days.

To perform these routine stock handling tasks a simple file is created with the fields -

CODE-NUMBER, TITLE, COUNT, DATE-FOR-RETURN

The CODE-NUMBER is a unique field given to the video when it is added to stock and the COUNT field is used to sum the number of loans.

(i) Justify why an indexed sequential file organization might be a suitable choice for the stock file and discuss the access methods available for each task. (3)

(ii) Outline briefly what extra processing will be carried out on the file during the weekly listing. (2)

(iii) Devise appropriate backup procedures to ensure that the shop is protected from a failure of the Winchester drive. (4)

ULSEB (June 1991) Paper 1

Q33. A water company uses computer controlled equipment to monitor and control the quality of drinking water. Sensors are placed in various positions on the equipment to take digital measurements every minute. The computer has been programmed to respond to feedback from the sensors and input from the operator.

(a) What data is likely to be captured by the sensors? (2)

(b) Describe situations in which the computer will respond to

(i) feedback

(ii) input from the operator. (4)

Program Design and Implementation

JMB (May 1990) Paper 2

Q34. The contents of a block of Immediate Access Store for a byte orientated computer is shown below in hexadecimal (hex), starting at 1700 hex:

location							contents								
1700	54	68	65	20	63	6F	6D	6D	6F	6E	20	43	6F	72	6D	6F
1710	72	61	6E	74	20	6F	72	20	53	68	61	67	2C	20	6C	61
1720	79	73	20	65	67	67	73	20	69	6E	73	69	64	65	20	61
1730	20	70	61	70	65	72	20	62	61	67	2E	20	54	68	65	20
1740	72	65	61	73	6F	6E	20	66	6F	72	20	74	69	73	20	74
1750	68	65	72	65	20	69	73	20	6E	6F	20	64	6F	75	62	74

In the following subroutine, AX, BX and CX are all 16 bit registers. Each register can be used as a pair of 8 bit registers referenced as the H(High) 8 bits and the L(low) 8 bits (e.g. BL means the 8 low-order bits of BX).

```
;Subroutine - retrieve pixel colour for video display.
START:
LD      BX,     (X-COORD)    ;load BL with contents of location X-COORD, set BH
                             ;to zero
SRL     BX,     2            ;shift right logical BX, 2 bit positions
LD      CX,     (Y-COORD)
MUL     CX,     50           ;multiply CX by 50 hex, result in CX
ADD     BX,     CX           ;add CX to BX, result in BX
ADD     BX,     1600         ;add 1600 hex to BX, result in BX
LD      AL,     [BX]         ;load AL with the contents of the memory byte whose
                             ;address is stored in BX
LD      BX,     (X-COORD)
AND     BX,     3            ;logically AND BX with 3
INC     BX                   ;add 1 to BX
SLL     BX,     1            ;shift left logical BX, 1 bit position
ROL     AL,     BX           ;rotate left AL by n bit positions where n is the
                             ;value stored in BX, result in AL
AND     AL,     3
RET                          ;return to calling routine
```

(a) If X-COORD contains the value 8E hex, Y-COORD contains the value 3 and the subroutine is called and executed once, what value is returned in AL? Use a trace table for AL, BX and CX to show clearly the working by which you obtained your answer. (10)

(b) If X-COORD is now set to the value 55 hex, Y-COORD set to the value 4 and the subroutine again called and executed once, what value is returned now in AL? (6)

(c) In this subroutine, X-COORD is the x coordinate and Y-COORD is the y coordinate of a pixel used by the video display of the computer. The value returned in AL represents the current colour setting of the pixel.

How many possible colours are there for each pixel? Explain how you obtained your answer. (4)

USLEB (June 1989) Paper 2

Q35.

(i)   Explain briefly why the process of sorting a file into key order is a common activity in data processing. Why is there a diversity of sorting algorithms available? (4)

(ii)

(a) A one dimensional array has been initialised to

a[1] = 2, a[2] = 9, a[3] = 8, a[4] = 7,
a[5] = 4, a[6] = 5, a[7] = 6.

The procedure *sort* given below has been designed to sort integer arrays into ascending order. The procedure includes calls to two other pre-defined procedures *display* and *swap* and to a pre-defined function *integer.part.of.*

The procedure *display* is called by a command of the form *display*(a) and it outputs the contents of the complete array starting on a new line.

The procedure *swap*, called by *swap*(x,y), exchanges the contents of locations x and y.

The function *integer.part.of* returns the largest integer smaller than, or equal to, its argument.

After a call *sort*(a,1,7) using the above data the first two lines of output are

2	6	5	4	7	8	9
2	4	5	6	7	8	9

Work through the procedure carefully to confirm this result and show clearly how you arrive at your conclusion. (7)

```
procedure sort(a,left,right);
(*comment: a is an array, left and right are integers*)
      i := left; j := right;
      mid := integer.part.of(left + right)/2);
      key := a[mid];

      repeat
            while a[i] < key do i := i + 1 endwhile;
            while a[j] > key do j := j - 1 endwhile;
            if i <= j then swap(a[i],a[j]);
                            i := i + 1;
                            j := j - 1;
            endif;
      until i > j;
      display(a);
      if left < j then sort(a,left,j);
      if i < right then sort(a,i,right);
endprocedure;
```

(b) Although the data has been sorted after two calls to the procedure *sort* explain why further calls will take place.

(2)

(c) What parameter passing mechanism has been used in the procedure *swap*? (2)

Welsh Joint Education Committee (May 1990) Paper 1

Q36.

(a) An application requires a large number of names held in an array in main store to be sorted. The current sorting algorithm used is an insertion sort, but it has been found to be too slow. Describe a sorting algorithm which would be suitable for carrying out this task much more quickly. Illustrate the operation of your algorithm by showing how it sorts into alphabetical order the following list of names (you may use the initial letters only if you wish).

Jones	Hammond	Burrows	David	Farthing	Lee Monson
Gledhill	Arch	Coulson	Khan	Evans	(10)

(b)   Describe an algorithm which determines the position of a key value in an ordered list by means of a binary search. Assuming that the twelve names above are A level examination candidates sitting, in alphabetical order, in seats 1 to 12 of the examination room, illustrate the operation of your algorithm to find the seat number of Hammond.   (10)

ULSEB (June 1990) Paper 1

Q37.

(a)   In the context of data structures, explain what is meant by a queue.   (1)

(b)   Briefly describe two distinct applications for which a queue is a suitable data structure.   (4)

(c)   Why are queues in computer systems usually implemented as circular queues?   (2)

(d)   Describe how a circular queue may be implemented using a one dimensional array. Give algorithms for inserting and removing items from this queue.   (5)

(e)   If these algorithms were written as procedures, what parameters would need to be passed between each of the procedures and the calling program?   (3)

Cambridge (May 1989) Paper 1

Q38.

(a)   Describe, with the aid of diagrams, how names may be stored in alphabetical order in a linked list structure by using arrays. Use the names Rachel, Majid, Sian, Mary, Jonathan as example data.   (4)

(b)   Show how the free space can be managed so that items can be easily added to or deleted from the linked list. Use as examples

(i)   adding the name Henry to the list;

(ii)   deleting the name Majid from the list.   (4)

ULSEB (June 1991) Paper 2

Q39.

(a)   Describe, with the aid of a suitable diagram, how a queue can be maintained using a linked list.

Outline an algorithm for removing an item from this queue including the manipulation of the free list. You may assume that the queue is not empty.

What are the advantages and disadvantages of linked storage to manipulate a queue?   (6)

(b)   The following tree structure is use to provide indexed access to a file. Each node of this tree can store 3 pointers and two sets of data in the order

(pointer, data, pointer, data, pointer),

where the data comprises a key value and the corresponding disc address. In the diagram below only the key values of the records are shown and pointers are drawn as arrows. An entry of -1 for a key implies that there is no data and an entry of nil for a pointer implies that there is no corresponding link.

If a node has the logical structure (p1, k1, p2,k2, p3) then, unless that pointers are nil,

> p1 points to a node containing keys with values <k1,
> p3 points to a node containing keys with values >k2,
> p2 points to a node containing values between k1 and k2 unless k2 = -1 when it points to a node with keys with values >k1.

The software always arranges the contents of a node so that k1 < k2 (unless k2 = -1).

Data has been added to the tree in the order of key values 20, 40, 10, 15, 30, 25, 14, 50 to give:

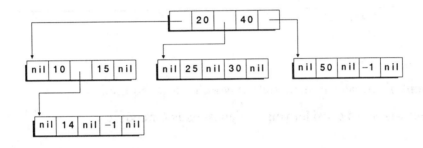

Figure 5

(i)   Draw diagrams of the tree after records with keys 38 and 12 have been added to the file.   (3)

(ii) How might the software reorganize the original tree if the record with key 30 has to be deleted?   (1)

(iii) How does the structure in the diagram above compare with the use of an ordered binary tree to perform the same task? By making appropriate assumptions compare the storage used and the average search time to locate an item. What happens if the record with key 12 is added? What might happen in the case of a very large file?   (5)

JMB (May 1990) Paper 1

Q40. A document file has been processed to produce a special text file consisting of words, each followed by a space, and with all punctuation removed.

The following list is the specification of user requirements for a word counting program.

> Read the text file and produce a list, in alphabetical order, of all the different words found with the number of occurrences of each word.

A 'word' consists of a sequence of characters followed by a space.

The text file is terminated by an end-of-file marker.

The list of different words produced is stored in an array called *word-data* which is kept in order while it is being built up rather than being sorted at the end. A linked list is NOT used.

Assume there is a function *find-word* that takes a word as its single argument and returns the position of this word in word-data, if found. If the word is not found, it returns the position where it should be inserted in word-data to maintain alphabetical order.

Ignore any problems concerning the size of the text file or the size of word-data.

(i)   Carefully describe the structure of word-data.   (2)

(ii) Derive a top down program design for these requirements by expanding Process Word in the following top level:

```
initialization
WHILE NOT eof DO
     ProcessWord
ENDWHILE
output word-data
```

No further refinement of 'initialization' or 'output word-data' is required.

Stop your refinement when you consider your design is ready for coding.   (14)

Index

Other computer textbooks from Business Education Publishers

Computer Studies for BTEC
Third Edition

Geoffrey Knott Nick Waites
Paul Callaghan John Ellison
608 pages May 1993 ISBN 0 907679 46 3
Size 290 x 200mm Soft Cover £19.50

This book has been written for BTEC National courses in Computer Studies and covers the following units
Core Units:
Information Systems, Introduction to Programming, Computer Systems, Quantitative Methods and Communication Skills.
Programming Stream:
Concepts and Practice Unit.
The third edition incorporates major revisions to the chapters on hardware and software keeping students fully aware of the most recent changes and developments. The book gives all the necessary source material for each unit and provides opportunities to develop understanding through a problem based assignment programme. It has been written in a way which allows students to gain a fundamental understanding of the technical and applicational areas of computing and makes no assumptions about the student's previous knowledge. It is ideally suited to form the basis for an active student centred approach and can be used in conjunction with **Small Business Computer Systems for BTEC** and **An Introduction to PASCAL.**

An introduction to PASCAL

James K Morton
June 1993 160 pages
ISBN 0907679 47 1 Size 252 x 200mm
Soft Cover £9.95

This book has been specially designed for those studying Pascal for the first time and assumes no prior knowledge of programming. The format of the book provides the student with a logical, step-by-step learning experience proven to be successful in practice. The material included covers the programming requirements of BTEC National and First Award, City & Guilds Modular Courses and GCE Advanced Level Computing syllabuses. BTEC National/First Award and City & Guilds students will find their requirements met by the material contained in chapters 1 to 5; Advanced Level students should include chapter 6 in their course of study. Undergraduate and HNC/HND students requiring a working knowledge of Pascal will find this an invaluable text. Chapters 1 to 5 provide the material necessary for a good, general understanding of the Pascal language and chapter 6 provides a platform for those students intending to pursue programming at a professional level.

The book contains a wealth of complete, ready-to-run programs along with numerous end-of-chapter practice programs, exercises and assignments designed to enhance understanding of the material presented in each chapter.

Small Business Computer Systems for BTEC

Geoffrey Knott September 1989 244 pages
ISBN 0907679 26 9 Size A4 Soft Cover £12.50

This book was written to cover the Small Business Computer Systems stream of the BTEC National courses in Computer Studies. It provides students with all the necessary source material for the Concepts and Practice Units. The programme of problem based assignments is specifically designed to consolidate students' learning at every stage of the course and to cover the BTEC specific objectives for these units.

Small Business Computer Systems - A Tutor's Guide

Geoffrey Knott September 1989 282 pages
ISBN 0907679 33 1 Size A4 Soft Cover £15.95

This text is a comprehensive support system for the planning and delivery of an assignment programme for the Small Business Computer Systems option on BTEC Computer Studies courses. Each assignment guide provides the BTEC Principal and Specific Objectives covered by the assignment, suggested aims of the assignment, suggestions for ensuring that students are adequately prepared for the assignment and suggested assignment content to provide a basis for assessment.